36: *British Novelists, 1890-1929: Modernists,* edited by Thomas F. Staley (1985)

37: *American Writers of the Early Republic,* edited by Emory Elliott (1985)

38: *Afro-American Writers After 1955: Dramatists and Prose Writers,* edited by Thadious M. Davis and Trudier Harris (1985)

39: *British Novelists, 1660-1800,* 2 parts, edited by Martin C. Battestin (1985)

40: *Poets of Great Britain and Ireland Since 1960,* 2 parts, edited by Vincent B. Sherry, Jr. (1985)

41: *Afro-American Poets Since 1955,* edited by Trudier Harris and Thadious M. Davis (1985)

42: *American Writers for Children Before 1900,* edited by Glenn E. Estes (1985)

43: *American Newspaper Journalists, 1690-1872,* edited by Perry J. Ashley (1986)

44: *American Screenwriters,* Second Series, edited by Randall Clark, Robert E. Morsberger, and Stephen O. Lesser (1986)

45: *American Poets, 1880-1945,* First Series, edited by Peter Quartermain (1986)

46: *American Literary Publishing Houses, 1900-1980: Trade and Paperback,* edited by Peter Dzwonkoski (1986)

47: *American Historians, 1866-1912,* edited by Clyde N. Wilson (1986)

48: *American Poets, 1880-1945,* Second Series, edited by Peter Quartermain (1986)

49: *American Literary Publishing Houses, 1638-1899,* 2 parts, edited by Peter Dzwonkoski (1986)

50: *Afro-American Writers Before the Harlem Renaissance,* edited by Trudier Harris (1986)

51: *Afro-American Writers from the Harlem Renaissance to 1940,* edited by Trudier Harris (1987)

52: *American Writers for Children Since 1960: Fiction,* edited by Glenn E. Estes (1986)

53: *Canadian Writers Since 1960,* First Series, edited by W. H. New (1986)

54: *American Poets, 1880-1945,* Third Series, 2 parts, edited by Peter Quartermain (1987)

55: *Victorian Prose Writers Before 1867,* edited by William B. Thesing (1987)

56: *German Fiction Writers, 1914-1945,* edited by James Hardin (1987)

57: *Victorian Prose Writers After 1867,* edited by William B. Thesing (1987)

58: *Jacobean and Caroline Dramatists,* edited by Fredson Bowers (1987)

59: *American Literary Critics and Scholars, 1800-1850,* edited by John W. Rathbun and Monica M. Grecu (1987)

60: *Canadian Writers Since 1960,* Second Series, edited by W. H. New (1987)

61: *American Writers for Children Since 1960: Poets, Illustrators, and Nonfiction Authors,* edited by Glenn E. Estes (1987)

62: *Elizabethan Dramatists,* edited by Fredson Bowers (1987)

63: *Modern American Critics, 1920-1955,* edited by Gregory S. Jay (1988)

64: *American Literary Critics and Scholars, 1850-1880,* edited by John W. Rathbun and Monica M. Grecu (1988)

65: *French Novelists, 1900-1930,* edited by Catharine Savage Brosman (1988)

66: *German Fiction Writers, 1885-1913,* 2 parts, edited by James Hardin (1988)

67: *Modern American Critics Since 1955,* edited by Gregory S. Jay (1988)

68: *Canadian Writers, 1920-1959,* First Series, edited by W. H. New (1988)

69: *Contemporary German Fiction Writers,* First Series, edited by Wolfgang D. Elfe and James Hardin (1988)

70: *British Mystery Writers, 1860-1919,* edited by Bernard Benstock and Thomas F. Staley (1988)

(Continued on back endsheets)

Dictionary of Literary Biography • Volume Eighty-two

Chicano Writers
First Series

Chicano Writers
First Series

Edited by
Francisco A. Lomelí
University of California, Santa Barbara

and

Carl R. Shirley
University of South Carolina

8062

A Bruccoli Clark Layman Book
Gale Research Inc. • Book Tower • Detroit, Michigan 48226

Manufactured by Edwards Brothers, Inc.
Ann Arbor, Michigan
Printed in the United States of America

Copyright © 1989
GALE RESEARCH INC.

Library of Congress Cataloging-in-Publication Data

Chicano writers, first series/edited by/Francisco A. Lomelí
and Carl R. Shirley.
    p.   cm.–(Dictionary of literary biography; v. 82)
"A Bruccoli Clark Layman book."
Includes index.
ISBN 0-8103-4560-9
    1. American literature–Mexican American authors–
Dictionaries. 2. American literature–Mexican American
authors–Bio-bibliography. 3. Mexican American authors–
Biography–Dictionaries. 4. Mexican Americans in
literature–Dictionaries. I. Lomelí, Francisco A. II. Shirley,
Carl R., 1943- . III. Series: Dictionary of literary biogra-
phy; v. 82.
PS153.M4C48 1989
810'.9'86872–dc19   88-36536
                                                 CIP

Contents

Contents

Plan of the Series

... Almost the most prodigious asset of a country, and perhaps its most precious possession, is its native literary product—when that product is fine and noble and enduring.

Mark Twain*

The advisory board, the editors, and the publisher of the *Dictionary of Literary Biography* are joined in endorsing Mark Twain's declaration. The literature of a nation provides an inexhaustible resource of permanent worth. We intend to make literature and its creators better understood and more accessible to students and the reading public, while satisfying the standards of teachers and scholars.

To meet these requirements, *literary biography* has been construed in terms of the author's achievement. The most important thing about a writer is his writing. Accordingly, the entries in *DLB* are career biographies, tracing the development of the author's canon and the evolution of his reputation.

The purpose of *DLB* is not only to provide reliable information in a convenient format but also to place the figures in the larger perspective of literary history and to offer appraisals of their accomplishments by qualified scholars.

The publication plan for *DLB* resulted from two years of preparation. The project was proposed to Bruccoli Clark by Frederick G. Ruffner, president of the Gale Research Company, in November 1975. After specimen entries were prepared and typeset, an advisory board was formed to refine the entry format and develop the series rationale. In meetings held during 1976, the publisher, series editors, and advisory board approved the scheme for a comprehensive biographical dictionary of persons who contributed to North American literature. Editorial work on the first volume began in January 1977, and it was published in 1978. In order to make *DLB* more than a reference tool and to compile volumes that individually have claim to status as literary history, it was decided to organize volumes by topic, period, or genre. Each of these freestanding volumes provides a biographical-bibliographical guide and overview for a particular area of literature. We are convinced that this organization—as opposed to a single alphabet method—constitutes a valuable innovation in the presentation of reference material. The volume plan necessarily requires many decisions for the placement and treatment of authors who might properly be included in two or three volumes. In some instances a major figure will be included in separate volumes, but with different entries emphasizing the aspect of his career appropriate to each volume. Ernest Hemingway, for example, is represented in *American Writers in Paris, 1920-1939* by an entry focusing on his expatriate apprenticeship; he is also in *American Novelists, 1910-1945* with an entry surveying his entire career. Each volume includes a cumulative index of subject authors and articles. Comprehensive indexes to the entire series are planned.

With volume ten in 1982 it was decided to enlarge the scope of *DLB*. By the end of 1986 twenty-one volumes treating British literature had been published, and volumes for Commonwealth and Modern European literature were in progress. The series has been further augmented by the *DLB Yearbooks* (since 1981) which update published entries and add new entries to keep the *DLB* current with contemporary activity. There have also been *DLB Documentary Series* volumes which provide biographical and critical source materials for figures whose work is judged to have particular interest for students. One of these companion volumes is entirely devoted to Tennessee Williams.

We define literature as the *intellectual commerce of a nation:* not merely as belles lettres but as that ample and complex process by which ideas are generated, shaped, and transmitted. *DLB* entries are not limited to "creative writers" but extend to other figures who in their time and in their way influenced the mind of a people. Thus the series encompasses historians, journalists, publishers, and screenwriters. By this means readers of *DLB* may be aided to perceive litera-

*From an unpublished section of Mark Twain's autobiography, copyright © by the Mark Twain Company.

ture not as cult scripture in the keeping of intellectual high priests but firmly positioned at the center of a nation's life.

DLB includes the major writers appropriate to each volume and those standing in the ranks immediately behind them. Scholarly and critical counsel has been sought in deciding which minor figures to include and how full their entries should be. Wherever possible, useful references are made to figures who do not warrant separate entries.

Each *DLB* volume has a volume editor responsible for planning the volume, selecting the figures for inclusion, and assigning the entries. Volume editors are also responsible for preparing, where appropriate, appendices surveying the major periodicals and literary and intellectual movements for their volumes, as well as lists of further readings. Work on the series as a whole is coordinated at the Bruccoli Clark Layman editorial center in Columbia, South Carolina, where the editorial staff is responsible for accuracy of the published volumes.

One feature that distinguishes *DLB* is the illustration policy–its concern with the iconography of literature. Just as an author is influenced by his surroundings, so is the reader's understanding of the author enhanced by a knowledge of his environment. Therefore *DLB* volumes include not only drawings, paintings, and photographs of authors, often depicting them at various stages in their careers, but also illustrations of their families and places where they lived. Title pages are regularly reproduced in facsimile along with dust jackets for modern authors. The dust jackets are a special feature of *DLB* because they often document better than anything else the way in which an author's work was perceived in its own time. Specimens of the writers' manuscripts are included when feasible.

Samuel Johnson rightly decreed that "The chief glory of every people arises from its authors." The purpose of the *Dictionary of Literary Biography* is to compile literary history in the surest way available to us–by accurate and comprehensive treatment of the lives and work of those who contributed to it.

The *DLB* Advisory Board

Foreword

Just a decade ago critics were still debating as to the nature of Chicano literature and whether it was a recent literary phenomenon without antecedents or if it had deep roots in the distant past. Today with its origins and character well established, Chicano literature as a field of study is no longer questioned. It is accepted as that literature produced by writers of Mexican descent born in the United States, living here permanently, or having lived in the territory which until 1848 was part of Mexico.

In the 1960s the term *Chicano* began to be used by Americans of Mexican descent to designate their culture. Some critics apply the term only to the literature produced since then, but one of the fundamental ideas of the movement toward recognition of a Chicano culture has been the search for a foundation in the indigenous and revolutionary aspects of Mexican culture. Chicanos are the heirs to a rich heritage extending back for several centuries and anteceding that established by the English at Jamestown, Virginia, in 1607.

During the 1960s Chicanos tended to find their origins in the great Aztec and Maya civilizations of Central and Southern Mexico. For example, in the essay "Mexican Culture and the Mexican-American," (*El Grito,* Fall 1969), José de Anda, after tracing the development of Mexican culture, concludes by saying that the Chicano is the inheritor of that culture: "It has been said that a man without a past has no future. Mexico has a past with great and noble traditions. Mexican-Americans will learn about this past in order to be able to determine their future." Given his legacy from Mexico the Chicano has had to reconstruct his own history to show that there has existed an uninterrupted line of descent from that distant past to the present. A historical reconstruction has not been easy, due primarily to the neglect of studies about the Mexican people in the United States. A few decades ago no researcher or critic even considered the study of Chicano literature because to the literary historian, it just did not exist. If the histories and anthologies of American literature are examined, until very recently, no Chicano writer is mentioned. Nor is one mentioned in the histories and anthologies of Southwestern literature. In his study, *The Early Novel of the Southwest* (1961), Edwin W. Gaston, Jr., states that "The Southwestern novel is predominantly the work of Anglo-American writers, and as such has a particular correspondence with its national counterpart. It borrowed certain patterns of form and thought from American novel writing. A brief survey of the American novel will suggest many of the basic fictional patterns discernible in the Southwestern novel." Gaston does not consider the possibility that the Southwestern novel could have been influenced also by the novel of Mexico or Spain, but when he enumerates the characteristics of the Western novel, the reader acquainted with the novel of the Mexican Revolution of 1910 to 1920 immediately sees a strong relationship between the two subgenres. The Chicano novelist José Antonio Villarreal, when asked by Juan Bruce-Novoa (1980) about the relationship of Chicano literature to Mexican literature, answered, "Mexican literature is not that different from American literature, excepting for the idiom, because in the development of literature in the western world, Spain contributed to the development of the English novel."

Chicano and pre-Chicano writers have been ignored because of Anglo-American ethnocentricity. According to Gaston Spanish-Mexican exploration and settlement of the Southwest, despite its historical significance, "failed to build adequate expression in the early novel. . . . Just why the novelists ignored the spectacle of Spanish-Mexican exploration and settlement cannot be ascertained. The most logical assumption is that the writers, most of them Anglo-Americans, were interested in the affairs of their own race. . . ." As early as 1891 Charles F. Lummis, in his book *A New Mexico David* (not published until 1902), complained of the absence of a history of the United States based on the knowledge that history "began in the great Southwest. . . . I hope to see such a history, which will do justice to perhaps the most wonderful pioneers the world has ever produced; but it has not yet come. Why, there is not even one history which gives the correct date of the founding of Santa Fe, which was a Spanish city more than a decade before the landing at Plymouth Rock!"

His complaint, extended to include literary history, was also expressed by Mabel Major, the author of *Southwest Heritage* (1938), who wrote, "It is annoying to find American history and letters continually described as a style tradition with its genesis in the Mayflower and the Massachusetts Bay Psalm Book.... Villagrá's account of the heroic capture of Acoma by Zaldívar and seventy men bears comparison with the scaling of the heights outside Quebec by Wolfe if one keeps all the circumstances in mind."

In the field of literature, Chicano scholars and critics have begun to research the past literary production of the Mexican people in the United States, in spite of the fact that most of the early books and manuscripts generally are not available. The present dictionary is an example of the advances accomplished by recent Chicano literary criticism, which had its origins during the late 1960s in publications such as *El Grito*, a periodical founded in 1967 "to provide a forum for Mexican-American self definition and expression." In the summer 1970 issue of *El Grito* Herminio Ríos and Lupe Castillo published a listing of 195 Mexican-American newspapers, going back to 1842. In 1972 Ríos and Castillo published an expanded list, noting their purpose was to contribute "towards the eradication of the commonly disseminated but erroneous notions of the non-literate, non-literary, and non-intellectual Mexican-American" (*El Grito*, Summer 1972). In his article, "Apuntes para la documentación de la cultura chicana" (Notes for the *Documentation of Chicano Culture*, Winter 1971-1972), Ray Padilla attempted to establish a date of origin for Chicano culture as 1848, saying that this year, the date of the Treaty of Guadalupe Hidalgo, was as good as any other. Luis Leal's article, "Mexican-American Literature: A Historical Perspective" (*Revista Chicano-Riqueña*, 1973) examined so-called pre-Chicano materials and argued that there is an uninterrupted production of literary works from the sixteenth century to the present by authors writing about the Southwestern region of the United States which is now called Aztlán by Chicanos. Put simply, the article says the literature produced in the Southwest before 1848 can be included in a history of Chicano literature–in spite of the fact that the area was part of Spain until 1821 and of the Mexican Republic from that year until 1848–because it contains a sensibility that is different from that of the writers of Central Mexico.

By 1848, during the Hispanic period, the people living in what is now the Southwestern United States had developed a culture much different from that of Spain and Central Mexico. The region was almost isolated from the governing metropolis and therefore developed new social institutions, customs, attitudes, and values which have been of great importance in determining the nature of the culture of the contemporary Chicano.

By the time of the Mexican wars of independence, the inhabitants of the borderlands, due to neglect by Mexico City, had attained a high degree of self-sufficiency. Therefore the sentiment for the establishment of an independent political entity was prevalent. As early as 1813 Bernardo Gutiérrez de Lara declared Texas independent. He did not succeed, for he was soon defeated by the Spanish armies sent from Mexico. But the desire for independence did not disappear, and by 1836 some Mexicans favored the idea of declaring Texas independent from the Mexican republic. Three prominent Mexicans, among them the writer Lorenzo de Zavala, attended the convention in Washington, D.C., where the independence of Texas was made a reality. Zavala became Texas's first vice-president. Unforeseen by the Mexicans living in Texas was the 1845 annexation of the Texas republic into the expanding United States, and the elimination of Mexicans from most government positions after the Mexican War ended in 1848.

After 1848 writers in the Southwest continued to use the Spanish language, but later generations began to transfer to the use of English. In 1889 the New Mexican poet Jesús María Alarid lamented the fact that the Spanish language was being supplanted by English. In one of his many Spanish poems he touches upon this topic:

> Hermoso idioma español
> ¿Qué te quieren proscribir?
> Yo creo que no hay razón
> que tú dejes de existir.
> (Are they going to banish you,
> my beautiful Spanish language?
> There is not a valid reason
> Why you should not endure)

Before 1910 the Spanish language in the Southwest was slowly disappearing, but the Mexican Revolution of 1910 to 1920, World War II, and agricultural and industrial expansion in the United States resulted in a massive emigration from Mexico to the borderlands, which reinforced the Spanish language and renewed other ties with Mexico. In the literary field, the influence of Mexican writers such as Ricardo Flores Magón, José Vasconcelos, and other exiled revolutionaries, some of whom founded Spanish language newspapers and publishing houses in the United States, was decisive. The 1920s marked the first period of pre-Chicano literary production. Unfortunately, this period has not been well researched. The large number of literary contributions which appeared in such newspapers as *La Prensa* in San Antonio, Texas, and *La Opinión* in Los Angeles, California, have not been collected and studied. The same can be said of books published in the period, which, with few exceptions, have not been identified.

The children of the immigrants that came to the Southwest from Mexico during the first two decades of the twentieth century formed a new society made up of native born Americans of Mexican descent, or Mexican-Americans, often called *pochos* by the people of greater Mexico, a term which, unlike the word *Chicano*, did not prevail. The writers of the 1930s and 1940s usually wrote in English and were influenced mostly by American and English letters. Typical of the literature of this period are the works of Fray Angélico Chávez, author of several books of poetry, a novel, and essays on cultural topics. During the same period literary criticism was born, although it was oriented toward the study of the linguistic problems of Mexican-Americans, as well as folklore. Among the pioneer scholars the names of Aurelio M. Espinosa and Arthur Campa stand out. Both writers gave great impulse to the study of the manifestations of popular forms of literature, such as the *romance* (popular narrative poem), the *corrido* (ballad) and the *décima* (stanza of ten octosyllabic lines). They also unearthed some important dramatic pieces of the early nineteenth century, thus documenting the existence of a theater in the Southwest. Espinosa also wrote a novel of early life in California, *Conchita Argüello* (1938).

With the zoot suit riots of 1942 in Los Angeles and World War II Mexican-Americans developed ethnic consciousness. Chicano veterans often felt that they were being excluded from the economic and social benefits which resulted from winning the war. To improve their lot they took advantage of the G.I. bill to further their education, participated in politics, and created organizations such as the American G.I. Forum, founded in Corpus Christi, Texas, in 1948, by Héctor García. From the postwar generation came the first important Chicano writers, who produced their best work during the late 1940s and the 1950s. In general the tendency of Chicano writers was to accept the idea of total assimilation into the majority culture. Significant writers were John Rechy, Floyd Salas, and Richard Vázquez—who wrote in English. Also representative of this period are the short stories of Mario Suárez, and the novels *El Coyote the Rebel* (1947), by Luis Pérez, and *Pocho* (1959), by José Antonio Villarreal, both published nationally. The hero in Pérez's novel is a young Mexican revolutionary who deserts and goes to Arizona where he works as a *campesino* (farmhand). He moves to California where he is able to study and finish high school. In Villarreal's novel the father of the hero goes to California when Francisco Villa, under whom he was fighting, is defeated. His son Richard, born there, becomes thoroughly assimilated, and the novel ends when he joins the navy.

Among the scholars of the postwar generation are Carlos Castañeda, Ernesto Galarza, Américo Paredes, George I. Sánchez, and Juan B. Rael, all of them active in supporting the Chicano cause with research in history, labor, folklore, and education. It was a brilliant generation whose works gave Chicano scholarship respectability and established the basis upon which contemporary Chicano studies have been built.

The year 1965 marks an event that was influential in the creation of a new political and literary trend in the history of the Chicanos. César Chávez and his National Farm Workers Association, frustrated by the growers in their effort to unionize farm workers, began a grape strike and marched from Delano, California, to the state capitol in Sacramento to bring the plight of the farm workers to the attention of the nation. Luis Valdez, who joined Chávez, organized the Teatro Campesino (Farm Workers' Theater) with the purpose of making the Chicano and Mexican farm workers politically conscious, as well as teaching them the advantages of joining the farm workers union. The literature produced during the late 1960s and 1970s is one of confrontation, motivated by the desire to help the Chicanos, especially the campesinos. At the same time, it tried to document life in the barrio (neighborhood) with the object of establishing communal identity. This is the literature that is properly called *Chicano*. In an essay published in 1982, "Chicano Literature: The Establishment of Community,"

Tomás Rivera (author of the novel ". . . *y no se lo tragó la tierra,*" 1971) stated that "in the last ten years Chicano literature has established community, myth and language. Or at a minimum, it has reflected the urge and desire to establish such elements of the Chicano ethnic group."

During the late 1960s an important change in ideology took place among Chicano intellectuals who, disillusioned with the attitude of the publishing houses, the periodicals, and the critics, decided to declare their independence and establish their own media outlets. In 1967 the editors of *El Grito* stated that they intended to reaffirm their identity by refusing to disappear into the great American melting pot. The editors of *El Grito* were successful in establishing their own editorial house, Quinto Sol Publications, and in editing the anthology *El Espejo/The Mirror* (1969), which for the first time brought to the attention of the general public the fact that Chicanos had a literature worth reading. Important also was the establishment of the Premio Quinto Sol, an award which gave impetus to the establishment of Chicano literature. The first prizes (1971, 1972, and 1973) were granted to three novels that opened new paths in Chicano narrative, and which are among the most representative contemporary Chicano novels. Two of them, Rivera's ". . . *y no se lo tragó la tierra*" (1971) and Rolando Hinojosa-Smith's *Estampas del valle y otras obras* (1973), are, significantly, written in Spanish, and the other, Rudolfo Anaya's *Bless Me, Ultima* (1972), in English. The example set by *El Grito* and the fact that Chicano writers now had their own publishing houses gave a tremendous impetus to the development of Chicano literature, which attained a high level of accomplishment both in creative writing and literary criticism. During the decade of the 1970s Chicanos reaffirmed their identity and became active producers of significant works in art and literature. The Chicano writer thus gained a new confidence in his ability to communicate to the public. He was proud to use both English and Spanish, and even a combination of both languages, to express himself, as Alurista (Alberto B. Urista) aptly demonstrated, without giving up aesthetic value. At the same time, the Chicano writer often found his inspiration in Mexico's ancient past, giving it form in his verse or prose through the use of myths, legends, and folktales as metaphors to express his contemporary place in American society.

Chicano literature in the 1980s has not been as fruitful as that of the 1970s, but its criticism flourishes. Significant fiction has been published indicating new trends. Most significant is the return to the use of English as a predominant means of expression. Some of the younger writers (for example, Gary Soto, Arturo Islas, and Richard Rodriguez) prefer English to Spanish. Even those who began writing in Spanish, as, for instance, Hinojosa-Smith, are now writing in English. Since the decade is not yet over, it remains to be seen if this trend will continue. There is no question, however, that the field of literary criticism, which had begun in the 1970s when critics were preoccupied with the reconstruction of the historical past, is now firmly established. The first bibliography dedicated exclusively to Chicano writers was that of Guillermo Rojas, "Towards a Chicano/Raza Bibliography: Drama, Prose, Poetry," published in *El Grito* (December 1973). In his introduction Rojas states after he examined bibliographies from the period 1965 to 1972: "We have reviewed more than 30 works of this nature and it is sad indeed that no discrimination was implemented in the preparation of these guideless guides. It is for this very reason that we decided to review all of the Chicano journals, newspapers, bulletins and newsletters published in the Southwest by Chicanos." Rojas's pioneer work has served as a model and has inspired others to amplify it. Not all bibliographers have followed his original plan to list only Chicano writers of literature. Presently, there is an extensive bibliography of Chicano creative writing (by Roberto G. Trujillo and André S. Rodríguez), and literary criticism (Ernestina N. Eger). These two bibliographies have done much to give Chicano literature a legitimate standing among world literatures. They are indispensable today for the literary critic whose task now is to search deeper to identify earlier writers and to reconstruct a complete history.

Dictionaries of Chicano literature are of very recent origin. Francisco A. Lomelí and Donaldo W. Urioste published what could be called the first in the field, *Chicano Perspectives in Literature* (1976). Although it is subtitled "A Critical and Annotated Bibliography," it is much more than that, since it includes information about the writers as well as short appreciations of their works. The format is that of a dictionary, as authors are listed alphabetically, according to genre. The volume lists thirty-nine poets, twenty-one fiction writers (novels and short fiction), four dramatists, twenty-three editors and compilers of anthologies, seven critics, and five authors of *literatura chicanesca,* a classification used here for the first time to refer to non-Chicano writers who write about Chicano life. An important characteristic of the book is the emphasis given to the literature published by Chicanos during the six years 1970 to 1976. Only eighteen of the works listed in the volume were published before 1970. Charles M. Tatum's *A Selected and Annotated Bibliography of Chicano Studies* was also published in 1976. In the section dedicated to literature he lists ninety-eight items classified by genre. None, however, is earlier than the late 1960s, and most belong to the 1970s. He does include useful lists of anthologies, bibliographies, and literary criticism.

Lomelí and Julio A. Martínez's *Chicano Literature: A Reference Guide* (1985) is much more extensive than Lomelí's first bibliography. In general the presentation is much more scholarly. Included are articles on Chicano poetry, literary criticism, philosophy, theater, the novel, women in Chicano literature, Chicano children's literature, and surveys tracing the development of Chicano literature from the sixteenth century to the present. In the introduction the editors state that they have accepted a broad definition of Chicano literature, regarding it as "the literary output of Mexican Americans since 1848, with backgrounds and traditions as far back as the sixteenth century." With the exception of Eusebio Chacón no early writers are covered in detail.

However, in the general surveys the background and traditions of Chicano literature are well documented. This large volume ends with a useful chronology of Chicano literature, a glossary of literary items, a bibliography of general works, an index, and a list of forty-one contributors, among whom are the leading Chicano critics.

Carl R. Shirley and Paula W. Shirley's *Understanding Chicano Literature* (1988) is a paperback survey of the field designed for students and non-academic readers. There is an extensive annotated reading list at the end of the volume.

The present *Dictionary of Literary Biography* represents another step forward in Chicano literary criticism. It will become an invaluable research tool for scholars and a source of information for the general reader of Chicano literature, principally due to the numerous authors included. Of particular importance is the large number of critics who have contributed to make this dictionary the most complete in the field. Although the methodology applied by each contributor may vary, in general the volume reflects a consensus of opinion regarding Chicano literary criticism. The objectivity, the effort to present accurate information, and the desire to arrive at a balanced portrait of the authors demonstrate that Chicano literary criticism has established a solid foundation.

–Luis Leal

Preface

Chicano Writers, First Series marks an important step in the evolution of Chicano literature and criticism. Although much research has been published in the field over the last few years, this volume gathers for the first time fifty-two biographical/critical essays representing a broad cross section of authors who have contributed to the growing body of Chicano literature. Included here are many of the leading writers–novelists, poets, short-story writers, dramatists–but not all. A second series "Chicano Writers" volume is in progress.

Since some readers may be unaware of what a Chicano is, a brief note of explanation is in order. Chicanos are people who live in the United States, citizens for the most part, who are of Mexican heritage. Some can trace their families' residence here for over four hundred years, while some are relative newcomers. The word itself is probably derived from *mexicano*, which comes from *mexica* (pronounced "meshica") who are generally known as Aztecs. The term was widely used by the 1950s, sometimes in a pejorative sense. As an ethnic term it became popular in the 1960s as Chicanos sought political and social reforms. For many, the designation Chicano has become a source of pride, while other people (including some authors) resent the label, still viewing it as pejorative or as linking them to a political movement with which they do not wish to be identified. Some writers of Mexican origin prefer other terms–Mexican-American, Latino, Californio, to cite a few; others who are of mixed ethnic heritage prefer not to be distinguished from the larger society of the United States. In addition, there is a handful of writers whose heritage is quite obviously not Mexican, but whose works are usually discussed by critics as related to Chicano (sometimes called Chicanesque). For example, Jim Sagel and Chester Seltzer (who wrote under the name Amado Muro) are Anglo writers whose work treats Chicano subjects and themes; consequently, most critics treat their writing as part of the corpus of Chicano literature.

Deciding exactly what constitutes Chicano literature can also be a troublesome task, as there

are varying opinions. Julio A. Martínez and Francisco A. Lomelí described it in *Chicano Literature: A Reference Guide* (1985) as literature "written since 1848 by Americans of Mexican descent or by Mexicans in the United States who write about the Mexican-American experience." In 1848 the United States obtained most of the southwestern states–Arizona, California, New Mexico, parts of Colorado, Nevada, and Texas–from Mexico, and the Mexicans living in those regions became American citizens. The editors of this volume have accepted Martínez and Lomelí's definition and, following the lead of the majority of scholars, have also included here other writers whose work is usually treated under the rubric Chicano.

Because of the distinct social and literary traditions of the Chicano people, the volumes on Chicano writers stand in marked contrast to other volumes in the *DLB* series. Chicano literature, the aesthetic principles that define it, and the body of criticism that supports it resist comparison to what may be called mainstream American literature; indeed, Chicano writing is an assertive declaration of cultural identity that frequently assumes validity by its independence from Anglo traditions and standards. Throughout the 140-year history of Chicano literature, its writers have been driven in large degree by their responses to social oppression and by their attempts to define and embrace their cultural heritage. The result is a literature that is written for the people it is written about and that is, as a result, often elusive to other readers.

The *DLB* volumes on Chicano writers are as significant for their value as social history as they are for their merit as literary history. The process by which literature is used by a people to declare their cultural identity is a complex one involving not only writers and their works but also readers, the means by which works are made available to them, the critical responses of ethnic scholars, and the reactions of what may be perceived as the literary establishment. Chicano writers have been criticized for their failure to adapt to mainstream standards. They answer by questioning the validity of a canon of national literature that excludes the Mexican experience in the United States and by denying the authority of an aesthetic standard that denies them their distinct voice. The debate about the viability of Chicano writing (as well as the criticism it stimulates) has often resorted to social and political issues and is still being resolved. Yet precedent teaches us that emerging ethnic literatures bear close scrutiny: they provide the energy and creative force that mold the future.

–Francisco A. Lomelí and Carl R. Shirley

Acknowledgments

This book was produced by Bruccoli Clark Layman, Inc. Karen L. Rood is senior editor for the *Dictionary of Literary Biography* series. Charles Lee Egleston was the in-house editor.

Production coordinator is Kimberly Casey. System manager is Robert A. Folts. Art supervisor is Susan Todd. Penney L. Haughton is responsible for layout and graphics. Copyediting supervisor is Joan M. Prince. Typesetting supervisor is Kathleen M. Flanagan. William Adams, Laura Ingram, and Michael D. Senecal are editorial associates. The production staff includes Rowena Betts, Charles D. Brower, Joseph M. Bruccoli, Amanda Caulley, Teresa Chaney, Patricia Coate, Mary Colborn, Sarah A. Estes, Brian A. Glassman, Cynthia Hallman, Kathy S. Merlette, Sheri Beckett Neal, and Virginia Smith. Jean W. Ross is permissions editor.

Walter W. Ross and Jennifer Toth did the library research with the assistance of the reference staff at the Thomas Cooper Library of the University of South Carolina: Daniel Boice, Cathy Eckman, Gary Geer, Cathie Gottlieb, David L. Haggard, Jens Holley, Dennis Isbell, Jackie Kinder, Marcia Martin, Jean Rhyne, Beverly Steele, Ellen Tillett, Carol Tobin, and Virginia Weathers.

For information on archival holdings the editors are grateful to Joanne Colley, Stella De Sa Rego, and Rose Díaz, special collections librarians, University of New Mexico, Albuquerque, General Library, Special Collections Department; Margo Gutiérrez, Mexican American Studies librarian, The General Libraries, University of Texas at Austin; Salvador Güereña, Chicano Studies librarian–unit head, Colección Tloque Nahuaque, University Library, University of California, Santa Barbara; Roberto G. Trujillo, curator, Mexican American Collections, Stanford University Libraries, Stanford University; Mary Ann Latham, secretary to Alumni Relations, University of Dubuque, Dubuque, Iowa; Geoffrey Rips, editor, *Texas Observer*, Austin, Texas; and Clifford Wurfel and Armand Martinez Standifird, Special Collections, University of California, Riverside.

For illustrative material the editors thank Karen Van Hooft, Bilingual Review Press, Arizona State University, Tempe, Arizona; Marina Tristán, Program Director, Arte Publico Press, University of Houston, Houston, Texas; Ellen Robertson, University of Colorado, Boulder; Lucy Coppel, University of California, Santa Barbara; Rosemary Catacalos, Literature Program Director, Guadalupe Cultural Arts Center, San Antonio, Texas; the University of California, Santa Barbara; and the University of California, Riverside.

Dictionary of Literary Biography • Volume Eighty-two

Chicano Writers
First Series

Dictionary of Literary Biography

Oscar Zeta Acosta
(8 April 1935?-)

Joe D. Rodríguez
San Diego State University

BOOKS: *The Autobiography of a Brown Buffalo* (San Francisco: Straight Arrow, 1972);
The Revolt of the Cockroach People (San Francisco: Straight Arrow, 1973).

OTHER: "Perla Is a Pig," in *Voices of Aztlán: Chicano Literature of Today*, edited by Dorothy E. Harth and Lewis M. Baldwin (New York: Mentor, 1974), pp. 28-48.

PERIODICAL PUBLICATIONS: "Tres Cartas de Zeta," *Con Safos*, 2, no. 6 (1970): 29-31;
"The Autobiography of a Brown Buffalo," *Con Safos*, 2 (Winter 1971): 34-46.

Oscar Zeta Acosta is a controversial Chicano author whose work focuses upon ethnicity and the ways that people of Mexican ancestry in the United States forge an awareness of themselves. His books evoke an extremely volatile period of United States history, the 1960s and early 1970s, when issues such as civil unrest, the Vietnam War, and social reform captured the attention of many artists and intellectuals. He was a lawyer as well as a writer, and he defended different groups of Chicano political activists during acrimonious and bitterly contested trials. His writing drew upon iconoclastic sources including Jack Kerouac, Henry Miller, and gonzo journalism and helped establish a polemical style of Chicano prose. Acosta constantly reminded readers of his intention to shock and engage them with his choice of subject and language as well as his sense of humor. Acosta often characterized writing as insurrection against the status quo.

Oscar Zeta Acosta (courtesy of Marco Acosta)

Any biography of Acosta has to acknowledge perhaps the only sure fact about him. In the early 1970s he went to Mexico and disappeared, an act so characteristic of him that it appears staged. Yet he has never resurfaced, and no one has explained what happened to him. His novels offer points for conjecture. He might have had a nervous breakdown and decided never to re-

3

turn to the United States. He may have over-dosed on drugs and alcohol. He made enemies because of his courtroom battles and political statements, and he could have been assassinated. Or he might have tried to make a quick fortune dealing drugs and met with foul play. Marco Acosta, his son, believes he was the last to hear from him. In May 1974 he telephoned from Mazatlán, Sinaloa. He told his son he was about to board a boat full of white snow. In his fiction Acosta uses his life story as a strategy, a means to put on different guises in order to play the literary anthropologist. He reminds readers that he is an anti-intellectual: statements about the world cannot be separated from the points of view of the people who make them, and symbols need to be tied to behavior.

The relationship between Acosta the writer and Acosta the subject in his novelistic autobiographies is difficult to unravel. Acosta's work is about himself. One of his major concerns is his own transformation from a confused and alienated person of Mexican descent to a Chicano lawyer-activist. Acosta presents himself as a champion of his people who demands fair treatment and equal opportunity. In using his life story as a means to convey his ideas and beliefs, his work sometimes ignores biographical information or alters it. Some details are imprecise. For example, his birth is recorded in El Paso, Texas, on 8 April 1935. On his application for the California bar, he recorded his birthday as 6 April 1935. In Acosta's first novel-autobiography, *The Autobiography of a Brown Buffalo* (1972), he offers 8 April 1934, 1935, and 1936. The reader who assumes that literature is fiction and distinct from the writer has difficulties with Acosta, who blends journalism and fiction in his works.

In *The Autobiography of a Brown Buffalo* Acosta mentions that his father was descended from Indians of Durango, Mexico. His mother, a naturalized Texan whose family was among the working poor, struggled to improve the quality of her life and encouraged him to better his position in society. When his father was drafted during World War II, Acosta helped take care of the household. The family moved to a small rural barrio in the San Joaquin Valley in central California near Modesto when he was a youngster. Acosta sometimes felt like an outsider, and there are signs in his works of alienation, mistrust, and a sense of dislocation which relate to childhood experiences. He was an intelligent and sensitive student who appears to have cultivated a streak of

Acosta's wife, Betty, circa 1957 (courtesy of Marco Acosta)

brashness and bravado. In high school he began to abuse alcohol. Around age eighteen he began to experience symptoms of ulcers that troubled him throughout his life. After high school Acosta joined the air force, demonstrating that he was able to accept discipline and adapt to regulations despite his later claims that he was a *vato loco* (wild street dude). He worked his way through college, went to law school, and was admitted to the California bar on 28 June 1966. In 1967 he was an attorney for an antipoverty agency in Oakland, California.

In the 1960s in Los Angeles there was a heightened interest in ethnicity. A group of Chicanos founded the magazine *Con Safos* in order to give Chicanos a forum and to call attention to their political and cultural agendas. Acosta's short story "Perla Is a Pig" (collected in *Voices of Aztlán*, 1974) was published by the magazine in 1970. "Perla Is a Pig" analyzes reverse discrimination, how people of Mexican ancestry discriminate against one of their own because of appearance and the refusal to conform. It reminds readers that simply being a victim of race prejudice does not automatically free someone of prejudiced behavior against others. At about the same time the story was published, Acosta added *Zeta* (perhaps taken from the name of a Mexican revolutionary he heard about in a film) to his name because he experienced a transformation. Assimilation to him had meant the rejection of Mexican culture and the Spanish language. For him the name signified that he had crossed a threshold in terms of identifying with Chicanos. The story shows that in spite of his new identity, Acosta had not given himself over to labels and slogans. There is another important biographical element in "Perla Is a Pig." During his tour of service in Latin America Acosta converted to Protestantism. He became a Baptist minister and proselytized among local people. Although at the end of *The Autobiography of a Brown Buffalo* he denounces Christianity as a "white man's religion," at the time he studied the Bible extensively. "Perla Is a Pig" can be interpreted as a story built upon the religious maxim about the futility of casting pearls before swine. Huero, the protagonist, sacrifices his pig Perla in order to gain the acceptance of the barrio community. He looks different from other Mexicans and is iconoclastic. However, malicious rumors and *chisme* (idle gossip) cause his plan to backfire, and he is driven into exile. In *The Autobiography of a Brown Buffalo* Acosta mentions a novel, "My Cart for My Casket," which was never published. "Perla Is a Pig" was probably excerpted from the novel. It is his most polished literary effort.

At about the time "Perla Is a Pig" was published, Acosta became involved with the Chicano Resurgence. He was engaged in battles over charges that education in the United States and grand jury selection in Los Angeles were culture-specific and discriminatory, and he was the lead attorney in the landmark case *Castro* v. *the Superior Court of Los Angeles*. Salvatorre Castro, a high-school teacher, and others were indicted on charges arising out of high school walkouts connected with protests against inferior education. Castro and others were charged with disturbing the peace and indicted on felony conspiracy charges for allegedly planning to disrupt various high schools. In a precedent-setting decision which involved constitutional first amendment rights of free speech and assembly, the California State Court of Appeals ruled that the felony conspiracy charges be quashed, because stricter standards of proof were necessary in order to protect first amendment rights. Acosta also was the lead at-

torney in the case of *Carlos Montez et al.* v. *the Superior Court of Los Angeles County*. He argued that Spanish-surnamed Mexican-American citizens had been systematically excluded from participating in the Los Angeles County grand jury.

After "Perla Is a Pig" Acosta's work changed dramatically. Undoubtedly, his courtroom work galvanized his political interests and shaped his art, but another important influence was the well-known gonzo journalist Hunter S. Thompson. In *The Autobiography of a Brown Buffalo* Acosta suggests that he first met Thompson (who appears as the pseudonymous journalist Stonewall in Acosta's second and last novel, *The Revolt of the Cockroach People*, 1973) in 1967 during a cross-country odyssey to find himself. Gonzo, a character based on Acosta, appears as Raoul Duke's three-hundred-pound Samoan attorney in Thompson's report-fantasy *Fear and Loathing in Las Vegas* (1972). In Thompson's book neither Raoul Duke nor his attorney are sympathetic characters. Acosta appears as a drug-addled, cynical, unpredictable, and dangerous buffoon. No trace of social conscience, no pride in ethnicity, and a lack of basic civility characterize the portrait.

The Autobiography of a Brown Buffalo is a Chicano odyssey of self-discovery in which Acosta fictionalizes his life story to show how an alienated lawyer of Mexican ancestry in an Oakland antipoverty agency with no sense of purpose or identity, and who survives on drugs, alcohol, and psychoanalysis, is transformed into a Chicano activist. He wants to write but is blocked. Bleeding ulcers, anxiety, and impotence drive him to despair, and he takes to the road to save his life. At the end of the book the protagonist adopts a new name, Zeta, which underscores that he is now an advocate for Chicanos and someone who affirms his Mexican roots. Acosta, the character, begins his odyssey in Oakland. Later he travels to Colorado, and then he goes to El Paso, Texas, his birthplace. As he travels, the protagonist learns who he is by reflecting upon his education and mulling over the lessons which the road presents. In grade school he was taught to feel inferior. In high school he suffered from racism. In college he had two interests, mathematics and writing, and these different ways of thinking remind him that there are distinct, sometimes irreconcilable, ways of considering experience. The protagonist tells the reader that he enjoyed the formal symmetry and symbolic precision of numbers. Euclidian geometry develops inexorably from a few precepts; axioms spring from these initial assump-

Acosta with his father and son on the day he graduated from law school, mid 1960s (courtesy of Marco Acosta)

tions with tautological or circular exactness. However, the protagonist comes to understand that creating a sense of peoplehood requires a different type of thinking. He wonders if there is a way of thinking and presenting ideas which can unify people who share a multiple sense of peoplehood and a syncretic sense of self. As a law student he was trained to think logically and dispassionately. As a lawyer for a poverty agency, however, he finds that the courtroom does not work like a textbook.

Even at the beginning of *The Autobiography of a Brown Buffalo*, before his transformation from the confused lawyer to the dynamic Zeta, Acosta (the main character) lives according to the Sapir-Whorf hypothesis. This model proposes that language and culture shape worldview so that the way people see the world is a function of the culture and language from which they spring. What is a hypothesis for social scientists is a fact for the character Zeta/Acosta. His sense of the world changes radically depending upon social context. For example, after meeting a gonzo journalist (a thinly disguised Thompson), he goes berserk. Because the Sapir-Whorf hypothesis ob-

sesses him, the main character is able only to construct an ethnic system of communicating ideas because he asserts that reality does not exist. Fact cannot be separated from a specific point of view. A mestizo has different cultural outlooks, and thus any outlook has to consider not only the vista that is opened but the blind spots as well.

While he is on the road, the confused protagonist considers different ways of interpreting experience and understanding who he is. He had suffered several nervous breakdowns, had been hospitalized, and had been seeing a psychiatrist, Dr. Serbin, a Freudian who told him that his problems with his sexuality and facing his Mexican background are the same. Also, the main character had been converted from Roman Catholicism to Protestantism and had sought converts in Panama as a Baptist minister. But he had a crisis of faith and gave up Christianity. He is extremely intelligent and able to write well and speak forcefully, and he wants to believe in a cause. He sorts through and tries various ideologies and systems of belief but is unable to find himself.

Only at the end of *The Autobiography of a Brown Buffalo* is the main character, Acosta, able

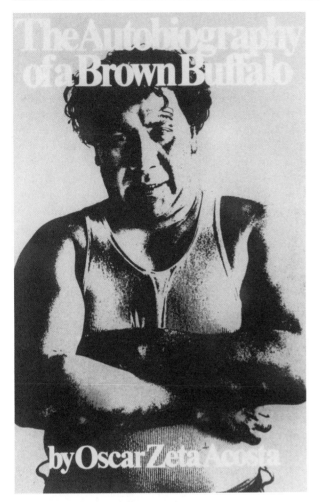

Dust jacket for Acosta's first autobiographical novel, which appeared in 1972

to give up alcohol and drugs and find a measure of peace. Abruptly the voice of Zeta proclaims that ethnic identity is his platform and program for health, selfhood, and social change. The main figure has had to address his mixed cultural legacy in order to negotiate his identity. He is the product of many distinct cultures and yet he has to live in the Anglo tradition because he is a citizen of the United States. He has dealt with paranoia and the fear that he is an outsider in his own country. Sometimes Acosta has to reconcile oppositions: for example, he has taken advantage of educational opportunities and has improved his standard of living, yet he realizes that many from his background are trapped. The character has had to construct who he is moment by moment. He determines that a mestizo has distinct cultural perspectives and reality is multiple for him. For example, at the end of the novel, when the protagonist visits Mexico to explore his

roots, he is told to learn his father's language (Spanish). When he tries to cross the border at El Paso/Juárez, an immigration agent tells him to prove that he is a United States citizen because he does not look American.

Acosta the writer draws upon diverse traditions: the Spanish picaresque novel, gonzo journalism, the folklore of the American Indian, the Mexican *corrido* (folk ballad), and the novels of Henry Miller and Jack Kerouac. Sometimes he uses certain legacies and ignores others. For example, when he considers the history of the Southwest, he adopts a Mexican perspective to critique the United States doctrine of Manifest Destiny.

When *The Autobiography of a Brown Buffalo* first appeared, reviews in *Choice* (May 1973) and by Joseph Kanon in *Saturday Review* (December 1972) hailed the book as a powerful manifesto of the Chicano Movement. Both reviews gave the work national exposure, treating *The Autobiography of a Brown Buffalo* as both an expression of a people and of a historical moment in the United States. Norman D. Smith's article in the *Latin American Literary Review* (Spring-Summer 1977) analyzes how the symbol of Aztlán, the mythical homeland of the Aztecs identified with the Southwest of the United States, ignited Acosta's demands for fairness and equal opportunity on behalf of Chicanos. An essay in *Explorations in Ethnic Studies* (July 1981) by Joe D. Rodríguez weighs Acosta's crisis of faith in the work and considers whether peoplehood replaces religious belief. Rodríguez's essay in the *Denver Quarterly* (Fall 1981) studies the structure of the work. Taking to the road is Acosta's version of a frontier saga. Instead of the wilderness or untamed open space, the protagonist must work with the premise that reality is constructed and that realization involves the fear and uncertainty that comes with uncharted territory. Rodríguez's essay in *Revista Chicano-Riqueña* (Spring 1984) considers parallels between the ways the Puerto Rican author Piri Thomas and Acosta use multiple cultural backgrounds to create the self in their novels.

At the end of *The Autobiography of a Brown Buffalo* the character Zeta Acosta abruptly cuts short his life story and proclaims that more will follow. *The Revolt of the Cockroach People* is the sequel. Published at about the time of Acosta's disappearance, the novel takes the ethnic and revolutionary credo at the end of *The Autobiography of a Brown Buffalo* into the political arena in Los Angeles during a period when the city is literally in flames. *The Revolt of the Cockroach Peo-*

Acosta in the early 1970s (photo copyright © Annie Leibovitz/ Contact Press Images)

ple is not as much a novel in the conventional sense as a first-person account of events from the perspective of a Chicano lawyer Buffalo Zeta Brown, whose day-to-day life is like surviving under siege. This book also poses the same dilemma as *The Autobiography of a Brown Buffalo:* how to distinguish the writer Acosta from his central figure, Buffalo Zeta Brown. For example, Oscar Zeta Acosta was the attorney who defended cases much like those which appear in the book. Acosta ran for sheriff of Los Angeles County as does his protagonist, Buffalo Zeta Brown. While Acosta's actual biography and the novel share many parallels, Acosta the writer never uses his name in *The Revolt of the Cockroach People*, as he does in *The Autobiography of a Brown Buffalo*. His motive appears to have been avoiding prosecution and civil liability. *The Revolt of the Cockroach People* conveys a powerful immediacy: challenges are raised to institutions such as religion, the courts, and schools. Demonstrations are

launched, bombs thrown, people killed. The distinction between fiction and actual events blurs. The work opens with a demonstration in a cathedral and closes with a murder in a courthouse. The Saint Basil Twenty-One are indicted for disrupting religious services on Christmas Eve 1968. Buffalo Zeta Brown not only handles this controversial case but many others. For example, he defends clients who protest against inferior education and represents the Tooner Flats Seven, who have been charged with rioting when parts of the Los Angeles barrio are put to the torch during demonstrations protesting the Vietnam War and the high numbers of combat casualties of Mexican-American descent. He also demands a coroner's inquest into the death of a Chicano prisoner. During the 1960s and early 1970s people of Mexican ancestry made up a significant percentage of the population in Los Angeles. *The Revolt of the Cockroach People* documents how this population was roused by small numbers of activists, typified by Brown, who wanted to attract the media and raise the consciousness of Latinos not just in Los Angeles but throughout the Southwest and the United States as a whole.

Buffalo Zeta Brown's state of mind and the story of his life literally come unglued in the course of the novel. Too much happens in court, in the community, and in his private life for him to function with equanimity. The wild, frantic, self-glorifying quality of the book intensifies the question of how much of the work is fact and how much is fiction. It is impossible to read *The Revolt of the Cockroach People* without looking for explanations for Acosta's actual disappearance in the early 1970s. At the end of the novel, during a disturbance in East Los Angeles, a police officer fires blindly through a doorway and kills a journalist, Roland Zanzibar. This incident closely parallels the actual shooting of the award-winning correspondent Reuben Salazar. The police have one version of the killing, justifiable homicide in the line of duty. They see what they consider a riot and feel caught up in urban guerrilla warfare. Buffalo Zeta Brown sees the streets of Los Angeles turn into Vietnam. In his eyes, Zanzibar is murdered and he fears genocide. Images of death appear everywhere. Early in the novel, he goes to Mexico to unwind. Instead, his twin brother tells him his work in the courtroom and organizing the community is posturing, and until he is willing to die for his beliefs, he is a charlatan. By the end of the book, Buffalo Zeta Brown's thinking appears to be frozen, and sanity deserts him. He is overwhelmed by the fact that people of Mexican ancestry do not automatically unite or see eye to eye. His sister, for example, is a consumer, not a Chicana. The protagonist finds out that Chicano groups are infiltrated by police informers. He feels personally betrayed and is unable to see why people who share the same ancestry, blood, or social standing do not necessarily see the world in the same way.

Sam Blazer's review of *The Revolt of the Cockroach People* (13 April 1974) suggests that at least three issues raised in *The Autobiography of a Brown Buffalo* are transformed by politics in latter work and are no longer simply personal or literary statements about ethnicity. Negotiating identity in terms of a mixed cultural legacy becomes a matter of brokering alliances in a multicultural society. The issue of finding one's voice as a member of a unique ethnic group becomes the task of constructing an ethnic discourse that sways distinct factions. The question of how to tie a sense of peoplehood to appropriate behavior becomes a discussion of how to improve society through group action.

The Los Angeles of *The Revolt of the Cockroach People* is a multicultural society, as Smith points out. Brown believes that social justice, equality, and fair treatment under the law should be the norm. He wins partial victories because a black woman finds merit in the argument that dissent must be protected even if church services are disturbed, because a Japanese-American coroner allows him to have a body exhumed when he questions the death of a Chicano prisoner, and because his friends include *vatos locos, cholos* (neighborhood buddies), and *pintos* (ex-convicts), as well as famous personalities.

Thompson's reminiscence about Acosta in *Rolling Stone* (15 December 1977) speculates why he vanished and never reappeared. He recalls Acosta's penchant for telling his life story to anyone within earshot: doubts about his masculinity, bouts of paranoia, and fears of being driven mad by society–nothing was held back. Scatological details, ribald remarks, and gallows humor were Acosta's way of conveying who he was, according to Thompson. Acosta demanded that his readers consider his life as his work. Thompson argues that Acosta's writing is as much a chronicle of actual experience as it is a sort of literary anthropology which treats self-awareness as a process of mutual discovery. Acosta's characters assume different personalities depending upon whom they are with. Thompson recalls that Acosta used

the label *Samoan* not only to protect himself from legal prosecution for some of his antics but also to avoid calling forth prejudice against Mexicans. Thompson wonders if Acosta needed a mask so that he could stand back and observe how people reflect their culture in spontaneous interactions and unedited relationships.

The strongest explanation for Acosta's disappearance, in Thompson's view, relates to his paranoia and his need to be a messiah. Drugs may have intensified his feelings about going off the deep end. Zeta Acosta lived in an "as if" world because he did not have one definition of himself or a singular sense of who he was. Ethnicity was a starting point, but no final destination was clear for Acosta. Such ideas are hard to explain and even harder to live. Thompson can imagine that Acosta became insane. Part of him wanted a final answer to the question of who he was. He was prone to conversions and sometimes grabbed at all-encompassing explanations for the meaning of life. Near the end, he wanted to be like Mahatma Gandhi or Martin Luther King, Jr. Yet his success as an attorney brought publicity which exacerbated his feelings of insecurity and self-doubt. Before he disappeared, Acosta sincerely believed that government groups were out to get him.

Acosta's standing within Chicano literary circles is problematic, in part because of the mixed nature of his message. The strident militancy in his novels about improving society commands attention. No Chicano author had more enthusiasm for the Chicano cause than Acosta. Both his books often denigrate women and seem not to include them in a Chicano agenda for full rights and equal privileges. Many Chicana (Chicano women) critics see his women characters as little more than sources of ego gratification and sexual release. Both books use derogatory labels for ethnics of color and those who happen to be white, which is odd in light of the sensitivity to reverse discrimination shown in Acosta's short story, "Perla Is a Pig." Acosta approaches *Chicanismo* (Chicano ethnicity) from the angle of the *pocho*, the Latino who speaks English and who has tried to assimilate. Not all Chicanos are immigrants. However, there is an old saying about the third generation of immigrant families needing to explore their roots, and there may be a resurgence of interest in him in the future. Ethnicity was Acosta's literary mission. His importance rests on whether or not readers are willing to go along. Like Acosta, the unnamed protagonist of Tomás

Rivera's novella "... *y no se lo tragó la tierra*"/"... *and the Earth Did Not Part*" (1971), experiences a crisis of faith, questions his parents, and rejects certain aspects of his Mexican background in order to develop his sense of identity. The central figure in Corky Gonzalez's epic poem *Yo Soy Joaquin* proclaims that he embodies all his legacies, Spanish, Indian, Mexican, and yet is different from them because he is Chicano. The contemporary novels of Sandra Cisneros, *The House on Mango Street* (1984), and Denise Chavez, *The Last of the Menu Girls* (1986), explore how Chicanas construct who they are as women and artists. In 1988 Rodríguez's *Oddsplayer*, the first Vietnam novel written by a Chicano, was published. Pérez, the Latino protagonist, recalls his life in the 1960s before he was drafted. He remembers the tumult in Los Angeles as groups of Chicanos from the barrios and universities protested against unfair elections, inferior education, and prejudice in the marketplace. As Pérez fights for his life in Vietnam, he considers each of his cultural legacies and realizes that he has to create his own identity if he survives, a philosophical position inspired by Acosta.

References:

Sam Blazer, "Justice Still Not Flowin'," *Nation*, 218 (13 April 1974): 469-471;

Choice, 10 (May 1973): 538;

Joseph Kanon, "Heavens on Earth," *Saturday Review*, 55 (December 1972): 67-69;

Luis Leal, "Mexican American Literature: A Historical Perspective," *Revista Chicano-Riqueña*, 1 (1973): 32-44;

Tomás Rivera, "Into the Labyrinth: The Chicano in Literature," *Southwestern American Literature*, 2, no. 2 (1972): 90-97;

Joe D. Rodríguez, "The Chicano Novel and the North American Narrative of Survival," *Denver Quarterly*, 16 (Fall 1981): 229-235;

Rodríguez, "God's Silence and the Shrill of Ethnicity in the Chicano Novel," *Explorations in Ethnic Studies*, 4 (July 1981): 14-21;

Rodríguez, "The Sense of Mestizaje in Two Latino Novels," *Revista Chicano-Riqueña*, 12 (Spring 1984): 57-63;

Antonia Castañeda Shular, Tomás Ybarra-Frausto, and Joseph Sommers, eds., *Literatura chicana: Texto y contexto/Chicano Literature: Text and Context* (Englewood Cliffs, N.J.: Prentice-Hall, 1972);

Edward Simmen, *The Chicano: From Caricature to Self-Portrait* (New York: Mentor, 1971);

Norman D. Smith, "Buffalos and Cockroaches: Acosta's Siege at Aztlán," *Latin American Literary Review*, 5 (Spring-Summer 1977): 85-97;

Hunter S. Thompson, "Fear and Loathing in the Graveyard of the Weird: The Banshee Screams for Buffalo Meat," *Rolling Stone*, 15 December 1977, pp. 48-54, 57, 59.

Papers:

Acosta's papers are held in the Colección Tloque Nahuaque, University of California, Santa Barbara.

Leonard Adame

(2 September 1947-   )

Donald Wolff

Pennsylvania State University at Harrisburg

BOOK: *Cantos pa' la memoria* (San Jose, Cal.: Mango, 1979).

OTHER: "Lost Together with Our Children," "On Sides of Tractor Paths," "Esperanza," "The White Theater," "Roberto en Kindergarten," and "My Grandmother Would Rock Quietly and Hum," in *From the Barrio: Chicano Anthology*, edited by Luis Omar Salinas and Lillian Faderman (San Francisco: Canfield, 1973), pp. 25-26, 105-108;

"El dolor de invisibilidad," "El manioso," "Warm Frost," "Prayers," and "My Grandmother Would Rock Quietly and Hum," in *Entrance: 4 Chicano Poets*, edited by Gary Soto (Greenfield Center, N.Y.: Greenfield Review, 1975), pp. 9-23;

"In Chihuahua, Villa Was Shooting Traitors" and "In December's Air," in *Speaking for Ourselves: American Ethnic Writing*, edited by Faderman and Barbara Bradshaw (Glenview, Ill.: Scott, Foresman, 1975), pp. 390-390-391;

"Canto pa' mis amiguitos," in *Fiesta in Aztlán: An Anthology of Chicano Poetry*, edited by Toni Empringham (Santa Barbara: Capra, 1981), pp. 37-39;

"Black and White," in *Literature, Structure, Sound and Sense*, fourth edition, edited by Laurence Perrine (San Francisco: Harcourt Brace Jovanovich, 1983), p. 770;

"My Grandmother Would Rock Quietly and Hum," "Once Again," "In December's Air," "For the Spine," and "Into Shadow," in *Piecework: Nineteen Fresno Poets*, edited by Jon Veinberg and Ernesto Trejo (Albany, Cal.: Silver Skates, 1987), pp. 6-15.

PERIODICAL PUBLICATIONS: "On Sides of Tractor Paths," *Backwash*, 11, no. 2 (1972): 1;

"Roberto en Kindergarten," "Prayers," "The Error of Rain and Me," and "My Grandmother Would Rock Quietly and Hum,"

Leonard Adame (photo by Maria Adame, courtesy of the author)

American Poetry Review, 2 (May/June 1973): 8-9;

"Basilio" and "Workshops and Ethnic Students," *American Poetry Review*, 2 (November/December 1973): 37, 38, 40;

"In Chihuahua, Villa Was Shooting Traitors," *Oyez Review*, 8, no. 1 (1973): 5;

"El Señor Arroyo," *Greenfield Review*, 3, no. 2 (1973): 6;

"El dolor de invisibilidad," "Black and White," and "La verdad," *American Poetry Review*, 6 (May/June 1977): 29;

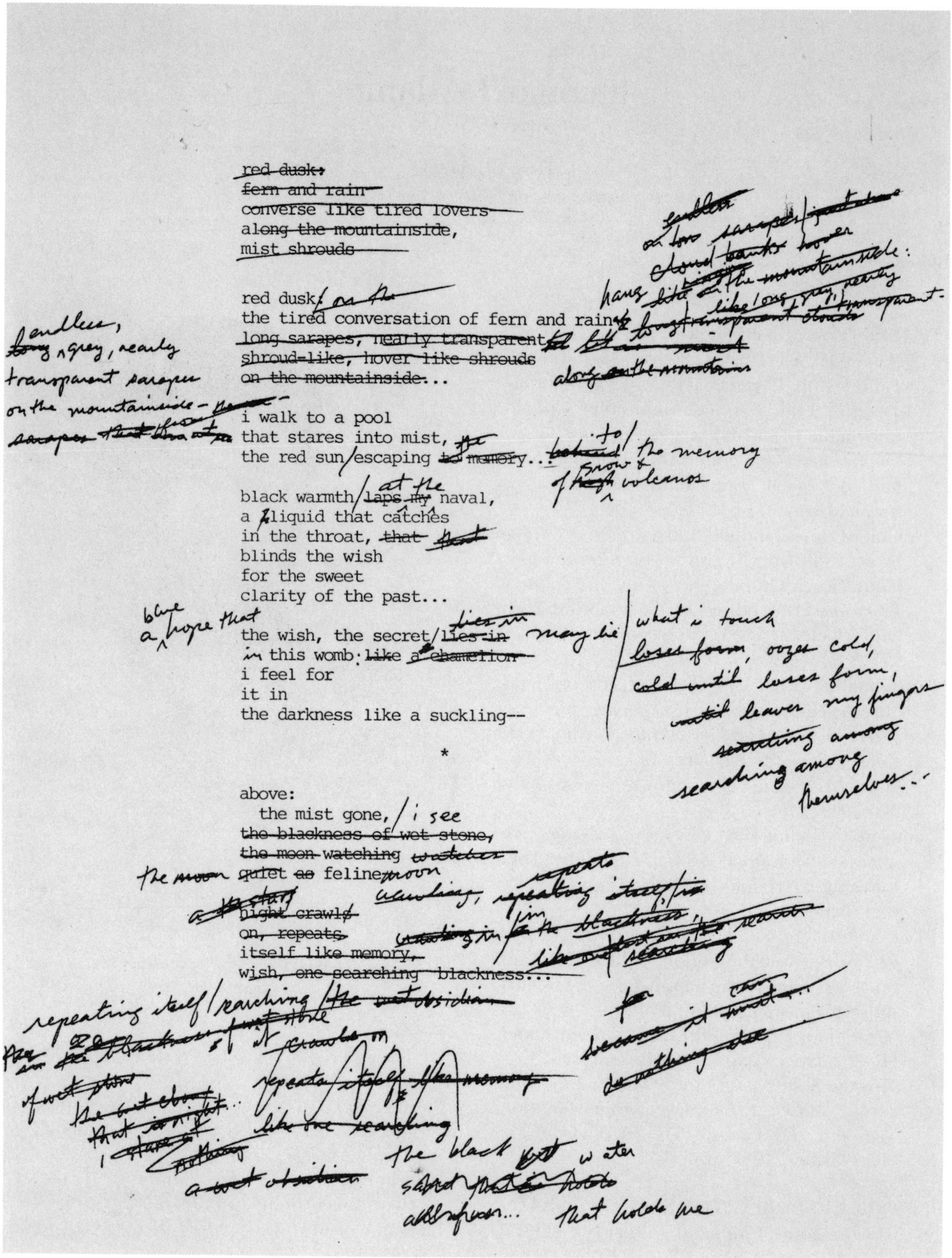

~~red dusk:~~
~~fern and rain~~
~~converse like tired lovers~~
~~along the mountainside,~~
~~mist shrouds~~

red dusk
the tired conversation of fern and rain
~~long sarapes, nearly transparent~~
~~shroud-like, hover like shrouds~~
~~on the mountainside...~~

i walk to a pool
that stares into mist,
the red sun/escaping ~~to memory...~~

black warmth/~~laps my~~ naval,
a liquid that catches
in the throat, ~~that~~

blinds the wish
for the sweet
clarity of the past...

the wish, the secret/~~lies in~~
in this womb: ~~like a chameleon~~
i feel for
it in
the darkness like a suckling--

*

above:
    the mist gone, / i see
~~the blackness of wet stone,~~
~~the moon watching~~
~~quiet as feline~~

~~night crawls~~
~~on, repeats~~
itself like memory,
~~wish, one searching blackness...~~

Rough draft and final version of a poem by Adame (courtesy of the author)

the feline moon

red dusk:
the tired conversation of fern and rain;
endless, grey, nearly
transparent sarapes
on the mountainside

i walk slowly to a pond
that stares into mist,
the red sun
excaping to
the memory of snow and volcanos

black warmth
at the naval,
a liquid that catches
in the throat,
blinds the wish
for the sweet
clarity of the past...

                    *

a blue hope that
the wish, the secret may
lie in this womb:
i feel for
it in
the darkness like a suckling:
  what i touch
oozes cold, loses form,
leaves my fingers
searching among themselves...

    above:
the mist gone;
i see the feline moon
repeating itself,
searching the black water
that holds me...

                         Leonard Adame

"Stillness" and "You to Life," *Backwash*, 20, no. 1 (1981): 12-15;

"Note for Omar," *Berkeley Poetry Review*, 11-12 (Fall 1981-Winter 1982): 29-31.

Leonard Adame is a poet of memory, family, and culture. His largely autobiographical poetry is full of the stories, characters, and lives of a precisely imagined and reified past. But if Adame is a poet of historical consciousness, he uses history for his own purposes in order not to be used by it.

Adame was born in Fresno, California, a city he remembers, as he puts it in an interview in *Piecework: Nineteen Fresno Poets*, 1987), in the images of "my grandmother's house, the park, my father's restaurant, a school across the street, and a drug store where I discovered comic books, the *Police Gazette, Playboy*, Steinbeck, Hemingway." High school was a particularly painful time for Adame, when he was forced to acknowledge his ethnic identity. At graduation a counselor told him he had no business going to college and taking the place of someone who truly deserved to be there. He earned first a B.A. and later an M.A. in English from California State University at Fresno, where he worked on his poetry under the tutelage of Peter Everwine and Philip Levine and came in contact with other Chicano poets including Gary Soto, Luis Omar Salinas, and Ernesto Trejo. Adame still lives in Fresno, which he feels "is not much different than most places on earth. People live and die here, bigotry and racism still abound, the weather is usually very hot or very foggy, and some pretty good restaurants have been opened."

Adame's poetry is predicated upon the past and present, never one without the other, a sense of history at once personal and social, concrete and universal, where memory is "shepherd / of an invisible / flock of acts," as he puts it in the title poem to his collection *Cantos pa' la memoria* (Songs for Memory, 1979). Like all of Adame's best work, *Cantos pa' la memoria* displays a seamless texture that carefully and rhythmically interweaves the dominant elements of his vision. Texture is readily apparent in the autobiographical "Canto pa' my hija" (Song for My Daughter), where Adame begins by remembering what his father told him and goes on to wonder what he might truly be able to say to his daughter:

—he'd just
tell me about the things he did . . . and
i've done the same with you. but
living with you, having seen you at

birth with blood in your eyes, with
your hair crusty with fluids, having
heard the first of your years of cries,

having seen how you looked at me your
first morning, how you couldn't recognize
me, having you grow so secretly through

your five years that i still hold you
like a baby, has made me need to tell
you something of myself . . . what can

i tell you?

Parallelism provides the means for connecting the father and son and then the son and his daughter, while still allowing the poet to explore what cannot be connected and to indicate by verbal gestures what cannot find its way into language. The result is a rich texture of association. Even so, one can see that the poet's life is related to his poetry.

"Canto pa' mi hermana Maria" (Song for My Sister Mary) shows how the larger context of social reality impinges on the simplest facts, how unlikely it is, in Adame's vision, that an image will maintain a pristine purity:

the priest's pale hands
the robes
that were finer
than your dress,

there should be
more.

It is not just memory and family that constitute Adame's subject but always the social context, the felt truths of everyday life precisely observed. The image of the priest does not merely limn a religious ritual but refers as well to poverty, subtly evoked by "finer," that weighs heavily on the poet's consciousness and leads to the sense of economic, moral, and even metaphysical deprivation of "there should be / more." Adame's sociological perspective comes out of his pride in his culture. In *Piecework* he says that Fresno was where he learned that "my Mexican background was not something to be hidden. I learned instead that the recurring miseries constituting much of the lives of Chicanos are not self-inflicted, that my

Spanish-speaking culture was a natural spring of identity and self-awareness, emotional support and rejuvenating creative impulses and motifs, motivation and resilience."

There are many places in Adame's poetry where the reader can feel the harshness of a metaphysical reality, a spiritual dread at the center of his vision. As he says in "toward":

> the horizon
> seethes behind
> the bruised hills, roils
> with pigments of dread
> and the unknown.

The unknown forms the metaphysical basis for his poetry. In his more recent work, which displays great economy, there is at the center a quintessential sadness which can affect even the landscape. However, this sadness does not override the poetry, as it might. He is saved from the enervating dangers of nostalgia and faithlessness by the facts of everyday life that most often provide the substance of his poetic meditations. He is capable of many moods. In "Basilio" (1973) everyday facts arrange themselves into an elegiac hymn for his grandfather:

> The morning's work done, he
> sat beneath the shade of the
> loquat tree, the ripe fruit
> hanging above him like
> ornaments. A radio in his
> pocket spoke of ballgames,
> the June weather and used cars—
> and he slept, his head leaning
> to his left side. . . .

Subtle but arresting combinations of the natural, human, and even commercial worlds are always maintained in Adame's poetry, brought together in the consciousness of the moment. It is as if there is no escape from quotidian truths, from the realities of everyday life that keep the poet focused on the concrete and particular, and that can sometimes provide the hopeful counterpoint to pervading sadness. But the inescapable cannot be comfortable either, and perhaps that is why Adame is currently turning his attention to inventing an "indigenous past," to use his phrase from the *Piecework* interview, where Fresno truths do not abide quite so absolutely.

Adame is a poet whose promise is yet to be fulfilled. The publication of a selection of his work in *Piecework* may lead to greater recognition of his talent and a place in the mainstream of contemporary poetry, for it identifies him with the remarkably talented group of poets whose work will continually claim critical attention for its wisdom, grace, and perspicacity. It is hoped that he will work toward that vision which he claimed for his students in "Workshops and Ethnic Students," an essay on poetry workshops published in 1973. For too long, he feels, Chicano culture had been considered culturally deprived, "as if our indigenous past were suddenly invisible, as if our customs . . . were worthless, . . . as if our tongues were incapable of expressing subtle thoughts, delicate emotions—as if it were an outcast roaming in and out of civilization." It is Adame's purpose to give voice and permanence to place, family, home, and memory in order to reify Chicano culture, past and present. It is an ambitious project, for he defines that history as broadly as he can, and he fights against the accumulated prejudice of the dominant Anglo culture, so antithetical to historical consciousness.

Alurista
(Alberto Baltazar Urista)
(8 August 1947-   )

Judith Ginsberg
Modern Language Association

BOOKS: *Floricanto en Aztlán* (Los Angeles: Chicano Cultural Center, 1971; revised, 1976);
Nationchild Plumaroja, 1969-1972 (San Diego: Toltecas en Aztlán, 1972);
Colección Tula y Tonán: Textos generativos, 9 volumes (San Diego: Toltecas en Aztlán, 1973);
Timespace Huracán: Poems, 1972-1975 (Albuquerque: Pajarito, 1976);
A'nque / Alurista: Acuarelas hechas por Delilah Merriman-Montoyah (San Diego: Maize, 1979);
Spik in Glyph? (Houston: Arte Publico, 1981);
Return: Poems Collected and New (Ypsilanti: Bilingual / Editorial Bilingüe, 1982).

OTHER: *El Ombligo de Aztlán: An Anthology of Chicano Student Poetry*, edited by Alurista, Jorge González, and others (San Diego: Centro de Estudios Chicanos, San Diego State College, 1972);
Herberto Espinoza, *Viendo morir a Teresa y otros relatos*, edited by Alurista (San Diego: Maize, 1983);
Southwest Tales: A Contemporary Collection, edited by Alurista and Xelina Rojas-Urista (Colorado Springs: Maize, 1986).

PERIODICAL PUBLICATIONS: "The Chicano Cultural Revolution," *De Colores*, 1 (Winter 1973): 23-33;
"Dawn," *El Grito*, 7 (June-August 1974): 55-84;
"La estética indígena a través del Floricanto de Nezahualcóyotl," *Revista Chicano-Riqueña*, 5 (Spring 1977): 48-62;
"El caso, la novela y la historia en la obra de Acosta: *The Revolt of the Cockroach People*," *Maize*, 2 (Spring 1979): 6-13;
"Boquitas Pintadas: Producción Folletinesca Bajo el Militarismo," *Maize*, 4 (Fall-Winter 1980-1981): 21-26.

A keen delight in language characterizes the work of Alurista, considered by many the poet lau-

Alurista (courtesy of the author)

reate of Chicano letters. Possessing a noteworthy agility in English, Spanish, Náhuatl, and Maya, Alurista is equally at ease with both standard usage and slang. In tune with the realities of the barrio–the Chicano neighborhood–and yet immersed in the broad cultural heritage of Náhuatl and Mayan cultures, Alurista is a remarkably versatile and powerful poet and one of the first to succeed in the creation of interlingual texts.

Born, as he told Juan Bruce-Novoa (1980), "in the lake of Texcoco in what is known today as Mexico City" on 8 August 1947, Alberto Baltazar Urista spent his early years in the Mexican states of Morelos and Guerrero. The oldest of six children of Baltazar and Ruth Heredia Urista, he was thirteen when his family immigrated to the United States and settled in San Diego, California. Alurista began to write poetry in the second grade, and he was soon reciting at school for special events. He recalled to Bruce-Novoa, "Communication became a very important thing to me in my early days. . . . Of course in those days I was playing or experimenting with the word. It is a discovery about which even to this day I am happy."

In San Diego the family language continued to be Spanish. Alurista's parents understood English but found it "a very dry, cold language, only suited for business transactions and things like that." His present home is deliberately bilingual. He has two children, Tizoc and Maoxiim, from his 8 August 1969 marriage to Irene Mercado, and two, Zamna and Zahi, from his 16 June 1977 marriage to poet Xelina Rojas (Xelina Rojas-Urista). He uses both Chicano Spanish and Mexican Spanish so that the children will be able to communicate with speakers of either dialect.

Alurista himself is completely at home with both Spanish and English, the result of a concerted effort. "Even when it comes to the question of writing," he comments, "I write and read in English and Spanish and I do it very deliberately, I try to read a book in Spanish and one in English." Aware of the ramifications of his decision to write in both Spanish and English, Alurista is committed to communicating with his people and has refused to make concessions to publishers who have wished to republish his works in English translations. Currently on the faculty of California State Polytechnic College in San Luis Obispo, California, he supports himself by teaching and not from his poetry.

Exceptionally well-read, Alurista uses a broad range of references: religious, political, historical, and cultural. One of the first topics he explored in depth was Catholicism. Briefly attracted to the priesthood, he spent about three months in his early teens in a preseminary school where he read religious literature. His interest in Catholicism was a way of finding himself, but he was soon disappointed. In his view, "the Church was a big business. They wanted to train me for something I didn't intend." His belief that much of the church is venal is perhaps most sharply reflected in "Candle Shuffle," from the collection *Nationchild Plumaroja, 1969-1972* (Nationchild Redfeather, 1972), in the portrayal of a greedy bishop demanding his tithe from the meek, working poor. In "Nuestra Casa - Denver '69" (Our House - Denver '69), from the same collection,

the poet demands: "no more rezos de rodillas / no more apologies por ser de carne / y de hueso" (no more prayers on bended knees / no more apologies for being of flesh / and of bone).

Disillusioned with the Catholic church, Alurista turned first to the study of Protestant religious figures: Luther, Calvin, and others; then he explored the texts of Buddhism, Hinduism, Taoism, Zoroastrianism, and Islam. He also learned much about pre-Columbian history and religious traditions which are of considerable importance in his poetry and often appear combined with aspects of the Christian tradition. In high school and in his first years of college he read a book every week in addition to his school assignments. His writings reveal a familiarity with contemporary Mexican writers such as poet Octavio Paz and novelist Carlos Fuentes.

After his graduation from high school in 1965 Alurista began studying business administration at Chapman College, in Orange, California. Realizing two years later how inappropriate this field was to his interests, he transferred to San Diego State College and switched to the study of religion. Finding his instructors very dogmatic, he again switched, this time to sociology, then to social welfare, because of a need to channel his energies "in a manner which would aid in the well-being of the rest. I wanted to change things. I wanted to help my brothers and my sisters." From 1965 to 1968 he worked as a counselor and psychiatric child-care worker in San Diego, later doing a brief stint with Volunteers in Service to America (VISTA) and the Brown Berets. He graduated with a B.A. in psychology from San Diego State in 1970.

Despite his success in formal education–he went on to earn an M.A. from San Diego State in 1978 and a Ph.D. from the University of California, San Diego, in 1983, writing a dissertation on the Chicano author Oscar Z. Acosta's novel *The Revolt of the Cockroach People* (1973)–Alurista has experienced what T. S. Eliot has spoken of as "the eternal struggle of art against education." Alurista has said that "schooling is where you are trained to follow directions, and as a poet, as a writer, as a creative person that is the last thing I wanted. I don't want to follow anyone else's structures, no path that anyone would mark for me. . . . Anything that has been accomplished has been in spite of formal schooling." He also reads less than he did previously. As he told Bruce-Novoa in 1980, "Now I try to learn more from people, from what I observe, more than from

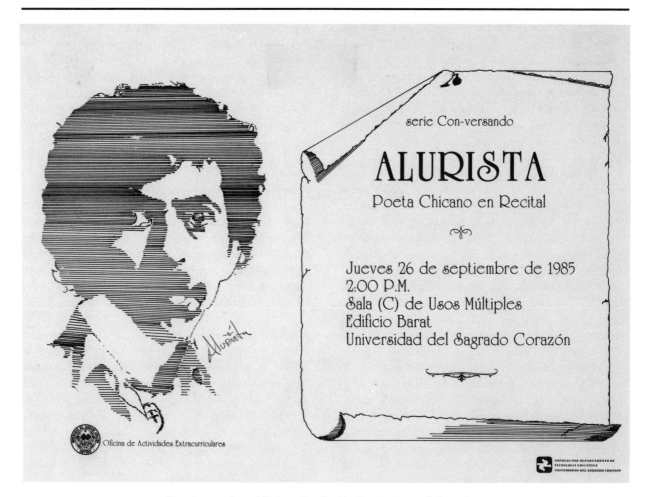

Signed poster for a 1985 reading by Alurista (courtesy of the author)

books. . . . It's very important for a writer to know how to listen and observe."

Although he had been writing continuously since childhood, Alurista marks 1966 to 1967 as the time when he began to take his poetry seriously and to prepare it for wider publication. As his attitude toward his writing underwent change, he began to use the pen name Alurista, a contraction of his first name, Alberto, and his surname, Urista. These were also the years when he became more aware of the culture shock involved in living as a Chicano in the United States. An important realization came to him that he spoke not just for himself, but for all the Chicano people.

César Chávez and the farm workers' strike exercised a profound influence on Alurista. In an interview with Tomás Ybarra-Frausto (1979), the poet recalls standing on a hill and watching the long line of farm workers and supporters as they moved along the highway singing behind red and black thunderbird flags: "It was the farmworkers who brought Chicanos to the forefront of national consciousness. As I watched the pilgrimage from Delano, I said to myself, that man Chávez is either a fool, a fanatic or a truly wise man. And very soon his genius was apparent."

In the wake of the struggle of the farm workers between 1965 and 1967, Alurista decided to use his writing to communicate and reflect Chicano experience. He sees himself as a weaver of words, images, metaphors, and symbols in which the Chicano people can see themselves reflected. His poem "el sarape de mi personalidad" (The Serape of My Personality) in the collection *Floricanto en Aztlán* (Flower and Song in Aztlán, 1971) captures his identification with the Chicano people, symbolized in the traditional woven shawl or serape, and provides an implicit elaboration on the notion of the poet as a weaver: "el sarape de mi personalidad / comes in fantastic colores / basic / essentially fundamentales." The spectrum of his wool "is life itself" and "La

RETURN

Poems Collected and New

Cover for Alurista's 1982 volume, which includes new poems and a revision of his earlier collection Nationchild Plumaroja, 1969-1972

esencia de mi Raza es fundamental" (the essence of my Race is fundamental): "basic / to the chromatic wheel of humanity / free to compound in secondary colors / retaining the basic texture / our woolen skin of color bronze."

In 1968 Alurista cofounded the Chicano Studies Department at San Diego State. He was a lecturer there from 1968 to 1974 and from 1976 to 1979. In 1969 he was also the cofounder of the Chicano Studies Center at San Diego State. These were no small accomplishments since the acceptance of any new field of study in academia is usually a slow and often tedious process. In addition to his many poetry readings at academic institutions, Alurista has served the cause of Chicano literature by editing works of other Chicano authors. He is the founder of the Chicano journal of literature and criticism, *Maize*, which he coedits with Xelina Rojas-Urista. In the mid 1970s Alurista was the chief organizer of the an-

nual Festival Floricanto which drew published and unpublished Chicano authors and their critics together with the Chicano community for several days of creative exchange. In 1967 he was the cofounder of the Movimiento Estudiantil Chicano de Aztlán (MECHA, Chicano Student Movement of Aztlán).

In the late 1960s Alurista was perhaps the first to establish the concept of Aztlán at the level of literature and formal ideology as a cultural, political, geographical, and mythical symbol of the aspirations of the Chicano people. In keeping with Náhuatl mythology as recorded by the sixteenth-century friar Diego Durán and other Spanish chroniclers of pre-Columbian civilization in Mexico, Aztlán is a lost paradise, the mythical ancient homeland of the Aztec people, roughly coincident with what is now the southwestern part of the United States. The concept is set forth in "El plan espiritual de Aztlán" (The Spiritual Plan of Aztlán), a document written largely by Alurista during the first Chicano Youth Liberation Conference held at the Crusade for Justice in Denver, Colorado, in 1969. Explicit in the concept is the notion that the land belongs to those who work it. When the "Plan" was published in both English and Spanish in 1970 in the first issue of the journal *Aztlán*, Alurista's "Poem in Lieu of a Preface" (later revised as "it is said" in *Nationchild Plumaroja*) appeared as the prologue. Although the poem's probable source of inspiration is Durán's *Historia de las Indias de Nueva España* (History of the Indies of New Spain, 1867-1880), its bilingual, politically aware presentation of Aztlán provides an excellent introduction to Alurista's early work. The poem's beginning, "it is said," places it in the realm of the oral tradition of the people. The Aztec heritage is highlighted throughout the work by the use of uppercase letters, hence the character "MOTECUHZOMA ILHUICAMINA" (Moctezuma I, 1440-1469), the renowned Aztec king and warrior who, during the height of the Aztec power, sent expeditions to search for the mythical Aztlán as a way of exalting his own historic origins. The Chicanos' daily experiences in the world of the dominant culture is consistently presented in lowercase letters, reflecting mundane sufferings. Gary D. Keller (1982), among other scholars, has noted that it is a common device in Chicano literature to write English in lowercase when the standard spelling would call for capitals: "The intention is usually to undermine the oppressive status of English, to put it on a par with Spanish, which rarely uses capitals."

Multilingualism, the use of pre-Columbian symbolism, and chantlike repetition found in "Poem in Lieu of a Preface" appear more fully developed in Alurista's first collection of poetry, *Floricanto en Aztlán*, the most widely read and influential of his works. The one hundred *cantos* (songs or chants) which comprise this volume were composed in 1968 and 1969, when the Chicano struggle for cultural self-determination was in an early and crucial phase, and many of the poems were recited before large crowds at rallies. Juan Gómez-Quiñones, in his introduction to the first edition, places the works in the context of the historical moment: "These writings parallel the altering dynamic within the Movement. The collection is poetry and testimony." At the time the poems were written, Alurista was studying pre-Columbian philosophy, especially that of the Náhua, and their concepts of poetry and art were incorporated. As he commented in a 1977 article in *Revista Chicano-Riqueña*, "We should note that in contrast to European poetry written by the privileged classes and destined for the same audience, Náhuatl poetry was publicly sung, dialogued and collectively danced as much by the nobility as by the working classes. And although much of it was written in elevated style with didactic intent, it never ceased being an object of tribal recreation and delight."

The expression *floricanto* (flower and song) is a Spanish version of the Náhuatl term for poetry which, in that system of thought, was considered the key to knowledge. It was through poetry that a *tlamatini* (philosopher or wise man) preserved the culture's wisdom and values. The preservation of many centuries of Chicano wisdom is, essentially, the goal of the poems in *Floricanto*, which highlight the humanitarian and spiritual values of pre-Columbian Mexico and of contemporary Chicano society. In "tizoc left us his hair" (Tizoc was an Aztec emperor, murdered in 1486, best known for his military campaigns against rebellious tribes and for the reconstruction of the largest temple in Mexico) the affirmation that "my ancestry" is a "sacred host" conveys the connection that Alurista has with his culture's past. The fact that Alurista's oldest son is named Tizoc further underlines this identification.

Much of the drama in *Floricanto* is a result of the fact that Chicano culture often stands in sharp contrast with and is often challenged by an antagonistic and oppressive Anglo society, personified as "the man" or "mr. jones." Yet in poems such as "la carne de tus labios" (Flesh of Your Lips), "flowers in the lake," "cantos de ranas viejas" (Songs of Old Frogs), and "el recuerdo de mis grillos" (The Memory of My Crickets), the heritage's affirmative and optimistic values are symbolized by such pre-Columbian deities as Quetzalcóatl, the most revered Aztec deity, source of love, art, agriculture, astronomy, and crafts; Tlaloc, the Aztec rain god; Tonantzin, the Aztec goddess of motherhood; and Ométéotl, the supreme creator representing male-female duality. Beginning with the first poem in the volume, the widely known and anthologized "when raza?" (When the People?), Alurista exhorts his fellow Chicanos to struggle for their freedom, their values, and their culture: "now, ahorita define tu mañana hoy" (now, define your tomorrow today). The poem sets the tone for the volume, with human values constantly in conflict with the strictly material values of the Anglo majority. For example, the second poem in the volume, "la canería y el sol" (the cannery and the sun), says "we pang / but mr. jones is fat / with money / with our sweat / our blood / why?"

During the years 1969 to 1972, the period when he produced the poems contained in his second collection, *Nationchild Plumaroja, 1969-1972*, Alurista helped organize (in 1971) a center for cultural workers called "Toltecas en Aztlán" (Toltecs in Aztlán) in San Diego. In addition to the study of indigenous teachings in literature, music, art, and life, the group trained what were termed "cultural guerrillas," individuals who were to use art as a weapon in the struggle for cultural change. Alurista joined Juan Felipe Herrera and Mario Aguilar in a music and theater ensemble named Servidores del Arbol de la Vida (Guardians of the Tree of Life). This group aimed at recreating, in a modern context, Indian dance forms, ritual singing, and chant. Alurista played the conch, a modern adaptation of a pre-Columbian instrument. As Ybarra-Frausto described it, Alurista "developed a style of recitation which is a cross between Gregorian chant and monotone. The intent is to locate poetry not only in the mind but also in the viscera."

Nationchild is composed of one hundred typically didactic poems divided into five Mayan *katunes* (units of twenty). Each *katun* uses the symbol of an animal or flower—*nopal* (prickly pear), *xóchitl* (flower), *serpiente* (serpent), *conejo* (rabbit), *venado* (deer)—to signify a particular mood. The poems in the *conejo katun*, for example, are to be read in a fast tempo while the poems in the *xóchitl* or *nopal katunes* are in a more reflective or lyrical style. As Alurista told Bruce-Novoa, he and many other Chicano authors are "talking about humanizing the social and economic order of earth." To do that, "we have to expel the Yankees from our heart. We have to give ourselves the responsibility of constructing a vision of the world that is truly ours, not a colonized version of the world . . . If we paint a more humanistic world to live in, we will construct that world. Literature is a healing art, not only a reflective art." For example, in "who are we? . . . somos aztlán: a letter to 'el jefe corky,' " the narrator claims justice as the Chicano community's weapon to "establish peace, / restore the earth, / and respect the sun. . . ." The message is that "peace, earth and sun / can bring liberation from / ignorance, war, disease, / . . . their violence must end / with our culture, our heart, and our peace." Similarly, the nationchild is exhorted in "Aquí Nomás" (right here) not to "dream / suicide, homicide / genocide or biocide / our hearts must find our spot / our place, our body / our family, our tribe / our nation and our motherearth / will welcome the return of her children. . . ."

There is general critical agreement that Alurista's *Floricanto en Aztlán* and *Nationchild Plumaroja* are major, vital works in the developing Chicano canon. His place as a literary leader is also undisputed. Luis Leal and Pepe Baron (1982) have declared Alurista "the best known and most prolific Chicano poet." Cordelia Candelaria (1986) describes him as a pioneer and a "seminal innovator," a view shared by Jesus Maldonado (1971) and others. Critics such as Ybarra-Frausto (1979) and Juan Rodríguez (1979) have placed him among a group of Chicano authors that they criticize for romanticizing the Amerindian past. Keller largely defends Alurista (1982), pointing out the important function the poet's treatment of Amerindian themes has had in terms of educating the Chicano community and providing a positive cultural referent at a crucial moment of the embryonic Chicano movement, while conceding that Alurista "is vulnerable to not representing the past as critically as he has engaged the present." Keller is also more enthusiastic about Alurista's more recent works and their verbal virtuosity than Alfonso Rodríguez (1981) or Candelaria, who says, "The fact that the poet has remained a respected figure among Chicano writers despite the dropping off in quality of these later volumes reconfirms the greatness of his earlier work."

In 1974 Alurista published "Dawn," a brief poetic drama, described by Keller as a "contemporary *Everyman*, an allegory of economic imperialism that makes extensive use of ritualized and ceremonial language." The characters include Mexicano, Chicano, Quetzalcóatl, Pepsicóatl, and Cocacóatl. The latter two, "magicians of colored / sugar water / and idiot box addiction" whose names Alurista has created from the popular Anglo-American soft drinks (Coca-Cola and Pepsi-Cola) combined with Náhuatl suffixes, are the villains and represent the Anglo-American people's exploitation of their neighbors. The dawn of the title, however, brings the death of these characters and "the blooming of humanity," inaugurating a new beginning for the Chicano people: "the return to our / beginning / walk on earth / again / forge our nation / . . . the children shall rise in justice. . . . " "Dawn" shares with much of Alurista's work of the late 1960s and early 1970s a fondness for musical forms, an assertive criticism of Anglo-American greed, and the hope for the "nationchild's" bright future. "Dawn" is in part liturgical rather than dramatic; it does not strive for realism but rather attempts to exalt through the use of pre-Columbian mythology the struggle for existence of the Indian and Mexican-American peoples who are threatened by the rapacity of Anglo-America and its pursuit of its manifest destiny. Alurista has not actively pursued his interest in writing for the theater since the publication of "Dawn."

Alurista's third book of poetry, *Timespace Huracán: Poems, 1972-1975* (Timespace Hurricane), published in 1976, has been termed "both a synthesis of previous thematic concerns and a new departure" by Ybarra-Frausto. The new departure involves the fact that all the poems are written in Spanish, and there is intensive experimentation with form. The title of the collection, like that of *Nationchild Plumaroja*, juxtaposes Spanish and English and includes a new word, *timespace*. In the interview with Bruce-Novoa, Alurista described three levels of "time-space" within which all individuals live and function: a historical or collective time-space "that describes reality as accorded by a consensus of people"; a personal, individual, psychological time-space; and a "mythological time-space that unifies the personal and historical time-spaces." Alurista draws on all three spaces, linking the Amerindian of history and mythology with the energy of the contemporary Chicano Movement. *Timespace Huracán* is characterized by considerable experimentation with form, including shaped poetry, serial poems, prose poems, and haiku. Chants, songs, rhythmic patterning, and acoustic effects appear frequently. In a discussion with Salvador Rodríguez del Pino he has termed his experimentation with basic poetic forms "lapidary poetry."

Among the more successful poems in *Timespace Huracán* is the spiral-shaped "In lak'ech," whose title comes from the Mayan word *in lak'ech* (you are my other self). The poem asserts the Mayan belief in the unity of the world in which all things are alive and unified, part of a larger univeral oneness.

A'nque / Alurista: Acuarelas hechas por Delilah Merriman-Montoyah (Even Though / Alurista: Watercolors done by Delilah Merriman-Montoyah) and *Spik in Glyph?* appeared in 1979 and 1981, respectively. Although neither collection is as compelling as *Floricanto* or *Nationchild*, and both are burdened by their often esoteric style, they deserve mention as indications of Alurista's continued commitment to innovation and experimentation. The title of *Spik in Glyph?* is a bilingual pun on the English verb *speak* and the derogatory epithet *spik* (referring to *Hispanic*), as well as a play on *in glyph* (in hieroglyphic), which can also sound like *English*. The titles of the first thirteen poems are puns, variously Spanish and English, on the numbers one through thirteen. The tenth poem in the collection, for example, is entitled "ten," the English number as well as the informal singular imperative form of the Spanish verb *tener*, to have. The extreme experimentation with English and Spanish that characterizes *Spik in Glyph?* is apparent in "birth": "in / corporated / anno / ni mous / lyvali / um / vali / um / um / a / um / valium / mmmmmmm / inc., ink? / think u / nut good / kill / ër / off payn? pain / pay in? / tax / es." But many readers may question the purpose and the point of the incessant wordplay that does not appear to lead anywhere. Among the more effective works in the collection, on the other hand, is "borinquen," which captures the sound and vocabulary of Puerto Rican Spanish with its characteristic dropped syllables and frequent use of *bro'* for brother.

Alurista's collection of poetry, *Dawn's Eye: 1979-1981*, has been published with a new edition of *Nationchild Plumaroja* in a volume entitled *Return: Poems Collected and New* (1982). The linking of these new works with one of his most successful earlier collections under a common title suggests a special relationship between them. The first two poems in *Dawn's Eye*, "apá" (Daddy)

and "baltazar," touching eulogies to the poet's father, suggest a reengagement with more accessible language and human themes and a movement away from the often brittle and obscure wordplay of *A'nque / Alurista* and *Spik in Glyph?*. One of the longest and finest poems in *Dawn's Eye*, "From Amsterdam," records Alurista's mixed reactions to a culture that both welcomes is filled with wonder that his picture appears in a Dutch newspaper, "debo estar soñando" (I must be dreaming); yet, with his dark complexion, he does not escape the racism of a nation in which passersby impassively watch a Turk drown in a canal but jump in to save a dog. His own physical appearance leads him to experience directly this racism: "me miran como turco, / suriname o indonesio / cuando bien soy amerindio / chicano moro maya con / salsa de país vasco los / taxis no me hacen caso / y me empapo en el / racismo de holanda / ni las prostitutas nos / ofrecen sus ombligos" (They look at me as if I were a Turk,/ or from Surinam or Indonesia / when I'm really Amerindian / Chicano, Moorish, Mayan with / sauce from the Basque country the / taxis pay me no heed / and I am soaked in the / racism of Holland / not even the prostitutes / offer us their navels.)

Alurista is a writer of considerable wit, culture, and energy who has produced an impressive amount of work since he began to write seriously in the mid 1960s. In addition to writing volumes of poetry, he has served Chicano letters as a publisher, editor, performer, scholar, and teacher. He has also written a collection of nine short volumes for children, *Colección Tula y Tonán: Textos generativos* (1973). Still a young writer, it is to be hoped that Alurista will continue to develop and refine his vision of Chicano culture and its place in the United States and beyond. It is to be hoped as well that he will reject a reliance on verbal pyrotechnics that have threatened to diminish the power of his expression.

References:

Elga Morales Blouin, "Símbolos y motivos nahuas en la literatura chicana," *Bilingual Review/ Revista Bilingüe*, 5 (January-August 1978): 99-106;

Juan Bruce-Novoa, *Chicano Authors: Inquiry by Interview* (Austin: University of Texas Press, 1980), pp. 265-287;

Bruce-Novoa, *Chicano Poetry: A Response to Chaos* (Austin: University of Texas Press, 1982), pp. 69-95, 212-214;

Cordelia Candelaria, *Chicano Poetry: A Critical Introduction* (Westport, Conn.: Greenwood, 1986), pp. 72-74, 78-99, 99-108, 155-156, 164-166;

Ernestina N. Eger, "Bibliography of Works by and about Alurista," in Alurista's *Return: Poems Collected and New* (Ypsilanti: Bilingual / Editorial Bilingüe, 1982), pp. 141-155;

Juan Gómez-Quiñones, introduction to the first edition of Alurista's *Floricanto en Aztlán* (1971);

Gary D. Keller, "Alurista, Poeta-antropólogo, and the Recuperation of the Chicano Identity," in Alurista's *Return: Poems Collected and New* (Ypsilanti: Bilingual / Editorial Bilingüe, 1982), pp. xi-xlix;

Keller, "The Literary Strategies Available to the Bilingual Chicano Writer," in *The Identification and Analysis of Chicano Literature*, edited by Francisco Jiménez (New York: Bilingual / Editorial Bilingüe, 1979), pp. 263-316;

Luis Leal and Pepe Barron, "Chicano Literature: An Overview," in *Three American Literatures,* edited by Houston A. Baker, Jr. (New York: Modern Language Association, 1982), p. 28;

Francisco Lomelí and Donaldo Urioste, "El concepto del barrio en tres poetas chicanos: Abelardo, Alurista y Ricardo Sánchez," *De Colores*, 3, no. 4 (1977): 22-29;

Jesus Maldonado, *Poesía Chicana: Alurista, el Mero Chingón* (Seattle: Centro de Estudios Chicanos, 1971);

Alfonso Rodríguez, "Review of Alurista's *A'nque: Collected Works, 1976-79,*" *La Palabra*, 3 (Spring 1981): 146-147;

Juan Rodríguez, "La búsqueda de identidad y sus motivos en la literatura chicana," in *The Identification and Analysis of Chicano Literature*, edited by Jiménez (New York: Bilingual / Editorial Bilingüe, 1979), pp. 170-178;

Salvador Rodríguez del Pino, "La poesía chicana: una nueva trayectoria," in *The Identification and Analysis of Chicano Literature*, edited by Jiménez (New York: Bilingual / Editorial Bilingüe, 1979), pp. 68-89;

Gustavo Segade, "Chicano *Indigenismo*: Alurista and Miguel Méndez M.," *Xalman*, 1 (Spring 1977): 4-11;

Daniel Testa, "Alurista: Three Attitudes Toward Love in His Poetry," *Revista Chicano-Riqueña*, 4 (Winter 1976): 46-55;

Tomás Ybarra-Frausto, "Alurista's Poetics: the Oral, the Bilingual, the Pre-Columbian," in his and Joseph Sommers's *Modern Chicano Writers* (Englewood Cliffs, N.J.: Prentice-Hall, 1979), pp. 117-132.

Papers:

Some of Alurista's manuscripts are held in the archives of the Nettie Lee Benson Collection, Latin American Collection, University of Texas at Austin.

Rudolfo A. Anaya
(30 October 1937-   )

Cordelia Candelaria
University of Colorado

BOOKS: *Bless Me, Ultima* (Berkeley, Cal.: Quinto Sol, 1972);

Heart of Aztlán (Berkeley, Cal.: Editorial Justa, 1976);

Tortuga (Berkeley, Cal.: Editorial Justa, 1979);

The Silence of the Llano: Short Stories (Berkeley, Cal.: Tonatiuh-Quinto Sol, 1982);

The Legend of La Llorona (Berkeley, Cal.: Tonatiuh-Quinto Sol, 1984);

The Adventures of Juan Chicaspatas (Houston: Arte Publico, 1985);

A Chicano in China (Albuquerque: University of New Mexico Press, 1986);

The Farolitas of Christmas (Santa Fe: New Mexico Magazine, 1987);

Lord of the Dawn: The Legend of Quetzalcoatl (Albuquerque: University of New Mexico Press, 1987);

Voces: An Anthology of Nuevo Mexicano Writers (Albuquerque: El Norte, 1987).

PLAY PRODUCTION: *The Season of La Llorona,* Albuquerque, El Teatro de la Compañia de Albuquerque, 14 October 1987.

MOTION PICTURE: *Bilingualism: Promise for Tomorrow,* screenplay by Anaya, Carlos and Jeff Penichet, Bilingual Educational Services, 1976.

OTHER: *A Ceremony of Brotherhood, 1680-1980,* edited by Anaya and Simon Ortiz (Albuquerque: Academia, 1980);

José Griego y Maestas, *Cuentos: Tales from the Hispanic Southwest,* translated by Anaya (Santa Fe: Museum of New Mexico Press, 1980);

Cuentos Chicanos, edited by Anaya and Antonio Márquez (Albuquerque: New America, University of New Mexico, 1980);

"Autobiography," in *Contemporary Authors Autobiography Series,* volume 4, edited by Adele Sarkissian (Detroit: Gale Research, 1987), pp. 15-28.

PERIODICAL PUBLICATIONS: "The Writer's Sense of Place," *South Dakota Review,* 13 (Autumn 1975): 66-67;

"*Mexico Mystique*–Another View," *New Mexico,* 53 (November 1975): 37;

"The Writer's Landscape: Epiphany in Landscape," *Latin American Literary Review,* 5 (Spring-Summer 1977): 98-102;

"A Writer Discusses His Craft," *CEA Critic,* 40 (November 1977): 39-43;

"Requiem for a Lowrider," *La Confluencia,* 2 (October 1978): 2-6;

"Cuentos de los Antepasados," *Agenda: A Journal of Hispanic Issues,* 9 (January-February 1979): 11;

"Myth and the Writer: A Conversation with R.A.," *New America,* 3 (Spring 1979): 76-85;

"The Light Green Perspective: An Essay Concerning Multicultural American Literature," *MELUS,* 11 (Spring 1984): 27-32;

"*The Silence of the Llano:* Notes from the Author," *MELUS,* 11 (Winter 1984): 47-57.

Principally because of his first novel, *Bless Me, Ultima* (1972), Rudolfo Anaya is considered a major contemporary Mexican-American writer. The book, one of the few Chicano literary bestsellers, appears on high school and college curricula, holds an important place in the landscape of Chicano literary criticism, and (with some of his other novels) has been translated into German and Polish. The book's merit and market success have allowed Anaya to enjoy popularity simultaneously with relative critical acclaim. Since 1972 he has published four more novels and coedited several anthologies.

Anaya was born to Martín and Rafaelita Mares Anaya on 30 October 1937, in Pastura, a village lying south of Santa Rosa in eastern New Mexico. He attended public schools in Santa Rosa and Albuquerque despite an extended hospitalization for a spinal injury he suffered as a youth. He earned a B.A. (1963) and M.A. (1968) in English from the University of New Mexico, and he

Rudolfo A. Anaya (courtesy of University of New Mexico, Albuquerque, Special Collections Department)

also has an M.A. (1972) in guidance and counseling from the same institution. In 1966 he married Patricia Lawless, who is also trained in guidance and counseling. From 1963 to 1970 Anaya taught in the Albuquerque public schools. He left to become director of counseling at the University of Albuquerque. His current appointment in the Department of English at the University of New Mexico began in 1974. He has received numerous awards and fellowships, including an honorary doctorate from the University of Albuquerque, the New Mexico Governor's Award for Excellence, and the President's National Salute to American Poets and Writers in 1980. Perhaps the most important of his honors is the Premio Quinto Sol awarded to *Bless Me, Ultima,* for it was his first national literary honor and a harbinger of later recognition, including grants from the National Endowment for the Arts and the National Chicano Council of Higher Education, and a Kellogg Fellowship.

To read Anaya's work is to encounter a preoccupation with, as he describes it (*MELUS,* Spring 1984), "instinct and the dark blood in which it dwells." The bringing of instinct to light is both

an artistic and a moral imperative for Anaya, who perceives the writer's role in shamanistic terms. He points this out with painstaking care in his gloss to his *The Silence of the Llano: Short Stories* (The Silence of the Plain: Short Stories, 1982):

> The storyteller tells stories for the community as well as for himself. The story goes to the people to heal and reestablish balance and harmony, but the process of the story is also working the same magic on the storyteller . . . [who] must be free and honest, and . . . must remain independent of the whims of groups. Remember, the shaman, the *curandero* [folk healer], the mediator do their work for the people, but they live alone.

Anaya is also concerned with integrating into his work the Jungian ideas associated with intuition and feeling. Nowhere in his work is the integration of subjective insight as effective or inspired as in his first novel.

Bless Me, Ultima takes place in the cultural richness of its author's native soil (New Mexico), one of the continent's oldest communities, a point that bears stressing because primal antiquity girds Anaya's mythic worldview. The novel

A PUBLICATION OF TONATIUH INTERNATIONAL

Cover for Anaya's first novel, which explores the relationship between seven-year-old Antonio Márez and his spiritual guide, Ultima

presents the maturation of Antonio Márez, a boy growing up in Guadalupe, a small New Mexico farm village. The book explores his relationship with his spiritual guide, Ultima, a *curandera*. Narrated in the first person by seven-year-old Antonio, the events in *Bless Me, Ultima* unfold as if in the present, but it is soon clear that temporal distance separates the narrator from the experiences he is describing. Anaya achieves this distance by opening the story with the boy's flashback to "the beginning that came with Ultima," a period of time that moves from the year he starts school to the end of the next year when he completes third grade after precociously skipping second. Anaya separates the narrative voice from the events narrated by endowing the narrator—not necessarily the boy in the thick of the plot—with a sensitivity and insight usually reserved for adult maturity. The distancing permits the maturity of the child's vision to work; otherwise the boy's sagacity would strain the reader's

disbelief beyond suspension, a concern that has nonetheless bothered some readers.

The moment Antonio's parents welcome Ultima, the *curandera* they respectfully call "la Grande," into their household in bucolic Guadalupe marks the boy's first clear awareness of time and signals the start of his rite of passage from a state of timeless innocence to one of adolescent understanding of the weight of time. On the first page Antonio observes that "the magical time of childhood stood still," while in the final chapter he muses, "sometimes when I look back on that summer I think that it was the last summer I was truly a child." Even the vast difference in ages between the boy and the elderly Ultima becomes an emblem of the temporal changes mirrored in the plot as he learns that "things wouldn't always be the same."

In the course of the novel Antonio enters public school where, despite the initial fear of leaving mother and hearth, he quickly excels academically and also successfully engages a social network outside his family. He is catechized into the Catholic church and struggles with his growing dismay at the artifice connected with its hierarchy and bureaucracy. Much of his struggle relates to his discovery of a genuine spirituality and legitimate morality outside the church—in nature, for example, and in the legends told by "Jasón's Indian." More traumatically, he encounters four deaths, including two violent killings and the drowning of his special friend, Florence, a young "heretic." Anaya balances the traumas of the deaths with Antonio's participation in the life-affirming *curanderismo* practiced by Ultima. She provides him with the one stable certain part of his life, satisfying both his intellectual curiosity and emotional needs and, as a result, inspiring his spiritual growth as well.

Anaya textures his main story with a subplot focusing on Antonio's life within his family (parents, three brothers, and two sisters). He shares the family's agony over the fate of his three brothers who, in their youthful machismo, appear wayward and irresponsible to him, and he also serves as the central figure in his parents' bitter conflict over his destiny. Embodied in his father's aggressive Márez (i.e., turbulent seas) characteristics and his mother's more subdued Luna (i.e., gentle moon) traits—the wild vaquero versus the settled farmer—the family conflict divides him by tugging his natural loyalties and affections in opposite directions. Ultimately, the evocative power of the book lies in the crossweaving of cultural, social, and psychological levels of action to form a seamless, holistic unity.

Anaya expresses his preoccupation with instinct and blood in the dream sequences which filter and mediate for Antonio the conflicts, violence, and other traumas he encounters. Signaling his intuitive grasp of the importance of his dreams, Antonio continually thinks about them even though his youth prevents his full understanding. Each of his dreams has a noticeable effect on his outlook, conduct, and ultimately on (in Jungian terms) the individuation of his personality. For example, as early as the end of chapter 1, Antonio's recollection is that his "dream was good"; and the disturbing dream at the beginning of chapter 9 leads the story directly into an argument between Antonio's parents and his brothers. Antonio's dreams and their effect on him are an index to his development.

Chapter 14 effectively illustrates the efficacy of dreams to Antonio's self-insight. From the hilarity of a school play plagued by calamities to the horror of Narciso's cruel murder and the apocalyptic furor of the concluding *pesadilla* (nightmare), the chapter obtains its power from the wide range of subjects thrown together with unusually vivid force. By uniting the children's innocent bedlam with Tenorio's sinister mayhem, Anaya sets the stage for the *pesadilla,* the dream apocalypse that will hurl Antonio's entire life before him, "the whole town," the wicked and the good, the sacred and the profane. The nightmare drowns Antonio with "its awful power" as major and minor figures from his life swirl up in a fiery, bloody chaos of symbols. Besides cataloguing various tortures and rituals suffered by his friends and family members, the nightmare also portrays the boy's own "withering" death after which his "bleached bones [are] laid to rest . . . in front of the dark doors of Purgatory."

Important to the novel's ultimate affirmation, the end of the dream shifts the tumultuous horror of the *pesadilla* into a soothing tranquil scene and a healing experience:

> Evening settled over the land and the waters. The stars came out and glittered in the dark sky. In the lake the golden carp appeared. His beautiful body glittered in the moonlight. He had been witness to everything that happened, and he decided that everyone should survive, but in new form. He opened his huge mouth and swallowed everything, everything there was, good and evil. Then he swam into the blue velvet of the night, glittering as he rose towards the stars. The moon

> smiled on him . . . he became a new sun . . . to shine its good light upon a new earth.

Anaya transmutes the nightmare's chaos, pain, and violence into the surreal beauty of a nature pure and uncontaminated by human strife, a nature preserved in the indigenous mythology and *curanderismo* of Indo-Hispanic—in other words, mestizo—America. By suggesting that good and evil are meaningless abstractions within the timeless power of nature embodied in the night's beauty and the carp's power, the book offers a pantheistic resolution to the nightmare's New Testament-like apocalypse. The story's social realism vanishes into the private realms of dream, fantasy, and primordial legend.

Antonio's dream, like all the others steeped within his subconscious, expresses ideas that he will only fully comprehend in the future when he sets about reconstructing his (and Ultima's) story, and his mature reconstruction enables him to give form to the events which he experienced desultorily as a child. Yet, the boy Antonio intuits wisdom from his dreams. In chapter 15 he shows a more loving tolerance of his father and brothers, and he also exhibits a more realistic acceptance of "the sons seeing the father suddenly old, and the father knowing his sons were men and going away." Throughout the novel dreams contribute to the individuation of Antonio's personality and the seasoning of his moral character.

Another central area of Antonio's life is his involvement with Jasón, Samuel, and Cico, the boys who introduce him to the legend of the golden carp which holds that the fish was once a god who "chose to be turned into a carp and swim in the river where he could take care of his people." The legend at first confuses Antonio because "everything he had ever believed in seemed shaken. If the golden carp was a god, who was the man on the cross? The Virgin?" But he eventually fathoms the legend's message regarding the spiritual force of aboriginal nature: "I knew I had witnessed a miraculous thing," he thinks when the fish swims by Cico, "the appearance of a pagan god. . . ; a sudden illumination of beauty and understanding flashed through my mind. This is what I expected God to do at my first holy communion!" The dream he has that night makes explicit the holistic meaning of the legend which probes "beyond into the great cycle that binds us all." A significant part of Antonio's development apart from his family and Ultima relates to his network of school and friends.

Cover for Anaya's 1976 novel, about the adjustments a Chicano family must make when they move from a rural New Mexico town to the city of Albuquerque

Through them he conquers many of the familiar fears common to boyhood, as well as those specific to rural Chicanitos (young Chicanos) like him who are teased for packing tortillas and beans instead of white bread sandwiches for school lunch. They "banded together" and in their "union found strength." Each boy has his special talent that adds to Antonio's expanding repertoire of worldly knowledge and experience, an expansion that edges him outside the family's orbit even as it helps him better to understand his family.

Bless Me, Ultima is essentially an extended flashback told in the first person by an involved narrator. Although it resembles a bildungsroman, the novel is technically not an apprenticeship novel because it is limited to only a couple of boyhood years and does not present Antonio's complete rite of passage to young manhood. Critic Daniel Testa (Spring 1977) notes that even though "the boy-hero of the story is only eight

years old at the end . . . we are convinced that his character has been formed in a radically profound way." If analyzed alongside the main character in Anaya's novel *Tortuga* (1979), the main character of *Bless Me, Ultima* is part of a composite bildungsroman protagonist. Such an approach takes into account Anaya's perception of his first three novels as a "New Mexico trilogy" (see "Autobiography"), making Clemente Chávez and his son, Jasón, of *Heart of Aztlán* another resonating part of the character. Antonio's retrospection begins with Ultima's visit, but its depth of insight derives from the artistic process of recalling, ordering, and then sharing the story with others.

Bless Me, Ultima has sold over two hundred thousand copies. Critical analyses and assessments have been extensive and largely favorable. Antonio Márquez (1982) asserts that Anaya's work, "especially *Bless Me, Ultima,* has inspired the largest body of criticism in contemporary Chicano literature." Among the noteworthy extended studies are several which discuss the dream sequences in the book. For example, Roberto Cantú (November 1974) perceives the "structure and meaning" of the dream sequences as integral to both theme and plot, whereas Vernon E. Lattin (Spring 1978) places his analysis of the dreams within the context of the novel's violence and "horror of darkness." Especially illuminating of the work's narration and presentation of time is Daniel Testa's 1977 discussion of its "extensive / intensive dimensionality." Studies which examine *Bless Me, Ultima* within the context of Anaya's entire work are Antonio Márquez's overview in *The Magic of Words* (1982) and Cordelia Candelaria's in *Chicano Literature: A Reference Guide* (1985), which examines his use of Jungian themes. Of more recent interpretations of the novel, José Monleón's "Ilusión y realidad en la obra de Rudolfo Anaya" (Illusion and Reality in the Work of Rudolfo Anaya, 1986), while negative in its appraisal, is still very effective in its unified treatment of Anaya's three novels. Most of the criticism of this novel praises it for what Antonio Márquez calls "Anaya's imaginative mythopoesis and his careful and loving attention to the craft of fiction."

Anaya's second novel, *Heart of Aztlán* (1976), depicts one year in the life of the Clemente Chávez family, who moves from the rural community of Guadalupe to the barrio of Barelas in Albuquerque. The family members respond differently to the pressures of the hostile urban environment. The oldest practical son manages adequately, but Benjie, the youngest, becomes a drug user and delinquent and eventually dies violently. Clemente, the father, shares with middle son, Jasón, a profound respect for "la tierra sagrada" (the sacred land), but Clemente abdicates his role as patriarch to Jasón because of unemployment and excessive drinking. Typical of Anaya's flat characterization of women, the two daughters, Juanita and Ana, school dropouts, are portrayed as sellouts, repudiating their Chicano heritage. While strong and courageous, the mother, Adelita, hovers in the background. Jasón must lead the family until Crispín, a blind poet (much like Ultima in Anaya's first novel), inspires Clemente to take on his natural role as a leader of his people.

While the changes wrought upon the Chávez family in their new environment constitute a major part of the plot of the novel, it is Clemente's personal growth and moral development which dominate the action. The move from the country to the city tests Clemente as husband, father, and human being; but despite the hardships and near ruin he experiences, he survives. He is guided somehow to the light that will lead him through the darkness of both his personal inferno and the social hell that surrounds the barrio and eventually accepts the community's call for his leadership in their opposition to the vast powers that exploit and shackle them.

The three major exploiters in *Heart of Aztlán* are technology, religion, and capitalism. The giants of technology and industry who enslave the workers are symbolized by the huge steel water tank overlooking the railroad (the tracks are like tentacles) where most of the men in Barelas work. Religion is represented by the Catholic church and Father Cayo. Both corrupt the masses who take refuge from their poverty in faith. The third oppressor is capitalism, which Anaya presents through the narcissistic and exploitive Mannie García, "el Super," the opportunistic owner of the barrio supermarket. Casting an ominous shadow over everything is the "black tower," the water tank with the words *Sante Fe* painted on its side. The giant letters proclaim the modern holy faith in profit which dominates American society. The steel tank's Spanish words denote a past sacredness now become profane and neatly fuses the three types of exploitation into one symbol.

Although *Heart of Aztlán* concerns the sociopolitical realities experienced in a Chicano ghetto, its characters and story line are not developed realistically. For example, the wide array of characters lack verisimilitude and are sketched as literary types–from traditional *machos* and *mamacitas*, to melodramatic healers and artists. Concerned primarily with questions of Chicano labor and barrio sociology, Anaya densely packs the novel's surface structure with several threads of action. Despite the overt social message, *Heart of Aztlán* is overlaid with the same Jungian motifs and mythological themes which gave *Bless Me, Ultima* its infrastructure (and where they were compatible with the idealism of the child narrator); the failed treatment of these yoked polarities lies at the heart of the second novel's failure. As Marvin A. Lewis noted (*Revista Chicano-Riqueña*, Summer 1981), "The novel attempts to accumulate and to assess the myths, legends, and social realities reflecting the totality of Chicanismo. Unfortunately, the author falls short of the mark due to a conceptual disparity between form, content, and overall meaning."

Consequently, the exact nature of the novel's conclusion and overall meaning are hard to gauge. The closing lines of the novel are " '¡Adelante!' They shouted without fear." If the ending is genuinely uplifting, what practical solutions explain the affirmation? If tragic, are Clemente's final exhortations "shouted without fear" only the mere ravings of a self-proclaimed messiah? Neither the story nor its subtext offers suitable answers. As María López Hoffman has noted (1980), "the feeling of a shared communal soul" is not enough to "destroy the chains" that the author has created to "bind" his oppressed characters, for myths and symbols are not "a real tool to correct social injustice."

Anaya has himself publicly faulted his execution in *Heart of Aztlán* (*New America*, 1979), pointing to his considerable difficulty in extricating Clemente from his hardships by way of a "visionary trip." The author also admits to toying with his readers, "especially critics," by indulging his tendency to engage in rhetorical flourishes and redundancies. Juan Bruce-Novoa's observation (1977) that *Heart of Aztlán* "is a disappointing novel" that "ring[s] false" primarily because of Anaya's "simplistic division of the world into positive and negative" instead of attending to the "total harmony of nature" and reality is generally shared by other readers of the novel.

Patterned in the mythic journey motif of classical literature, *Tortuga*, recipient of the 1980 Before Columbus Foundation American Book

José Griego y Maestas
&
Rudolfo A. Anaya
award-winning author of *Bless Me, Ultima*

Bilingual Stories in Spanish and English

Cover for the 1980 collection that includes tales by José Griego y Maestas with English translations by Anaya

Award, completes Anaya's New Mexico Trilogy. The protagonist is a paralyzed sixteen-year-old boy identified only by the nickname Tortuga (turtle) given to him by his peers because his body is encased in a shell-like cast. Like *Bless Me, Ultima*, *Tortuga* is the first-person story of a journey from ignorance to enlightenment. The novel traces Tortuga's long recovery from a near-fatal accident. He encounters many other crippled children and Salomón, an Ultima-like paralytic mute who communicates with him telepathically. Salomón introduces him to Tortuga Mountain, a place of *agua bendita* (holy water) which has curative power like the waters inhabited by the golden carp in *Bless Me, Ultima* and the cave spring in *Heart of Aztlán*. During his recovery Tortuga falls in love with Ismelda, a nurse's aide. The novel's most important theme is that physical health is inextricably fused with emotional and spiritual well-being and that both types of well-being derive from the con-

scious recognition of the self's place in the universe.

Tortuga's literal journey consists only of his travel from home across a stretch of New Mexican desert past the mountains to the Crippled Children and Orphans Hospital (probably patterned after the Tingley Hospital in Truth or Consequences, New Mexico, where Anaya was treated as a young man for a near-fatal accident like that of his protagonist). The trip and one-year confinement are meant to signify the manifold passages of the boy's personal development. Suffering the agony of immobility within the plaster body cast as well as the pain of physical therapy, Tortuga develops the emotional maturity produced by suffering. The novel traces the process that transforms him from a withdrawn teenager lacking self-awareness to someone who discovers his mystical destiny as "the singer, the man who would not only feel the misery of the hell we lived in, but also return to sing about it." The book ends with Tortuga's bus ride away from the hospital, "going home."

The framework of symbolism dominates the narrative and nearly overshadows the lives of the characters. In a dichotomy of good and evil, the symbols divide into two clusters, one relating to the harmony of nature outside the hospital and the other concerned with disease and distress within the hospital. Tortuga, the title symbol, relates to the harmony of nature, for even though it refers to the protagonist's body cast, it also refers to Tortuga Mountain, the "magic mountain" situated "right by the hospital." Emblematic of both the boy's psychological shell and physical cast, the turtle image is carried out to the end of the novel when Tortuga leaves the hospital without crutches to begin his trek back across the desert (an allusion to the persistent turtle in John Steinbeck's *The Grapes of Wrath*, 1939).

Important symbols in *Tortuga* suggesting the harmony of nature are butterflies and Filomón and Ismelda, two of the novel's sympathetically drawn characters. Closely associated with Salomón, an iron lung patient who resides in the ward for the most severely handicapped, the butterfly symbolizes beauty, hope, and love, which emerge through a difficult metamorphosis. The characters Filomón and Ismelda, who live outside the hospital, function primarily as symbols of mysticism. Filomón, an ambulance driver who drives a converted hearse, is supposed to "be over a hundred years old." Filomón's age links him directly to Anaya's other ancient characters, Ultima and

Crispín, for example. Like them, he represents the important guides of youth. The beautiful young nurse's aide, Ismelda, has an immediate and profound effect on Tortuga, who instantly falls in love with her. Late in the novel, Ismelda's idealized feminine perfection, described as "the lizard woman," typifies Anaya's one-dimensional fictional characterizations of women.

The symbols associated with the hospital and the crippling diseases within it embody the negative side of humanity: hate, envy, and greed. Like the settings of Katherine Anne Porter's figurative *Ship of Fools* (1962) and Aleksandr Solzhenitsyn's *Cancer Ward* (1968), the hospital serves as a microcosm of a stagnant humanity which has been corrupted away from fundamental truth. Evil parts of the hospital are the committee which oversees the hospital, and Danny's withered arm. Both are agents of sinister purpose within their surroundings as are Tenorio in *Bless Me, Ultima* and Mannie in *Heart of Aztlán*.

The critical reception of *Tortuga* was generally negative, although Johnson observed, "*Tortuga* is a tour de force in which Anaya creates a memorable hell of suffering humanity . . . , from [which] flower hope and a conviction in the sanctity of human life." Others found the novel's themes and symbols quickly becoming predictable and faulted its execution. Candelaria (*MELUS*, Summer 1983) found the portrayals of women as either "predictable idealizations of femininity" or "predictable renderings of feminine undesirables." Angelo Restivo (*Fiction International*, 1980), in an echo of complaints made about *Bless Me, Ultima,* was bothered by the clumsy intrusions of the author's voice which "tries to explain precisely what . . . doesn't *need* explaining," as well as by the stylistic "rough spots" and a self-conscious use of Indian myth not sewn effectively into the narrative.

The thematic interconnection of *Tortuga, Bless Me, Ultima,* and *Heart of Aztlán* occurs on several levels and much cross-referencing between books occurs. One of the most notable allusions concerns poet Crispín's bequest of his magical blue guitar to Tortuga, a legacy that will assure that the boy will "take his turn" as the community's singer-shaman-prophet. Accordingly, Anaya has observed (*MELUS*, Winter 1984),

I define myth as the truth in the heart. . . , that we as human beings have carried all of our history, going back to the cave, pushing it back to

THE SILENCE OF THE LLANO

short stories

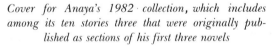

Rudolfo A. Anaya

Cover for Anaya's 1982 collection, which includes among its ten stories three that were originally published as sections of his first three novels

the sea. It seems to me that . . . in order to come to a new conscious awareness [people] need to separate necessarily from a social, political context.

Certainly his created heroes and their sage old guides, his mythic narratives and themes, his fantastic imagery and symbolism, all convey the same fundamental scheme in one form or another. His concomitant concern for "instinct and the dark blood in which it dwells," and his ability to evoke it powerfully with the limited tools of fiction explain much of what works in *Bless Me, Ultima.* As Ron Arias has said, "part of [that] novel's attraction" has been "its 'feeling' of authenticity, of [the] trueness" of its "fictional world." Conversely, Anaya's Jungian perspective applied formulaically in *Heart of Aztlán* and *Tortuga* also explains their weakness. The author "tries to include too much [myth, dream, and fantasy]," writes Restivo, who goes on to say, "some of his motifs aren't developed . . . [and] he sometimes loses control of his narrative voice." One of the most developed and tightly argued criticisms of Anaya's Jungian viewpoint is by Monleón who challenges the validity of the author's philosophy both within Anaya's fictive universe and within our literal shared reality: "Por qué quiere perpetuar, en nuestra sociedad tecnológica-industrial de segunda mitad del siglo XX, la noción de magia? . . . ; Este es un elemento básico . . . que no debe perderse de vista: el mundo referencial que sustenta su narrativa es el medieval." (Why, in our technological, industrial society in the second half of the 20th century does [Anaya] wish to perpetuate the notion of magic? . . ; This is a basic element . . . that must not be lost from sight: the actual world that sustains his narrative is the medieval.)

The Silence of the Llano is a collection of ten short stories. Three of the stories were first published as sections of chapters in each of Anaya's first three novels ("The Christmas Play" from *Bless Me, Ultima;* "El Velorio" from *Heart of Aztlán;* and "Salomón's Story" from *Tortuga*). With the exception of "The Apple Orchard," a weak story, the seven remaining stories primarily deal with either the subject of mythmaking and the nature of fiction, or with the llano's silence.

The collection opens with the two stories about the "silence of the llano," a concept that, in the voice of the first story's narrator, refers to "the loneliness of the llano . . . the silence of the endless plain [which] grew so heavy and oppressive it became unbearable." "The Silence of the Llano" and "The Road to Platero" are both about incest. The title story focuses on Rafael's isolation after the death of his beautiful wife during childbirth. Foreshadowed by dreams, visions, and the fecundity of nature, the union of Rafael and his equally isolated and mute daughter finally occurs on the last page. Anaya expresses the incest symbolically through the image of Rafael's phallic-like ax and his final words to the daughter he calls by his wife's name: "The spring is the time for the garden. I will turn the earth for you. The seeds will grow." Developing the theme further in "The Road to Platero," Anaya addresses the palpable nature of the guilt and revenge which haunt incest-troubled souls. In the story these agonies take the form of the "ghost [that] rides the road to Platero" tormenting the strange lives of the boy narrator and his beautiful mother, Carmelita. In an apocalyptic solution to this suffering, the "ghost of the past" can only be conquered by violent death; in this case Carmelita and a vaquero murder each other in front of the

boy. But like other Anaya protagonists–Antonio, Jasón, and Tortuga, who at different times face death and catastrophe with a stoic calm remarkable in boys so young–the unnamed narrator is not traumatized by his mother's murder. Instead he feels "death enter the room" and "settle a strange peace" over him as the "gentle moonlight shimmers" in the night.

The four stories in *The Silence of the Llano* which explore mythmaking and the nature of fiction and its relation to lived experience contain the most effective writing in the volume. In "Place of the Swallows" and "The Village which the Gods Painted Yellow" Anaya examines fictiveness in the context of primitive myth. "Place of the Swallows," for instance, deals with the way shared experience changes form when it is later retold. The story describes the power of language and fiction to reify and to transmute the dynamic relationship between life and art.

"A Story" and "B. Traven Is Alive and Well in Cuernavaca" also examine fictiveness but situate it in contemporary time and space. The creation of a story, any story as well as the writing of these two works themselves, serves as framework for both their self-reflexive plots. Anaya's persona in "A Story" appears as the character "The Writer," who encounters *actual* people from his fictive life along with *fictional* characters seeking to ingratiate their way into his writing. Employing theatrical motifs (for example, stage directions and a cast of characters) to underscore the inevitably staged effects of all literature, Anaya also incorporates humor into "A Story." The title "B. Traven Is Alive and Well in Cuernavaca" immediately brings into focus the historical but elusive writer Berick Torsvan who immigrated to Mexico, took the Traven pseudonym, and became one of his adopted country's most mysterious celebrities. From this enigmatic beginning the story calls into question the precise nature of the reader's and writer's shared reality. What keeps Traven "alive and well," the narrative ultimately concludes, is his art, the canon of fiction that represents a host of surrogate lives.

The one story in *The Silence of the Llano* that does not fit in either category discussed above is "The Apple Orchard," a slight piece constructed around the puerile practical joke of a glued mirror on a boy's shoe to sneak a glimpse under an attractive teacher's skirt. The story's major flaw is the author's chronic problem in portraying women credibly. He uses terms for women like "big, luscious" and "hot and lonely and ready for

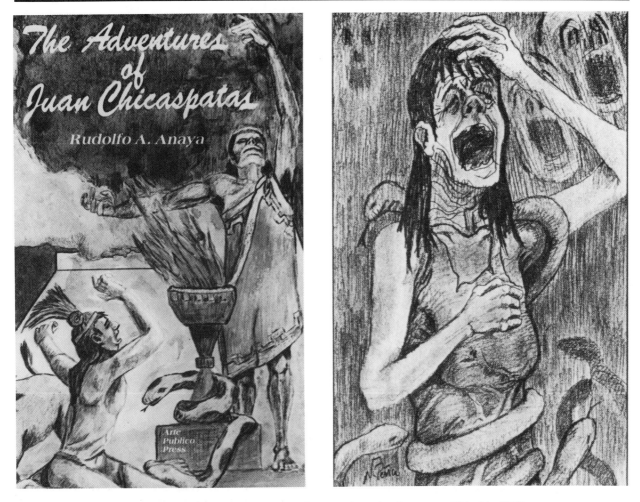

Cover and illustration by Narciso Peña for Anaya's mock epic poem, published in 1985

company" without trace of irony or of possible psychological or social nuance. But the story fails even within its own terms because the narrative climax, the teacher's disrobing in the classroom, lacks any plausibility on every level of the fiction itself.

The fascinating and complex life and legend of La Malinche (Doña Marina), the Aztec interpreter-consort of the Spanish conqueror Hernan Cortés, is the subject of Anaya's fourth novel, *The Legend of La Llorona* (1984). In less than seventy-five pages of narrative, the book fictionalizes her life from the start of the conquest to the fall of Tenochtitlán in 1521 and the beginning of the colonial era of New Spain. Without persuasive historical, folkloric, or internal novelistic logic, the novella asserts La Malinche to be the indisputable basis of La Llorona, in the weeping woman myth. In general Anaya handles the rich, vital, well-researched material (see, for example, Candelaria's "La Malinche, Feminist Proto-

type" [*Frontiers: A Journal of Women Studies*, Summer 1980] for discussion of over a dozen important treatments) in the same reductive manner of his post-*Bless Me, Ultima* style. Unlike Carlos Fuentes, Haniel Long, Gustavo Rodriguez, Margaret Shedd, and other writers who have worked both the Malinche and Llorona material in fresh creative narratives, Anaya's *The Legend of La Llorona* reduces the history and folklore of the original sources considerably.

The Adventures of Juan Chicaspatas was published in 1985. A slight work consisting of approximately forty short pages of parodic incantations and slangy humor, it is a mock epic poem about Aztlán and *chicanismo* (the philosophic concept of Chicano culture). In the course of the adventures of Juan Chicaspatas and Al Penco (whose name is an anglicization of *el penco*, meaning useless nag), a mixed bag of Chicano history and folklore are presented: from La Malinche and Cortés to Zapata, Villa, and Hidalgo; from Huitzilopochtli to

Coatlicue; from Don Cacahuate to La Llorona, and so on. Anaya parodies such well-known staples of the Chicano literary renaissance as the poetry of Alurista; *I Am Joaquin*, the 1967 poem by Rudolfo "Corky" Gonzales; and Sergio Elizondo's *Perros y antiperros* (1972). His protagonists, Juan and Al, also serve as serious vehicles for the narrator's basic message conveyed in the work's closing lines. "And so Juan Chicaspatas and Al Penco / became folk heroes, traveling across the Land of the Chicanos, helping those in need, / singing the songs of la raza / and reminding the people of their history / and the covenant with the earth / of Aztlán."

Primeval antiquity and myth, the pain and promise of chicanismo, the literature and legends of mestizo America especially in its U.S. context– these are the subjects of Anaya's fiction. They are his principal sources, but not his only ones, for his literary imagination roams wide. Repeatedly, his stories dramatize the conflicting claims made on his protagonists by family, nature, church, and art, and repeatedly they portray a struggle that ends in personal harmony, a clearcut search that always finds its uplifting grail of enlightenment and happiness. Alienation, irony, ambiguity, and the myriad uncertainties of a dynamic cosmos, whether ancient or modern, seem to lie beyond the boundaries of his fictive universe.

References:

Juan Bruce-Novoa, "Rudolfo A. Anaya," in his *Chicano Authors: Inquiry by Interview* (London & Austin: University of Texas Press, 1980), pp. 183-202;

Bruce-Novoa, "The Space of Chicano Literature," *De Colores*, 1, no. 4 (1975): 22-41;

Bruce-Novoa and Karl Kopp, "Two Views on *Heart of Aztlán*," *La Confluencia*, 3 (July 1977): 61-63;

Hector Calderón, "Rudolfo Anaya's *Bless Me, Ultima*: A Chicano Romance of the Southwest," *Critica*, 1 (Fall 1986): 21-47;

Cordelia Candelaria, "Los Ancianos in Chicano Literature," *Agenda: A Journal of Hispanic Issues* (November 1979): 4-5, 33;

Candelaria, "On La Llorona," *Agenda: A Journal of Hispanic Issues* (July 1977): 46-47;

Candelaria, "Rudolfo Alfonso Anaya," in *Chicano Literature: A Reference Guide* (Westport, Conn.: Greenwood Press, 1985), pp. 34-51;

Roberto Cantú, "Degradación y regeneración en *Bless Me, Ultima*: el chicano y la vida nueva," *Caribe*, 1 (Spring 1976): 113-126;

Cantú, "Estructura y sentido de lo onírico en *Bless Me, Ultima*," *Mester*, 5 (November 1974): 27-40;

John R. Chávez, *The Lost Land: The Chicano Image of the Southwest* (Albuquerque: University of New Mexico Press, 1984);

Alan Cheuse, "The Voice of the Chicano: Letter from the Southwest," *New York Times Book Review*, 11 October 1981, pp. 15, 36-37;

Reed Way Dasenbrock, "Intelligibility and Meaningfulness in Multicultural Literature in English," *PMLA*, 102 (January 1987): 10, 15-17;

Edward Elías, "*Tortuga*: A Novel of Archetypal Structure," *Bilingual Review / Editorial Bilingüe*, 9 (January 1982): 82-87;

Robert F. Gish, "Curanderismo and Witchery in the Fiction of Rudolfo A. Anaya: The Novel as Magic," *New Mexico Humanities Review*, 2 (Summer 1979): 5-12;

César A. Gonzáles-Trujillo, ed., *Rudolfo A. Anaya: Focus on Criticism* (Wellesley Hills: Massachusetts Bay Press, forthcoming, 1989);

Armando Gutiérrez, "Politics in the Chicano Novel: A Critique," in *Understanding the Chicano Experience through Literature*, edited by Nicolás Kanellos (Houston: Mexican American Studies, University of Houston, 1981), pp. 7-14;

María López Hoffman, "Myth and Reality in *Heart of Aztlán*," *De Colores*, 5 (Spring 1980): 111-114;

Richard S. Johnson, "Rudolfo Anaya: A Vision of the Heroic," *Empire* (2 March 1980): 24-29;

Charles R. Larson, "Books in English from the Third World," *World Literature Today*, 53 (Spring 1979): 245-247;

Vernon E. Lattin, "The 'Horror of Darkness': Meaning and Structure in Anaya's *Bless Me, Ultima*," *Revista Chicano-Riqueña*, 6 (Spring 1978): 50-57;

Lattin, "The Quest for Mythic Vision in Contemporary Native American and Chicano Fiction," *American Literature*, 50 (January 1979): 625-640;

Lattin, ed., *Contemporary Chicano Fiction: A Critical Survey* (Binghamton, N.Y.: Bilingual / Editorial Bilingüe, 1986), pp. 33-44, 171-199;

Antonio Márquez, "The Achievement of Rudolfo A. Anaya," in *The Magic of Words: Rudolfo A. Anaya and His Writings*, edited by Paul Vassallo (Albuquerque: University of New Mexico Press, 1982), pp. 33-52;

Teresa Márquez, "Works by and about Rudolfo A. Anaya," in *The Magic of Words: Rudolfo A. Anaya and His Writings,* edited by Paul Vassallo (Albuquerque: University of New Mexico Press, 1982), pp. 55-81;

Rebecca Martin, "Focus: Rudolfo Anaya," *Albuquerque Monthly,* 1 (November 1981): 26-28;

José Monleón, "Ilusión y realidad en la obra de Rudolfo Anaya," in *Contemporary Chicano Fiction,* edited by Vernon E. Lattin (Binghamton, N.Y.: Bilingual Press / Editorial Bilingüe, 1986), pp. 171-199;

Raymond A. Paredes, "The Evolution of Chicano Literature," *MELUS,* 5 (Spring 1978): 71-110;

Ishmael Reed, "An Interview with Rudolfo Anaya," *San Francisco Review of Books,* 4 (June 1978): 9-12, 34;

Cecil Robinson, *Mexico and the Hispanic Southwest in American Literature* (Tucson: University of Arizona Press, 1977), pp. 324-328;

Jane Rogers, "The Function of *La Llorona* Myth in Rudolfo Anaya's *Bless Me, Ultima,*" *Latin American Literary Review,* 5 (Spring 1977): 64-69;

Daniel Testa, "Extensive / Intensive Dimensionality in Anaya's *Bless Me, Ultima,*" *Latin American Literary Review,* 5 (Spring 1977): 70-78;

Albert D. Treviño, "*Bless Me, Ultima*: A Critical Interpretation," *De Colores,* 3 (Fall 1977): 30-33;

Paul Vassallo, ed., *The Magic of Words: Rudolfo A. Anaya and His Writings* (Albuquerque: University of New Mexico Press, 1982);

Amy Waggoner, "Tony's Dreams—An Important Dimension in *Bless Me, Ultima,*" *Southwestern American Literature,* 4 (1974): 74-79;

Carter Wilson, "Magical Strength in the Human Heart," *Ploughshares,* 4 (June 1978): 190-197.

Papers:

Anaya's papers through publication of *Bless Me, Ultima* are held at the Zimmerman Library, Special Collections, University of New Mexico.

Rudy S. Apodaca

(8 August 1939-   )

Nasario García
New Mexico Highlands University

BOOK: *The Waxen Image* (Mesilla, N.M.: Tital, 1977).

Rudy S. Apodaca was born in Las Cruces, New Mexico. He grew up on the east side of town, where most Chicanos lived and where his parents owned a grocery store. His father's family, who settled in Las Cruces in the nineteenth century, came from Socorro, Texas, a small town southeast of El Paso. There are at least five generations of Apodaca's family still living in Las Cruces. In 1957 Apodaca graduated from Las Cruces High School. He earned a B.S. in mathematics in 1961 from New Mexico State University and a J.D. from Georgetown University Law Center in 1964. He and his wife, Nancy, have three daughters and one son. Apodaca has been general counsel and bank attorney for Citizens Bank of Las Cruces, while maintaining a part-time law practice and overseeing his family's business ventures. In an unpublished interview granted in 1984, Apodaca commented: "growing up Hispanic in New Mexico subconsciously drove me to become an attorney and to fight for civil rights and causes which I believe to be just."

The Waxen Image, his only book, is a mystery-suspense novel in which Apodaca mixes fantasy with reality. Much of the novel is set north of Albuquerque, in the fictitious town of Esperanza (possibly modeled on Bernalillo), where witchcraft is common. Andrew Borlin, an old and eccentric American scientist, invents a drug which transforms him into a virile young man. Borlin takes the name of Conrad and as a professor at the University of New Mexico becomes the leader of a pervasive drug cult. Esperanza, which serves as the retreat for the cult members' drug escapades, is the site of a series of deaths and mysterious disappearances. These include the murder of Carol Lockwood, the disappearance of her daughter, and the death of Andrew Borlin, who turns out to be Carol Lockwood's father. Ross Blair, Carol's ex-husband, travels to Esperanza to try to locate his missing daughter, but he too becomes a

Rudy S. Apodaca (courtesy of the author)

victim of the decadent atmosphere that pervades the town. The various mysteries are finally resolved in Mexico.

The Waxen Image is an interesting but flawed novel. Most of the characters lack depth, and often their language seems not to correspond to their social or educational backgrounds. In its fall 1978 issue *Rocky Mountain Review* published one assessment of *The Waxen Image;* otherwise the novel has received little critical attention.

Apodaca is also the author of an unproduced screenplay entitled "A Rare Thing." This work, which is partly autobiographical, according to Apodaca, is the story of Javier García, a New

36

Mexico teenager who lives in the fictitious town of San Carlos in south central New Mexico during the 1960s and early 1970s. His father, Nicolás García, an alcoholic, is married to Ramona, Javier's stepmother (his natural mother died when he was six years old). As Nicolás's marriage deteriorates and his drinking increases, Javier, lonely and forlorn, falls in love with Deborah Perkins, a non-Hispanic who has moved into his neighborhood.

To escape from the problem of his father's alcoholism and from the guilt he feels as a result of his relationship with an Anglo, Javier enlists in the army. He and Deborah continue their relation-

ship as he waits to be sent to Vietnam. She becomes pregnant. After an introspective examination, he is able to reconcile within himself that he indeed loves Deborah. He plans to marry her when he returns from Vietnam, but he is killed in combat. Deborah decides to raise her son in San Carlos so that he can carry on the García name in the town.

As of this writing, Rudy S. Apodaca is an appellate judge of the New Mexico Court of Appeals in Santa Fe, serving an eight-year term from January 1987 to December 1994. However demanding his new position may be, it is doubtful that he will forsake his interest in creative writing.

Ron Arias

(30 November 1941-   )

Cordelia Candelaria
University of Colorado

BOOK: *The Road to Tamazunchale* (Reno, Nev.: West Coast Poetry Review, 1975).

OTHER: "The Barrio" and "We're Supposed to Believe We're Inferior," in *The Chicanos: Mexican American Voices*, edited by Ed Ludwig and James Santibáñez (Baltimore: Penguin, 1971), pp. 123-126, 173-176;
"The Wetback," in *First Chicano Literary Contest Winners*, edited by Juan Villegas (Irvine, Cal.: University of California Spanish & Portuguese Department, 1975), pp. 15-23.

PERIODICAL PUBLICATIONS: "El mago," *El Grito*, 3 (Spring 1970): 51-55;
"Chicano Books a Rare Item," *El Chicano*, 5 (November 1971): 3, 10;
"The Interview" [short story] and "Stoop Labor," *Revista Chicano-Riqueña*, 2 (Winter 1974): 2-6, 7-14;
"A House on the Island (Or, The Story of a Poetry Teacher Who Seduces Her Students)" and "The Story Machine," *Revista Chicano-Riqueña*, 3 (Autumn 1975): 3-8, 9-12;
"The Castle," *Bilingual Review/Revista Bilingüe*, 3 (May-August 1976): 176-182;
"El señor del chivo," *Journal of Ethnic Studies*, 3 (Winter 1976): 58-60;
"Chinches," *Latin American Literary Review*, 5 (Spring-Summer 1977): 180-184;
"The Interview" [play], *Revista Chicano-Riqueña*, 7 (Winter 1979): 1-7;
"The Boy Ate Himself," *Quarry West*, 13 (1980): 23-27.

With the 1975 publication of his novel, *The Road to Tamazunchale* (republished in 1978), Ron Arias joined the short list of major Chicano writers in the twentieth century. The book has attracted critical praise, including the top award in the 1975 University of California, Irvine, Chicano literary competition and a National Book Award nomination. Like his literary icon, Mexican writer Juan Rulfo, whose international eminence rests primarily on his masterpiece, *Pedro Páramo* (1955), Arias is not a prolific writer. He is a post-modernist who integrates in his fiction a keen eye for actual Mexican-American experience. His literary style has been influenced by pop-

Ron Arias

ular Latin American writers of the latter half of the twentieth century. He is concerned with chronicling the urban Chicano experience in all its bittersweet contradictions, and his major themes are the struggle between imagination and rationalism and the transcendent possibilities of ethnic pluralism. His themes reveal Arias to be a well-read student of both Anglo and Latino histories and mythologies of the Americas. His fusion of North and South American identities has produced a remarkable *mestizaje* (a term for the admixture of Spanish and Indian blood once used pejoratively) that philosopher José Vasconcelos has recognized as the dynamic synthesis of racial, historical, and cultural products of the hemisphere's indigenous (Indian) and immigrant (European and African) roots.

Ronald Francis Arias was born in Los Angeles, California, 30 November 1941. His mother was originally from El Paso, Texas. His childhood was itinerant because of his stepfather's career in the U.S. Army, which took the family

throughout the United States and Europe. Arias received his high-school diploma from the American high school in Stuttgart, Germany, in 1959. In a 1976 interview with Juan Bruce-Novoa he has described spending much time as a child with his maternal grandmother, with whom he spoke Spanish, and he has also indicated that he "identified with both my real father [from Juárez, Mexico] and my stepfather [from Nogales, Arizona]." As soon as he could, he left home for the summers and hitchhiked in Spain, Argentina, Peru, and all over the United States.

Arias traces his genesis as a writer to a notebook his mother gave him when he was in the hospital for a tonsillectomy at the age of nine. Her instructions were for him to record all his observations and thoughts in it, and from that start, he told Bruce-Novoa in 1980, he "continued writing for high school and college newspapers," eventually going on to write for large city dailies and wire services, including the Associated Press. Although he earned both a bachelor's degree in Spanish (from the University of California, Berkeley) and a master's in journalism (from the University of California, Los Angeles), he believes his "true education–at least where writing is concerned" came from his travels and his newspaper work, which forced him to learn how to adapt readily to new places and circumstances while instilling in him the ability to separate the trivial from the serious. Examples of such circumstances during his apprenticeship as a writer include being caught in combat crossfire while reporting on Latin American politics as well as encounters with Ernest Hemingway, Jorge Luis Borges, and Indira Gandhi. One of Arias's first stories, "El mago" (1970), which anticipates most of the themes and techniques of his later fiction, emerges from his many experiences. The title character in "El mago" is the old *mago* (magician) and *curandero* (a practitioner of herbal medicine) Don Noriega. He lives in a decrepit house containing a bohemian assortment of herbs, "thick Moroccan rugs, plaster sphinxes, pictures and figurines from pre-Columbian cultures." Set in Glendale, California, the story describes how two girls, Luisa and Sally, meet and how (over Sally's objections) Luisa befriends the old man. When the girls make the bizarre discovery of a mummy among his odd possessions Don Noriega explains that the mummy is simply a reminder for "the living of those once known and loved." The reader knows that Noriega's function in the girls' innocent lives is to teach them that the aged and decrepit are not always useless, ugly, or narrowminded like Sally's grandmother. He also functions symbolically, as Arias's *ancianos* (old people) usually do, as a trickster figure and guide to discoveries beyond the commonplace.

Arias borrows the device of incorporating death as a literal presence among the living from Rulfo's *Pedro Páramo* and Carlos Fuentes's *The Death of Artemio Cruz* (1962), and it is a technique that he repeats in later stories and ultimately refines in *The Road to Tamazunchale*. The everpresence of death in "El mago" is found not only in Noriega's mummy but also in his "shabbylooking," eventually "burned down" house. In a final twist of strangeness, Luisa discovers that the object she had originally seen and heard in the company of the *curandero* as a magical music box becomes (with Sally present) a mere piece of charred wood. Readers realize that Noriega's power resides as much in Luisa's "innocent curiosity" as it does in his being a tale-spinner, "hypnotist, [and] a soothsayer and doctor of sorts."

"The Interview" (1974) is the comic story of Antonio Chávez, a young man earning money by conducting surveys in the barrio, who interviews the wino Jess instead of the person on his assigned list. He fails to realize it, however, until after he has been duped by Jess and his pal Pete. Interest in this story, besides the fact that it was later adapted into a play, lies in the clever way that Arias transforms a simple situation into an examination of the basic urge to improve one's circumstances and self-image by fabricating alternatives to them.

Arias likes to repeat names and types in his work. "Stoop Labor" (1974) presents another befuddled character named Chávez. A college student working as a janitor for a sorority house, Chávez is beset by the weather (rain from "the sky, gray and hateful") and the dreary prospect of an evening in his dismal job. The narrative follows that evening and everything in it to its troublesome end, which echoes the myriad disappointments of his day. The day began with his landlady mistakenly accusing him of pot smoking, a professor complaining about his paper's footnotes, his student loan application being rejected, and his trouser cuffs getting soggy in the rain, among other problems—all recollected with more comedy than sympathy. While "The Interview" balanced a simple, humorous plot with symbolic and thematic depth, "Stoop Labor" is virtually plotless and remains no more than an extended, amusing portrait of Chávez having a

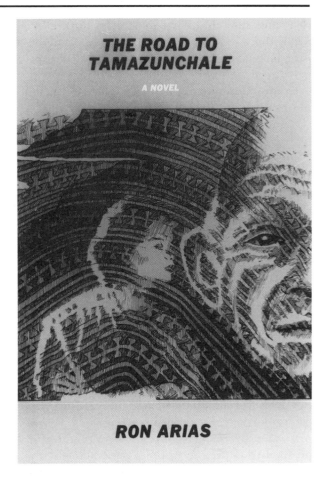

Dust jacket for the 1978 edition of Arias's novel, influenced by the writings of Gabriel García Márquez

bad day. Consequently, the possibilities of black comedy promised by the careful portraiture and carefully wrought style remain undeveloped at the end.

"A House on the Island (Or, The Story of a Poetry Teacher Who Seduces Her Students)" (1975) is an excellent narrative, one that has much in common with *The Road to Tamazunchale*. Its well-developed plot and characterizations and, especially, its multiple viewpoints and multilayered dimensions of time and space anticipate the novel. Depicting the timeless dynamics of a love triangle, "A House on the Island" relates the seduction of Nan's boyfriend Ricardo by their Spanish teacher, Elena Alvarez, after the trio have become friends in the last days of a "relentlessly" driven semester. Described as "beauty title" pretty, Nan is unwaveringly prosaic, always concerned with the literal, practical consequences of every action and "timidly" fearful of taking even small risks. Spontaneous Elena, unlike girdled, eye-shadowed Nan, is described as "soap-clear and smooth." What makes the story effective is the way Arias skillfully shifts the scene before the reader, subtly changing temporal and spatial directions in the middle of a paragraph or even in midsentence. For example, the action moves from the classroom, where the story opens and ends, to island exploration sequences, and climaxes in a lovemaking scene in the forest. Also enriching the story's texture are the flashbacks that reveal Elena and Ricardo more fully, while the love poem discussed in class, which opens and closes the story, gives added emphasis to art (the beauty of art is a theme central to Arias's masterpiece, *The Road to Tamazunchale*).

Omnisciently narrated in the third person, *The Road to Tamazunchale* tells the story of the last week of Fausto Tejada's mortal life, a time span conceived not in simple chronological terms but experientially. This approach to real time seeks to convey the total experience of memory, fantasy, the nonverbal subconscious, as well as the periods of consciousness during which language dominates the social construction. Within a temporal context the novel presents Fausto's response to the certainty of his dying–his rejection of, escape from, and ultimately his acceptance of death. In his preface to the 1978 edition of the novel, José Armas says it is not only about a man "confronting physical death," it is also "a story about man in relationship to the concept of death."

A widower and retired encyclopedia salesman, Fausto lives in Los Angeles with his niece, Carmela (whom he and his deceased wife, Evangelina, have raised from childhood), and with their parakeet Tico-Tico. Old and physically ailing, Fausto depends on the dutiful, good-humored Carmela for most of his basic needs, but, like his namesake Faust and his spiritual forebear Don Quixote, he digs deeply into his memory and imagination for emotional and spiritual solace. The novel is written in the manner of Latin American "magic realism," a form which Gabriel García Márquez has described (in a February 1983 *Playboy* interview) as "adult fairytales." The book transports readers back in time, forward to the future, and among several layers of present experience, in addition to a myriad array of places, including Peru and Mexico. The fairy-tale quality of Fausto's adventures combined with the narrator's lively tone explains how *The Road to Tamazunchale*, despite its solemn subject, remains consistently cheerful, humorous, and playful.

Because of his age and poor health, most of Fausto's travels occur within his mind and imagination, but–and this is an important point–they are no less real for being interior ramblings instead of physical excursions. For example, when he quixotically dons "the fragile, pink cape" his wife "used to wear on cold nights," takes his "hoe by its rusty head" to use as a staff, and then catches the bus to town, his adventures with the tough *vato* (dude) Mario have an aura of lunatic unreality about them even though they are supposedly actual happenings. The two characters interrupt a funeral procession, then become centrally part of it, after which they encounter a herd of Peruvian alpacas whose shepherd, Marcelino, they rescue. In contrast, Fausto's imagined trips to Cuzco, the "Navel of the World," and to Mexico, once the source of Evangelina's worst misery, are depicted realistically; the images of the jungle and mountains, of the city's rush and squalor, of sociopolitical inequity, all serve to vivify concretely Fausto's mental encounters with his personal ancestry and cultural heritage. The road weariness, dirty toilets, crowd of *mojados* (wet ones), and other mundane realities thus transform Fausto's recollections and imaginings into a journey into a collective Chicano past.

To guide the reader through the multitudinous range of narrative time, space, and experience, Arias relies primarily on a structure of intertextuality. To begin with, he bases his protagonist in part on the Faust legend as it has been variously interpreted in literature. Retired from making his living through books, Fausto, like his namesake, wishes to experience life fully, but unlike his prototype he seeks no alliance with either the devil or his infernal agents. In the face of death he shares Faust's desire to extend his life to complete unfinished business and realize his loftiest goals, but his is a quest which also forces him to confront the mortal weaknesses he has hitherto overlooked in himself. For instance, while cleaning Tico-Tico's cage, he hastily decides to go looking for an unusual snow cloud sailing over Los Angeles, but Carmela must remind him that his shoelaces need tying before the two of them can go out. Similarly, when he seeks to save some *mojados* by leading them across the desert to freedom, he is shaken out of his noble but impossible dream by Carmela's nervous death-vigil conversation with their friends about his fever and delirium. Arias's protagonist also shares intertextual affinities with the most famous of all Iberian heroes, Miguel de Cervantes's Don Quixote, the world's archetype of idealism and the redemptive imagination. Arias portrays Fausto as quixotic first in his insistence on diverting himself from death's nearness through his self-indulgent but uplifting wanderings in the labyrinth of memory and imagination—as when he seeks his origins in Peru or when he engages his dead wife in extended bedside chats. Arias also exploits the quixotic possibilities of comedy throughout the novel, which begins with a startling scene in which the old man removes his skin, wads it into a fistful of physical self, and then accidentally drops it on the floor to become, through Carmela's entrance, a crumpled Kleenex tissue. The humor here, as elsewhere, derives from such bizarre associations as linking Fausto's epidermis to chicken skin, nylon hose, and the wadded tissue that remind the credulous reader that skin-peeling is absurd, even in view of the scene's implied reference to an ancient Aztec Xipe Totec ritual. Another of the book's quixotically funny episodes occurs on a Hollywood motion picture set where Fausto and his Sancho Panza of the moment, the alpaca shepherd Marcelino, stumble upon a revolution scene and are mistaken for acting extras.

Crucial to the structure of intertextuality are the novel's embedded allusions to Latin American fiction. The opening scene described above recalls Fuentes's *A Change of Skin* (1967). Other aspects of *The Road to Tamazunchale* bring to mind *Pedro Páramo* and Fuentes's *The Death of Artemio Cruz*. The work and style of Colombian García Márquez is a major influence on Arias. "I'll always remember," he told Juan Bruce-Novoa in 1980, "my sense of pleasure and wonder when I first discovered, page-by-careful-page, *Cien años de soledad* [1967; translated as *One Hundred Years of Solitude*, 1970], transformed, *deepened* reality in so many of its aspects—tragic, humorous, adventurous, wondrous." Chapter 7 of *The Road to Tamazunchale*, for example, tells the story of the handsome drowned man whom Mrs. Rentería adopts as the husband she never had ("everyone called her Mrs. out of respect"). In outline, tone, effect, and many details, the chapter—originally published as a separate story—recalls García Márquez's "The Handsomest Drowned Man in the World, A Tale for Children" (published in English in 1971). Similarly the episode of Fausto's near burial after he first interrupts, then joins, a funeral procession resembles García Márquez's "The Other Side of Death" (1948), which records a firsthand description from the grave of postmortem sensation. Arias also echoes the Colombian's

narrative tone, which is always light, humorous, inquisitive, and filled with childlike wonder. Arias's allusive framework works because it is grounded in Mexican-American culture. His symbolism in *The Road to Tamazunchale* blends allusions from myth and literature with vivid details of Mexican-American life. It serves to unify his two central themes, the struggle between rationalism and the imagination and the transcendent possibilities inherent in a well-defined ethnic identity.

Of the many key symbols in the novel the journey motif provides the emblematic fulcrum of the narrative. From buses, trains, vans, and hearses, to Jess's Chevrolet Impala, Carmela's horse experience, and bookstore shopping carts, travel imagery appears in nearly every scene. In the same way, from the title's reference to "the road," to Fausto's constant journeying, to the recurrent procession images, to the motif's eloquent culmination in the bus trip that constitutes "The Road to Tamazunchale," the play-within-a-play, the journey as process and lived experience, as self-expression and self-discovery, dominates the novel. This idea is summarized aptly in the book's most frequently quoted lines, spoken by the play's bumbling emcee:

> Under his wife's coaching, he rambled to the end of his speech, explaining to the audience how they were all either coming from or going to Tamazunchale. "And we are too," he added. "We may not know it, but it's the same road. Everyone is on that road. Sí, compadres, everyone! But as you'll see, Tamazunchale is not what you think it is. . . ."

Another key symbol in the novel derives from the myth of Orpheus. In the first chapter Fausto is seized by "the monstrous dread of dying," and, just as suddenly, he is calmed and beckoned by "the faint, soft sound of a flute." When flutist Marcelino finally appears, he functions as a fusion of the Orphic god with his "song of life" and Hermes, guide of departed souls to Hades. Marcelino gives Fausto the will to keep trying until, even in the face of death, "nothing can make you fall." Fausto himself also represents Orpheus in the characteristics of the Greek hero's loyalty to his wife, Eurydice, by the magical-musical powers embodied in his imagination, in his fascination with his body parts and his association with water. Although she is mentioned earlier, readers first meet the dead Evangelina in chapter 3 while Fausto "listened to a few tango records . . . [then] the liveliest Mariachi song in his

"... if you truly believe you can, you place one more stone on top. If it stays and does not fall, you will be as stong as that last stone."

At the intersection leading to the freeway on-ramp the frightened alpacas blocked a row of funeral cars, headlights on. Fausto, shouting and waving his hoe stumbled up the ramp ...

The column, led by the old man and the girl, quickly formed and wound up into the sky ... eventually all were lost, diminished, gone between the horizon and the stars.

Fausto watched the changes ... Now a stork, now a bear, one minute a horse, the next minute the rider, one moment a dog's howl, the next moment the rustle of wind through the highest trees.

Illustrations by Desolina in the 1978 edition of The Road to Tamazunchale

collection." Responding to his "exhaustion" and anxiety about dying expressed early in the novel, Evangelina attends him and gives the "small, stooped man with a dopey smile" a comforting kiss that puts him deeply to sleep. After her introduction Evangelina frequents the novel's pages like a Eurydice, a living part of her husband's reality. She is part of the composite female figure, Carmela-Ana-Evangelina, that haunts Fausto's consciousness until the very last lines, when he set "himself down beside his wife, clapped some life into his cold hands, then crossed them over his chest and went to sleep." Fausto recalls the dismembered Orpheus of myth in his preoccupation with assorted body parts. He fusses over his detached skin, spidery varicose veins, his toe, and other organs and appendages. And just as Orpheus is associated with bodies of water, so too is Fausto repeatedly linked with rivers and streams, sources of tangible life as well as archetypal emblems of the human journey through it.

The chorus of voices celebrating *The Road to Tamazunchale* includes Juan Bruce-Novoa in his *Chicano Authors*, Cordelia Candelaria in the *American Book Review* (April 1983), Carlota Cárdenas de Dwyer in *Bilingual Review/Revista Bilingüe* (September-December 1977), Willard Gingerich in Julio A. Martínez and Francisco A. Lomelí's *Chicano Literature: A Reference Guide* (1985), Vernon E. Lattin in *Revista Chicano-Riqueña* (Summer 1982), Eliud Martínez (Spring 1977) and Judy Salinas (Spring-Summer 1976) in the *Latin American Literary Review,* and Eva Margarita Nieto in Lattin's *Contemporary Chicano Fiction: A Critical Survey* (1986). Focusing on the novel's experiments with "textual interpolation," Nieto lauds the compelling way that "it constructs a dialectic between the reader and itself." Gingerich stresses how "Arias shows the promise of . . . *chicanismo*" which fuses "all the currents of indigenous, colonial (Spanish and Anglo), and modern Yankee identities into one being" and in so doing "appropriates all that is American in experience for itself, free to move at will among genres, languages, and techniques." Most readers also comment on the author's mastery in creating a work that, while telling a gripping story, is also richly textured and intertextual. Eliud Martínez summarizes the critical favor by praising Arias's "simple, joyful, story-telling gifts–in the most praiseworthy sense–and for his commitment to art and truth which transcends but does not preclude social commentary on facets of the Chicano Experience. . . . In terms of craftsmanship and artistry

no Chicano novel before *The Road to Tamazunchale* has tapped the artistic resources of the modern and contemporary . . . arts in a comparable way. . . ; it is a pace-setter and marks a new direction . . . , [and] is a significant contribution to American literature."

After *The Road to Tamazunchale* Arias has published four significant works. In "The Castle" (1976) Sam, an old, homeless derelict, lives atop a hill in an abandoned unfinished building he calls his castle. He befriends a youth named Carlos, a pensive boy made acutely sensitive by the three-year absence of his prisoner-of-war father. A tender story of the depth of friendship and love which loneliness inspires, the story's fantasy-inclined, outcast protagonists bring to mind several Arias characters, notably "el mago" and the stranger in "The Story Machine," a story published in 1975. Similarly, Arias took the essentials from the short fiction "The Interview" and adapted them into a play by the same name (1979). The most significant alteration for the play is the rendering of student-interviewer Chávez as an explicitly pathetic fall guy to the more dynamic and aggressive winos.

"El señor del chivo" (1976) repeats Arias's common themes in a personal essay. The piece describes the author's fascination with a sidewalk vendor of goat-meat tacos during a trip through Michoacán, Mexico. What enchants him is the skillful way the vendor balances his taco-making routine with delightful repartee with his customers, who usually function both as friendly audience and as scapegoats. "This style of expressing language and experience," writes Arias, "this game-playing with reality, of course occurs frequently in speech . . . it might be Cantinflas or Groucho . . . [or] your crazy neighbor always putting you on, killing time by making time." For Arias, the taco-seller's life-style becomes a metaphor for the writer's view of life and art. Like the vendor who combines his quotidian reality with an enchanting style of "jiving, cabuleando [yarn-spinning], enlarging our perception of experience," Arias prefers fiction that "has many points, stimulates many responses, presents truth from several angles." He concludes the essay with an appeal to all writers, whatever their background: "stay in touch with [your] ethnicity. If you stay in touch, you've got a unique lifeline to another world . . . another perspective on people and even on physical reality."

"Chinches" (1977) is a terse but dramatic story of Gabriela, a young schoolteacher who attempts "escape into nowhere." Arias succeeds in his depiction of her by providing plausible motivation for her troubled state: her exhaustion from "teach[ing] those kids, I'm tired of gray streets and loud noise, I'm tired of watching my mother's little knife plunge itself into [my father's stony silence]." She is also tired of her boyfriend, Roberto. For Gabriela literal reality has become infested with nasty, biting chinches [bedbugs] just as its atmosphere has become "brown" and "muggy" after three days of rain. In common with most of Arias's outcasts her only hope lies in some form of escape, whether through travel, writing, tours of "burial caves," or diversions of the mind through memory (to Roberto) or imagination (her notebooks).

"Chinches," like Arias's other short stories, is a sound, well-written contribution to Chicano prose. His fame, however, rests with *The Road to Tamazunchale*, a recognized masterpiece.

Interviews:

Juan Bruce-Novoa, "Interview with Ron Arias," *Journal of Ethnic Studies*, 3 (Winter 1976): 70-73;

Bruce-Novoa, "Ron Arias," in his *Chicano Authors: Inquiry by Interview* (Austin: University of Texas Press, 1980), pp. 235-252.

References:

Cordelia Candelaria, "Los Ancianos in Chicano Literature," *Agenda: A Journal of Hispanic Issues*, 9 (November 1979): 4-5, 33;

Candelaria, *Chicano Poetry, A Critical Introduction* (Westport, Conn.: Greenwood Press, 1986), pp. 4, 74-75;

Candelaria, "Hang-up of Memory: Another View of Growing Up Chicano," *American Book Review*, 5 (April 1983): 4;

Gabriel Cano, "Letras chicanas," *Plural*, 62 (November 1976): 84;

Carlota Cárdenas de Dwyer, "International Literary Metaphor and Ron Arias: An Analysis of *The Road to Tamazunchale*," *Bilingual Review/Revista Bilingüe*, 4 (September-December 1977): 229-233;

Willard Gingerich, "Chicanismo: A Rebirth of Spirit," *Southwest Review*, 62 (Summer 1977): 302-304;

Vernon E. Lattin, "The 'Creation of Death' in Ron Arias' *The Road to Tamazunchale*," *Revista Chicano-Riqueña*, 10 (Summer 1982): 53-62;

Lattin, "The Quest for Mythic Vision in Contemporary Native American and Chicano Fiction," *American Literature*, 50 (January 1979): 625-640;

Marvin A. Lewis, *Introduction to the Chicano Novel* (Houston: Arte Publico, 1984);

Francisco A. Lomelí and Donaldo W. Urioste, *Chicano Perspectives in Literature* (Albuquerque: Pajarito, 1976), pp. 41-42;

Eliud Martínez, "Ron Arias' *The Road to Tamazunchale*: A Chicano Novel of the New Reality," *Latin American Literary Review*, 5 (Spring 1977): 51-63;

Eva Margarita Nieto, "The Dialectics of Textual Interpolation in Ron Arias' *The Road to Tamazunchale*," in *Contemporary Chicano Fiction: A Critical Survey*, edited by Vernon E. Lattin (Binghamton: Bilingual/Editorial Bilingüe, 1986), pp. 239-246;

Cecil Robinson, *Mexico and the Hispanic Southwest in American Literature* (Tucson: University of Arizona, 1977), pp. 330-331;

Judy Salinas, "*The Road to Tamazunchale*," *Latin American Literary Review*, 4 (Spring-Summer 1976): 111-112.

Fausto Avendaño
(5 June 1941-   )

Jorge Santana
California State University, Sacramento

BOOK: *El corrido de California* (Berkeley: Editorial Justa, 1979).

OTHER: "Historia de un mundo: fragmento," in *Nueva narrativa Chicana*, edited by Oscar U. Somoza (Mexico City: Editorial Díogenes, 1983), pp. 49-52;
"El forastero," in *Palabra nueva: Cuentos Chicanos*, edited by Ricardo Aguilar, Armando Armengol, and Somoza (El Paso: Texas Western, 1984), pp. 45-50;
"Juan González, poeta," in *Saguaro*, edited by Armando Miguélez (Tucson: Mexican American Studies, University of Arizona, 1985), pp. 43-46;
"Carpe diem," in *Palabra nueva*, edited by Aguilar, Armengol, and Sergio D. Elizondo (El Paso: Dos Pasos, 1985), p. 33;
"Los buenos indicios," in *Cenzontle*, edited by Helena Viramontes (Binghamton: Bilingual/Editorial Bilingüe, 1987);
Literatura hispana de los Estados Unidos, edited by Avendaño (Sacramento: ETL-Hispanic, 1987).

PERIODICAL PUBLICATIONS: "La mujer desnuda," *El Grito*, 2 (Fall 1971): 33-37;
"The Feud," *Obsidian*, 1 (Winter 1972): 13-15;
"La riña," *Revista de la Universidad de México*, 27 (February 1973): 27-28;
"Historia de un mundo capítulo 10," *Revista Chicano-Riqueña* (Spring 1978): 43-47.

Fausto Avendaño (courtesy of the author)

Fausto Avendaño stands among the most learned of contemporary Chicano writers, one who demonstrates exceptional skill in the short story and drama. Having published many short stories in the United States and Mexico, he is fluent in both Spanish and English, though most of his publications are in Spanish. His historical play, *El corrido de California* (The Ballad of California, 1979), is a good example of his dramatic talents. In it he gives life and shape to historical facts, creating an interesting and compelling plot.

Born in Culiacán, in the Mexican state of Sinaloa, Avendaño came to California with his parents at the age of four. He grew up in Southern California, primarily in the San Diego area, where he attended school and four years of college. As a student his first love was art. He had wanted to study painting, hoping eventually to do so in Paris, but soon realized that languages and literature were more to his liking. His studies were interrupted by two years in the United States Army, serving in Hawaii when the Vietnam War was in its first stages. Once home he re-

45

sumed his studies at San Diego State University and the National University of Mexico and eventually found himself in Tucson, Arizona, where he enrolled in a doctoral program. By this time Avendaño knew he would dedicate his life to literature—especially Hispanic literature. Recipient of a Ford Foundation Fellowship and a grant from the Gulbenkian Foundation, Avendaño traveled to Europe to study at the University of Lisbon, finishing his doctorate in Hispanic and Luso-Brazilian languages and literatures in 1973. During these years he became proficient in Portuguese and French. The recipient of a Fulbright Fellowship (1983) and a grant from the California State University Foundation, Avendaño has lived and traveled in Mexico, South America, and Europe, especially France, where he was an exchange professor (1983-1984). He has published numerous articles, essays, and translations. In an unpublished 1987 interview he said, "I had always considered academic publications necessary in my case because they gave me the necessary skills for more creative writing." He will no doubt continue to produce academic work, but he says he limits it more and more in order to dedicate his time and energy to creative work.

Although Avendaño began publishing in the early 1970s, he acknowledges he was not prepared to produce a major work until the late 1970s and early 1980s. He has finished two novels. Two plays and various short stories are also in the process of completion. "I sometimes feel that I should be further along as a writer," says Avendaño. "And I am sure some colleagues expect more from me, but the truth is I am where I should be, considering the circumstances. I started late—as so many of our [Chicano] writers. My high school education was almost nil with respect to literature and zero when it came to Hispanic literature. I didn't start reading our fundamental works till two or three years into college. Had I been raised with literary magazines, novels, plays; had there been *tertulias* (improvised discussions) and poetry readings at home—as is the case with so many of our leading Hispanic writers—perhaps it would have been a different story. I had to catch up, make up for lost time."

Avendaño's play, *El corrido de California*, has a compelling plot and interesting characters, some based on historical figures. The play explores psychological and social changes within a Mexican family in Alta California during the American invasion of 1846. The focus is on the emotional and intellectual strain experienced by

Don Gerónimo, a dynamic character who in a short time has to assimilate drastic changes in his life. Although—like many Mexicans of his time—he admires the United States and its Constitution, he is torn by his son's obstinate decision to resist the American presence. Don Gerónimo, the *alcalde* (mayor) of a small town, tries to remain apolitical, arguing that the affairs of nations, including war and annexation, are the concerns of those at the seat of power, namely Mexico City and Washington. However, his son Rafael and many of the townspeople believe that they as men can do no less than resist open aggression, no matter the outcome. "Por mi parte," says Rafael, "mil veces prefiero la muerte que recibir, encogido y melindroso, al enemigo triunfante, sin disparar una sola bala ni lanzar una sola cuchillada. No. Perderíamos más que la vida. ¡Perderíamos el derecho de llamarnos hombres!" (As for me, I prefer death a thousand times over than to shrink obligingly before a triumphant enemy, without firing a shot nor raising a blade. No. We would lose more than our lives. We would relinquish the right to call ourselves men!). In the end Don Gerónimo realizes that his son has been right all along. The circumstances call for sacrifice and determination, not passive acceptance of a new order. No amount of accommodation with the American presence will change the facts of war. Resistance, no matter the outcome, is essential for the very survival of his people. Don Gerónimo learns that Americans are not invincible and Mexicans, regardless of political change in California, need not accept subjugation. Rafael defeats Kearny's forces in the Battle of San Pascual but is killed in the process. As the play comes to a close, Don Gerónimo is completely transformed. He joins the resistance and leads his fellow citizens into battle.

Although his play has not yet been produced, Avendaño is attempting to raise ethnic awareness with *El corrido de California*. As such, the play can be related to the work of Chicano historians Rodolfo Acuña, Fernando Rivera, and Juan Gómez-Quiñones. Although he never allows readers to lose sight of his didactic purpose, Avendaño's characters are well drawn. His use of allegory (to explain, for example, the concept of Manifest Destiny) and *corrido* (ballad) are well integrated. The play has been praised by Armando Miguélez, who says that in it historical fact is meshed with dramatic tension so that the political and philosophical thought of the time is presented clearly. Oscar U. Somoza, too, asserts that

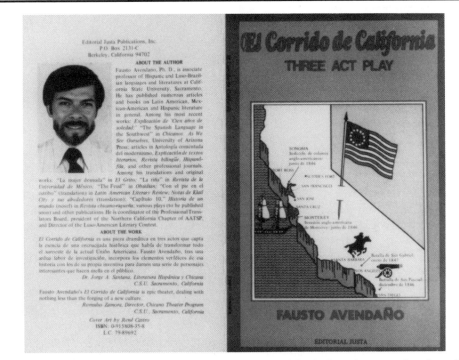

Covers for Avendaño's play which examines the 1846 invasion of Alta California from the perspective of one California family

Avendaño helps create the foundations for Mexican-American historical theater in the United States.

Avendaño's stories provide readers with a good assortment of interesting characters from farm workers and bureaucrats to actors and poets, among others. "Juan González, poeta" (1985) and "El forastero" (1984) are perhaps among his best. In the first story Juan González, an aging poet, though mocked by his peers, doggedly clings to his dream of publishing his first book. Raw talent and a deep love of poetry, however, fall short of the demands of art. González, instead of delighting audiences, bores them with his ghastly verse. Yet, as the story comes to a close, González emerges triumphant, at last recognized by all as a true poet. The protagonist of "El forastero" must alter her perception of reality in order to cope with life. The young Raquel is the bride of an older man who fails to provide the companionship she needs. In desperation she finds refuge in a dream world that eventually becomes her torment. Nebiros, a stranger, appears from nowhere to dissipate her every frustration, but reality is harsh, and in the end she must face the fact that her lover is not real.

In general, Avendaño's work emphasizes Chicano culture over political considerations. "Of course," he says, "there is political content in my writing—politics exists in most literature to some degree—but I don't want to force ideology or dogma down people's throats. As a writer, I ultimately want to entertain. I am inclined toward culture and wish to preserve it for future generations because, without it, we would disappear as a people; I think political gains may, therefore, depend on a collective awareness and appreciation of our cultural heritage."

If Avendaño were to stop writing today he would still hold an important place among Mexican-American writers, for *El corrido de California* is among the first and most effective examples of Chicano historical theater. However, his importance as a writer will probably lie in the works he has yet to publish. He is in the process of completing a play, "Abrahán Salazar," and a novel, "The Chicken Tenders," about the world of *polleros* (smugglers of aliens).

References:

Armando Miguélez, "Aproximaciones al nuevo teatro chicano de autor único," in *Literatura hispana de los Estados Unidos*, edited by Avendaño (Sacramento: ETL-Hispanic, 1987), pp. 8-18;

Oscar U. Somoza, Review of *El corrido de California*, *Explicación de textos literarios*, 9 (Spring 1981): 204.

Raymond Barrio

(27 August 1921-   )

John C. Akers
North Carolina State University

BOOKS: *Experiments in Modern Art* (New York: Sterling, 1968);

Art Seen (Sunnyvale, Cal.: Ventura, 1968);

The Plum Plum Pickers: A Novel (Sunnyvale, Cal.: Ventura, 1969);

Mexico's Art and Chicano Artists (Sunnyvale, Cal.: Ventura, 1975);

The Devil's Apple Corps: A Trauma in Four Acts (Sunnyvale, Cal.: Ventura, 1976);

Barrio's Estuary (Guerneville, Cal.: Ventura, 1981);

A Political Portfolio (Guerneville, Cal.: Ventura, 1985).

PERIODICAL PUBLICATIONS: "*Macho*–A Pitiful Effort," *Tecolte*, 4 (22 February 1974): 9;

"The Day Tlaloc Reigned," *Nuestro*, 1 (October 1977): 46-50;

"Rolling Up the Tortilla Curtain," *Nuestro*, 3 (January-February 1979): 8;

"Into Each Life a Little," *Nuestro*, 3 (August 1979): 38-43;

"Pushing the Button," *Revista Chicano-Riqueña*, 9 (Winter 1981): 27-33;

"Resurrection–1999," *Nuestro*, 7 (May 1983): 50-51.

Raymond Barrio's social protest novel *The Plum Plum Pickers* (1969) remains the most anthologized work of Chicano fiction. Selections from it have appeared in more than twenty high-school and college-level textbooks. Barrio is not Chicano by birth; he was born in West Orange, New Jersey, of Hispanic parentage. His parents immigrated to the United States from Spain in 1920. His father, Saturnino Barrio, born in Seville, was killed by poisonous fumes in a chemical factory in New Jersey; his mother, Angelita Santos Barrio, was from Algeciras and is living today in San Francisco. In unpublished correspondence Barrio explained that he and his brother lived with foster families while their mother pursued her career as a Spanish dancer, giving him a "very inde-

pendent United States Protestant education, despite a Catholic birth and upbringing." He identifies with both Protestant and Catholic religious traditions. In Mazatlán, Mexico, he met Yolanda Sánchez, whom he married 2 February 1957. The couple have five children. He is comfortable being called Hispanic because he has grown up in America as a descendant of Latin peoples.

Barrio has lived in California since 1936 (excepting time for military service in Europe from 1943 to 1946). His academic degrees are from the University of California, Berkeley (B.A., 1947), and the Art Center College of Los Angeles (B.F.A., 1952). Besides his devotion to art and writing, Barrio has taught a variety of courses (art, creative writing, Chicano studies and literature, and Mexican art) in eight California institutions (San Jose State University; Ventura College; the University of California, Santa Barbara; West Valley College; De Anza College; Skyline College; Foothill College; and Sonoma State University). In 1964 he was awarded the Creative Arts Institute Faculty Grant by the University of California. He lives in Guerneville, California, where he owns and operates Ventura Press.

Barrio has asserted that his vocation is art, and his avocation writing (his teaching has provided his family's financial security); his early publications deal with art. *Experiments in Modern Art* (1968) is an introduction to the basics of abstract painting, where readers are encouraged to "practice bold, confident, accidental strokes," always enjoying the process. *Art Seen* (1968), whose title is an evident play on the words *art scene*, is introduced by Barrio as "a kind of graphic compendium of loose sketches, comprising ideas, irrelevant commentaries, irreverent coincidences, wry observatorios, and prehensile pretensions . . . in: line, brush, block, letter and collage; in short *The Art Scene* as seen, gleaned, and executed by Ray Barrio." *Art Seen* contains about fifty pages of graphics. His search is for denuded essence in art and word. What little text there is in *Art Seen* is anecdotal description exemplifying his career-

Raymond Barrio in Guerneville, California, 1985 (courtesy of the author)

long tendency to bury pretension–whether in himself or another–sarcastically, cleverly, and humorously with wordplay, hyperbole, and oxymoron.

The Plum Plum Pickers is primarily a study of exploitation of migrant laborers by Northern California agribusiness. Barrio examines the lives of Mexican, Anglo, and Chicano farm workers, showing how their marginal existences as fruit pickers are dictated by ruthless overseers–both Anglo and Chicano–and ultimately by a system embodied in the growers' relentless striving for economic power and control. He was writing and publishing *The Plum Plum Pickers* when César Chávez's movement to unionize farm workers was becoming national news. Barrio learned that the major U.S. publishing houses were reluctant to back his novel, which was perceived as being too limited and regional in scope. His manuscript was initially rejected by every publisher he approached, and it was not until Barrio had the work published himself and had sold over ten thousand copies in five printings (in less than two years) that Harper and Row approached him for publishing rights.

Barrio frequently writes of people he has known: *The Plum Plum Pickers* was inspired by the writer's friendship with a migrant family he met in Cupertino, California, in the Santa Clara Valley–the setting of his novel. The personalized slant of the novel is manifested in Barrio's sensitive and realistic portrayal of many of the downtrodden characters he creates.

The principal figures of *The Plum Plum Pickers* may be divided into migrants, overseers, and owners. The migrant workers include Ramiro Sanchez, the protagonist, a Chicano farm worker who vociferously proclaims opposition to the exploitive grower's system; Manuel Gutierrez and his family (Chicanos from Texas); and Zeke Johnson and his wife (Anglos from the South). The overseers are Morton J. Quill and his Mexican assistant, Roberto Morales. The owner of the Western Grande migrant compound is Frederick J. Turner. There are also many important minor characters, including Phyllis Ferguson, the compound's prostitute; Jim Schroeder, a local nursery owner who defies Turner and supports the workers; Turner's wife, growing mad in her en-

Front cover for a later printing of Barrio's 1969 novel,
which explores the hardships faced by migrant workers

trapped, meaningless existence; the Delgados, a worker's family whose fortunes have supposedly improved (they are no longer dependent on migrant farm work for a livelihood but their menial employment at the compound results in alcoholism and cultural despair); Rat Barfy, an outspoken, bigoted radio broadcaster; and Howlin Mad Nolan, governor of California.

The plot of *The Plum Plum Pickers* is deceptively simple and is for the most part secondary to the social protest contained in the work. The opening of the book deals with a threat during the night on the life of the compound manager, the merciless Quill. The novel revolves around the relationship of Quill and his subordinates (the pickers), while it reveals the greed of the owner (Turner), the unfulfilled dreams of the workers, and the external and internal challenges to the false peacefulness of the migrant compound system. The novel exposes injustice, deception, disillusionment, self-destruction, and resis-

tance, finally resolving itself in the murder of Quill, apparently by the workers. The novel's discourse is by Barrio's design fragmented and irregular.

The reader of *The Plum Plum Pickers* is constantly aware of a certain spirit–Barrio's sense of a great cause–that pervades the novel. Following the threat on Quill's life early in the novel, Barrio begins an exposé of life in the compound, barely disguising his condemnation of the system that backs it, and using simple, often-staccato prose that regularly unleashes unabashed, strident criticism:

> Well, whatever had been out there hugging the darkness was gone now. The Western Grande was slowly coming awake again, all set to rip another beautiful day to shreds. All the families were in various stages of wakeful destruction. A baby bawled. A pot banged. A candle sagged. A rectangle of yellow light shone spectacularly out of a black wall, signaling the start of a new campaign of terror.

The novel gains momentum as it progresses. Fragments of dialogue, interior monologue, narration, and intermittent description are effectively supplemented with graffiti, verses of popular songs in both Spanish and English, radio broadcasts, bulletin-board announcements for the pickers, newspaper articles, and even picking instructions from a government pamphlet. The effect of Barrio's style is to bring the reader into closer contact with the world of the picker.

Barrio's novel adeptly links social protest with literary technique. Admittedly difficult to read because of the loose narrative design (the novel covers almost thirty-five episodes or fragments, some of which are no longer than a paragraph or are even broken down again into smaller units), *The Plum Plum Pickers* is nevertheless a carefully structured and coherent whole. It comes across as being a complete treatment of migrant life. The title of the novel itself echoes the routine drudgery of the stoop pickers' day, and there are lyric and poetic qualities in the repeated descriptions of the endlessly ripening plums. Barrio attempts to reproduce the speech patterns of some of his protagonists. A quote of one minor character, Jesús Avila, shows a native Spanish speaker struggling in English: "But how is it done, hombre? Damn, I moss know. Where you go sign up, man? I want sign up bad, man. Just tell me. I never realize how this was sotch a goddamn wonnerful contry all right just until this minute, pop." Along with syntactical parallels–the speaking of English with typically Spanish word order–Barrio offers immediate translations of Spanish phrases in his text. On occasion he will also indulge in code-switching–alternating Spanish and English in the same sentence or paragraph.

Critical reception of *The Plum Plum Pickers* has been favorable though disappointingly limited. In a critical essay for *Aztlán*, Fall 1970, Teresa McKenna analyzed Barrio's style. Patricia Geuder, in *Aztlán*, Fall 1975, detailed the complex relations among characters through a classification of the ways they address each other. A study by Vernon E. Lattin (April 1975) emphasizes Barrio's theme of unfulfilled promise, symbolized by ever-ripening plum trees that contrast with the barren lives of the workers who pick them. Francisco Lomelí, in his recent introduction to the Chicano Classics edition of the novel, has developed further the dichotomy between promise and reality for the farm workers.

In the development of the Chicano novel over the past fifteen years, *The Plum Plum Pickers* occupies a pivotal role. It was the first of a series of works that discovered the potential for novelistic development of Chicano social issues via the use of innovative literary techniques and a distinctive style. The Bilingual Press has selected the novel as one of the first of its Chicano Classics series. Also, it has been translated into German.

Barrio has continued his output. He has published editorials (*A Political Portfolio*, 1985) and art studies (*Mexico's Art and Chicano Artists*, 1975). His *The Devil's Apple Corps, A Trauma in Four Acts* (1976) is a mock trial of the reclusive billionaire Howard Hughes with Gore Vidal as a public defender. Barrio presents an outspoken critique of his exploitive characters, supplemented with dozens of drawings. The result is an obvious condemnation of a justice system that allows the unscrupulous machinations of financiers. Barrio has alluded to working on two novels, "Carib Blue" and "Americus," but to date the only evidence of these projects has been the publication of an excerpt from "Americus" in a 1977 issue of the journal *Nuestro* and the inclusion of three selections from "Carib Blue" ("The Caribbean Empire," "Tri-Dimensional Chess," and "Does Diane Matter?") in his collection *A Political Portfolio*.

References:

Ernestina N. Eger, "Bibliography of Works by and about Raymond Barrio," in Barrio's *The Plum Plum Pickers* (Tempe: Bilingual Review/Press, 1984), pp. 227-232;

Patricia A. Geuder, "Address Systems in *The Plum Plum Pickers*," *Aztlán*, 6 (Fall 1975): 341-346;

Vernon E. Lattin, "Paradise and Plums: Appearance and Reality in Barrio's *The Plum Plum Pickers*," *Selected Proceedings of the 3rd Annual Conference on Minority Studies*, 2 (April 1975): 165-171;

Francisco A. Lomelí, "Depraved New World Revisited: Dreams and Dystopia in *The Plum Plum Pickers*," introduction to Barrio's *The Plum Plum Pickers* (Tempe: Bilingual Review/Press, 1984), pp. 9-26;

Teresa McKenna, "Three Novels: An Analysis," *Aztlán*, 1 (Fall 1970): 47-56;

Philip D. Ortego, "The Chicano Novel," *Luz*, 2 (May 1973): 32-33.

Vicente J. Bernal

(15 December 1888-28 April 1915)

Erlinda Gonzales-Berry
University of New Mexico

BOOK: *Las primicias*, edited by Luis E. Bernal and Robert N. McLean (Dubuque, Iowa: *Telegraph-Herald*, 1916).

Vicente J. Bernal's poetry marks the beginning of bilingualism for Hispanic New Mexicans. He was educated in the Midwest, and his writing reflects the work of a young man who made a clean transition from a Hispanic cultural milieu to an Anglo environment. Bernal is one of the first Hispanics of the American Southwest to publish a text of creative literature in English. He does not ignore his mother tongue, however, as half of his collection is written in Spanish, and the entire text bears the Spanish title *Las primicias* (The First Fruits, 1916).

Bernal was born in 1888 in the isolated mountain village of Costilla, New Mexico. His was not to be a long life. On 28 April 1915, he died of a brain hemorrhage in Dubuque, Iowa, where he attended Dubuque German College and Academy (now University of Dubuque). Edited by his brother, Luis E. Bernal, and a faculty member of Dubuque German College and Academy, Robert N. McLean, Bernal's single collection of poetry and ten brief pieces of prose and oratory was published posthumously by the *Telegraph-Herald* of Dubuque in 1916. The little that is known of Bernal's life comes from McLean's preface to the book and from the introduction by W. O. Rouston, dean of the college. An article on Bernal by John B. Sánchez which appeared in the *LULAC News* in 1938 draws on this introduction for its information. Another article, by Fred Abben, appearing in *La Aurora* (18 January 1939) adds a few new details: Bernal was "known for his diligent and conscientious spirit of getting the best from his tasks. He was quiet and unassuming but with a beauty of character that remains to this day strong in the memories of his classmates and teachers." Bernal was buried in the Linwood cemetery, where "a granite cylinder, given in his memory by the members of his class of 1916, marks his grave." That Bernal

Vicente J. Bernal (Archives, University of Dubuque)

was indeed respected by his classmates is borne out by the fact that on 2 June 1936, at their twentieth class reunion, they gathered at his graveside to conduct a ceremony in his memory.

Spending the early part of his life with his grandparents in Costilla rather than with his parents in San Pablo, Colorado, Bernal worked on sheep ranches with his uncles and helped care for his grandfather's farm. These experiences left a deeply imprinted love and appreciation of nature which surfaces in Bernal's poetry. Not infrequently Bernal found in nature a source of comfort and revelation: "Two birds I spied on verdant hill; / Their heads were near, their breasts more near; / I heard no warbling, heard no trill. / But was inflamed with God's own love." Bernal's education began in the Presbyterian mission school of Costilla, continued in 1907 at the Menaul Presbyterian school in Albuquerque; and he planned to enter Dubuque Seminary upon graduation from Dubuque College in the class of 1916.

Religion, death, and love of life are common themes in Bernal's poetry. For example, "To ———" reveals a contemplative view of life and a highly lyrical sense of the precarious nature of human existence:

But why should I desire to scan
more thorny hills, if life's a breath
which seeks an ampler sphere!
A flickering flame, the life of man
Extinguished by the breath of death,
Which lurks forever near.

He loves life–"Oh let me kiss thy brow and locks, / And draw thee to my side, my life"–and he lives it (he says in "Prelude") heeding the words of his grandfather:

My grandpa, filling well his pipe would say:
"Well done, my child! we'll rest, and then keep
    on,
for God has said that we shall work as if
forever we should live, and by our toil."

Poems of love or of admiration for young women, who are frequently not identified, appear sporadically, as do poems dedicated to classmates. Of the thirty-four English-language poems, three are songs dedicated to the college. One of these became Dubuque's alma mater, as Abben says: "The poem written in 1914, was set to music by Mr. Mark James, who was instructor of Music, in Commercial Education and treasurer of the school at the time. The song was enthusiastically received by faculty and students and has been our Alma Mater ever since." The school still uses the Bernal alma mater.

Those who knew Vicente Bernal appreciated his sense of humor. Commenting on Bernal's youth in New Mexico, McLean observes: "In his association with men, the boy showed a ready wit, which made him an acceptable companion, and his jokes often furnished entertainment for the neighbors. . . . Indeed, humor was one of his

chief intellectual qualities and enabled him always to keep a cheerful outlook." His humor occasionally takes on a biting edge, as when he satirizes behavior which he finds objectionable. In a poem called "A Teacher" he chastises a young man who prospers at his mother's expense, taking money from her so that he may better himself: "But years brought greater needs / and greater needs more money. / Till mother lived on weeds, / while he was saying 'Honey.' " In the last lines he suggests the effects of this self-centered behavior: "Four years did laugh for him / And now has his profession. / And thousands follow him, / Nor stops the great procession."

A question of interest to readers of Bernal's work might be whether or not, given his ethnic and class background, he may have felt alienated during his tenure at Dubuque. The issue seems valid given that the historical reality of the time made for strained relations between Hispanics and Anglos in the Southwest, as Hispanics felt the ever-increasing pressure of displacement and marginalization. The village of Costilla must have been extremely isolated and contacts between its inhabitants and Anglo citizens limited if not rare. Through the mission schools Bernal came into contact with members of the dominant class; the home environment, however, was apparently heavily Hispanic. When Bernal arrived in Iowa in the fall of 1910, New Mexico had not yet achieved statehood, because of the "foreignness" of its Spanish-speaking population. The battle for statehood had produced a virulent campaign of defamation against Hispanic citizens of the territory. Yet Bernal's English-language texts, the majority of which were written between 1913 and 1915, show no evidence of social alienation. Perhaps Bernal's Presbyterianism may have alienated him from Hispanics who, in the main, were Catholics; certainly his religion provided him contact with Anglo culture. That Bernal was, in fact, socially accepted by his peers is borne out by the fact that he served as president of the college literary society, treasurer for the YMCA, and editor-inchief for his class.

It remains curious that the nostalgia one would expect to find in the poetry of one immersed in a foreign culture is minimized in Bernal's work. There are few allusions in his poetry to his family or to the village of Costilla. One lone dark-haired girl, scant generic references to the mountain and desert landscapes of the West, a poem in honor of his mother, a short verse prompted (says the editor's note) "by a postal re-

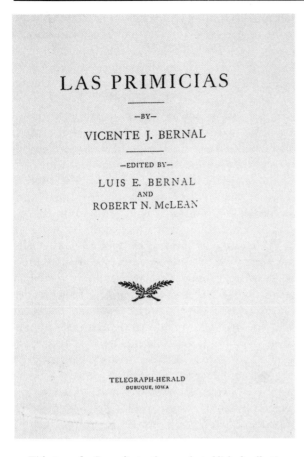

LAS PRIMICIAS

—BY—

VICENTE J. BERNAL

—EDITED BY—

LUIS E. BERNAL
AND
ROBERT N. McLEAN

TELEGRAPH-HERALD
DUBUQUE, IOWA

*Title page for Bernal's posthumously published collection
of poetry and prose*

ceived from home bearing a picture of a house and the word 'Bonita' " exhaust the inventory of references to his homeland. Only once, in his English texts, does he draw upon his cultural roots for thematic inspiration. In a short prose piece called "The Wedding Feast," the names of the characters, the description of the wedding party procession from the bride to the groom's house are undoubtedly Hispanic. Furthermore, the manner in which Bernal portrays the behavior of the emotionally wounded Bernardo upon the marriage of Estrella to the rich Porfiro and the description of his subsequent death conjure up the voices of New Mexico village *viejitas* (old ladies) spinning *brujería* (witchcraft) and folk tales.

Nowhere is evidence of Bernal's desire to assimilate the new cultural experiences offered by Dubuque German College and Academy more apparent than in his immersion in his secular studies, the fruits of which inspire much of his poetry. He frequently employs classical allusions and often engages in poetical dialogues with English-language writers. "Rubayat," "To Tennyson," "To

Burns," "Elvira by the Stream," "To Miss Self and Jimmy" are examples of the homage he paid those whose literary works inspired him.

Though Bernal's poetry suggests a conscious attempt to gloss over his cultural roots, there remains one very clear indication that Bernal did not totally deny his Hispanic background: his poetry written in Spanish. In his Spanish poems, there is some expression of a longing for the past which is absent in the rest of his work. One trace of that nostalgia is to be found in his frequent mention of correspondence. In "Parte de una carta" (Part of a Letter), nostalgia and even a sense of alienation (while not explicit) form the nucleus of the poem in which the speaker expresses frustration with the typical Midwestern repast that lacks beef, is eaten with a fork rather than a spoon, and includes a triple daily ration of potatoes. Bernal seems to miss the basic New Mexican staple of beans eaten with a spoon or with a tortilla used like a spoon.

In the Spanish poem "TRADUCCION The Barefoot Boy," the simple education of a barefoot youth under the tutelage of nature is described by Bernal in personal terms: "Parabienes jovencito! / Yo tambien fui descalcito" (Congratulations barefoot boy! / For I too was one of you). This poem, together with "A Teacher" and "Dishwasher," a humorous verse, suggest that Bernal was painfully aware of his social position.

Robert McLean observes in his preface to *Las primicias* that "Vicente Bernal was a child of the hills and plains of New Mexico, and when we are most deeply stirred, we speak the language of our birth. The artificiality of an acquired tongue can never really measure the deep things of the soul." Yet there is little evidence in the poetry of Bernal to support his statement. Bernal's Spanish-language poems, while they include a few more examples of his sense of longing for the past than those written in English, are in the main occasional poems which seek easy but tedious rhyme. The rich intertextuality found in his English verse is not echoed in his Spanish poems though his editors say that he studied both English- and Spanish-language literatures. Furthermore, his English poems truly aspire to universality.

It does not seem inappropriate to say that Vicente Bernal lived the last five years of his life in exile. Judging from his poetry, his exile was not of the sort that sharpens the vision of the homeland, nor did it engender nostalgia for the pastoral life of northern New Mexico. It was, rather, an exile which virtually obliterated his past, opening the door to an experience "which taught so many of strange tongue the syllables of liberty and brotherhood, guiding their first steps to higher plains of usefulness" (to quote the dedicatory note of the editors of *Las primicias* to Dubuque Seminary). The title of Bernal's collection appropriately captures the essence of his work.

His poems are, in fact, the "first fruits" of his creative endeavors.

References:
Fred Abben, *La Aurora* (Dubuque College newspaper), 18 January 1939;

John B. Sánchez, *LULAC News*, 5 (September 1938): 7-9.

Juan Bruce-Novoa
(20 June 1944-   )

Juanita Luna Lawhn
San Antonio College

BOOKS: *Inocencia perversa = Perverse Innocence* (Phoenix: Baleen, 1977);

Chicano Authors: Inquiry by Interview (Austin: University of Texas Press, 1980);

Chicano Poetry: A Response to Chaos (Austin: University of Texas Press, 1982).

OTHER: "Genesis," in *Christmas Anthology* (Bloomington: Backstage, 1975);

"The Space of Chicano Literature," in *The Chicano Literary World-1974*, edited by Felipe Ortego and David Conde (Arlington, Va.: ERIC Kress, 1975), pp. 29-58;

"L.A. Cantos," in *Canto al pueblo: An Anthology of Experiences II*, edited by Leonardo Carrillo and others (San Antonio: Penca, 1978).

PERIODICAL PUBLICATIONS:

FICTION

"To Carola, With Love," *La Luz* (April 1973): 57-59;

"Satisfaction," *Tejidos*, 3 (Spring 1976): 40-44;

"El extraño e increíble caso de la misteriosa desaparición del profesor K," *Caracol* (August 1977): 12-14;

"Autobiowishfulography," *Cambios Phideo*, 3 (April 1978): 15;

"Entry Into Matter," *Cambios Phideo*, 4 (Spring 1979): 20-21;

"Origen," *Plural*, 123 (December 1981): 5-10;

"Intervalo," *La Opinión* (17 January 1982): 8-10;

Juan Bruce-Novoa (photo by David Valentin)

"Aparición invisible," *El Gallo Illustrado* [Mexico City], no. 1034 (1982): 12-15;

"El paraíso terrenal," *La Opinión* (27 June 1982): 11.

POETRY

"String of Tears," *Literata* (April 1974): 7;

"Mystery," *Cambios Phideo*, 1 (April 1976): 22;

"Recuerdos del 20 sacrificio," *Cambios Phideo*, 1 (April 1976): 35-36;

"Expulsed," *Cambios Phideo*, 1 (April 1976): 38;

"Viajaré por tu cuerpo," *Mango*, 1 (Fall 1976): 28;

"Streets of New Haven," *Cambios Phideo*, 2 (April 1977): 14;

"Artist's Proof 1/1," *Cambios Phideo*, 2 (April 1977): 15;

"Metaphor," *Cambios Phideo*, 2 (April 1977): 16;

"Puerta," *Mango*, 1 (Winter 1977): 29;

"Motif No. 5," *Cambios Phideo*, 3 (April 1978): 41-42;

"Patron Saint of Lost Generations," *RiverSedge*, 2 (1978): 10;

"Epiphany," *RiverSedge*, 2 (1978): 36;

"Response to Disbelief," *Xalmán*, 2 (Spring 1978): 12;

"Settle," *Xalmán*, 2 (Spring 1978): 14;

"Preguntas a la distancia," *Cambios Phideo*, 5 (1980): 12-14;

"Grass," *International Poetry*, 18 (Spring 1981): 1;

"Poetim," *International Poetry*, 19 (Summer 1981): 1;

"La leche," *Cambios Phideo*, 6 (1981): 19-20;

"Connecticut, 91-95," *Cambios Phideo*, 6 (1981): 23-26;

"hAmOR," *Cambios Phideo*, 6 (1981): 13;

"Self-Portrait of Editorial Board," *Cambios Phideo*, 6 (1981): 31;

"Because Between," *RiverSedge*, 4 (1982): 39;

"In Your Long Absence," *RiverSedge*, 4 (1982): 39.

Juan Bruce-Novoa, the fourth son of Dolores Novoa and James H. Bruce, was born 20 June 1944 in San Jose, Costa Rica, where his father worked with the Ottis McAllister coffee importers. When the family returned to the United States in 1945, James H. Bruce joined the United States Army. During his absence, the family resided in San Antonio, Texas. In 1948 the reunited family moved to Denver, Colorado, where Bruce-Novoa was raised and where he attended Holy Family High School. He often spent summers with an uncle in Mexico City. In 1966 he graduated with a B.A. from Regis College. He received an M.A. in 1968 and a Ph.D. in 1974 from the University of Colorado at Boulder. His formal education has been multidisciplinary. He majored in European history and psychology as an undergraduate, studied twentieth-century Spanish literature for his M.A., and specialized in contemporary Latin American literature for his doctorate.

Bruce-Novoa has taught since the 1960s. From 1967 to 1974 he taught Spanish and Mexican-American studies at the University of Colorado at Boulder and Denver. In 1974 he joined the Yale University faculty. As director of undergraduate studies in Latin American Studies, he assisted the Yale Latin American Studies Center in grant writing, represented the center in Washington, D.C., secured the establishment of Bildner Grants for research on Latin America, and organized three national and international conferences on Latin American literature. He was faculty adviser of the student literary magazine, *Cambios Phideo*. He also instituted and funded an annual prize for the best student essay on Chicano literature and created a Chicano library.

In his essay "The Space of Chicano Literature" (1975) Bruce-Novoa stated that while Chicano literature had been influenced by both the American and Mexican literary canons, its literary space was neither American nor Mexican. Rather it occupied the space between the two literatures: "no one would deny the predominance of the Mexican and the American influences; yet, we are neither, as we are not Mexican-Americans. I propose that we are the space (not the hyphen) between the two, the intercultural nothing of that space. We are continually expanding that space, pushing the two out and apart as we build our own separate reality, while at the same time creating strong bounds of interlocking tension that hold the two in relationship. Each Chicano work opens a space for its existence and adds to the total space of Chicano art as well as Art itself. No Chicano represents all Chicano art, yet each does manifest, in the particular, the impersonal totality of it. Each addition, be it traditional or an extreme departure, has legitimate place, and each enters into the process of continuity. Chicano art is the space created by the tensions of all its particular manifestations. It is the nothing of that continuous space where all possibilities are simultaneously possible and all achieved products are simultaneously in relationship, creating one unit. We may concentrate on one, but it is only a particular surface leading to the space of all: the impersonal, continuous nothing."

Each piece of Bruce-Novoa's fiction constitutes a facet of his literary theory concerning the space of art, and consequently, of Chicano literature. For example, in his short story "To Carola, With Love" (1973) he uses the metaphor of translating a poem to develop the thesis that the sacredness of art is somewhere between the art piece and the spectator. In this case, it is in the process of translation. The narrator states, "The words flowed into phrases and phrases into each other as she flowed into him and together they flowed into the room. Her words, his words. Her poem, his poem. One and still two. It didn't matter to whom she had written it because now they wrote it anew." In the act of translating the poem, the narrator transcends his aloneness and enters an impersonal union with the loved one. In "Intervalo" (Interval, 1982), he illustrates his idea that the ideal space in which to exist is between two extremes, "pushing the two out and apart as we build our own separate reality. . . ." He develops his thesis by creating a story of a man who exists inside a hollow egg. At first the man, whose body is molded to the curvature of the egg, is able to keep track of day and night by the seven- or eight-hour cyclical changes of light and dark coloring of the surface and the gradual change of temperature, but when the entire surface changes to a pink tone and the temperature changes to a constant warm temperature that resembles that of his body, he loses his ability to monitor time and to map his position within the egg. Because he is unable to distinguish any differences in the surface, he creates a pleasurable game of trying to visualize the exact point at which the pressure creates a half-moon under the nail of his ring finger. Once the game has been perfected, to augment the level of difficulty and the sense of pleasure, he abstains from playing. When he resumes the game, he learns that he has lost the ability to visualize that exact point of the pressure. Horrified at the lack of sensation, he pulls his hands away from the wall, closes his eyes, and, gradually begins to feel the return of a slipping-away sensation. In the end, the man disappears into the surface of the onyx egg. He becomes nothing since he has become part of the egg. In "El paraíso terrenal" (Terrestrial Paradise, 1982), Bruce-Novoa develops a thesis that Chicano literature should not be limited to its own social or ethnic space, but that it should have an intertextual dialogue with all literatures.

Bruce-Novoa has stated that "a man's biography is what he reads and his autobiography is what he writes." Consequently, *Inocencia perversa = Perverse Innocence* (1977), a collection of poetry written in English and Spanish, can be read as a literary autobiography which reveals the relationship of Bruce-Novoa's poetry to the work of Mexican novelist Juan García Ponce, American

psychologist Norman O. Brown, and French writer George Bataille. His book of poetry demonstrates a philosophy that eroticism can be an alternative to confront the threat of death. The book establishes three types of relationships. In poems such as "The Coffee House," one of the partners moves away to save the relationship. Other poems, such as "When she really arrives," show a relationship in which one partner tries to dominate and entrap the other individual. The third type of relationship examined in the book is one governed by a pure pleasure that is guided by the perverse innocence of the woman. This type is best exemplified in the poem "Perverse Innocence":

> and you gave me no idea,
> though I felt it obscurely,
> that you had imagined
> the thirteen possible positions
> you wanted to try the first time,
> seeing us in them
> from all the corners of the room
> and even reflected
> in the mirror you inclined
> to see us from there
> from here
> not knowing you would no longer see
> anything but yourself
> drowning in the perverse innocence
> of the last of your children's games
> the first of your childish games;

Inocencia perversa = Perverse Innocence received favorable reviews. Francisco A. Lomelí and Donaldo W. Urioste state in *Chicano Perspectives In Literature* (1976) that "Juan Bruce-Novoa, showing signs of Octavio Paz' influence, develops fine erotic poetry." Arthur Ramírez in *Revista Chicano-Riqueña* (Fall 1977) characterized the volume thus: "a first rate collection of twenty-one poems, in Spanish and English language versions on opposing pages in which the Spanish-language poems are superior to the English-language versions. Bruce-Novoa's poetry is not Chicano poetry in the sense that there are no social concerns, no specific Chicano themes or brown consciousness. Instead, the substructure of this splendid collection is found in more universal erotic and metaphysical concerns." Judy Salinas in *Hispamérica* (1978) focused on the unifying theme of the poetry: "Categorizar esta primera publicación de poesía del autor chicano Bruce-Novoa como simplemente una colección de poemas seria un error. Es una novela-poema cuyo tema central es la mujer-diosa-inspiración creativa. El protagonista-hombre del libro reacci-óna pasivamente ante las acciones de las tres protagonistas-mujeres cada una de las cuales es y representa en realidad ese ser femenino: el proceso creativo de escribir–la diosa universal y eterna del escritor" (To categorize the first work of the Chicano author Bruce-Novoa simply as a collection of poems would be an error. It is a novel-poem whose central theme is the woman-goddess-creative inspiration. The male protagonist of the book reacts passively to the action of the three women protagonists, each one of which is and represents in reality that enigmatic feminine being: the creative process of writing).

In 1983 Bruce-Novoa received a Fulbright to teach American and Hispanic Studies at Johannes Gutenberg University in Mainz, West Germany. While in West Germany he organized and directed the first international conference on Chicano culture and literature, and in 1986 he organized and directed the second international conference on Hispanic culture in the United States, which was held at the University of Paris. From 1983 to 1985 he was affiliated with the University of California, Santa Barbara, where, in addition to teaching, he was associate director for the Center for Chicano Studies. In 1985 he accepted a tenured position in the Foreign Language Department at Trinity University, San Antonio, Texas.

Interviews:

Jesse Cardona, "San Antonio Ambiente: 'Chicano Literature is a response to threat,'" *River City Press* (21 August 1980): 7;

Patricia Dorame, "Un chicano y su inocencia perversa: Entre-vista a Juan Bruce-Novoa," *ecosEPESA*, 1 (November 1982-February 1983): 19-23.

Papers:

Bruce-Novoa's manuscripts are in the Nettie Lee Benson Collection, Latin American Collection, University of Texas at Austin.

José Antonio Burciaga

(23 August 1940-   )

Patricia De La Fuente
Pan American University

BOOKS: *Restless Serpents* (Menlo Park, Cal.: Diseños Literarios, 1976);
Drink Cultura Refrescante (San Jose, Cal.: Mango,
1979);
Versos Para Centroamerica, by Burciaga and Emy López (Menlo Park, Cal.: Diseños Literarios,
1981);
Weedee Peepo: A Collection of Essays (Edinburg,
Tex.: Pan American University Press, 1988).

OTHER: "Río Grande, Río Bravo," in *Canto al Pueblo: An Anthology of Experiences*, edited by Leonardo Carrillo, Antonio Martínez, Carol Molina, and Marie Wood (San Antonio: Penca,
1978), pp. 13-14;
"Romantic Nightmare," "Letanía Al Tomate,"
and "Chico and the Man," in *Flor y Canto IV
and V: An Anthology of Chicano Literature from
the Festivals Held in Albuquerque, New Mexico,
1977, at Tempe, Arizona, 1978*, edited by José
Armas, Bernice Zamora, and Michael Reed
(Albuquerque: Pajarito, Flor y Canto V Committee, 1978), pp. 37-39;
"Españotli titlan Englishic," in *Linguistics for Students of Literature*, edited by Elizabeth Closs
Traugott and Mary Louise Pratt (New York:
Harcourt Brace Jovanovich, 1980), pp. 390-
391;
"El Corrido de Pablo Ramírez" and "La verdad
es que me canso" in *Chicanos: Antología histórica y literaria*, edited by Tino Villanueva
(Mexico City: Fondo de Cultura Económica,
1980), p. 260;
"Sammy y los Del Tercer Barrio," in *Nueva Narrativa Chicana*, edited by Oscar U. Somoza
(Mexico City: Editorial Diógenes, 1983),
p. 46;
"La Sentencia," in *Palabra Nueva: Cuentos Chicanos*, edited by Ricardo Aguilar, Armando Armengol, and Somoza (El Paso: Texas Western, 1984), p. 133.

PERIODICAL PUBLICATIONS:
FICTION AND POETRY
"Verdad es que me canso," *Mango*, 1 (Fall 1976):
8-9;
"It's the Same Guy," *Revista Chicano-Riqueña*, 5
(Spring 1977): 16-17;
"Smelda" and "Río Grande," in *Vórtice: Literatura,
Arte y Crítica*, 2 (Spring 1978): 32-36;
"Pasatiempos" and "There's a Vulture," *Revista
Chicano-Riqueña*, 6 (Summer 1978): 21-24;
"World Premiere," *Grito del Sol: Chicano Quarterly*,
3 (July-September 1978): 34-35;
"Ghost Riders," *Maize*, 2 (Fall 1978): 46-47;
"To Mexico with Love," *Escolios*, 3 (May-Novem-
ber 1978): 71;
"Letanía en Caló," *Semana de Bellas Artes* (Mexico
City) (18 June 1980), p. 15;
"Dear Max" and "Without Apologies," in *Revista
Chicano-Riqueña*, 8 (Summer 1980): 6-11;
"The Care Package," *Revista Chicano-Riqueña*, 8
(Winter 1980): 45-48;
"I Remember Masa," *Texas Monthly* (July 1981):
120;
"For Emmy," *Denver Quarterly*, 16 (Fall 1981): 94;
"El Retefemenismo" and "El Juan Cuéllar de San
Jo," *Imagine*, 1 (Winter 1984): 116-117.

NONFICTION
"The Care of Tortillas Requires Finesse," *San Jose
Mercury News*, 11 April 1980, C14;
"Three R's and Two Cultures," *San Diego Union*,
6 June 1980, B9;
"Aquellos días en que no podíamos hablar españ-
ol," *El Miami Herald*, 1 September 1980,
p. 10;
"Convalescing from a Hispanic Heritage Hang-
over," *El Universal*, 2 October 1980, p. 3;
"La creación de la Margarita," *El Observador*, 10
December 1980, p. 4;
"Yule with the Shul Gang: Celebrating a Mexican-
Jewish-Anglo Christmas in El Paso," *San Jose
Mercury News*, 25 December 1980, B7;
"An Anglicized Nightmare in Official English,"
San Jose Mercury News, 27 April 1981;

José Antonio Burciaga (courtesy of the author)

" 'Weedee Peepo' or 'We the People,' the spirit is the same," *San Jose Mercury News*, 5 October 1981, B7;

"The New Year's Flaco Diet," *Nogales International*, 30 December 1981;

"Buzz of a Fly, Whine of a 747," *San Francisco Chronicle*, 24 February 1983, p. 45;

"Bilingual Study Could Ease Culture Shock," *Christian Science Monitor*, 3 February 1984, p. 21;

"Death and Humor in Chicano Drama," *San Francisco Chronicle Review*, 11 March 1984, p. 5;

"Cinco de Mayo Affirms an Indomitable Spirit," *San Jose Mercury News*, 6 May 1984, C7;

"New Plays of the Southwest: Review of Carlos Morton Play," *Pawn Review*, 9 (1985): 146.

A successful muralist, José Antonio Burciaga's importance as a poet, journalist, and humorist lies in his versatility and virtuosity with language; he writes in Spanish, English, and combinations of the two to express social criticism and his deep feelings of alienation. Francisco Lomelí and Donaldo Urioste, in their review (*De*

Colores, 1977) of *Restless Serpents* (1976), say that his poetry "is powered by an incisive sense of irony with the purpose of criticizing set or ignored truths. . . . His critical approach becomes effective because his attacks avoid demagogic or abstract declarations." Burciaga's appeal as a writer lies in his sense of humor, which he uses to satirize the rigidity of a system still clinging to traditions of racism and discrimination. With few exceptions his themes are eminently political and social, echoing the early militant voices of poets like Ricardo Sánchez, Abelardo Barrientos Delgado, and Raymundo "Tigre" Pérez, although Burciaga is distinctly more sophisticated than the latter two and avoids Sánchez's strident anger and provocative license with language.

Burciaga was born and raised in the border town of El Paso, Texas. It was in the small Texas cow town of Mineral Wells near Fort Worth, where he worked for a time from 1969 to 1970 as an illustrator in a civil service job, that Burciaga acquired a first-hand experience of the racism and discrimination he condemns in his poetry. As he says in "Without Apologies," "In Mineral Wells, Texas / mah memories lie dormant / in the pot holed streets / where people carry / bibles in their belts / and bias in their blood." In many ways, his childhood in El Paso laid the foundations for his future as a writer. During the summer he often read biographies, his favorite pastime. His mother, who had been a schoolteacher in Mexico, used to read to him as a child. Storytelling was an integral part of his family life. His youth was also influenced by the fact that his family lived in the basement apartment of a synagogue, where his father worked as a caretaker for forty years. This circumstance exposed him to a different culture at an impressionable age, and in the 1950s his group of friends became known as the Temple Gang. When Burciaga moved to California in 1974 and became a journalist, these early experiences provided abundant anecdotes for essays like "Yule with the Schul Gang: Celebrating a Mexican-Jewish-Anglo Christmas in El Paso" (25 December 1980). During these boyhood years, and in the absence of television, Burciaga was an avid reader of newspapers; in particular, his admiration for El Paso journalist Rubén Salazar may have stimulated his own career as a writer.

In 1960 Burciaga joined the United States Air Force. After spending a year in Iceland, where he wrote extensively as part of his job, he was sent to Zaragoza, Spain, for three years. There he discovered the work of Spanish poet, Federico García Lorca. After completing his military service, he earned a B.A. in fine arts from the University of Texas at El Paso in 1968 and started work as an illustrator and graphic artist, first in Mineral Wells, Texas (an experience he later recorded in an "Hispanic Link" column called "Mineral Wells–A Near and Distant Memory"), and then in Washington, D.C., where he began his participation in the Chicano Movement and where he met Cecilia Preciado, whom he married in 1972. The couple have two children. After a move to California in 1974 Burciaga started writing reviews and columns for local journals and newspapers. In 1985 he became a freelance contributor to the syndicated column "Hispanic Link" and the Pacific News Service. Burciaga is the founder of Diseños Literarios, a publishing company in Menlo Park, California. At present he lives in Stanford, California.

His collection *Restless Serpents* contains twenty-nine poems and short prose pieces. In terms of theme and style, the poems fall into two distinct categories. The smaller group contains poems which are written mostly in Spanish and contain nonpolitical, philosophical, or romantic themes. Of these Spanish poems, which tend to be somber and meditative, one of the best is "Hojas muertas" (Dead Leaves). The narrator contemplates the fallen leaves, pressed close together on the earth, and imagines them sharing the stored warmth of their time in the sun. The narrator regrets the death of his dreams and sees an uncertain future in contrast to the natural death of the leaves. Dated November 1969, written in Mineral Wells, the poem's theme is extreme loneliness and alienation from the natural order of things. This theme recurs in varying degrees of intensity in "La despedida" (The Good-bye) and "I've Yet to Cut My Lawn," although the latter does foresee an end to loneliness.

The second group of poems in *Restless Serpents* focuses on social and political issues, and the tone is satirical, often verging on the sarcastic. Many of the poems directly address the theme of the 1976 U.S. bicentennial celebration or use this event as a backdrop for probing into social injustice. The poems often highlight unfavorable comparisons between the revolutionary ideals of 1776 and the reality of 1976 oppression, as in "El corrido de Pablo Ramírez" (The Ballad of Pablo Ramírez), in which the famous ride of Paul Revere is effectively parodied to reflect a Chicano perspective of historical events. In "Amerika! Amerika!," "The Freedom Train," and "The Liberty Bell" Burciaga exposes such ideals as freedom and democracy as designed to benefit the few rather than the many. Burciaga also ridicules the Anglo settlers of California, as in "In Commemoration of the American Bicentennial," which looks back with bitter nostalgia to a time two hundred years ago when the Christians came to "civilizar y educar / pero sólo conquistaron" (civilize and educate / but they only conquered). Other poems in this group deal with specific contemporary issues such as welfare in "It's The Same Guy" and police brutality and racism in "World Premiere," "The Last Bastion," and "Obituario de Uncle Sam" (Obituary for Uncle Sam).

Although his poems, short stories, and art have been widely published in small literary journals and also in elementary level bilingual readers, Burciaga has perhaps achieved greater exposure as a muralist and illustrator and as a contributor to local and national syndicated newspaper columns than as a creative writer. In his column "Up Front," published in the *El Paso Times*

"Bullcycle" and "The Three Wise Men," note cards designed by Burciaga in 1979 (courtesy of the author)

Burciaga, 1988, standing next to his mural Chicano Last Supper *in the Stern Hall dining room at Stanford University (photo by Edward W. Souza, Stanford University News Service)*

(December 1980), Ed Foster acknowledges Burciaga's growing influence in national news circles: "One of the Chicano authors now gaining prominence, whose views I find interesting, is José Antonio Burciaga of Menlo Park, Calif., a former El Pasoan." In another "Up Front" (October 1980), Foster praises Burciaga's "Three R's and Two Cultures" (published in the *San Diego Union* in June), noting especially the author's sense of humor: "A piece of writing that came my way recently catches the 'humorous tone' that I like to think is truly American." And indeed, Foster has put his finger on one of the main ingredients of Burciaga's success as a journalist: his seemingly effortless ability to create, as Foster puts it, "a funny piece of writing . . . drawn from the depths of humiliation and pain like so much good humor . . . as American as apple pie." Coming from a fellow journalist, this is praise in no small measure, and Burciaga's prose fully deserves it.

Unlike his early poetry, which tends to fall into categories, Burciaga's essays range over a wide variety of topics. The most striking thing about them, however, is the facility with which he enlivens mundane subjects with humorous personal anecdotes, often at his own expense. For example, an essay on tortillas, "The Care of Tortillas Requires Finesse" (*San Jose Mercury News*, 11 April 1980), opens with Burciaga telling how he used to play with tortillas at the dinner table, biting holes in them. This idea leads him to poke gentle fun at himself: "By biting holes, I learned to make many interesting designs. My family claims that I owe my career as an artist and designer to the tortillas. That early, informal training, they say, provided me with the essential motivation and foundation, although sometimes I wore tortillas on my head, like yarmulkes, and never had any great urge to convert from Catholicism to Judaism." This is a typical example of Burciaga's sense of humor, and he uses it to advantage in essays that deal with serious subjects, as in "Convalescing from a Hispanic Heritage Hangover" (*El Universal*, 2 October 1980), in which Burciaga looks at some of the hazards of being a Chicano.

In "Living Astride the Line Between Two Cultures Can be Difficult" (*Denver Post*, 8 December 1980), he examines some of the differences between English and Spanish expressions and speculates on the meaning of cultural bias. His "An Anglicized Nightmare in Official English" (*San Jose Mercury News*, 27 April 1981) satirizes the idea of English as the official language of the United States by exaggerating the kinds of name-changing this amendment, proposed by Senator S. I. Hayakawa, would entail: Boca Raton becomes highly unappetizing as "Rat Mouth"; Yerba Buena would become "Good Weed"; and Aromas would become "Smells." Equally satirical is Burciaga's approach to "The New Year's Flaco Diet" (*Nogales International*, 30 December 1981), which laments the lack of an ultimate Mexican diet and shares various ideas on how to eat Mexican food and not get fat. The technique of taking a purely personal topic and using it as an approach to a more serious issue is one of Burciaga's favorite and most successful gambits. In "Texas-California Pair: Mixed Marriage" (*San Antonio News*, 29 June 1984), he talks of his own marriage to a Californian but manages to include interesting asides about "pachucos" and the vast number of transplanted Texans in California.

Burciaga has expressed a desire to write his autobiography. Not only does he have a vast store of fascinating experiences but, more significantly, he is blessed with the sensitivity and humor required to tell a successful story. From his early days when he ravaged the urban trash cans of El Paso in search of discarded issues of *Life*, *Look*, *Saturday Evening Post*, *Colliers*, and other reading matter, Burciaga has now won recognition as a writer himself. From his beginnings as a starving artist, working for two dollars an hour painting "furniture store art" as he calls it, Burciaga now paints controversial murals as the resident artist at Stanford and has exhibited his work in Washington, D.C., Atlantic City, San Francisco, Mexico City, Tijuana, Juárez, El Paso, as well as at many local shows. Besides the projected autobiography, Burciaga still feels the pull of his favorite writers Edgar Allan Poe and Federico García Lorca and continues to write poetry. His own favorite work is his short story "The Care Package" (*Revista Chicano-Riqueña*, Winter 1980), which he says was inspired by an actual dream. As yet there have been no in-depth critical studies done on Burciaga's writing; some early reviews of *Restless Serpents*, which is hardly representative of his later work, have been notably superficial. Juan Bruce-Novoa (*Caracol*, September 1977) finds Burciaga's poems lacking in imagery but entirely overlooks the playful irony of Burciaga's narrative voice. Lomelí and Urioste focus on themes rather than evaluation of technique and style. If asked to identify his best work, Burciaga would say that the best is always still to come, a good indication that as a visual artist and writer, José Antonio Burciaga looks forward to professional growth and development and to the exploration of new outlets for his dynamic and versatile creative energy.

References:

Alfred Frankenstein, "One Artist's Self-Defense," *San Francisco Chronicle*, 9 March 1978;

Jesús Rangel, "Heirs of José Posada: Revolution Lives in Chicano Art," *San Diego Union*, 24 February 1980, D4;

"RC Artists Hurl Paint at Mural," *San Mateo Times*, 27 February 1978, B7;

Ricardo Sánchez, "Non-Introduction," in Burciaga's *Restless Serpents* (Menlo Park, Cal.: Diseños Literarios, 1976), pp. 7-13.

Cordelia Candelaria
(14 September 1943-   )

Margarita Tavera Rivera
California State University, San Bernardino

BOOKS: *Ojo de la cueva/Cave Springs* (Colorado Springs: Maize, 1984);
Chicano Poetry: A Critical Introduction (Westport, Conn.: Greenwood, 1986);
Baseball in American Literature (Westport, Conn.: Greenwood, 1989).

OTHER: "Argument Against the Sublime," in *International Poetry Yearbook,* edited by Teresinha Pereira (Boulder: International Book, 1985), p. 33;
Multiethnic Literature of the United States: Critical Introductions and Classroom Resources, edited by Candelaria (Boulder: University of Colorado, 1989).

PERIODICAL PUBLICATIONS: "The Flowers Said" and "Loss," *Alas: The South Bend Indiana Women's Collective Newsletter* (Spring 1973);
"Voyeur," *Denver Post,* 25 February 1979, p. 22;
"Face," *Denver Post,* 13 January 1980;
"Wait Watcher," *Denver Post,* 17 August 1980, p. 63;
"Sin raices hay flor?" and "Fresh Mint Garden," *Revista Chicano-Riqueña,* 11, no. 3 (1983): 65-66;
"Festival of the Winds," *Imagine: International Chicano Journal of Poetry,* 1 (Winter 1984): 140.

Cordelia Chávez Candelaria was born in Deming, New Mexico, in 1943, the fifth of eight children of Ray Chávez and Addie Trujillo Chávez. Her father, who worked in road construction, had to travel frequently, and her family moved with him. She continues this pattern, commuting to her job as associate professor of English at the University of Colorado at Boulder from the working ranch she and her husband have in Ojo de la Cueva in northwestern New Mexico. She attended Fort Lewis College in Durango, Colorado, graduating in 1970 with an honors de-

gree in English and French. She received an M.A. in English from the University of Notre Dame in 1972 and a Ph.D. in American literature and structural linguistics in 1976, also from Notre Dame. She was married in 1961 to José Fidel Candelaria, and they have one son, Clifford.

Candelaria's fondest childhood memories are of being immersed in reading, participating in a world made up of words. It is not surprising that she decided to write. Her earliest poems appeared in 1973, and her first collection, *Ojo de la cueva/Cave Springs,* was published in 1984.

In the epilogue to her book *Chicano Poetry: A Critical Introduction* (1986) Candelaria speaks of the "eyes" of Chicano poetry; in an unpublished 1986 interview, when asked whether this concept evolved from her own poetry or from her critical studies, Candelaria answered that it was a combination of both. Examining her poetry, the reader can find the initial definition of the concept; it is the *"I"* of the artistic persona which focuses on another (similarly pronounced) *hay* (there), the geographical location that represents, in Candelaria's words, the "poet's locus of interest."

Candelaria's poetry is largely autobiographical. It can be said to have two major themes, an affinity for the land and an acknowledgment of her feminine identity. Her work is not one of a search for identity; rather it is reaffirmation of identity forged from and with the land. A series of early poems entitled "Thoughts of my Desert Home," which originally appeared in *El Grito* in 1976 and later were included in *Ojo de la cueva/Cave Springs* under different titles, places the poet in close relation to the land, expressing a nostalgic awareness both of the importance of identification with the land and the fact that the land can be acknowledged only from a distance. The land is the source of both life and death, as in "Cliffs," and is something yearningly recalled from a distant and very different present, as in "Within" and "Desert Blues." In "Within," for example, the poet writes:

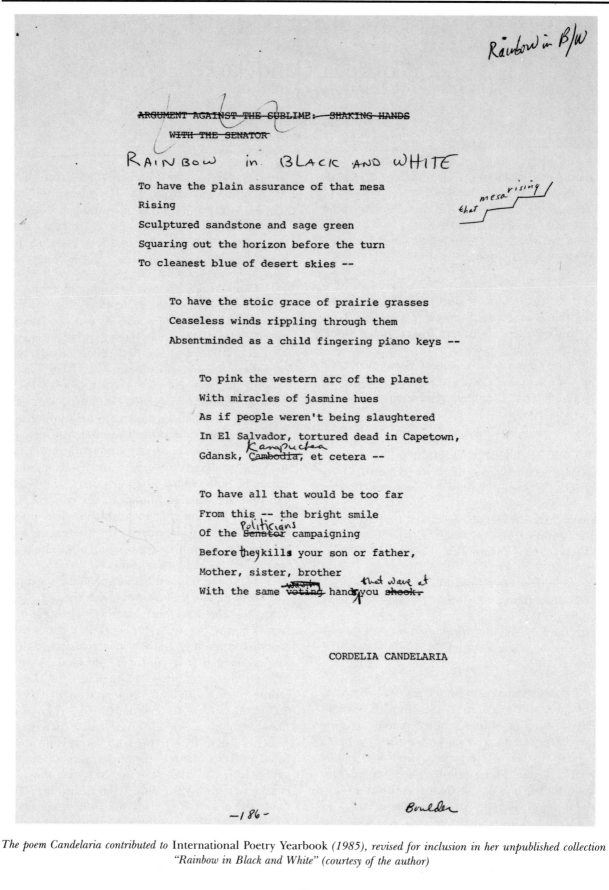

ARGUMENT AGAINST THE SUBLIME: SHAKING HANDS
WITH THE SENATOR

Rainbow in B/W

RAINBOW in BLACK AND WHITE

To have the plain assurance of that mesa
Rising
that mesa rising
Sculptured sandstone and sage green
Squaring out the horizon before the turn
To cleanest blue of desert skies --

To have the stoic grace of prairie grasses
Ceaseless winds rippling through them
Absentminded as a child fingering piano keys --

To pink the western arc of the planet
With miracles of jasmine hues
As if people weren't being slaughtered
In El Salvador, tortured dead in Capetown,
Kampuchea
Gdansk, Cambodia, et cetera --

To have all that would be too far
From this -- the bright smile
Politicians
Of the Senator campaigning
Before they kills your son or father,
Mother, sister, brother
that wave at
With the same voting hands you shook.

CORDELIA CANDELARIA

-186-

Boulder

The poem Candelaria contributed to International Poetry Yearbook *(1985), revised for inclusion in her unpublished collection*
"Rainbow in Black and White" (courtesy of the author)

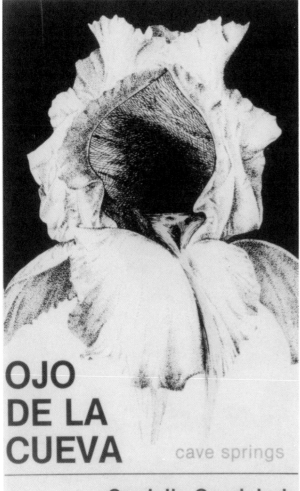

Cover for Candelaria's 1984 poetry collection

That far-off fresh aridity
pure exact meticulously alive

beckons the itching barefoot squirming
inside my damp dull heart—
so like the unwonted sludge without.

Uniting the themes of Candelaria's poetry are the recurring motifs of the spring and el ojo (the eye) as the sources of life, captured in the volume's title. The cover of the collection merges those two images for the reader. It is a drawing of a type of lily that suggests the female genitals and the spring that flows therefrom. The feminine persona expresses a positive view of motherhood and of family. Candelaria explores both images by naming them in "Graffitti Semiotics," which rebels against the fact that men and women are identified as only sexual parts. In "You" she reminisces about a sexual encounter, saying it was not a conquest or violation, but a sharing: "Like love it lingers to compel a smile / Now and then and will long outlive the pain."

"Ojo de la cueva" presents the cactus plant as a symbol of hardiness, of survival. The cactus sends roots down to the cave springs in search of life-giving water, an image which functions for Candelaria as a metaphor for the Chicano writer, who has managed to survive the aridness of the desert of inattention, and which surprises the observer with the vividness and beauty of its blossoms.

Candelaria has of late been concentrating on academic research such as that which appears in her book *Baseball in American Literature* (1989). When asked about her future publications, she mentions two completed poetry collections: "Warts and Frogs" and "Rainbow in Black and White."

Nash Candelaria
(7 May 1928-)

Paula W. Shirley
Columbia College

BOOKS: *Memories of the Alhambra* (Palo Alto, Cal.: Cibola, 1977);
Not by the Sword (Ypsilanti: Bilingual/Editorial Bilingüe, 1982);
Inheritance of Strangers (Binghamton: Bilingual/Editorial Bilingüe, 1985);
The Day the Cisco Kid Shot John Wayne (Tempe: Bilingual/Editorial Bilingüe, 1988).

PERIODICAL PUBLICATIONS: "Tio Ignacio's Stigmata," *Puerto del Sol*, 16 (Spring 1981);
"The Retribution," *Revista Chicano-Riqueña*, 9, no. 3 (Summer 1981): 37-45;
"Carnitas y huesitos," *De Colores*, 5, no. 3-4 (1981);
"Mano a mano," *Bilingual Review/Revista Bilingüe*, 8 (May-December 1981): 153-161;
"The Prowler," *Bilingual Review/Revista Bilingüe*, 9 (January-April 1982): 66-71;
"Be-bop Rock," *RiverSedge*, 4 (May 1982);
"The Day the Cisco Kid Shot John Wayne," *Revista Chicano-Riqueña*, 11 (Summer 1983): 52-64;
"The Price of an Ice Cream Sundae," *Revista Chicano-Riqueña*, 12 (Spring 1984): 5-14.

Nash Candelaria standing in front of a statue by Taos, New Mexico, wood-carver Patrocinio Barela (photo by Victor Samoilovich)

A historical novelist of the Hispanic people of New Mexico, Nash Candelaria has brought a special perspective to Chicano literature. His trilogy *Memories of the Alhambra* (1977), *Not by the Sword* (1982), and *Inheritance of Strangers* (1985) explores the relationship between historical incident and individual destiny.

Although born in Los Angeles, California, Candelaria told Juan Bruce-Novoa in a 1980 interview that he considers himself a New Mexican. His family was among the founders of Albuquerque in 1706, and one ancestor, Juan Candelaria, dictated a history of the New Mexico territory in 1776. His parents, Ignacio N. and Flora Rivera Candelaria, were born and raised in that state, and he and his sister spent their summers with family in Los Candelarias, a rural area of Albuquerque. These summer vacations were

crucial to Candelaria's strong identification with New Mexico because he was able to observe and develop a feeling for the special way of life of the New Mexican Hispanics as well as their unique identity.

Candelaria grew up in Catholic Anglo neighborhoods of Los Angeles. Participation in Anglo and Hispanic life made him feel part of both cultures yet gave him a certain objectivity that has to a great extent determined the course of his writing. Candelaria was encouraged to go to college after completing high school and received a B.S. degree in chemistry in 1948 from the University of California, Los Angeles. While working for a pharmaceutical company in Glendale, California, he found himself attracted to writing, an activity that had interested him for several years. Determined to make a career change, he did so after completing air force service during the Korean War. He took a position as a science writer-editor with a firm that made nuclear reactors and later went into science advertising and sales promotions.

During his air force service Candelaria wrote his first novel. Over the years he wrote several more, but the first to be published was his eighth novel, *Memories of the Alhambra*. Candelaria says that inspiration for it came quite suddenly while he was listening to an Andrés Segovia recording of "Recuerdos de la Alhambra." As he told Bruce-Novoa, "A mood, a feeling came over me and the idea for the story came to me in a flash. It was a chilling, exhilarating experience–like having a visitation from an archangel. The book would be a culmination of much I had gone through myself and much that I saw in my own family and others from New Mexico. It would be about 'Mexicanness' and the acceptance of it."

Candelaria originally planned his history of the Rafa clan to be a trilogy depicting the family from the Mexican War of 1846 to the present but now projects it as a tetralogy. *Memories of the Alhambra* lays the foundation for the saga by exploring the contemporary conflict of the Hispanic New Mexican who identifies with the Spanish and European past more than with his Indian and mestizo heritage. The novel opens with the death of the patriarch, the father of protagonist Jose Rafa. Although now cast in the role of head of the family, old family tensions and the ending suggested by his father's death cause Jose to experience a strong sense of alienation. The realization that he too will die one day forces him to think back to the beginnings–back to the conquistadores–back to the hidalgos, "hijo de algo, son of someone.... He was *someone*." Jose leaves his wife and home without a word and embarks on a journey to recover the past. He hopes that knowledge of his origins will give meaning to a life full of insults and pain brought on by ethnic prejudice.

Jose's quest to find his ancestral past is a tragic one because it is rooted in his aversion to Mexicanness. Although his search begins in Mexico, this leg of the journey is only a necessary stopover in the route of the conquistadores. He yearns to find the genealogical key that will prove that he is indeed Spanish and not Mexican. He is tortured by dreams of his own death, suffers from diarrhea, and is present at a cantina

shooting that unnerves him. After a brief but troubling stay Jose decides to leave Mexico, thinking, "This was the wrong place. To hell with the missing links in Mexico. To Spain! To the beginnings of the exploration of the Indies. And of himself."

Several flashbacks to Jose's childhood and youth reveal those moments that open his character to the reader. For it is the painful memories of the racist taunts and police roundups of "Mexicans" that included anyone with dark skin that illuminate the need for the quest. In her summer 1968 review of the novel in *Western American Literature,* Carlota Cardenas de Dwyer comments on Jose's journey: "... the tragedy of Jose's flight from himself is that it is not so much an attempt to escape what he is, as it is an effort to elude the false stereotypes created by others."

Jose continues to be frustrated in his search for a credible heritage. He travels to Granada and Seville, hoping to discover proof of the identity he craves, and continues to deny a clear historial reality, as he insists, "No taint of those dark races that pollute the blood and make a man a slave. I'm Spanish. Pure Spanish." Heeding the suggestion of a genealogist to look in the Estremadura region of Spain if he wants to find conquistadores, Jose sets out to find "in the family tree that limb that said he was all right and that the pain had all been a mistake." He regards the bronze statue of Hernán Cortés, conqueror of Mexico, and finally faces something he has always known: "If Cortes was your father ... then your mother was–He did not want to think the next words. They popped out anyway. Malinche. Never mind that the Spaniards called her Dona Marina. It was Malinche. An Indian. And you, child of the Old World and the New, are Mexican." Jose dies of a heart attack on the bus ride back to Seville, disappointed and unfulfilled.

Jose's son, Joe, reaps the benefits of his parents' struggle to establish themselves in California away from the restricting Rafa clan: he graduates from the university and marries an Anglo. He believes that his father has earned for him the right to succeed but now wants for his children the right to fail and still be accepted. As Bruce-Novoa commented in a 1985 article in *La Opinión,* (31 March 1985), "In other words, first one has to play the game of the master, winning–even though it may cost our very self–in order to then say that it doesn't matter."

In the main, *Memories of the Alhambra* received a very positive reception. Vernon E. Lattin stated in a review in *De Colores*, September 1980,

Covers for Candelaria's three novels about the Rafa family

that "Candelaria adds a new page to the Chicano novel, testifying to the fact that Chicano fiction is not limited to certain ideological themes or certain stock answers to questions of identity and ethnicity."

Not by the Sword, the second novel in the Rafa family saga, covers the years of the Mexican war with the United States (1846 to 1848) to depict the historical and social background suggested in *Memories of the Alhambra*. The opening lines of the novel uttered by the protagonist, José Antonio Rafa III, "Well, Grandfather. They say that we are to become Yankees now," establish the themes of the struggle to discover heritage and identity explored in the first novel of the series. The historical moment is fraught with confusion and conflict, as the New Mexicans try to preserve their lands, their traditions, and their identities.

José Antonio Rafa III, also known as Tercero, and his twin brother Carlos follow the traditional roles laid out for them by previous generations. The elder, Carlos, becomes a soldier-rancher and heir to the land, while Tercero becomes a priest. José Rafa's homecoming from his seminary in Mexico City takes place on the eve of the Mexican-American War. His ministry is to serve the poor, but he is immediately in conflict with the priest in charge, who holds with the custom that only those who can pay fees may receive the sacraments of the Catholic church.

Although Carlos has a great responsibility as heir to the family's land, his hot-headedness and domestic unhappiness put him on a disastrous course. His inability to pay a huge gambling debt to an Anglo gnaws at him until he commits murder and becomes a fugitive. He enters the conflict between the native New Mexicans and the Americans and is finally killed during the Taos Rebellion. After the death of Carlos, Tercero decides to leave the priesthood, for now it is his duty to continue the family name. He falls in love, marries, and takes up the ancestral responsibilities of the landed gentry.

Tradition and the continuing struggle to preserve it are concerns of *Not by the Sword*. The breaking of tradition within the family (Tercero's sister's refusal to accept an arranged marriage and Carlos's dishonorable acts), the questioning of tradition within the church by Tercero, and the weak hold of the landed families in the face of the Americans reflect a society on the verge of collapse. Candelaria makes it clear that the struggle has happened before. Tercero's grandfather re-

minds his grandson that he was born a citizen of the Spanish empire in New Mexico and that the Spanish took the land from the Indians. Nevertheless, echoing the sentiments of Jose Rafa generations later, he affirms, "The right people are Spanish and they own land."

Inheritance of Strangers was written during a three-year hiatus Candelaria took from his business-writing career. This third novel in the Rafa series continues to plot the course of the New Mexican-Anglo antagonism and rivalry in the forty years following the 1848 Treaty of Guadalupe Hidalgo. Tercero Rafa is again the protagonist, although considerably older than in *Not by the Sword*. He continues to live on Rafa land with his wife, their son, and the son's family. This novel begins with a conversation between grandfather and grandson, providing a framework for the lengthy narrative to follow. Temporal as well as spatial elements in *Inheritance of Strangers* are divided between present and past, New Mexico and California.

The narrative concerns a local election and the efforts of Anglos and Hispanos to control the outcome. Tercero meets with the biggest landowner in Los Rafas, the Anglo James Smith, to discuss the upcoming election, their candidate, and getting the people to vote for him. The system had been arranged primarily to the benefit of the Anglos, with the support of Hispanics whose votes were routinely bought. But this time dissension within the Hispanic community leads to violence and the formation of a vigilante group, los Hijos de la Libertad (the sons of liberty), in order to dissuade Benito Duran, the Anglos' choice as a puppet sheriff, from continuing his candidacy. Tercero's son, Francisco, is brutally beaten by Duran's men. The antagonism eventually leads to a tragedy when Francisco's son, Leonardito, is killed in a confrontation.

An alternate narrative is the one related by Tercero to Leonardito before his death in an effort to teach him of his family's (and by extension, his people's) past. Leonardito hears a tragic tale of land grabbing, murder, dispossession, and madness. Insane Uncle Pedro, who lives locked up in a shack on the small Rafa farm, is the embodiment in the novel of the fruits of injustice. As Tercero tells the story, Leonardito sees through his imagination the enormous, lovely California ranch where Pedro spent an idyllic childhood. But he also hears of the westward expansion and disregard of the old Spanish land grants. Tercero voices an attitude repeated elsewhere in the Rafa

Characters in Rafa Novels

The Rafas of New Mexico

Francisco Rafa	b. 1641 Río Abajo d. 1680 Río Abajo (Taos Rebellion)				
m. 1667 Madalena Gutiérrez	b. 1653 Río Arriba d. 1720 Los Rafas				
(2) José Antonio Rafa I	b. 1675 Río Abajo d. 1770 Los Rafas	(2) m. 1700 Maria Trujillo	b. 1680 Santa Fe d. 1725 Los Rafas		
(2) Concepción (Navajo chief's daughter)	b. approx. 1710 d. Unknown				
Félix Blas Rafa (out of wedlock)	b. 1725 Los Rafas d. 1765 Buffalo Country				
m. 1750 Juana Armijo	b. 1732 Río Abajo d. 1784 Los Rafas				
(2) José Antonio Rafa II	b. 1755 Los Rafas d. 1850 Los Rafas				
m. 1775 Rosalía Baca	b. 1759 Los Rafas d. 1829 Los Rafas				
(2) Francisco Juan Rafa	b. 1781 Los Rafas d. 1857 Los Rafas				
2 m. 1807 Estela Lucero	b. 1791 Alameda d. 1873 Los Rafas				

(3)(2) José Antonio Rafa III	b. 1821 Los Rafas d. 1906 Los Rafas	(2) Carlos 1821-1847	Josefa 1809-1883	Clara 1811-1889	(2) Andrea 1829-1909
(3)(2) m. 1854 Gregoria Sánchez	b. 1831 Los Rafas d. 1898 Los Rafas				
(3) Francisco Leonardo Rafa	b. 1856 Los Rafas d. 1916 Los Rafas	Carlos José 1858-1903	Consuela 1863-1934	José Blas 1865-1898	Andrea 1869-1937
(3) m. 1875 Florinda Chávez	b. 1859 Los Chávez d. 1920 Los Rafas				
(3) Carlos Antonio Rafa	b. 1881 Los Rafas d. 1971 Los Rafas	(3) José Leonardo 1876-1890	Rosa Florinda 1882-1948	Gregoria 1883-1923	Juanita 1885-1951
m. 1896 Matilda Griego	b. 1879 Los Griegos d. 1974 Los Rafas				
(1) José Hernando Rafa	b. 1906 Los Rafas d. 1971 Spain (on bus to Sevilla)	Tomás 1895-1950	Carlos 1899-1976	Juana 1908-	
(1) m. 1927 Theresa Maria Mathilda Trujillo	b. 1911 Albuquerque	Eufemia 1896-1977	Gregoria 1901-	Daniel 1911-1960	
(1) Joseph Rafa, Jr. (1) m. 1954 Margaret Winston	b. 1931 Los Angeles, CA b. 1932 Chicago, Illinois				
	Joseph III b. 1955 Anaheim, CA	William b. 1959 Fullerton, CA	Theresa b. 1961 Newport Beach, CA		

(1) *Memories Of The Alhambra*
(2) *Not By The Sword*
(3) *Inheritance Of Strangers*

Candelaria's annotations on the Rafa family genealogy, which was published in Inheritance of Strangers
(courtesy of the author)

family series: "In a way it was retribution. What the Spanish had taken from the Indians, the Yankees took from their Spanish/Indian descendants." When Gregoria, Tercero's wife, chides her husband for telling the boy their tragic history, he justifies his action by saying: "He'll never know what happened to him and his family in California. So how can he appreciate New Mexico if he does not know what terrible things happened to our people in other places? How can he learn what to watch out for so that these terrible things never happen again?"

After Leonardito's death Tercero begins again the tale of Rafa/New Mexico history by turning to another grandson, Carlos. The novel draws to a conclusion with a new beginning, as Tercero starts the story: "Once upon a time . . . there was a land called New Mexico."

Candelaria's Rafa trilogy is a novelistic representation of his view of culture as steadily evolving. Through his work he rejects the notion "that there is a fixed Chicano culture that we can go back to, like Eden, when in reality it is changing all the time." This appears to be a repudiation of the myth of Aztlán in favor of acceptance of the inevitability of radical change and assimilation. Instead he embraces a long view of cultural evolution whereby "we will all evolve into a common culture, an American culture, in this country, or perhaps a world culture on this planet." Despite this broadly assimilationist view, Candelaria vividly depicts the present in which his characters live and their natural resistance to change. As a historical novelist he contributes a view of historical reality which enhances the reader's understanding of the Chicano experience.

References:

Juan Bruce-Novoa, "An Interview," *De Colores*, 5 (September 1980): 115-129;

Bruce-Novoa, "Nash Candelaria: Novelista, 1," *La Opinión* (Los Angeles), 31 March 1985, pp. 6-7;

Vernon E. Lattin, "Time and History in *Memories of the Alhambra*," *De Colores*, 5 (September 1980): 102-114.

Lorna Dee Cervantes
(6 August 1954-   )

Roberta Fernández
Occidental College

BOOK: *Emplumada* (Pittsburgh: University of Pittsburgh Press, 1981).

The gulf in life between that which is desired and that which is real is the predominant theme in the poetry of Lorna Dee Cervantes. Culture and locale play a primary role in her poetry collection, which presents a young woman in the process of coming of age. By dealing with the inner and outer conflicts in the Chicano world amid the greater American context, the poet as narrator finds resolutions for herself through the act of writing. In an unpublished 1986 interview she fully identifies with her narrator: "My color and my class are intermingled in my poetry," she says, "I don't have a psychological separation from who I am because materially there is no separation."

Lorna Dee Cervantes was born 6 August 1954 in the Mission District of San Francisco, California, into what she described in an unpublished 1982 interview as the "welfare class." Her maternal Mexican ancestors intermarried with the Chumash Indians of the Santa Barbara, California, area, and her paternal ancestry is Tarascan Indian from Michoacán, Mexico. When she was five years old her parents separated, and she and her mother and brother went to live with her grandmother in San Jose, California. As a child she discovered the world of books in the houses which her mother cleaned. First she read Shakespeare, then the English Romantic poets. By the time she was twelve she was reading Byron, Keats, and Shelley over and over aloud, getting a feel for the cadence of the English language. At home her fascination with the rhythmic possibilities of language were further enhanced through the music of her brother, Steve Cervantes, who has become a professional musician. She started writing poetry when she was eight years old, and at fifteen she put together her first manuscript, to date unpublished. At Lincoln High School in San Jose she published some of her poems in the high school paper.

Emplumada

Lorna Dee Cervantes

UNIVERSITY OF PITTSBURGH PRESS

Title page for Cervantes's 1981 poetry collection

Cervantes's introduction to poetry reading was auspicious and truly dramatic. In 1974 she went to Mexico City to the Quinto Festival de los Teatros Chicanos, accompanying her brother, who played with the Teatro de la Gente (Theater of the People) of San Jose. Realizing that they needed to add to their repertoire, the group asked Lorna Cervantes to read some of her poetry as part of their performance. "Barco de refugiados" / "Refugee Ship" (the only poem which she has published both in a Spanish and an English version), which renders the Chicano dilemma of not belonging to either the American or the Mexican culture, was her selection to read before thousands in the open-air venue.

> Mama raised me without language.
> I'm orphaned from my Spanish name.
> The words are foreign, stumbling
> on my tongue. I see in the mirror
> my reflection: bronzed skin, black hair.
> I feel I am a captive
> aboard the refugee ship.
> The ship that will never dock.
> El barco que nunca atraca.

The poem was picked up by *El Heraldo*, a Mexico City newspaper. Soon after, her poetry appeared in *Revista Chicano-Riqueña* and, subsequently, in many journals and reviews.

That same year, 1974, Cervantes began to devote her full attention to writing and to helping other writers. She learned the trade of printing and with her savings bought herself an offset printing press. One of her projects was *Mango*, a literary review which she edited. Through her association with the Centro Cultural de la Gente (People's Cultural Center) of San Jose and through Mango Publications she soon began to publish chapbooks of the work of Chicano writers. By 1978 she was beginning to gain national recognition. That year she received a grant from the National Endowment for the Arts. The following year she spent nine months at the Fine Arts Workshop in Provincetown, Massachusetts, where she completed the manuscript for *Emplumada* (1981).

Emplumada is a created word which testifies to the personal and cultural nature of the poems. It is an amalgam of the participle *emplumado* (feathered; in plumage, as after moulting) and the noun *plumada* (a pen flourish). The title furthermore has allusions to Quetzalcóatl, the Mexican god of creativity, in his guise as the plumed serpent–symbol of nature's balance and the full potential of human experience. Bird imagery appears frequently throughout the book. *Emplumada* is divided into three sections, each depending on the other two for their full context. The first section deals with the social environment that has been given to Cervantes and with the choices that she and others make about the pattern of their lives, and is introduced by the epigraph: "Consider the power of wrestling your ally. His will is to kill you. He has nothing against you." Bárbara Brinson-Curiel (1982) says that "the ally is the person's childhood, family and early-life friends. The wrestling is a coming

to terms with experiences of loss, separation and grief, and with the mixed joy of formation into adulthood."

The opening poem of the first section, "Uncle's First Rabbit," is a feminist poem about the social determination of sex and class roles and focuses on how these prescribed roles affected a male relative. The narrative traces an individual, presumably the poet's uncle, through fifty years of male aggression and the male rituals of hunting and war. He associates a dying rabbit's scream with the violence which he has already witnessed–that of his father kicking his pregnant mother, resulting in the death of his baby sister.

> . . . She had a voice
> like that, growing faint
> at its end; his mother rocking,
> softly, keening.

Committed to being a gentler man than his father, ironically he winds up taking the "man's vow" and goes to war. Much later he has nightmares about that experience, and in fighting them off he "pounds their voices out of his head" only to find himself "Slugging the bloodied / face of his wife." By the end of the poem the reader can infer that this man will not escape but will stay where he is, continuing the momentum of misery in his life. Thus, the poem is about the inability of one individual to break out of the sex and class roles into which he has been born. "Cannery Town in August" continues with the description of a deterministic social milieu, capturing the moment when the female cannery workers leave their job at the end of the day. Describing the bleakness of their situation, the poet spotlights the silent, anonymous line of workers with the headlights of the trucks that await them.

> . . . I listen, while bodyless
> uniforms and spinach specked shoes
> drift in monochrome down the dark
> moon-possessed streets. Women
> who smell of whiskey and tomatoes
> peach fuzz reddening their lips and eyes[.]

The class status of the women condemns them to the deadening life at the cannery, and the harshness of their situation is first underlined by the silent ghostlike qualities of their presence; then the quiet is contrasted with the earlier noise of the clamor of the cans which by day's end has "dumbed" them. Like "Uncle's First Rabbit" this poem presents the realities of class and gender, which form the background of the poet.

For Cervantes escape is to be found in nature. "The Anthill," the third poem in the first section, balances the burden of ancestry and milieu by presenting the poet as a child frolicking with another child in fields of wild mustard, "[the] friend's throat / ringed with daisies." Together they explore the dank recesses of an anthill, observing the "array of soldiers" and kicking in the nests to find the queen and "the soft white packets / of her young." Exuberance, curiosity, and a sense of self characterize the child as she romps in broad daylight, not in alienation but with a friend, in open spaces of fields of flowers.

"Beneath the Shadow of the Freeway," another poem in the first section of *Emplumada*, is Cervantes's most celebrated poem. It describes her grandmother and her mother–the progenitors of her female self–and acknowledges the directions which each offers the poet in her quest for selfhood. The grandmother becomes a symbol of traditional female wisdom, and the mother becomes a symbol of an unhappy struggle with threatening urban forces. The grandmother's wisdom is expressed through her strong sense of self: "She believes in myths and birds. / She trusts only what she builds / with her own hands." Rejecting her mother's sardonic urban advice, the poet turns to the heritage steeped in folk culture which her grandmother offers and in the final lines of the poem turns the grandmother's actions into symbols of rituals which the poet will incorporate into her own life: "and in time, I plant geraniums. / I tie up my hair into loose braids, / and trust only what I have built / with my own hands."

"For Virginia Chávez" is a poem about reclaimed female friendship. Its main focus is on the writer's awareness of the opposing paths which she and the friend with whom she shared exploits in adolescent sexual awakening have chosen. Books, leading to Cervantes's diploma, made the difference in their lives. The author as an adolescent reads to her friend "the poems of Lord Byron, Donne, / the Brownings; all about love." Having already chosen for herself an identity as writer, Cervantes let "the child in [her] die that summer." Virginia Chávez, on the other hand, "was proud of the woman blooming out of [her] fourteen lonely years." Chávez chose her path and kept her child only to have the poet find her years later battered and bloodied by the man with whom she had chosen to live.

He did this.
When I woke, the kids
were gone. They told me
I'd never get them back.

The poet reestablishes her friendship with Chávez, "ignoring what / the years had brought between us: / my diploma and the bare bulb / that always lit your bookless room."

The first six poems of section 2 of *Emplumada* show the poet's harmonious relationship with the world of nature. The next seven poems focus on deprivation and contrast. In "An Interpretation of Dinner by the Uninvited Guest" Cervantes contrasts "the feast," on which a family dines every night, with the meager "voting booth room" from which the uninvited guest, alone and hungry, observes them. What is a routine dinner for a middle-class family is seen as a "Punch and Judy farce" by the person who does not have what they have.

In "Poem for the Young White Man Who Asked Me How I, An Intelligent, Well-Read Person Could Believe in the War Between Races" the poet reacts and becomes a participant in the world through the act of writing. Although she feels wounded with a "stumbling mind, [an] 'excuse me' tongue, and [a] nagging preoccupation / with the feeling of not being good enough," she confronts the world with her poetry albeit not with the romantic poetry she would prefer to write about if she did not think that a race war were going on in the United States. Thus, the poem contains Cervantes's *Ars Poetica* which binds the social poems of the first two sections to the lyrical poems of the third section. The poems "Barco de Refugiados" (Refugee Ship) and "Oaxaca, 1974" deal with her loss of the Spanish language: "I'm orphaned from my Spanish name. / The words are foreign, stumbling / on my tongue." Her loss of cultural continuity is lamented in "Poemas para los Californios Muertos" (Poems for the Dead Californios): "In this place I see nothing but strangers. / On the shelves there are bitter antiques, / yanqui remnants / y estos no de los Californios" (and these not pertaining to the Californios).

Resolution for the various losses the poet has articulated is finally achieved in the eighth and last poem of section 2, "Visions of Mexico While at a Writing Symposium in Port Townsend, Washington." Cervantes divides the poem into two parts, "Mexico" and "Washington." In

Mexico she is no longer threatened with the feeling of not belonging but rather is fascinated with her observations of the people and their subtle connections to ancient cultures. She is aware of who she is—a Chicana—and is comfortable with her identity. Thus, she acknowledges the oral culture which has connected her to her past:

> I don't want to pretend I know more
> and can speak all the names. I can't.
> My sense of this land can only ripple through my
>   veins
> like the chant of an epic corrido.
> I come from a long line of eloquent illiterates
> whose history reveals what words don't say.

From Mexico and her newly found sense of cultural identity Cervantes goes to the writing symposium in the state of Washington. "I don't belong this far north," she begins, once again feeling out of place. In this section she combines both her concern with her identity as a Chicana and her concern with her identity as a woman by describing how in a painting, which hangs above a bar in a tavern where she finds herself, "dark-skinned men [. . .] were drooling in a caricature of machismo." Even as she is disturbed at the racist portrayal of the men in the painting she sees the reenactment of the portrait in the scene below where some Chicano men "fiddled with [the] asses, absently" of two Chicanas at the bar. But instead of getting upset at what she sees, the author recedes to her identity as poet and tells the reader that she can control her world with her songs. In Washington, as in Mexico, she comes to terms with herself, finding resolution for the many conflicts in her life and in her role as poet: "as pain sends seabirds south from the cold / I come north / to gather my feathers / for quills."

Section 3 is entitled "Emplumada." Cervantes is no longer concerned with what she does not have; instead, she enters a harmonious state of being in which dreams, love, and nature abound, for she is now in a completely new cycle of life. The first poem of section 3 is called "This Morning," a clear reference to a beginning. The poet is still observing, but now she is admiring a hundred robins playing in the winter light and rain. No longer is she a captive in a refugee ship; instead, she dares to dream "all I could ever be / all I would dare describe."

In the last poem in the volume, the title poem, Cervantes witnesses the passing of time from one season into another, and although she hates to see the flowers go, she is accepting of the cycles of nature. In place of the flowers will later be peaches. Life prevails: "two hummingbirds, hovering, stuck to each other, / arcing their bodies in grim determination / to find what is good, what is / given them to find." Like the hummingbirds, Cervantes has found what is good in her life. Like them, whom she sees as "warriors distancing themselves from history," she finds peace and harmony for herself. She accepts the dimensions of her life, immerses herself in her various realities, and comes of age as a woman, as a Chicana, and as a poet.

The poems in *Emplumada* form a tightly knit unit which shows readers the environment into which the poet was born, the social realities against which she must struggle, and the resolutions she finds for these conflicts. Written in a controlled language and with brilliant imagery, *Emplumada* is the work of a poet who is on her way to becoming a major voice in American literature.

A new collection titled "Bird Ave," from which Cervantes has been reading since 1985, promises a more mature voice. Since the publication of *Emplumada* Cervantes has undergone major transformations in her life. In 1982 her mother was brutally killed in San Jose. In a 1986 interview she said, "I had no more poetry left. I thought I had given it up forever." However, after a long period of grief and introspection, she resumed control of her life. She finished her B.A. from California State University at San Jose and began a Ph.D. program in the History of Consciousness at the University of California, Santa Cruz, where she is concentrating on philosophy and aesthetics. Her dissertation will be on the aesthetics of black music.

"Bird Ave" will continue with the issues of identity found in *Emplumada*. Binding them all together is Cervantes's preoccupation with her role as poet. As in *Emplumada* she has refused to be limited in her thematic possibilities, and she goes back and forth, weaving together her conflicting experiences spanning all the voices we all have. She refuses to distance one world from another—the world of the barrio and the world of the mind—for she has lived in both and has been shaped by both. It is this synthesis of the private and the public voice which gives Cervantes's poetry a depth in thematic expression and a scope in imagery that have made her one of the most intelligent poets currently on the American scene.

References:
Bárbara Brinson-Curiel, "Our Own Words: *Emplumada*," *Tecolote* (San Francisco), 3 (December 1982): 8;
Marta Ester Sánchez, "The Chicana as Scribe: Harmonizing Gender and Culture in Lorna Dee Cervantes' 'Beneath the Shadow of the Freeway,'" *Contemporary Chicana Poetry* (Berkeley: University of California Press, 1985);
Lynette Seator, "*Emplumada*: Chicana Rites-of-Passages," *MELUS*, 11 (Summer 1984): 23-38.

Eusebio Chacón
(16 December 1869-3 April 1948)

Francisco A. Lomelí
University of California, Santa Barbara

BOOK: *El hijo de la tempestad; Tras la tormenta la calma: Dos novelitas originales* (Santa Fe, N.M.: *El Boletín Popular*, 1892).

OTHER: "A Protest Rally in Las Vegas, 1901" and "The Tempest's Son," in *Las Vegas Grandes on the Gallinas, 1835-1985*, edited by Anselmo F. Arellano and Julián J. Vigil (Las Vegas, N.M.: Editorial Teleraña, 1985), pp. 50-55, 74-76.

PERIODICAL PUBLICATIONS: "Descubrimiento y conquista de Nuevo México en 1540 por los españoles," *Las Dos Repúblicas* (Denver, Colo.), 7 March 1896-23 May 1896;
"Los hispano-americanos y la sangre de Cuauhtémoc," *El Progreso* (Trinidad, Colo.), 30 July 1898, p. 2;
"El pueblo hispano-americano," *El Progreso* (Trinidad, Colo.), 27 August 1898, p. 2;
"Elocuente discurso," *La Voz Del Pueblo* (Las Vegas, N.M.), 12 November 1901, p. 2.

Eusebio Chacón represents an important link in the development of early Hispanic literary tradition, particularly with respect to the novel and the essay. As a person of multiple talents, he was also fully conscious of contributing to the preservation of written literature from the Southwest. Not only was he a writer of certain distinction; his reputation was greatly enhanced by his keen interest in bibliographical listings of original works, collections of manuscripts on cultural his-

Eusebio Chacón (Miguel A. Otero Collection, Special Collections, General Library, University of New Mexico, Neg. No. 000-021-0168)

tory, and the dissemination of old texts relevant to the region. He is generally credited for publishing the first novels in Spanish in his native state, New Mexico, and in his adopted state, Colorado. He also promoted a wide gamut of literary activities. As a Hispanic leader and spokesman he contributed to efforts to document extant Hispanic expression such as a reprinting of Gaspar Pérez de Villagrá's *Historia de la Nueva México* (History of New Mexico, 1610).

Born in Peñasco, New Mexico, Chacón was the son of an illustrious and distinguished family of pioneers and colonists: Rafael Chacón and Juanita Páez. His father was a career military man who had experienced frontier life from the Mexican period in the 1830s to the territorial period (between 1848 and 1912). Both parents endured the hardships of frontier life, moving constantly from one military fort to another while suffering Indian raids, bureaucratic blunders in army assignments, diseases, or simply bad luck. Just before Chacón's first birthday, his family moved permanently from northern New Mexico to the town of Trinidad in southern Colorado.

Chacón's primary- and secondary-level schooling took place in Trinidad, but his New Mexican association was renewed when he was sent to the Jesuit Las Vegas College in Las Vegas, New Mexico, where he completed an undergraduate degree in 1887. He earned a law degree from Notre Dame University in 1889. Especially adept at public speaking, he was invited in 1889, when he was only nineteen years old, to deliver the welcoming address in Spanish to the Pan American Congress at St. Paul, Minnesota. For part of the next two years, he taught English and served as assistant director at the Colegio Guadalupano in Durango, Mexico. Health reasons forced him to return to Trinidad in 1891, and after he passed his Colorado bar exam that same year he began to practice law. His career peaked early when he was appointed official interpreter and translator for the United States Court of Private Land Claims, the official mediator of land grant settlements stemming from Spanish and Mexican rule. He also served as deputy district attorney in Las Animas County in southern Colorado, and, according to his father's biographer Jacqueline Dorgan Meketa (1986), he was "known as a scholarly man fluent in all the Romance languages who was also capable of reading books written in Aramaic." In November 1891 he married Sofía Barela, daughter of the well-known Colorado senator and Mexican consul Casimiro Barela. The Chacóns moved freely between northern New Mexico and southern Colorado, but the family al-

ways regarded Trinidad as their home.

Chacón enjoyed a remarkable reputation as a public speaker, civic figure, and man of letters. In a political meeting in 1898 for the newly founded Union party, a reporter commented:

El joven Chacón probó con su discurso lo que tantas veces se ha dicho de él: que es uno de los mejores oradores que tiene el país. Fluido en su lenguaje y pulido en su modo de expresarse, encantó con su discurso á cuantos tuvieron la feliz suerte de oírle.

(The young Chacón proved with his speech what has been said so often about him: that he is one of the best orators that the country has. Fluid in his language and polished in his way of expressing himself, he delighted with his speech whomever had the lucky fortune to listen to him.)

Chacón's relationship with his father-in-law permitted him to participate extensively in journalism for Spanish-speaking people. He served as an associate with José Escobar in the newspaper *El Progreso* (The Progress) from Trinidad, and he contributed articles to *Las Dos Repúblicas* (The Two Republics) from Denver, a paper controlled by Barela. In January 1890 he announced the future founding of *La Epoca* (The Epoch), a newspaper which never materialized because of a lack of subscribers. Being a man of fervent convictions, he frequently lent his name to social causes on behalf of Hispanics. For example, in November 1901, after a series of slanderous articles appeared in Las Vegas (New Mexico) newspapers about local Hispanics, especially Catholics, Chacón wrote the first rebuttal, "Elocuente discurso," in what became known as "La Junta de Indignación 1901" (The Indignation Meeting of 1901):

El sentido . . . es que los Hispano-Americanos somos una gente sucia, ignorante y degradada . . . a quienes la falta de luz evangélica tiene siempre en retroceso, y a quienes la fiebre sectaria reclama para espiritualizar con sus dogmas. . . . [Y] aunque todavía el nombre de ningún Neo-Mexicano haya llenado el orbe con su fama, no estamos tan dejados por Dios por acá como nos pintan algunos escritores que pasan por entre nosotros como caballeros apocalípticos, con la copa de hiel en una mano y la guadaña del odio en la otra.

(The sense [of the articles] . . . is that we Spanish-Americans are a dirty, ignorant and degraded people . . . whose lack of evangelical light puts us in a backward motion, and whose sectarian fever clamors for spiritualization with its dogmas. . . . [And] although as of yet no New Mexican has achieved fame in the world, we are not as abandoned by God around these parts as some writers portray us, passing among us like apocalyptic gentlemen with the cup of bile in one hand and the scythe of hate in the other.)

Chacón had a deep interest in supporting Hispanic literature. Besides writing a novel and essays, he also wrote poetry (which has been lost). He sometimes used the pseudonym "Romeo" for his most provocative essays. Not aspiring to be a critic, he nevertheless contributed to the bibliographical documentation of works for posterity and particularly to the dissemination of Southwestern classics in Spanish. As the owner of a rare copy of the first American epic poem, *Historia de la Nueva México* by Gaspar Pérez de Villagrá, he was instrumental in making it known by including it, in serial form, in two Colorado newspapers, *El Progreso* and *Las Dos Repúblicas* in 1898 and 1899. Other important works of valuable cultural content that he possessed in his personal library were Pedro Baptiste Pino's *Noticias históricas y estadísticas sobre la antigua provincia del Nuevo-México* (Historical News and Statistics on the Old Province of New Mexico, 1812) and Manuel Alvarez's unpublished manuscript titled "New Mexico History of the First Half of the XIXth Century." He announced several times that he was writing a history of New Mexico using the rare documents at his disposal, but the project was never completed because of his career obligations.

One of Chacón's principal goals was to establish Hispanic literary expression in the Southwest. He saw a flourishing tradition and believed it needed only recognition and acceptance independent of Anglo-American circles. He set out to appropriate a tradition from his cultural background to create an autochthonous novel. Believing himself to be an initiator, he tried to lay the groundwork for the novelistic genre in Spanish in his region. In the dedication to his two novel-ettes, *El hijo de la tempestad; Tras la tormenta la calma: Dos novelitas originales* (Son of the Storm; Calmness after the Storm: Two Original Novelettes, 1892), which operates as a manifesto or prologue, Chacón bluntly puts into perspective the significance of his writings:

Son creación genuina de mi propia fantasía y no robadas ni prestadas de gabachos ni extranjeros. Sombre el suelo Nuevo Mexicano me atrevo á cimentar la semilla de la literatura recreativa para que si después otros autores de más feliz ingenio que el mío siguen el camino que aquí trazo, puedan volver hacia el pasado la vista y señalarme como el primero que emprendió tan áspero camino.

(They [the novels] are a genuine creation of my own fantasy and not stolen nor borrowed from *gabachos* [Anglos] or foreigners. I dare lay the foundations or the seed of an entertaining literature on New Mexican soil so that if other authors of a more fortunate ability later follow the road I hereby outline, may they look back on the past and single me out as the first to undertake such a rough task.)

Presented in a romantic mode of sharp contrasts and ominous elements, *El hijo de la tempestad* traces the impact Son of the Storm, an outlaw, has in an unspecified area in the last part of the nineteenth century. Although the story is filled with ambiguities, the indirect allusions add up to structure a political allegory, says Francisco A. Lomelí (1987), that shows ". . . the genesis of an outlaw and associates him with the underground that becomes institutionalized in a political system." The romantic figure of the bandit here does not figure as a victim but as a victimizer who terrorizes people for no other apparent reason than being predestined to do so. The protagonist is called Son of the Storm because he is born during a storm and his mother dies giving birth. His father also dies, figuratively, when he gives the newborn to a wandering gypsy woman who is viewed as a witch. According to popular tradition, a child who grows up under those conditions will become evil. The story switches from the gypsy woman's efforts to retain the rights as surrogate mother to the child's development into a pillager and terrorist. The basic plot acts out the predictions as a self-fulfilling prophecy. The Son of the Storm, with his one hundred thieves, operates out of a system of labyrinthine caves to sack surrounding communities. His evil deeds and his enslavement of innocent people lead to his downfall and death when a cavalrylike group of men attack the cave. The novel, fueled by techniques of oral tradition, such as hyperbole, fantastic events, chronological leaps, and popular beliefs presented as truth, unravels a quick succession of episodes. Folklore contex-

```
        SANTA TERESITA DE LISIEUX.                    SANTA TERESITA DE LISIEUX.

          (As originally written)-                      (As now revised)-

          -------------------                          -------------------

   Como botón de Amor entre azucenas,           Símbolo del Amor entre azucenas,
   Le contemplaste en brazos de María;          Lirio del valle, en el tranquilo día,
   Era el Niño Jesús, que sonreía,              Así le viste en brazos de María,
   Despertando en las albas nazarena.           Sombreado por las palmas nazarenas.

   Después, años después, en las escenas        Después,lustros después,en las escenas
   De su terrible y trágica agonía,             De su terrible y trágica agonía,
   Le volviste a encontrar,y ya tenía           Le volviste a encontrar,y ya tenía
   Su corona de espinas y de penas.             Su corona de espinas y de penas.

   Y por eso, paloma del Carmelo,               Y por eso, paloma del Carmelo,
   Puso en tu corazón su marca santa,           Puso en tu corazón su marca santa,
   Y te dotó de angelical belleza:              Y te dotó de angelical belleza:

   Y por eso del mundo se levanta,              Y por eso del mundo se levanta,
   Interminable la plegaria al cielo,           Interminable la plegaria al cielo,
   Cuando de hinojos te saluda y reza.          Cuando de hinojos te saluda y reza.

                      E.Chacón                                   E.Chacón.
```

Typed copies of the first and revised versions of a poem by Chacón (courtesy of A. Lonteen and the Chacón family)

tualizes this evildoer in a process of damnation, but the novel implies that the protagonist is a minor villain in comparison to petty politicians. The novel functions as a social commentary on the rampant lawlessness of the 1890s and its main perpetrators. As a political allegory *El hijo de la tempestad* represents an early antecedent to a common theme often found in later Chicano literature.

Tras la tormenta la calma is something of an experiment in literary fancy. In it Chacón combines British and Spanish influences, including the Don Juan legend, the romanticism of Gustavo Adolfo Bécquer and George Gordon, Lord Byron, with a discussion of honor, the favorite theme of the Spanish Golden Age theater. Chacón incorporates points of each in creating a regional novel that also includes another valuable local source, narrative aspects of oral tradition. The characters appear as intertextual embodiments that are combined with archetypes from popular lore.

According to Lomelí (1987), *Tras la tormenta la calma* "can best be understood as a nineteenth-century Hispanic dime novel." The pursuit of honor and sentimentality is presented as a dangerous social game, particularly when characters of contrasting social class are involved. The fantasy-filled love triangle involves two humble persons, Lola and Pablo, and the higher-class Luciano (a Don Juan figure). Chacón avoids simplicity in plot structure through a third-person narrator who comments on the events with a great deal of attachment and sympathy and who contributes to the melodrama. The point of the story is not only the plot itself but also how it is told. The narrator moralizes about the dangerous games of love while he consciously establishes the characters and the events in New Mexico, specifically Santa Fe. The location is portrayed as significant to the action, almost suggesting that New Mexico is an extension of the Old World with its regionally adapted values. As stock characters, the figures in the story fulfill predictable roles because of their known flaws: Pablo, the noble poor man, does not assert himself to retain Lola's attention; Lola, meanwhile, surrenders to Luciano's advances; and Luciano's mockery of love and honor rebounds on him to put an end to his sexual exploits. Irony, more than poetic justice, places each character in a situation contrary to what he or she originally wished. Honor is presented as a code of behavior equally demanding. The title,

Title page for Chacón's only volume of fiction (Special Collections, General Library, University of New Mexico)

"Calmness After the Storm," hints at Chacón's desire for a reconstructive period for the moral fiber of New Mexico.

Contemporary newspaper editors and reporters were particularly complimentary of Chacón's ability to focus cultural and historical issues from a Hispanic point of view. More than a polemicist, he was viewed as an authority with insight into the past who had narrative talents. He was not singled out for his literature until Benjamín

Read wrote about him in *Historia ilustrada de Nuevo México* (Illustrated History of New Mexico, 1911). Read focused on Chacón's skill as an essayist, praising especially his historical revisionism in "Descubrimiento y conquista de Nuevo México en 1540 por los españoles" (Discovery and Conquest of New Mexico in 1540 by the Spanish, 1896). In 1975 Anselmo Arellano highlighted his fame as an orator by reproducing "Elocuente discurso" in a special issue of the journal *De Colores*. In 1976 Lomelí and Donaldo Urioste situated him within the development of Chicano fiction: "Chacón's collection supports the theory that novels (or short fiction) written by Chicanos did exist in the nineteenth century." Critics Cosme Zaragoza and Lomelí have both concentrated on analyzing Chacón's novels within their proper historical context while demonstrating his literary relevance. Clearly Chacón is a significant figure in early Hispanic literary history.

References:

Francisco A. Lomelí, "Eusebio Chacón: A Literary Portrait of 19th Century New Mexico," in *Chicano Literature: A Reference Guide*, edited by Lomelí and Julio Martínez (Albuquerque: Southwest Hispanic Research Institute, University of New Mexico, 1987), pp. 1-60;

Lomelí, "Eusebio Chacón: Eslabón temprano de la novela chicana," *La palabra,* 2 (Spring 1980): 47-55;

Lomelí and Donaldo W. Urioste, "Eusebio Chacón," *Chicano Perspectives in Literature: A Critical and Annotated Bibliography* (Albuquerque: Pajarito, 1976), pp. 41-42;

Jacqueline Dorgan Meketa, *Legacy of Honor: The Life of Rafael Chacón, a Nineteenth Century New Mexican* (Albuquerque: University of New Mexico Press, 1986), pp. 327-332;

Benjamín Read, "Eusebio Chacón," *Historia ilustrada de Nuevo México* (Santa Fe, N.M.: Compañía Impresora del *Nuevo Mexicano,* 1911), p. 460;

Cosme M. Zaragoza, "Del XIX al XX: La novela aztlanense en español," Ph.D. dissertation, University of Arizona, 1984, pp. 68-97.

Felipe Maximiliano Chacón

(1873-?)

Doris Meyer
Connecticut College

BOOK: *Obras de Felipe Maximiliano Chacón, "el cantor neomexicano": poesía y prosa* (Albuquerque, 1924).

Knowledge of Chacón's life and work is limited to the information found in a single volume, *Obras de Felipe Maximiliano Chacón, "el cantor neomexicano": poesía y prosa* (1924, Works of Felipe Maximiliano Chacón, the New Mexican Bard: Poetry and Prose). Only 183 pages long and written entirely in Spanish, the book was published by the author in his native state of New Mexico. Fortunately, it contains a ten-page prologue by the legislator and historian Benjamin M. Read, a highly respected man of letters at the time. In this prologue Read introduces the work of his friend, Chacón, to the reading public, providing biographical and literary information for those unfamiliar with his work. When the Historical Society of New Mexico purchased the Benjamin Read Collection in 1936, one of the very few copies of this volume was found. The book's value is that it preserves the literary efforts of an early Mexican-American author and that it documents a pride in ethnic identity as expressed by both the author and his friend.

Felipe Maximiliano Chacón was born in Santa Fe, New Mexico, in 1873, to Urbano Chacón, a newspaper publisher in several towns in northern New Mexico and southern Colorado, and Lucía Ward de Chacón. As was the custom among affluent Mexican-Americans in New Mexico in those days, Chacón received a public school education in Santa Fe and then attended the local College of San Miguel. After college he apparently decided to follow his father's example and make journalism his career. Between 1911 and 1918 he was an editor for various Spanish-language newspapers in Las Vegas, Bernalillo, Albuquerque, and Mora, New Mexico. He left journalism for a short time, perhaps to try another field, but in 1922 he returned to Albuquerque to work for *La Bandera Americana* (American Flag), a popular newspaper during that time. When his

Felipe Maximiliano Chacón

book was published in 1924 he was the paper's editor and general manager. This is virtually all that is known of Chacón's professional training and personal life. One could conclude that he was a man of better-than-average means, more extensively educated and literarily aware than most of his fellow New Mexicans, yet committed to the development of the Spanish-speaking community.

His own words in a brief preface to his book confirm a sense of social responsibility. Chacón claims that his aim as an author is to

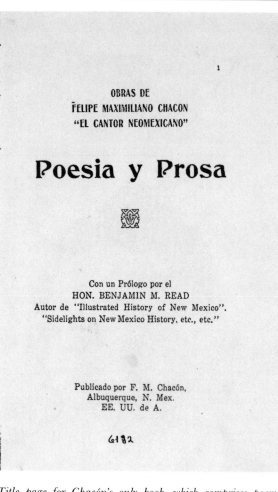

1

OBRAS DE
FELIPE MAXIMILIANO CHACON
"EL CANTOR NEOMEXICANO"

Poesia y Prosa

Con un Prólogo por el
HON. BENJAMIN M. READ
Autor de "Illustrated History of New Mexico".
"Sidelights on New Mexico History, etc., etc."

Publicado por F. M. Chacón,
Albuquerque, N. Mex.
EE. UU. de A.

6182

*Title page for Chacón's only book, which comprises poems,
short stories, and translations of poetry by others*

make "una simple contribución a la Lectura Recreativa, para las masas populares de los pueblos, con debidas apologiías a Teólogos, Filósofos, Retóricos y Lógicos" (a simple contribution to Recreational Reading, for the popular masses, with due apologies to Theologians, Philosophers, Theoreticians and Logicians). He made no pretensions to being a learned writer. Indeed, he preferred to follow the current taste in popular verse, which was traditional in both style and subject. According to Read, Chacón had been writing poetry since the age of fourteen but had been content to share it with friends or to publish here and there in newspapers. He must have touched a common chord–choosing inspirational themes of universal appeal–as his work was well known in the area and widely praised. Chacón was apparently quite modest and reluctant to acknowledge his talent; in Read's opinion, " . . . es un genio, y como todos los genios, no se sabe estimar a sí mismo" (he is a genius, and like all geniuses, he

does not know how to value himself).

Read goes on to describe Chacón as "un genio netamente americano, el primero que diera lustre a su Patria en el bello idioma de Cervantes" (a genuinely American genius, the first to honor his Country in the beautiful language of Cervantes). This observation may be somewhat exaggerated, but Read was ahead of his time in recognizing the multilingual foundations of United States history and the importance of a writer such as Chacón, who was equally adept in Spanish and English. His bilingualism is admirable considering the lack of Spanish educational facilities at that time. Not only was English the only official language of the territorial states, but the use of Spanish was looked down upon by many racially biased educators. Read was clearly aware of this problem when he wrote: "El poeta Chacón no debe ninguna apología por haber escogido la lengua castellana para dar forma a las brillantes producciones de su talento" (The poet Chacón owes no apology for having chosen the Spanish language to express the brilliant products of his talent).

Chacón's book is divided into three parts: a section of fifty-six poems, another of prose, containing three short stories, and seven translations into Spanish of poems by authors such as Henry Wadsworth Longfellow, John Dryden, and George Gordon, Lord Byron. The original poetry, written over several decades, reflects a wide range of themes, from the universal (love, family, religious faith, youth) to the topical (local and national political events). Stylistically, it reflects the popular Hispanic preference for octosyllabic and hendecasyllabic verse; poetry of this type was commonly found in Spanish-language newspapers published in New Mexico in the territorial period. It was written primarily to appeal to the reader's moral values and sentiments. In this sense, Chacón was a people's poet who used literature to foster a spirit of communal purpose and identity, much in the tradition of the medieval Spanish bard. The value of such work lies in its documentation of the concerns of a whole community, particularly one that had previously been overlooked in the annals of American history.

In spite of the prejudice suffered by Mexican-Americans, many were very vocal in their patriotism, especially after New Mexico was granted statehood in 1911. Chacón's response was typical. His poem commemorating the fourth of July, 1918, and entitled "A la Patria" (To the Fatherland), contains lines which are effusive in their rhetoric:

> Quisiera yo la esplendorosa lira
> Que ha labrádole a Homero eterna gloria
> Para cantaros lo que al alma inspira
> Ese nimbo brillante de tu historia;
>
> (Would that I had the splendorous lyre
> With which Homer gained eternal glory
> To sing for you what that bright glow
> Of your history inspires in my soul;)

In several of Chacón's poems, there is a vivid concern for social and political justice which comes from knowledge of disillusionment and defeat. For example, an excerpt from a long poem in honor of New Mexican statehood:

> Por fin habéis logrado, suelo mío,
> De lauros coronar tu altiva frente,
> Alcanzando del cielo del estío
> Una estrella gloriosa y esplendente;
> ....
> Honor para tus hijos, que han sufrido
> Contigo numerosos desengaños
> Y con ellos tan sólo conseguido
> El injusto baldón de muchos años
>
> (You have finally achieved, land of mine,
> The laurels that crown your lofty forehead,
> Plucking from the summer heaven
> A glorious and shining star;
> ....
> An honor for your sons who have suffered
> With you numerous disappointments,
> And from them have only reaped
> The unjust insult of many years).

Chacón's prose—two very short stories and a thirty-page story—is uneven in its literary merit. The longer piece, entitled "Eustacio y Carlota" (Eustace and Carlota), is the saga of a brother and sister, orphaned and separated early in life, who miraculously recognize each other by matching birthmarks, just as they are about to consummate their marriage. Chacón claimed that this was a true event, much publicized in New Mexico and Colorado some years earlier. In any event it was a plot found in many nineteenth-century literary works, appealing to the romantic inclination of the time. His shorter stories are more successful, as they tend to be picaresque in flavor, mirroring more realistically the sociohistorical period in which he lived. One, for example, called "Don Julio Berlanga," tells of the experience of a shepherd in Las Vegas, New Mexico, in 1918. Its narrative structure is a forerunner to the currently popular "novel of testimony" in Latin America: a bystander-narrator recounts a story told to him by a certain Don Julio, in town for the roundup, about a short-lived love affair with a faithless woman. In its unencumbered language and style it is an authentic reflection of Mexican-American life.

Like other newspaper editors and part-time authors in his day, Chacón was a writer whose literary impact was transitory. His work is of interest today principally as historical documentation of a marginalized society. However florid his poetry may sound today, it is written in a style extremely popular in the late nineteenth and early twentieth centuries, both in Mexico and in the United States. His work fits well into the kind of recreational literature he intended to write.

References:
Doris Meyer, "Felipe Maximiliano Chacón: A Forgotten Mexican-American Author," *New Scholar*, 6 (1977): 111-126.

Fray Angélico Chávez

(10 April 1910-)

Clark Colahan
Whitman College

BOOKS: *Clothed with the Sun* (Santa Fe: Writer's Editions, 1939);

Seraphic Days; Franciscan Thoughts and Affections on the Principal Feasts of Our Lord and Our Lady and All the Saints of the Three Orders of the Seraph of Assisi (Detroit: Duns Scotus College, 1940);

New Mexico Triptych; Being Three Panels and Three Accounts: 1. The Angel's New Wings; 2. The Penitente Thief; 3. Hunchback Madonna (Paterson, N.J.: St. Anthony Guild, 1940);

Eleven Lady-Lyrics, and Other Poems (Paterson, N.J.: St. Anthony Guild, 1945);

Our Lady of the Conquest (Albuquerque: University of New Mexico Press, 1948);

The Single Rose; the Rose Unica and Commentary of Fray Manuel de Santa Clara (Sante Fe: Los Santos Bookshop, 1948);

La Conquistadora: The Autobiography of an Ancient Statue (Paterson, N.J.: St. Anthony Guild, 1954);

Origins of New Mexico Families in the Spanish Colonial Period. In Two Parts: The Seventeenth (1598-1693) and the Eighteenth (1693-1821) Centuries (Santa Fe: Historical Society of New Mexico, 1954);

Archives of the Archdiocese of Santa Fe, 1678-1900 (Washington, D.C.: Academy of American Franciscan History, 1957);

From an Altar Screen / El retablo: Tales from New Mexico (New York: Farrar, Straus & Cudahy, 1957); republished as *When the Santos Talked: A Retablo of New Mexico Tales* (Santa Fe: Gannon, 1977);

The Virgin of Port Lligat (Fresno, Cal.: Academy Literary Guild, 1959);

The Lady from Toledo (Fresno: Academy Guild, 1960);

Coronado's Friars (Washington, D.C.: Academy of American Franciscan History, 1968);

Selected Poems, With an Apologia (Santa Fe: Press of the Territorian, 1969);

The Song of Francis (Flagstaff: Northland, 1973);

Fray Angélico Chávez (Special Collections, General Library, University of New Mexico)

My Penitente Land: Reflections on Spanish New Mexico (Albuquerque: University of New Mexico Press, 1974);

But Time and Chance: The Story of Padre Martínez of Taos, 1793-1867 (Santa Fe: Sunstone, 1981);

Très Macho-He Said (Santa Fe: Gannon, 1985);

The Short Stories of Fray Angélico Chávez, edited by Genaro M. Padilla (Albuquerque: University of New Mexico Press, 1987).

OTHER: *Missions of New Mexico, 1776, A Description by Fray Francisco Atanasio Domínquez With Other Contemporary Documents*, edited and translated by Chávez and Eleanor B. Adams (Albuquerque: University of New Mexico Press, 1956);

Archives of the Archdiocese of Santa Fe, 1678-1900, compiled by Chávez (Washington, D.C.: Academy of American Franciscan History, 1957);

The Oroz Codex; or Relation of the Description of the Holy Gospel Province in New Spain and the Lives of the Founders and Other Note-worthy Men of Said Province Composed by Fray Pedro Oroz: 1584-1586, edited and translated by Chávez (Washington, D.C.: Academy of American Franciscan History, 1972);

Ted J. Warner, ed., *The Domínquez-Escalante Journal: Their Expedition Through Colorado, Utah, Arizona, and New Mexico in 1776*, translated by Chávez (Provo, Utah: Brigham Young University Press, 1976).

Recognized as one of New Mexico's most distinguished writers and officially honored by the state's governor and three of its universities, artist, poet, and historian Angélico Chávez was born 10 April 1910 in Wagon Mound, New Mexico. He was named Manuel Chávez by his parents, Fabián Chávez and Nicolasa Roybal Chávez. In unpublished 1986 correspondence he described his one real distinction as being born "the day when Halley's comet appeared the brightest over our northern hemisphere." He grew up and attended school in the town of Mora, New Mexico. As a boy he loved to read, particularly histories of New Mexico and the great writers of English literature. Although he had never met a Franciscan friar, he was attracted to the order because of its importance in the region's history. He attended St. Francis Seminary in Cincinnati and colleges in the Midwest and in 1937 became the first native New Mexican to enter the priesthood as a Franciscan. Because he liked to paint, his teachers gave him the name Angélico after Fra Angelico, the Florentine painter of the late Middle Ages. Fray (Friar) Angélico Chávez has been his pen name ever since.

From the time he returned to New Mexico to be ordained at age twenty-seven until his amicable parting with the Franciscan order at age sixty-two, he devoted himself to his duties as pastor of several towns and Indian pueblos in New Mexico, including Peña Blanca, Cochiti, Santo Domingo, Domingo, Sile, La Bajada, San Felipe, Jemez, and Cerrillos. He served as an army chaplain both in World War II, when he was with the

New York Infantry Division (in the Pacific), and the Korean War, during which he was stationed in Germany. No matter what his work involved, he made time for his art and his writing. In Peña Blanca he painted the stations of the cross, taking his parishioners as models. He did restoration work and frescoes at Domingo and, while at Cerrillos, did more restoration, including the old chapel at nearby Golden, New Mexico. His skill as a writer and his knowledge of southwestern history has led to posts as Southwest book review editor for *New Mexico Magazine*, regent of the Museum of New Mexico, board member of the Franciscan Academy of History, and official archivist for the Archdiocese of Santa Fe. Since 1972 he has lived in Santa Fe, and on major occasions he concelebrates with Archbishop Robert Sánchez.

Chávez has written a large body of work, varying in form yet unified by three elements that characterize practically all of it to some degree: New Mexico's past, the region's Franciscan Catholicism, and the stamp of his own New Mexican Catholic personality. He has produced so much that it is easiest to think of his work occurring in two time periods. Until the early 1950s he was essentially a religious poet. However, in the late 1940s he had begun writing historical fiction. In the years immediately prior to his withdrawal from his religious order and active ministry he published little, but soon thereafter his *My Penitente Land: Reflections on Spanish New Mexico* (1974), a historical essay and spiritual autobiography and his most discussed book, was published. His subsequent works have all been on colonial history, but like *My Penitente Land*, they are consistently concerned with the nature of being a New Mexican Hispano.

In his first two books of verse, *Clothed with the Sun* (1939) and *Eleven Lady-Lyrics, and Other Poems* (1945), Chávez strives with uneven success to write artfully simple lyrics that attempt to recreate moments of intense emotion, as in his "Symphony in C: the Rite of Ordination" ("In unison we feel it throbbing through the chancel / prone before the grave archbishop in his pallium, / whose extended hands, as on an unseen console, / conjure from celestial lofts a strain more solemn. / / What pentecostal bellows blow from woods of Eden, / or Gethsemane's, to thrill us to what vision"). While there are New Mexican settings in some of these poems, they are not local-color pieces but sketches of his own inner life. The title *Clothed with the Sun*, for example, refers above all to the rebirth, like that of the burning phoenix, of the Christian soul in God, and only secondarily to the physical or spiritual ambience of New Mexican life.

Chávez's third and fourth books of poetry, *The Single Rose; the Rose Unica and Commentary of Fray Manuel de Santa Clara* (1948) and *The Virgin of Port Lligat* (1959), are complex and intellectually ambitious, revealing the presence, as he said in his apologia to the *Selected Poems, With an Apologia* (1969), of his early "haunting finds in Blake and Donne and all their star-crossed fellows down the years." *The Single Rose*, published with Chávez's own commentary, recalls the biblical *Song of Songs*, a book taken by the Church as a metaphor for the love binding the Creator to his chosen people. Like St. Francis of Assisi, the narrator talks to God through his creation, comparing himself to hedge birds, field mice, chicks, and foxes and likening their natural longings to his own for the warmth of enfolding love: "Say how long must I yet yearn / until I, too, find cover." Beginning with Chávez's own verses in old Spanish, the book gave readers the impression it was a translation of a fifteenth-century poem, a confusion abetted by his publishing it as if it were by Fray Manuel De Santa Clara. In fact *The Single Rose* does with some success continue the late medieval tradition of exploring human and divine love through an allegory centered on the rose, though naturally from Chávez's modern perspective. *The Virgin of Port Lligat* was inspired by a Salvador Dali painting that expressed concern with man's access to atomic energy. The poem, which was praised by T. S. Eliot, offers, according to Chávez in the apologia, a vision of Western man's condition at that time and addresses the question of man's place and significance in the modern scientific view of the cosmos. The narrator sings of the world as God's creation, whose playful Maker lovingly dazzles human understanding "to fill the hungry with good things."

Several critics and anthology editors were supportive of Chávez's work during this period. Robert Hunt, in the summer 1946 issue of *Southwest Review*, praised Chávez's "winged mounting style," and an unnamed contributor to Matthew Hoehn's *Catholic Authors: Contemporary Biographical Sketches, 1930-1947* (1948) called him "one of the great hopes of Catholic poetry." In 1963 he received the annual poetry award of the Catholic Poetry Society of America. His last poetry collection, *Selected Poems, With an Apologia*, published ten years after *The Virgin of Port Lligat*, brings to-

gether and regroups earlier poems he and others felt to have been the most successful. In his apologia he candidly attributes the end of his poetic creation both to changing fashions in poetry that left his traditional manner outmoded and the fading of the continuous excitement that had moved him to write in verse.

Chávez's four works of historical fiction are something of a bridge between his poetry and his historical studies. Still avowedly original creations, often accompanied by his own artwork and bearing titles from the vocabulary of religious art, they are at the same time stories with the anonymous, traditional feeling of legend and folklore. He began writing historical narrative because, as he told Robert Huber (1970), he loves to write: "I took up history because it's there and makes my writing readable. There was a drama to the colonial life, and I have found its records." *New Mexico Triptych; Being Three Panels and Three Accounts: 1. The Angel's New Wings; 2. The Penitente Thief; 3. Hunchback Madonna* (1940), as though bringing to life a medieval altar screen, portrays the Nativity, the Crucifixion, and the Madonna as they might have been imagined by early Hispanic New Mexicans. *La Conquistadora: The Autobiography of an Ancient Statue* (1954) imagines the story that might be told by the famous image of the Virgin (unofficial patroness of colonial New Mexico) which was carried at the head of his company by Diego de Vargas in his reconquest following the 1680 Pueblo Indian revolt. *From an Altar Screen / El retablo: Tales from New Mexico* (1957), illustrated by New Mexico artist Peter Hurd, presents symbolic incidents revealing the close ties of rural New Mexicans to their patron saints. As Albert Duhamel observed (*New York Times*, 15 December 1957), *From an Altar Screen* successfully recalls the style of a colonial *retablo*, "authentic but simple, sincere but stiff, colorful but without perspective."

The Lady from Toledo (1960) retells the events culminating in the catastrophic revolt of the New Mexico Indians against the Spanish in 1680. The principal characters—a sickly girl miraculously cured, the malevolent mastermind behind the rebellion, a native convert caught between conflicting loyalties, a martyred missionary—are carefully drawn and plausibly fleshed out from period documents, and the narrating of each character's story one after another is the occasion for a short biography representing an anecdotal summary of the life and times of one sort of colonial New Mexican. The characters' only relationship, though, is not to each other in a structure of cause, effect, and personalities, but rather to the central historic event. Indeed the lady in the title is not a person at all, but a small statue of the Virgin Mary said by legend to have foretold the rebellion a few years earlier, and her woodenness is shared to some degree by each of the sketchily developed figures.

The voluminous documentation included in the historical volumes Chávez began writing in his mid forties bears witness to the intensity of his interest in New Mexican history. His intent in the histories is to construct an accurate understanding of Hispanic New Mexicans—clearly presented as his people, for whom he feels respect and affection. *Our Lady of the Conquest* (1948), his first book on history, is a collection of articles. *Origins of New Mexico Families in the Spanish Colonial Period. In Two Parts: The Seventeenth (1598-1693) and the Eighteenth (1693-1821) Centuries* (1954) uses his unsurpassed familiarity with original documents to trace genealogies, including his own. New Mexico readers have made it perhaps his most popular book. *Missions of New Mexico, 1776, A Description by Fray Francisco Atanasio Domínquez With Other Contemporary Documents* was edited and translated by Chávez and Eleanor B. Adams, editor for many years of the *New Mexico Historical Review*. A large and richly documented study, illustrated with sketches by Chávez, *Missions of New Mexico* was designated the state's official book for the national bicentennial celebration in 1975, when a facsimile reprint appeared. Chávez translated and edited *The Domínquez-Escalante Journal: Their Expedition Through Colorado, Utah, Arizona, and New Mexico in 1776*, which was published by the bicentennial commissions of the four states in 1976. His *Coronado's Friars* (1968) resolved four centuries of confusion and contradiction about the role of the Franciscans who participated in the first Spanish exploration of New Mexico. *The Oroz Codex; or Relation of the Description of the Holy Gospel Province in New Spain and the Lives of the Founders and Other Note-worthy Men of Said Province Composed by Fray Pedro Oroz: 1584-1586* (1972), which grew out of the research for *Coronado's Friars*, corrects numerous errors about sixteenth-century Mexico. In the dedication Chávez describes his father and mother as "both heirs of ten generations of cultural and economic disadvantage in their native New Mexico," and speaks of the pressure on their children "to compete successfully within an alien modern culture in our century."

Critical response to Chávez's histories has recognized his familiarity with sources, his attention to detail, and his propensity to formulate new answers to long-standing historical questions. "History is all down in black and white," he commented to Robert Huber in the March-April 1970 issue of *New Mexico Magazine*, "and if a person bothers to look it all up there is little to be controversial." Praise by professional historians was sometimes glowing, as when Eleanor B. Adams, in her 1969 review of *Coronado's Friars* in *American Historical Review*, wrote that "Chávez' attempt to solve an old problem was no easy task. He has performed it admirably, returning to his sources and formulating his conclusions on the basis of meticulous textual comparison and critical evaluation." But Chávez did not follow academic trends, and his methodology was sometimes criticized. Bruce Glasrud wrote in *Journal of the West* (October 1974) that *Origins of New Mexico Families* was "not a modern investigation, utilizing new social science techniques."

The autobiographical *My Penitente Land* had its origin in Chávez's lifelong curiosity to know his heritage and to understand his parents' pride in being Spanish, not Mexican, while they were unable to articulate for him the nature of the difference. ("The thoughts of the young are long, long thoughts.") The book is an interpretive history of his "falling in love with God." He traces the operation of God's grace through time to the Spanish New Mexico that shaped his inheritance. The book intertwines biblical episodes, historical anecdotes, and personal memories. For example, the opening superimposes the image of the ceremony held when the first settlers crossed the Rio Grande over that of the Israelites' entrance into the Promised Land and his own birth and christening. He finds his roots in the historical circumstances that kept New Mexicans apart both from the culture of the indigenous peoples and the rest of changing Spanish America, conditions, he insists, that made them remain *castizo* (pureblooded) while Mexicans mixed with the Indians and produced a new and different culture. It is for this reason that he chooses to call himself *Hispano* (Spanish) instead of *Chicano*, a name he associates with the struggle of people of Mexican culture living in the United States.

The clarity and force of *My Penitente Land* have allowed its ideas to be understood, though not always seconded. Reviewers generally gave the book favorable overall evaluations. Typical was Raoul E. Isais, who described it in the July

1976 issue of *Catholic Historical Review* as "a classic study." In a 1975 issue of *Journal of Ethnic Studies* Kenneth R. Weber called it "a personal odyssey." Francisco A. Lomelí (1982) said the book belonged to the Hispanic genre of the lyric essay, especially as practiced by Miguel de Unamuno y Jugo (1834-1936) who "mixed poetry and sociology" to write a history of Spain that sought to go beyond the sort of superficial collection of facts more cautious writers often try to pawn off as knowledge. Isais said much the same thing. For him it shows the Hispanic New Mexican's world view "at its most lucid. Whether one agrees or disagrees with Fray Chávez's views, they are the views of his people, and no one has expressed these attitudes and values with such honest intensity." In a complete genealogy on which Chávez is working, "Chávez, A Distinctive American Clan of New Mexico," he points out specific instances in which native American blood has come into all New Mexico families through four centuries of residence.

With *But Time and Chance: The Story of Padre Martínez of Taos, 1793-1867*, published in 1981, Chávez returned to documented history. The work is a defense of Antonio José Martínez, one of New Mexico's Hispanos most committed to the state's cultural autonomy and one whose reputation suffered both during his life and after death with the coming of the Americans. Martínez resisted the non-Hispanic church government brought to the state by John Baptist, Archbishop Lamy (1814-1888). Although novelist Willa Cather portrayed Martínez negatively in *Death Comes for the Archbishop* (1927), Chávez shows he is a figure of importance. Reviewers such as G. L. Seligmann, Jr., in the October 1983 issue of *Western Historical Quarterly*, and J. Manuel Espinosa, in the October 1984 issue of *The Americans*, felt that Chávez's treatment of Martínez, though in a few instances marked by subjective explanations and personal affirmations reminiscent of *My Penitente Land*, was a valuable corrective to the usual anti-Hispanic view of New Mexico's French prelates and clergy.

Chávez's latest work to date, *Très Macho-He Said* (1985), is a biography of José Manuel Gallegos (1815-1875) of Albuquerque, New Mexico's first United States congressman. The title and the political subject of the book confirm the evolution of Chávez's writing toward the goal of reaching a popular audience with the story of the achievements of New Mexican Hispanos. In addition, *The Short Stories of Fray Angélico Chávez*, edited by Genaro M. Padilla, appeared in 1987. This collection includes fourteen examples of Chávez's early short fiction, some previously unpublished. Of special interest is the selection of narratives written while Chávez was a student at St. Francis Seminary.

Accurately called a twentieth-century Renaissance man, Chávez's achievements as artist, poet, storyteller, archivist, and historian have given a wide audience to the land and the people of and for which he has written. His affirmation of the rich cultural tradition inherited by Hispanic New Mexicans, while different from the focus on the present and future characteristic of many Chicano writers, has clarified and articulated the region's distinctive sense of connection to the best of Spanish civilization.

References:

Robert Huber, "Fray Angélico Chávez: 20th-Century Renaissance Man," *New Mexico Magazine*, 48 (March-April 1970): 18-23;

Robert Hunt, "Fray Angélico Chávez and His Lady Lyrics," *Southwest Review*, 31 (Summer 1946): 267;

Francisco A. Lomelí, Review of *My Penitente Land*, *New Scholar*, 8, no. 1-2 (1982): 495-498;

Phyllis S. Morales, *Fray Angélico Chávez: A Bibliography of His Published Writings (1925-1978)* (Santa Fe: Lightning Tree, 1980);

Kenneth R. Weber, Review of *My Penitente Land*, *Journal of Ethnic Studies*, 3, no. 2 (1975): 119-121.

Lucha Corpi

(13 April 1945-)

Barbara Brinson Curiel
University of California, Santa Cruz

BOOKS: *Fireflight: Three Latin American Poets,* by Corpi, Elsie Alvarado de Ricord, and Concha Michel, bilingual edition, with translations by Catherine Rodríguez-Nieto (Berkeley: Oyez, 1976);

Palabras de mediodía/Noon Words, bilingual edition, with translations by Rodríguez-Nieto (Berkeley: El Fuego de Aztlán, 1980);

Delia's Song (Houston: Arte Publico, 1989).

OTHER: "The Marina Poems" in *The Other Voice: Twentieth-Century Women's Poetry in Translation,* translated by Corpi and Rodríguez-Nieto, edited by Joanna Bankier and others (New York: Norton, 1976), pp. 154-156;

"Keeping Still" in *Contemporary Women Poets: An Anthology of California Poets,* translated by Rodríguez-Nieto, edited by Jennifer McDowell and M. Loventhal (San Jose: Merlin, 1977), pp. 95-96;

"A mi padre," "Romance Marino," "Romance Chicano," "Un minuto de silencio," and "Músico Amigo," in *Chicanos: Antología histórica y literaria,* edited by Tino Villanueva (Mexico City: Fondo de Cultura Económica, 1980), pp. 263-268;

"Denuncia," "Lamento," in *A Decade of Hispanic Literature: An Anniversary Anthology,* edited by Nicolás Kanellos (Houston: Revista Chicano-Riqueña, 1982), pp. 59-60;

"Dark Romance," in *Women Poets of the World,* edited by Bankier, Dierdre Lashgari, and Doris Earnshaw (New York: Macmillan/London: Collier, 1983), pp. 324-325;

"Los cristos del alma," in *Palabra nueva: cuentos chicanos,* edited by Ricardo Aguilar and others (El Paso: Texas Western Press, 1984), pp. 3-12.

PERIODICAL PUBLICATIONS: "Tres mujeres," *De Colores,* 3, no. 3 (1977): 74-89;

Lucha Corpi (courtesy of the author)

"Predicamento," "Mariposa negra, mariposa negra," and "Poema en obscuridad," *El Fuego de Aztlán,* 1 (Summer 1977): 45-50;

"La casa de los espejos," "Receta de invierno," and "Protocolo de verduras," translated by Catherine Rodríguez-Nieto, *Prisma,* 1 (Spring 1979): 10-12;

"Romance liso" and "Romance tejido," *La Palabra,* 1 (Fall 1979): 33-34;

"Puente de cristal," *Semana de Bellas Artes,* 133 (18 June 1980): 12;

"Voces," "Mariana," and "Ámbito y jornada," *Imagine,* 1 (Winter 1984): 80-82;

"Martyrs of the Soul," translated by Elizabeth Ladd, *Boston Review,* 10 (April/May 1985): 19-21;

"City in the Fog," *Poetry San Francisco,* 3 (Winter 1985): 7;

"Alguna fe adorable," *El Tecolote,* 6 (December 1985): 12-13.

Lucha Corpi was born 13 April 1945 in Jáltipan, Veracruz, Mexico, and immigrated to the United States as a newlywed at the age of nineteen. Since that time she has lived and worked in the San Francisco Bay Area and is a vital part of the Chicano literary world in California. She is a founding member of two significant Chicano arts organizations, Aztlán Cultural (1971) and the Centro Chicano de Escritores (Center for Chicano Writers, 1980), and has served as an officer of both groups. She holds a B.A. from the University of California, Berkeley, and an M.A. in comparative literature from San Francisco State University. Her poetry and fiction have appeared in numerous journals and anthologies, in the United States as well as in Mexico. She has also been the recipient of numerous awards, among them first place in the tenth Chicano Literary Contest at the University of California, Irvine, in 1984 for her short story "Shadows on Ebbing Water"; first place in the *Palabra nueva* literary contest for her story "Los cristos del alma" (Martyrs of the Soul) in 1983; as well as a creative writing fellowship from the National Endowment for the Arts from 1979 to 1980.

Corpi is recognized primarily for her work as a poet, although in recent years she has also been recognized as an accomplished prose writer. Her poetry, produced mainly in Spanish and published with translations by Catherine Rodríguez-Nieto in the collection *Palabras de mediodía/Noon Words* (1980), is characterized by an imagistic lyricism combined with a controlled and direct use of language. Thematically her work examines love, feelings of isolation and loneliness, and social topics, especially the role of women in the home and in society, political commitment, and the experiences of the marginalized.

The poems in *Palabras de mediodía/Noon Words* draw from Corpi's life in three distinct geographical places (Jáltipan, San Luis Potosí, and the United States) and are organized loosely into chronological order. She described Jáltipan in *Fireflight: Three Latin American Poets* (1976) as "a rush of dense green, full of the smell of mango blossoms and the clean petticoats of Indian women." The poem that most clearly addresses her view of Jáltipan in *Palabras de mediodía*, is "Solario" (Sunscape) which describes it and her early life in images that are tropical, sensual, and warm. The poem begins with a portrait of night-

fall: the orange trees "habían guardado/sus trajes de bodas para mañana" (had put away /their bridal gowns for morning). Mango trees are "cúpulas verdes/de catedrales selváticas" (the green cupolas/ of jungle cathedrals). The environment is beautiful, magical, and sacred. In the third section of the poem, there is a unity of the poetic voice and the tropical environment. The narrator recounts how Tirso, the water carrier, taught her to curse "cuando apenas tres años/angostos pero hondos/ abrían paso/entre el verde añejo/de las sabanas" (when barely three years/narrow but deep/were opening their way/between the ancient greens/of the savannahs). In the same vein, recalling how, as a small child, she repeated her new words, the speaker explains that half of the hearers "lo celebró con risas" (laughed) and that "la otra mitad/me podó la selva/de la lengua/con navaja de lejía" (the other half/pruned the jungle/on my tongue/with the razor/of laundry soap). The narrator and nature remain one; as she explains in the final section of the poem:

Algo del mar
se me quedó en las venas:
La salada emancipación
de las aguas inquietas

(Something of the sea
stayed in my veins:
The salty freedom
of restless water).

Corpi moved with her family at the age of nine to San Luis Potosí, a colonial city in central Mexico. In a 1979 interview she said San Luis Potosí was "closed, grey; the climate was temperate and the people suspicious of each other, critical." "Solario nocturno" (Nocturnal Sunscape) portrays San Luis Potosí as the polar opposite of Jáltipan. The first section of "Solario nocturno" invokes the city "con su alma de piedra/cincelada/ por los cascos indómitos/del sol" (with its soul of stone/chiseled/by the untamed hoofs/of the sun). The city, obsessed by the rote ritual of the Catholic church, is cold, sanctimonious, and hypocritical. Whereas in "Solario" Corpi describes "aquella soleada casa/de amplio patio exterior/y grietas azules" (that sunlit house/with its broad patio/and blue cracks), noting warmth and the fecundity of vegetation, in "Solario nocturno" the narrator searches for "verde/entre las grietas/ de las canteras" (green/in the cracks/of quarried hillsides) and finds only "gris" (gray). The inhabitants of Jáltipan and San Luis Potosí have different attitudes toward life. San Luis brings the persona an awareness of sin and also of society's hatred of self-expression:

> Ahí conocí
> por primera vez
> el terrible pecado
> del silencio.

> (It was there
> I first discovered
> the terrible sin
> of silence.)

The poems in *Palabras de mediodía/Noon Words* set in the United States mostly focus on domestic life. In "De mi casa" (My House) domestic images impart feelings of comfort and familiarity; the day ends "derramado de café/y naranja" (spilling coffee/and oranges). In the same poem dishwashing is a "sonata/de cristal y jabón/agua y porcelana" (a sonata/of glass and soap/water and china). In "Labor de retazos" (Patchwork) ironing triggers thoughts of authenticity:

> Mientras plancho
> una voz adentro
> me avisa:
> "El alma necesita
> arrugas
> necesita pliegues
> alforzas y otros
> motivos de edad."

> (While I iron
> a voice inside me
> warns:
> "The soul has need
> of wrinkles,
> need of pleats,
> tucks and other
> signs of age.")

The narrator struggles to fit her life into her domestic role. In "Protocolo de verduras" (The Protocol of Vegetables) domesticity takes precedence:

> . . . debo atender
> los asuntos
> del día de plancha
> y escribir versos
> cuando puedo
> entre el ir y venir
> de la tempestad
> en el lavadero

> (. . . I must tend
> to the affairs
> of ironing day,
> and write poems
> when I can
> between the shifting winds
> of the tempest
> in the laundry).

"Segundo dos de noviembre" (Second Day of the Dead) ends on a note of black humor: "alguien traspapeló a hoy/entre ayer y mañana/y no hay tiempo de buscarlo/porque la comitiva ya llega/y la cena no se ha preparado;/y vámonos, que ya voy tarde/a mi propio funeral" (someone has misfiled today/between yesterday and tomorrow/and there's no time to look for it/because the committee is here/and supper isn't ready;/and let's go, because I'm already late/for my own funeral).

Corpi's best known work is the series of four poems, "The Marina Poems": "Marina madre" (Marina Mother), "Marina virgen" (Marina Virgin), "La hija del diablo" (The Devil's Daughter), and "Ella (Marina ausente)" (She [Marina Absent]) which first appeared in English translation in *The Other Voice: Twentieth-Century Women's Poetry in Translation* (1976). They were also published in the original Spanish with accompanying English translation in *Fireflight*. Both the English and Spanish versions also were included in *Palabras de mediodía/Noon Words*. "The Marina Poems" have been widely anthologized and reprinted. The subject of the poems is the historical character referred to in various contexts either as Malintzin Tenepal, her indigenous name, Doña Marina, her Christian name (and the one Corpi chooses to call her); and by the pejorative La Malinche, which in modern Mexico is synonymous with *traitor*. As a girl Marina had been traded from tribe to tribe, and therefore knew enough languages to act as one of two translators to Hernán Cortés in his conquest of Aztec Mexico. Marina gave birth to Cortés's son Martín, who was taken from her and raised in Spain after Cortés married her off to one of his officers. Corpi portrays Marina as an individual rather than as a sorceress who through her evil caused the downfall of her people. She sees her as a victim caught between an old world and a new world, a woman who had journeyed from one culture and society to another and yet who had no home. In a footnote in *Fireflight* she offers the Marina poems "by way of vindication." Marina reflects the experiences of many women

MARIANA

Lugar más bello ha de existir
en este mundo
que esta ciudad despiadada,
gentes más felices quizá,
allá, al otro lado de la bruma.

5 sp.

Mas ella ha escogido vivir aquí,
entre los antiguos pinos
~~combatiendo la furia implacable~~
~~del viento occidental.~~

Criada en las barriadas del amor,
desposeída de todos:
El marido sacrificado en Korea
y en Viet Nam el único hijo,
dos cruces separadas por un mar,
dos medallas en una bolsa raída.

Mas ella ha escogido vivir aquí,
entre los antiguos pinos
~~combatiendo la furia implacable~~
~~del viento occidental.~~

Ya ha pagado su deuda
~~me ha dicho,~~
aunque nunca debió nada
~~y así todavía~~ Aún así su nombre
~~su nombre~~
cuyas vocales abiertas
el sol pintó morenas
su nombre es solamente
un ~~extraño juego de palabras~~ un diseño ~~borroso~~ ~~obscuro~~ borroso
~~para aquel que espera~~   en la negativa del tiempo.
~~en medio de la niebla~~

Mas ella ha escogido vivir aquí,
entre los antiguos pinos
~~combatiendo la furia implacable~~
~~del viento occidental~~

Lucha

Revised typescript for a poem by Corpi (courtesy of the author)

from many cultures through time. Through her Corpi reinterprets the historical circumstances which have fostered the devaluation of all Mexican women. Her narrator goes back into history to act as a witness to what truly happened in Marina's life. She echoes the chronicler of the conquest Bernal Díaz del Castillo, who in his *Historia verdadera de la conquista de la Nueva España* (The True History of the Conquest of New Spain) refers to her as Doña Mariña, "tan excelente mujer" (an excellent woman). Díaz del Castillo notes that it is Cortés who the Indians refer to as "Malinche."

The first poem in the series, "Marina madre" describes the naming of Marina, the creation of her destiny by "los viejos" (the oracular elders). She is for them a shell or a mask of "barro" (clay), a deliberate creation linked with the earth. Like the Indian goddess Cuatlicue, Marina is given the attributes of fecundity (in her role as the mother of modern Mexico) and also of death (in her role as a temptress figure). The old men write Marina's name, full of negative meaning, on a tree with the blood of a lamb: she is destined to be sacrificed, and her naming fixes her destiny of ill-fortune. There is a remarkably similar scene in the play *Todos los gatos son pardos* (All Cats are Gray) by Mexican writer Carlos Fuentes, but while he accepts her destiny as something fixed and permanent, Corpi sees it as something which, although significant, is ultimately fragile and thin, like the ceramic that was used to create her. The first two lines of the second stanza delineate the critical tension between the image of Marina, and the reality of her situation: "Húmeda de tradición, mística/y muda fue vendida. . ." (Steeped in tradition, mystic/and mute she was sold–). For the elders Marina is a slave worn down by abuse that is both general and sexual (from hand to hand, night to night,/denied and desecrated). In the meantime "el alba" (the dawn), her rescue, never comes. On the contrary, her condemnation by the Indians is adopted by Cortés (her lover), her son Martín, and the Mexican people (the "te" [you] of the third stanza). All call her "la chingada" (whore).

The title of the second poem of the series, "Marina virgen," encapsulates a comparison which is key to the analysis of all the Marina poems. The adjective "virgen" implies Marina's innocence while strengthening the theme of Marina as creator. As the Virgin Mary was the mother of Christ, the goddess-victim, Marina, is the mother of the postconquest, victimized Mexi-

can people. Marina loves Christ whose suffering is similar to that of her children, and he becomes the point of reference for everything she does:

> Como ella te amó, veía solamente
> al ser sangrante. Y amaba en él
> tu recuerdo secreto y enlutado
>
> (Because she loved you, she only saw
> the bleeding man, and loved in him
> her secret and mourning memory of you).

Marina's condemnation comes from her people, not from God. She tries to "lavar su pecado/con agua bendita" (wash away her sin/with holy water) and dresses herself in "una manta gruesa/y nítida" (a long, thick cloth) so that "no supieran que su piel/morena estaba maldita" (no one would ever know/that her brown skin had been damned), for it is her "brown skin" (that is, the physical circumstances of her life) that condemns her. At the end of the poem Marina plants her clean soul in the earth, cultivates it, and in so doing gives life to the people of Mexico:

> Alguna vez te detuviste a pensar
> en dónde estaba su alma escondida.
> No sabías que la había sembrado
> en las entrañas de la tierra
> que sus manos cultivaban–
> la tierra negra y húmeda de tu vida
>
> (Once, you stopped to wonder
> where her soul was hidden,
> not knowing she had planted it
> in the entrails of that earth
> her hands had cultivated–
> the moist, black earth of your life).

In "La hija del diablo" Marina's death is a cataclysm which destroys the shell-like myth of her life. The "mística pulsación" (mystic pulsing), an echo from the first poem of the series, is silenced. The clay mask created by the elders, the "ídolo/de barro sucio y viejo" (ancient idol), shatters. The wind carries her name–not the name the Indians used to condemn her, nor her son's epithet, but the name that carries her essence "tan parecido a la profundidad/salina del mar" (so like the salt depths of the sea). Corpi chooses "Marina" from the varied names used to identify her. The destruction of the myth of Marina and the liberation of her essence through her Christian name become a vehicle of hope, of a new beginning. All that is left is "una semilla/a medio germinar" (a half-germinated seed), the unrealized possibilities of a whole being.

The last poem in the series, "Ella (Marina ausente)," is an enumeration of the essential elements that make up Marina which are absent (translated as *distant*) because they were carried away by the wind in "La hija del diablo." She is natural beauty, made of clay while at the same time a prisoner trapped in an imposed clay image. She is also a sad part of Mexican historical consciousness, "la sombra enlutada de un recuerdo/ ancestral" (mourning shadow of an ancestral memory). However, the final image describes her liberation, when the superficial is rejected. Marina achieves the dawn. Crossing the bridge into death, she leaves her sad life behind, and in an image of fecundity and of power, her hands are "llenas de sol y de tierra" (full of earth and sun).

One of Corpi's early works of short fiction, "Tres mujeres" (Three Women, 1977), demonstrates a dilemma similar to that faced by Marina. The story, which Corpi describes as both "autobiographical and allegorical," is about a young woman with a son who takes a trip looking for her destiny: "She finds three women, Guadalupe, Amerina, and Justina. Guadalupe says she can come back to her, but the woman can't accept that, as I at that time couldn't accept going back to Mexico. Things were no longer the same, I couldn't go back to being 'una hija de familia' (a good daughter). Amerina offers a dream, an illusion, but it was not the woman's as it was not mine. In the U.S. I felt like a fish out of water. This was not my culture, these were not my people, and yet I couldn't go home. It is Justina who says at the end, " 'I can't resolve this for you. You have to find your own answers, your own road.' "

Corpi's recent fiction is characterized by its portraits of women in untenable situations who choose a course of action and who follow it, often with tragic consequences. The story "Los cristos del alma" is a monologue narrated by Paula, an old woman on her deathbed, who tells her brother's son of the circumstances that brought them from Mexico to the border city of Juárez thirty-five years before, and which has determined the shape and circumstance of both their lives. Her life has been jarred from the predictable track of the life of anonymous women: "Hubo veces en que hubiera querido ser como ellas. Perderme en esa insensatez mundana de pecado y confesión y avesmarías y padresnuestros; y regresar a casa después de misa de cinco, limpiecita y olorosa a santidad como esta

mañana. No. Yo tendré que llegar al cielo arrastrándome, sangrante, y quizá ni así me dejen entrar" (There were times when I wished I could be like them. To lose myself in the mundane foolishness of sin and confession and Hail Marys and Our Fathers, to come home after five o'clock Mass smelling of saintliness and as clean as the morning. No. I will have to drag myself up to heaven bloodstained, and even then they might not let me enter).

She relates that her brother Roberto and her father supported a candidate for mayor who was not endorsed by the ruling party. Salvador Romero, the local political boss and the father of Roberto's wife Sara, fixed the election in favor of the party candidate, prompting a riot. Romero and the mayor initiate a plan to arrest the rioters, including Roberto's father, which Roberto learns about through Sara. When he tries to warn his father, the message is intercepted, and both Roberto and his father are arrested for disloyalty to the party. Up until this point the story's actors are men; as Paula tells her nephew, "tu madre era buena mujer, pero de nada valía porque las mujeres ni contaban en eso" (your mother was a good woman, but it wasn't any help because women didn't count in such matters).

After the arrest, however, the brunt of the action shifts to women, and to Paula in particular. The women of the prisoners stand vigil outside Romero's house waiting to ask him for clemency. While they are waiting, Romero comes out and announces that five of the prisoners, including Roberto and his father, have been sentenced to die. Paula seeks out Enrique Acosta, the defeated candidate, a man she has secretly loved for years. She quickly realizes, however, that he is powerless to help her. Paula returns to Romero, who offers to save one of her loved ones. He tells her she must choose which of the two will die. Although shocked and anguished, Paula discovers the strength to respond affirmatively, saying she must see them both first. She tells her nephew that it was as if "una voz adentro dictara lo que iba diciendo" (a voice from inside was dictating what I was saying). Although she is in a position from which there can be no successful resolution, Paula tells her nephew that she refuses to be defeated. She resolves to kill her father and brother. She rationalizes the action by telling herself that even if one of her loved ones lived, he would be stripped of all dignity and humanity.

When they see the gun, her father and brother affirm her decision. Her brother charges her with the welfare of his son, and her father instructs "No falles" (Don't miss). Paula fires two shots, at which time she says "tres corazones dejaban de latir" (three hearts stopped beating). At the sound of the shots, the soldiers capture, torture, and rape her, by order of Romero, who sentences her to death.

Three earthquakes topple the train carrying her to her execution causing massive death and destruction. She makes her way out of the train and meets up with Acosta, who was there in an attempt to free her from the soldiers. They go back to her hometown where all the parties involved in the case, including Romero, have been killed. She finds her injured nephew, the responsibility for whom becomes her "salvación." Acosta helps them both to hide and then to make their way to Ciudad Juárez, where they pass their lives in exile cut off from all that they had known before in what she describes as a "purgatorio frente al río" (purgatory on the river).

At the end of the story Paula, about to die, expresses her constant uncertainty as to whether she did the right thing. She also contemplates what would have happened if the earthquakes had come sooner and taken the responsibility of choice away from her. She says salvation comes only when all actions have been taken and when the victim has surrendered herself to her fate:

> La tierra tiembla sólo cuando los cristos del alma yacen inertes en la cruz, atentos al segundo advenimiento del hijo del hombre

> (The earth trembles only when the martyrs of the soul lie motionless on the cross, listening for the second coming of the son of man).

The work of Corpi is distinguished. Accomplished and recognized both as a prose writer and as a poet, she has used discernible thematic patterns. Two particularly prominent concerns are women cornered by the circumstances of their lives and a notion that fate is inescapable. She speaks for the powerless unable to speak for themselves.

References:

Francisco Alarcón, "Lucha Corpi: Poeta Solar," *Metamorfosis*, 3/4 (1980/1981): 111-113;

Barbara Brinson-Pineda, "Poets on Poetry: Dialogue with Lucha Corpi," *Prisma*, 1, no. 1 (1979): 4-9.

Nephtalí De León
(9 May 1945-)

Jean S. Chittenden
Trinity University

BOOKS: *Chicanos: Our Background and Our Pride* (Lubbock, Tex.: Trucha, 1972);
5 Plays (Denver: Totinem, 1972);
Chicano Poet: With Images and Vision of the Poet (Lubbock, Tex.: Trucha, 1973);
I Will Catch the Sun (Lubbock, Tex.: Trucha, 1973);
I Color My Garden (Shallowater, Tex.: Tri-County Housing, 1973);
Coca Cola Dream (Lubbock, Tex.: Trucha, 1973);
Hey, Mr. President, Man!: On the Eve of the Bicentennial (Lubbock, Tex.: Trucha, 1975);
Tequila Mockingbird, Or the Ghost of Unemployment (San Antonio: Trucha, 1979);
El Segundo de Febrero, by De León, Carlos González, and Alfredo Alemán (San Antonio: Centro Cultural Aztlán, 1983);
Guadalupe Blues (San Antonio: Privately printed, 1985);
Sparky y su Gang (San Antonio: Nosotros, 1985);
Artemia: La Loca del River Walk (An Allegory of the Arts in San Antonio) (San Antonio: Educators' Roundtable, 1986);
El pollito amarillo: Baby Chick Yellow (San Antonio: Educators' Roundtable, 1987).

PLAY PRODUCTIONS: *The Flies*, El Paso, University of Texas at El Paso, 1973;
¡Chicanos! The Living and the Dead, Hagerman, N.M., 1974;
Play Number 9, Boulder, University of Colorado, 1976;
El tesoro de Pancho Villa, Lubbock, Tex., 1977;
La muerte de Ernesto Nerios, San Antonio, San Pedro Playhouse, 1978;
I Will Catch the Sun, San Antonio, Thiry Auditorium, Our Lady of the Lake University, 1979.

OTHER: "Of Bronze the Sacrifice," in *We Are Chicanos: An Anthology of Mexican-American Literature*, edited by Philip D. Ortego (New York: Washington Square Press, 1973), pp. 155-162;

Nephtalí De León (courtesy of the author)

"Tengo Mucho Miedo," "The Girl I Never Knew," "Juanito el Piojo," "Jaimito the Louse," "Los pájaros ya no lloran," and "Cuatro escudos," in *El Quetzal Emplumece*, edited by Carmela Montalvo and others (San Antonio: Mexican-American Cultural Center, 1976), pp. 56-66;
"Llevan flores," "Pulga," and "No No No," in *Festival de Flor y Canto: An Anthology of Chicano Literature*, edited by Alurista and others (Los Angeles: University of Southern California Press, 1976), pp. 61-62;
"In the Plaza We Walk," in *Dále Gas* (Houston: Contemporary Arts Museum, 1977); in *Patterns in Literature: America Reads*, seventh edition, edited by Edmund J. Farrell and others (Glenview, Ill.: Scott, Foresman, 1985), p. 158;
"Himno dedicado a los comercios chicanos," in *Chicanos: Antología histórica y literaria*, compiled by Tino Villanueva (Mexico City: Fondo de Cultura Económica, 1980), pp. 309-311;
"Mamá" and "A los graduados," in *Hispanics in the United States: An Anthology of Creative Litera-*

ture, edited by Gary D. Keller and Francisco Jiménez (Ypsilanti: Bilingual/Editorial Bilingüe, 1980), pp. 115-120.

PERIODICAL PUBLICATIONS: "How Chicanos Came to Be, or History of Modern Man," *La Luz*, 1 (January 1973): 56-57;

"Los Tres Little Pigs" and "Las fiestas patrias," *Caracol*, 2 (October 1975): 8, 10;

"Tamales," *Caracol*, 2 (November 1975): 7-8;

"*Caracol*: Un Año Después," *Caracol*, 2 (December 1975): 13;

"Sábado Trip," "Sangre," "Babe," and "My Midnight Cross," *Caracol*, 2 (February 1976): 13;

"Fresh Tomato Soup," *Caracol*, 2 (May 1976): 16;

"Por favor no me entierren vivo," *Caracol*, 2 (July 1976): 6, 23;

"No, Mr. Boa" and "Raquel and the Umbrellas," *Caracol*, 3 (March 1977): 22-23;

"El libro de Isaiah," *Caracol*, 3 (May 1977): 22;

"Chile" and "Día de elecciones," *Caracol*, 4 (November 1977): 20;

Review of *Tiempo Artesano/Time the Artesan*, by Mireya Robles, *Rayas*, 1 (January-February 1978): 10;

"Así como la lluvia," "Llevan flores," and "Día de elecciones," *Grito del Sol*, 3 (July-September 1978): 50-53;

"La Llorona," *Caracol*, 5 (January 1979): 16-17;

"Que lo sepa tu mamá," *Caracol*, 5 (July-August 1979): 25;

"Así como la lluvia," "El libro de Isaiah," and "Chile," *New Blood*, 6 (April 1982): 65-70.

One of the most prolific Chicano writers, Nephtalí De León is principally known as a poet, although his literary production includes dramatic works, children's stories, and essays. De León also is highly regarded as a painter and illustrator; nearly all of his books contain his illustrations.

De León writes mainly to express the dreams, desires, and aspirations of the Chicano people. His motivation in writing is to give an honest and truthful representation of the plight of the Chicano, which he sees as the result of a historical process. His inspiration, as he described it in an unpublished interview granted in 1985, comes from the realization that Chicanos have been held in a "psychological and spiritual bondage," that they are "cultural and intellectual hostages" in American society.

Born 9 May 1945, in Laredo, Texas, De León is the son of migrant workers. His father,

Francisco De León Cordero, a Mexican citizen, and his mother, María Guadalupe De León-González, a United States citizen, both had little formal education, but De León credits them with having exposed him, his two brothers, and his sister to literature at an early age. In the introduction to his selections in the anthology *El Quetzal Emplumece* (1976) he said, "One early surprise: one evening we arrived exhausted and dusty from the fields to find that a truck had delivered a whole set of encyclopedias! Nobody slept that night." His oldest brother, Francisco, introduced him to Hispanic writers, including poets such as Federico García Lorca and Amado Nervo, while his mother interested him in non-Hispanic writers such as Leo Tolstoy, Rabindranath Tagore, and Kahlil Gibran.

His early years of moving from one small town to another in south Texas while working in the fields picking tomatoes, cabbage, green peppers, and other vegetables made a profound impression on the young De León. In a profile of him in *Víaztlán* (Summer 1985) San Antonio journalist Rafael C. Castillo speaks of De León's vivid recollection of an event which took place at a ranch where he and his family were working in the fields with several illegal aliens from Mexico. Some border patrolmen arrived and fired at the group and then chased them. Finally the patrolmen caught the aliens and, according to De León's description, "tossed them into a truck like sacks of potatoes." Shortly after that experience De León began to write.

The family settled for a while in Rio Grande City, Texas, where De León attended junior high school. During one of their trips to the Texas Panhandle to work in the fields near Lubbock, the family car broke down, and they decided to remain in Lubbock. De León recalls their difficulties in adjusting to the urban setting. In order to survive in the city the various family members took whatever menial jobs they could find. In 1962 De León graduated from Lubbock High School and enrolled at Texas Tech University, where he began a major in psychology. He remained only a short period of time and subsequently studied in Mexico City and at the Instituto de Alianza Francesa in Vera Cruz, Mexico. During the next few years he spent a brief period in the U.S. Army, traveled throughout the United States, Mexico, and the Virgin Islands, and finally returned to Lubbock, where from 1968 until 1973 he edited a bilingual weekly journal, *La Voz de los llanos* (The Voice of the Plains).

During this period he also published his first book, *Chicanos: Our Background and Our Pride* (1972), a volume of essays dealing with the origins, culture, problems, and contemporary situation of Chicanos. This book was published by Trucha Press, which was created in Lubbock in 1970 by De León and others from the Lubbock barrio who felt the need for an outlet for their literary and artistic productions. The endeavor was begun with only fifteen hundred dollars, contributed by "street people" such as dishwashers, janitors, and farm workers.

In his prefatory remarks to *Chicanos: Our Background and Our Pride* De León defines a Chicano as "a very real person." He continues: "Beyond the person, Chicanismo is a way of life, a spiritual calling, a love, a respect, and a duty." He explains the background of the book and his inability to get it published under the Emergency School Assistance Program in Lubbock because the program director deemed it "a divisive work." The book comprises twenty-five essays and covers such topics as how the ancient Asians crossed the Bering Strait to North America; a definition of Aztlán (the mythical homeland of Chicanos in the Southwest); the founding of Tenochtitlán; a brief history of the Aztecs; the arrival of the Spaniards; the revolution against Spain; and the "Rape of Mexico" by the United States during the nineteenth century. De León also includes essays on border folk-hero Gregorio Cortez (1875-1916), who symbolizes the conflict between Mexican-Americans and Anglos in Texas; contemporary Chicano activist Reies Tijerina; Mexican-born journalist Ruben Salazar, who was shot by a sheriff's deputy during a 1970 protest against the Vietnam War; the shooting of Chicano youth Ernesto Nerios by Lubbock police on 14 August 1971; and a "March of Faith" by fifteen hundred people in Lubbock on 7 November 1971, during which grievances and demands of the Chicano community were presented. The book ends with the optimistic prediction that change will come, in spite of the fact that the system is "stubborn" and "narrow," but that La Raza (the Race) must continue in the effort to bring justice to all.

Although *Chicanos: Our Background and Our Pride* was clearly written with a message in mind, the artistic merit of the work is also apparent. De León's style is concise, eloquent, and at times quite poignant, particularly when he writes about children. His love for his people and his respect for his fellow human beings are evident through-

out. De León's drawings of Aztecs, Spaniards, Los Niños Héroes (The Child Heroes of the 1846 United States invasion of Mexico), and Pancho Villa are cleverly done and provide interesting complements to the text.

Reaction to *Chicanos: Our Background and Our Pride* was generally favorable. Although written with a Chicano audience in mind and published by a small press the book sold several thousand copies within a short period of time. Reviewers noted the sincerity of De León's writing. Arnulfo Trejo, in *Bibliografía Chicana* (1975), observed that there are "more profound and comprehensive" writings on the subject but that "this booklet has special merit because the writing emanates from the heart and displays deep feelings which come from bearing long years of social injustice." Charles Tatum, in *A Selected and Annotated Bibliography of Chicano Studies* (1979), called it "a personal and enlightening interpretation of the origin, history, and present status of his [De León's] people," adding that "His tone is overtly and unabashedly militant as he tries to instill pride in his Chicano readers."

De León's *5 Plays*, a collection of bilingual dramas, was published in 1972. In his introduction to this volume the author speaks of having studied "how to do it" books on drama and the stage before discovering "that there was greater drama in the streets where I grew up; there was also greater drama in the mind–in its wakeful hours and its nightly travels in multipathed worlds." The first play, *The Death of Ernesto Nerios* (produced in 1978 as *La muerte de Ernesto Nerios*), tells of the 1971 murder of the young Chicano. In a note De León explains that the account of Nerios's death is factual but that the rest of the play is his own invention, designed "to depict the suddenness and the intensity with which injustice and misfortune pursue us in the barrio" as well as "the frustrations and backlash that we are often prey to." Ernesto, who has served with honor in Vietnam, finds himself in financial straits with a sick baby and an employer who is threatening to fire him. After he and a friend spend most of the night drinking, he enters a convenience store, gets into an argument with the clerk, and is subsequently shot to death by the police, who are pursuing him. A mysterious voice calling periodically for Ernesto, his wife's premonitions about his going out that night, and six strange figures symbolizing death heighten the play's sense of tragedy and of supernatural events beyond man's control.

Illustrations by De León for his first collection of verse, Chicano Poet *(courtesy of the author)*

¡Chicanos! The Living and the Dead (produced in 1974) was written at the request of a high-school girl, a friend of De León. The first two scenes depict a Chicano protest rally, with a list of grievances, followed by a dialogue between X and Y, who voice complaints against the injustices of the American system and call for humanization of the government and reforms in the educational process. Then comes a scene that takes place in Limbo, where two champions of the downtrodden, Ernesto "Che" Guevara (1928-1967) and Manuel (who represents Ruben Salazar), speak of their violent deaths and of the plight of California's farm laborers. Che explains that his revolution was based on love of his fellowman and on the teachings of Christ. The action then returns to the Chicano rally of the first scene. The topic of conversation is Manuel's death, and there is another recitation of abuses against Chicanos, interrupted by a young woman who suggests that rather than fomenting hate for the gringo the protesters should be urging their people to better themselves through education. The play ends with a plea for love and tolerance but leaves open the possibility that if reforms are not brought about by peaceful means, those seeking justice may be pushed to rebellion and killing.

In *Play Number 9* (produced in 1976) De León uses the Prometheus myth to draw a parallel between the man who stole the secret of fire from the gods and the Chicano who tries to ignite a spark to bring about reforms in American education. The universality of the struggle for equality is clearly portrayed as Prometheus longs for freedom from his chains, just as the Chicano longs to escape from a system which keeps him in bondage. The failure of the educational process to meet the needs of Chicano children (because of linguistic and cultural shortsightedness) is the theme of this play, which juxtaposes the board meeting of a group of white, black, and Chicano citizens who are to implement a project to improve the education of Chicanos with a scene in which a young Chicano encounters Prometheus and explains the problems of his contemporaries when they attend schools which are dominated by English-speaking teachers and administrators. Prometheus remarks on the similarity between his situation and that of the Chicano. The final act consists of a monologue by Prometheus, who speaks from behind a curtain, proclaiming himself a Chicano and swearing to break his chains and gain his freedom.

The fourth play in the collection, *The Judging of Man*, is more abstract than its predecessors. It takes place "beyond time and space," and its characters are personifications of death, destiny, beauty, faith, and virtue. A narrator explains that the earth has been destroyed by war and that the time has come for the judging of man. Death claims that all mankind is his, but the other characters argue that they are immortal and that destiny, not death, is the omnipotent force. Finally Destiny decrees that man shall live and asks that his "folly and dark ignorance end with this atrocious act of war." Beauty, Faith, and Virtue are then reconstituted in animal shapes, making it impossible to tell if they are humans or beasts. Their last statement is one of thanks to Destiny for permitting them to live and praying that they may "grow to be worthy mysteries of your kingdom." Through abstract personages De León expresses his hope for a world of peace in which men can learn to love each other.

De León writes in his introductory statement that the last play of this volume, *The Flies* (produced in 1973), was written one night after he had killed three flies in succession. His "flyicide" began to prey on his mind, as he thought how "men have killed other men with the same ease and thoughtlessness with which I had killed these flies." This drama, which he describes as "timeless," relates the story of two boy flies and one girl fly who meet, converse, and ultimately are threatened by a voice which shouts, "I'm coming to get you . . . you little punks." At the end of the play the reader learns that one of the boy flies has been squashed, while the other two flies remain, vowing their love for each other. Of this work, De León said in the 1985 interview, "I am asked if it is a comedy. Everyone roars with laughter each time it is performed. I remain silent and grim." The analogy of the flies with the Chicano people, who are "squashed" with equal cruelty, forms the basis for this symbolic play. The dialogue is witty, but there is a deep compassion for society's victims which underlies the humor.

The year 1973 saw the publication of four books by De León—*Chicano Poet: With Images and Vision of the Poet, Coca Cola Dream, I Will Catch the Sun,* and *I Color My Garden.* The first two are volumes of poetry and the other two are children's books.

Chicano Poet is the first book-length collection of poetry by De León. Illustrated with surrealistic woodcuts by the author, it is composed of twenty-nine poems, of which nineteen appear only in English and ten appear in both an English and a Spanish version. According to De León, he began to compose poetry when he was quite young as a means of escaping from his oppressive and nearly intolerable life as a migrant worker. In his preface to *Chicano Poet* he admits that he cannot "flaunt a banner of disgust" in his poetry, because "The realm of poetry is too sacred, too lovely to profane." He concludes that this "does not mean that rage is not proper for a poem, but rather that a poem is not proper for rage." His purpose in writing poetry is "as an expression of my insane world where happiness could be, free from the interminable caravan of Amerika's travesties and wrongs."

In this poetry De León gives free reign to his imagination to create a world full of plastic, sometimes sensuous, imagery. In "And Thus Came Down" ("Y así bajó") the moon becomes "a star/of raving light/as treasure chests/of gold it oozed–" ("una estrella/de luz divina/menguante y rubia/como un joyar–"). The effect of the poems is heightened by the illustrations, which are integrated into the work in such a way that the combination of poetry and visual art provides an escape from reality into fantasy. Underlying many of the poems, such as "Child of the Wind" ("El niño del viento"), is the desire for peace and love for the Chicano people. The first stanza of "Alone" addresses De León's own personal dilemma and suffering, "Alone,/I wander through the universe,/Vast, real/and unreal,/A cosmic vagabond am I–/a derelict in space."

One of the most impressive poems of *Chicano Poet* is "Coca Cola Dream," which was published as a separate volume, with additional illustrations by the author, in 1973, went through three printings, and was published in a second edition in 1976. The theme of this lengthy poem is the poet's disillusionment with what he refers to as "Gringolandia" and the commercialism and lack of human understanding which it symbolizes. At first the sparkling bubbles and the shape of the bottle lift his thoughts to Jesus and to what might be, but the empty bottle brings him back to reality, where "My Coca Cola dream/ becomes once more–/an empty bottle green/a glass,/and one fantastic fool . . ."

De León's concern for the education of Chicano children and for the inability of the education system to provide an effective means of keeping them in school led him to write the two children's books, published in 1973. Seeing Chica-

nos not as "dropouts" but as "kickouts," De León wanted to provide school materials that would inspire young Chicanos to have pride in their heritage. Although his writings occasionally have been termed "too radical" for use in some school districts, several of his works, including *Chicanos: Our Background and Our Pride*, *I Will Catch the Sun*, and *I Color My Garden*, have been used by schools in California, Colorado, New Mexico, Nebraska, Minnesota, Wisconsin, and Utah, and one of his poems, "In the Plaza We Walk," is included in the 1985 edition of *Patterns in Literature: America Reads*, for use in junior high schools.

I Will Catch the Sun is the story of Raúl, a young Chicano who is the object of ridicule because when his teacher asks him what he wants most of all, instead of responding like the other children, who want to be doctors or lawyers, he answers, "I will catch the sun." With the help of a frog he discovers that he can catch the sun by using a pan of water to reflect its image, thereby earning the respect of his fellows. Reviewing this work, Larry Tjarks writes (in *Children's Literature: The Great Excluded*, 1974) that it "deals realistically with the harshness and ridicule that barrio-Spanish speaking children all too often must endure in some schools." Tjarks takes note of De León's use of the barrio Spanish-English spoken in many Chicano homes and comments on his reference to various Chicano customs and foods. "Most important, however," he concludes, De León "credibly captures the intuitive genius of all children, transcending narrow ethnic traditions."

De León's second children's book published in 1973, *I Color My Garden*, is a bilingual, bicultural edition "dedicado a toda nuestra Raza who know what it's like to work in the fields." De León explains how the book can be used for teaching reading, numbers, writing, spelling, art, and science, and he includes suggestions for activities in these areas. The book includes seventeen poems, each of which appears in an English version and a Spanish version; each is about a different vegetable. Accompanying every poem is a drawing of the vegetable made by the author's brother, Francisco, and designed to be colored by the children. Cultural information is included whenever possible, as in the poem on corn, which is described as being good for tamales, tortillas, enchiladas, tacos, and Fritos, and as being found in all Mexican and Chicano towns. The poems (in which the vegetable characters carry on dialogues with the reader) and the drawings provide a creative and imaginative way for chil-

Cover and illustrations by De León for one of his children's books (courtesy of the author)

dren to learn about nature while increasing their cultural awareness and developing academic skills as well.

During the decade of the 1970s De León continued to write in a variety of forms. *Hey, Mr. President, Man!*, subtitled *On the Eve of the Bicentennial*, was published in 1975. Addressed to President Gerald Ford, it constitutes one of De León's most bitter and vitriolic attacks on the United States government. Calling the president a "presumptuous ass," he depicts the Statue of Liberty as crying for help as she observes what is going on in her country. To Ford he says, "So putrid is your breath/ which violates with death/la Santa Raza/cómica y presente." Finally, speaking to the president, Congress, and other officials, he says, "I do declare/ officially, unofficially,/categorically/and quintessentially/that yes,/your hour,/your day,/your worthless funeral,/–has come!" Here the poet, through his bombastic language, reveals an impatience with the injustices he perceives.

From 1975 to 1979 several poems, short stories, plays, and essays by De León appeared in journals specializing in Chicano writing, most notably *Caracol*. By 1979 De León had moved from Lubbock to San Antonio; Trucha Press relocated as well. De León still resides in San Antonio, but the press has been inactive since 1980; De León's 1979 play *Tequila Mockingbird, Or the Ghost of Unemployment* is the most recent work to carry its imprint.

Like some of De León's earlier plays, *Tequila Mockingbird* is on the surface a comedy, but it has as its basis the struggle of the Chicano to exist in a hostile world. In his introduction to this work, Rafael Castillo writes, "it is through the vehicle of expression called Satire that Nephtalí adroitly creates the unifying spirit of Chicanismo: being able to laugh in the face of adversity." The play deals with unemployment and its effects on Chicanos. Mr. Fruitloop, owner of Jumbo Sugar Fruitloops, Incorporated, a breakfast-cereal manufacturing company, replaces his Chicano workers with a robot. However, two border patrolmen, Red and Boots, appear and mistake Fruitloop, his assistant Springs, and Uncle Sam (who has come to collect taxes from the employees' last paychecks) for undocumented workers and send them to Mexico. The three try unsuccessfully to buy their way back into the United States. Eventually Red and Boots, too, are taken for illegal aliens and sent to Mexico, where they meet the others. They all suffer the psychological effects of unemployment and, bronzed by the Mexi-

can sun, are taken as compatriots by Fruitloop's former employees. At the end the Virgin of Guadalupe appears to redeem her Mexican people; the former employers and the two border patrolmen become Brown Berets; and a demonstration shows the emergence of a "mythic invisible minority." The ending, then, shows optimism for the future, with the appearance of the Mexican Virgin stressing the role that religion plays in the hope for a better life for Chicanos.

In 1980 De León's daughter, Aidé, became ill with leukemia. She was five years old at the time and had already suffered a near-fatal automobile accident at age two that left her in a coma for three months. In spite of the doctors' gloomy predictions, she had made an excellent recovery from the accident. Her death from leukemia in 1985 left De León devastated. During the five years of her illness he had continued to write, paint, and lecture, but he has been profoundly affected by the tragic life of his child.

A play, *El Segundo de Febrero* (The Second of February), coauthored by De León, Carlos González, and Alfredo Alemán, was published in 1983. Designated "a historical play for young people," it is an account of the history of Mexico and the American Southwest written from a point of view sympathetic to the Mexican government in its territorial struggles with its neighbor to the north and giving special prominence to the Treaty of Guadalupe Hidalgo, which was signed on 2 February 1848 ceding a large part of Mexico to the United States. The last scene of the play shows the emergence of the new person, the Chicano, as a result of the political changes depicted in the first part of the play.

In the spring of 1985 De León published *Guadalupe Blues*, a volume of poetry dedicated to Open Dialogue, a group of Chicano-Hispanic artists in San Antonio. One of these poems, "San Antonio de Bexar," boasts of the Chicanos who have come to prominence through their own efforts and the sacrifices of their parents, and promises the emergence of yet more Chicano leaders in San Antonio.

De León's literary output has decreased in the last few years as he has turned to lecturing and painting as well as writing. He has maintained his interest in the education of Chicano children and spends much time working in various school systems within and outside of Texas in an effort to provide better materials and to serve as a role model for these children. Although several of his works for children remain unpublished, several fables by De León have appeared in journals. At Christmas 1988 he directed Bidal Agüero's play *El traje de Santo Clos* (Santa's Suit) in San Antonio.

The motivation to bring about justice for his people has caused De León to declare himself "first an activist and then an artist." He sees the Chicano literature as a nascent one but believes that it can grow and survive. As he continues to write, he will no doubt contribute even more to that literature.

Interviews:

"Entrevista con Nephtalí De León," *Caracol*, 5 (May 1979): 12, 13, 19;

"La Entrevista del *Visitante Dominical* con: Nephtalí De León," *El Visitante Dominical* (5 August 1979);

"Nephtalí De León," *El Bravo* (Matamoros, Tamaulipas), 15 December 1985, II: 1, 4.

References:

Reyes Cárdenas, "Nephtalí's Purple Shirt," *Caracol*, 2 (February 1976): 21;

Rafael C. Castillo, "Naphtalí De León: A Profile," *Víaztlán*, 3 (Summer 1985): 7-8;

Ricardo Sánchez, "A Literature by Chicanos: Recapturing a Lost Voice," *Texas Circuit Newsletter* (February-March 1982).

Abelardo Barrientos Delgado

(27 November 1931-)

Donaldo W. Urioste

California Lutheran University

BOOKS: *Chicano: 25 Pieces of a Chicano Mind* (Denver: Barrio, 1969);

The Chicano Movement: Some Not Too Objective Observations (Denver: Colorado Migrant Council, 1971);

Mortal Sin Kit (El Paso: Barrio, n.d.);

Reflexiones . . . (N.p., n.d.);

Bajo el sol de Aztlán: 25 soles de Abelardo (El Paso: Barrio, 1973);

It's Cold: 52 Cold-Thought Poems of Abelardo (Salt Lake City: Barrio, 1974);

A Thermos Bottle Full of Self Pity: 25 Bottles of Abelardo (Arvada, Colo.: Barrio, 1975?);

A Quilt of Words: 25 Quilts of Abelardo (N.p.: Barrio, 1976?);

Reflexiones: 16 Reflections of Abelardo (Salt Lake City: Barrio, 1976);

Here Lies Lalo: 25 Deaths of Abelardo (Salt Lake City: Barrio, 1977; revised, Arvada, Colo.: Barrio, 1979);

Under the Skirt of Lady Justice: 43 Skirts of Abelardo (Denver: Barrio, 1978);

Totoncaxihuitl, A Laxative: 25 Laxatives of Abelardo (Arvada, Colo.: Barrio, 1981);

Letters to Louise (Berkeley: Tonatiuh-Quinto Sol International, 1982);

Unos perros con metralla (Some Dogs with Machinegun): 25 Dogs of Abelardo (Arvada, Colo.: Barrio, 1982).

OTHER: *Los cuatro*, edited by Delgado and Ricardo Sánchez, includes work by Delgado (Denver: Barrio, 1971), pp. 4-14;

Aztlán: An Anthology of Mexican American Literature, edited by Luis Valdez and Stan Steiner (New York: Knopf, 1972), includes poetry by Delgado, pp. 394-397;

Literatura chicana: Texto y contexto, edited by Antonia Castañeda Shular, Tomás Ybarra-Frausto, and Joseph Sommers, includes poetry by Delgado (Englewood Cliffs, N.J.: Prentice-Hall, 1972), pp. 249, 264;

We Are Chicanos: An Anthology of Mexican American Literature, edited by Philip D. Ortego, includes poetry by Delgado (New York: Washington Square Press, 1973), pp. 216-220;

Festival de Flor y Canto I: An Anthology of Chicano Literature, edited by Alurista, F. A. Cervantes, Juan Gómez-Quiñones, Mary Ann Pacheco, and Gustavo Segade, includes poetry by Delgado (Los Angeles: University of Southern California Press, 1976), pp. 33-34;

Abelardo Barrientos Delgado, July 1987 (courtesy of the author)

Mexican-American Anthology II: Prose, Essays, Stories, Songs, Dichos, Corridos, Art, edited by Joy Hintz, includes poetry by Delgado (Lansing, Mich.: E. Renacimiento, 1976), pp. 202-205;

El quetzal emplumece, edited by Carmela Montalvo, Leornado Anguiano, and Cecilio García-Camarillo, includes poetry by Delgado (San Antonio: Mexican American Cultural Center, 1976), pp. 70-75, 328-336;

"Mictlán," in *Nahualliandoing: Poetry in Español/Nahuatl/English*, edited by Cecilio García-Camarillo and Mía García-Camarillo (San Antonio: Caracol, 1977), p. 8;

Canto al pueblo: An Anthology of Experiences, edited by Leonardo Carrillo, Antonio Martínez, Carol Molina, and Marie Wood, includes poetry by Delgado (San Antonio: Penca, 1978), pp. 9, 32, 36, 46, 67, 89-90;

"Ejele," in *Festival de Flor y Canto II: An Anthology of Chicano Literature from the Festival held March 12-16, 1975, Austin, Texas*, edited by Arnold C. Vento, Alurista, and José Flores Peregrino (Albuquerque: Pajarito, 1979), p. 113;

Face of Poetry, edited by LaVerne Harrell Clark and Mary MacArthur, includes poetry by Delgado (Arlington, Va.: Gallimantry, 1976), p. 67;

Canto al Pueblo: Antología, edited by Justo S. Alarcón, Juan Pérez Aldape, and Lupe Cárdenas, includes poetry by Delgado (Mesa: Arizona Canto al Pueblo IV, Comite Editorial, 1980), pp. 49-56;

Chicanos: Antología histórica y literaria, edited by Tino Villanueva, includes poetry by Delgado (Mexico City: Fondo de Cultura Económica, 1980), pp. 274-277;

Flor y Canto IV and V: An Anthology of Chicano Literature From the Festivals held in Albuquerque, New Mexico, 1977 and Tempe, Arizona, 1978, edited by José Armas, Bernice Zamora, and Michael Reed, includes poetry by Delgado (Albuquerque: Pajarito, Flor y Canto V Committee, 1980), pp. 62-64;

"Orate Frates," in *A Ceremony of Brotherhood, 1610-1980*, edited by Rudolfo A. Anaya and

Simon J. Ortiz (Albuquerque: Academia, 1981), p. 119;

"Walls of Silence," in *Impressions: A Collection of Poetry*, edited by Shirley J. Mikkelson (Minot, N.D.: Quill, 1986), p. 90.

PERIODICAL PUBLICATIONS: "El árbol de navidad es naranjal. . . ," *Ya mero*, 1 (27 December 1969): 5;

"El jefe," *El Gallo*, 2 (January 1970): 4, 6;

"Ash Wednesday" and "El Splash," *El Gallo*, 2 (February 1970): 6;

"The Chicano Manifesto," "Lali," "Mellow Melo," "El chisme," "Bilingual Babe," "One Hundred Dollar Bill," "I Was Just," "La hembra," and "At Dawn," *El Pocho Che*, 1 (April 1970): 17-20, 50-55;

"Raymundo Pérez," *El Chicano*, 4 (11 September 1970): 3;

"El primer cumpleaños de la huelga," *Ahora*, 2 (30 July 1971);

"1972, el año del orgullo," *Ahora*, 3 (25 December 1971);

"From El Chuco to Albu," *La Voz Mexicana*, 1 (February 1972): 4;

"Yo soy chicano," *La Voz Mexicana*, 1 (March 1972): 10-11;

"The Chicano Movement" and "White Napkin," *El Gallo*, 4 (May 1972): 8;

"Los desraizgados," *La Luz*, 1 (March 1973): 46;

"Aurum," "The Next Eon," "Abati," and "La revolución," *Caracol*, 1 (May 1975): 19;

"Me dicen que sabes español," *Xalmán: Alma Chicana de Aztlán*, 1 (July 1975): 7;

"Red or Black Lace," "El compadre más correlón," "Critical Incident Reports," "Universo," and "Ejele," *Caracol*, 2 (April 1976): 8;

"Escritor," *Colorado-North Review*, 12 (Spring 1976): 44;

"Such is the Punishment," "From Garden City to Hayes," "Wild," and "Where?," *Southwest Woman's Poetry Exchange*, 4 (January 1977): 44-50;

"Ambassador," "From Garden City to Hayes," "Parliamentary Procedure," "Updated Prayers for Novochristians," and "El Fundi," *Revista Chicano-Riqueña*, 5 (Spring 1977): 11-15;

"Por eso," *Caracol*, 3 (July 1977): 20;

"El encimoso," "De Yakima para Seattle," and "De Jamestown to Aberdeen," *Caracol*, 4 (November 1977): 12;

"Anclas de desunidad," "La barraca," and "Samartina," *Caracol*, 4 (February 1978): 20;

"No tengo papeles" and "To Ana and Alicia," *Metamorfosis*, 1 (February 1978): 25-27;

"For Men Only" and "The Last Wow," *Revista Chicano-Riqueña*, 4 (Spring 1978): 25-26;

"From Lewiston to Boise" and "I'm Going to Dedicate this Poem," *Grito del Sol*, 3 (July-September 1978): 25-27;

"Ten Peanuts for Five Cents," *Caracol*, 4 (August 1978): 5;

"Miss Emily A. Lewis" and "Operation Wine," *River-Sedge*, 2, no. 2 (1978): 21, 39;

"Amador," *Revista Chicano-Riqueña*, 9 (Spring 1981): 17-18;

"From Garden City to Hayes" and "The Last Wow," *Revista Chicano-Riqueña*, 10 (Winter-Spring 1982): 62-65;

"Walls of Silence," *Wide Open Magazine*, 3 (July 1986): 43;

"Feliz cumpleaños, esposa mía" and "Three Margaritas Later," *Rocky Mountain Arsenal of the Arts: Denver's Literary Magazine*, 7 (May-June 1987): 6, 20;

"Exit the Frogs / Salida de las ranas," *Americas 2001*, 1 (September-October 1987): 40-46.

Autobiographical poet, critic, and short-story writer Abelardo "Lalo" Delgado is among the most prolific of the Chicano writers who first came to prominence in the late 1960s and early 1970s. Because of his literary productivity, his thematic versatility, and his social commitment, he has served as a model for many current Chicano poets, becoming known in some literary circles as "el abuelito" (the grandfather).

Born in La Boquilla de Conchos, Chihuahua, Mexico, on 27 November 1931, Delgado spent his early childhood years in this rural village and in the cities of Parral and Juárez in northern Chihuahua. In 1943, at the age of twelve, he and his mother, Guadalupe Díaz Delgado, immigrated to El Paso, Texas, and settled in the impoverished neighborhood known as *el segundo barrio* (The Second Neighborhood), where he lived until 1969. He attended Aoy Grammar School, where at first he had some difficulties because of his unfamiliarity with English, but he quickly excelled in his studies. While at Aoy he was promoted twice and in two years advanced to Bowie Junior-Senior High School. At Bowie he enrolled in college preparation course work and was selected vice-president of the National Honor Society. He was involved in extracurricular activities such as ROTC and was coeditor of the school newspaper, for which he received an award in journalism. Shortly after his graduation from Bowie in 1950 in the top 10 percent of his class, he married Dolores Estrada. The couple have eight children.

From 1950 to 1955 Delgado held various jobs, mostly in construction and restaurant work. Early in 1955 he was employed as special activities director at Our Lady's Youth Center in El Paso, Texas, where he was to spend the next ten years working with deprived youths from El Paso's barrios. In an unpublished July 1987 interview with Donaldo W. Urioste he claimed that it was at the youth center that he had his "formative years in the [Chicano] Movement," and that he "pledged a lifetime commitment of love and struggle for those afflicted with the social illness of poverty." He returned to school at the University of Texas at El Paso, where he received a B.S. in secondary education in 1962. He has been employed continuously since then in the areas of health and social services, working on behalf of juveniles, migrant farm workers, and undocumented workers in the states of Colorado, Washington, Utah, and Texas. He has also taught one year of high school and one year of elementary school and has been an instructor and lecturer at various universities. He currently lives in Arvada, Colorado, where he is the director of the Adult Basic Education Program for the House of Neighborly Services. He also teaches on a part-time basis at Aims Community College in Fort Lupton.

While the primary objective of the Chicano Movement of the 1960s and 1970s was to promote civil and human rights and to affirm a positive cultural identity for Chicanos, it also encouraged writers, artists, and musicians who set out to present the Chicano point of view. Among the first of the writers to emerge was Delgado. Like the writing of his contemporary poets in the Chicano Movement (for example, Alurista, Sergio Elizondo, José Montoya, Luis Omar Salinas, Raúl Salinas, Ricardo Sánchez, Raymundo Pérez, and Tino Villanueva), much of Delgado's early poetry is social in its content and focus and reflects many of the ideological concerns of the movement. He told Juan Bruce-Novoa that he has considered himself a sort of *cronista* (chronicler) of the Chicano experience, or, as he states, "a recorder of Chicano events, happenings, victories, defeats, and struggles from a poetic perspective absent from newspapers and prose journals," and an "animator to give spirit and . . . philosophical direction and criticism." His poetry is typically

written in a bilingual (Spanish and English) format with a resonant, declamatory style. Francisco Lomelí and Arcadio Morales note in Julio A. Martinez and Lomelí's *Chicano Literature: A Reference Guide* (1985) that while many of Delgado's contemporaries have condoned violent resistance to racism, oppression, and other social inequities, his "relentless search for justice" is usually approached by appealing to common interests of love and understanding.

With the exception of *The Chicano Movement: Some Not Too Objective Observations* (1971) and *Letters to Louise* (1982), all of Delgado's books have been self-published by Barrio Publications, a publishing house he established in 1970. Faced with the reluctance of major publishing houses to accept Chicano writers because they saw little chance for profit, he set up Barrio Publications to print his own works as well as those of new writers. The publishing house operates on a buy-in share system whereby supporters, including writers interested in having their works published, invest their resources to finance the company. Unfortunately, due to the restricted budget resulting from this system of operations, Barrio has at times been forced to forsake quality (many works have appeared in photocopy form) and quantity (limited runs of one hundred to two hundred copies). This, in turn, has resulted in a limited exposure of Delgado's own work. Nevertheless, he has still managed to develop a following through his many personal appearances at readings throughout the United States.

Delgado's first and perhaps best-known collection of poetry is *Chicano: 25 Pieces of a Chicano Mind* (1969). Published during the height of the Chicano Movement, the collection is composed of twenty-five poems that generally promote social change and aspire to arouse social awareness among Chicanos. Delgado focuses on some of the main social, political, and cultural concerns of the movement. He takes up the cause of the economically deprived and the socially disenfranchised such as the *campesino* (farm worker), the undocumented immigrant, and the barrio dweller. He also explores Chicano identity and devotes himself to themes and concepts of a more cultural nature, such as *chicanismo, carnalismo* (brotherhood), machismo, *el compadrazgo* (family links through godparents), *la tierra* (the earth), the sixteenth of September (Mexican Independence Day), and the Virgin of Guadalupe. Delgado is at his best when he advocates social justice, human dignity, and equality for Chicanos, and when he

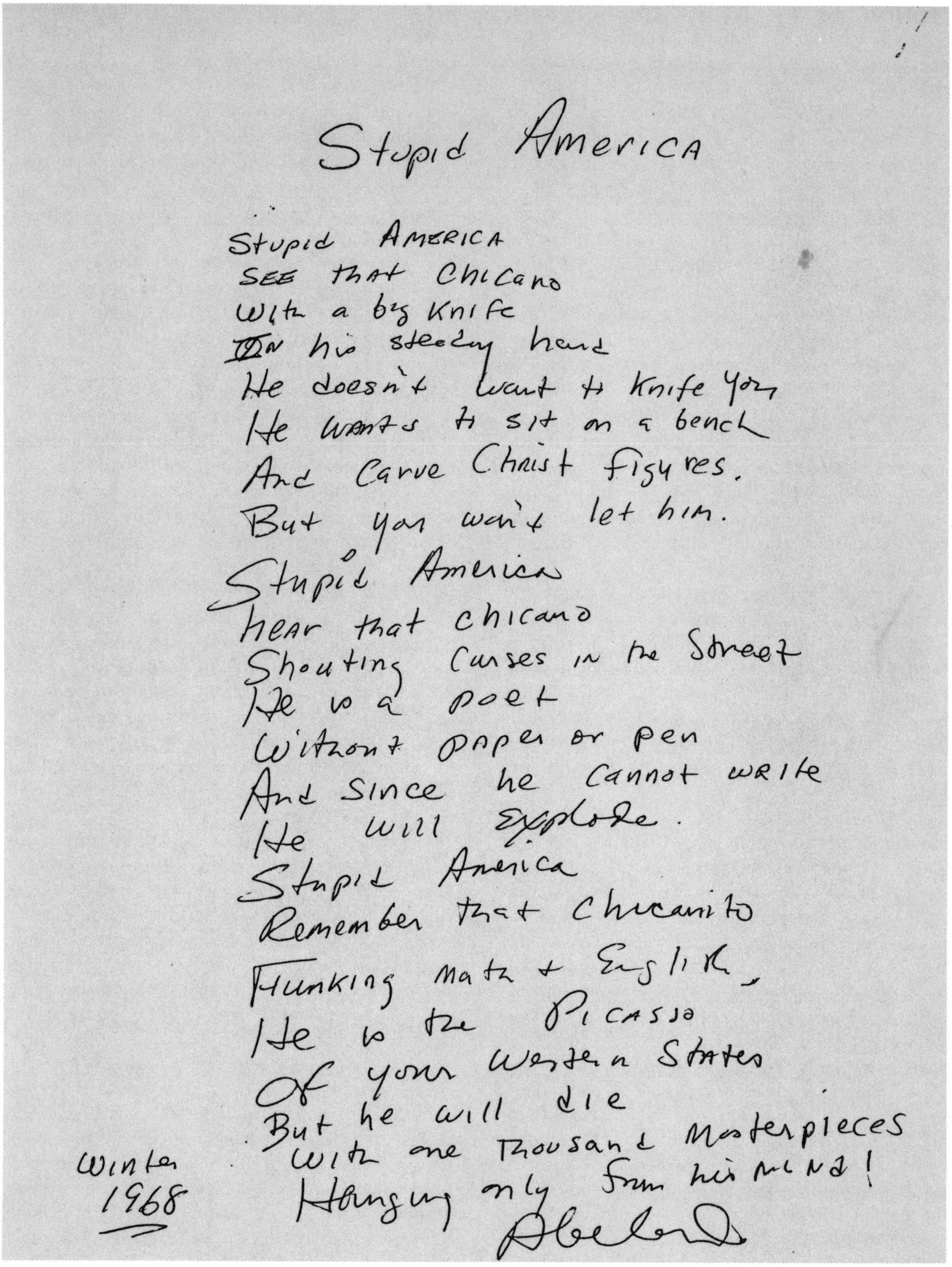

Stupid America

Stupid AMERICA
SEE that Chicano
With a big knife
In his steady hand
He doesn't want to knife you
He wants to sit on a bench
And carve Christ figures.
But you won't let him.

Stupid America
hear that chicano
Shouting curses in the street
He is a poet
Without paper or pen
And since he cannot write
He will explode.

Stupid America
Remember that Chicanito
Flunking math & English,
He is the Picasso
Of your Western States
But he will die
With one thousand Masterpieces
Hanging only from his mind!

Abelardo

Winter
1968

Fair copy of Delgado's best-known poem (courtesy of the author)

angrily condemns those forces–be they social or cultural, Anglo or Chicano–that work against these ideals. In "Stupid America," the most acclaimed of all of his poems, he censures Anglo-America's unwillingness to recognize the intellectual and artistic abilities of the Chicano:

> stupid america, see that chicano
> with a big knife
> on his steady hand
> he doesn't want to knife you
> he wants to sit on a bench
> and carve christfigures
> but you wont let him.
> stupid america, hear that chicano
> shouting curses on the street
> he is a poet
> without paper and pencil
> and since he cannot write
> he will explode.
> stupid america, remember that chicanito
> flunking math and english
> he is the picasso
> of your western states
> but he will die
> with one thousand masterpieces
> hanging only from his mind.

In an unpublished interview with Urioste, Delgado gave an account of the circumstances under which he wrote "Stupid America": "Like many of my early poems, I wrote 'Stupid America' out of anger and frustration. At the time [1969], I was at a conference in Warrenton, Virginia, in which Anglo educators blamed Chicanos for their lack of success in school. It never occurred to them to ask whether or not the *chicanitos* [Chicano children] were being challenged and encouraged in the schools. Later, back in my hotel room, I felt frustrated by their attitudes, and the words of the poem began to flow. At the time kids everywhere were using the words 'dumb' and 'stupid' in phrases such as 'stupid school,' 'stupid books' and 'stupid teachers,' and it is in the same spirit that I use the term in my poem."

Los cuatro (1971), which contains the work of Delgado, Ricardo Sánchez, Raymundo "Tigre" Pérez, and Juan Valdez (Magdaleno Avila), is a collection of Chicano Movement social-protest poetry representing a joint effort on the part of the four poets to awaken, sensitize, and, when necessary, condemn Anglo-American society for its injustices and destruction of Chicano culture. The militant purpose and confrontational tone of the collection are best described by Sánchez in the work's introduction:

> let us then see, amerika, if you can stomach the desperation in our voices, if you can read us ojos-abiertos [open-eyes] style and objectively take our words and ideas; if after you have read you still do not make the effort to understand what we say, then perhaps it will be time for amerika to disappear once and for all . . . amerika must be informed that La Raza will never have a watts so that los gringos can have their cheap thrills at our expense . . . la verdad es que [the truth is that] we shall not burn down our own–for if we burn, it is simply: LOOK OUT, GRINGO, LA RAZA SHALL BURN YOU DOWN.

Delgado's poetry in the volume is of three types. In poems such as "Icon" he presents the image of a cold, dehumanized society whose mechanization and technology have created an ambiance in which alienation and loneliness reign. He takes up the plight of the migrant farm worker and the hungry in "Total Conclusion" and "Dicho y Echo" (Said and Done). "Rojo" (Red) and "Metamorphosis" express his concern about issues such as police brutality and racism in the United States, calling on all Americans "to prove our human nature wrong / designing square coins so they / won't rule and role, / a world map with no dividing lines our full accord / thereby delaying forever the coming of the lord."

Delgado's *The Chicano Movement: Some Not Too Objective Observations* represents an early attempt by a Chicano intellectual to analyze the then fervent Chicano Movement. Written in the form of an essay organized into twenty-four brief chapters, the work describes the movement as a nationwide affair whose primary goals include social and political justice, economic independence, self-determination, community control, better educational opportunities, the abolishment of poverty, better housing, land reform, and adequate job training for all Chicanos. Delgado's objective is to inform and provoke Chicanos into taking a more active role in the Chicano Movement so that it might achieve its goals. He explores the movement's strengths and weaknesses, along with its politics and leaders, discussing its various ideologies and strategies. He predicts recent worldwide sensitivity to traditional values will make it possible for the movement "to fit in a greater perspective of man's struggle to be free of the bondage he oftentimes sets on another."

Delgado's collections *Mortal Sin Kit* and *Reflexiones . . .* (Reflections) are undated, but both are known to have been published prior to 1973, the date of publication of his *Bajo el sol de Aztlán: 25 soles de Abelardo* (Under the Sun of Aztlán: 25 Suns of Abelardo), in which both are mentioned. They mark the beginning of a new direction in his work in that they contain mostly poetry that is personal, intimate, and introspective, with little mention of the Chicano Movement or its concerns. In his introduction to *Mortal Sin Kit* Delgado says his turn toward intimacy is his attempt to allow others to see and feel his mortality and his humanity: "I purposely let a few windows open inviting readers to touch, lick, or kiss my soul-wounds, which after all are his own wounds, too." Though the general tone of *Mortal Sin Kit* is light-hearted and playful, "Maria" laments the death of a young child. "Out There" likens life in American society to life in prison, suggesting that the imprisoned, despite their confinement, might be psychologically freer than those on the outside. In "Sábado de Gloria" (Holy Saturday), "Francisco y Angela," and "Rosalinda y Héctor," Delgado reaffirms his marriage vows and his love for his spouse as he joyfully celebrates the nuptials of intimate friends. *Reflexiones . . .* consists of thirteen mental reflections on such themes as affectionate love for mothers, the intimacy of sex, the horrors of a nuclear holocaust, and expressions of solitude and disillusionment about the deteriorating condition of mankind. Delgado sees himself–like his cultural forefathers Quetzalcóatl and Don Quixote–as one of the redeemers who can right wrongs, radiate hope and goodness, and bring new life to the world. In "Today" he says, "we, you, i, are desperately / looking for fools, maniacs who / dare to speak of hope."

Bajo el sol de Aztlán is written Spanish, English, and sometimes a combination of both languages. With the exception of a few poems that focus on the Chicano Movement and ideas of a social and ideological nature (for example, "Aquí" [Here]; "Why am I Here?"; "Museum Piece"; "Metamorphosis"; "Twin Falls"; "Happy 200th Anniversary"; "Uanetl, indio sin regalo" [Uanetl, Indian Without a Gift]; and "Cream or Sugar"), the work is personal and philosophical. Confiding in the reader as if he were a close friend, Delgado shares his thoughts and feelings on themes such as love and sexual desire, the passing of time and the bygone days of childhood, solitude (for example, "Espinas" [Thorns]), and his love for his spouse (as in "Feliz cumpleaños, esposa mía" [Happy Birthday, Dear Wife]). In "My Unborn Sons (or Daughters)" he metaphorically equates poetry to his offspring, born to embellish, beautify, and vitalize life, while in "Ya no" (No Longer) he anxiously fantasizes his desire to write of beauty, happiness, and enjoyment rather than the grim and chaotic nature of human existence. As he says, "ya no quiero escribir / de lo que veo sino de lo que sueño" (No longer do I wish to write / about what I see but about what I dream).

In "The Poet as a Mirror" Delgado envisions the poet as a godlike figure who, at rare moments, "creates . . . something out of nothing." He is a "human x-ray machine / *para el alma*" (for the soul) or a mirror who sees through objective reality, interprets it, and reflects it back to the reader as a more permanent image: "the poet / mirror interprets / what's not there / visible to the unpoetic eye. / . . . measures the fleeting moment-love / and makes it stand still on paper / for the slow, non poet / to come and stare at / as long as he / she wants to."

Delgado's next collection, *It's Cold: 52 Cold-Thought Poems of Abelardo* (1974), by and large marks his return to a social mode of writing, although there are many poems about love and brotherhood. In his previous social writing he focused mostly on Chicano causes and on the Chicano Movement; in this work he seeks a more universal justice. The underlying tone of much of the work is established in the first poem, "From Lewiston to Boise," where Delgado presents the human condition as chaotic and waning. Through the continuous repetition of the refrain "I'm worried about my soul . . . it's cold," he accentuates American society's indifference and insensitivity toward humanity and highlights the Vietnam War, Watergate, police brutality, and the like as indicative of its loss of human values. The poem ends with a chaotic, stream-of-consciousness-like description:

i'm worried about my soul . . . it's cold.
may lay . . . a million jews,
that's o.k., drop the bomb . . . hiroshima, nagasaki,
27 bodies discovered buried, homosexual crimes,
arab liberation . . . irish struggle,
infanticide up two points, dow averages,
prostitutes return to seattle
15th smashing month of deep throat
a bottle of listerine to the first 100 patrons,
hitler, custer, hirohito, mussolini, mitchell . . .
de colores . . . ale . . . alelu . . . aleluya . . . ajúah,

right on, the sacred number four . . . shazam . . .
three blind mice . . . see how they run . . . row, row,
    row.
i'm worried about my soul . . . it's cold.

The poems about love in *It's Cold*—be it sexual, sensual, maternal, or fraternal love—say that it is a way of combating and escaping solitude and alienation. For example, in "Back to the Sun," the narrator compares his loved one with the sun, indicating that she, like the heavenly body, warms his spirit and life in times of loneliness and coldness: "with her caresses / store the heat of her love / in the marrow of my bones /in case the sky darkens / light up once and for all / my spirit / so i can survive / the lack of light. . . ." Similarly, the mother figure and her capacity to love are seen as a healing source for the insensitivity and isolation encountered in society. In the poem "Ya volví mamá" (I Returned Mother), after experiencing a life of emptiness, hurt, and solitude, the defeated and distraught narrator turns to his mother and asserts, "con sólo verte comienzo a sanar, / tú eres, mamá, el único remedio que tengo que buscar . . ." (Just in seeing you I begin to heal, / you, mother, are the only remedy that I need . . .). These poems, as well as several others dispersed throughout the work, suggest that humanity can avoid alienation and total destruction by unselfishly nurturing and seeking solace in love, companionship, and brotherhood. The volume also contains seven essays on Chicano culture and Delgado's life.

In *Reflexiones: 16 Reflections of Abelardo* (1976) Delgado returns to subjective poetry. Though there is an occasional mention of the Chicano Movement and other social causes (in poems such as "The Survivors," "The Twin Falls Three," "El 16 de septiembre" [The 16th of September]), most of the poems address such themes as loneliness, solitude, alienation, anguish, death, and the difficulty of life in general. In "Reflexiones" an anxious poetic voice desirous of delivering peace and hope indicates that all he shares with his fellowmen are feelings of solitude: "I have also / frozen in those / cold temperatures of sheer loneliness / and watched myself reflected, / old movie like . . . reruns of time, / in the eyes without light, lips without sound, / compañeros, todos ellos / de mi soledad" (Companions, all of them, of my solitude). In "Fatigado" (Fatigued) the narrator's solitude becomes outright weariness with life as he contemplates death:

Véome y me pregunto,—¿por qué me voy a acostar
deseando nunca más volverme a levantar,
    por qué quiero en mi dormir morir
    y dejar por siempre de todo existir?—

(I see and ask myself,—why am I going to sleep
wishing nevermore to awaken,
    why do I want in my sleep to die,
    and relinquish forevermore all feelings of life?)

Based on Delgado's childhood memories and conversations with his grandmother, the first of two short stories in *Reflexiones: 16 Reflections*, "Pieces for the Jig-saw Puzzle Memory" is about the legendary revolutionary Francisco "Pancho" Villa and his personal system of justice. In "My Father Hijacked a Plane" a first-person child-narrator recalls the events and conditions that compelled his father, a good and hardworking family man, into hijacking an airplane. He neither condones nor condemns the actions of his father, but as the tale unfolds, the narrator—as well as the reader—comes to understand and accept how the man was driven by his desperation over his economic condition.

Sometime prior to the publication of his next dated work (*Here Lies Lalo*, 1977), Delgado released two special editions of poetry: *A Quilt of Words: 25 Quilts by Abelardo* and *A Thermos Bottle Full of Self Pity: 25 Bottles by Abelardo*. Both works appear in limited numbers, eighty and one hundred copies respectively, and are low-grade photocopies of new and previously published poetry. *A Quilt of Words* is a collection of uneven poems with no particular unifying theme or consistency of tone, except perhaps existential pessimism. In *A Thermos Bottle Full of Self Pity* the narrator promotes justice, human warmth, love, and compassionate solidarity among all mankind while at the same time condemning those forces throughout the globe that impede these principles and values. For example, in "Breaking Bread," the work's introductory poem, he addresses the theme of world hunger and urges all people to take part in its eradication; and in "Occupied" he expresses his wish to travel the world over to spread the "Jerusalem kind of love" he feels toward his fellow man. In one poem he speaks to the issue of human rights ("Human Rights"), and in others he links his passion for justice to the events of El Salvador and Central America ("¿Qué sé yo del Salvador?" [What Do I Know About El Salvador?]).

In terms of quality, *Here Lies Lalo: 25 Deaths of Abelardo* is the least impressive of Delgado's literary works. With the exception of some love poems dedicated to his wife, Dolores ("Te acuerdo Lola" [I Remember you, Lola] and "Esposa" [Wife]), and poems in which he considers his own existence ("Here Lies Lalo"), contemplates the existence of God ("La Navidad" [Christmas] and "Catechism"), satirically examines the state of the Union on the celebration of the bicentennial ("Its Buy Cent Anal Time, Carnales"), or addresses the more general existential circumstance of mankind ("Baile de disfraces" [Dance of Costumes] and "We are Leaving the Earth Behind"), the work represents a rather "low level of accomplishment," to quote Lomelí and Morales. "Here Lies Lalo," the opening poem, seems to be an elegy to the gradual demise of the Chicano Movement. Of it Lomelí and Morales say, "The symbolic portrayal of his own death admits that both his audience–and by extension, the movement–and its informant (the poet) have reached a stage of dangerous quietude or possibly apathy."

Under the Skirt of Lady Justice: 43 Skirts of Abelardo (1978) returns to the forms, themes, and strengths of Delgado's earlier writing. He takes up the plight of the migrant farm worker, the undocumented worker, and the poor in general. "No tengo papeles" (I Don't Have Any Papers) is probably its most popular poem. In a monologue, an undocumented worker desperately describes his plight to an unidentified listener:

> usté dispense, cuál es el nombre desta ciuda?
> tengo necesidá.
> no tengo papeles.
> quiero trabajar.
> me quiero mejorar.
> no tengo papeles.
> el hambre
> no tiene fronteras
> ni reconoce rios.
> no tengo papeles. . . .
> tengo frío, tengo miedo.
> no tengo papeles.
> busco por acá
> lo que no hay en mi patria
> por la misma culpa
> de tanta explotación americana . . .
> sí, mi espalda está mojada
> pero de sudor.
> mis huevos también
> no tengo papeles.
>   no tengo papeles.
> no tengo papeles.

> (Excuse me, what is the name of this city?
> I am needy.
> I don't have any papers.
> I want to work.
> I want to better myself.
> I don't have any papers.
> Hunger
> has no boundaries,
> nor recognizes rivers.
> I don't have any papers. . . .
> I am cold. I am afraid.
> I don't have any papers.
> I am looking around here
> for that which doesn't exist in my country
> because of so much American exploitation . . .
> Yes, my back is wet
> and so are my balls
> because of sweat.
> I don't have any papers.
>   I don't have any papers.
> I don't have any papers.)

Delgado's *Letters to Louise* is an autobiographical epistolary novel for which he was awarded the first annual Tonatiuh Prize for literature for 1977 and 1978. The letters are written by the protagonist-narrator, Santiago Flores, and directed toward Louise, an unknown correspondent. In the letters Santiago, a forty-four-year-old Chicano poet, social worker, and administrator, searches for his own identity. The book is divided into three sections–July, August, and September–each of which symbolically represents a year of his adolescence. He tells of his emigration from Mexico into the United States, of his life in el segundo barrio, his school years in El Paso, Texas, his first kiss and sexual experiences, and so on.

Interwoven with the story of his adolescence, Santiago tells Louise of his travels throughout the land, advocating for and solving the problems of migrant workers as the director of the Colorado Migrant Council, and attending literary conferences and seminars as a poet and promoter of Chicano literature. In most instances his life parallels that of Delgado, suggesting that author and character are the same. At one point in the text, while the protagonist is examining his thoughts about death and eternity, he cites poetry taken from Delgado's *It's Cold*, claiming it to be his own. Richard Johnson comments (3 March 1985) on the similarities between the two: "Like Santiago, Lalo is extraordinarily open about his life. He says that *Letters* is a mixture of autobiography and fantasy, but he acknowledges that in it he deals with his own passionate, odd, funny and sometimes painful experiences–including love affairs."

Delgado's two most recent collections of poetry reflect his social activism. Generally speaking, in *Totoncaxihuitl, A Laxative: 25 Laxatives of Abelardo* (1981) the world is presented as a place of chaos, evil, and ugliness, with much need of a cosmic laxative to rid it of such maladies. In the work's title poem the narrator finds himself surrounded by epidemics of social afflictions, contemporary despair, and ugliness, to which he reacts: "Totoncaxihuitl, / there is no one around me and yet I'm in the middle. / There is no doubt our world needs a laxative. / An enema will be better./ God can administer/with bullfighter accuracy. . . ." Similarly, in "Navidad" (Christmas) and "What did Love Die of ?," the narrator sadly points to a contemporary world in which people no longer believe in or care about the Christ child. Also found in *Totoncaxihuitl, A Laxative* are several selections of prose which point to Delgado's interest in short fiction. Two of the selections ("10-4-77" and "10-6-77") represent examples of letters from a manuscript titled "Letters to Mindy." *Unos perros con metralla (Some Dogs with Machinegun): 25 Dogs of Abelardo* (1982) is basically a repeat of many of the poems from previous collections, but it does include several new selections that demonstrate Delgado's passion for justice, be it in his condemnation of the Ku Klux Klan ("To Hell with the Klan") or his censure of Reaganomics ("Perdió Reagan" [Reagan Lost]). Other than writing new verses and reworking or polishing some of his previous works, Delgado dedicates much of his time to prose. He is presently working on two separate manuscripts, "Letters to Mindy" and "Life as an Art Form." Directed toward Chicano youth, the second manuscript is a collection of short philosophical essays discussing such themes as life, love, death, and drug abuse. He is also busy creating short stories around a Christ-like wonder-boy, Bubuluj (immaculately conceived and born to a ninety-year-old woman), whose purpose on Earth is to help Chicanos and Mexicans find the sixth sun (See "Cuento" in *Totoncaxihuitl*.)

Despite his prolific literary output over the last twenty-plus years, Delgado still remains one of the least acclaimed of Chicano writers. In the 1987 interview with Urioste he said his lack of recognition by the critics does not bother him. Acknowledging that much of his literary production is raw and unpolished, he stated, "los poemas son como los hijos, no se debe esconder a los feos" (Poems are like children, one shouldn't hide the ugly ones). He recognized himself as a people's poet rather than a poet for literary critics: "La comunidad es lo que cuenta y he estado en muchas partes del país leyendo poesía" (The community is what counts and I have been in many parts of the country reading poetry). Delgado has been, and continues to be, a vital force and an important source of inspiration in Chicano letters. Over the last twenty years he has remained steadfast in his quixotic idealism and his social commitment.

References:

Juan Bruce-Novoa, *Chicano Authors: Inquiry by Interview* (Austin: University of Texas Press, 1980), pp. 95-114;

Reyes Cárdenas, "Abelardo's Poetry," *Caracol*, 2 (October 1975): 15, 22;

Richard Johnson, "Abelardo Delgado: The Don of Chicano Poetry," *Empire: The Denver Post Magazine*, 3 March 1985, pp. 6-9, 15, 19;

Francisco A. Lomelí and Donaldo W. Urioste, "El concepto del barrio en tres poetas chicanos: Abelardo Delgado, Alurista y Ricardo Sánchez," *De Colores*, 3 (Summer 1977): 22-29; translated by Sonia Zúñiga and Lomelí as "The Concept of the Barrio in Three Chicano Poets: Abelardo Delgado, Alurista and Ricardo Sánchez," *El Grito del Sol*, 2 (October-December 1977): 9-24;

Urioste, "Donaldo Urioste entrevista a Abelardo Delgado," *Caracol*, 2 (April 1976): 9.

Papers:

Delgado's papers are held in the Nettie Lee Benson Collection, Latin American Collection, University of Texas at Austin.

Sergio Elizondo

(29 April 1930-   )

Ana Perches
California State University, Hayward

BOOKS: *Perros y antiperros; una epica chicana* (Berkeley: Quinto Sol, 1972);
Libro para batos y chavalas chicanas, bilingual edition, with translations by Edmundo Garcia Giron (Berkeley: Editorial Justa, 1977);
Rosa, la flauta (Berkeley: Editorial Justa, 1980);
The Characters, Plots, and Settings of Calderon's Comedies, by Elizondo and Richard W. Tyler (Lincoln, Nebr.: Society of Spanish and Spanish-American Studies, 1981);
Muerte en una estrella (Mexico City: Tinta Negra Editores, 1984).

Born in El Fuerte, Sinaloa, Mexico, on 29 April 1930, Sergio Danilo Elizondo Domínguez was the ninth son. His mother died when Elizondo was five, and he lived unhappily with his father and stepmother until his father's death six years later, after which he lived with various relatives.

His father, Cristino Elizondo, was a teacher and school principal who interrupted his career to fight in the Mexican Revolution. According to Elizondo, in an unpublished 1986 interview, his father was "la otra cara de Artemio Cruz," that is, the opposite of Artemio Cruz, the selfish bourgeois protagonist of Carlos Fuente's novel *La muerte de Artemio Cruz* (1962), who turned his back on the people after he fought for their ideals. Elizondo was not one of his father's favorite sons, nor was he his mother's favorite either: "mi madre estaba hasta el copete de cabroncitos, de machos; cuando nací yo, aparentemente, ella ya estaba cansada y dijo, '¡este cabrón va ser mujer!' . . . a la edad de tres o cuatro años, todavía me vestía muy femeninamente, no creo que esto haya influido lo de hoy. . ." (My mother was up to here with little bastards when I was born. Apparently, she was tired and said: "this one is going to be a girl!" . . . at around age three or four she still dressed me as a girl. I don't think this had any consequences . . .).

Although Elizondo does not remember his mother well, he recalls that she was an industri-

Sergio Elizondo

ous, hardworking, and independent woman who engaged in various business activities from renting rooms in her house to raising mules. After her first husband abandoned her and their two sons during the revolution, she met Cristino Elizondo, with whom she had seven more boys. Elizondo alludes to the nature of their relationship in "Grito," a poem in *Perros y antiperros; una epica chicana* (Dogs and Antidogs, A Chicano Epic, 1972), declaring: "Mis padres no se casaron, solo se amaron" (My parents never married; they only made love).

Despite the fact that Elizondo's father was an educator, he did not encourage his children to attend school. Sergio was the only son who showed an interest in education, and even so he turned to his studies only after he immigrated illegally to the United States, working at menial jobs such as dishwashing while studying for a high school diploma. In 1953 Elizondo turned himself in to the U.S. Immigration and Naturalization Service and obtained status as a legal resident. He earned a B.A. at Findlay College in Ohio in 1958 and an M.A. (1961) and a Ph.D. (1964) at the University of North Carolina, Chapel Hill. He has been married twice and has two sons, Mark and Sean.

Elizondo taught Spanish and Chicano literature at New Mexico State University, where he was promoted to professor of foreign languages. He considers himself a teacher-apprentice first and a writer after that. His impulse to write comes, he says, from his desire to teach his readers–Chicanos, primarily–a sense of self-esteem and to denounce Anglo hegemony. He is fluent in Spanish and English, and, having traveled extensively in Europe, he has conversational knowledge of German and French.

Elizondo's four literary works differ substantially in technique from one another despite the similarities in certain aspects of language and tone. They all seek to establish the importance of traditional Chicano culture to the Chicano people, and at the same time they express contempt for the Anglo. This stance dominates *Perros y antiperros,* in which the perros (dogs) are the Anglos and the antiperros are the Chicanos. The Chicano is portrayed as a nature-loving, down-to-earth, family-oriented person who retains courage even when times are difficult. The Anglo is seen only superficially and is portrayed negatively. He is a symbol of oppression. To a Chicano reader, the message of the book is to trust his fellow Chicanos and to learn (or relearn) his history, heritage, and the Spanish language so as to reject the Anglo world.

According to Carey McWilliams (*North from Mexico,* 1949), there exists a fantasy heritage that overstates the importance of Spanish peninsular legacy to the Mexican-American people and relegates to a minor role their Mexican and Indian roots. Proponents of this fantasy heritage espouse the idea that the Spanish conquistadors were heroic models whose descendants still live in the Southwest in a selective group of people, specifically Hispanics from northern New Mex-

Elizondo in 1953 (courtesy of the author)

ico. The Chicano Movement did much to reverse this notion, emphasizing, with some exaggeration, the Chicano's Mexican and Indian heritage. Unlike some Chicano poets–Alurista, for example–Elizondo does not endorse the movement's attempt to glorify the Indian myths. He does, however, admire Alurista's way of incorporating his vast knowledge of Aztec culture into his poetry and feels that the Chicano "tuvo que recuperar, reconsiderar o revalorizar ciertas palabras como *Aztlán* aunque Aztlán no exista más que en muestras conciencias" (had to recuperate, reconsider or revalue such words as *Aztlán* even though Aztlán [the mythical pre-Columbian homeland] exists only in our consciousness). A collector of pre-Columbian artifacts, Elizondo construes the term *mestizo* in a Mexican way: being Indian is part of the eclectic nature of the Mexican, not something separate. His work can be said to recognize the complexity that arises from a people who themselves were part conquered, part conqueror, but his protagonists' identities come from their ties to the working class rather than from their subracial group. Rather than speaking directly of Aztlán, Elizondo creates a mythical setting, such as Ur in *Rosa, la flauta* (Rosa, the Flute, 1980). *Aztlán* thus becomes a way of thinking rather than a precise geographical area. He accepts the term *Chicano* as one that expresses the synthesis of Spanish and Indian peoples, coupled with a new American identity, as expressed in *Perros y antiperros:*

> yo, señor, pues soy Chicano,
> porque asi me puse yo.

> (Yes, sir, I am Chicano,
> because that's what I chose to name myself.)

Chicano heritage is deliberately glorified and even fantasized by Elizondo in *Perros y antiperros.* The poet-singer combines various elements that make up the Chicano mystique: his love of family, his attachment to nature and to his land, his contribution to American history, his racial mixture, migrant and/or barrio status, his Guadalupean religion, and his linguistic originality–all realities at one time or another either ignored, neglected, misunderstood, or degraded. Part of the theme in *Perros y antiperros* is Chicano awareness. The Chicano of today no longer accepts being treated as a second-class citizen:

> Tengo estos ojos, Apá,
> que ora si ven derecho,
> no se bajan ni a chingazos
> cuando el otro brinca en parejo.

> (These eyes you see here, Dad,
> finally see straight,
> they don't look down not even by force
> when the other guy jumps at me.)

Elizondo pays homage to the Chicano's past, emphasizing the struggles, arduous physical labor, and the tragic loss of land. The tone is that of a martyr, of the conquered and not of the heroic conquistador often portrayed in Southwest history books. The Chicano is not seen entirely as a victim since this would only generate a fatalistic attitude; instead he is given a voice by which he can express his inner frustrations, anger, and energy:

> Mire, Apá, ya ve, ya no soy pendejo.
> Palabras fuertes, Apá.
> Lo siento, hágase a un lado,

> ahora si quiero, con valor
> hablo claro, hablo, hablo, hablo y hablo,
> si no me hacen caso entonces hasta fusil y fuego como
> soldado.

> (Look, Dad, you see, I am no longer a fool.
> Strong words, Dad.
> I'm sorry, please step back,
> Now I want to speak with courage
> I'm speaking clearly, I speak, speak, speak and speak,
> If they don't listen then even the rifle and the fire will be my
> soldiers.)

Perhaps Elizondo does portray Chicanismo as something sublime and perfect, but such a Chicano fantasy heritage is justified by him in that it delivers an optimistic tone of hope.

Although Elizondo often expresses contempt for Spain due to her past imperialistic activities, he does not regret Spain's cultural impact on the Chicano people. As Erlinda Gonzales-Berry has pointed out in a 1980 article in *De Colores*, stylistically speaking, *Perros y antiperros* renders homage to the Hispanic literary tradition. Its rhythm and tone are reminiscent of pre-Renaissance Spanish *romances*. In "Polka," a poem about the 12 December celebration of the Virgin of Guadalupe, most stanzas contain seven or eight syllables, the vocabulary is simple, and repetition of phrases such as "dos cuetes suelto, dos" (I throw two fire-crackers, two) emulate speech patterns. The speaker speaks tenderly about the virgin, whom he calls "Lupita." She resides in a house of gold (the church), which also belongs to him. The tone is optimistic in that Elizondo portrays religion as a pure and loving expression. In "España" the voice of Federico García Lorca comes to mind except that Elizondo twists the tone to render a colloquial, playful, and virtually untranslatable rhyme: "garabato, caresapo, culoalto, chilesin, Putin, hijo de Rintintin."

To achieve vernacular accuracy, Elizondo employs code-switching in *Libro para batos y chavalas chicanas* (A Book for Chicano Guys and Girls, 1977). Code-switching appears in this book as the main discourse, in contrast to *Rosa, la flauta* and *Muerte en una estrella* (Death on a Star, 1984), in which Spanish is used about 80 to 90 percent of the time. Many of the expressions are not translatable. The word *bato* in Spanish, for example, is not as neutral as the term *guy*. *Bato* carries the connotation of bravery. It also implies solidar-

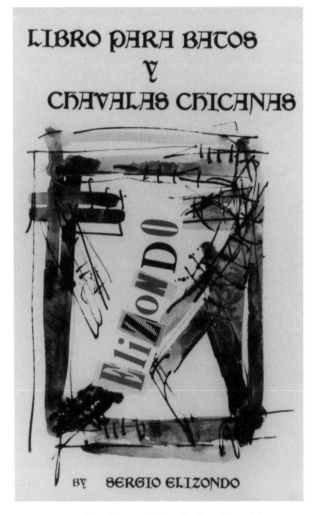

*Cover for a later printing of Elizondo's 1977
poetry collection*

ity and brotherhood as does the word *brother* in black English. The book opens with a poem titled "Canción de cuna para batos" (Cradlesong for Guys), in which the speaker uses a lullaby tone to show his affection toward the young Chicanos while he offers them his sapient advice. A lullaby usually tells a story of good versus evil. Elizondo deconstructs the lullaby by making it erotic and including religion and politics. The affection is coupled with an objective not found in the usual children's lullaby, that of arousing protest feelings vis-à-vis socioeconomic realities. The childhood rhyme in an adult context at the beginning of *Libro para batos y chavalas chicanas* sets the seriocomic tone of the book as a whole. As in many lullabies, the threat of an antagonistic person, animal, or thing is ever present.

The poet's voice assumes three major roles: one of wise parent-teacher, another of lover, and the third, that of the philosopher who contemplates his inner and outer worlds. This work is Elizondo's most autobiographical expression; it was inspired by the love of a real woman who went away, as seen in "A una chavala chicana que se alejó sin explicación" (To a Chicano Girl Who Went Away Without Explanation).

In *Rosa, la flauta,* says Charles M. Tatum in *Chicano Literature* (1982), Elizondo "explores two realms–realism and fantasy–with a sensitivity and narrative skill unusual considering it is this writer's first prose work." Regarding this book, Elizondo commented: "es muy Elizondo todo" (it is all very Elizondo). This collection is modern in that many of the protagonists are voices of a multidimensional author-narrator who exposes his inner self through the use of fantasy and stream of consciousness. The story "Rosa, la flauta" has an elegant discourse typical of that found throughout the book. Despite the use of certain colloquial expressions, such as "amá" for "mamá," the dialect that Rosa uses is one characteristic of the middle class. By having Rosa, who is a member of the lower class, speak in middle-class dialect, Elizondo suggests that she is in between the two classes, as many contemporary Chicanos are. The middle-class character is a new phenomenon in Chicano literature, which has tended to portray the social reality of the barrio and glorify the characteristics of the proletariat.

Rosa, la flauta is Elizondo's most metaphysical work. The narrator wishes to find a place of solitude, an original and individual place filled with "round" and "soft" energy and harmony. As he expresses in "Soledad con palabra intrusa" (Solitude with an Intrusive Word), one can make something out of nothing in the way that a child digs a hole in the dirt and gradually makes a well.

Notwithstanding his Chicano ethnocentricity, Elizondo has stated that he had first been a Mexican, then became a gringo, and finally, a Chicano, an experience he shares with many Chicanos. The gringo stage responds to societal pressures to assimilate into the Anglo-conformity model and is a tool with which to combat discrimination. Efforts at assimilation are almost always futile as are attempts to become "mexicano" again. The most logical alternative is to become Chicano: a United States citizen of Mexican descent. Whereas most Chicanos are born Chicanos, first-generation Mexicans such as Elizondo must undergo a process of chicanoization. Elizondo expressed his own experience in the following way: "yo creo que soy chicano porque estoy en-

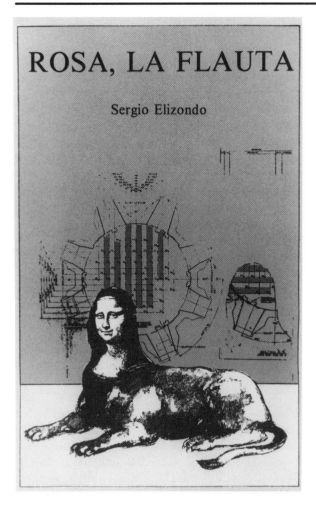

Cover for Elizondo's first volume of prose, a collection of eleven brief stories published in 1980

frentado al sistema americano y al sistema mexicano y siento el rechazo de la sociedad mexicana incluyendo mi propia familia. Soy chicano porque creo que puedo demostrarlo y me siento chicano" (I believe I am Chicano because I am confronted with the American and the Mexican systems and I feel rejected by Mexican society, including my own family. I am Chicano because I believe I can prove it and because I feel Chicano). Chicanos constitute a heterogeneous group primarily because they belong to so many different generations, ranging from first to tenth and beyond. The type of Chicano that Elizondo portrays most often is the migrant farm worker who is originally from Mexico and thus first-generation, or the Chicano whose parents are from Mexico and thus second-generation. His characters generally speak Spanish.

In his *Muerte en una estrella*, the two young protagonists are second-generation Chicanos and

are a good example of the rapid chicanoization process which can occur from one generation to the next. The difference between these youths and, say, fourth- or fifth-generation Chicanos is that the second generation still is aware of their parents' nostalgic view of the native homeland and their hopes in the new land, the United States. While the first generation accepts its inferior social status, the protagonists in *Muerte en una estrella* feel that as Americans they are being cheated. *Muerte en una estrella* consists mainly of dialogues and stream of consciousness, and the action is limited, despite the fact that the death (muerte) of the title is based on a true story. Oscar Balboa and Valentín Rodríguez, two Chicano youths (sometimes referred to by their ages, sixteen and nineteen) who are enrolled in a Job Corps program in Camp Gary, Texas, go to a circus in Austin, Texas, one night, allegedly to steal a car and participate in a Chicano march. They are shot in a bank by policemen. Little detail is given of the crime involved; it is the death scene in which Oscar and Valentín lie dying on the grass and communicate telepathically which constitutes a major focus of the novel.

There is perhaps a third character, the anonymous narrator who sometimes merges with the voice of Oscar. At other times the narrator becomes an unidentified observer or participant. This narrator identifies himself from the beginning as a folk bard or singer of "corridos" (folk ballads). The use of the second-person singular, "tú," in passages throughout the text involves the reader and makes the novel a collective endeavor in which the reader is both receptor and participant because he must enter into the confusion of events.

Most of the narration, aside from the dialogue scenes, is in the first person, but progressively it focuses on Oscar's life, including his migrant experiences and his parents' outlook on life. It is through Oscar that the novel's thematic unity manifests itself, rendering an intimate and romanticized portrait of the migrant worker's experience. The social commentary which is evident throughout the novel is expressed directly as well as indirectly. The individual voice which most of the time can be identified as Oscar's relates past experiences as if they were part of his present state of mind. Most of the events of the novel occur on the same day. The middle part of the novel provides the social setting which in turn helps to explain the psychological framework of the protagonists. The protagonists reconstruct past dialogues with their parents and friends. Other voices, such as those of Texas police, onlookers, and German-American characters, are deliberately rendered in a stereotypical fashion.

Valentín and Oscar are distinct in character but resemble one another in their intimate ties with family and land. Valentín is portrayed as a tough, macho troublemaker. Readers come to know him through his dialogues with Oscar. His parents were poor, and he wore diapers and ate dirt at age three. Oscar is more complex. His parents were migrant workers, and he worked the fields. His persona begins in his mother's womb from where he speaks to readers. His parents are hardworking and loving folks who accept their bleak social condition for fear of losing what little they have. Oscar, their only child, is a love child. He shows signs of being nonconformist. His consciousness is stimulated during a farmers' union strike in which he and his father disagree on whether or not to join the *huelguistas* (strikers). His decision to join the Job Corps shows his determination to learn a trade.

In many ways the novel is about Oscar's quest for identity. One of his metamorphoses includes his transformation into a woman, which he considers a natural phenomenon. He tells Valentín: "Pues ya veremos algún día cuando yo sea mujer; y no te rias porque lo veo como la cosa más natural del mundo" (We'll see some day when I become a woman; and don't you laugh, I see it as the most natural thing in the world). Another time Oscar takes the form of a cello, managing to sneak into Antonín Dvořák's cello case. He further imagines being placed between Dvořák's legs, being hugged by him while watching his beautiful smile as he places his left hand on Oscar's neck. Music is also part of the scene during the march to Austin when Oscar carries an accordion and a guitar. The analogy of a musical movement to the Chicano Movement is made subtly in the description of a concert that Oscar attends through the invitation of his father's German boss, Miss Schaeffer.

Elizondo considers a hero anyone who disturbs Anglo authority. Oscar and Valentín are not prototypical heroes who fight for ideology and honor; they have not been exposed to ideas, only to actions. It is through the voice of Oscar's father that the reader hears of the injustices, hardships, and hopes found in the Chicano community. It is also his father who voices the dichotomy of conformity versus nonconformity.

During a farmers' strike Mr. Balboa feels fear and embarrassment (but not shame) to see his own people marching and ponders what the gringos are going to think of his people: "Ayer los vi por la 281, . . . salieron temprano de Linburgo y no sé que sentí, me dio como vergüencita ver a tanta raza junta. No sé pa qué andan haciendo eso. No sé pa qué lo hacen, a mi me da no sé qué; como que me da miedito que los mexicanos anden haciendo eso, que dirán los gringos. Los gringos dirán que no sé qué . . . que somos no sé qué . . . desordenados y que nomás somos buenos pa hacer borlote; . . . a poco no estamos bien asi, cada quien que busque su trabajo y no se anden metiendo en nada, no se vayan a enojar los gringos y si se enojan quién sabe que va a pasar; andan poniendo la gente en vergüenza . . . (I saw them yesterday on 281, . . . they started early from Linburgo and I felt funny, hard to explain, sort of embarrassed to see so many Mexicans together. I don't know why they get into those things. I don't know why they do it, it makes me feel like, I don't know; sort of afraid when Mexicans do that, what are the gringos going to think. The gringos will say we're this or that . . . that we're disorderly and that the only thing we're good at is at being rowdy; . . . Aren't we fine the way we are, everyone should just do their job and not get into trouble, or else the gringos are going to get angry and then who knows what would happen; all they do is put our people to shame . . .). Old Balboa is against social injustice, but he keeps his opinion to himself.

In *Muerte en una estrella* Elizondo returns to the tone of protest of his first work. Ignacio Trejo Fuentes, reviewing the novel in *Excelsior* (28 May 1985), discussed the author's narrative technique: "cada uno de los procedimientos novelisticos que en un principio llegan a confundir e incluso a irritar son totalmente deliberados por parte del autor" (each one of the novelistic techniques that at the beginning confuse and irritate the reader is used deliberately by the author). The same critic concludes by classifying Elizondo's work as an example of "la más nueva novelística chicana" (the newest Chicano writing).

Although Elizondo's work is varied, several generalizations in terms of themes and style can be drawn. He has an ethnocentric view of Chicano culture which he has defended: "Somos etnocéntricos porque es una manera de demostrar que tenemos algo válido, que somos humanos, que valemos algo o que somos atractivos, bonitos, lo que sea" (We are ethnocentric because it is a way of showing that we have something valid, that we are human, that we are worth something or that we are attractive, good-looking or whatever). The process of idealization is necessary in order to call attention to a neglected sector of society. Tied to his ethnocentricity, Catholicism is presented as a sensual experience for Chicanos. The Virgin of Guadalupe reminds the Chicano that he is loved, as seen in "Domingo Bright Morning," from *Libro para batos y chavalas chicanas:*

> Lupe, Lupe, Lupe,
> ángeles prietos siempre supe,
> que me quieres la quieres,
> nos quieres
> Virgen de flores virgen de amores.

> (Lupe, Lupe, Lupe,
> swarthy angels I always knew,
> that you love me love her,
> love us
> Virgin of flowers virgin of lovers.)

Furthermore, the Virgin conveys the idea that the church belongs to the Chicano and not to the Anglo: "por esta puerta pasan los mejores cristianos" (through this door pass the best Christians). Like many Chicanos the Virgin of Guadalupe has black eyes and dark skin. The angels in the icon are dark as well, "ángeles prietos," and the church is a mixture of elements that together form the Chicano faith: "Dios Judio,/Virgen india, /iglesia Chicana" (Jewish God, Indian Virgin, Chicano Church).

Elizondo is not an easy writer, in part because of the many contradictions in his work. Such contradictions include writing about romantic love when, in fact, he does not believe in it and glorifying the Virgin of Guadalupe, though he criticizes superstition and submission to authority. In Elizondo's words, "yo admiro mucho la integridad; y el aguante. La integridad y el valor son atributos muy especiales en la vida" (I greatly admire integrity and endurance. Integrity and valor are very special attributes in life). It is the intregrity and endurance that he finds in the Chicano people to which he pays homage.

References:

Juan Bruce-Novoa, "Sergio Elizondo," in his *Chicano Authors: Inquiry by Interview* (Austin: University of Texas Press, 1980), pp. 67-82;

Bruce-Novoa, "The Heroics of Self-Love," in his *Chicano Poetry: A Response to Chaos* (Austin: University of Texas Press, 1982);

Ignacio Trejo Fuentes, "*Muerte en una estrella:* De la más nueva novelística chicana," *Excelsior,* 28 May 1985;

Erlinda Gonzales-Berry, "*Perros y antiperros:* The Voice of the Bard," *De Colores,* 5, no. 1-2 (1980): 45-80;

Charles M. Tatum, *Chicano Literature* (Boston: Twayne, 1982).

Lionel G. García
(20 August 1935-)

Patricia De La Fuente
Pan American University

BOOKS: *Leaving Home* (Houston: Arte Publico, 1985);

A Shroud in the Family (Houston: Arte Publico, 1987);

Hardscrub (Houston: Arte Publico, forthcoming, 1989).

OTHER: "The Wedding," in *Cuentos Chicanos*, edited by Rudolfo A. Anaya and Antonio Márquez (Albuquerque: University of New Mexico Press, 1984).

PERIODICAL PUBLICATIONS: "The Day They Took My Uncle," *Revista Chicano-Riqueña*, 13 (Spring 1985): 5-13;

"The Sergeant," *Americas Review*, 15 (Spring 1987): 7-26.

The importance of novelist and short-story writer Lionel G. García is his ability to create plausible characters whose pain and joy can be vividly shared by readers. Although he has been writing since the early 1950s, García published his first novel, *Leaving Home*, in 1985. As a work in progress, it won the 1983 P.E.N. Southwest Discovery prize.

García was born to Gonzalo Guzmán García and Maria Saenz García in 1935 in San Diego, Duval County, Texas. He grew up in San Diego, where he enjoyed a close relationship with his grandparents and the many aunts and uncles who made up his extended family circle. As a child he lived and worked with his grandfather on a ranch near San Diego, herding goats and working in the fields. Later he worked in his father's paint and body shop. García admits that much of his fictional material stems directly from these early family ties which included a rich tradition of oral story telling by his elders and family friends. In 1959 he married Noemi Barrera; they have three children. His studies at Texas A&M University, where he majored in biology, brought him into contact with English professors who encouraged him to write. After serving in the U.S.

Lionel G. García (courtesy of the author)

Army, he went back to Texas A&M and graduated from the College of Veterinary Medicine in 1965. He taught anatomy at the university for three years and in 1969 set up his veterinary practice in Seabrook, Texas, where he presently lives.

García's short story "The Day They Took My Uncle" (1985) is typical of his narrative style and reveals how he successfully integrates his childhood experiences into his fiction. In his

Covers for García's two novels

early years he was cared for by an uncle and aunt who were quite insane. In the story a small boy recalls his experiences with his uncle, an alcoholic who suffers from insanity and must eventually be taken away by the sheriff. His "bedevilment," as the grandmother tells it, was provoked by drinking the dregs of someone else's beer, which happened to be laced with a powerful potion. García creates intensely vivid and compassionate portrayals of family members coping in their different ways with the embarrassing situation seen and evaluated through the eyes of the young narrator.

In his novel *Leaving Home*, García develops the flair for story telling and character development revealed in his shorter fiction. Set in southern California in the late 1930s and 1940s, the novel explores Adolfo Argüelles's struggle to cope with the harsh reality of extreme poverty. True to its title, the novel examines the anxiety, nostalgia, fear, and soul-searching inherent in the act of breaking family ties, of leaving a safe if

impossible present for an unknown, uncertain future. The down-and-out protagonist, Argüelles, sustains his old age on the strength of his reputation as a famous baseball pitcher for the New York Yankees and the St. Louis Cardinals. Adolfo moves from one sexual entanglement to another in a perpetual search for love and acceptance. The reader is torn between feeling that Adolfo deserves all the grief he gets and feeling sorry for him. In a sequence of episodes in which a variety of women use and misuse him, Adolfo resembles a picaresque hero.

In his novel *A Shroud in the Family* (1987) García explores the intergenerational conflicts and humor-filled situations of a Mexican-American family living in modern Houston. He loses none of his satirical humor in this move from the small-town life of *Leaving Home* to the urban environment of the big Texas city. Andy García, protagonist of the story, spends his time between working at his erratic law practice, seeing a psychiatrist with a talking parrot, and dealing with his feuding family, situations which the author examines with unfailing and slightly wacky humor. In her review in the *Houston Post* (September 1987) Mitzi Brunsdale states, "García is almost too successful in skewering a wide range of personalities and situations." Another novel,

Hardscrub, has been scheduled for publication in the summer of 1989.

While little substantial criticism has yet appeared on either of García's novels, reviewers have reacted favorably to his work. García promises to become a major new voice in American ethnic literature.

César A. González-T.
(17 January 1931-   )

Ernesto Chávez Padilla
California State College, Bakersfield

BOOK: *Unwinding the Silence* (La Jolla: Lalo, 1987).

OTHER: "A Ver, Hijo . . .," in *First Chicano Literary Prize*, edited by Juan Villegas and others (Irvine: Department of Spanish and Portuguese, University of California, Irvine, 1975), pp. 67-78;

What You Want to Know About English Grammar But Are Afraid to Ask: English Grammar for College Students, edited by González-T. and others (San Diego: San Diego Community College District, 1978); bilingual edition, 2 volumes, with translations by Ramon Merlos and others (San Diego: San Diego Community College, 1978);

Real Writing: English Composition for College Students, edited by González-T. and others (San Diego: San Diego Community College District, 1979); republished as *Escritos veraces: La Composición en inglés para los estudiantes universitarios*, bilingual edition, with translations by Maria Betancourt and others (San Diego: San Diego Community College District, 1980);

"Sol Invernal," "Ancient Youth," "Corrientes," and "Going Home," in *Flor y Canto IV and V: An Anthology of Chicano Literature from the Festivals Held in Albuquerque, New Mexico* (Albuquerque: Pajarito, Flor y Canto Committee, 1980), pp. 71-74;

"Hay Cosas," "Plange Lingua," "Sueños Desbarajados," and "Lugareños," in *Literatura Fron-*

teriza: Antología del Primer Festival, San Diego-Tijuana, May 1982, edited by Alurista and others (San Diego: Maize, 1982), pp. 68-71;

"The Wizard or Things That Go Bump in the Night," in *Palabra Nueva: Cuentos Chicanos*, edited by Ricardo Aguilar, Armando Armengol, and Oscar U. Somoza (El Paso: University of Texas, Texas Western Press, 1984), pp. 87-96;

"Toño," in *Southwest Tales: A Contemporary Collection*, edited by Alurista and Xelina Rojas-Urista (Colorado Springs: Maize, 1986), pp. 81-87;

Fragmentos de Barro: The First Seven Years, edited by González-T. and Luis Alberto Urrea (San Diego: Tolteca, 1987);

Rudolfo A. Anaya: Focus on Criticism, edited by González-T. (Wellesley Hills: Massachusetts Bay, forthcoming, 1989).

PERIODICAL PUBLICATIONS: "José," "The Women of Zúñiga," and "Balboa Park," *Maize*, 1 (Fall 1977): 57-60;

"La Jolla," *Paperback Edition*, 22 (13 February 1978): 3;

"Black Velvet Lady," *Paperback Edition*, 22 (15 May 1978): 3;

"Blessed Be the Raza," *Caracol*, 4 (August 1978): 5;

"Rag Bells," *Citybender* (San Diego), 2, no. 3 (1978);

"Feliz Cumpleaños," "Untitled," and "In Washington, D.C.," *Mesa Press*, 2 (17 March 1980): 3;

César A. González-T. with his wife, Bettie (photo by Robert Waltrous)

"A Monument to Madness," *Revista Literaria de El Tecolote*, 4, no. 3 (1983): 6;

"South by Southwest," "Reasons Unremembered," "Pisac," "Ese," and "The Question," *Imagine*, 1 (Spring 1984): 38-44.

Seldom can a creative writer concretely identify the first experience that has given direction to his work. Cesár A. González-Trujillo remembers that experience and the two incidents that triggered it quite vividly. At the age of three, in the midst of the Great Depression, he heard his elders talking about a job distributing phone books. Some forty workers were needed, but hundreds showed up, resulting in fights among the desperate men. The second incident occurred within weeks of the first. The author remembers hearing shouting in the street below while he and his mother were in the Lowe's State Building on Seventh and Broadway in downtown Los Angeles. Rushing to the window, he caught a glimpse of workers surrounding a streetcar and rocking it. The conductors, angry because of low wages, had driven streetcars into downtown Los Angeles

and blocked traffic. The streetcar company had called for strikebreakers, and the men began to fight. In an unpublished 1987 interview González recalls lying in bed shortly after both incidents weeping "at the sadness of life, seeing how hard life was. And I had a little ritual, I would sit at the back door, in my little short pants and look out at the back toward the left where there was an old, leaning, faded, blue fence. There was a little *matita, no era yerba buena, era otra parecida, larga, no sé qué* [plant, it was not a mint plant, it was something similar but long, I don't know what], and I said to myself, '*Ya nos vamos a pasar*' [Soon all things will pass]. And that's already been published in a poem, so at age three, you might say, I wrote my first line of poetry, a sense of '*todo se pasa*,' almost an Aztec sense, a sense of 'everything passes,' but is there anything that abides? And, as a child, I had a great sense of this, almost philosophical, of the sadness of the world, of the evil in the world, of the pain in the world, of how everything passes." The major themes of González's poetry and short stories are the struggle between good and evil, the need to establish good through beauty and honesty, and the attempt to understand evil through philosophy.

González was born in Los Angeles, California. His contemplative nature was reinforced by the positive role-modeling of his parents, José A. González, a cook, and Camerina Trujillo de González, a seamstress, both of whom had been born in central Mexico in the state of Colima. According to González, people in his parents' hometown of Comala say that his maternal great-grandfather, Gabriel Valencia, was the *cacique* (local chief) on whom Mexican novelist Juan Rulfo modeled the protagonist of his *Pedro Páramo* (1955). When González started first grade at St. Vincent's Catholic School in Los Angeles he could not speak English. The school anticipated it would take him two years to learn English, but by the end of the first grade he had finished the second-grade reader. His success was a result of his sister's help and his father's love for story telling. José González told family stories about the adventures of uncles, aunts, and grandparents, including stories about the Mexican revolution, the *Villistas* (the soldiers of Pancho Villa), the *Carrancistas* (the government soldiers who followed Venustiano Carranza), and the *Cristiada* (the persecution of the Catholic church from 1927 to 1929 under the government of Plutarco Elías Calles). Both parents read to the children in Spanish, his father from the Sunday supplement of *La Opinión*, which always included poetry. These stories turned González into a voracious reader. At about age nine he had already exhausted all the fairy-tale books, both in English and Spanish, at the Twenty-third and Wall Street branch of the Los Angeles Public Library.

González became an academic anomaly, entering high school at age twelve. As a result of an early inspiration to excel in logic, philosophy, and literature, he began his university studies at sixteen with the Jesuits at the University of Santa Clara. He received his B.A. in Spanish literature in 1951 and obtained his M.A. and Ph.L. (licentiate of philosophy) in philosophy from the University of Gonzaga in Spokane, Washington, which he attended from 1951 to 1954. He taught in Chihuahua, Mexico, from 1954 to 1957. He earned an M.S.T. (master of sacred theology) and an S.T.L. (licentiate of sacred theology) from the University of Santa Clara, which he attended from 1957 to 1961. In the early 1960s he studied for a Ph.D. in sociology at the University of California, Los Angeles. He decided, however, that sociology was not his calling, and he opted for working at community development projects in Mexico City. Early in 1968 Chicano youths in Los Angeles refused to attend high school in protest against what they perceived as a racist system. He returned to Los Angeles to work in the Chicano community for one year. He moved to San Diego in 1969, married Bettie Beattie, and accepted his present position at San Diego Mesa College, where he helped create the Chicano Studies Department. González feels that he has been "called to serve" at Mesa College, as he writes in his 1980 poem "Sol Invernal" (Winter Light), collected in *Unwinding the Silence* (1987):

> Y le doy gracias a mi creador
> porque voy al trabajo a labrar
> el campo de la juventud Chicana.
>
> (And I give thanks to my Creator
> for I am on my way to till
> the field of our Chicano youth.)

González has written most of his poetry and short stories since 1970. In addition he has collaborated on two college composition textbooks, written several critical articles on Chicano literature, and edited the literary journal *Fragmentos de Barro* (Fragments of Clay), which is the source of material for the anthology *Fragmentos de Barro: The First Seven Years* (1987), compiled by González and Luis Alberto Urrea. His most important contribution in the field of literary criticism is *Rudolfo A. Anaya: Focus on Criticism*, a collection of critical articles on Anaya's novels.

González is best known as a poet, but his first published work was a short story, "A Ver, Hijo . . . " (Let's See, Son). Carlota Cárdenas de Dwyer (*De Colores*, 1977) called it the "most rewarding of the seven short stories" which were published in the anthology *First Chicano Literary Prize* (1975). His first published poem, "José" (*Maize*, Fall 1977), in common with much of Chicano poetry of the late 1960s and early 1970s, asserts the beauty of brown skin:

> The peacock, with its
> blue-gold, mother-of-pearl
> opalescent satin sheen,
> saluted the sparrow
> rejoicing in the proliferation
> of its beautiful, brown being.

His first poems reflect a commitment to the Chicano struggle to establish a strong sense of self based on Chicano/Mexican/Indian cultural values. At this point González's verse fits well with other Chicano Movement poetry of the late 1960s, for example, Rodolfo Gonzales's *Yo Soy Joaquín* (I Am Joaquín) and Alurista's "Mis ojos hinchados." These poems are a part of the relatively unsophisticated, first-wave Chicano renaissance of the 1960s and constitute a period which is now referred to as the "culturalist/nationalist" phase.

González's poem "Rag Bells" markedly contrasts with his first, socially oriented writing. This 1978 work clearly indicates the author's preference for themes with philosophical overtones:

> Mute beggars
> still aspiring
> ring rag bells
> secular sacristans
> deaf with desperation
> clap hammer hard tongues
> appeal dampened absolutes
> rung yesterday
> cast-off verities
> told now
> in private purgatorios.

Here the bell is the key figure in a lament over the loss of absolute values. Those that espoused (and, it is implied, also imposed) those absolutes are portrayed as sinners now paying for their ideological despotism. The poem is a mute, understated celebration of unnamed progressive values that have liberated humanity from the past. The most significant aspect of this early poem is the poet's treatment of a philosophical/ideological issue.

Some of González's early poetry appearing in journals is collected in his 1987 volume *Unwinding the Silence*. In the introduction to this collection Luis Leal notes that González's poetry "reflects multiple states of soul, dominated by an outstanding, profound human sensibility, along with a heart-rending yearning to decipher the beyond. Hence, his work achieves breadth and universality." Leal sees in the poetry González's search for universal absolutes; he also notes the preoccupation with good and evil and the sadness and empathy for human suffering that reflect the poet's early life.

The phrase "unwinding the silence" refers to González's own achievement of bursting forth with his first sustained effort to project his poetic consciousness. And yet this unwinding serves as metaphor for a larger group, as Leal points out:

"The title of the book, *Unwinding the Silence*, gives us the key image, which tells us that silence must give way, that there must be an end to the limits which Chicanos impose upon themselves or which society compels them to maintain."

In philosophical terms González is concerned with antipodes: "love and unlove, heaven and hell, affirmation and negation, stasis and dynamos. . . . I have pondered in terms of absolutes, of good and evil, of being, becoming, and non-being, trying to make some kind of unity for myself." "Ancient Youth," from *Unwinding the Silence*, elucidates his vision of how good and evil, chaos and order are transformed into a unity:

> The Quetzal Tlamatinime ask:
> Is there any truth on earth?
> Is it perhaps that we are on this earth
> Only for a little while to dream?
> Only for a little while?
>
> Ya nos vamos a pasar.
>
> Every mountain will be leveled.
> Every sea dried up.
> Every wind grow weary.
> Every fire die.

And although each individual human must die, humanity continues. The only thing that redeems man from the brutalizing realization of "ya nos vamos a pasar" (everything will pass) is "redeeming companionship."

His are songs of innocence and experience that probe life with the logical mind of the philosopher; and yet, in the end, González abandons the rigor of philosophy for the mystical precept that man can sustain contraries in his approach to the perfection of love. In "Quetzalcóatl and Christ," in *Unwinding the Silence*, he writes:

> You and I
>   are the processional imperfect bearers
>   of the sacred flame.
>
> Instinct and reason
> unlove and love
>   are wedded
>   in eternal antinomies
>   within us.

According to González, "perfection equals love and truth. Our destiny is to affirm, to evoke and create love. St. Irenaeus speaks of his theory of recapitulation, that each successive level of reality includes the perfection of the lower level and transcends it. And so the organic has all the perfection of the mineral and transcends it, and the sensate has all the perfection of the anorganic and the organic and transcends them. You have plants at the level of primitive consciousness. There is a continuity that leads to human consciousness, through a state of evolution. Add to this physical reality the dimension of faith, and we are led to divine love. . . . [The] most important message in poetry is not to lose faith despite all of the brutality and dehumanization that we see in the world."

González's expression of philosophical concerns is a distinguishing attribute of his poetry; yet, as fascinating as his purely philosophical poetry is, his more modest statements—"Rag Bells," for example—have greater power and show his image-making at its most persuasive. Leal also comments on the strength of the personal and the local in González's poetry: "The poet's voice is the voice—let there be no doubt about this—of a Chicano rooted in the barrio, but whose sights are set on the world which surrounds him."

In several poems González renders the experience of what it is to be Chicano. For example, "Hay qu'ir" (You Gotta Go) is about the food offered at Las Cuatro Milpas, a humble Mexican-style restaurant in the barrio, but at the same time the poem brings to life the experience of a culture. In all of his work González demonstrates the relatedness of nature, culture, and language and celebrates them with an attitude of contemplation and respect.

References:

Carlota Cárdenas de Dwyer, "First Chicano Literary Prize," *De Colores*, 3, no. 4 (1977): 70-71;

Luis Leal, Introduction to González-T.'s *Unwinding the Silence* (La Jolla: Lalo, 1987), pp. xii-xxiii.

Rolando Hinojosa-Smith

(21 January 1929-   )

Charles M. Tatum
University of Arizona

BOOKS: *Estampas del valle y otras obras: Sketches of the Valley and Other Works* (Berkeley: Quinto Sol, 1973); English version revised as *The Valley* (Ypsilanti: Bilingual, 1983);

Klail City y sus alrededores (Havana: Casa de las Américas, 1976); republished as *Generaciones y semblanzas* (Berkeley: Justa, 1977); translated as *Klail City: A Novel* (Houston: Arte Publico, 1987);

Korean Love Songs from Klail City Death Trip (Berkeley: Justa, 1980);

Mi querido Rafa (Houston: Arte Publico, 1981); revised and translated by the author as *Dear Rafe* (Houston: Arte Publico, 1985);

Rites and Witnesses (Houston: Arte Publico, 1982);

Partners in Crime: A Rafe Buenrostro Mystery (Houston: Arte Publico, 1985);

Claros varones de Belken: Fair Gentlemen of Belken County (Tempe: Bilingual/Editorial Bilingüe, 1986);

Tomás Rivera, 1935-1984: The Man and His Work, by Hinojosa-Smith, Gary D. Keller, and Vernon E. Lattin (Tempe: Bilingual/Editorial Bilingüe, 1988).

OTHER: "Chicano Literature: An American Literature in Transition" and "Literatura Chicana: Background and Present Status of a Bicultural Expression," in *The Identification and Analysis of Chicano Literature*, edited by Francisco Jiménez (Binghamton: Bilingual/Editorial Bilingüe, 1979), pp. 37-40; 42-46;

"This Writer's Sense of Place," in *The Texas Literary Tradition: Fiction, Folklore, History*, edited by Don Graham, James W. Lee, and William T. Pilkington (Austin: University of Texas at Austin & the Texas State Historical Association, 1983), pp. 120-124.

PERIODICAL PUBLICATIONS: "Por esas cosas que pasan," *El Grito*, 5 (Spring 1972): 26-36;

"The Mexican American Devil's Dictionary, I," *El Grito*, 6 (Spring 1973): 41-53;

Rolando Hinojosa-Smith (courtesy of the author)

"Voces del barrio," *El Grito*, 6 (Summer 1973): 3-8;

"E pluribus vitae," *Revista Chicano-Riqueña*, 1 (Fall 1973); 14-16;

"Mexican American Literature: Toward an Identification," *Books Abroad*, 49 (Summer 1975): 422-430;

"Epigmenio Salazar" and "Enedino Broca López," *Hispamérica* (1975): 4, 11-12;

"Con el pie en el estribo," *Bilingual Review/Revista Bilingüe*, 3 (January-April 1976): 64-65;

"From the Mexican American Devil's Dictionary, II," *Revista Chicano-Riqueña*, 4 (Spring 1976): 2-5;

"Excerpts from *The Mexican American Devil's Dictionary*," *Revista Chicano-Riqueña*, 4 (Fall 1976): 45-46;

"Feliz cumpleaños, E.U.A.," *La Palabra*, 1 (Spring 1979): 54-56;

"Conversations on a Hill," *Mester*, 10, nos. 1 and 2 (1981): 93-97.

Rolando Hinojosa-Smith intends each of his works, regardless of genre, to form a part of a life-long novel which he has called "Klail City Death Trip." He has created a fictional world, Klail City, Belken County, Texas, located somewhere in the lower Rio Grande valley–filled with memorable characters whose ordinary lives take on tragicomic proportions as they go about their daily tasks, dealing with conflicts arising out of generations of racial strife and cultural misunderstanding.

Born in Mercedes, Texas, Hinojosa-Smith is the son of Manuel Guzman Hinojosa, a Mexican-American, and Carrie Effie Smith, an Anglo. His paternal grandparents were born in the United States. Their ancestors arrived in the lower Rio Grande valley in 1749 as part of the expedition of José Escandón when the area was part of Spain's northern frontier known as Nuevo Santander. After Mexico's independence from Spain in 1821, the Hinojosas gave their loyalty to the newly established Mexican government and continued to identify strongly with Mexico even after the 1848 Treaty of Guadalupe Hidalgo.

Carrie Smith's family was from Illinois. Her father was a Union veteran of the Civil War. Arriving in the valley in 1887, she was raised among Mexicans. Comfortably bilingual and bicultural, she spoke, read, and wrote both English and Spanish, a common experience for Anglos in the valley. Hinojosa-Smith's father had spent time in Mexico during different phases of the Mexican Revolution of 1910 to 1920.

The youngest of two sisters and one surviving brother, Hinojosa-Smith had a peaceful childhood and adolescence in Mercedes. He first attended private schools taught by Mexican exiles paid by the town's Spanish-speaking parents which provided him with an intensive reinforcement of Mexican culture. To illustrate how thoroughly Mexican these schools were, their day would begin with the singing of the "Himno Nacional," the Mexican national anthem.

At age six Hinojosa-Smith began attending public schools where the vast majority of the children were from the Mexican-American neighborhoods of Mercedes, but where the teachers were exclusively Anglo. He did not come to know Anglo children until junior high school, where adolescents from all neighborhoods came together.

It was in high school at fifteen that Hinojosa-Smith began writing seriously, publishing his first pieces in English in an annual literary magazine called *Creative Bits*. During high school he played football and was a member of the science club, the Pan-American club, and the board of governors of the school's little theater. He acted in several plays and authored an essay, "So You Want to be an Actor."

The years he spent living in the valley form the substance of most of Hinojosa-Smith's later works. He heard the old people telling stories about their early lives, the difficulties of survival, the conflicts and tension between Hispanics and Anglos, and their joys and disappointments. In an essay reprinted in *The Rolando Hinojosa Reader, Essays Historical and Critical* (1985) he observes that the valley was a place of sharing: "the sharing of names, of places, of a common history, and of belonging to the place; one attended funerals, was taken to cemeteries, and one saw names that corresponded to one's own or to one's friends and neighbors, and relatives."

After graduating from high school in 1946, Hinojosa-Smith stopped living in the valley, but he returned there hundreds of times in the ensuing years. He joined the army at seventeen and served two years, spent a short time attending the University of Texas, and was reactivated in 1950 when the Korean conflict erupted. Besides serving in Korea–an experience about which he is reluctant to talk but its horror is reflected in *Korean Love Songs from Klail City Death Trip* (1980)–he was stationed at Fort Eustis, Virginia, where he edited a camp publication. Sent to the Caribbean, he became a radio announcer and the editor of the Caribbean Army Defense Command newspaper, which enjoyed wide distribution throughout the region. He graduated from the University of Texas in 1954 with a degree in Spanish, having been a student employee in the reserve section of the university library, which provided him a marvelous opportunity to read widely and avidly.

After graduation Hinojosa taught government, Spanish, history, Latin, and typing for a short time at Brownsville High School, located at the southern tip of the Rio Grande valley. He soon quit to earn more money as a common laborer in a chemical processing plant. During this period (1954 to 1958), he wrote little but did continue reading voraciously, especially Russian novelists and Spanish literature. In 1959 he went to work for a clothing manufacturer in Brownsville, then spent two more years as a high-school teacher.

During the summer of 1960 he decided to quit high-school teaching to begin graduate studies, selecting Highlands University in Las Vegas, New Mexico, at the urging and support of the dean of humanities. He spent 1962 to 1963 there as a graduate dormitory supervisor, reading during the day and attending classes at night. He married Patricia Louise Mandley in 1963. The couple has three children.

After finishing an M.A. in Spanish at Highlands, Hinojosa entered the Spanish doctoral program at the University of Illinois at Urbana. Most of his writing efforts there were expository—for example, seminar papers and a doctoral dissertation on the prolific nineteenth-century Spanish novelist Benito Pérez Galdós. After receiving his Ph.D. in Spanish in 1969, he taught at Trinity University in San Antonio, Texas, for two years.

In 1970, while serving as chairman of the modern language department at Texas A & I University in Kingsville, Texas, Hinojosa-Smith began to write *Estampas del valle y otras obras: Sketches of the Valley and Other Works* (1973). In 1971 he began a close friendship with Tomás Rivera, the highly regarded Chicano writer, academic, and university administrator who died in 1984. Rivera, whose novel: " . . . *y no se la tragó la tierra"/" . . . and the Earth Did Not Part*" (1971) won the Quinto Sol prize for literature in 1970, was instrumental in encouraging him to submit his writings. In fact he sent Hinojosa-Smith's manuscript of *Estampas del valle y otras obras* to Quinto Sol Publications, who printed excerpts from it in *El Grito*, an important early Chicano journal of the humanities and the social sciences, marking the beginning of Hinojosa-Smith's success as a published writer. Soon after the appearance of several pieces in *El Grito*, he was notified in 1973 that he had received the third annual Quinto Sol prize for *Estampas del valle y otras obras*.

Hinojosa-Smith's first book does not fit easily within the traditional concept of a novel because it lacks a plot. There is no denouement nor does it provide a sense of completion or resolution. It is, rather, a series of *estampas* (sketches)

that forms a rich tapestry of the Chicano community in and around the fictional town of Klail City, located in Belken County—clearly meant to represent the lower Rio Grande valley, where the author grew up. Each sketch forms an integral part of the complex of lives, joys, struggles, and tragedies of the community. The author warns readers at the outset of the work that the sketches are individual strands of hair matted together with the sweat and dirt of generations of human toil. To separate them would interrupt the flow of vitality and spontaneity which surges through the work.

Estampas del valle y otras obras is characterized by a wide range in tone, from a terse, direct presentation to a rich and subtle folk humor. The voice in the work alternates between omniscient author and a first-person narrator. The first sketch begins at an indefinite point in time and place with the marriage of Roque Malacara and Tere Tapia; in every sketch, a new character is added or a different facet of one already presented is revealed. Over twenty-five characters appear in the work's relatively few pages.

Hinojosa-Smith intentionally obscures relationships between characters, does not identify the narrator until late in the work, and blurs characterization in order to create an overall impression of the collective nature of the community of Klail City. A few characters reappear throughout the pages of the novel, serving as threads of unity among the many sketches. The reader does not discover for several pages the general location of the fictional community nor the time period in which it is set. Hinojosa-Smith's intent seems to be to place the focus on the shared traditions, values, language, and history.

Estampas del valle y otras obras was generally well received. The Quinto Sol prize signaled to readers that the novel merited serious consideration. Teresinha Alves Pereira, in *Revista Chicano-Riqueña* (Winter 1975), commented that the novel's movement, themes, and structure indicated that the writer had learned well from the literary vanguardists. She also noted that the black humor which abounds throughout goes far in providing release for the reader from the hard reality the characters suffer at the hands of both Hispanics and Anglos. Salvador Rodríguez del Pino, in his book *La novela chicana escrita en español: cinco autores comprometidos* (The Chicano Novel in Spanish: Five Socially Committed Writers, 1982), praised Hinojosa-Smith for having gone beyond regionalism. José David Saldívar, in a critical intro-

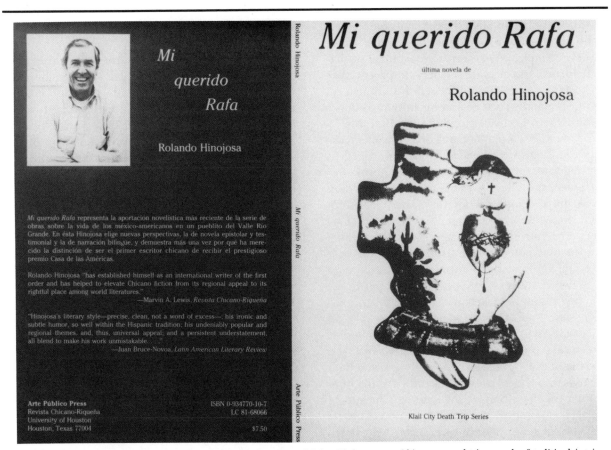

Covers for Hinojosa-Smith's 1981 novel, which tells the story of Jehú Malacara, a Chicano caught in a web of political intrigue and financial manipulation

duction to Hinojosa-Smith's *Klail City Death Trip* for *The Rolando Hinojosa Reader* (1985), considered *Estampas del valle* as the important first work in a "sensitive and skillful literary metahistory of the Rio Grande Valley, one of the most important dialogical productions of narrative in the Southwest today." Luis María Brox, however, in his review essay (*Mester*, April 1974), was of the opinion that *Estampas del valle y otras obras* is flawed by the author's choice, especially in the first part of the book, of the *costumbrista* form, that is, the superficial description of typical characters mouthing typical language. He saw this choice as unnecessarily limiting because it depicted a static and closed society in which change and response to exterior influences were not possible. The nontraditional form of *Estampas del valle y otras obras* created a dilemma for some critics who seemed confused about how to classify the work. Because it obviously did not fit within a neat general framework, it was often identified as a collection of interrelated sketches. This identification was to carry over to Hinojosa-Smith's other works as well, an unfortunate development

that affected critical appreciation of his subsequent publications.

In 1976 Hinojosa-Smith was promoted to vice-president for academic affairs at Texas A & I University. In the meantime he had placed many short pieces (several of which would later become integrated into his novels) in journals and magazines such as *Bilingual Review, Mester, Revista Chicano-Riqueña, Caracol,* and *Hispamérica.* In 1976 he received the prestigious Premio Casa de las Américas for his second novel, *Klail City y sus alrededores* (1976; translated as *Klail City: A Novel,* 1987). In an unpublished 1986 interview he recalled that he had been encouraged by a friend to submit the manuscript to the annual international competition held in Cuba and sponsored by the state-supported Casa de las Américas publishing house. One day he received a telegram and a letter–sent weeks earlier but circuitously routed to avoid the U.S. embargo on Cuba–notifying him of the judges' decision. The distinguished group of intellectuals who formed the prize committee–Domingo Miliani (Venezuela), Juan Carlos Onetti (Uruguay), Lisandro Otero

(Cuba), and Lincoln Silva (Paraguay)–commented on his skillful use of dialogue, descriptive vigor, richness of imagery, extraordinary control of dialectal forms, and overall aesthetic impact. Other meritorious comments addressed his innovative use of time and structure and his humor in documenting the collective struggle of the Chicano.

Klail City employs many of the same techniques as *Estampas del valle y otras obras*, particularly methods of fragmentation, but in the second novel, the effect is richer. Structurally, *Klail City* is more complex than the earlier work. In this relatively short novel over one hundred characters are introduced, and the author weaves them in and out of the narrative in a way that leaves the impression of naturalness and spontaneity. A few characters in *Klail City* stand out in relief: for example, Esteban Echevarría, an old-timer with a prodigious memory, who is Klail City's wise man and storyteller; Jehú Malacara, who recalls his youthful adventures with the fundamentalist preacher Tomás Imas; Rafa Buenrostro, an ever-present narrator from whom we learn of the struggles of a young Chicano in school and later in the military; Don Manuel Guzmán, ex-revolutionary-turned-cop who is respected by the Chicano community for his role as a counselor and friend of drunks and other "down and outers"; Choche Markham, the opportunistic Anglo politician who becomes a benevolent Chicano-lover during elections; the greedy Leguizamón family, which was responsible for the violent death of Rafa's father, Jesús, and which consorts with Anglo power brokers to further its own financial interests; and a few others such as Pedro Zamudio and Celso Villalón.

These few central characters give the work its continuity, but they possess little of the stuff of protagonists. They are not literary heroes or even antiheroes; on the contrary, Hinojosa-Smith makes an effort to convince readers how plain his characters are: "Aquí no hay héroes de leyenda: esta gente va al escusado, estornuda, se limpia los mocos, cría familias, conoce lo que es morir con el ojo pelón, se cuartea con dificultad y (como madera verde) resiste rajarse. El que busca héroes de la proporción del Cid, pongamos por caso, que se vaya a la Laguna de la Leche" (There are no legendary heroes here: these people go to the bathroom, sneeze, wipe their noses, raise their families, know how to die without a cent, to give in a little with difficulty and [like green wood] to resist giving up. If you're looking for heroes of El Cid's dimensions,

for example, you had better go looking around the Lagoon of Milk).

Hinojosa-Smith said in the 1986 interview that he wrote *Klail City* in order to keep alive the memory of his youth in light of a new and changing world that removes him further and further from his past. He keeps his memory alive by suppressing the role individual characters play in the novel and by highlighting the function of the collective protagonist of Klail City. Readers can relate more readily and more personally to a multitude of names, relationships, places, and happenings. The multiplication of points of view breaks down the barriers between reader and character, reducing the narrative distance between them.

Klail City first was published in the United States in 1977 as *Generaciones y semblanzas* and in 1980 appeared in German translation. Most reviewers and critics have responded favorably to the novel. Marvin Lewis, for example, in his review appearing in *Revista Chicano-Riqueña* (Summer 1978), concluded: "In this work Hinojosa sets high literary standards for which subsequent authors must strive. With *Generaciones y semblanzas* the author has established himself as an international writer of the first order and has helped to elevate Chicano fiction from its regional appeal to its rightful place among world literatures." Saldívar in *The Rolando Hinojosa Reader* called it "his most finished piece of fiction," noting that it is "a compendium of the formal and ideological achievements that the author discovered in the creative illuminations of *Estampas* and that he would relentlessly pursue throughout his early literary career."

Yolanda Guerrero's comments were representative of some of the negative criticism the novel received. In *La Palabra* (Fall 1979) she said that his treatment of Chicano life was superficial and misleading in that it did not sufficiently highlight the conflictive nature of Chicano-Anglo relations and the contradictions inherent in Chicano culture itself.

In 1976 Hinojosa-Smith resigned his administrative position at Texas A & I to accept an appointment as professor of English and chair of the program in Chicano studies at the University of Minnesota, responding in part to his wife's decision to enter law school. During the early part of his stay in Minnesota, he immersed himself in reading the great war novelists and poets such as Siegfried Sassoon, Evelyn Waugh, and Robert Graves in preparation for the drafting of *Korean Love Songs*, a book of poems. In *The Rolando*

Cover for Hinojosa-Smith's 1985 translation of
Mi querido Rafa

Hinojosa Reader he said he had originally tried to write about Korea in Spanish but "since the experience wasn't lived in Spanish," he switched to English.

Through Rafa Buenrostro, the poem's narrator, readers view the brutalization of young Chicanos—Rafa himself, David "Sonny" Ruiz, José Vielma, Rosalío "Charlie" Villalón, and, later, Jacob Mosqueda and Cayo Díaz Balderas—assigned to the 219th Field Artillery Battalion. Rafa is wounded, recovers in an army hospital, and is given medical leave to Japan. In a key scene he meets "Sonny" Ruiz who, having gone AWOL, is trying to assimilate into Japanese culture. Rafa reflects on his own impending return to Klail City, "to the valley, and home. Home to Texas, our Texas,/That slice of hell, heaven,/ Purgatory and land of our Fathers." He realizes that "Sonny" Ruiz is probably better off in Japan and decides to lie to a board of inquiry to protect his friend. Having witnessed the deaths of his friends on the Korean battlefields, Rafa returns

to Belken County to take up where he left off, but now, in the early 1950s, life in the valley is changing rapidly. José David Saldívar, in an essay in *The Rolando Hinojosa Reader*, noted that *Korean Love Songs* falls in the tradition of British World War I poetry. Ramón Saldívar (writing also in *The Rolando Hinojosa Reader*) was of the opinion that it falls within the Mexican/Chicano *corrido* tradition but with important differences: "I suggest that, like *El Corrido de Gregorio Cortez* [a well-known border ballad], Hinojosa's *Korean Love Songs* has its underlying impulse—albeit in symbolic and unconscious form—in some of our deepest fantasies about social life, both as we [Chicanos] live it and as we would like to have it be. The difference is that in the earlier song this impulse can be expressed directly and literally, whereas in the latter song the impulse can be expressed only indirectly and figuratively."

Hinojosa-Smith left the University of Minnesota in 1981 to accept a position in the department of English at the University of Texas at Austin, where he is currently located. His work since *Korean Love Songs* traces the changes that have occurred in the valley since the 1950s. *Mi querido Rafa* (1981; revised and translated as *Dear Rafe*, 1985) received the Southwestern Conference on Latin American Studies prize for best writing in the humanities in 1982.

Mi querido Rafa is divided into two parts, the first consisting of twenty-two letters that Jehú Malacara writes to his cousin Rafa Buenrostro who, having been wounded in Korea, is recovering in a veterans hospital. Malacara has become a loan official at the Klail City Savings and Loan. Important characters in the novel are Noddy Perkins, president of the savings and loan; his daughter, Sammy Joe Perkins; and the Klail-Blanchard-Cooke families, which control most of the capital in the valley. Toward the end of the first part, Jehú Malacara suddenly resigns his position at the bank to attend the University of Austin, leaving the reader and many of the townspeople wondering why. Most of the second part of the novel consists of speculation about Malacara's mysterious departure. His letters reveal his disillusionment with valley politics in which he had become involved for a short time. P. Galindo, a local writer, interviews several Anglo and Chicano characters who all contribute to solving the puzzle of his departure. Readers learn that Jehú Malacara had been having an affair with Sammy Joe, who has discovered her husband's homosexual relationship with a former congressman and one of Noddy Perkins's sidekicks; that Malacara and Perkins had had a frank interchange prior to his leaving; that Malacara has had an affair with Becky Escobar, the wife of an aspiring Chicano politician; and that Malacara sidetracked a land deal involving Don Javier Leguizamón and Noddy Perkins. In the end it is evident that Malacara is held in general disfavor by all but a few who sympathize with his difficult position as a Chicano caught in a complicated web of political intrigue and financial manipulation. While Jehú Malacara is not depicted as either totally good or totally bad, he does emerge as a sympathetic character. Margarita Cota-Cárdenas in *The Rolando-Hinojosa Reader* called him a Chicano Everyman, an antihero who is neither idealized nor condemned.

While *Mi querido Rafa* received little attention in the press–probably because Spanish-language works published in the United States are not accessible to most readers–*Dear Rafe*, Hinojosa-Smith's revision and translation of it, was reviewed enthusiastically. For example, Robert Houston, in the *New York Times Book Review* (18 August 1985), commented: "Although his sharp eye and accurate ear capture a place, its people and a time in a masterly way, his work goes far beyond regionalism. He is a writer for all readers.... " Lyman Grant, writing in the *Dallas Morning News* (1 September 1985), said that the novel "makes one eager for the next novel. Can more be said for a book?" The reviewer for *Choice* (16 April 1986) concluded that *Dear Rafe* was "a feast for scholars in American and Latin American Studies."

In *Mi querido Rafa* Hinojosa-Smith experimented with the epistolary form and reportage. In *Rites and Witnesses* he employs reportage, dialogue, and vignettes, focusing on Klail City toward the end of the 1950s and the beginning of the 1960s and the world of the Korean War reflected in the bitter experiences of Rafa Buenrostro. While in *Mi querido Rafa* readers were given a glimpse of the inner workings of Anglo financial and political life in the Valley, in *Rites and Witnesses*, published in 1982, they are shown alcoholism, promiscuity, sexual exploitation, and a pervasive financial and political dishonesty. Another narrative line has to do with Rafa's and others' tours of duty in Korea nine years prior to the events of the novel, going back to the wounding of Rafa on the battlefield and his subsequent evacuation to an Army hospital prior to being transported stateside to the veterans hospital.

The camaraderie of Anglo and Chicano soldiers in Korea is contrasted with the racism and antagonism between them once they returned to the valley. *Rites and Witnesses* is written in English perhaps because its settings and characters are essentially Anglo and because the Chicano characters' integration into the English-speaking world now takes on greater importance for them than their relationship with their own culture and language. While *Rites and Witnesses* is a well-constructed novel, it elicited little substantive critical response.

In 1983, the year he was inducted into the Texas Institute of Letters, Hinojosa-Smith published *The Valley*, a revision of the English version of *Estampas del valle*. In 1985 *Partners in Crime: A Rafe Buenrostro Mystery* appeared. Also written in English, it is significantly different from Hinojosa-Smith's previous works in several respects. It lacks their collective focus, narrative structure, and close affiliation with oral tradition. It is instead a work that follows in formulaic fashion the pattern of many modern detective stories. The familiar characters and scenes that formed an essential part of the earlier works have disappeared. For example, gone are Esteban Echevarría and P. Galindo, the narrators who had provided a unifying thread in the complicated tapestry which Hinojosa-Smith's readers had come to know as Belken County. Also missing are references to the Buenrostro, Malacara, Támez, and Leguizamón families and their links to the early history of the valley. To be sure, Rafa Buenrostro and Jehú Malacara both play an integral part in the novel, but they have become professionals–Buenrostro a lieutenant detective on the Belken County homicide squad and Malacara a vice-president at the Klail City First National Bank. They move comfortably in and out of the world dominated by Anglo capital and political power.

Most of the novel takes place in the squad room of the Belken County Building as Rafa and his fellow detectives go about the often tedious work of solving homicides, answering phone calls, and filling out endless reports. The reader is also taken into Malacara's office at the bank, into a local insane asylum, several bars, and a restaurant in Barrones where American and Mexican police officials cooperate to solve a horrible crime, the brutal slaying of Gus Elder and two Mexican nationals. Basically, *Partners in Crime* is good detective fiction. Its main interest consists in revealing, from circumstances largely physical,

PARTNERS IN CRIME

ROLANDO HINOJOSA

Partners in Crime: A Rafe Buenrostro Mystery is the latest work in Rolando Hinojosa's heterogeneous novel, *Klail City Death Trip Series*. As Hinojosa's subtitle suggests, *Partners in Crime* follows the conventional patterns and motifs of the popular cultural murder mystery genre: shrewd detectives, naive disciples, and the misleading of genuine clues. Hinojosa's sleuths are Lt. Rafe Buenrostro of the Belken County Homicide Squad and Captain Lisandro Goméz Solís, Cuerpo de Policía Estatal, Sección del Orden Público of Barrones, Tamaulipas. An unnamed narrator tells the story, and his curiosity and growing awareness of the complexity of the murders underscores Hinojosa's concern with truth and falsity.

Rolando Honojosa is the author of *Estampas del valle y otras obras, Klail City y sus alrededores, Korean Love Songs, Claros varones de Belken, Mi querido Rafa, Rites and Witnesses, The Valley,* and *Dear Rafe.* Presently, Rolando Hinojosa is Ellen Clayton Garwood Centennial Professor in Creative Writing and English at The University of Texas at Austin.

Arte Público Press
University of Houston
University Park
Houston, TX 77004

ISBN 0-934770-37-9
LC 84-072298

PARTNERS IN CRIME

A Rafe Buenrostro Mystery

ROLANDO HINOJOSA

An Arte Público Press Book

Covers for Hinojosa-Smith's 1985 mystery novel, set in his fictional Belken County

the true order and meaning of events that to the reader have been partly disclosed and partly concealed.

Through dogged detective work, cooperation between American and Mexican officials, and luck, twin mysteries–the illegal banking of drug money and the slayings–are solved. The process of setting upright the world of Belken County occupies two-thirds of *Partners in Crime.* Valley Mexicans, valley Anglos, and Mexican nationals all band together to rid from their midst profoundly corrupt and evil outside forces who are smuggling cocaine. The last scene is a classical detective story ending as tranquillity and predictability return once again to the valley, the forces of order having triumphed over the forces of chaos.

Reviews of *Partners in Crime* have been overwhelmingly positive. For example, Tom Pilkington, writing in the *Dallas Times Herald* (11 August 1985), praised Hinojosa-Smith for having done his homework on police procedures and crime in the valley. He cites the author's clipped, hard-boiled style as being appropriate to the detective

genre. Bryce Milligan comments in the *Dallas Morning News* (11 May 1986) that the novel "reads like Dashiell Hammett with a Texas Twang," and he compliments Hinojosa-Smith for his gift for conversational lyricism. Louis Dubose believes that *Partners in Crime* serves to cement Hinojosa-Smith's reputation as a major novelist (*Texas Observer,* 7 February 1986).

Claros varones de Belken: Fair Gentlemen of Belken County was not published until 1986 although it was written earlier. It forms the fourth part of the *Klail City Death Trip* series, *Estampas del valle, Klail City y sus alrededores,* and *Korean Love Songs* being the first three. The work is a collection of dialogues and monologues in which four of Hinojosa-Smith's principal characters– Rafa Buenrostro, Jehú Malacara, P. Galindo, and Esteban Echevarría–remember the immediate or distant past or comment on their or others' present circumstances. As in the other works, the multiple perspective serves to provide unity to the many loose strands that are found within *Claros varones.* In the prologue readers learn that the young Jehú Malacara finally separated himself

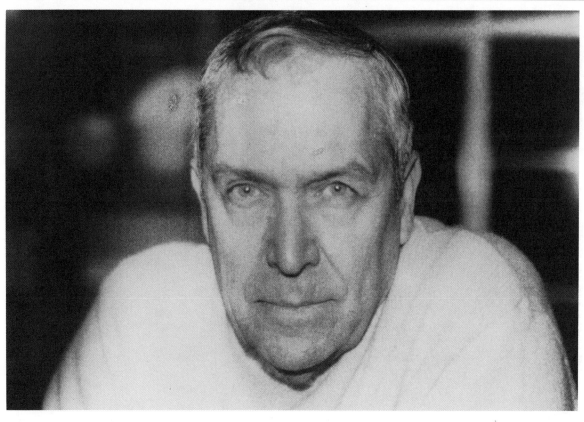

Hinojosa-Smith, February 1986 (courtesy of the author)

from Brother Tomás Imás, a traveling evangelical preacher, to join the army. He was stationed at Fort Eustis, Virginia, and after serving out his tour of active duty, his reserve unit was activated during the Korean conflict. Malacara served as a chaplain's assistant in Korea. The work's first section focuses on the post-Korea years. Buenrostro, the narrator there, tells readers that after returning from Korea he and Malacara went to college in Austin at the University of Texas. Buenrostro graduated four years later as a Spanish major; Malacara specialized in history. Both became teachers at Klail City High School. This first section is followed by a short section in which Jehú comments on some lesser-known characters. In the third section the focus shifts again as Galindo recalls a few humorous and not-so-humorous incidents from Klail City's immediate past: Malacara's traumatic recovery from strangling the snake which had bitten Tomás Imás; Ignacio Loera's entrapment of his adulterous wife Rita and her lover Moisés Guevara; the death of Melitón Burnias; the marriage of the colorful la güera Fira; Buenrostro's visit to the family of Chale Villalón, a valley boy killed in Korea; the various fortunes and misfortunes of the Vielma

clan; and the last days of Esteban Echevarría. The novel then goes back to Buenrostro's return from Korea, the year he spends with a family on El Rancho del Carmen, and his healing from the physical and emotional wounds of war. In the last section Echevarría comments sardonically on his people's history of allowing themselves to be exploited by both Anglos and their own kind: "Raza pendeja. Nunca aprendemos" (Screwed-up people. We never learn). The critical response to *Claros varones de Belken* has been positive. Reviewer E. A. Mares, writing in *Southwestern Discoveries* (June-August 1988), comments that the work's series of vignettes "has the impact of a fine novel on the reader." He feels that its publication bodes well for American literature. Alejandro Morales comments enthusiastically on the novel's "beautiful, witty tapestry" in which the novelist "captures the intra-history of the collective experience of the Chicano" (*Los Angeles Times Book Review*, 12 April 1987). Salvador Rodríguez del Pino's review in *American Book Review* (March-April 1988) is equally positive.

Although Rolando Hinojosa-Smith is among the best-known and most celebrated Chicano writers in the United States, he is much better known in Europe and Latin America than in his own country. His *Klail City Death Trip* series presents a vast panorama of Chicano and Anglo life in South Texas, depicted with sensitivity and skill. Chicano literature is enriched by his contributions.

References:

Luis María Brox, "Los límites del costumbrismo en *Estampas del valle y otras obras,*" *Mester*, 5 (April 1974): 101-104;

Yolanda Guerrero, "Literatura y sociedad: Análisis de *Generaciones y semblanzas,*" *La Palabra*, 1 (Fall 1979): 21-30;

Robert Houston, review of *Dear Rafe*, *New York Times Book Review*, 18 August 1985, p. 9;

Teresinha Alves Pereira, "*Estampas del valle y otras obras,*" *Revista Chicano-Riqueña*, 3 (Winter 1975): 57-58;

Salvador Rodríguez del Pino, *La novela chicana escrita en español: cinco autores comprometidos* (Ypsilanti: Bilingual/Editorial Bilingüe, 1982), pp. 117-137;

José David Saldívar, "Rolando Hinojosa's *Klail City Death Trip*: A Critical Introduction," in *The Rolando Hinojosa Reader, Essays Historical and Critical*, edited by José David Saldívar (Houston: Arte Publico, 1985), pp. 44-63;

Ramón Saldívar, "*Korean Love Song*: A Border Ballad and its Heroes," in *The Rolando Hinojosa Reader, Essays Historical and Critical*, p. 144.

Papers:

Hinojosa-Smith's papers are in the Nettie Lee Benson Latin American Collection, University of Texas at Austin.

Angela de Hoyos

(23 January 1940-   )

Gwendolyn Díaz
Saint Mary's University

BOOKS: *Arise, Chicano: and Other Poems*, poetry in English by de Hoyos, Spanish translations by Mireya Robles (Bloomington: Backstage Books, 1975);

Chicano Poems for the Barrio (Bloomington: Backstage Books, 1975);

Selecciones, poetry in English by de Hoyos, Spanish translations by Robles (Veracruz, Mexico: Universidad Veracruzana, 1976); republished as *Selected Poems/Selecciones* (San Antonio, Tex.: Dezkalzo Press, 1979);

Woman, Woman (Houston: Arte Publico, 1985).

When considering the entire body of work of award-winning poet Angela de Hoyos readers can note changes and constants. Initially her work expressed anger and frustration toward unjust circumstances, particularly the plight of the Chicano. More recently she has become satirical and <u>views</u> issues with a distant and caustic tone, reflecting her maturation not only as a poet, but also as a person. She has maintained a concern for those groups society has marginalized (be they Chicano or female) and a desire to verbalize the inner workings of the individual. She interprets the world from a dualistic point of view, effectively re-creating the tensions, for example, between male and female, Anglo and Hispanic, and compassion and apathy. De Hoyos's most significant merit is her ability to perceive the follies and virtues of human nature with sensitivity and a Spartan style.

De Hoyos was born in the state of Coahuila, Mexico. Her father owned a dry-cleaning establishment, and her mother was a talented matriarch with an artistic penchant she sought to instill in her daughter. The poet's early childhood was a traumatic one because at the age of three she was burned on the neck and chest by a gas heater and suffered a long convalescence. Smoke inhalation caused further complications, forcing her to spend many months in bed where she began an interior monologue of rhymes and verses to entertain herself and to draw attention

Angela de Hoyos (courtesy of the author)

away from the pain. While she was still a child, the family moved to San Antonio, Texas, where de Hoyos has since resided. Preferring to prescribe her own course of studies and eschewing the need to follow a degree plan, she took courses at the University of Texas at San Antonio, San Antonio College, the Witte Museum, and the San Antonio Art Institute, where she pursued her interest in fine arts and writing. De Hoyos's poetry has appeared in literary journals, anthologies, magazines, and newspaper literary supplements in the United States and also in several Latin American and European countries. She is active in both the artistic and literary communities in San Antonio and in Austin, Texas, and also serves as general editor for M&A/ Manda Publications and as a coeditor for M&A Editions. She is director and general editor of *Huehuetitlan* magazine.

140

What de Hoyos strives to do in her poetry is to represent the concerns of those who are not able to express themselves, yet who have much to say: for example, a hungry child, a teenage spray-paint sniffer, or a poor mother from the barrio. For her, poetry is a social activity; it entails understanding all types of people and melding with them to achieve a product that represents not only the poet's inner self, but also the multiplicity of characters that populate her milieu: people from the barrio, Chicanos with a cause, women in need, and all those who feel that life is unfair.

Arise, Chicano: and Other Poems (1975), written between 1969 and 1975, deals with the social and political issues relevant to the plight of the Chicano living in an Anglo-dominated society. The title poem, "Arise Chicano!," sets the tone for the entire collection; it is a prophetic call for change which the Chicano himself is responsible for achieving and an exhortation to reinstate the dignity of a race which has been slighted. The poem presents a series of images and ideas which gives a critical view of the Anglo yet avoids being moralistic. In the first stanza the predominant images are those of the poverty of migrant workers whose only reward for strenuous manual labor is physical nourishment: "In your migrant's world of hand-to-mouth days/your children go smileless to a cold bed." The next stanza alludes to the prostrate position of the Chicano, oppressed by the Anglo employer ("under the shrewd heel of exploit"); his "brutal sweat" is with "ignoble pittance crowned." The narrator calls for her people to arise, to rebel against the exploitative "mocking whip of slavehood" which is causing a loss of dignity and even of dreams. The poet places the responsibility of liberation on the shoulders of those oppressed, who must be their own redeemers: "there is no one to succor you/You must be your own messiah." The poet's mission is to give voice to those who cannot express themselves: "How to express your anguish/when not even your burning words are yours." Also here is the idea that the Chicano is oppressed by language, for his Spanish is impoverished by living in an English-speaking society and English is the language of those who alienate him. The poem is representative of a dialectical view which is characteristic not only of de Hoyos's poetic structure, but also of her thematic and conceptual world. Antithetical ideas such as past and present, life and death, physical and spiritual, supine and erect are juxtaposed throughout this poem.

"The Final Laugh," which won the 1972 Diploma de Benemerenza, the second prize of the Academia Leonardo Da Vinci in Italy, is concerned with the issue of race as a cause for discrimination. Race becomes an obstacle to achieving equal standing, and in so stating this poem presents a pessimistic view of the future of the Chicano in society. The irony of the situation is highlighted by de Hoyos's choice of understated terms: "the necessity being of white/the advisability of mail-order parents." Having white parentage is equated with having power and freedom. Yet, there is sarcasm in these lines as well; the term "mail-order parents" connotes the idea of stereotyped, homogenous personalities lacking in individuality. The Chicano is criticized, for his dignity has only afforded him a "grumbling belly" and "shivering flesh." The poem gives two solutions to racism. The less preferable one is to continue being subordinated, being "content with the left-overs of a greedy establishment." The preferred alternative is to burst the shackles of oppression so as to take a rebellious stance against the "alien white world."

"Brindis for the Barrio" (A Toast for the Barrio) was written in response to a poem by the Peruvian César Vallejo. Vallejo's poem, "La cena miserable" (The Miserable Supper), poses the question of how long man must suffer on earth. De Hoyos contrasts the fatalism of Vallejo's poem with her hope for "a promise of gold for tomorrow."

De Hoyos's second book, *Chicano Poems for the Barrio* (1975), deals mainly with the threat of loss of identity within the barrio, a place where both Mexican and American cultures become fused. The collection can be seen as an inventory of Chicano life experiences such as discrimination, alienation, poverty, loss of traditions, and the acquisition of alien Anglo values. Whereas her first book is written almost entirely in English, *Chicano Poems for the Barrio* uses Spanish terms and concepts within an English text (code-switching). Following the Chicano poet Alurista, this integration of both languages to express a bicultural reality is a conscious effort on the poet's part to express the melding of two different ways of examining life.

A significant element in *Chicano Poems for the Barrio* is the reexamination of history from the perspective of the subjugated. The poem "Hermano" (Brother) begins with an epigraph which refers to the battle of the Alamo, in which Mexican forces defeated a small company of besieged Texans. To the call "Remember the Alamo," which

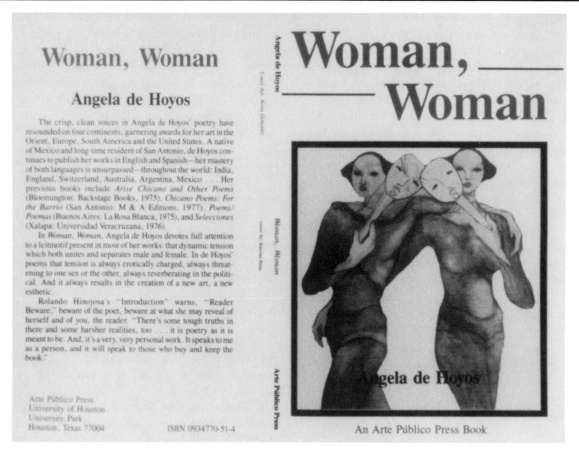

Covers for de Hoyos's 1985 poetry collection, which focuses on the individual and social experiences of women

spurred the Texans on to ultimate victory at San Jacinto soon after the Alamo defeat, de Hoyos adds ". . . and my Spanish ancestors that built it." The epigraph encapsulates the fact that Anglos have forgotten that the land and people they conquered are of Hispanic heritage. The poem sets up a tension between the Anglo and Hispanic cultures and juxtaposes the Spanish and English languages. The narrator laments the fact that Texas's Hispanic heritage has been ignored by the Anglo, whose ethnocentricity leads him to say to the Chicano: "Why don't you go back where you came from?" The narrator indicates that to do so the Hispanic would need to resurrect Columbus's *Niña, Pinta,* and *Santa Maria;* yet the Anglo also arrived from European shores in the *Mayflower,* and therefore this land belongs simultaneously to neither and to both. As the poem ends the Chicano is waiting: "I must wait for the conquering barbarian/to learn the Spanish word for love: Hermano," the implication being that the Chicano will overcome his present victimized status only when the Anglo learns the meaning of brotherly love.

The fear of losing Hispanic heritage and traditions is the theme of "Para una ronda agridulce" (For a Bittersweet Round) and "Small Comfort." Both are nostalgic in tone, for the barrio portrayed in the poems is beginning to disintegrate under the pressure to become Anglicized and accept the values of the establishment. In "Small Comfort" a Chicano laments forgetting the Spanish vocabulary as well as the customs, the special foods, and the social events that are "little by little/becoming buried in the land of the gringo." The first verse becomes the poem's conclusion: "So much for ethnic ties." Becoming Americanized, learning to integrate into the dominant society, is "small comfort" for having lost one's cultural patrimony.

"Blues in the Barrio" links faith and hunger as common denominators of the economically oppressed. A mother "rolls out tortillas/paper thin/ as her hope," so that there will appear to be more. To the poor mother in the barrio hunger is as real a presence as that of the Catholic religion she has inherited from the centuries: "Tonight she will kiss/with the flame of her faith/the warm crucifix at her throat."

The concern for the individual and his personal struggles parallels de Hoyos's social themes and becomes the main focus of her next two books, *Selecciones* (1976) and *Woman, Woman* (1985). *Selecciones* includes poems written between 1965 and 1973. The success of the Mexican edition led to a republication with a bilingual title in 1979. In *Selecciones* there is a dialogue between life and death, which de Hoyos considers to be two sides of the same experience. For example, in the poem "Mi dolor hecho canción, mi canción hecho dolor" (My Sorrow Made Song, My Song Made Sorrow) the urge to die is perceived as a desire to ". . . feel my way/back into the warm/painless/womb of earth/from whence I came." However, the narrator claims "but everything/binds me to you, Life/–even these illusions:/Love/Peace/Happiness." Dawn finds the narrator "bravely singing,/waving/my worn-out flag of truce," concluding that life is a series of compromises that hinder the death instinct. In "One Ordinary Morning" there is compassion for those surprised at the finiteness of life. Even as satisfaction with life has begun to be felt, "at the zenith" death is discovered "with her diligent hoe/insidiously scraping away at . . . your body."

In *Woman, Woman*, her most recent book, de Hoyos experiments with style and language. Though most of the poems are written in English, many are in Spanish, and there is also a noticeable use of code-switching. One interesting linguistic feature of this volume is the use of pre-Columbian terminology. De Hoyos feels that many expressions lose their original impact and significance when translated and prefers to use, for instance, the Mayan term *in-lak ech* (my other self) because it sounds and feels more authentic. Another stylistic device used frequently in this collection is the combining of an English and a Spanish word to form a new term with special connotations or the combining of two words of the same language to form a new one.

Woman, Woman focuses on the individual and social experiences of women, projecting a balanced, intimate perspective of them by adopting various personas and portraying images and reactions which are specific to their gender. For example, two poems which give voice to distinctly feminine ways of experiencing rejection and disappointment are "Ex Marks the Spot" and "Fairy-Tale: Cuento de Hadas." "Ex Marks the Spot" is a poem about a woman who has been abandoned by her companion. She says she was left "dan-

De Hoyos (courtesy of the author)

gling from a limb," yet she "learned to hang and saved my skin." "Fairy-Tale: Cuento de Hadas" depicts a naive young girl who learns that romance is only a dream when she realizes her "Prince Charming" is "stepping out on the sly." Her disillusionment leads her to "never never never again/blindly believe/in deities, or in men."

The poems "Two Poems: Inebrieties" and "Mona Lisa: Marguerite" are noteworthy because of the syncretism of Spanish and English languages. "Inebrieties" appears to be two poems, one in English and the other in Spanish. However, the messages of both are combined to form two different perspectives, one Anglo, one Hispanic, of the same issue: the unsettling feeling one experiences when falling passionately in love. The first half of each stanza in "Mona Lisa" is in English and is echoed in the second half by a Spanish counterpoint.

The critical response to de Hoyos's work has been fairly extensive and mostly favorable. Her poetry has caught the attention of critics not only in the United States and Mexico, but also in Europe. Franca M. Bacchiega (September-December 1987) comments that de Hoyos's poetry possesses acute intelligence, subtle irony, and the power to enter into the depths of reader's souls. Naomi Lindstrom (1984) points out that the poet's work addresses quite directly the issue of economic deprivation while it effectively celebrates basic Chicano values and the truthfulness of cultural traditions.

De Hoyos is currently completing her fifth book, titled "Dedicatorias" (Dedications) and has all but completed a manuscript for her sixth, "Gata Poems" (Cat Poems). "Dedicatorias" is a collection of poems dedicated to people who have affected the poet's life and work, such as Rodolfo Anaya, Rolando Hinojosa-Smith, and Willie Velasquez. In "Gata Poems" she says that human beings are not civilized until they learn to laugh at themselves. The tone of this collection is both philosophical and ironic, although at times it is simply humorous.

The work of de Hoyos develops from the angered protests of a socially conscious activist, apparent in *Arise, Chicano* and *Chicano Poems for the Barrio*, to a more introspective tone and individualistic focus in *Selecciones* and *Woman, Woman*. Stylistically, her later poems display more complexity, particularly regarding code-switching and other experiments in bilingual writing. Much of the merit of Chicano literature lies in its objective of recuperating and reappropriating its cultural and historical past. Angela de Hoyos takes it upon herself to reconstruct the history of the Chicano from his own perspective. Her cultural images have helped perpetuate a society which is in danger of losing its ethnic identity to the mainstream Anglo world. She also posits an unresolved or unresolvable tension between the male and the female, yet her dialectical worldview breaks the boundaries of gender and ethnicity to tap into universal archetypes of injustice, disrespect, insecurity, and fear.

References:

Marcela Aguilar-Henson, *The Multi-Faceted Poetic World of Angela de Hoyos* (Austin, Tex.: Relámpago Books, 1985);

Franca Minuzzo Bacchiega, "Poesia Dall'Estremo Ovest," *L'Ozio: Rivista di Letteratura*, 5 (September-December 1987): 90-102;

Naomi Lindstrom, "Four Representative Hispanic Poets of Central Texas: A Portrait of Plurality," *Third Woman*, 2, no. 1 (1984): 64-70;

Luis Arturo Ramos, *Angela de Hoyos, A Critical Look (Lo Heroico y lo antiheroico en su poesía)* (Albuquerque: Pajarito, 1979).

Gary D. Keller

(1 January 1943-   )

S. Daydí-Tolson
University of Wisconsin-Milwaukee

BOOKS: *España en el siglo veinte*, by Keller and Antonio Regalado (New York: Harcourt Brace Jovanovich, 1974);

¡Viva la lengua!, by Keller and Francisco Jiménez (New York: Harcourt Brace Jovanovich, 1975);

Cuentos españoles concertados, by Keller and Gonzalo Sobejano (New York: Harcourt Brace Jovanovich, 1975);

Mi escuela (Chicago: Science Research Associates, 1976);

The Analysis of Hispanic Texts: Current Trends in Methodology, by Keller, Mary Beck, and others (New York: Bilingual/Editorial Bilingüe, 1976);

Bilingualism in the Bicentennial and Beyond, by Keller, Richard V. Teschner, and Silvia Viera (New York: Bilingual/Editorial Bilingüe, 1976);

The Significance and Impact of Gregorio Marañón: Literary Criticism, Biographies, and Historiography (New York: Bilingual/Editorial Bilingüe, 1977);

Spanish Here and Now, by Keller, Nancy Sebastiani, and Francisco Jiménez (New York: Harcourt Brace Jovanovich, 1977);

Bilingual Education for Hispanic Students in the United States, by Keller and Joshua A. Fishman (New York: Teachers College Press of Columbia University, 1981);

Leo y entiendo (New York: Teachers College Press of Columbia University, 1984);

Tales of El Huitlacoche (Colorado Springs: Maize, 1984);

Chicano Cinema: Research, Reviews, and Resources (Binghamton: Bilingual/Editorial Bilingüe, 1985);

Tomás Rivera, 1935-1984: The Man and His Work, by Keller, Vernon Lattin, and Rolando Hinojosa-Smith (Tempe: Bilingual/Editorial Bilingüe, 1988).

Gary D. Keller (courtesy of the author)

OTHER: *Hispanics in the United States: An Anthology of Creative Literature*, two volumes, edited by Keller and Francisco Jiménez (Ypsilanti: Bilingual/Editorial Bilingüe, 1980-1982);

"Real Poetría," in *Five Poets of Aztlán*, edited by Santiago Daydí-Tolson (Binghamton: Bilingual/Editorial Bilingüe, 1985), pp. 98-116.

Gary Keller, known as a fiction writer and poet under the pen name of El Huitlacoche, was born in San Diego, California, to Jack Keller and Estela Cárdenas Keller. He grew up on the United States-Mexican border as his father's different occupations required his family to travel between the two countries. From an early age Keller worked to support his family. Although his schooling was affected by the many moves, he was an avid reader and developed an early enthusiasm for literature. He supported himself teach-

Cover for Keller's short-story collection, published in 1984

ing English in Mexico City while attending the Universidad de las Américas, where, in 1961, he obtained a B.A. in philosophy. A skillful Jai Alai player, Keller could have become a professional athlete, but he preferred to continue with his graduate studies in language and literature. He moved to New York City, where in 1967 he received an M.A. in Hispanic literature and linguistics and in 1971 a Ph.D. in the same field, both from Columbia University. Also in 1971 he received an M.A. in experimental psychology from the New School for Social Research. His writing interests have developed parallel to his career as an educator and founder and director of the Bilingual Press/Editorial Bilingüe. Presently he is Arizona Board of Regents' Professor at Arizona State University in Tempe.

Underlying the popular and humorous tone of Keller's poems and short stories is a profoundly critical, and frequently cynical, view of society as seen by his literary alter ego, El

Huitlacoche, a young Chicano man who cares deeply for his people but keeps the seemingly detached perspective of a sarcastic observer. The ingenuity and persistence of a people who need to survive in a largely foreign and inimical society is a central theme with Keller, whose pen name pays homage to a popular Mexican boxer of the 1950s who was loved by many because of his concern for the poor.

Keller's fourteen poems are collected in *Five Poets of Aztlán* (1985) under the title "Real Poetría". The title is an untranslatable mix of English and Spanish. Two of the poems are translated from the work of the medieval philosopher Sem Tob. In the other poems the objective of El Huitlacoche, the speaker, is to help himself and the Chicano people forced to live under oppressive circumstances. "Searching for La Real Cosa" is a poetic treatise on Chicano problems and concerns, starting with the need to find the final, evasive truth: "¿Quién es La Real Cosa?/ ¡Dime, dime por favor!" (Who is the Real Thing? Tell me, please tell me!). The poem is an extended question that examines the basic personae associated with the Chicano search for identity and sociopolitical strength, including the "radical chic,/ the poverty pimp" at the universities, the father who fights daily for survival within the system, the "vato loco" (wild dude) in the streets of the barrio, and the poet who becomes the representative of his people in the eyes of the literary establishment. "The Urban(e) Chicano's 76" examines the chance that Chicanos will have to participate in political decision-making. The attitude is that of a man who hopes–rather impulsively and with a strong sense of ironic criticism–to change things drastically: "Pues [well] I'm just a vato loco man/ but if I had my way again/I'd ask for 'Miliano Zapata's rise." "From the Heights of Macho Bicho," dedicated to Chilean poet Pablo Neruda, is a poem written in response to the U.S. Marine presence in Cuba, Vietnam, and other places around the world. "My Man, Bobby K, Lying in the Kitchen" is a brief elegy to Robert Kennedy, assassinated in 1968, who had represented values which minorities had embraced.

Tales of El Huitlacoche (1984) contains four short stories that depend on each other for their effectiveness and full meaning. Rosaura Sánchez (in "The Comic Vision in *Tales of El Huitlacoche*") says these narratives form a macrotext "in that there is a common thematic and formal element running through all the texts." The collection is best known for "Papi Invented the Automatic

- 6 - Gary D. Keller

over an archaic jukebox and fired me a negative grin. "¡Gueros!"

"What does that mean?"

"It means you've got blonde hair. You'll get used to it."

A pilgrimage from the countryside swept down the main drag, the Promenade of Institutionalized Revolution, to the cathedral. Herds of goats and turkeys and geese, bullied by trotting boys and mongrels. Then crests of cyclists congruous to paramilitants. Legions of grey benedicts, huffing and chanting Ave Maria, each village headed by a priest and ikon. The peddlers followed hawking tamales with green and red sauce, sweet potatoes and guava. Jesting and cursing in the militant sun the pilgrims marched and peeled corn husks, smearing the tender grain with colored sauce. A supplicant came by on bloody knees, bearing the indrawn vision.

All this mysticism gave me a manic indigestion. I became giddy and exhibited my coloratura. "Up the mystic eddy. Fa, la, la, la, la. Down your rainbarrel, fo, lo, lo, lo, lo. And we'll be friends for ever more."

He clenched me warmly. This is what he wanted to hear.

"Imagine Zorich. You've made it in a foreign patrimony. Beachhead at Anzio, as it were. Let's teach each other tag."

Suddenly I was at the hem of an embankment. I turned chill and legalistic. A psychedelic of excrement. Shit, tin, piss, paper waste, everything flowed equally, without privilege. A dead man rippled beneath a cloud of insects. I almost retched the noodles forthwith.

"You bastard!"

He smiled disarmingly. "I've dealt with hysterical potheads before."

A significant impromptu happens and you seek to anchor it to your mealy normalcy. Days are like that. You'll grizure them to their inevitabilities on the prompting of some perfectly coincidental revelation. People make the most binding resolutions on a mere shred of intensity. At the Jai Alai we got drunk. He debated how best to gamble away my money. I felt secure.

"The timeless syndrome, youth vs. experience. Only a poet or saint will win this match."

Page from a draft for Keller's story "The Raza Who Scored Big in Anáhuac," included in Tales of El Huitlacoche
(courtesy of the author)

Jumping Bean," which tells the story of how El Huitlacoche's father filled a medicine capsule with mercury from a thermometer and invented the automatic jumping bean. The father is an idealist, struggling against an unjust society. The narrator belongs to the generation of those who received an education and freed themselves from the social and cultural constraints of his father and his other older relatives. The subtle alternation of tone, from humorous to nostalgic, from sad to irate, from ironic to sentimental, is enriched by a narrative structure which stresses repetition. Under the title "The Man Who Invented the Automatic Jumping Bean" the story won a 1977 Pushcart Prize for being one of the best stories published by a small press.

The two central stories in the volume are narrated by El Huitlacoche in his college years. "The Mojado Who Offered Up His Tapeworms to the Public Weal" tells of El Huitlacoche's encounter with a prankster who calls himself Rompeculos (ass-thrasher), while both are traveling by Trailways bus across the Southwest. El Huitlacoche and Rompeculos indulge in asides and wordplay very much in accord with folkloric tradition. At the end of the story the unmasking of the Rompeculos's identity corresponds, to a certain extent, to the unmasking of the narrator himself. "The Raza Who Scored Big in Anáhuac," set at the Universidad Nacional Autónoma (National Autonomous University) in Mexico City tells of El Huitlacoche's experiences as a Chicano among Mexicans.

In the last story of the book, "Mocha in Disneyland," El Huitlacoche is a college professor, divorced from an Anglo woman, and father of Pancholin, called Mocha. The story recounts the narrator's feelings of loneliness and inadequacy when he receives a card from his son saying that he is low on the boy's loving list. To remedy the situation El Huitlacoche asks his former wife to let him keep the boy for a weekend. The father takes his son to Disneyland, where they spend the night illegally in a treehouse. As a counterpart to "Papi Invented the Automatic Jumping Bean," in which filial love makes the father a quixotic figure, this story develops the deep feelings of the father for the son. The bond is established when El Huitlacoche tells his child the story of Golden Carp, a myth about the origin of the Chicano people from Rudolfo Anaya's *Bless Me, Ultima* (1972). Under the spell of the story the boy becomes engrossed in his father's dreams and hopes to be accepted in the Order of the Golden Carp.

Gary Keller's work represents an important contribution to Chicano literature. Rosaura Sánchez has pointed to humor and sociopolitical concerns as the salient characteristics in Keller's narratives; her judgment can also be applied to his poetry, which reflects the attitudes and mood of the Chicano Movement of the late 1960s.

References:

Santiago Daydí-Tolson, "Voices from the Land of Reeds," in *Five Poets of Aztlán*, edited by Daydí-Tolson (Binghamton: Bilingual/Editorial Bilingüe, 1985), pp. 31-36;

Rosaura Sánchez, "The Comic Vision in *Tales of El Huitlacoche*," in Gary Keller's *Tales of El Huitlacoche* (Colorado Springs: Maize, 1984), pp. vii-xviii.

Sylvia S. Lizárraga

(3 November 1925-   )

Clara Lomas
Colorado College

WORKS: "El movimiento chicano," *El Nuevo Sonorense* (Hermosillo, Sonora, Mexico), 26 June 1971, p. 2;

"El sacerdote comprometido con problemas sociales," *El Nuevo Sonorense* (Hermosillo, Sonora, Mexico), 2 August 1971, p. 3;

"El proyecto de la frontera," *El Nuevo Sonorense* (Hermosillo, Sonora, Mexico), 19 December 1971, p. 5;

"Protestan los estudiantes chicanos de la Universidad de California," *El Nuevo Sonorense* (Hermosillo, Sonora, Mexico), 12 May 1972, p. 3;

"Poetry in Chains," *North Star* (San Diego) (March-April 1975): 13;

"A lo mejor . . . ," *Caracol*, 3, no. 12 (1977): 18-19;

"From a Woman to a Woman," in *Essays on la mujer*, edited by Rosaura Sánchez and Rosa Martínez (Los Angeles: Chicano Studies Research Center, 1977), pp. 91-95;

"Camino del lago/Silver Lake Road," "Quinceañera/Coming Out," "Management," "Monarquía / Monarchy," "Doña Lola," "El regreso/Returning," and "El momento/The Moment," in *Requisa treinta y dos*, edited by Sánchez (La Jolla: Chicano Research, University of California, San Diego, 1979), pp. 29-49, 119-140;

"La importancia del bilingüismo," *Chispas* (Berkeley: Chicano Studies, University of California), 9, no. 2 (1980);

"Don," in *Nuevos Horizontes*, edited by José B. Fernández and Nasario García (Lexington, Mass.: Heath, 1981), pp. 7-10;

"Chicana Woman Writers and Their Audience," *Lector* (Berkeley, Cal.), 1 (June 1982): 15-18;

"Observaciones acerca de la crítica literaria chicana," *Revista Chicano-Riqueña*, 10, no. 4 (1982): 55-64;

"An Analysis of the Double Exploitation of Women in the Short Story by Tomás Rivera,"

CHIPEC: *Chicano Political Economy Collective Working Papers Series*, no. 110 (1983);

"La mujer ingeniosa en *There Are No Madmen Here*," *FEM* (Mexico City), no. 34 (June-July 1984): 41; translated as "The Resourceful Woman in *There Are No Madmen Here*," *Third Woman*, 2, no. 1 (1984): 71-74;

"Un día común y corriente," in *Suplemento Literario* to *La Opinión* (Los Angeles), 22 February 1985;

"Images of Women in Chicano Literature by Men," *Feminist Issues: A Journal of Feminist Social & Political Theory*, 5 (Fall 1985): 69-88;

"La mujer doblemente explotada," *Aztlán*, 16, no. 1-2 (1985): 197-215;

"El otro lado," in *Palabra Nueva: Poesía Chicana*, edited by Ricardo Aguilar, Armando Armengol, and Sergio D. Elizondo (El Paso: Dos Pasos Editores, 1985), p. 79;

"The Patriarchal Ideology in 'La noche que se apagaron las luces,' " in *International Studies in Honor of Tomás Rivera*, edited by Julian Olivares (Houston: Arte Publico, 1985), pp. 90-95;

"De recuerdos," *FEM* (Mexico City), no. 48 (October-November 1986): 34;

"¿Qué tenía que ver con ellos?," in *Memorias: Colección de cuentos* (Chula Vista, Cal.: Editorial Juventud Chicana, 1987), pp. 119-123;

"Hacia una teoría para la liberación de la mujer," in *In Times of Change: Chicanos and Chicanas in American Society*, Mexican American Studies Program Monograph Series, no. 6, edited by Juan García, Julia Curry, and Clara Lomas (Houston: University of Houston, 1988), pp. 25-31.

Sylvia Lizárraga's abiding concern with sociopolitical issues and the struggle for social change has been her major preoccupation as a creative writer, essayist, and teacher. Born in Mazatlán, Sinaloa, Mexico, Lizárraga is the daughter of Pedro M. and Carmen Sarmiento. A successful blacksmith in Mazatlán, Pedro Sarmiento be-

Sylvia S. Lizárraga (courtesy of the author)

lieved in the value of education and secured math and English tutors for his children. According to Lizárraga in an unpublished 1986 interview, the strong emphasis on education in her early childhood encouraged her to begin high school at the age of thirty-two.

In 1940, at the age of fifteen, Sylvia Sarmiento married Roberto Lizárraga, and their first two children, Alba and Bobby, were born before their move to San Diego, California, in 1946. Their two younger children, Marta and Esteban, were born in California. In 1957, when their youngest child started kindergarten, Lizárraga enrolled full-time at Midway High School for adults, beginning an uphill battle against her husband, family, and friends, who thought her desire "to go to school was definitely a sign of insanity." She completed high school in two years and graduated along with her oldest daughter. At the suggestion of one of her teach-

ers she applied to San Diego State University and entered in September 1959; but an automobile accident in November made it impossible for her to continue.

It was not until 1968, after Alba married, Bobby left for Vietnam, and Marta moved to her own apartment, that Sylvia Lizárraga, at the age of forty-three, returned to college. Her intense interest in all subjects prompted her to take every introductory course offered at Southwestern Junior College in Chula Vista, California, graduating in 1970 with highest honors and twice the required number of units. That summer she traveled throughout Europe and upon her return decided to continue her education. She completed a B.A. in Spanish at San Diego State University in 1972 and an M.A. and Ph.D. at the University of California, San Diego, in 1976 and 1979 respectively. She held a Ford Foundation Fellowship from 1973 to 1978 and has taught at the University of California, Berkeley, since 1979.

El otro lado

El deseo,
  Entrar, llegar, vivir.
La esperanza,
  Arriesgarse, trabajar, aprender.
El viaje,
  Peligros, sinsabores, Temores.
El encuentro,
Desconocimientos, dificultades, barreras.
La realidad,
  Miseria, discriminación, explotación.

Sylvia S. Lizárraga

Fair copy of a poem by Lizárraga (courtesy of the author)

One of Lizárraga's first published short stories, "De recuerdos" (From Memories), won first place in the 1972 San Diego State University Literary Contest. The story juxtaposes the playful world of children—in which a young brother insists that his sister be treated as an equal by the neighborhood boys—and the harshly realistic, although metaphorical, world of the town's madwoman who cannot understand the basis of inequalities.

While participating in the Chicano Literary Workshop at the University of California, San Diego, Lizárraga produced the majority of her seven short stories that appear in the anthology *Requisa treinta y dos* (Requisition of 1932, 1979). The underlying theme of the collection is life and the working conditions in the Southern California border region. Lizárraga focuses primarily, though not exclusively, on women in various social roles: mothers, adolescents, documented and undocumented workers, community organizers. The skillful narration of small, apparently insignificant, everyday occurrences in the lives of these characters reveals a complex yet subtle treatment of socioeconomic factors that affect their lives: physical and psychological abuse, social inequities, racial and sexual discrimination. Characteristic of Lizárraga's narrative is its attempt to draw a critical and analytical response from the reader, prompted by the juxtaposition of a character's perception of his or her situation to an omniscient narration exposing a multidimensional, objective reality which reveals the contradictions. Interior monologues and stream-of-consciousness techniques enable the characters to arrive at self-knowledge through an understanding of their circumstances.

For example, the protagonists of "Silver Lake Road" and "Management" are indigent single mothers who struggle daily to make ends meet. The pressing economic considerations of the single mother in "Silver Lake Road" provide the background to her rape by a young man she has compassionately given a lift to the border. Her economic straits and their alleviation pall next to the violence and helplessness she experiences as she is raped. In "Management" the protagonist reflects on the details of an interview for a job as a waitress at a prosperous Mexican restaurant owned by an assimilated Mexican and his Anglo wife. She realizes that dressing in a "Mexican costume" while enduring condescending attitudes and ill-treatment was too high a price to pay for the meager salary.

Some of the consequences of the socioeconomic and psychological problems confronted by adolescents are dealt with in Lizárraga's short stories "Coming Out," "Monarchy," and "The Moment." In "Coming Out" a dying fifteen-year-old orphan girl reveals in a stream of consciousness her innocent assessment of her adoptive mother and pimp boyfriend. The questions asked of her by a hospital employee as the girl is being admitted to the hospital trigger thoughts of a childhood of love with her parents but also of deprivation. "Monarchy" is an anecdote which, through irony and satire, comments on the inequities of social class and their perpetuation through seemingly insignificant extracurricular activities in school. The story reveals how these activities are devised to favor economically advantaged girls and to keep poorer girls distracted from their studies with a competition they will never win. "The Moment" describes the alienation suffered by a young student due to language barriers and lack of support from his teachers. As the story develops, the student reaches a level of consciousness which permits him to realize he is not entirely at fault for his lack of comprehension in the classroom.

"Doña Lola" reflects the active and dynamic role of an elderly woman in her community. Fed up with the substandard quality of food sold by a local merchant, Doña Lola organizes the neighborhood residents to stop buying from him.

In these short stories in *Requisa treinta y dos* Lizárraga's characters are not militant nor do they speak about massive social protest. Rather, by means of a strong narrative and deft portrayal of her characters, she exposes discrimination and its effects on them. She comments metaphorically on the effects of discrimination on the consciousness of those discriminated against in the widely published 1981 short story "Don." The story centers on a young girl's mysteriously acquired capacity to remain invisible before the world in spite of her attempts to have others acknowledge her presence. Perplexed by the fact that some people "genuinely" cannot see her, the anonymous narrator wonders how she could have inadvertently acquired this curious talent.

Lizárraga's most recent creative work includes two short stories, "¿Qué tenía que ver con ellos?" (What Did It Have to Do With Them?, 1987) and the unpublished "Unidos" (United), in which she experiments with narrative technique by taking on the forceful and critical tone characteristic of her essays. Those essays examine the limitations of various critical methods, especially when applied to Chicano literature ("Observaciones acerca de la crítica literaria chicana" [Observations Concerning Chicano Literary Criticism], 1982) and the portrayal of Chicanas in literature by Chicano male authors ("Images of Women in Chicano Literature by Men," 1985), among other topics. Her 1988 study, "Hacia una teoría para la liberación de la mujer" (Toward a Women's Liberation Theory), contributes to the developing dialogue of feminist theory which takes into account gender, class, and race.

Lizárraga's writings, creative and critical, depict an oppressed minority and argue for a reexamination of reality in order to change it. They challenge readers to rethink their perceptions and understanding of reality. Unfortunately, Lizárraga's work has received scant critical at-tention. But, as María Herrera-Sobek has noted in her essay-review of *Requisa treinta y dos*, Lizárraga's literary contributions stand out both for her excellent artistic elaboration as well as for the perspective she offers.

References:

María Herrera-Sobek, "Literatura y sociedad: la problemática del chicano/mexicano en los Estados Unidos a través de la obra literaria," *Bilingual Review*, 11 (September-December 1984): 83-87;

Rosaura Sánchez, "Chicana Prose Writers: the Case of Gina Valdés and Sylvia Lizárraga," in *Beyond Stereotypes: The Critical Analysis of Chicana Literature*, edited by María Herrera-Sobek (Binghamton: Bilingual/Editorial Bilingüe, 1985), pp. 60-70.

Max Martínez
(10 May 1943-   )

Patricia De La Fuente
Pan American University

BOOKS: *The Adventures of the Chicano Kid and Other Stories* (Houston: Arte Publico, 1982); *Schoolland* (Houston: Arte Publico, 1988).

PERIODICAL PUBLICATIONS: "The Necessity of Chicano Literary Critics," *Caracol*, 2 (May 1976): 18-19;
"Max Interviews Max: A Wild, Weird Thing. . . ," *Caracol*, 3 (November 1976): 4-5;
"Prolegomena for a Study of Chicano Literature," *De Colores*, 3, no. 4 (1977): 12-14;
Review of *Below the Summit*, by Joseph Torres-Metzgar, *Caracol*, 3 (April 1977): 20-22;
"Los Mejores Escritores de Aztlán," *Rayas*, 2 (March-April 1978): 3;
"Chicano Literature and the Critic," *Rayas*, 6 (November-December 1978): 8,10;
"Max-y-más," *Carta Abierta*, 13-14 (December 1978): 3;
"Max-y-más," *Carta Abierta*, 15 (Summer 1979): 8-9.

Max Martínez (courtesy of Arte Publico Press, Houston)

Max Martínez's short stories, which focus on those who exploit others, are often brutal yet just as often compassionate in their portrayals of human needs and failings. He does not subordinate his art to political ideology. His concern for style and structure, for the infinite shades of meaning in language, makes him a writer who looks for human beings beneath stereotypes. His protagonists are usually men and women who struggle to know themselves and to understand others in a vain and desperate attempt to survive with some dignity in an inhospitable, unjust world.

Maximiano Martínez was born in Gonzales, Texas. He has led a varied life which has included farm and ranch work while living with his uncle in Gonzales County and a period with the U.S. Navy. He attended St. Mary's University and East Texas State University, earning an M.A. from the latter in 1972. He taught creative writing at the University of Houston from 1977 to 1982.

Martínez's most famous story, although perhaps not his best, is the novelette *Faustino*, first published by *Caracol* as a special issue in January 1977, and later included in his collection *The Adventures of the Chicano Kid and Other Stories* (1982). *Faustino* is notorious for its raw, almost oppressively explicit sexual descriptions, the violence of which is perhaps justified as a metaphor for the main theme of physical and psychological exploitation. The central character is Faustino, a simple, almost primeval figure of a man whose distorted relationships with his Anglo boss, Buster Crane, with young Mrs. Crane, and with his own wife María are explored in excruciatingly vivid detail. Racial tension is implicit in the setting, a South Texas ranch owned by Anglos who exploit Faustino's natural attachment to the land where he was born. This obvious Anglo-versus-Chicano theme is complicated by sexual conflicts in the development of relationships between Buster and Mrs. Crane and Faustino and María. Faustino's manhood is inextricably tied to his sexual prowess. Unable to respond emotionally to a crudely blatant seduction attempt by the voracious, sex-starved Mrs. Crane, he rushes home to have intercourse with his wife, fully expecting in this way to bolster his faltering self-image. Impotence with María so threatens the only dignity and pride Faustino possesses that he rapes and beats her. The ambiguities in the situation are richly suggestive. At first glance the impotent Anglo rancher and his sexually aggressive wife compare unfavorably to the virile Faustino and the sensitive María. The aborted encounter with Mrs. Crane, in which Faustino becomes a surrogate for the impotent rancher, is a victory for Faustino against the attempted exploitation of his body by the aggressive Mrs. Crane. On another level, his impotence is a loss of face for him; if he had been confident about anything, it was his sexual prowess. With the rape and beating, the central theme of exploitation assumes an added dimension of perversity which extends beyond superficial racial stereotype.

The theme of aggressive users who impose their values and standards on others is one of the basic concerns in Martínez's fiction. In "Doctor Castillo" and "Portal," for example, marital exploitation is a central issue. The wealthy Doctor Castillo, secure in his male role of provider, condescendingly thinks of his wife as oversexed, "reading entirely too many grocery store magazines which contained the latest information on sexual responses and techniques." He is unable to recognize his wife's need to live her life as something other than an appendage to his. The destruction of their bedroom during a hurricane signals the end of their mechanical relationship. When Susan Castillo disappears, her husband's search for her is perfunctory, and he soon falls back into his dull, orderly routine. The central concern of emotional and sexual exploitation is fully explored in their confrontation ten years later, at which time Castillo's lack of self-awareness, his smug arrogance, his sexual exploitation of his secretary, and his inability to think of anything but his own ordered existence are contrasted with Susan Castillo's new life as a real woman rather than the failed ideal wife Castillo had created to fulfill his preconceived notions. In "Portal" Martínez's treatment of the theme of marital exploitation is less elaborately philosophical and more compassionate, perhaps because of his choice of a less conspicuously biased central character. The observer of disharmony between Marta and Eduardo Macías is Jerónimo Portal

Cover of Martínez's 1982 collection, which includes stories originally published in Caracol *and* Revista Chicano-Riqueña

(Eduardo's father-in-law), through whose perceptive and sensitive consciousness the process of Eduardo's struggle to survive with dignity and his ultimate suicide are filtered and evaluated. Portal's daughter, Marta, becomes the predator–a female counterpart of Doctor Castillo–who victimizes her husband in trying to force him to live up to her standards: "she's always been very good about convincing [Eduardo] that what she wants [he] wants."

The collection's most dramatic example of the tragedy that an aggressive breach of respect can unleash occurs in "Doña Petra." The story is a familiar one–a young Chicano is shot by Texas Rangers in a careless show of authority. Doña Petra's life is filled with humility and gentle love for her only son. She finds the strength to confront his murderer, and in the final scene of the story, shocking in its stark and ugly racism, she reveals dignity and determination in killing him.

Two stories in *The Adventures of the Chicano Kid* are Western stories with Chicano heroes. The title story, subtitled "A Dime Novel," is a parody of an Old West saloon shoot-out, told with wit and humor and sprinkled with liberal comments and exhortations to "Dear Reader." The story follows the traditional, racist Western theme of the straight-shooting hero and the "greasy Meskin" villain except that the roles are reversed and thus ridiculed. The hero is the Chicano Kid, a "true, stout-hearted knight of the desert" who "has journeyed far and wide rooting out the evil lurking in the hearts of men." The villain is an Anglo with the improbable name of Alf Brisket, "the scurrilous scourge of the Southwest." The story "La Tacuachera," describes the events leading up to a confrontation between a Chicano hero, Chango, and an Anglo bully, Ambrose Tench, in a local bar. The abyss separating their two cultures is established in the name of the bar, which is known by the Anglos as Pleasant Hill Tavern. The Chicanos, however, "mindful of some legendary or mythical occurrence . . . referred to it as La Tacuachera." Martínez examines the interaction between the two cultures and the gradually changing patterns of discrimination as evidenced in the progressive encroachment by Chicanos into a traditionally Anglo stronghold. In the shared family environment of the tavern social rituals of discrimination are rigidly observed; even the rare fights adhere strictly to the segregated seating arrangements. Martínez deftly conveys the reality and irrationality of the ingrained, unspoken laws which erect invisible barriers between human beings. "La Tacuachera" is the story of one small yet significant breach in that invisible wall. The confrontation between Chango and Ambrose Tench effectively dissipates some of the misconceptions. The story does not end with a regular shoot-out. Chango uses laughter instead of violence, and his victory involves a psychological blow against discrimination. In 1988 Martínez produced a novel, *Schoolland*, about a Mexican-American family living in Texas during the 1950s.

Although his creative work has generated little criticism, Martínez is widely known for his uncompromising stance on the nature and quality of Chicano literature. In his review of *Below the Summit* (1976), a novel by Joseph Torres-Metzgar, published in the April 1977 issue of *Caracol*, he says that the work "is not properly a Chicano novel because it is anti-Chicano in perspective, in

Cover for Martínez's 1988 novel, which examines the life of a Mexican-American family in Texas during the 1950s

execution, and in intention." Although he elaborates on the defects of the novel, Martínez's notion of an anti-Chicano perspective and his insistence on the required presence of "chicanismo" to justify the label of Chicano literature suggest arbitrary limitation. More balanced is his claim that "much of Chicano literature is unartistic in terms of aesthetics." In an article in *De Colores* (1977), "Prolegomena for a Study of Chicano Literature," he calls for works that "display a sensitivity, a technical mastery, a universality, which deserve consideration as the output of a specific culture, but which . . . [make] significant statements . . . extending far beyond the barrio." His article "Chicano Literature and the Critic" (*Rayas*, November-December 1978) chastises Chicano authors for their lack of education and for attempting to isolate themselves from the Western cultural tradition to which they belong. "This cultural elitism," he claims, "is nothing more than pure . . . laziness." He also points out that in avoiding so-called contamination with gringo thought, Chicano critics have cut themselves off from a rich European source of critical theory which could well be adapted to analyze and explicate Chicano writings.

Reference:
Evangelina Vigil, Introduction to Martínez's *Faustino, Caracol*, 3 (January 1977): 3.

Miguel Méndez M.
(15 June 1930-   )

Salvador Rodriguez del Pino
University of Colorado at Boulder

BOOKS: *Peregrinos de Aztlán* (Tucson: Editorial Peregrinos, 1974);

Los criaderos humanos y Sahuaros (Tucson: Editorial Peregrinos, 1975);

Cuentos para niños traviesos: Stories for Mischievous Children, bilingual edition, with translations by Eva Price (Berkeley: Justa, 1979);

Tata Casehua y otros cuentos, bilingual edition, with translations by Price, Leo Barrow, and Marco Portales (Berkeley: Justa, 1980);

De la vida y del folclore de la frontera (Tucson: Mexican American Studies and Research Center, University of Arizona, 1986);

El sueño de Santa María de las Piedras (Guadalajara, Mexico: Universidad de Guadalajara, 1986);

Cuentos y ensayos para reír y aprender (Tucson: Miguel Méndez M., 1988).

OTHER: "Taller de imágenes: pase," "Workshop for Images: Come In," "Tragedias del noroeste: Tata Casehua," "Tragedies of the Northwest: Tata Casehua," in *El Espejo/The Mirror*, edited by Octavio I. Romano and Herminio Riós-C. (Berkeley: Quinto Sol, 1969), pp. 30-74.

PERIODICAL PUBLICATIONS: *Génesis de la palabra, La Palabra*, 1 (Spring 1979): 1-2;

"Little Frankie" and "Lluvia," *Revista Chicano-Riqueña*, 2, no. 2 (1974): 8-11;

"Mr. Laly," *La Palabra*, 1 (Autumn 1979): 38-43;

"Luna," "El hombre pequeño," "No," "El hombre más feo del mundo," "Huachusey," "El tío Mariano," and "Muerte y nacimiento de Manuel Amarillos," *La Palabra*, 3 (Spring-Fall 1981): 87-120.

Chicano literature has in Miguel Méndez M. one of its finest and most sensitive writers. His prose, rich in imagery, is a challenge to readers because he demands literary awareness and erudition. The fact that much of his work is only available in Spanish and is difficult to translate makes him virtually unknown to English-speaking readers. His first novel, *Peregrinos de Aztlán* (Pilgrims of Aztlán, 1974), has yet to be translated into English.

In 1969 two of his short stories, "Tata Casehua" and "Taller de imágenes" (Shop of Images), were collected in *El Espejo/The Mirror*, an anthology of Chicano literature. These short stories, written in poetic prose by a bricklayer with only a sixth-grade education, left a profound impression on readers and critics.

Méndez was born in Bisbee, Arizona, scarcely five miles from Mexico, on 15 June 1930. Five months after his birth, because of the Great Depression and Mexican repatriation, the Méndez family moved to El Claro, an *ejido* (government-owned farming community), in Sonora, Mexico. El Claro formed part of a conglomeration of communities in which the total population barely reached one thousand. His father, Francisco Méndez Cárdenas, who had gone to Arizona as a miner, found it difficult, with his wife and five children, to return to farm work. In a 1976 videotaped interview at the University of California in Santa Barbara, Méndez said that he was taught to read by his mother, Maria Morales,

Miguel Méndez M. (courtesy of the author)

who grew tired of his continuous insistence that she read to him. The local elementary school and its teachers were "just as poor and needy as the community we lived in," recalled Méndez, "but the teachers were so dedicated and human that I owe them the strong sense of responsibility they ingrained in me. They would hide their hunger behind their books." From his parents, Méndez inherited the blood and traditions of the Yaquis, an ancient and proud people from the desert of Sonora who were not brought under Mexican domination until the beginning of the twentieth century. The stories and traditions of his parents fascinated him. The years that Méndez lived in El Claro served as an introduction to the mysterious voices of the desert and the Yaquis.

At the age of fifteen Méndez left his family to look for work and adventure along the Arizona-Sonora border. He worked as a hired hand picking fruit and vegetables. It was during this time that he began to meet the different kinds of people that he later portrayed in his stories, such as prostitutes, indigent workers who had no papers, car washers, and people with "illusions of work

and food to be found in the land of the dollar," as he said in the videotape interview. Méndez believes that the region along the United States-Mexico border is different from the countries it divides, and his fiction is often set in the border area.

Méndez finally settled in Tucson, Arizona, in April 1946 where he became a bricklayer. It was during this time in Tucson that he began to write seriously. In spite of the hardships of construction work in 115-degree weather, he wrote after work until well into the morning. He completed his first novel when he was eighteen years old. For fifteen years Méndez wrote stories that were not published, yet he kept writing. During the 1960s the Chicano Movement came to Tucson. Méndez found that much of what he had been writing was consistent with the movement's goals and ideology. Méndez sent "Tata Casehua" to *El Grito*, one of the magazines that flourished during the Chicano literary renaissance of the 1960s; the story was published in 1968.

"Tata Casehua" (later collected in *Tata Casehua y otros cuentos* [Tata Casehua and Other Stories, 1980]), an allegorical tale of the plight of the Yaqui Indians of Northwest Mexico, is Méndez's most successful and popular short story. Juan Manuel Casehua, an old Yaqui warrior, whose real name is Tetabiate, wanders among the dunes of the Sonoran desert searching for an heir to whom he can transmit the history and traditions of his tribe, a group dispersed by the arrival of the *yory* (a Yaqui term for the white man). He loves the desert, which he views as "forever pregnant but never giving birth." José Manuel Casehua, the first heir chosen by Juan Manuel Casehua, is drowned during the initiation rites; the new heir, Jesús Manuel Casehua, survives the ritual, winning the right to be the transmitter of his people's history and traditions. "Tata Casehua" is a social indictment of the yory for destroying a way of life and converting its humiliated survivors into marginal misfits left to wander in the land that once was theirs.

As his literary reputation grew, Méndez was invited to lecture in universities and in literary organizations. A mature and humble man, he was unaccustomed to celebrity. His life as a construction worker and fruit picker had not trained him to be a public speaker, but he spoke well. His mastery of language, he said, was the fruit of long hours of writing in solitude by candlelight. In 1976 he described his writing habits: "Hace mucho tiempo que escribo. Fue una necesidad

NOVELA

Peregrinos de Aztlán
LITERATURA CHICANA
MIGUEL MENDEZ M.

Cover for Méndez M.'s 1974 novel, narrated by Loreto Maldonado, an old indigent who washes tourists' cars in the streets of Tijuana

grande, pero con las reservas de autodidacta traté de conquistar un lenguaje. Posiblemente me falta mucho camino para dominarlo en su amplitud necesaria para crear literatura. Sin embargo, he escrito porque me apasiona la literatura y después que he escrito, examino mis escritos para ver qué contienen y veo que lógicamente viene de lo social. Claro, puesto que yo he pasado trabajando muchos años en las zonas agrícolas y en la construcción. . . . En cuanto a la inquietud artística, está latente en cualesquier parte en donde haya un núcleo humano que sufre y que tiene necesidad de expresar su historia. La técnica no se la he pedido prestada a nadie. Como autodidacta he hecho lo que he podido, y así, tengo inquietudes estéticas igual que muchos autores" (I've been writing for a long time. It was a great need, but with the restrictions of being a self-taught man, I tried to conquer a language. It is possible that I have a long way to go before I master the language well enough to create literature. Neverthe-

less, I write because literature is a passion with me. After I have written, I examine my writings to find out what they contain and I see that, logically, they spring forth from a social context. Of course, this is true, because I've been working for many years in farming areas and in construction. . . . As for artistic aspirations, I think they are latent wherever there are human beings who suffer and have the need to express their history. I have not borrowed my technique from anyone. As a self-taught man, I've done what I could, and I have artistic aspirations just like other authors).

The literary interest awakened by his stories gave Méndez the evidence he was waiting for that his stories of the oppressed had found an audience. He continued working in construction until 1970, when he was offered a job at Pima College in Pima, Arizona. He has taught Hispanic literature there since then; he has also taught at the University of Arizona in Tucson.

In Méndez's novel *Peregrinos de Aztlán* the main characters are poor people whose lives are manipulated by the rich and unscrupulous. The novel is an intricate mosaic of fragmented stories emanating from the feverish memory of Loreto Maldonado, an old and indigent car-washer in the streets of Tijuana. A once-proud revolutionary who rode with Pancho Villa, Maldonado wanders through the city wringing out a meager existence washing the cars of tourists. He recollects the stories of the people with whom he comes into contact: prostitutes, drug addicts, white-slavers, poets, hippies, politicians–all victims of a sordid and perverse socioeconomic order. The two-thousand mile border between the United States and Mexico is represented as a war zone separating two cultures and two economic systems.

In the preface to *Peregrinos de Aztlán* Méndez discusses his purpose for writing and his use of language: "De estos antiguos dominios de mis abuelos indios escribo esta humildísima obra, reafirmando la gran fe que profeso a mi pueblo chicano, explotado por la perversidad humana" (From these ancient lands of my Indian ancestors I write this very humble work, reaffirming the deep faith that I have in my Chicano people exploited by human perversity). He warns that the language of his novel might be offensive to some, but that he had no choice, to paraphrase his Spanish, because the language of the oppressed was the faithful expression of a living language.

The text of *Peregrinos de Aztlán* is divided into three parts. In the first part all the characters are introduced through the main character, Maldonado. The second part elaborates and develops some of the characters, providing details about their tragic lives, which are products of social injustice. Revolution and war is the setting of the third part, in which the lives of the characters Cuamea and Frankie are paralleled within a context of personal and psychological struggle. The theme of the novel is articulated by Colonel Cuamea, who observes that even in Mexico, where most of the population are Mestizos, "estaban sentenciados por nacencia, no por el agravio de ser revoltosos; el ser indio significaba el olvido, el oprobio, el desprecio, la inicua sentencia de las más vil de las miserias, y el afrentoso desdén hacia sus pieles prietas" (they were sentenced by birth, not by being renegades but by being Indian, which signifies oblivion, opprobium, scorn, the unequal sentence of the worst miseries, and the blatant disdain for their dark skin).

Peregrinos de Aztlán is a hopeful book which sees reaffirmation of man through honor and honesty, an end served through confronting evil: "!Miente! No hay poesías ni poetas, todo es una mascarada para no ver la tragedia humana; sólo los holgazanes que ignoran el dolor y el crimen, le cantan a las flores" (Lies! There is no poetry nor poets, everything is a masquerade that prevents looking into human tragedy; only the good-for-nothings, who ignore pain and crime, sing to the flowers).

On its publication in spring 1974, *Peregrinos de Aztlán* was admiringly reviewed. Evodio Escalante, one of Mexico's leading literary critics, compared *Peregrinos de Aztlán* to *La región más transparente* (1958) by Carlos Fuentes and said that Mendez's novel is to Chicano literature what Mariano Azuela's *Los de abajo* (1927) is to the Mexican Revolution.

Méndez's epic poem, *Los criaderos humanos y Sahuaros* (The Human Breeding Grounds and Saguaros), was published in 1975. The subject of the two-part poem is *los humillados* (the humiliated ones), the people of the desert who are mocked and despised, those people dominated by the white race. In the first part of the poem, set in the mythic homeland of Aztlán, "Los criaderos humanos" (The Human Breeding Grounds), the narrator takes readers on a journey in which he finds his origins in a long-exploited people. Allegorically, Méndez introduces three groups of exploiters of these people: men of crystal, plunderers, and stingers:

"!Ay señor!
Los más grandes explotadores de criaderos
humanos
son los hombres de Cristal
Los Rapiña de muchos pueblos
son tributarios de los de Cristal . . .
. . . Los Aguijón
con garras
dientes
puñales y rifles
desollaban la carne de los rebeldes
que osaban levantar los puños cerrados

(Alas, Gentleman!
The greatest exploiters of these
human breeding grounds
are the Men of Crystal
The Plunderers from many nations
are vassals of the Men of Crystal . . .
. . . The Stingers with claws teeth
daggers and rifles
peeled the flesh off the rebels
who dared lift their fists).

Within a tragic and bleak scenario lie the human breeding grounds surrounded by a crystal wall, where there is no hope of escape and where the visions of prosperity beyond the wall are unattainable.

In the second part of the poem, "Sahuaros" (Saguaros), "el peregrino" (the pilgrim), who wanders for eternity, takes readers into the mythical Aztlán where redemption will take place and where the desert's people, the sons of Tonatiuh (The Sun), "nadando contra la corriente" (swimming against the current), will return ragged, tired of fighting, and bring forth the rebirth of the desert: "Esta tierra/este paisaje/todo es Aztlán/con el alma universal del indio" (This land/this view/everything is Aztlán/with the universal soul of the Indian). The *Sahuaros*, desert cacti resembling human figures which are compared to the original inhabitants, are the guardians of the sacred land where the renaissance of Aztlán will take place. In an interview published in *La Palabra* (Spring-Fall 1981), Méndez concedes that of all his books, *Los criaderos humanos y Sahuaros* has received the least attention from critics. It is his favorite book–the one to which he dedicated the most work and the longest hours. He is sure that one day it will be deemed his best work. He says it has been reviewed and studied in Peru and Italy, where it is being translated by Franca Bacchiega.

In Méndez's first short-story collection, *Cuentos para niños traviesos: Stories for Mischievous Children* (1979), he departs from his usual theme of oppression to draw from the rich oral history of the Hispanic tradition. The stories and fables of the *Libro de Calila y Dimna*, Spanish-language tales translated from the Arabic in 1251 by order of King Alfonso X of Castile, serve as the model for Méndez, who transcribes six of the stories to the American-Hispanic Southwest, thus linking them with the Chicano oral tradition.

Some of the fables in the original collection are narrated by animals, but in others the narrators are human. Méndez reminds readers in his prologue that the stories from the *Calila y Dimna* were inherited through the Hispanic oral tradition, and it is his intention to share them with the English-speaking world since Anglo-American culture is one of the pillars that sustains Mexican-Americans.

Méndez skillfully adapts the ancient tales and fables to a Chicano frame of reference. Ubiquitous symbols of Chicano folklore like tequila, mariachis, and the religious symbol of the Virgin of Guadalupe enrich the stories, transforming and placing them inside a predominant southwestern ambience. He uses the regional Spanish dialect of the Southwest. The original characters become familiar figures like the cowboy, the illegal alien, and rich Anglos. Even the Castilian flora and fauna are transformed into saguaros, mesquites, coyotes, and roadrunners. Méndez transforms the old Medieval tales into modern anecdotes more meaningful to the contemporary reader than the original ones. For example, in the tale of a holy man the story is placed in Arizona where the local priest, Nazario, is given some rich garments by the governor to replace his old and tattered robes. Sangaruto, the local tailor, learns of the fabulous gift and immediately runs to the church to pray to Saint Dimas (patron saint of thieves) to find a way of talking Nazario out of his gift. Nazario soon places Sangaruto under his protection as a sexton. Then the priest has to go to Tucson, "a place walled in by giant saguaros and cursed with a climate so hot that it forced its inhabitants to sin." During his absence, Sangaruto steals the clothes and runs away to Yuma, a place so hot that it functions as a branch of hell. Nazario follows Sangaruto, not to catch him, but to save his soul. During his quest for the sexton the priest witnesses many strange happenings. He sees a fight in the desert between two mountain goats with

CUENTOS
PARA NIÑOS TRAVIESOS

Miguel Méndez-M.

EDITORIAL JUSTA

Cover for Méndez M.'s first volume of stories, several of which are modeled on fables from the medieval Spanish collection Libro de Calila y Dimna

massive horns who bleed so much in their encounter that a destitute and hungry fox, attracted by the blood, tries to lick some of it and ends up flattened by the gigantic horns of the goats. Arriving in Yuma the sexton settles in a hotel where an old hag sells her daughter as a prostitute. The daughter has a lover who has taken over her earnings and some of her mother's money. The old hag plans to murder the lovers by making them drunk with tequila and, while they are asleep, placing a reed in their nostrils to insert poison. Her plan backfires when she places the reed in the nose of the young man, tickling him and causing him to sneeze so hard that he reverses the poison into her mouth. The old hag dies with curses and fits unbeknownst to the drunken couple. The priest witnesses the attempted murder in surprise and disbelief. The story concludes with the priest in court condemning not the crimes but the follies of imprudence. Méndez elaborates and enriches the original tale into a modern satire and protest against social injustice. The stories in *Cuentos para niños traviesos* not based on *Calila y Dimna* are traditional folk tales from the Southwest retold with contemporary imagery and up-to-date characters such as hippies, drug addicts, and rock-and-roll figures. Respecting the form of the ancient tales and modernizing the oral tradition, Méndez brings forth a contemporary piece of story telling so that the traditional moral message is revived.

Méndez's next collection of short stories, *Tata Casehua y otros cuentos*, is composed of nine stories published in a bilingual format. The stories have no apparent central theme. One of the best in the collection is "Esteelio," a metaphorical character study of modern man alienated in a material society. Esteelio is the unwanted son of a couple of television watchers who conceive him after watching an erotic movie. After various attempts at abortion, the mother decides to let Esteelio live. After he is born, he is ignored by his parents, who watch television. Esteelio grows up without any love whatsoever, surrounded by cheap toys and learning about life through television commercials. His parents die while he is in his teens, and he inherits their insurance money. Esteelio becomes a successful salesman of birth-control pills and marries a beautiful woman who soon divorces him because of his habit of watching television instead of making love to her. He takes a mistress but his affair also fails, after which he joins the army and leaves for Vietnam where he views the reality of war through his television experiences. When the war is over he comes back to an alienated world of loneliness hoping to regain his divorced wife and start his life anew. Esteelio's appearance is appalling: long stringy hair, unkempt clothes, and a look of desperation. He goes to spy on his former wife and witnesses a sexual encounter through an open window. Realizing that she has found someone else whom she loves, Esteelio crushes a pet frog which he constantly carries in his pocket, and his complete deterioration occurs. He is transformed into a catlike figure dashing and darting among the city's cars. He roams the city in complete disregard for his looks. He becomes like a beast unable to live in a civilization and a reality for which television has not prepared him. Méndez leaves no hope for people like Esteelio. He indicts society for producing consumer addicts who have lost touch with human values.

Five of Méndez's short stories and two of his poems were published in an issue of *La Palabra* (Spring-Fall 1981) dedicated to him. The issue also includes critical articles on his work and an interview with Méndez by Justo Alarcón, the editor of *La Palabra*.

In May 1984 the University of Arizona conferred on Méndez the honorary degree of doctor of humanity, an honor that was supported by Camilo José Cela, the well-known Spanish novelist. He has recently published three new books. The first, *De la vida y del folclore de la frontera* (From Life and Folklore Along the Border), was published in 1986. It is a collection of short stories, some previously published in journals, such as "Ambrosio Ceniza" and "Mr. Laly," as well as new character studies such as "El güero Paparruchas" and "Los viejos mexicanos de los Estados Unidos" (Old Mexican Men from the United States). In the latter story Méndez introduces readers to old men who meet in the town square to recollect stories and remember characters who have shaped the history of Santa María de las Piedras, a town that gossip and hearsay declare lies near the border in the desert of Sonora but which does not appear on any map. The old men figure prominently in Méndez's novel *El sueño de Santa María de las Piedras* (The Dream of Santa María of the Stones, 1986) which was published in Mexico. The story of Santa María is told by the old men of the town who bicker among themselves. Their recollections of the town's history are shaky, but they reinforce themselves by throwing barbs at each other, touching on their physical infirmities or personal indiscretions. The old men become unforgettable as the town comes alive in fantasy and memory. *El sueño de Santa María de las Piedras* has not yet received much critical attention in the United States. It has been reviewed in Mexico and by friends of Méndez who have read the novel and comment on it through personal correspondence. A review by María Luisa Puga that appeared in a regional magazine, *Provincia y Metrópoli* (Pátzcuaro, Mexico, 1988) compares the novel to Gabriel García Márquez's *Cien años de soledad* (1967). In an unpublished letter written to Méndez, Cela said of the novel "muy hermosa y refleja con muy eficaz maestría ese mundo apasionante" (It is very beautiful and reflects that exciting world with mastery).

Cuentos y ensayos para reír y aprender (Stories and Essays for Laughing and Learning, 1988) is a Spanish reading textbook for Hispanic children in the Southwest. It includes Méndez's favorite

JUANROBADO

Entre aquel mar de naranjas se mueven más de cien mexicanos . Debajo de los
árboles improvisan viviendas . Acondicionan cajas de madera para guarecerse de
la intemperie . Cuando llueve se resguardan como ratas . Trabajan a sus cuerpos
como si se tratara de máquinas ajenas , hasta dejarlos como vil bagazo . Para
contentar al perro que los vigila y merecer así los billetes que les otorga el
gringo . Lana que no hallan en su misma patria por causas que hasta los gatos sa-
ben . Es leyenda que allí han muerto mojados extenuados por la labor, incruenta
el asedio ponzoñoso del sol que recuece hasta los tuétanos . También se dice
sin que se sepa a ciencia cierta , que entre esos zurcos , bajo las arboledas ,
han parido a sus escuincles algunas mujeres que siguen a sus hombres como soldada-
deras .

Cuando está en fruto el naranjal , saturado de múltiples esferas doradas , se
ve desde arriba como un mar de oro burbujeante , o quizá como una noche muy verde
plagada de estrellas anaranjadas .

Desde hace cosa de un mes que Juanrobado pizca naranjas . Sus brazos huesudos se
mueven certeros.¡Órale naranjas sanjas , acá mangas y remangas ! Se suceden las cajas llenas de jugosos cítricos .Allá andan la bola de mojarrines encaramados en es-
caleras .Se retuercen y se estiran como changos. ¡ Pícale Juanrobado ! ¡Malditos ces-
tos dijo el de los canastos !

Acá en la Finiquera se siente el calorcito , pa que lo sepas , si se te duerme
la paloma te vuelves empanada , camarada , desde que amanece te pega el sol con el
puño cerrado . Lo ves y no tienes otra más que echarle de la madre. Tú que le en-
tras al jale y el sudor que te chorrea y entonces sí es una sola exprimidera de la
retostada . ¿ La migra ? ¡ Nombre ! aquí te hace los mandados y se come los pilones.
Dicen que todo esto es del hermano de un coyote grande con dientes de lobo y cola
de perro .

Juanrobado no tiene pelos en la cara como buen indio , es de natural prieto ,
requemado además por la tatema , más flaco que una bicicleta , por eso tiene aires
de chamaco , pero ya le peina los treinta . Sobre su gran tristeza le hormiguea siempre una sonrisa . Sus compañeros le hacen bromas , a veces se pasan de la raya , pero
él sonríe de continuo. ¡Órale ! Juanrobado , ya sé cómo vinites . Como el peso anda
flotando y no vale una tiznada de tan liviano , pos ticites una alfombra de billetes

Page from the revised typescript for "Juanrobado" (courtesy of the author)

stories from his previous collections plus essays intended to interest school children in literature and language. He had been asked repeatedly by educators to edit a book of his favorite stories that could be used as a textbook to teach language. In a different format from his previous collection of short stories, *Cuentos y ensayos* is completely in Spanish with no English translations.

Interview:

Justo Alarcón, Interview with Méndez, *La Palabra,* 3 (Spring-Fall 1981): 3-17.

References:

Miriam Bornstein, "*Peregrinos de Aztlán*: Dialéctica estructural e ideológica," *Cuadernos Americanos,* 39 (July-August 1980): 23-33;

Aresteo Brito, "El lenguaje tropológico en *Peregrinos de Aztlán,*" *La Luz,* 4 (May 1975): 42-43;

Juan Bruce-Novoa, "Miguel Méndez M.," in *Chicano Authors: Inquiry by Interview* (Austin: University of Texas Press, 1980), pp. 83-93;

Bruce-Novoa, "La voz del silencio: Miguel Méndez," *Diálogos,* 13 (May-June 1976): 27-30; translated as "Miguel Méndez: Voices of Silence," *De Colores,* 3, no. 4 (1977): 63-69;

Evodio Escalante, "La obra fundamental de Miguel Méndez," *Sábado* (Mexico City), 23 January 1988;

Lauro Flores and Mark McCaffrey, "Miguel Méndez: El Subjetivismo frente a la historia," *De Colores,* 3, no. 4 (1977): 46-57;

Elaine D. Johnson, "El papel de la naturaleza en *Peregrinos de Aztlán,*" *La Palabra,* 3 (Spring-Fall 1981): 50-57;

Luis Leal, " 'Tata Casehua' o la deseperanza," *Revista Chicano-Riqueña,* 2 (Spring 1974): 50-52;

Leal, "Méndez y el Calila y Dimna," *La Palabra,* 3 (Spring-Fall 1981): 67-76;

Marvin Lewis, "*Peregrinos de Aztlán* and the Emergence of the Chicano Novel," in *Selected Proceedings of the Third Annual Conference on Minority Studies,* edited by George R. Carter and James R. Parker (La Crosse, Wis.: Institute for Minority Studies, 1976), pp. 143-157;

Mariana Marín, "*Pocho y Peregrinos de Aztlán:* Contradicciones textuales e ideologia," *Revista Chicano-Riqueña,* 6 (Autumn 1978): 59-62;

María Luisa Puga, "*El sueño de Santa Maria de las Piedras,* de Miguel Méndez," *Provincia y Metrópoli* (Pátzcuaro, Mexico), March 1988;

Roberto R. Quiroz, "The Images of Miguel Méndez M.," *Raza Art & Media Collective Journal* (University of Michigan, Ann Arbor), 1 (1 March 1976): 1-2;

Salvador Rodriguez del Pino, "Miguel Méndez y el compromiso con el pueblo," in his *La novela chicana escrita en español: cinco autores comprometidos* (Ypsilanti: Bilingual/Editorial Bilingüe, 1982), pp. 37-63;

Rodriguez del Pino, *Interview with Miguel Méndez M.* (Center for Chicano Studies, University of California, Santa Barbara, 1976);

Gustavo V. Segade, "*Peregrinos de Aztlán:* Viaje y Laberinto," *De Colores,* 3, no. 4 (1977): 58-62.

Cherríe Moraga
(25 September 1952-)

Yvonne Yarbro-Bejarano
University of Washington

BOOKS: *Loving in the War Years: (lo que nunca pasó por sus labios)* (Boston: South End, 1983);
Giving up the Ghost: Teatro in Two Acts (Los Angeles: West End, 1986).

PLAY PRODUCTION: *Giving Up the Ghost*, Seattle, Front Room Theater, 27 March 1987.

OTHER: *This Bridge Called My Back: Writings by Radical Women of Color*, edited by Moraga and Gloria Anzaldúa, with a preface by Moraga (Watertown, Mass.: Persephone, 1981);
Cuentos: Stories by Latinas, edited by Moraga, Alma Gómez, and Mariana Romo-Carmona (New York: Kitchen Table/Women of Color, 1983).

Cherríe Moraga's work as poet, essayist, editor, storyteller, and playwright is considered courageous and polemical in both Chicano and feminist communities. Speaking from her commitment and experiences as a Chicana feminist lesbian, she has broken the silence surrounding taboo topics such as sexuality and lesbianism; sexism and homophobia in Chicano culture; racism and classism in the white women's movement; and the urgent need for a feminism of color, not just in theory, but in a practice leading to real social change. In all her writing, and particularly in her poetry, Moraga is committed to the search for an original voice, one that does not imitate white literary norms, but empowers the disenfranchised. Her essays stretch the boundaries of the conventional form, combining the poetic and the expository, the subjective and the objective, intellectual analysis and visceral knowledge. Her effort to think out what it means to be Chicana and lesbian in essays that are collages of dreams, journal entries, and autobiographical reflection represents an important foundation on which to continue to build a Latina feminist theory.

By coming out as a lesbian in print, by writing poetry that springs from and gives imaginative expression to lesbian experience, by putting

Cherríe Moraga (courtesy of the author)

the Chicana lesbian onstage for the first time in the history of the Chicano theater movement, by calling for a Chicana feminism that includes commitment to Chicana lesbians, Moraga has given voice and visibility in Chicano writing to those who have been silenced. For many Chicana lesbian activists her writing and editorial work have broken the taboo about raising their own issues within the community.

Born in Whittier, California, Moraga is the daughter of a Chicana, Elvira Moraga, and an Anglo, Joseph Lawrence. Elvira Moraga was born in Santa Paula, California, in 1914, and has lived primarily in California, though she resided for a time in Arizona and Tijuana. Her parents were from Sonora, Mexico. Joseph Lawrence was born in San Francisco in 1926, the son of a Canadian father and a mother from Missouri. During Moraga's early years her family changed residences frequently, but when she was nine, the family moved to the San Gabriel Valley and still lives in the town of San Gabriel.

In the Los Angeles area Moraga grew up in the environment of her mother's family. A poor reader as a child, she affirms that her appreciation of language has always been "through her ears," and that the hours spent at the kitchen table listening to the women of her extended family tell stories had a profound influence on her. It was this oral tradition that instilled in her her love of words, the art of telling a story with an eye to details, and her sense of the blend of Spanish and English. This is a well she still draws from, especially in her dramatic work.

Moraga, her sister, and her brother were the first in the family to earn college degrees. She completed undergraduate studies at a small private school in Hollywood. Attending this nonsectarian, progressive college was influential in Moraga's development because it was there that she was first exposed to the "mysterious alchemy" of art, as she said in an unpublished 1988 interview. Although she took some writing classes it was primarily the experience of being around people dedicated to making art that agitated her, intimidated her, and attracted her at the same time. She ignored her fascination with art for a while, determined to accomplish her practical goal of finishing college and getting a good job as a teacher as was expected of her.

After receiving her B.A. in English in 1974 Moraga taught English at a private high school in Los Angeles for two years. During this time she enrolled in a writing class through the Women's Building in Los Angeles, and for the first time she became excited about her writing. This change she attributes to having simultaneously come out as a lesbian, revealing from the beginning the intimate mesh between her sexuality and her writing. The difference between what she was now writing and the stories she had produced during college while she was still "writing with secrets" was dramatic. As she sees it, "something opened up" when she stopped lying to herself. Her first poems were lesbian love poems and were characterized by openness.

Ironically, in the flush of her self-discovery as lesbian and poet, in her writing group she came up hard against attitudes and values concerning voice and sexuality that she has wrestled with ever since. She was told that her vocabulary was too small, that she needed to read more. This discouraged her, especially since by the standards of her social and cultural context someone with a B.A. was considered very well educated. Years later she would realize that for her, "good" writing did not mean a bigger or more "literate" vocabulary, but "having your ear finely tuned to the many voices inside you." Moraga read a love poem to the class that referred to her lover as "she." She was told by the group that she could not say "she" because readers would expect her to write to a man. Her response to them was that people need to expand not only how they write, but also how they read. She has remained loyal to this fundamental commitment to writing from her own identity.

After two years of teaching Moraga realized that since she did feel fulfilled in this role, if she continued to teach she would never become a writer, would never inhabit the mysterious world of art that held out such an allure. She decided to give herself the space of one year to find out if she did in fact have what it takes to be a writer. In 1977 she moved to the San Francisco Bay Area. This change of residence was also motivated by her need to become more public about her lesbianism, which would have been more difficult in the city where her family lives. During her trial year Moraga formulated her relationship to writing in terms of priorities and professional commitment. She decided not to work full-time, living on unemployment and odd jobs in order to devote herself to her writing. Besides writing a great deal during that year, she also followed the advice of her writing group and read voraciously, but with a twist. Tailoring their advice to meet her own needs as a lesbian writer, she immersed herself in writings by Anglo lesbians, from Radclyffe Hall's *The Well of Loneliness* (1928) to the works of Djuna Barnes. At the end of that year she and Los Angeles poet Eloise Klein Healy read together in a woman's coffeehouse. The reading was well attended, and Moraga recalled that she felt affirmed in her identity as a writer. One of the poems she wrote during this time, "For the Color of My Mother," was published in *Loving in the War Years: (lo que nunca pasó por sus labios)* [what never passed her lips], her first book of collected poetry, in 1983. From that time on Moraga applied herself to her writing with increased determination.

At the same time, working as a lesbian in the highly charged political climate of the Bay Area in the late 1970s made her increasingly aware of the fusion of literature and politics, especially the intricate relationship between race, sexuality, class, and writing. Moraga recounted that the discovery of the poem "A Woman Is Talking to Death" (1974) by working-class lesbian poet Judy Grahn crystallized her need to write not only as a lesbian, but also as a woman of color conscious of class differences. Moraga was struck by Grahn's skill in using simple, ordinary language to talk about complex political realities, and by her definition of lesbianism as an act of love, a definition that confirmed her own feelings. When Moraga arranged to meet her and showed her some of her poems she recalls that Grahn advised her "to do what nobody else can do, which is to write exactly from your own voice, the voices you heard growing up." The contact with Grahn and her work was a pivotal experience in Moraga's politicization as a writer, and it opened her writing further, ridding her language of a constricted quality she felt came from imitation of white, privileged voices.

Moraga had met other women of color writers while working at San Francisco State University on a master's degree in feminist writings, which combines creative writing with the study of feminist literature. It was at this time that Gloria Anzaldúa approached her about putting together a collection of writings that would address the ways in which women of color writers' voices are silenced and denied. Moraga's advisers agreed to accept the manuscript as fulfilling the thesis requirement for the degree, which she received in 1980; the book, *This Bridge Called My Back: Writings by Radical Women of Color*, appeared in 1981.

This Bridge Called My Back, which was republished in 1983, is a collection of writings by radical women of color: poetry, stories, but mainly essays. The overarching vision provided by Moraga and Anzaldúa is one of defining a feminism by women of color that would incorporate an analysis of racial, cultural, and class oppression as well as addressing issues of sexuality, gender, and heterosexism. The writers included are all radical, having in common a belief in the end of all oppressions, which they see as interlocking systems.

It is difficult to overestimate the timeliness and importance of *This Bridge Called My Back* in the 1980s because it coincided with the coalescing of the organizing activity of women of color, particularly lesbians of color, at the same time that it helped coalesce that activism. The book grew from the need of women of color to express their rage and frustration with the racism and classism of the predominantly white feminist movement. At the same time, it marked the emergence of new connections among Chicanas, Latinas, Afro-American, Native-American, and Asian-American women, firmly establishing the term "woman of color" in the political vocabulary. In the late 1970s gatherings of women of color were still marked by mutual suspicion based on racial and cultural differences. By 1981 women of color were realizing that their bonding point was their common experiences of oppression and racism. *This Bridge Called My Back* was a catalyst in the process of bringing women of color together. It is a book that changed people's lives, as Moraga avowed that working on it with other women of color changed her life.

Moraga's work is represented in the collection by two poems and an essay. She also wrote a preface in which she develops the image of the bridge to envision the possibility of women of color coming together in spite of their differences: "How can we–this time–not use our bodies to be thrown over a river of tormented history to bridge the gap?" The poem included in the first section, "For the Color of My Mother," expresses the connections between light-skinned daughter and dark mother and, through her, with other women of color:

> I am a white girl gone brown to the blood color
>   of my mother
> speaking for her
> as it should be
> dark women come to me
>   sitting in circles
> I pass through their hands
> the head of my mother
> painted in clay colors
>
> touching each carved feature
>   swollen eyes and mouth
> they understand the explosion the splitting
> open   contained within the fixed expression
>
> they cradle her silence
>   nodding to me[.]

"The Welder" uses the metaphor of welding to trace the relationship between writing and the possibility of transformation:

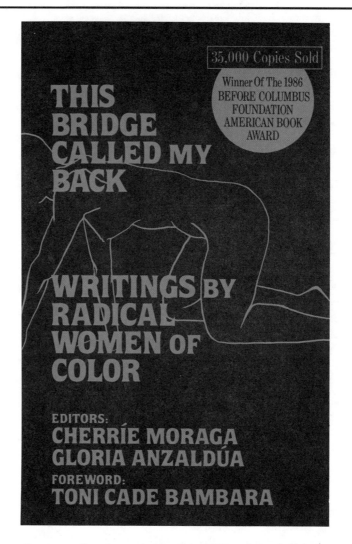

Front cover for a later printing of the 1981 anthology which explores the ways in which the voices of "women of color" are ignored

I am a welder.
Not an alchemist.
I am interested in the blend
of common elements to make
a common thing. . . .

I am the welder.
I understand the capacity of heat
to change the shape of things.
I am suited to work
within the realm of sparks
out of control.

I am the welder.
I am taking the power
into my own hands.

For the second section of *This Bridge Called My Back* Moraga wrote an essay called "La Güera" (the fair-skinned girl or woman). Because her light skin allowed her to "pass," it was only when she "lifted the lid" to her lesbianism that she understood what oppression was and was able to identify with her mother's oppression as a poor, uneducated Chicana. The essay documents her painful journey to "my brown mother–the brown in me," while it calls for all feminists to confront the ways they have "taken the values of the oppressor into our hearts and turned them against ourselves and one another." The essay is written in a remarkably honest voice and employs raw, poetic language. Moraga recalls that when she was working on this essay, every time she sat down at the typewriter she thought she was going to be sick because what she was trying to say was so private, yet her need for communication on the topic was urgent. As she says in the essay, "the only thing worth writing about is what seems to be unknown and, therefore, fearful." It was courage that enabled her to get in touch with internalized racism, classism, and homophobia and to put it in print: "The object of oppression is not only someone outside of my skin, but the someone inside my skin. . . . the real battle . . . begins under the skin."

This Bridge Called My Back has sold over thirty-five thousand copies and was the winner of the Before Columbus Foundation American Book Award in 1986. The book was reviewed in virtually every feminist publication in the United States, though it took longer to appear on the pages of Third World publications. It sparked considerable controversy due to its breaking open the topic of racism within the women's movement. It is widely used as required reading in women's studies and Third World studies courses across the nation, and, not least of all, it introduced the work of some thirty women of color writers to the national scene (well-known contributors such as Audre Lorde and Barbara Smith were the exception, not the rule).

It was in her search for a publisher for *This Bridge Called My Back* that Moraga first went to the East—to Boston, then to New York—where she stayed for over four years. Moraga's stay on the East Coast was a time of intense literary and political activity for her. Besides cofounding Kitchen Table/Women of Color Press with other women of color writers, she was involved in women of color organizing against sexual violence. This active involvement with the press and other women of color writers and activists, such as Lorde and Smith, heightened her growing consciousness about the relationship between art and politics.

In 1983 Kitchen Table/Women of Color Press published *Cuentos: Stories by Latinas*, edited by Moraga with Alma Gómez and Mariana Romo-Carmona. This collection was the first anthology by creative writers who were both Latinas and feminists. In terms of Moraga's own personal evolution it reflects the next step in the journey "back to my brown mother—to the brown in me" referred to in "La Güera." Having made the transition from seeing herself primarily as a lesbian writer to her identification with women of color, at this time it became increasingly important to her to work more closely with other Latina writers.

In their introduction the editors outline their principal concerns. Most importantly, *Cuentos* represents the first step in the creation of a written literary tradition that grows directly out of the specific realities of first-generation Latina writers living in the United States. Another concern of the editors and contributors of *Cuentos* is to break the silence around sexuality, especially Latina lesbianism, and explore what it means to be Latina and female, putting the "struggles of the Latin woman first." A third related concern of the editors of *Cuentos* is language. The collection validates the originality of Latina writers by including work in Spanish and in English as well as pieces that mix English and Spanish.

Moraga has two stories in the section that deals with breaking the taboos surrounding female sexuality. "Sin luz" (Without Light) is a frank depiction of a young girl's attitudes about sexuality. Married at fourteen by her family to an old man, she is indifferent to sex, thinking only of the baby growing inside her whose conception she thinks she ensured by imagining "a pin of light, penetrating her rib cage, piercing her heart where the love would begin, inflaming her belly where the baby would grow." The one time she has an orgasm her mind remains silent. She attributes her miscarriage at seven months to the fact that "no light had shown." Moraga leaves it up to the reader to interpret the story in relation to the separation of love and sex, pleasure and procreation for the young protagonist, as well as the feelings of guilt that may run beneath the surface of her assuming responsibility for the death of her son. "Pesadilla" (Nightmare) presents the relationship between a Chicana and a black woman. Their private world is invaded by what they call the "animal," a man who breaks into their apartment, trashes it, and writes homophobic insults on their walls. In the nightmare at the end of the story the "animal" returns, but the threat to their union does not come only from the hostile "outside." The most frightening aspect of the *pesadilla* has to do with the barriers between women of color, the things within Cecilia, the Chicana protagonist, that keep her from "letting Deborah in."

In addition to coediting *Cuentos* in New York, Moraga continued to work on her writing. In 1983 she collected several essays and her poems, some dating back to 1976, in *Loving in the War Years: (lo que nunca pasó por sus labios)*. It was while she was immersed in the multicultural, multiracial milieu of New York that Moraga became more aware of the uniqueness of Chicano culture and began to feel more and more the need for a Chicano context. Surrounded by the rhythms of Puerto Rican Spanish, she felt a need for the Chicano community that prompted her to write "A Long Line of Vendidas" (Sellouts), a major essay in *Loving in the War Years*. As in "La Güera" (republished in *Loving in the War Years*), Moraga's cultivation of the essay form stems from the private urge to make sense of the contradictions of her identity as both Chicana and lesbian. But at the same time her sense of books as organizing tools also motivated her to turn to the essay form in an attempt to break things down and explain them for specific readerships. Paradoxically it was the isolation from the Chicano culture on the East Coast that made it possible for her to write the essay, at a safe distance from the critical voices she felt would attack her for her feminism and explicit lesbian identity.

In "A Long Line of Vendidas" Moraga addresses the dialectical relationship between Chicanas' sexuality and cultural identity, tracing the ways in which women are both damaged and empowered by their cultural experience. In order to understand Chicanas' sense of self as sexual beings, Moraga analyzes the pervasive influence of the myth of "La Malinche" in the definition of masculine and feminine gender roles. During the conquest of Mexico, the noble Aztec woman Malintzin Tenepal (also called by her Spanish name, Doña Marina) acted as Cortés's mistress, translator, and tactical advisor. "La Malinche" is "La vendida"–equating female sexuality with betrayal–as well as "La chingada" (the violated one), contributing to the Chicano cultural construction of the gender of woman as passive object. Under the pressure of the conflation of her sexuality with betrayal, Moraga argues, the Chicana must "prove" her fidelity through commitment to the Chicano male, "putting the male first" from a subordinate position of servitude and obedience within the heterosexual structures of the family and the culture.

Moraga personalizes the title of the essay in reference to her own specific racial, cultural, and sexual identity: "My mother then is the modern-day Chicana, Malinche marrying a white man, to produce the bastards my sister, my brother and I are. Finally, I–a half-breed Chicana–further betray my race by *choosing* my sexuality which excludes all men, and therefore most dangerously, Chicano men. I come from a long line of Vendidas." The sword over the Chicana's head

has two edges: fear of being "sold out" by other women who put men first, and fear of being labeled a "sellout" for questioning traditional gender roles and organizing her sexuality independently, whether lesbian or heterosexual. To break the long line of vendidas means revisioning the family structure: "Family is *not* by definition the man in the dominant position over women and children. Familia is cross-generational bonding, deep emotional ties between opposite sexes, and within our sex. It is sexuality, which . . . springs forth from touch, constant and daily."

The position Moraga outlines in "A Long Line of Vendidas" is not separatist, but woman-centered. Chicana feminism means putting women first, "making bold and political the love of the women of our race." This can only be accomplished if Chicanas first learn to love themselves as female and *mestiza*. The political commitment to women must include a political commitment to lesbians as well: "There will be no change in heterosexual relations, as long as the Chicano community keeps us lesbians and gay men political prisoners among our own people. Any movement built on the fear and loathing of anyone is a failed movement." The essay is a cornerstone text in the development of a Chicana feminist analysis of sexuality and gender. While it illuminates Moraga's creative writing, it refuses the rigid distinction between theoretical discourse and personal voice.

The themes that unify the poetry, stories, and essays of *Loving in the War Years: (lo que nunca pasó por sus labios)* are suggested by the two parts of the title. When Moraga first contemplated the idea of publishing her collected poetry, in 1979, the idea of "loving in the war years" referred to lesbian love. Two women who love each other find themselves at war with the rest of the world and at times with each other; they are besieged from without as well as from within the relationship, as in "Pesadilla." When Moraga came back to her project after finishing *This Bridge Called My Back*, she realized that the new poems and essays she had written in the interim had extended the theme, broadening its political implications. In effect, these are war years for everyone; in a death-dealing culture, any act of love is an act of resistance. The second part of the title, "lo que nunca pasó por sus labios," refers to breaking the silence, violating the taboos surrounding the topics of lesbianism, gender roles, and sexuality within Chicano culture and the dominant culture. In a 1986 interview with Luz María Umpierre,

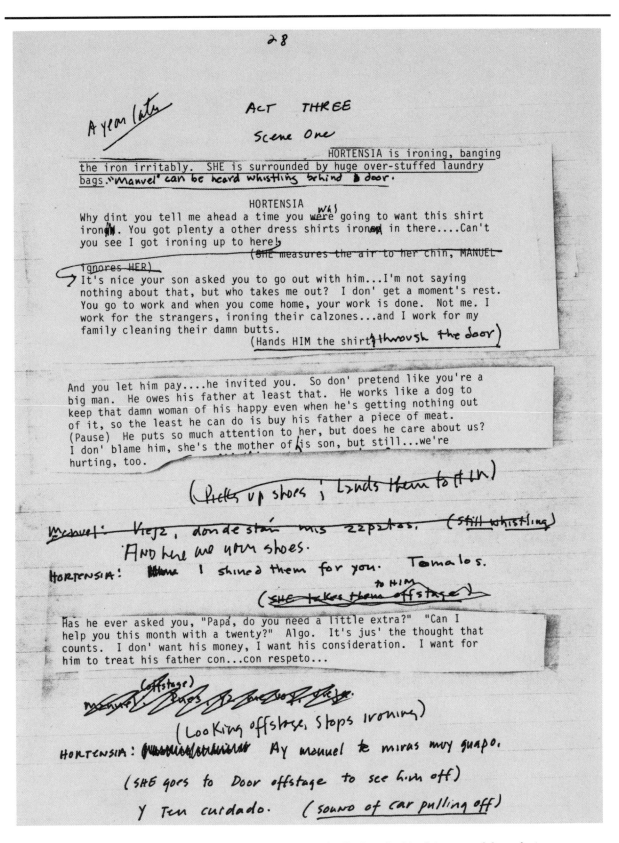

28

A year later

ACT THREE

Scene One

HORTENSIA is ironing, banging the iron irritably. SHE is surrounded by huge over-stuffed laundry bags. "Manuel" can be heard whistling behind the door.

HORTENSIA

Why dint you tell me ahead a time you was going to want this shirt ironed. You got plenty a other dress shirts ironed in there....Can't you see I got ironing up to here!

(SHE measures the air to her chin, MANUEL ignores HER)

It's nice your son asked you to go out with him...I'm not saying nothing about that, but who takes me out? I don' get a moment's rest. You go to work and when you come home, your work is done. Not me. I work for the strangers, ironing their calzones...and I work for my family cleaning their damn butts.

(Hands HIM the shirt through the door)

And you let him pay....he invited you. So don' pretend like you're a big man. He owes his father at least that. He works like a dog to keep that damn woman of his happy even when he's getting nothing out of it, so the least he can do is buy his father a piece of meat. (Pause) He puts so much attention to her, but does he care about us? I don' blame him, she's the mother of his son, but still...we're hurting, too.

(Picks up shoes; hands them to HIM)

MANUEL: Vieja, donde stan mis zapatos. (still whistling)
And here are your shoes.

HORTENSIA: Here I shined them for you. Tomalos.

(SHE takes them to HIM offstage)

Has he ever asked you, "Papá, do you need a little extra?" "Can I help you this month with a twenty?" Algo. It's jus' the thought that counts. I don' want his money, I want his consideration. I want for him to treat his father con...con respeto...

MANUEL: (offstage) Bags ... vieja.

(Looking offstage, stops ironing)

HORTENSIA: Ay Manuel te miras muy guapo.

(SHE goes to door offstage to see him off)

Y Ten cuidado. (sound of car pulling off)

Page from a draft for Moraga's play in progress, "The Shadow of a Man" (courtesy of the author)

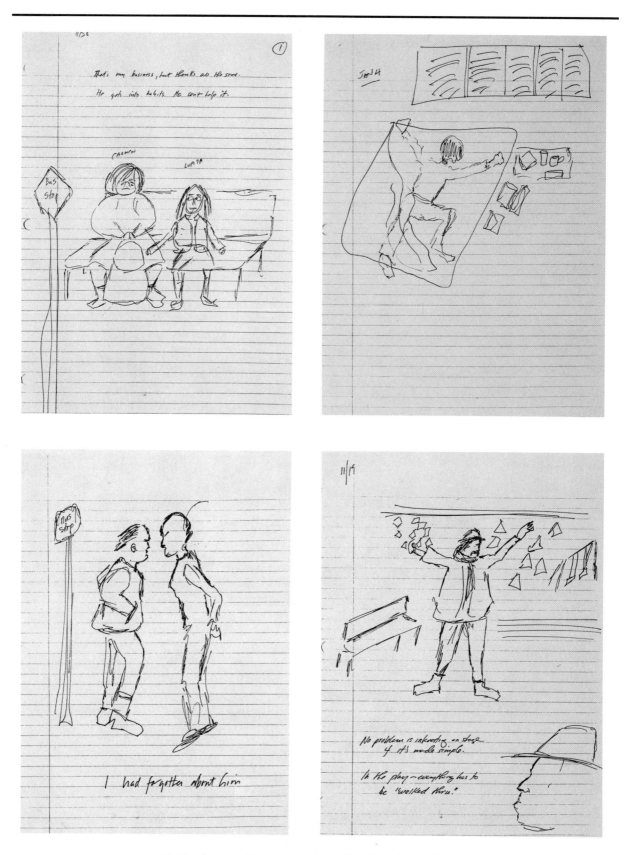

Sketches drawn by Moraga to work out ideas for "The Shadow of a Man" (courtesy of the author)

feminism, as in the title poem "Loving in the War Years":

I've got to take you
as you come, battle bruised
refusing our enemy, fear.

We're all we've got. . . .

In the final poem of the collection, a poem that embodies the second half of the book's title, there is the sense that in spite of the disappointments and failures, communication does occur: "profundo y sencillo/lo que nunca pasó/por sus labios/but = was/utterly/utterly/heard" (profound and simple/what never passed/her lips . . .).

Loving in the War Years represents the first published book of writing by an avowed Chicana lesbian. The twin modality of the book–the making sense of what it means to be Chicana and lesbian in the essays mirrored in the imaginative configurations of the poems and vice versa–as well as the power and originality of the language and the vision conveyed by it make it an invaluable contribution to the development of Chicana and women of color literature and to the development of the feminist movement.

While she was in New York, Moraga recalled, some of the poems she was working on started turning into monologues, or characters would come to her while she was writing in her journal. She attributes the emergence of the theatrical form in her writing to the experience of finishing the essay "A Long Line of Vendidas." After working on such an intensely autobiographical piece, she felt a need to broaden her perspective as a writer. She also felt the need to write something that would be heard, to hear the language spoken. The result was the two-act verse play *Giving up the Ghost* (1986). On 16 June 1984 the feminist theater At the Foot of the Mountain in Minneapolis gave the play a staged reading. Moraga had never worked in the theater before, and this experience intrigued her. The opportunity to work with actors and a director made her see the possibilities of a less isolated mode of writing, a connection between collective and private work, as well as the potential to reach a Chicano audience who might never read her books.

In 1984, with the script, she was accepted into a playwright residency directed by María Irene Fornes at INTAR (Hispanic-American Arts Center), a Hispanic and Latino theater group in New York City. During her residency Moraga worked on two other plays besides *Giving up the Ghost*, one of them a musical theater piece. Eight of the nine other playwrights in the program were Cuban and Puerto Rican (one was a Chicano). The experience on the whole was very positive, especially the opportunity to work with Fornes, whose poetic sensibility made Moraga feel that there was a place for the poet in theater. On the other hand, she felt that she was not receiving the feedback on the nuances of Chicano culture or language that she needed. Her desire for a community of Chicano writers and audiences motivated her return to California at the end of 1985. *Giving up the Ghost* was published in Los Angeles by West End Press in 1986.

In *Giving up the Ghost* there is no clear story with a beginning, middle, and end. Instead, the spectators listen to the "narratives" of three characters: Marisa, a Chicana in her late twenties; Corky, Marisa's younger self at eleven and seventeen; and Amalia, a Chicana in her late forties, born in Mexico. Moraga also includes The People, those viewing the performance, in the cast of characters. The stage is basically empty and black, with few props; lighting is the most important feature in the setting. The actors' monologues are for the most part directed to the audience; they rarely interact with one another, though the playwright indicates that they hear what the others are saying. In *Giving up the Ghost* Moraga uses more Spanish than in her previous writings. It is the language that makes the play: intensely poetic, yet spare, capable of both lyric flights and visceral power. The characters are typified by their language: Corky uses a mixture of Spanish, English, and Caló (Chicano slang), revealing the class and *cholo* subculture to which she belongs; Amalia uses more Spanish than Marisa and is responsible for the most lyrical passages in the play; Marisa's language is similar to Corky's and ranges from anger to great tenderness, humor, and lyricism.

Three strong actors are needed who can exploit the language and provide the interpretive delivery necessary to carry the play given the paucity of onstage action. The monologues of the characters are their memories, primarily memories of desire. Through these remembered stories they explore with The People their relationship to each other, to their own desire, and to the culture which has shaped them as sexual beings. In many ways *Giving up the Ghost* is the dramatic representation of the ideas developed in the essay "A Long Line of Vendidas." The play explores the ways in which women have been damaged by

Moraga referred to the difficulty of saying what has never been said: "If it hasn't been said, it's not supposed to exist." By "trying to make it *be* said, to come out of your mouth" the writer validates the experience, gives voice and visibility to what has been silenced and made invisible. Mirtha N. Quintanales, in her 1985 interview with Moraga, connects the fundamental importance of the task of saying with the pervasive imagery of mouths, lips, and throats in Moraga's writing, especially her poetry. While the need to speak the unspoken lends special weight to images of the mouth, tongue, lips, and throat, Moraga's poetry constantly constructs, destructs, and reconstructs the entire female body in the recognition of how it has been colonized, and in the attempt to reclaim it. Virtually every poem in the collection hinges on some part of the body: the "brown knotted knees . . . that begin to crack" in "The Pilgrimage"; "the part of the eye/that is not eye at all/but hole" in "Fear, a Love Poem"; "the very old wound in me/between my legs" in "Passage." In "The Voices of the Fallers" Moraga uses the metaphor of falling to explore the perils of lesbian existence:

> I was born queer with the dream
> of falling
> the small sack of my body
> dropping
> off a ledge
> suddenly.

One by one, the parts of the body fragment and fall through space, to reassemble in the impact with the ground:

> *Listen.*
> Can you hear my mouth crack
> open   the sound
> of my lips bending
> back against the force
> of the fall?
>
> *Listen.*
> Put your ear deep
> down
> through   the opening
> of my throat and
> *listen.*
>
> . . . . her   shoulder first
> tumbling
> off
> the cliff   the legs
> following

> over
> her head. . . .
>
> her body's
> dead
>
> silent
>
> collision
> with the sand.

The fear of betrayal by women, the myriad ways women fail to come through for each other, is echoed throughout *Loving in the War Years*. In the introductory essay Moraga, recalling sitting at the deathbed of her *abuela* (grandmother), feels that she has let her down: "Y yo nunca le hablé en la lengua que entendiera" (and I never spoke to her in the language she would understand). A counterbalance to her regret is provided by a desire to believe in the possibility of faithfulness to one another. The dynamic of betrayal and loyalty begins at home, in the relationships between mother and daughter; the title of one of the sections asks, "what kind of lover have you made me, mother?" It is from the mother that the daughter learns about faith. Moraga's work is steeped in Catholicism, but as she says in the preface to *This Bridge Called My Back*, she does not embrace the resigned faith of institutionalized religion, but the "faith of activists" that "we have the power to . . . change our lives." In "The Pilgrimage" the poetic voice makes the connection between the mother's faith and the daughter's faith in a vision of women bonding, a transition accomplished through communication, both the oral tradition (the mother's mouth) and, ultimately, the act of writing itself:

> She saw women
> maybe the first time
> when they had streamed in long broken
> single file
> out from her mother's tongue—
>
>> "En México, las mujeres crawl
>> on their hands and knees
>> to the basilica door.
>> This proves their faith."

Many of the pieces in the collection explore this need for women to "prove their faith," not in God, but in each other. For Moraga the lesbian couple is the microcosm in which the dynamic of faith works itself out, becoming a metaphor for

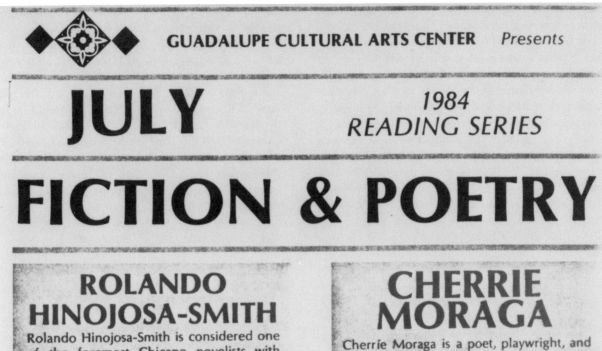

their culture's definition of masculine and feminine in terms of active subject and passive object.

Corky, a tough *cholita*, rejects socialization in her culture's notion of normal femininity at an early age and identifies with an active male role, thereby internalizing the values and attitudes attached to gender roles as assigned in the culture. Her erotic attraction to women is played out in contexts of violence and dominance, and she sees women as other, an object from which she disassociates herself. Yet she confesses that "deep down inside" she knew she was female and realizes that her toughness stems from the wound inflicted on her: "I knew/always knew/I was an animal that kicked back/cuz it hurt." Corky is forced to confront her internal split between identification with the subjugating male and her repressed self-knowledge as female when she is raped. The rape brings Corky's sexuality home to her as an inescapable fact, confirming her culture's definition of female as "being taken." With the shout "he made me a hole" she disappears from the play.

Corky's experiences have shaped Marisa's sexual choices and limitations. She is locked into her anger, which can reveal itself only in her painfully knotted legs. Anger, the primary obstacle to her liberation, is associated with her feelings of sexual betrayal by women, a reflection of the culture's insistence on putting men first. She defines her passion "to beat [men] at their own game" as her prison. She is unable to believe that "a woman capable of loving a man/was capable of loving a woman/me."

Amalia, too, is tormented by her "private miseries." She is tired of being used sexually by men, tired of using men to recover Mexico through them. She feels dead. By including a heterosexual character, Moraga widens the scope of the play to show how the sexuality of both lesbian and heterosexual Chicanas emerges from the same source. Amalia's sexual relationship with Marisa demonstrates her freedom to express her sexuality independently of cultural restrictions. That it is not easy to go against the grain of what is culturally accepted is shown in her dream that she and Marisa are Indians in a Mexican village where Marisa has broken a sacred taboo. Amalia does not fear the punishment so much as knowing that the taboo could be broken. Like Marisa she is engaged in a struggle between her internalized cultural attitudes and her desire to organize her desire independently.

The play does not give any easy answers nor indicate how the struggles of Marisa and Amalia end. The fact that Marisa and Amalia are no longer together suggests that Amalia's fears were stronger than her desire for Marisa, or that the damage already done to Marisa's sexuality cannot be healed. But the theme of salvation in the play hinges on the relationship between the two women. Through Amalia's desire for her, Marisa may learn to complement her active role as lover of women with the ability to be loved, to open herself to feel loved by women. Marisa's love might save Amalia, make her feel again and cure her wounds. Through her desire for Marisa, Amalia does come to life again in the play, but she expresses her desire in terms of her dead male lover being born in her. The unresolved contradictions persist in the ending lines of the play. While Marisa "prepares herself for the worst," she is finally able to love her female self ("I put my fingers/to my own/forgotten places"). It is this self-love that makes possible the hope for, in the idea of community of women, "making familia from scratch."

Besides the staged reading by At the Foot of the Mountain, *Giving up the Ghost* has enjoyed two full-scale productions, one in San Francisco on 5 April 1987 at the Mission Cultural Center, directed by Anita Mattos with the playwright Lourdes Portillo playing Marisa, and one in Seattle by Front Room Theater, directed by Laura Esparza. For the San Francisco production Moraga made substantial revisions to the published text.

Since her return to the Bay Area Moraga has continued her work in theater, poetry, and editing. Since 1986 she has been a part-time writing instructor in Chicano studies at the University of California, Berkeley. Besides working on the production of *Giving up the Ghost*, she attended a script analysis class to further her knowledge of the form and is revising a play she began in the INTAR residency, called "The Shadow of a Man." "The Shadow of a Man," like *Giving up the Ghost*, employs an all-female cast. It explores the effects of Catholicism on the formation of a girl's sense of herself and her sexuality. The play dramatizes this process within the Chicano family, for, as Moraga pointed out in the Umpierre interview, the family is the source of the private voice, "the heart of everything": "The family is this private place, so anything is allowed to happen there, any kind of power exchanges, any kind of control; it's . . . the first place where you learn to suffer and also the first place where you learn to love."

Moraga is working on a collection of poems tentatively entitled "Dreaming of Other Planets." She still feels that poetry is her primary love and the form with which she feels most comfortable, but she confesses her fascination with theater and her desire to learn more about it. She has edited, with Ana Castillo and Norma Alarcón, a special issue of *Third Woman* on Latina sexuality. *This Bridge Called My Back* has been revised for Latin American relevance and translated into Spanish as *Esta puente, mi espalda: Voces de mujeres tercermundistas en los Estados Unidos* (1988). The motivation behind the translation has to do with Moraga's faith in books as means to provoke and organize in the hope that it may be helpful for Latin American women in building their own feminist movement. At the same time, the translation is intended to correct the Latin American perspective of U.S. feminism as an exclusively white movement, by making the women of color movement more visible to them.

Moraga continues to grapple with issues of race, class, culture, and sexuality, but she feels she is now grounded in Chicano culture. She is concerned with the personal integration of all the facets of her identity and also "how those things live themselves out on our planet." She feels that in some ways her writing always precedes her, finds a way of expressing things on the page that she perhaps has not yet said to herself; as she puts it, "it knows before I do." For example, she feels that she is only now testing out in a Chicana and Chicano context what she wrote in "A Long Line of Vendidas" back in New York. Her writing continues to be centered on her lesbianism, in part because lesbianism is about love. She remains committed to exploring in her writing all the structures that inhibit the right to love.

Interviews:

Mirtha N. Quintanales, "Loving in the War Years: An Interview with Cherríe Moraga," *off our backs* (January 1985): 12-13;

Norma Alarcón, "Interview with Cherríe Moraga," *Third Woman*, 3, nos. 1 and 2 (1986): 127-134;

Luz María Umpierre, "With Cherríe Moraga," *Americas Review*, 14 (Summer 1986): 54-67.

Reference:

Yvonne Yarbro-Bejarano, "Cherríe Moraga's *Giving Up the Ghost*: The Representation of Female Desire," *Third Woman*, 3, nos. 1 and 2 (1986): 113-120.

Alejandro Morales

(14 October 1944-)

Marvin A. Lewis
University of Missouri-Columbia

BOOKS: *Caras viejas y vino nuevo* (Mexico City: J. Mortiz, 1975); translated by Max Martínez as *Old Faces and New Wine*, revised and edited by Alurista and José Monleón (San Diego: Maize, 1981);

La verdad sin voz (Mexico City: J. Mortiz, 1979); translated by Judith Ginsberg as *Death of an Anglo* (Tempe: Bilingual Review Press, 1988);

Reto en el paraíso (Ypsilanti: Bilingual/Editorial Bilingüe, 1983);

The Brick People (Houston: Arte Publico, 1988).

Alejandro Morales is regarded as one of the leading Chicano novelists because of his skill as a writer and his understanding of culture. He has published three quality works of fiction: two in Mexico City, because at the time he could not find a United States publisher, and later one in Michigan.

Alejandro Dennis Morales was born in Montebello, California, in the barrio of Simons to which his parents, Delfino Morales Martínez and Juana Contreras Ramíriz, had emigrated from Guanajuato, Mexico. Morales grew up in East Los Angeles where he attended elementary and secondary schools. He married H. Rohde Teaze 16 December 1967. He earned a B.A. from California State University at Los Angeles and an M.A. (1973) and Ph.D. (1975) from Rutgers University in New Brunswick, New Jersey. Morales is presently a full professor in the Spanish and Portuguese Department at the University of California, Irvine.

Morales is a consistent chronicler of the Chicano experience. His novels explore the urban barrio, rural strife along the border between Mexico and the United States, and conflicts between Chicanos and Anglos in California and Texas. There has been a definite progression in the evolution of his craft from his first interpretation of the barrio milieu in *Caras viejas y vino nuevo* (1975; translated as *Old Faces and New Wine*, 1981) to his evaluation of the impact of Manifest Destiny upon

Alejandro Morales (photo by Galal Kernahan)

Chicanos in *Reto en el paraíso* (Challenge in Paradise, 1983). Violence, eroticism, and the affirmation of *chicanismo* (the Chicano way of life) are prevalent motifs in his work.

Caras viejas y vino nuevo examines the Chicano experience with the barrio as the focal point. Characterization is sketchy in the novel. Enough is told about each character to understand his motives but that is all. Lives are reconstructed basically through hearsay and allusion. Females are especially underdeveloped as protagonists and appear to be present solely for the benefit of the macho, dominating males. Events in the novel are presented from the perspectives of Mateo and Julián, two teenagers. For Mateo the barrio offers the respect and protection lacking for him in the Anglo world. Julián is presented as a victim of both hereditary and environmental circumstances. He was born bad, and he cannot possibly overcome his faults after dropping out of school because of his father (Don Edmundo) and because of Anglo prejudice. Even his marriage to Virgy does not save him from his destiny. The conflict between generations is a central issue in the novel. Julián belongs to the new breed of urban delinquents referred to by Don Edmundo as "cabrones," "sinvergüenzas" (shameless), "místicos" (addicts), and "malas astillas" (misdirected). Don Edmundo expects unwavering respect and discipline; Julián and his father have a lack of respect for each other as well as mutual guilt feelings about accusations surrounding the death of Doña Margo (Julián's mother). Hatred is intensified when Doña Matilde is brought in to serve as Don Edmundo's companion and to care for his younger son, Ramón. The conflict is left unresolved until a drugged Julián, at the prompting of his friends, los Buenasuerte, forces entry into his father's house, attacks Doña Matilde, and dies in the subsequent police automobile pursuit which opens the novel. His earlier actions are told in retrospect.

The barrio residents in *Caras viejas y vino nuevo* maintain a sense of solidarity which includes a generally negative image of the Anglo world, often referred to as "otro lado" (the other side). Important Anglo characters include Cohen the bus driver; "la maestra" (the schoolteacher); and Barbara, the prostitute. Cohen and the teacher are presented in a positive light because they empathize with and relate to Chicanos. They teach order and respect to the young. Barbara is brutally caricatured. She is the recipient of some of the hate and frustration which promiscuous male barrio residents feel toward the Anglos. The primary Anglo representative is the local policeman, "la pistola loca" (crazy pistol), and his vehicle, "la llorona" (the wailing one, a term which is also applied to the Anglo emergency vehicles). An air of tension permeates relationships between residents and the police. The arrival of "la llorona" usually signals tragedy for barrio residents. Positive aspects of the barrio existence are brought out during the Christmas season, a time of mutual friendship and respect. A constant interchange between friends and family takes place and family ties are renewed. Christmas is viewed as a time of intense activity and togetherness where people reinforce their values and reflect upon their plight. Shared homes, food, religion, and customs help to create a sense of *carnalismo* (solidarity and identity). Tragic aspects of the barrio are embodied in the older "vatos" (dudes) and "veteranos" (veterans) who are portrayed as useless winos after having lived productive lives, and, to a certain extent, in the *palomilla* (peer group), a youth gang which func-

tions both positively and negatively to initiate youth into the larger society. Drugs, sex, and violence are characteristics associated with adulthood by the gang people. Morales uses highly figurative language to reflect the promiscuous attitude of gang members in dealing both with friends and the opposition.

As an interpretation of internal functions of the barrio *Caras viejas y vino nuevo* is a success. Morales is able convincingly to portray people cut off from the mainstream of United States society but nevertheless progressing because of their own positive values which are not overshadowed by negative influences. Yet the limitations imposed by this closed environment are strongly felt as revealed in the failures of so many people.

La verdad sin voz (1979; translated as *Death of an Anglo*, 1988) is a continuation of *Caras viejas y vino nuevo* in that it explores the life of Dr. Michael Logan who is Dr. Nagol in the earlier work. The novel is complicated, focusing on negative aspects of Mexico (guerrilla activity, drug trafficking, the petroleum industry, espionage, the dominant political party, assassination attempts, and problems incurred during Mexican President Luis Echeverría's administration because of his identification with Third World causes) and Mathis, Texas, which provides the backdrop for the action. The initial pages of the novel cover the defeat and expulsion from town of Dr. Leroy Hales, an Anglo physician, who has come to provide medical services for Chicanos. The novel terminates with the burial of Dr. Michael Logan, who replaced Hales and successfully delivered health care for a brief period. Both Hales and Logan are threats to the Anglo establishment because they help Chicanos. Logan, the idealist and leftist sympathizer, dies at the hands of Pistola Gorda, the Anglo policeman, who dominates the barrio through fear and intimidation although he is supposed to be a vehicle of communication between the two communities.

La verdad sin voz is divided into three sections. In the first section the two poles of the narrative are Mathis, Texas, and an unnamed city. The basic dichotomy between Chicanos and Anglos is drawn here and the protagonists are introduced. In Mathis, Hales is expelled by Pistola Gorda and his cohorts, while in medical school Michael Logan is emerging as an idealist with strong moral convictions. Mathis, their common ground, is a place of powerlessness and frustration for Chicanos. In the second section of the book, in addition to the triumphs and failures of

Covers for Morales's four novels

Michael Logan, the reader is informed of the experiences of a Professor Morenito, who is fighting a tenure battle with the university system and who eventually pens the novel *La verdad sin voz*. Morenito, who survives the blatant individual and institutional racism, is contrasted with Dr. Ignacio Pato Martínez, token member of a medical firm. Logan and his friend Casimiro, a Mexican anarchist, are killed (Logan supposedly because he is providing arms for Casimiro and the rebels in Mexico). Section 3 is an epilogue that sums up individual destinies and ties together loose narrative threads. Logan's deeds are kept alive in the popular imagination through Doña Gertrudis, a gossip who functions as an oral historian. There is no justice surrounding Logan's murder or any other atrocity committed against Chicanos. De la Sorre, a Chicano elected representative and a sellout, warns the people not to react violently. At the novel's end no progress has been made in human rights or human services.

Morales's novel *Reto en el paraíso* incorporates more than a century of Chicano history and myth. It is the story of the fall from grace of the Coronel family, rich *californios* (original Spanish California landowners), and the rise of the Irish immigrant Lifford family to the pinnacle of wealth and power. As a work of art which interprets social reality *Reto en el paraíso* assesses the negative impact of Manifest Destiny upon native Californians, primarily those of Mexican and Native American descent. *Reto en el paraíso* is divided into eight "Configuraciones" (configurations) which, for the most part, alternate between present and past. In the segments dealing with the present, the narrator is Dennis Berreyesa Coronel, while in the past, Dennis's great-grandfather Antonio Francisco Coronel and his descendants narrate their histories. Dennis is an architect and a witness to the turbulent 1960s, while Antonio Francisco bears the brunt of violence, discrimination, and treachery perpetrated by the gold- and land-hungry gringos who invade California beginning in the 1840s.

Reto en el paraíso has a very complex narrative structure. The Land Law of 1851 successfully challenged the legality of land titles held by the *californios* to the degree that they were relatively landless within three decades. Morales in his acknowledgments gives credit to Father Felisberto Imondi Bianca, who gave him permission to read the manuscript "Reto en el paraíso" which was penned by Antonio Francisco Coronel

and discovered by Bianca in Monte de Carmela church in Simons, California. The novelist is supposedly told by the priest that he is reading probably the most important novel of the many written by the Mexicans who lost California. Whether or not such a manuscript exists, it becomes apparent that there are elements of the historical novel incorporated in the work to the extent that it places the multiple characters in a clearly defined historical framework and interprets their reactions to a concrete set of circumstances. *Reto en el paraíso* interprets the impact of the transition from landowners to the landless upon the descendants of Don Ignacio and Doña Francisca Coronel: Antonio Francisco Coronel, Manuel Damián Coronel, and Refugio Coronel. The central event in the novel involves Antonio Francisco Coronel. He is a miner with aspirations of being a schoolteacher who offers to double the amount of gold allegedly stolen by two men in order to save them from the gallows. His efforts are in vain. He marries Marina Rodilla in his old age, and they do not have any children. Refugio Coronel marries Nicolás Berreyesa, and they have a son, Antonio Berreyesa. Manuel Damián Coronel and his wife Rafaela are the parents of two children, Beatriz and Jaime. Antonio Coronel marries his first cousin Beatriz Coronel, and they are expelled from home. Antonio Berreyesa and Beatriz Coronel are the parents of Antonio Berreyesa Coronel who marries his cousin María Coronel Martínez; this couple produces two children, Virginia and Dennis Berreyesa Coronel, the contemporary protagonist of *Reto en el paraíso* whose birth occurs in September 1944 as the novel ends. Ironically Dennis Berreyesa Coronel works for the Lifford Company, whose founders cheated his descendants out of the very land upon which they are constructing a model city.

Reto en el paraíso combines elements of contemporary psychology with the fantastic to produce interesting studies of characters and their circumstances. Many of the male protagonists seem to suffer from psychological problems. Dennis Berreyesa Coronel, the main modern character, is a hopeless neurotic who is looking for a return to the womb. He is obsessed with his own urine and feces. He spends much time in his darkened home, naked, in the fetal position seeking shelter in a pyramid which he has constructed of earth and flowers. Unable to cope with the everyday world—and women in particular because his mother, Beatriz Coronel, is reputed to have been a

Morales, late 1980s

prostitute–Dennis is obsessed with his own identity and his failure to cope with life. He becomes completely insane when he sees Rosario, his fantasized virgin, kiss another man (in Dennis's mind this equates her with a prostitute). Fantastic elements in the novel include a wolf plague; an albino shepherd who mates with his sheep and supposedly appears only to the Chosen, but who is equated with the Devil; and the Black Ball Widow, his grandmother Refugio Coronel Berreyesa, who disappears and suffocates in the mass of clothing she wears appearing as if she were a mountain of cloth. Some of her madness seems to have been passed on to Dennis Berreyesa Coronel.

The central episode in which Antonio Francisco Coronel acts to save the thieves is grounded in history. In *Occupied America: A History of Chicanos* (1981) Rodolfo Acuña narrates how, in 1851 after the passage of the Foreign Miners Tax, Antonio Coronel, a schoolteacher, intervened in the lynching of five men accused of stealing gold. Three of them were whipped and two were eventually hanged.

Reto en el paraíso displays some characteristics of metafiction. The novel is self-referential to the degree that it refers to itself and the manner in which it is constructed and communicated. Among other salient metafictional features outlined by Patricia Waugh in her book *Metafiction: The Theory and Practice of Self Conscious Fiction* (1984) are that it displays "an extreme self con-

sciousness about language, literary form and the act of writing fictions" as well as "a pervasive insecurity about the relationship of fiction to reality," evident in the references by Antonio Francisco Coronel to the manuscript he is writing which is incorporated into the fiction of Morales. Echoes of the work of "magic realist" Gabriel García Marquez include the metafictional elements, a preoccupation with sex, particularly incest, the search for and expulsion from Paradise, and insanity. As in his *Cien años de soledad* (1967) there is a rain of butterflies and other insects.

Reto en el paraíso is a very rich novel which, due to its complexity, leaves many loose threads. It is a work which treats some of the major themes of the Chicano experience, such as the search for identity embodied in the character of Dennis Berreyesa Coronel, dislocation, and migration. The novel maintains its internal coherence through the manipulation of language, symbols, and images encountered in the dialectic between Chicanos and Anglos. The principal accomplishment of *Reto en el paraíso* is to interpret convincingly the transition from Paradise to economic dependency in California.

In *The Brick People* (1988) Morales traces the interactions of the Chicano employees of the Simon Brick Factory with the Anglo owners. Beginning in the 1800s, this fictionalized account is based on factual events.

Morales's work is culturally based but not limited. That is, he possesses both an intimate knowledge of Chicanos and their circumstances and an excellent command of literary theory and technique as well. Recent articles by Oscar U. Somoza, John C. Akers, and Judith Ginsberg stress technical aspects of Morales's novels in relationship to form and theme. Akers (*Revista Chicano-Riqueña*, 1985) discusses perceptively the inept job of translation that was done on Morales's first novel. The readings by Somoza (1986) and Ginsberg (*Americas Review*, 1986) would have profited from a better understanding of the historical context from which Morales writes; the same is true for the review article on *Reto en el paraíso* by Victor N. Batiste (*Revista Chicano-Riqueña*, 1985).

References:

John C. Akers, "Fragmentation in the Chicano Novel: Literary Technique and Cultural Identity," *Revista Chicano-Riqueña*, 13, no. 3-4 (1985): 124-127;

Victor N. Batiste, "A Kaleidoscope on Many Levels: A Review Article of *Reto en el paraíso*," *Revista Chicano-Riqueña*, 13 (Spring 1985): 91-94;

Judith Ginsberg, "*La verdad sin voz*: Elegy and Reparation," *Americas Review*, 14 (Summer 1986): 78-83;

Marvin A. Lewis, *Introduction to the Chicano Novel* (Milwaukee: Spanish Speaking Outreach Institute, 1982), pp. 31-38;

Oscar U. Somoza, "Choque e interacción en *La verdad sin voz* de Alejandro Morales," in *Contemporary Chicano Fiction: A Critical Survey*, edited by Vernon Lattin (Binghamton: Bilingual/Editorial Bilingüe, 1986), pp. 299-305;

Charles M. Tatum, *Chicano Literature* (Boston: Twayne, 1982), pp. 126-128.

Amado Muro
(Chester E. Seltzer)
(17 September 1915-3 October 1971)

William Rintoul

BOOK: *The Collected Stories of Amado Muro* (Austin: Thorp Springs, 1979).

OTHER: "Mala Torres," in *Forgotten Pages of American Literature*, edited by Gerald W. Haslam (Boston: Houghton Mifflin, 1970), p. 222;
"Cecilia Rosas," in *The Chicano: From Caricature to Self-Portrait*, edited by Edward Simmen (New York: New American Library, 1971), p. 279;
"Maria Tepache," in *The Chicanos: Mexican American Voices*, edited by Ed Ludwig and James Santibáñez (Baltimore: Penguin Books, 1971), p. 127; translated into Russian and republished in *I Believe in Humanity* (Moscow: Raduga, 1986), pp. 339-342;
"Going Short," in *California Heartland: Writing from the Great Central Valley*, edited by Haslam and James D. Houston (Santa Barbara: Capra, 1978), p. 124.

PERIODICAL PUBLICATIONS: "Big Bill Strecher," as Seltzer, *New Mexico Quarterly Review* (November 1941);
"Man with a Guitar," as Seltzer, *Southwest Review*, 27 (Summer 1942): 459-462;
"San Antonio Matthews," as Seltzer, *Decade of Short Stories*, 8, no. 2 (1947): 36-38;
"Sunday in Little Chihuahua," *Americas*, 7 (November 1955): 22-25;
"Ay, Chihuahua," *Americas*, 9 (March 1957): 22-24;
"My Father and Pancho Villa," *Americas*, 10 (April 1958): 34-35;
"My Grandfather's Brave Songs," *Americas*, 12 (December 1960): 11-13;
"My Aunt Dominga," *New Mexico Quarterly*, 30 (Winter 1960-1961): 359-364;
"Cecilia, I Loved You," *Americas*, 13 (June 1961): 23-27;
"Street of the Crazy Women," *New Mexico Quarterly*, 31 (Autumn 1961): 195-203;

Amado Muro with one of his sons in Chihuahua, 1950s

"Going to Market," *Arizona Quarterly*, 18 (Autumn 1962): 209-216;
"Chihuahua Capirotada," *Arizona Quarterly*, 20 (Summer 1964): 142-146;
"Hobo Sketches," *Arizona Quarterly*, 20 (Winter 1964): 335-360;
"Sunday in Little Chihuahua," *New Mexico Quarterly*, 35 (Autumn 1965): 223-230;
"More Hobo Sketches," *Arizona Quarterly*, 21 (Autumn 1965): 255-260;
"Road Buddy," *Arizona Quarterly*, 22 (Autumn 1966): 269-273;

"Something About Two Mexicans," *New Mexico Quarterly*, 36 (Autumn 1966): 258-266;

"Hungry Men," *Arizona Quarterly*, 23 (Spring 1967): 34-38;

"Night Train to Fort Worth," *Arizona Quarterly*, 23 (Autumn 1967): 250-254; reprinted as "Night Train," *Mexican-American* (El Paso), no. 10 (December 1968): 1, 8;

"Sister Guadalajara," *Mexican-American* (El Paso), no. 11 (February 1969): 1-3;

"Something About Two Hoboes," *Arizona Quarterly*, 25 (Summer 1969): 12-24;

"Hobo Jungle," *Arizona Quarterly*, 26 (Summer 1970): 158-163;

"Blue," *Arizona Quarterly*, 27 (Spring 1971): 74-78;

"Homeless Man," *Texas Observer*, 63 (4 June 1971): 10-11;

"Two Skid Row Sketches," *Arizona Quarterly*, 27 (Autumn 1971): 259-263;

"The Gray-Haired Man," *Texas Observer*, 64 (21 January 1972): 14-15;

"Helping Hands," *Arizona Quarterly*, 28 (Autumn 1972): 225-230;

"Soledad Castillo" and "Something About Fieldhands," *Arizona Quarterly*, 34 (Autumn 1978): 205-216.

Born in Cleveland, Ohio, Chester Seltzer, who is best known as a writer under the name Amado Muro, was the son of Louis B. Seltzer and the grandson of author Charles Alden Seltzer. His father was the editor of the *Cleveland Press* and an influential journalist who was a guest in the White House of every president from Woodrow Wilson to Lyndon Johnson. Charles Alden Seltzer wrote forty-nine novels with romanticized western themes, including some that were made into motion pictures with such stars as William S. Hart.

Chester Seltzer rode freight trains, was a farm worker, went to sea, lived on skid rows, sometimes worked on newspapers, and, from age twenty until his death, he wrote short stories—perhaps among the best of their kind—about men on the road, in the fields, at the missions, and in the villages of Mexico. His stories talk about such things as how hungry men share stews they cooked in hobo jungles ("Hobo Jungle"), how poor shopkeepers feed wanderers too destitute to pay ("Maria Tepache"), and how simple men make hungry children smile ("Sunday in Little Chihuahua"). He chose to celebrate people helping other people.

After graduating from Cleveland's University School around 1932, Seltzer attended the University of Virginia for one year, where he majored in journalism and played guard on the freshman football team. He transferred to Kenyon College, where he took a course in creative writing taught by John Crowe Ransom. He graduated from Kenyon in 1936. Seltzer's first job after college was working as a sports reporter for the *Miami Herald*, where he covered professional boxing, a sport in which he maintained a lifelong interest.

While working in Miami, Seltzer began to submit short stories under his own name. He was not an orderly man who kept records, and so it is difficult to list with certainty where and when his stories, or how many, were published. According to available information, his first published story was "Big Bill Strecher," which appeared in the *New Mexico Quarterly Review* November 1941 issue. Other stories followed, perhaps a dozen or more, in periodicals such as *Southwest Review, Crescendo*, and *Decade of Short Stories*.

These stories anticipate those he wrote as Muro in their preoccupation with society's underdogs. They offer a sympathetic portrayal of poor people victimized by racial injustice and harassed by police acting as agents of the affluent. Written in the traditional third person, these stories reflect the keen ear and eye of a skilled reporter. The only evidence that critics took note of the stories published under Seltzer's name is the listing of "A Peddler's Notebook," published by *Southwest Review*, among the "Distinctive Short Stories" in *Best American Short Stories* (1944). At the time Seltzer was in prison.

In 1942 when Seltzer was twenty-seven and working on the *San Antonio Express*, he refused to comply with the Selective Service Act and was jailed until 1945. He spent six months at El Reno, Oklahoma, and from there was sent to a camp for conscientious objectors in Mancos, Colorado, where he met Pietro di Donato, the author of *Christ in Concrete* (1939). He was sent in 1943 to work at a mental hospital in Norwich, Connecticut. The job involved locking up patients in the ward for the criminally insane, including Louis "Kid" Kaplan, a former featherweight boxing champion. Seltzer told authorities he would rather go back to prison than be a jailer himself. He was sent to the federal penitentiary at Lewisburg, Pennsylvania, where he began a hunger strike that lasted twenty-nine days; during the last nine he claimed he was force-fed with a "garden hose" by the doctor the prisoners called Dr. Faustus. The hose, Seltzer said, was an instrument of torture, cutting his nose badly and forcing him to breathe like a dog. After that the warden put him to work, first in the quarry and then breaking rock for a guards' parking lot. Three months later he joined another hunger strike organized by a fellow prisoner, political activist David Dellinger, against racial discrimination in the prison. That strike lasted sixty-six days, and Seltzer was again force-fed.

After a year in Lewisburg he was paroled to wash walls and carry ice and garbage at a hospital in Harrisburg, Pennsylvania. From there he was sent to a Chicago hospital to shave men for operations. From Chicago he went to Houston and from there to Texarkana prison. He did six more months, went on another hunger strike, and finally was released.

Seltzer went home to Cleveland in 1945 to live with his parents and sister briefly before hopping a freight train heading west. In time Seltzer returned to work as a reporter, which he described as the only trade he knew. He worked for about two years in the late 1940s for the *New Orleans Item.*

He went to sea for a while, sailing as an ordinary seaman on long trips to Greece and South America. At Corfu a White Star Line freighter on which he was a seaman was on the hook about a mile from the wharves when a group of affluent Greeks came out to confer with the captain, who was a Greek. On that particular day Seltzer was mopping up on a sanitary detail. The visitors were in the forecastle, and not knowing this, he blundered in with his mop and bucket. The captain ordered him out, and in making his exit, Seltzer inadvertently spilled soapy water on an affluent Greek's shoe. The captain upbraided him crudely. His pride injured, he wrote a poem about the captain. The ending went: "With an ice pack for a pillow and a straitjacket for a bed / He'll lie supine as his keepers gently massage his head / For he is not a normal man. He delights in discord and strife / And a lunatic asylum is the proper stage for his life."

He gave the poem to a friend, who posted it on the bulletin board, breaking a promise not to do this until the ship docked at New Orleans. The twenty-five-day return trip on the old Liberty ship was unpleasant. He recalled the poem as his only literary success, since the seamen said they liked the poem.

While working for the *El Paso Herald-Post,* Seltzer met Amada Muro, a native of Chihuahua City, Mexico, who had grown up in El Paso and at the time they met was working in the El Paso office of Lamsa, a subsidiary of United Airlines. The two were married on 17 November 1950 in Las Cruces, New Mexico. The couple had two sons, Charles and Robert.

The masculinization of his wife's maiden name subsequently provided Seltzer with his pen name. Years later, in explaining why he changed his name, Seltzer said he was not doing well under his own name and thought the change might improve his luck. Also, he added, who would believe the kind of stories he wanted to write if they were written by someone named Chester Seltzer? The first story published under the name Amado Muro appeared in the November 1955 issue of *Americas* (the official cultural organ of the Organization of American States). In the month following its publication in English, the story appeared in the Spanish and Portuguese editions. Like stories that would follow, "Sunday in Little Chihuahua" is narrated in the first person by a character, Amado Muro. The main character in Muro's first story is Don Ignacio Olvera, "a short, pudgy man with deeply embedded eyes that kept blinking constantly as though trying to beat their way out of the morass of soggy flesh that surrounded them." Don Ignacio reads philosophy and writes literary, informed accounts of Ciudad Juárez bullfights as an unpaid correspondent for a Mexico City magazine while his wife earns the family's living running a tiny café in the Little Chihuahua district of El Paso. On Sundays Don Ignacio stages mock bullfights in a corral in back of the café with his dog that has been trained to play the role of the bull, bringing smiles to the faces of hungry children.

"Sunday in Little Chihuahua" was the first of at least twenty-nine stories that would be published under the name Muro. Many of his stories are set in Parral, Chihuahua, Mexico, in such places as a Street of the Crazy Women, which "held more poor Mexicans than jails do" ("Sister Guadalajara") and where gossiping housewives talk of their husbands ("Mala Torres"). Others are told against such El Paso backgrounds as La Perla de Jalisco café, which served "the delicate wispy tortillas, the largest and thinnest in all Mexico, that are among the great prides of Sonora" ("Sunday in Little Chihuahua"), and La Feria Department Store, where working in ladies' wear had two compensations for the young narrator,

Amado Muro: "Earning three dollars every Saturday was one; being close to the Señorita Cecilia Rosas was the other" ("Cecilia Rosas"). Still other stories are played out against changing scenes on the road and in the fields, including Maria Tepache's place "that was like all the homes of poor Mexicans that I'd seen in Texas. There was a broken-legged woodstove, a shuck-tick bed, a straight-back chair, a mirror with the quicksilver gone, and a table covered with oilcloth frayed and dark at the edges. . . . On a tiny shelf in a corner there was a gilt-framed picture of Maria Guadalupana and a crucified Christ" ("Maria Tepache"). A hobo jungle at Big Spring, Texas, is "a clearing in a stand of low-twisted mesquite trees within a stone's throw of the railroad . . . strewn with blackened cans and broken lugboxes" ("Hobo Jungle").

The Muro stories are peopled with an array of well-drawn characters ranging from Cecilia Rosas, whose "husky whisper, gentle as a rain breeze, was like a tender caress" ("Cecilia Rosas"), to C and O Dad, who "hustled toy flags attached to placards with 'Lest We Forget' in big letters and 'Sold by a Disabled Veteran' in smaller letters" and said, "You'll go a long way before you find a prettier little grift than flag hustling" ("More Hobo Sketches"). No less a character is the narrator who speaks as Amado Muro, whose feelings of wonder and discovery readers share through his youth in Parral, his coming of age in El Paso, and his progression to the life of a field hand following the crops when he grows up. He is a realistic but always sensitive observer of the world of freight trains, fields, and missions. While the persona of the fictional Amado Muro emerges clearly and appealingly in the stories, an outline of his life, equally fictitious, is drawn in short biographical notes that accompany published stories. Through notes, the reader is informed that Amado Muro was born in and grew up in Parral, Chihuahua, that his family moved to El Paso when he was a youngster, that he sometimes works on the ice docks in El Paso and has worked in crops through the Southwest.

One aspect of the critical attention Seltzer's stories drew was the listing of five of the Muro stories as "Distinctive Short Stories" in the annual *Best American Short Stories*, including "My Aunt Dominga" (1962), "Going to Market" (1963), "Maria Tepache" (1970), "Blue" (1972), and "Helping Hands" (1973). The work of Muro was exposed to a wider audience with the publication in the 1970s of various Chicano anthologies. In

the introduction to *The Chicano: From Caricature to Self-Portrait* (1971) Edward Simmen, the editor, described Muro as a man "who seems to have written more good short fiction than any other young Mexican-American." In *Forgotten Pages of American Literature* (1970) Gerald W. Haslam described Muro as "one of the most promising Mexican-American writers." In the *New York Review of Books* (31 August 1972) John Womack, Jr., in an article on Chicano writers, said, "Amado Muro was the funniest, brightest, most moving, accomplished, and prolific 'Mexican-American' writer, a veritable Isaac Babel of the Southwest."

In the later Muro stories there is a shift in setting from Parral and Little Chihuahua to the road and skid row. It seems a normal enough progression in the life of the fictitious Amado Muro, grown from childhood to labor in the fields. (Fourteen of the twenty-nine published Muro stories can be included in this category, starting with "Hobo Sketches" in 1964 and concluding with "Something About Fieldhands," published posthumously in 1978.) The reader is introduced to men with "eyes so deep-set that the shadows around them looked like bruises" ("Two Skid Row Sketches"), whose clothes were "so ragged they tied them on with binder twine" ("Hungry Men"), and who "bleached the four-dollar blood bank's finger marks off with Clorox so they wouldn't have to wait six weeks to put down again" ("Night Train to Fort Worth").

It is a world in which "The redball hummed the high-speed track's heavy rails without slowing. It stayed on the hot rail and never went into the hole. The noise of rolling cars rumbled and the rails vibrated" ("Road Buddy"). Near Pecos, New Mexico, "The freight train thundered over a highball stretch so fast it skipped on rail joints, and the rocking boxcars hit back on their coupling pins with a wrenching jerk" ("Night Train to Fort Worth"); and "Somewhere a long way off we heard a train whistle and after awhile the straight yellow finger of its headlight poked out of the east. We watched in silence as the engine came nearer and nearer and we heard the heavy coughing of its exhaust die away and knew it was going to stop" ("Hobo Jungle").

While there was nothing in Seltzer's life to indicate he felt any particular interest in what critics might think of his work, on at least one occasion he solicited the opinion of those who were the subjects of what he wrote. He once took a copy of a literary quarterly with a Muro story on a train trip to Big Spring, Texas, roughing up the magazine to look as if it had been discarded. One of the hoboes to whom he showed the story pronounced it a true-to-life account except for one detail. The hobo pointed out there was no mention of water, and that without it, the character in the story could not have lived through the long ride across the desert. In "Road Buddy," a story which he then wrote, a hobo with a Barbary pirate's mustache carried an empty wine bottle filled with water.

The editors of quarterlies often worked at a slow pace, holding stories for as long as a year or more before they accepted or rejected them. They sometimes paid Muro twenty or twenty-five dollars a story, but more often paid nothing. Sometimes they thought they knew better than he how men spoke, so one of his stories would appear in print with words changed, and he would take the complimentary copies they sent him and carefully cross out the word the editors had put in and put back his own. In one story the editors changed the words of a hobo who said of the fare in the Kern County Road Camp, "there was plenty of turnip greens and I eat a lot of roasting ears too." The editors changed "eat" to "et." He crossed out "et" and wrote over it "eat." "I sure seem like a tremendous intellect caviling about 'et,' " he wrote in an unpublished letter, "but as you say most Southerners who are roughly circumstanced use 'eat' in the past tense frequently. I've heard plenty of guys use 'et' but not in this case, and I think some educators equate incorrect grammar with simple-mindedness, and I sure don't think that's the case. In fact, I've met many men . . . who don't use pure grammar and are still superior intellectually, morally and every other way to guys who do simply, I think, because they've had more experience of life and learned some lessons. Anyway I'm no grammarian."

Self-described as an obscure journalist, Muro worked for at least fifteen newspapers, including the *St. Louis Post-Dispatch.* Among towns in which he worked were Las Cruces, New Mexico; San Diego and Bakersfield, California; New Orleans, Louisiana; Prescott, Arizona; and Dallas, San Antonio, Galveston, Wichita Falls, and El Paso, Texas.

Around 1965 Jim Day, managing editor of the *Bakersfield California,* a paper for which Seltzer wrote a Spanish-language column from about 1963 to 1966, assigned Seltzer to write editorials. In the autumn of 1965 Day asked Seltzer to write an editorial condemning student protesters, but he refused. He was soon replaced on the editorial page. "When a man hires out to express a publisher's views, and not his own," he once wrote, "he's in a bad fix. A streetwalker is more respectable."

Of writing short stories he said, "Short stories mean ragged pants and a like pocket and occasional fillips to vanity." The most money he received for a story was $150, late in his career, from Houghton Mifflin for printing "Mala Torres" in the anthology *Forgotten Pages of American Literature.* To write about people meant being with them, living the lives they lived, and so he never gave up riding the freights and spending time at the missions, working in the fields, and living on skid rows. He said all he did was tell the stories of these men.

On a Sunday morning early in October 1971 Seltzer died of a heart attack at Zamora's News Stand on Paisano Street in El Paso. He had gone there to look at magazines from Mexico City. Two days later he was buried in El Paso's Evergreen Cemetery, which is bordered by the main railroad lines. On 11 April 1987 Seltzer was posthumously inducted into the "Authors of the Pass: *El Paso Herald-Post* Writers' Hall of Fame."

References:

Elroy Bode, "The Making of a Legend," *Texas Observer,* 65 (30 March 1973): 1-5;

Albert F. Gegenheimer, "Amado Muro," *Arizona Quarterly,* 34 (Autumn 1978): 197-203;

Gerald Haslam, "The Enigma of Amado Muro," *Western American Literature,* 10, no. 1 (1975): 3-9;

William Rintoul, Introduction to Muro's *The Collected Stories of Amado Muro* (Austin: Thorp Springs, 1979), pp. 5-11.

Miguel Antonio Otero

(17 October 1859-7 August 1944)

Luis Leal
University of California, Santa Barbara

BOOKS: *My Life on the Frontier, 1864-1882* (New York: Press of the Pioneers, 1935);

The Real Billy the Kid: With New Light on the Lincoln County War (New York: R. F. Wilson, 1936);

My Life on the Frontier, 1882-1897, foreword by George P. Hammond (Albuquerque: University of New Mexico Press, 1939);

My Nine Years as Governor of the Territory of New Mexico, 1897-1906, edited, with a foreword, by Marion Dargan (Albuquerque: University of New Mexico Press, 1940).

Collection: *Otero. An Autobiographical Trilogy* (New York: Arno, 1974).

OTHER: "Early Recollections of Colonel Chaves by Former Governor Miguel Antonio Otero," in *Colonel José Francisco Chaves, 1833-1924*, edited by Otero, Paul A. F. Walter, and Frank W. Clancy (Santa Fe: Historical Society of New Mexico, 1926), pp. 11-16.

Miguel Antonio Otero's three-volume autobiography is one of the best documentations of life on the American frontier during the last half of the nineteenth century. His recollection of his life from his childhood until the end of his term as governor of the Territory of New Mexico in 1906 is written in the tradition of chronicles of the Southwest. His aim in writing it, he tells readers, was to provide future generations with a firsthand account of what really happened during that interesting period of his life. No less important, since he knew the subject personally, is his 1936 book on William H. Bonney, Billy the Kid, which he wrote because, according to him, all the others were "pure fiction, wholly devoid of fact." His, on the other hand, is "based entirely on actual fact."

Born 17 October 1859 in St. Louis, Missouri, Otero was the son of the famous Miguel Antonio Otero (1829-1882), professor of Latin and Greek at Pingree College, Fishkill on the Hud-

Miguel A. Otero (Miguel A. Otero Collection, Special Collections, General Library, University of New Mexico, Neg. No. 000-021-0004)

son, for two years (1847-1849) and three-time delegate to the United States Congress (1855, 1857, 1859) from the Territory of New Mexico. President Lincoln offered him an appointment as minister to Spain, which he refused because he wanted to retire from public life and dedicate himself entirely to his banking business, the firm of Whiting and Otero. He did, however, accept the position of secretary of the Territory. In 1857 he married Mary Josephine Blackwood, born in New Orleans and brought up in Charleston, South Carolina. The couple raised two boys, Page Blackwood (born 4 January 1858) and

Miguel Antonio, and two girls, Gertrude Vicenta (1865-1876) and Mamie Josephine (1867-1928).

The Otero family moved freely in the Midwest and the Southwest, living in Missouri, Kansas, Colorado, Arizona, and New Mexico. In 1866 the two brothers were sent to a boarding school in Topeka, Kansas, where they underwent unpleasant experiences. "The school proved to be a detestable place and its horrors are still fresh in my memory, though nearly seventy years have passed since then. I can only compare my experiences at the frontier boarding school with those which Dickens relates in *Oliver Twist*."

In 1867 the family moved to Ellsworth, Kansas, where Otero's father had a business. There Miguel Antonio was introduced to the "rough life of the frontier towns." Later they moved to Hayes City, "a wild and woolly town" whose main street was "almost a solid row of saloons, dance halls, restaurants, barber shops, and houses of prostitution kept by such notorious characters as 'Calamity Jane,' 'Lousy Liz,' 'Stink-foot Mag,' and 'Steamboat.'" To cope with lawlessness the city hired as town marshal the famous James Butler "Wild Bill" Hickok, who, according to Otero, was "one of the most perfect specimens of manhood I have ever seen." He met Wild Bill in 1868 and took "a great fancy to him and greatly enjoyed his company.... He often took my brother and myself on buffalo hunts." On the other hand, Otero did not have a very high opinion of William Frederick "Buffalo Bill" Cody, whom he considered too cautious to be brave. Nonetheless, Otero called Cody "a gentleman and a good business man." In spite of his love for life on the frontier, Otero was able to leave it in order to study, first at St. Louis University and then at Notre Dame, where he was trained in business administration.

After returning to the frontier from college, Otero joined his father's firm in the capacity of accountant. In 1886 he was elected probate clerk of San Miguel County, and on 19 December 1888 he married Caroline Virginia Emmett, with whom he had a son in 1891, Miguel Antonio III, who died a few days after birth. The following year his second son, Miguel Antonio IV, was born. In 1891 Otero represented New Mexico at the Republican National Convention, and there he met the future president William McKinley, who was to name Otero governor of the Territory of New Mexico in 1897. As governor Otero organized a powerful Republican political machine. His power and influence at the White

House continued under President Theodore Roosevelt. Historian Ralph Emerson Twitchell summarized Otero's incumbency with these words: "The political policies and methods advocated and pursued by Governor Otero are susceptible of adverse criticism. This cannot be said of his administration so far as the business interests of New Mexico were involved. Calling to his aid in the conduct of his office the business methods with which he was familiar and in which he had received a thorough education, he accomplished much for the welfare of New Mexico."

Otero's works consist of several reports written during his tenancy as governor; a six-page sketch of Colonel José Francisco Chaves; his autobiography in three volumes; and the biography of Billy the Kid. Otero was a friend and admirer of Colonel Chaves, whom he met in 1872 at his home in Valencia County, New Mexico. Eight years were to pass before he met him again, this time at the twenty-fourth legislative assembly in Santa Fe. From that year (1880) on they met often, as Chaves was the presiding officer of the Territory of New Mexico. While Otero was governor he named him superintendent of public instruction twice, in 1901 and 1903. The cowardly assassination of the colonel on 26 November 1904 for political reasons moved Otero deeply.

It was not until he had retired that some of his friends asked former Governor Otero to write his memoirs. He accepted the advice, and in 1935 he published the first volume of what turned out to be the trilogy. The first part ends with the death of his father, which occurred on 30 May 1882, when the author was twenty-three years old. This volume contains stories his mother had told him about the Old West, observations about life on the frontier as seen first through the eyes of a boy and then of a young man, and descriptions of local types, some of whom, such as Hickok, Cody, and Bonney, became famous nationally.

Like Bernal Díaz del Castillo, the chronicler of the conquest of Mexico, Otero had an excellent memory and late in life made use of his early impressions to elaborate the early part of his memoirs. The first volume of his life appeared when the author was already seventy-six years old. The reader, however, is impressed with the vividness of the narration and receives the impression that it was written shortly after the mentioned events took place, a circumstance that leads to the assumption that Otero wrote some of his pages well before publication. He

Otero as a child (Miguel A. Otero Collection, Special Collections, General Library, University of New Mexico, Neg. No. 000-021-0001)

does not, however, rely entirely on memory, as he often quotes the newspapers of the period. His main preoccupation was to confine his writing to actual facts "and adhere strictly to the truth, [and] let the chips fall where they may." This task was difficult to accomplish, since he wanted first of all to hold the attention of the reader. It is for this reason that in his life he gives emphasis to those images of the West that during his youth were already becoming the material out of which the myth of the frontier was to be woven. As George P. Hammond says in the foreword to the 1939 life, "Otero pictures a young, ribald, resourceful, and unregenerate West."

In the first volume of the trilogy the presence of the popular western heroes predominates. Much space is given to relate the lives of Wild Bill Hickok, Buffalo Bill, and Billy the Kid. To the last one he dedicated an entire book, *The Real Billy the Kid*, published in 1936, between the first and second volumes of *My Life on the Frontier*. To write the biography of the famous west-

ern outlaw Otero collected an enormous amount of material, "both as a youth and then as an official of the State of New Mexico." He also availed himself of all the written information about his subject, especially the books of Sheriff Pat Garret (the killer of Bonney). Firsthand information collected by Otero came from M. A. (Ash) Upon, a close friend of Bonney's from early youth to the time of his death, and other contemporaries. Otero met Bonney when the outlaw was taken prisoner in December 1880 and conducted to Santa Fe by train. "My brother and I were so much interested that Father permitted us to go along on the train to Santa Fe. On the way we talked to Billy the Kid. . . . In Santa Fe we were allowed to visit the Kid in jail. I was just one month older than Billy. I liked the Kid very much. In looking back to my first meeting with Billy the Kid, my impressions were most favorable and I can honestly say that he was a man more sinned against than sinning."

The second volume of *My Life on the Frontier* covers a period of fifteen years, from 1882 to 1897. In style and content it is very much like the first volume, except that the experiences related are those of a man in his prime. Here and in the last volume he makes greater use of quotations from newspapers and even books, such as that of Twitchell, to document his statements. He gives less emphasis to personal experiences and more to territorial matters: land grants, politics in the late 1890s, and frontier problems. Of particular interest is the chapter dedicated to the political organization known as *Partido del Pueblo Unido* (The United People's Party), under the leadership of Sheriff Lorenzo López. According to Otero, it was a well-known fact that this organization was supported by two allegedly criminal organizations, the *Gorras Blanco* [*sic*] (The White Caps) and *La Sociedad de Bandidos de Nuevo Mexico* (The Society of New Mexican Bandits). There is little mention of individual outlaws, although a chapter is dedicated to "the frontier ruffian" Dick Rogers. Also of interest is the chapter on the secret order *Los Penitentes*.

References to personal happenings, although less frequent, continue to form an important part of the second autobiography, especially those about his trip to Europe, his marriage in the Episcopal church, and an incident typical of life on the frontier: upon his return from Europe some of his many enemies hired Johnnie Carroll, "a reputed killer," to assassinate him. Carroll was sent to the Harvey House saloon, where

Otero with unidentified military officers (Miguel A. Otero Collection, Special Collections, General Library, University of New Mexico, Neg. No. 000-021-0181)

Otero was playing a game of billiards, "to try his best to get me into an argument and then shoot me." The plot, of course, failed, and Otero lived to become governor of the territory.

The second volume of the autobiography ends with an account of how President McKinley came to name Otero governor of New Mexico in 1897. The president asked him not to mention the fact of his appointment, "not even to your wife, for if it got out I would, perhaps, receive a thousand telegrams advising me not to appoint you." The day the president sent the appointment to the Senate for confirmation, Senator George L. Shoup of Idaho received the following telegram from a Thomas Brannigan: "Hold up confirmation of Otero for Governor of New Mexico. He is a dangerous and unscrupulous man. Documentary evidence will follow." Shoup gave the telegram to Otero, saying that his committee was not going to consider it. The Senate confirmed Otero's appointment, and he became the first Hispanic to be appointed governor of a southwestern territory.

The last volume of Otero's autobiography is the least interesting. *My Nine Years as Governor of the Territory of New Mexico, 1897-1906* was published in 1940, when the author was eighty-one years old. In it he gives a detailed account of his administration during his two terms as governor (he had been reappointed in 1901, in spite of his political enemies); the part he took in the movement for statehood; and his relations with Theodore Roosevelt, with whom he helped organize the military regiment known as the Rough Riders. When Roosevelt was still governor of New York, he sent Otero the following telegram: "To you, more than any other man, we owe the getting up of the regiment." However, he says, his relations with Roosevelt lacked the kind thoughtfulness for others which always characterized William McKinley.

Not an intellectual but rather a politician and a man of action, Otero was able to leave an autobiography that is vigorous, warm, and full of life. His writings reflect his personality, which was that of a man of strong convictions who did not hesitate to fight those who opposed him, nor to help his friends. He enjoyed the company of men of strong character and did not veil his sympathy for men who lived outside the law. As Hammond observes in his introduction to the second volume of the trilogy, "not all readers will agree with everything Mr. Otero has written . . . but few will deny that he has drawn a striking picture of that phase of life in New Mexico of which he was a leading actor."

It must be added that Otero was aware of a principle of primary importance in writing for the public, be it in fiction or nonfiction: whatever is related must be interesting. Realizing, however, that it is difficult to write an autobiography of interest "without having an appearance of indulging in much self-adulation," he endeavored, to the best of his ability, to confine himself "wholly to actual happenings." However, some of the events narrated are recorded as being remembered and are often embellished by imagination. Nevertheless, the trilogy remains one of the most important sources of information about life in the Southwest during a critical period. Otero's autobiography is one of the most important and worthy antecedents of a genre that has been a favorite among contemporary Chicano writers.

References:

F. L. Stanley Crocchiola, *The Otero, New Mexico, Story* (Pantex, Tex., 1962);

"Governor Miguel A. Otero's Plea for New Mexican Statehood," in *A Documentary History of the Mexican American*, edited by Wayne Moquin (New York: Bantam, 1972), pp. 324-327;

Ralph Emerson Twitchell, *The Leading Facts of New Mexican History* (Albuquerque: Horn & Wallace, 1963), pp. 309-310.

Papers:

Otero's papers are held in the Miguel A. Otero Papers, Special Collections, General Library, University of New Mexico.

Leroy V. Quintana

(10 June 1944-)

Douglas K. Benson
Kansas State University

BOOKS: *Hijo del pueblo: New Mexico Poems* (Las Cruces, N.M.: Puerto del Sol, 1976);
Sangre (Las Cruces, N.M.: Prima Agua, 1981).

OTHER: Gary D. Keller and Francisco Jiménez, eds., *Hispanics in the United States: An Anthology of Creative Literature*, includes poems by Quintana (Ypsilanti: Bilingual/Editorial Bilingüe, 1980), pp. 6-8, 107, 128;
"The Reason People Don't Like Mexicans" and "What Can They Do, Send Us to the Nam?," in *Five Poets of Aztlán*, edited by Santiago Daydí-Tolson (Binghamton: Bilingual/Editorial Bilingüe, 1985), pp. 117-136.

PERIODICAL PUBLICATIONS: "Marihuana"; "A Wooden Don Quijote," *Revista Chicano-Riqueña*, 2 (Spring 1974): 22;
"Untitled" [7 Poems], *Contact/II*, 6 (Winter-Spring 1984-1985): 48-49.

Rather than focusing on the political, philosophical or linguistic aspects of Chicano experience, communicated in abstract schemes or through a conglomerate speaker, poet Leroy V. Quintana draws upon oral tradition to introduce readers to a wide range of characters and their reactions to their social and natural environment. In this aspect his books resemble more the novels of Tomás Rivera and Rolando Hinojosa-Smith than they do those of other Chicano poets. His models come from the traditions of his grandparents and from his intense interest in psychology.

Quintana was born in Albuquerque, New Mexico, on 10 June 1944. He never knew his father and spent his early years moving between small northern New Mexico towns such as Ratón and Questa, where the old *cuentos* (tales) had not yet been displaced by Anglo influence. In a 1985 interview with Douglas K. Benson, published in 1987, he talked about his reverence for the aged and his fascination with their stories: "I remember grandmother making candy on the old firewood-burning stove and telling us all the old cuentos deep and long into the night, and grandfather telling me the tales of walking to Wyoming and sheepherding as a kid, along with the traditional cultural stories of *brujas* [witches], *casas despobladas* [abandoned houses], buried *tesoro* [treasure] and *la Llorona* [the legendary ghost-woman who cries out for her children on the night wind]."

Quintana speaks fondly of his parents and grandparents, yet he characterizes his childhood as "rootless," in part because he lived first with his grandparents (until third grade), then with his mother and stepfather. Summers were spent alternating between parents and grandparents, and for a year the family lived in a hotel in El Paso, Texas, while Quintana's stepfather worked as a roofer at nearby Fort Bliss. He suggests transience as a possible reason why the protagonist in his books never seems fully able to understand and participate in the stories he hears. The nostalgia he feels for the unity and harmony of the world of the aged storytellers is palpable, most tellingly in the final poem of *Sangre* (Blood, 1981), entitled "A Legacy." The speaker, "a poor fool/who went to college," realizes how little he really knows and how much he would like to find his way back "to the center of the world/where Grandfather stood that day." The poignancy of this wish is enhanced by the use of the ancient Spanish terms for the four compass directions his grandfather taught him—"Norte, Sur, Oriente, Poniente"—and the American Indian concept of the center of the world. Both traditions of the narrator's legacy are disappearing as the modern world increases his distance from them.

From the fifth grade, when Quintana moved back to Albuquerque, to the time he graduated from high school in that city in 1962, he did little writing and did not finish anything he wrote. After graduation he worked for a time as a roofer with his stepfather. In 1964 he began to study anthropology at the University of New Mexico. His college career was interrupted by a tour of duty in the army (1967 to 1969), with one

Leroy V. Quintana (courtesy of the author)

year in Vietnam. Upon his return he wrote a few rough drafts about his experiences and those of his buddies; these would later become the core of an important cycle of Vietnam poems in *Five Poets of Aztlán* (1985) and his manuscript "Interrogations." In 1970 he married Yolanda Holguin, a nurse from Silver City, New Mexico. The couple have three children.

Quintana returned to college at the University of New Mexico in 1969, declared a major in English, and, as he said in the interview, "began to haphazardly write things down." He became the poetry editor for the university's literary journal, *Thunderbird*, and sent poems off for publication. David Apodaca accepted some of them for a new periodical, *Puerto del Sol*, at New Mexico State University. In 1971 Quintana finished the B.A. in English, then worked as an alcoholism counselor at St. Joseph's Hospital in Albuquerque. In 1972 he began an M.A. at the University of Denver, then changed his plans when Apodaca sent him the first issue of *Puerto del Sol*, along with a New Mexico State University catalog and the news that noted American-Indian author

N. Scott Momaday would be a visiting professor. He applied for an assistantship at New Mexico State University, won it, and moved there after one quarter at Denver. He considers this move to be one of the most fortunate decisions of his life. It put him under the guidance of noted poet-professor Keith Wilson, who got him writing again and provided him the time to finish a book of poetry. He became poetry editor for *Puerto del Sol*, finished the M.A. in English in 1974, and taught for one year as an instructor at New Mexico State. Puerto del Sol Press published his *Hijo del pueblo* [Son of the People]: *New Mexico Poems* (1976) in an edition of five hundred copies.

Most of *Hijo del pueblo* consists of impressions of small-town New Mexico life as seen and heard by a young boy, although one entire section explores the impact of modern society on the American Indian. Much is left unrevealed in these poems, as much a mystery to the young speaker as to the reader. The speaker uses the rhythms of *cuenteros* (storytellers): "Grandfather used to say"; "I have been told." Thus, the objective perspective of the young listener is tempered

Cover for Quintana's second poetry collection, winner of an American Book Award in 1982

by the subjective impressions of the old ones, and readers are gradually pulled into the community with its sense of shared meanings. Quintana recasts ancient subject matter and form into the patterns of narrative technique which much contemporary poetry draws upon: multiple voices, speaker self-characterization, unreliable narrators, and conversational structure. There are no regularized metrics. The tension comes from the reader's organization of the intratextual allusions throughout the volume and the ambiguities which result. Characters include the elders who are both wise and naive, a pilgrim who goes on foot up Tortugas mountain to the shrine of the Virgin Mary of Guadalupe while admitting that "Mañana bailo Indio" (Tomorrow I dance as an Indian), a young woman participating in the Navaho Night Chant, and the shell-shocked soldiers of the Korean War who returned to live in the village.

As the book progresses the narrator becomes more pessimistic, revealing in gentle but ironic anecdotes the devastating effects the outside, modern Anglo world is having on his people. He never becomes strident as he tells of his mother's reactions to "Sterling, Colorado": "On Saturdays we would go into town/after picking potatoes all week/and the Anglos would laugh at us/ and call us dirty Mexicans." But as she "loops and loops the laughter" into "yet another doilie," readers can sense her hurt and understand that her crocheting is one way of overcoming her frustrations.

The critical reception of *Hijo del pueblo*, while limited largely to New Mexico writers, was positive. Karl Kopp in the *American Book Review* (December 1977) stresses the effectiveness of the book's understatement, irony, and sense of mystery. Whereas American culture is losing contact with its heritage and the earth, he says, "these poems are as deep and as full and as clear and as miraculous as a glass of mountain water." Frank Waters's introductory letter to the book notes that " 'Chicano' writing, prose and poetry, is fortunately emerging as a grassroots literature of a people, place, and time too long neglected." Leroy Quintana's present poems are a "new and valid record of this tradition." In a blurb for *Hijo del pueblo*, Keith Wilson praises the book's verisimilitude: "just a quick shadow of fear for the mountain's darkness, the long winters of the hill country, the laughter and the deaths of the old and of the children. It's all here–puro Nuevo Mexico–in the high quiet of these fine poems."

In 1975 Quintana was hired as English instructor at El Paso Community College, where he was coordinator of the poetry series. He was able to finish many of the poems for *Sangre* and rework and expand the Vietnam poems which he had begun after his return from the war. In 1978 he won a creative writing fellowship from the National Endowment for the Arts. His poems began to appear in many journals, and in 1980 his work was included in Gary D. Keller and Francisco Jiménez's anthology *Hispanics in the United States*. The poems, mostly about *vatos* and *pachucos* (dudes and street toughs), reveal an ambivalent attitude toward these young men who are the emblem of rebellion in Texas and California. In "Taps" the vato is a hero pitting himself against the social strictures and condescension of the nun who criticizes him. In others, such as "The Pachuco's Wedding," he appears pathetically out of place in the church where he has come to be wed, although the pettiness and righteousness of the speaker and the other churchgoers reveal more about themselves than about the pachuco whom they criticize: "they were afraid of us–they were in our barrio now." "Blasphemy" and "Leonardo" examine the disturbing psychological underpinnings of the macho exterior displayed by their protagonists.

In 1980 Quintana and his family moved to Albuquerque where he taught at the University of New Mexico. After a year he became a feature writer and sportswriter for the *Albuquerque Tribune*. He stopped writing except for his newspaper work, not having the time and privacy he needed to rework earlier poems and to come up with new material.

Quintana's *Sangre* is a more cohesive book than *Hijo del pueblo*, with a greater variety of poetic voices and a stronger feel for the gossip, puns, and mysteries of village life. In many poems Quintana creates a striking new metaphor, reminiscent of American Indian poetry, out of the anecdotal material. The grandmother's blood "flows through the family tree/as simple and quiet as stones." An old, familiar mystery becomes an entirely new, more chilling one in the poem "Sangre 3." The narrator tells of his grandfather, a wise man with the strength to withstand terrible adversity, including the amputation of his legs. This prepares the reader to accept grandfather's tale of the night he spent in an abandoned house, "frozen with fear," as a group of brujas danced in the next room. Nevertheless, the final stanza is surprising: "These stories about grandpa have been told/in the rooms of my family's homes/across the years, while the brujas/of our haunted blood dance/in the next room, dance in the next room." The third section of *Sangre* deals with the modern world: the Vietnam War, the twin mysteries of love and mathematics in school, the disillusionment of discovering that boyhood wrestling heroes were actually faking, a father's pride in his two daughters, and the sense of longing for the old ways of the speaker's grandfather. The family closeness of the world of the elders is gone.

In 1982 *Sangre* won the American Book Award for poetry and the El Paso Border Regional Library Association award. Criticism has been slight and mixed. Jerry Bradley in the *New Mexico Humanities Review* (Spring 1982) commends Quintana's talent for innuendo, comparing him to "a magician who refuses to explain the simplicity of his tricks." But Phillip Foss, Jr.,

writing in *Contact/II* (Winter/Spring 1984-1985), laments the absence of elements crucial to poetry. He wishes that the poems were more developed and more dramatized, or had been made into stories. In the (1985) interview Quintana agreed with Foss to a point; the rhythms of *Sangre* are too prosy.

In 1982 Quintana went to Western New Mexico University at Silver City to study under psychiatrist Humberto Quintana. He earned an M.A. in counseling in 1984. During the last six months of his stay in Silver City he finished the Vietnam poems which make up the second half of his section in the anthology *Five Poets of Aztlán*.

The poems in *Five Poets of Aztlán*, which has an introductory critical essay with personal information about Quintana, are of two different types. Quintana's "The Reason People Don't Like Mexicans" is similar to *Sangre* in theme and structure but depends more on humor and irony for effect. He introduces a stock character, Don José Mentiras (Lies), who offers comments such as this one on hot chile: "Chicanos have suffered so much/ . . . we're so used to it/we like to suffer/ even when we eat." The Vietnam War poem in *Five Poets*, "What Can They Do, Send Us to the Nam?" (from Quintana's manuscript "Interrogations"), deals with the terrible effects of the war on the narrator and his buddies as well as on Vietnam and its people. The unified world of Quintana's New Mexico youth is gone: "Some to get back to the world sooner/threw away their malaria pills/Tried to turn/green as government issue."

In Santiago Daydí-Tolson's introduction to Quintana's poetry in *Five Poets*, he praises Quintana's ability to focus without digressions, his mastery of nuance, and his compassion laced with irony.

In 1984 Quintana moved to San Diego, California, where he works as a counselor for the National City Family Clinic. In the (1985) interview with Douglas K. Benson, Quintana said he attends few conferences, though he is beginning to do readings again. "I suppose that at the base I'm a writer who is a counselor more than a counselor who writes." He is curious about the effect that life in California will have on his work. Currently he is reworking a novel and writing a collection of impressions of middle-age life. He hopes to try screenwriting and may go back to teaching, with the increased awareness of student needs that he feels he now has, or he may go on for a doctorate in psychology. His focus is still on individ-

April 13/85

November 22nd   JFK

I was 19 and working as a roofer
the moon St. apts in Albuquerque
I was ~~still~~ laying shingles on a gable
An old lady ~~walked across the street~~
~~and told us - no I think~~ asked us
if we knew that the president had been shot
~~I can't remember now if she said anything else~~
It was about three o'clock
~~I didn't know what to think~~ She mentioned Dallas
~~I think she discussed the details~~
and walked back across the street
Shortly after that the chuckwagon came
~~I don't remember getting down~~ men gathered around
I recall my step-father walking up fires, talked
to me, sadly saying some black guy a carpenter,
had told him he had lost a friend
as if he didn't know what else to say
~~We went back to work~~, the world somehow had
begun to fall apart and all the men and all the nails
and all the mexican bricklayers at a penny a brick
could never put it together again.

(over)

Drafts for Quintana's poem about the death of President John F. Kennedy (courtesy of the author)

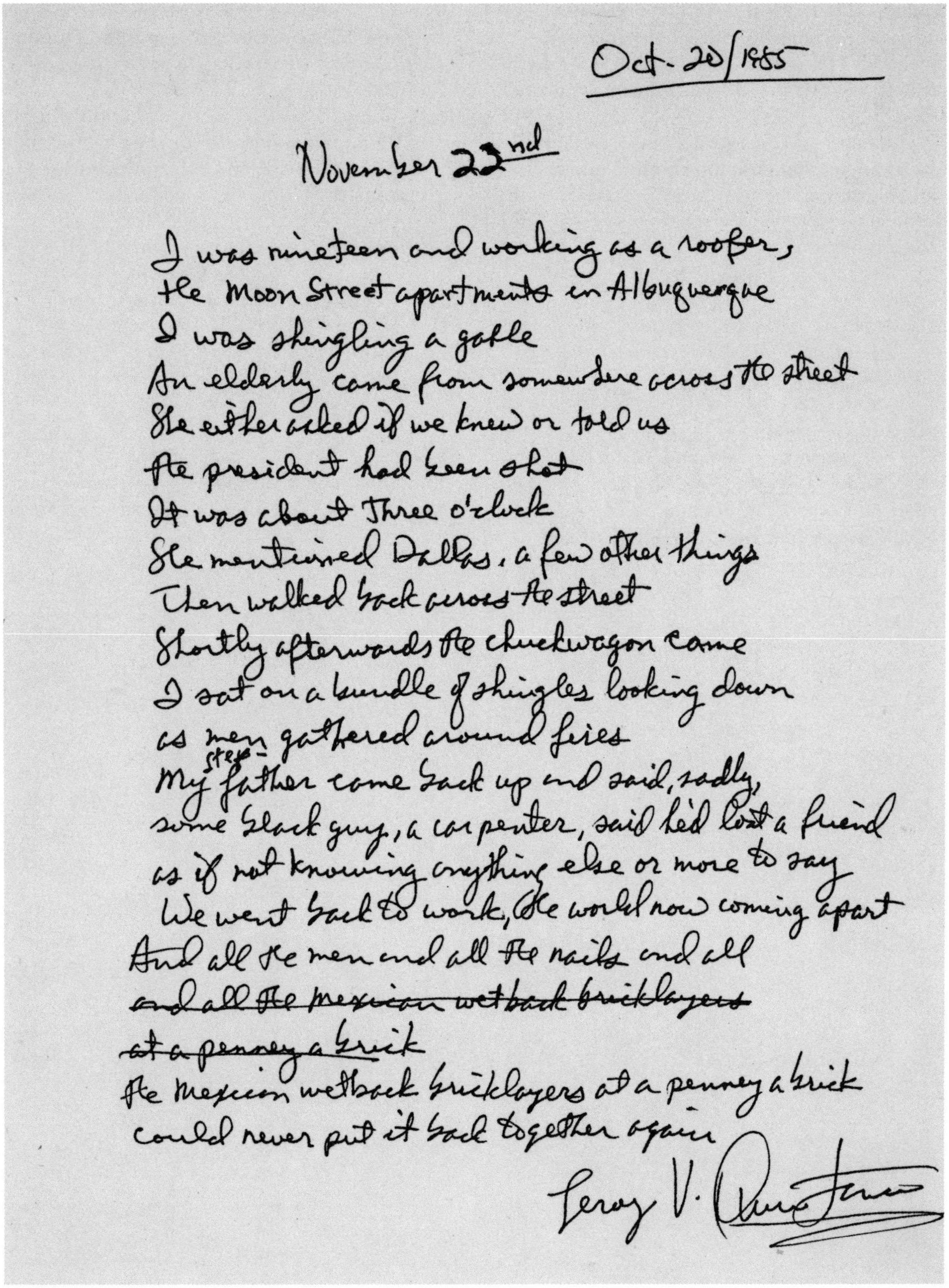

Oct. 20/1985

November 22nd

I was nineteen and working as a roofer,
the Moon Street apartments in Albuquerque
I was shingling a gable
An elderly came from somewhere across the street
She either asked if we knew or told us
the president had been shot
It was about three o'clock
She mentioned Dallas, a few other things
Then walked back across the street
Shortly afterwards the chuckwagon came
I sat on a bundle of shingles looking down
as men gathered around fires
My father came back up and said, sadly,
some black guy, a carpenter, said he'd lost a friend
as if not knowing anything else or more to say
We went back to work, the world now coming apart
And all the men and all the nails and all
~~and all the mexican wetback bricklayers~~
~~at a penney a brick~~
the mexican wetback bricklayers at a penney a brick
could never put it back together again

Leroy V. Quintana

ual reactions, perhaps due to his interest in psychology and perhaps because of the traditions of his boyhood. "In many ways, I'm still basically a smalltown New Mexico boy carrying on the oral tradition."

Quintana is well regarded in New Mexico and by an increasing number of critics elsewhere. His unique combination of the oral tradition with modern narrative technique speaks not just to Chicanos but to all readers.

Interview:

Douglas K. Benson, "A Conversation with Leroy V. Quintana," *Bilingual Review/La Revista Bilingüe*, 12 (1987): 218-229.

References:

Douglas K. Benson, "Inner and Outer Realities of Chicano Life: the New Mexican Perspective of Leroy V. Quintana," *Perspectives on Contemporary Literature*, 12 (1986): 20-28;

Benson, "Intuitions of a World in Transition: the New Mexico Poetry of Leroy V. Quintana," *Bilingual Review/La Revista Bilingüe*, 12 (1987): 62-80;

Jerry Bradley, "*Sangre*: Leroy V. Quintana," *New Mexico Humanities Review* (Spring 1982): 90;

Santiago Daydí-Tolson, "Introduction: Voices from the Land of Reeds," in *Five Poets of Aztlán*, edited by Daydí-Tolson (Binghamton: Bilingual/Editorial Bilingüe, 1985), pp. 9-58;

Phillip Foss, Jr., "Familial Portraits," *Contact/II*, 6 (Winter/Spring 1984-1985): 33;

Karl Kopp, "*Hijo del pueblo*: Leroy V. Quintana," *American Book Review*, 1 (December 1977): 19-20.

Papers:

Quintana's papers are held at the Zimmerman Library, Special Collections, University of New Mexico.

Isabella Ríos
(Diana López)

(16 March 1948-)

Annie Olivia Eysturoy
University of New Mexico

BOOK: *Victuum* (Ventura, Cal.: Diana-Etna, 1976).

Diana López, writing under the name of her maternal grandmother Isabella Ríos, holds a distinguished place in contemporary Chicano literature. Her novel *Victuum* (1976), a bildungs-roman, is one of the earliest Chicana novels and the first Chicano work to deal with the world of a psychic. *Victuum* experiments with both form and content, thus foreshadowing a trend which has characterized much Chicana fiction succeeding it.

López was born in Los Angeles, California, the oldest of nine children. Her father, an American Indian, is a descendant of a northern New Mexican tribe on his father's side and Chihuahua Indians on his mother's side but grew up within the Hispanic cultural heritage in Las Cruces, New Mexico. During the Depression, at the age of fourteen, he traveled with his family to California in search of employment and settled in Camarillo to work in the fields. He later became a contractor and started a business which he still owns. On her mother's side López is a descendant of an early Californio family. Her mother was born in Oxnard, California, and grew up in a large family in a Hispanic community. She became a beautician but later gave up her profession for marriage and a growing family.

López spent her early years in the small Hispanic community of Meta Street in Oxnard where her Hispanic cultural roots were established and her creative imagination received its initial influences. As a child she loved listening to stories. Her mother told her fairy tales and the family's historical anecdotes. There were stories of big ranches and orchards that had once been in the family's possession; of the famous California bandit Joaquín Murrieta, who would come to her great-grandfather's ranch with his men and leave a sack of gold for a pot of beans, while the

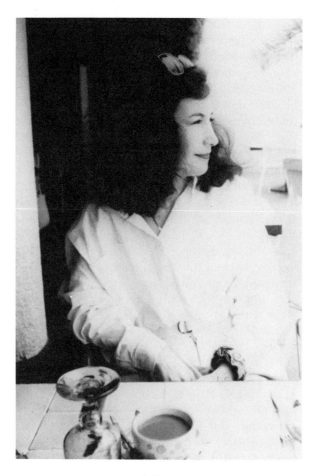

Isabella Ríos

women had to be hidden away for protection. Her great-aunts, many of whom lived to be over one hundred years old, provided an unending flow of stories about the family and of California's Hispanic past. It was from her great-aunts that López heard about the arrival of the Anglos, the eastern "pirateers" (as her great-aunts called them), and what that arrival meant to her own and many other Hispanic families. She heard the story of her great-great-uncle who was hanged from a tree in his own orchard because he re-

201

fused to relinguish his land to the newcomers. These oral accounts of her background not only fueled her imagination but also provided her with a cultural and historical consciousness which was to influence much of her political and creative activities in her adult years.

In 1952, when Diana López was four, the family moved from Oxnard to Ventura. Although Ventura is only eight miles from Oxnard the move proved to be a culture shock for López. Left behind was the security and comfort of a Spanish-speaking community. In Ventura Spanish was spoken only within the family. Racial remarks from neighborhood children became a daily occurrence, leaving her with a lasting sensitivity to prejudice. Despite these obstacles, López describes her childhood in Ventura as basically healthy and happy. Her creative impulse first found an outlet in caricatures and cartoons, and later she wrote plays and skits which she would have her sisters and brothers and neighborhood children perform. Her initial experiences with the American educational system were less than successful. She failed kindergarten since she only spoke Spanish, and the assumption was that inability to speak English represented mild retardedness. She was treated accordingly. After intense parental tutoring she learned English and spent twelve successful years at the Academy of St. Catherine in Ventura. In high school López often participated in dramatic performances and excelled by winning first place in the Shakespeare Drama Festival for three consecutive years. She loved to write, act, and direct plays, and a dramatic influence is easily recognizable in the writing style she later chose for her novel. During her high school years she also received much encouragement for her short stories and poems, some of which were published in school newsletters and yearbooks.

After high school López entered San Francisco State where she earned a B.A. in English literature and in 1969 an M.A. in English and creative writing. In 1970 she obtained a teaching position in English at Moorpark College in Ventura. López earned an Ed.D. degree in bilingual higher education from Nova University in 1979.

Throughout her high school years López was increasingly aware of the social conditions around her. The racism she had experienced as a child in an all-Anglo community she now saw reflected in society. When she entered San Francisco State she became involved in various political activities on campus. There were only six other Chicano students, yet they organized themselves and joined the Third World Liberation, a coalition of all campus minority groups. One of the objectives of this group was to bring more Chicano students to the university. They visited all the high schools in the area trying to encourage more young Chicanos to go to college. López worked for organizations which supported César Chávez (the leader of the United Farmworkers) and created a tutorial program for minority students.

Her involvement and commitment to the Hispanic community continued after she left San Francisco State and obtained her position at Moorpark College. There she started working for Los Hermanos (The Brothers) and the Pinto Program (Prisoner Program) which were designed to help veterans and former convicts (most of whom came from backgrounds of socioeconomic deprivation, drugs, and long periods of incarceration). In an attempt to bridge the wide gap which existed between the Hispanic community and Moorpark College, López started the Bilingual Center, a liaison which met the needs of many people by improving their proficiency in both English and Spanish.

López's many activities during her student years reflect a commitment to the Hispanic community which also forms the backbone of her writing. Although she had come to San Francisco State with the intent to study law, she gradually became more and more involved with writing because of the influence and encouragement of writer Kay Boyle and critic Wilder Bentley who were teaching there.

She entered the graduate creative writing program under their sponsorship. Her poetry and short stories reflecting the political mood of the era were published in local Chicano newspapers and campus literary magazines. Since she would give pieces of her writing to anyone interested in publishing them and never kept records, she does not know how much of her writing has actually been published, or where. She also gave many readings during her student years and continued to do so into the 1970s.

When López first started working on her novel, her objective was to write a Chicana bildungsroman and in the process provide the reader with a sense of a Hispanic family's history and cultural background. She interviewed one of her relatives over a period of almost two years, and the novel was going to be the relative's story,

CHAPTER 1

I watch. I listen. For sound am I, silenced ~~by~~ the human ear at present; shaped matter unseen by the human eye at present.

The cycle of fetal development completes its virtue of creation, and a small struggling body awaits my entrance. Since conception, I have observed the nurtured embryo...since webbing lessened and weighty water became a splendorous discovery between each appendage...since the torso would twist and press against the fleshy walls of warmed womb...swimming in constant movement...from ripples and flagulations...to the voluntary production of muscle control...each turn a spacial conquest in time, for now positioned at outlet, the small body conjurs strength to force its every element through its mother's birth canal.

How the woman moans with pain:

[Wet...Wet...Wetness...the water bag is broken...Oh, it is time!...What is the time?...It is so dark...just soft moonlight against the shade...let me see... it is two o'clock...Oh, now to move out of this wetness...Oh, I can feel it pour out...each time I shift...Oh, how there's pressure between my legs...Oh, the weight...for sure its a boy...I'm so big!...I must get up...go to the restroom... Oh...the struggle...Oh, at last the time has come...I am so anxious...How sad I was to learn that again I was pregnant, but I grew accustom to my womb's constant stretching, and knowing that a human being was miraculously developing with my help...How the little thing depended on me so...detachment will soon part our nearness and the babe will be its own...Oh so large...I am anxious for its birth...A boy?...A girl?...Oh!...the pains are far apart, but...Oh!...Oh!...

I better pad the bed...the water... I have had so many...but each one is different; some were easy...some, difficult, but...Oh... this one I fear...Oh! I'll need Susie...as soon as I see sunlight; I'll ask someone to go pick her up! Oh!...Oh!...Oh!...that pressure...yes, Susie!...early in the morning...they'll

1

First page of the revised typescript for Victuum, *Ríos's "Chicana bildungsroman" (courtesy of the author)*

recorded and translated into literary form by López. Her initial title was "Aguila descalza" (Barefooted Eagle), as the subject used to be called this by her aunts. In the course of the interviews the relative began relating dreams, visions, and psychic phenomena of extraordinary character. The project of writing a Chicana bildungsroman based on biographical information thus took on a quite different dimension as the woman's story went far beyond ordinary experience. Told in dialogue, *Victuum* is a fictionalized version of a life, encompassing both ordinary and extraordinary dimensions of that life. The woman whose story is told insisted that the novel be given the title *Victuum* as a tribute to her psychic guide (whom she called by that name) who had played such an important role in her development.

The protagonist, Valentina Ballesternos, appears on the opening page of *Victuum*, and the reader taps into her stream of consciousness while she is still in the fetal stage: "I watch. I listen. For sound am I, silenced by the human ear at present; shaped matter unseen by the human eye at present." The unborn, preconscious fetus reflects on its own coming into being: "My only regret is that I will begin life again. For as I sip nutrients from the soft warmth of my mother's breast, the knowledge I have gathered over centuries, epochs, will slip back into the sleeping silence of my conscience; it will be decades before they'll possess the strength to pull from the depths of my brain the knowledge of yesteryears. All will be forgotten. I will cling close to instinct and intuition, yet my tongue will lack the maneuverability to express all that I feel. My eyes will exist in darkness until enlightenment chooses to blaze from their enclosed profundity." The fetus, as a link in a long process of reincarnation, foreshadows the course of her own life in the process of coming into possession of psychic powers.

Part 1 of *Victuum*, which is two-thirds of the novel, continues to cover Valentina's development from birth to marriage. Through historical anecdotes, events of daily life, and the effects of contemporary developments such as Prohibition, the Depression, and the beginning of World War II, a picture emerges of the social and cultural environment of a Hispanic community.

In part 2 of *Victuum* the strong intuitive faculties which Valentina has had all through her childhood develop into elaborate visions as she comes into maturity. After her marriage she gives birth to nine children, events that are almost parenthetical as the focus is almost exclusively on her grow-

ing psychic powers. In dreams and visions she comes in contact with historical and mythical figures such as Isaiah, Ulysses, William Wordsworth, and Pope Eusebius, all of whom become her teachers. She is introduced to different areas of human thought of which she has no prior knowledge, notions which challenge her self-perception and her mental capacities. Her primary guide is Victuum, a prince from another solar system, who takes her on a journey into the past to demonstrate the infinite powers of the human brain and humanity's infinite abilities for survival through reincarnation. The second part of the novel renders almost exclusively Valentina's visions as they come to her, without incorporating them into her ordinary daily life, and when the novel ends, the reader is left wondering if Valentina has retreated completely into a world of visions to the exclusion of everything else. López explains that these visions represent the epitome of Valentina's state of mind. She wanted to create an atmosphere in which the reader is forced to question the nature of reality. López had plans for continuing with Valentina's dreams and visions in a second volume, a fact which may explain the abrupt conclusion of the novel. She is currently revising *Victuum* with the intention of changing the two separate parts of the novel into a more complete and cohesive whole.

Since its publication *Victuum* has received scant critical attention, possibly due to both subject matter and style. In choosing to write the story in a manner which would best communicate her relative's experience to the reader, López challenges literary categories. As critic Francisco Lomelí points out in a review in *Minority Voices* (Spring 1980), *Victuum* defies any single classification within literary genres. In an unpublished interview López said she sees *Victuum* as a nonfiction novel and drama. Rather than trying to fit her material and her creativity into a specific genre, López organized her information into a form much like a script. That the novel is written almost exclusively in the first person and in present tense further underscores its dramatic quality. López points out that she wanted to draw the reader into Valentina's environment. Through her use of dialogue López tries to draw the attention away from the individual in favor of the community and present the individual as an integral part of the collective whole.

López did not know her maternal grandmother personally but drew inspiration from her through the stories she heard from her great-aunts. Their voices from the past and their stories become part of *Victuum*, as they are an integral part of the world of her protagonist. By weaving together stories from the past and the present López translates into fictional form the cultural and social context of an extraordinary Chicana. She follows the tradition of her storytelling great-aunts and keeps the oral tradition alive; in this she affirms her commitment to her community and cultural heritage.

Interviews:

John Strobol, "Bridging the Gap," KBBQ (Ventura/Oxnard, Cal.), 1977, radio interview with López;

Fernando del Río, "Community Feedback," 13 May 1978, television interview with López;

Francisco A. Lomelí, "Voces Chicanas," University of California, Santa Barbara, May 1979, television interview with López.

References:

José Armas, "A Classical Biographical Novel by Isabella Ríos," *De Colores*, 4 (1980): 1-2;

Jess Gutiérrez, "A Novel that Grew in the Streets of Oxnard," *Star Free Press* (Ventura, Cal.), 9 January 1977;

Francisco A. Lomelí, "Isabella Ríos and the Chicano Psychic Novel," *Minority Voices: An Interdisciplinary Journal of Literature and the Arts*, 4 (Spring 1980): 49-61.

Tomás Rivera
(22 December 1935-16 May 1984)

Luis Leal
University of California, Santa Barbara

BOOKS: *". . . y no se lo tragó la tierra"/". . . and the Earth Did Not Part,"* novel in Spanish by Rivera, English translation by Herminio Ríos C. (Berkeley: Quinto Sol, 1971); translated by Rolando Hinojosa-Smith as *This Migrant Earth* (Houston: Arte Publico, 1985);
Always and Other Poems (Sisterdale, Tex.: Sisterdale, 1973).

OTHER: "Into the Labyrinth: The Chicano in Literature," in *New Voices in Literature,* edited by Edward Simmen (Edinburg, Tex.: Pan American University, 1971), pp. 18-25;
"On the Road to Texas: Pete Fonesca," in *Aztlán: An Anthology of Mexican American Literature,* edited by Luis Valdez and Stan Steiner (New York: Vintage Books, 1972), pp. 146-154;
Octavio I. Romano-V. and Herminio Ríos C., eds., *El Espejo/The Mirror,* includes work by Rivera (Berkeley: Quinto Sol, 1972), pp. 16-40, 238-244;
Philip D. Ortego, ed., *We Are Chicanos: An Anthology of Mexican-American Literature,* includes work by Rivera (New York: Washington Square, 1973), pp. 184-185, 187;
"Mexican American Literature," in *Spanish Speaking American Challenge: A Report of the Chicano Conference Held at BYU in 1974,* edited by Sid Shreeve and Merwin G. Fairbanks (Provo: Brigham Young University, Latin American Studies, 1975), pp. 104-115;
Carmela Montalvo, Leonardo Anguiano, and Cecilio Garcia Camarillo, eds., *El Quetzal Emplumece,* includes poetry by Rivera (San Antonio: Mexican American Cultural Center, 1976), pp. 246-253;
"Chicano Literature: Fiesta of the Living," in *The Identification and Analysis of Chicano Literature,* edited by Francisco Jiménez (New York: Bilingual/Editorial Bilingüe, 1979), pp. 19-36;
"Chicano Literature: The Establishment of Community," in *A Decade of Chicano Literature*

Tomás Rivera, 1982 (photo by Steve Walag)

(1970-1979): Critical Essays and Bibliography, edited by Luis Leal and others (Santa Barbara: Editorial La Causa, 1982), pp. 9-17;
"My Son Doesn't See a Thing," in *Fiesta in Aztlán: Anthology of Chicano Poets,* edited by Toni Empringham (Santa Barbara: Capra, 1982), p. 91.

PERIODICAL PUBLICATIONS: "Eva y Daniel," *El Grito,* 5 (Spring 1972): 8-25;
"Looking for Borges" and "The Child," *Revista Chicano-Riqueña,* 1 (Spring 1973): 2-4, 18;
"Alone," *Café Solo,* 8 (Spring 1974): 31;
"Las salamandras," *Mester,* 5 (November 1974): 25-26;

"El Pete Fonesca," *Revista Chicano-Riqueña*, 2 (Winter 1974): 15-22;

"Recuerdo, descubrimiento y voluntad en el proceso imaginativo literario/Remembering, Discovering, and Volition in the Literary Imaginative Process," *Atisbos: Journal of Chicano Research*, 1 (Summer 1975): 66-77;

"Inside the Window," *Caracol*, 3 (August 1977): 17-18;

"On American Literature," *Texas Books in Review*, 1, no. 1 (1977): 5-6;

"The Searchers," *U C Riverside*, 2 (June 1984): 22.

Besides his public life as an administrator of the University of California, Riverside, Tomás Rivera was well known in literary circles as a writer of prose and poetry. Although he published only two books and some scattered poems, short stories, and literary essays and left parts of an unpublished second novel, he was able to influence greatly the trend that Chicano literature was to take during the 1970s and into the 1980s. His most important work, "*. . . y no se lo tragó la tierra*"/"*. . . and the Earth Did Not Part*," a novel composed of short narratives, was awarded the Premio Quinto Sol in 1970 and published in 1971. Critics have praised the novel for its original structure, its terse style, and its faithful presentation of life among Chicano migrant workers. Less well known is his collection *Always and Other Poems* (1973), in which there is the same faith in the future of the Chicano community.

Born in Crystal City, Texas, the son of Florencio Rivera and Josefa Hernández, Rivera spoke Spanish at home since both his parents had emigrated from Mexico to Texas. His father had come to El Paso from the central state of Aguascalientes at age fifteen. He migrated to the Midwest, where he had several jobs, mostly on the railroad. On his way back to Mexico during the Depression, he stopped in Crystal City, where he met his future wife, whom he married there in 1930. As a young woman she had come to Texas with her family from the state of Coahuila and had lived in several cities in Texas. Her father had been an officer during the Mexican Revolution.

Before attending public school in his home town, Rivera learned to read and write Spanish in the barrio school. Although his family had to travel yearly to the Midwest to work in the fields he was able to graduate from high school. However, in order for him to be able to continue his studies at Southwest Texas Junior College, Rivera's parents let him work only three months so that he could come home in September. As he told Juan Bruce-Novoa in a 1980 interview, "My parents were still working in Iowa, but I would only work three months and then I had to return to complete the year at the college."

From junior college Rivera went on to Southwest Texas State University where he majored in English and received a B.A. degree in 1958. That same year he began to teach art in elementary schools. He married Concepción Garza in the late 1950s. He also continued his studies at Southwest Texas State, where he received an M.Ed. in administration in 1964. In 1969 Rivera earned an M.A. in Spanish literature and a Ph.D. in romance languages and literature from the University of Oklahoma. At Oklahoma he specialized in Spanish literature and for his dissertation wrote about León Felipe, a Spanish poet who lived in exile in Mexico from the end of the Spanish civil war in 1939 until his death in 1954. In 1967 Rivera's poem "Me lo enterraron" (They Buried Him), in which he remembered the death of his father in 1959, was published. Immediately after receiving his doctorate from Oklahoma, Rivera returned to Texas to accept a position at Sam Houston University, Huntsville, where he remained until 1971.

Rivera moved to the University of Texas, San Antonio, as a professor of Spanish in 1971. In 1973 he was appointed dean, and in 1976 he was appointed vice-chancellor for administration. He discovered that he could benefit the Chicano people more as a university administrator than as a professor. It was for that reason that Rivera later accepted the position of executive vice-president of Academic Affairs at the University of Texas, El Paso. In 1979 he was appointed chancellor at the University of California, Riverside, where he remained until his death in 1984. In a special issue of *Revista Chicano-Riqueña* dedicated to Rivera (Fall-Winter 1985), Rolando Hinojosa-Smith said that perhaps too much has been made of the fact that Rivera was the first Mexican-American to serve as chancellor in the University of California system. "It's a fact and undeniable, and it may also be a reflection upon the State of California. But look at these facts: Tomás Rivera won his Ph.D. from the University of Oklahoma in 1969, and he was named Chancellor less than ten years later. Now *that* was an accomplishment."

Rivera's administrative ability and his great concern for the educational problems of students earned him several honors. He was named a member of the board of the Carnegie Foundation for the Advancement of Teaching in 1976, received a presidential appointment to the Board of Foreign Scholarships (which directs and administers the Fulbright program), and was named member of the board of the National Chicano Council on Higher Education. In 1980 he served on the presidential commission established with the purpose of identifying the educational problems that the nation was to face during the 1980s. He was also a corporate officer of the Times-Mirror Corporation and a member of the board of directors of the Ford Foundation.

Rivera's success as a writer and administrator was due to his personal qualities. He had a great reserve of physical energy, a well-defined objective in life, and an unusual sense of human and social values. Most important he was unfailingly optimistic. His poem "The Searchers" reveals his hopeful sentiments:

> We were not alone
> after many centuries
> How could we be alone
> We searched together
> We were searchers
> And we will continue
> to search
> because our eyes
> still have
> the passion of prophesy.

Hinojosa-Smith observed that "a careful reading of 'The Searchers' will illustrate those strong, enduring human values which he [Rivera] possessed and which all of us admire, if not exactly follow and set for ourselves."

Rivera's desire to write came from the advice of his maternal grandfather, who told him that writing and art were the most important things in life. Although he wrote stories and poems, Rivera did not publish any until the late 1960s, when they began to appear in Chicano periodicals. In 1969 the editors of a Berkeley, California, periodical, *El Grito*, decided to establish an editorial house—which they called Quinto Sol Publications—and to offer prizes to the best works submitted by Chicano writers. Rivera had not published some of his early poems and stories because, as he told Burt A. Folkart in the *Los Angeles Times* (17 May 1984), they were written in English, and he felt they did not reach into his sub-

conscious. "But when I learned that Quinto Sol accepted manuscripts in Spanish, it liberated me. I knew that I could express myself as I wanted." He completed *". . . y no se lo tragó la tierra"* and sent it to Quinto Sol. The novel received the first prize in 1970; it was translated into English by Herminio Ríos C. and published in a bilingual edition in 1971.

Rivera's essay, "Chicano Literature: Fiesta of the Living" (1979), is preceded by a quotation from Octavio Paz's book *El laberinto de la soledad* (1950; translated as *The Labyrinth of Solitude*, 1961), which reads, "Every poem we read is a re-creation, that is, a ceremonial ritual, a fiesta." Rivera's essay focuses on Chicano literature "as a ritual, a fiesta of the living." For him the most important characteristic of Chicano literature is the striving on the part of the writer to conserve past experiences, real or imagined, in "a ritual of cleansing and a prophecy." The ritual of remembering is based on two common images, the house and the barrio, and on the concept of struggle. With the three elements Rivera presents a unique view of the Chicano world: "The ritual is simple yet complex. The bond is there, the cleansing is there, both for the Chicano writer and for his reader. These effects of the ritual are produced through simple forms as *la casa* and *el barrio* and by the transgressive and ingressive concept of *la lucha*," or struggle. It is relatively easy to find examples of the narrative technique of remembering in Rivera's work. In "Me lo enterraron" the speaker establishes the relationship between dead father and living son by remembering recurrent, and therefore ritual, actions carried out by the father. The poem is structured around the assumption that the persons who buried the father did not know about the intimate relationship that had existed between father and son, while the son did and could therefore remember:

> They did not know
> that he taught me
>   how to cry
> and how to love
> ....
> They did not know it
>   that is why
> they buried him.

The boy regrets his father's death; the burial is a ritual action that he wanted to prevent, but could not:

Covers for the 1977 edition of Rivera's novel, winner of the Premio Quinto Sol in 1970

> Not I, they
> they buried him.
> ....
> I refused to do it
> I didn't bury him.

In the issue of the journal *El Grito* which appeared during the fall of 1969 Rivera published, besides "Me lo enterraron," six other poems. One of them is "The Rooster Crows en Iowa y en Texas," a composition that can be traced to the days when, with his family, the author was a migrant worker making the yearly journey from southern Texas to the Midwest during the early summer and returning in the fall. In an article in *Atisbos: Journal of Chicano Research* (1975) he remembered that during those days "there was always someone who knew the old traditional stories–'el gigante moro,' 'el negrito guërin,' etc. Then there were always those who acted out mov-

ies, told about different parts of the world and about Aladdin and his magic lamp. An oral literature was, in that way, developed in migrant camps. People find refuge not only in the Church or with their brothers but also by sitting in a circle, listening, telling stories and, through words, escaping to other worlds as well as inventing them. It was natural that a type of narrative world developed in the children and worlds were crystallized because of the tedium of every-day work." He did not forget those stories, and in his fiction, as well as in his poetry, Rivera makes reference to them.

> The rooster crows.
> The alarm rings.
> They eat and go to work.
> "Aladín y su lámpara maravillosa."
> The snow falls.
> The truck runs full of people.
> And we return . . . . home.

The use of English and Spanish in this poem places the composition in the popular trend of the late 1960s among Chicano poets, who tried to create a new means of expression by combining the two languages, thus reflecting more accurately a Chicano vision of the world. The use of motifs common among the rural people, in this case the rooster, was also common at that time. In Rivera's poem the rooster symbolizes the monotony of life in the fields, where the only entertainment is the telling of stories around the bonfire after the day is done.

In Rivera's collection *Always and Other Poems* there is a brief poem, "Past Possessions," which is significant for the simplicity with which the poetic voice remembers and gives expression to childhood days through the listing of toys associated with a boy in the barrio or rural environment:

> A piece
> of string
> A broken top
> A crooked kite
> A wooden gun
> A mop . . .
> Quiet . . . noise
> A long thin weed a lance
> A few large cans a dance
> Boxes
> For cars and houses
> Such trivial things[.]

The poem "The Overalls," which again makes use of a common image, expresses the void and the emptiness felt as a result of the death of a member of the family and, at the same time, shows how the experience of remembering the ritual of the burial leads to personal discovery:

> Frightening
> as the attic hole
> the overalls in the garage, hanging
> and the vapor from the train
> swung to my face
> as the cross that
> shouted the lump
> in the cemetery
> and the sounds of clods
> of earth hitting the coffin
> reminded me of something
> I knew nothing about
> the glancing of tearful eyes
> embracing
> as I sensed
> that I had been born
> the crushing vapor
> and the overalls, hanging

> in the garage
> never to be filled again[.]

Rivera best succeeds in giving form to the life of migrant workers in his novel "*. . . y no se lo tragó la tierra.*" As he told Bruce-Novoa, "In . . . *tierra* and those stories, I wrote about the migrant worker in that period of ten years [1945-1955]. During that period I became very conscious, in my own life, about the suffering and the strength and the beauty of these people. I was more conscious of their strength when I was living with them. Later, 1967-68, I'm writing. The Chicano Movement was a complete power already in the university and so forth. I wanted to document, somehow, the strength of those people that I had known. And I was only concerned about the migrant worker, the people I had known best. . . . So I began to see that my role–if I want to call it that–would be to document that period of time, but giving it some kind of spiritual strength or spiritual history. Not just this and this happened, but to give a spiritual dimension to the people of that time. I see my role more as a documentor of that period of time when the migrant worker was living without any kind of protection. There was no legal protection, and without legal protection, there is nothing. I saw a lot of suffering and much isolation of the people. Yet they lived through the whole thing, perhaps because they had no choice. I saw a lot of heroic people and I wanted to capture their feelings." In the novel Rivera exalts the values of the Chicano family (*la casa*), the community (*el barrio*), and the struggle to obtain justice. As he said in his *Atisbos* article, "the political and economic structures which surrounded the lives of these families will always appear in history as something brutal, outrageous and inhuman. . . . Migrant workers still exist today [1975], but in fewer numbers and now have some protection by the law. But, in the long run, the migrant worker was and always will be exploited." In the novel he tries to re-create those conditions under which the migrant worker was living during the 1940s and 1950s, and this is what gives the work a sense of tragedy, found especially in such episodes as "The Children Were Victims," "Little Children Burned," and "When We Arrive." What saved the Chicano from being dehumanized was, according to Rivera, his relationship with his own people, with the land he cultivated, and his rejection of the system that exploited him, since he realized that the system did not offer any rewards "for acting human or for

Rivera with his family, Riverside, California, 1979 (photo by Steve Walag)

loving his neighbor unselfishly. This is the type
of character I tried to portray in my novel."

The Chicano novel published before the
1970s was, as a rule, a work of social protest or
based upon personal experiences somewhat fictionalized. No attempt was made to present the realistic materials in an innovative form. Rivera,
following the example of previous Chicano novelists, develops in "*. . . y no se lo tragó la tierra*" the
theme of social protest, but, unlike his precursors, and following in the steps of contemporary
Mexican and Latin American novelists, he uses a
fragmented structure. At the same time, the action is observed from a limited point of view,
that of a young boy who does not completely understand the meaning of what he observes.

The technique of remembering used by Rivera is best exemplified in the last chapter of the
novel, entitled "Under the House," where the
boy hides and remembers. Rhetorically, the ritual
of remembering on the part of the boy under
the house serves to recapitulate and give structural unity to the episodes that form the novel,

the experiences that have been remembered in
the previous twelve central chapters, symbolic of
the twelve months of the year. The boy thinks, "I
needed to isolate myself in order to understand
many things. From here on all I have to do is
come back here in the dark and think about
them. And I have so much to think about, and so
many years to catch up on. I think that today I
wanted to remember this past year. But that's
just one year. I'll have to come here to remember all the others." The fragmented structure of
Rivera's novel has led some critics (Daniel P.
Testa and Juan Rodríguez, for example) to consider the work as a collection of short stories, yet
there are unifying elements. A frame unites the
stories. Short introductions to each chapter function to set the mood for the story that follows.
For example, "The Prayer," in which the mother
implores the Virgin Mary to protect her son who
is fighting in Korea, is preceded by an anecdote
about a visit by several mothers to a medium to
find out the fate of their sons in Korea, some of
whom have been lost in action. Interrelated mo-

Rivera with President David Saxon at Rivera's 1980 inauguration as chancellor of the University of California, Riverside (photo by Steve Walag)

tifs make "... *y no se lo tragó la tierra*" an organic work composed of integrated stories preceded by related anecdotes or comments and framed by encompassing chapters at the beginning and the end.

The criticism of Rivera's work has been extensive and very favorable. Most of it, however, deals with his novel. Herminio Ríos C., who translated the work in 1971, places "... *y no se lo tragó la tierra*" in a historical context and says that the novel "reflects the multiple experiences of the Mexican-American and explores a multiplicity of Mexican-American themes." Rivera's work is examined from different perspectives in the special issue of *Revista Chicano-Riqueña* dedicated to him. Narrative techniques are studied by Lauro Flores (the discourse of silence), Luis Leal (the ritual of remembering), and Eliud Martínez (Rivera as witness and storyteller). The use of language and dialogue are examined by Nicolás Kanellos, while Julián Olivares traces the characters' search for identities. All this is complemented by Patricia De la Fuente's study of the presence of women in Rivera's narrative and Sylvia S. Lizárraga's thematic study of patriarchal ideology in one of the chapters of Rivera's unpublished novel, "La

noche que se apagaron las luces" (The Night of the Blackout). Other critics have undertaken comparative studies of "... *y no se lo tragó la tierra.*" Representative of this critical method is the study of Erlinda Gonzáles-Berry and Tey Diana Rebolledo, who compare the novel to Sandra Cisneros's *The House on Mango Street* (1983), from the perspective of growing up Chicano. John C. Akers includes "... *y no se lo tragó la tierra*" in a study of fragmentation in the Chicano novel.

Rivera transcended the political. He had a deep sympathy and respect for humanity, especially for the migrant workers from whom he drew his inspiration to write and to work building a better society in the Americas. As he told Bruce-Novoa, "To me they [the migrant workers] were people who searched, and that's an important metaphor in the Americas. . . . I hope I can also be a searcher." His search, unfortunately, ended with his early death. His life has been commemorated in many ways. The main library at the University of California, Riverside, now bears his name, as does the Tomás Rivera Center at Claremont, California, and the elementary school which he first attended in Crystal City, Texas. The University of California, Riverside, has estab-

212

lished the Rivera Archives in order to preserve and make available to researchers his papers as a writer and an administrator.

Rivera would have been honored by the poem that a native of his hometown in Texas, Isidro H. Ríos, read during the ceremony when Airport Elementary School was named the Dr. Tomás Rivera Elementary School, which says in part:

> En las escuelas del pueblo
> él estudió desde niño
> por eso lo recordamos
> lo hacemos con gran cariño.
>
> (In the schools of this town
> he studied as a boy
> that's why we remember him
> we remember him with love.)

Biography:

Rolando Hinojosa-Smith, Gary Keller, and Vernon E. Lattin, *Tomás Rivera, 1935-1984: The Man and His Work* (Tempe: Bilingual/Editorial Bilingüe, 1988).

References:

Juan Bruce-Novoa, "Tomás Rivera," in his *Chicano Authors: Inquiry by Interview* (Austin: University of Texas Press, 1980): 137-161;

Ralph F. Grajeda, "Tomás Rivera's '. . . *y no se lo tragó la tierra*': Discovery and Appropriation of the Chicano Past," *Hispania*, 62 (March 1979): 71-81;

Sylvia S. Lizárraga, "Cambio: Intentó principal de '. . . *y no se lo tragó la tierra*,'" *Aztlán*, 7 (Fall 1976): 419-426;

Francisco A. Lomelí, "Tomás Rivera: The Writer as Creator of Community," *Vortex: A Critical Review*, 1 (Spring 1986): 5-6, 13-14;

Armand Martínez-Standifird, "The Archives of Tomás Rivera," *Books at UCR*, 10 (Winter 1986): 1-2;

Frank Pino, "The 'Outsider' and 'el otro' in Tomás Rivera's '. . . *y no se lo tragó la tierra*,'" *Books Abroad*, 49 (Summer 1975): 453-458;

Pino, "Realidad y fantasía en '. . . *y no se lo tragó la tierra*,'" in *Otros mundos, otros fuegos*, edited by Donald A. Yates (East Lansing: Michigan State University, 1975), pp. 249-254;

Francisca Rascón, "La caracterización de los personajes en '. . . *y no se lo tragó la tierra*,'" *La Palabra*, 1 (October 1979): 43-50;

Revista Chicano-Riqueña, special issue on Rivera, edited by Julián Olivares, 13 (Fall-Winter 1985);

Marcienne Rocard, "The Code of Chicano Experience in '. . . *y no se lo tragó la tierra*,'" in *Annales de l'Université de Toulouse/Le Mirail*, 10, fascicule 1 (1974): 141-151;

Juan Rodríguez, "Acercamiento a cuatro relatos de '. . . *y no se lo tragó la tierra*,'" *Mester*, 5 (November 1974): 16-24;

Rodríguez, "La embestida contra la religiosidad en '. . . *y no se lo tragó la tierra*,'" *Pacific Coast Council on Latin American Studies Proceedings: Changing Perspectives in Latin America*, 3 (1974): 83-86;

Rodríguez, "The Problematic in Tomás Rivera's '. . . *y no se lo tragó la tierra*,'" *Revista Chicano-Riqueña*, 6 (Summer 1978): 45-50;

José David Saldívar, "The Ideological and the Utopian in Tomás Rivera's '. . . *y no se lo tragó la tierra*' and Ron Arias' *The Road to Tamazunchale*," *Crítica: A Journal of Critical Essays*, 1 (Spring 1985): 100-114;

Joseph Sommers, "Interpreting Tomás Rivera," in *Modern Chicano Writers*, edited by Sommers and Tomás Ybarra-Frausto (Englewood Cliffs, N.J.: Prentice-Hall, 1979), pp. 94-107;

Oscar U. Somoza, "Grados de dependencia colectiva en '. . . *y no se lo tragó la tierra*,'" *La Palabra*, 1 (Spring 1979): 40-53;

Daniel P. Testa, "Narrative Technique and Human Expertise in Tomás Rivera's '. . . *y no se lo tragó la tierra*,'" in *Modern Chicano Writers*, edited by Sommers and Ybarra-Frausto (Englewood Cliffs, N.J.: Prentice-Hall, 1979), pp. 86-93;

"Tomás Rivera: Words and Pictures," *UC Riverside*, 2 (June 1986): 17-22;

Javier Vázquez-Castro, "Entrevista con Tomás Rivera," in his *Acerca de literatura (Diálogo con tres autores chicanos)* (San Antonio: M&A, 1979), pp. 39-52;

Diana Vélez, "The Reality of the Chicanos," *Bilingual Review/Revista Bilingüe*, 2 (January-August 1975): 203-207;

Papers:

Rivera's papers are held in the Rivera Archives, University of California, Riverside.

Richard Rodriguez

(31 July 1944-)

Richard D. Woods
Trinity University

BOOK: *Hunger of Memory: The Education of Richard Rodriguez: An Autobiography* (Boston: Godine, 1981).

PERIODICAL PUBLICATIONS: "A Minority Scholar Speaks Out," *Forum* (November 1982): 2-5;
"California Christmas Carols," *California*, 8 (December 1983): 99;
"The Head of Joaquin Murrieta," *Nuestro*, 9 (November 1985): 30-36;
"The Mexicans Among Us," *Reader's Digest*, 128 (March 1986): 171-176;
"Mexico's Children," *American Scholar*, 55 (Spring 1986): 161-167.

In 1981 Richard Rodriguez burst onto the publishing scene with his autobiography, *Hunger of Memory: The Education of Richard Rodriguez*. Its success can be attributed to the author's antagonism to bilingual education and affirmative action and the media's attention to these issues. Beyond its notoriety, however, the book is significant because Rodriguez reveals himself with frankness and sensitivity.

Prior to 1981 Rodriguez published portions of *Hunger of Memory* in the *Columbia Forum* (1973), *American Scholar* (1974), *College English* (1978), and other journals. In recent years he has written several articles. "The Head of Joaquin Murrieta" (*Nuestro*, November 1985) takes as its subject the nineteenth-century California folk bandit supposedly shot by rangers who verified their deed by placing his severed head in a jar of alcohol. In his account of the legend and its survival, Rodriguez wryly interprets California and its search for a past. In "California Christmas Carols" (*California*, December 1983), a vignette reminiscent of episodes in *Hunger of Memory*, he gives a brief, poignant account of an early Christmas and his request for an unusual gift. In his article "The Mexicans Among Us" (*Reader's Digest*, March 1986) he compresses the history of the relationship between Mexico and the United States,

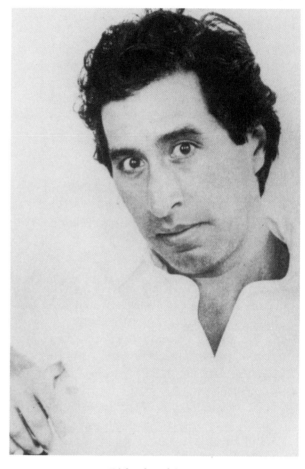

Richard Rodriguez

and, although he emphasizes the survival of the Mexican-Americans with their dignity and spirituality, he continues to lament linguistic fragmentation. A 1986 essay in *American Scholar*, "Mexico's Children" (also the title of a projected book), is a more complete analysis of this issue; there Rodriguez synthesizes and interprets the dilemmas of Hispanics both in Mexico and in the United States.

The son of Leopoldo Rodriguez and Victoria Moran Rodriguez, both Mexican immigrants, Rodriguez was born on 31 July 1944 in San Francisco, California, where he now resides as a full-time writer. As a child he moved with his parents to Sacramento–their purchase of a small house on the edge of an Anglo neighborhood is described in *Hunger of Memory*. He worked at a variety of jobs as a teenager, and in his book he describes the physical pleasure of labor and social interaction with workers from Mexico. He notes that although like them he had dark skin, because of his education he was distinguished from them. His working-class father observed that Richard would never know the meaning of hard work.

Rodriguez, a Roman Catholic, devotes an entire chapter of *Hunger of Memory* to his religion. As an altar boy he loved the church with its ceremony and sounds. As an adult he deplores the changes in liturgy and feels separated from it. Even the experience of religion marks a distinction between the Anglo and Mexican worlds: "I was un católico before I was a Catholic. That is, I acquired my earliest sense of the Church . . . through my parents' Mexican Catholicism. It was in Spanish that I first learned to pray. . . ."

Educated in Catholic primary and secondary schools, Rodriguez received his B.A. from Stanford in 1967 and his M.S. from Columbia University in 1969. He did graduate work at the University of California, Berkeley, and at the Warburg Institute in London and received a Fulbright Fellowship (1972-1973) and a National Endowment for the Humanities Fellowship (1976-1977).

The prologue and six chapters of *Hunger of Memory* chart the fragmented course of Rodriguez's education. For him *education* refers equally to formal training and maturing experiences. Rodriguez says his education (which he calls "radical self-reformation") and his revelations have alienated him from his family: "I am writing about those very things my mother has asked me not to reveal. Shortly after I published my first autobiographical essay seven years ago, my mother wrote me a letter pleading with me never again to write about our family. 'Write about something else in the future. Our family life is private.' And besides: 'Why do you need to tell the gringos about how "divided" you feel from the family?' " He points out that Latino culture practices autobiography in a restrained form. Nothing unfavorable is disclosed about the family, and childhood is consequently idealized or vaguely rendered. Furthermore, in Mexico the most favored autobiographical form is the memoir, which allows the writer to concentrate on others rather than on himself.

Cover for Rodriguez's 1981 autobiography, which he describes in the prologue as "a book about language"

Rodriguez's positions on language and affirmative action have sparked most of the public discussions. In brief, he feels that all Americans must learn English, a public language, as opposed to Spanish, a private language used in the home. Condoning the brash Irish nuns who invaded his home to insist that the Spanish-speaking Rodriguezes use only English, he attributes his success to this wrenching move toward assimilation. He attacks affirmative action, feeling that government programs accelerate the success of middle-class Chicanos like himself to the detriment of the targeted group, barrio Chicanos. To him affirmative action should be based on class, not ethnic group. In an interview in *People* magazine given shortly after the publication of *Hunger of Memory*, he synthesized his feelings on ethnic identity: "I refuse to accept my generation's romanticism about discovering 'roots.' The trouble with that is it somehow holds children accountable for maintaining their culture, and freezes them into thinking of themselves as Mexicans or as Chinese or as blacks. But culture is an extraordinary progression of ancestral memories and individual experience. People have accused me of losing my heritage. That assumes heritage is this little suitcase I carry with me, with tortillas and a little Mexican cowboy suit inside, and that one day I lost it at a Greyhound depot. The fact is, culture survives whether you want it to or not."

Rodriguez says that his autobiography "is a book about language." In chapter 1, "Aria," Rodriguez says he learned English to the exclusion of Spanish; his parents struggled with English but remained comfortable only in Spanish. The two languages merge in the child: "At the age of five, six, well past the time when most other children no longer easily notice the difference between sounds uttered at home and words spoken in public, I had a different experience. I lived in a world magically compounded of sounds. I remained a child longer than most; I lingered too long, poised at the edge of language–often frightened by the sounds of los gringos, delighted by the sounds of Spanish at home."

Rodriguez discusses his use of language as an author in the final chapter, "Mr. Secrets," in which he analyzes the act of writing and its motivation. A writer's feelings, he says, "are capable of public intelligibility. In turn, the act of revelation helps the writer better understand his own feelings. Such is the benefit of language: By finding public words to describe one's feelings, one can describe oneself to oneself. One names what was previously only darkly felt." As reviewer Paul Zweig observed, *Hunger of Memory* "is not only about the language adventures of a Mexican American child, . . . it is also about the coming into being of the remarkable language in which it is written."

Through the concept of language Rodriguez explores the processes of alienation, assimilation, growing up, and, of course, education. Through growth in language Rodriguez increasingly alienates himself from his family, the comfortable childhood with warm Spanish sounds, as he enters an adult world of superficial communication. The wedge between him and his family was caused mainly by education, a linguistic process that he describes as "radical self-reformation."

Reviewers have given Rodriguez more attention than any other Mexican-American author. Even the *New York Times Book Review*, indifferent to the literary creation of the Chicano Movement

since its beginnings in the 1960s, gave front-page recognition to *Hunger of Memory* (28 February 1982). Approximately fifty other periodicals, from professional newsletters to library journals to the *New Yorker* and *Atlantic Monthly*, have reviewed Rodriguez's autobiography. Some Mexican-Americans, such as Arturo Madrid (*La Red/ The Net*, 23 April 1982), saw in Rodriguez a betrayal of the goals of the Chicano people as evidenced by the government programs he attacked. Sarcastically deriding Rodriguez's angst, these detractors have been rarely moved by his style or convinced of the universality of his experience. They felt that he spoke only for himself to a white audience. Yet Antonio C. Marquez, a professor of Chicano literature, argued that "there is a level of artistry in *Hunger of Memory* that should not be shunned simply because Rodriguez does not meet the Procrustean bed of 'cultural awareness' of any other ideology. I contend that its ultimate value lies in its literary qualities and the uniqueness of the autobiographical form."

However controversial it may be, *Hunger of Memory* belongs to the mainstream of American autobiography. Indeed the universality the author achieves through his sensitive examination of the complexities of language is arguably the most notable accomplishment of the book. Presently Rodriguez's canon is small, distinguished by his thoughtful, outspoken stance on issues related to the Chicano experience and his skill as a stylist. One can look forward with anticipation to his future work.

References:

"'¿Habla español?' (Do You Speak Spanish?) Author Richard Rodriguez Does, but He Wishes the Schools Would Stop," *People*, 18 (16 August 1982): 75-79;

Patricia Holt, "Richard Rodriguez," *Publishers Weekly* (26 March 1982): 6-8;

Antonio C. Marquez, "Richard Rodriguez's *Hunger of Memory* and the Poetics of Experience," *Arizona Quarterly*, 40 (Summer 1984): 130-141;

Julio Marzan, "Richard Rodriguez Talks to Himself," *Village Voice*, 27 (27 April 1982): 46-47;

Tomás Rivera, "Richard Rodriguez' *Hunger of Memory* as Humanistic Antithesis," *MELUS*, 11 (Winter 1984): 5-12;

Paul Zweig, "The Child of Two Cultures," *New York Times Book Review*, 28 February 1982, pp. 1, 26.

Arnold R. Rojas

(25 September 1896-8 September 1988)

Gerald Haslam
Sonoma State University

BOOKS: *California Vaqueros* (Fresno: Academy Library Guild, 1953);
Lore of the California Vaqueros (Fresno: Academy Library Guild, 1958);
Last of the Vaqueros (Fresno: Academy Library Guild, 1960);
The Vaquero (Santa Barbara: McNally & Loftin, 1964);
Bits, Bitting, and Spanish Horses; The Chief Rojas Fact Book about Successful Horse Training and The Proper Use of Equipment (Goleta, Cal.: Kimberly, 1970);
Vaqueros and Buckeroos (Shafter, Cal.: Privately printed, 1979).
Collection: *These Were the Vaqueros: The Collected Works of Arnold R. Rojas* (Shafter, Cal.: Privately printed, 1974).

Arnold R. Rojas has the distinction of chronicling the life and lore of California's vaqueros in a series of books that are acknowledged to be regional classics. The vaqueros whose stories he told were Mexican cowboys who employed the Spanish *la Jineta* style of horsemanship in which a rider's body directed his mount; in the more conventional American cowboy style, reins are used to control a horse. This is an important distinction because the riding style symbolized a heritage; as Rojas explains in his 1974 collection, *These Were the Vaqueros: The Collected Works of Arnold R. Rojas,* "By vaquero I mean the man who brought the cattle to the West and herded them for a hundred years or more before the United States took possession of half of Mexico's territory." He said further that "the vaquero was a westerner, a Californian" whose "influence went north and east while the cowboy never got west of the Rockies. These are two cultures and their ways are very different. The vaqueros were driving cattle north to Canada in 1836, long before the Gold Rush which is so richly catalogued."

Although his formal education did not progress beyond the third grade, "Chief" Rojas received rigorous if informal training on huge *ran-*

Arnold R. Rojas

chos (ranches) early in this century while working as a vaquero, and his books capture the sense of those places and that time. He was one of those rare literary talents who blossomed without formal instruction. His weaknesses as a writer—repetition that sometimes borders on redundancy, an occasional lack of coherence, and a tendency to overgeneralize when dealing with historical matters—were products of his rigorous but unsystematic self-education. He was at his best when employing devices of oral literature, writing about his fellow riders, and when discussing the gear and techniques of the vaquero.

217

Although as an author and, to a degree, as a man Rojas harkened to an earlier time, he is an important figure in Mexican-American writing because of his uncompromising pride in his heritage and his tolerance of the diversity implicit within it. His perspective on social matters is wise. For example, in what may be the most succinct observation ever made on the subject, Rojas explains the ironic genesis of "pure Castilian" Californios, Hispanic natives of Alta California who supposedly have no Indian blood. Anglo-Americans entered the area in the 1840s and sought title to its riches. In *Vaqueros and Buckeroos* (1979) Rojas states: "The only way to acquire the land was to marry a daughter of the landowner. But they [the gringos] had already started a campaign of discrimination. They very neatly solved that problem by creating 'Old Spanish Families' and marrying into them. But those who had no lands left became Mexicans, doomed to work for cheap wages and to suffer discrimination."

Rojas was born in Pasadena, California, in 1896 into a family whose ancestors had migrated to the state from western Mexico in the 1820s. His mother's grandparents came from Alamos, in the state of Sonora, while his father's people were from San Miguel Horcasitas, Sonora, and Mazatlán, Sinaloa. His Indian ancestors were Yaquis and Mayas, while his Spanish progenitors were Sephardic Jews who migrated to the Americas to escape the Inquisition.

Following the death of his parents Rojas was placed in an orphanage in San Luis Obispo in 1902. He ran away when he was twelve. "I wanted to come to the San Joaquin Valley and I did," he explained in an April 1985 interview. He wanted to be a rider, not a fruit picker, and the San Joaquin, along with the mountains that surround it, was cattle country. But there was an underlying social reality: "The only work a man of my race could get in those days was as a mule skinner or vaquero, both cheap labor."

He rode first for the V7 Ranch in San Luis, then on the massive San Emideo Ranch operated by the Kern County Land Company, and for the fabled rancher José Jesús López on the Rancho Tejon. Until 1935 Rojas worked horses and cattle on the California range, meeting its denizens and learning its legends.

When Rojas was a teenager living with an uncle in Soledad Canyon near Acton an old homesteader—"He was starving out," said Rojas—borrowed food from them. The old man noticed that Rojas was reading an O. Henry "Heart of

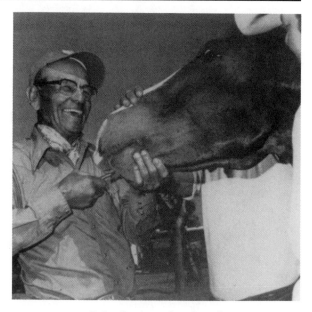

Rojas floating a horse's teeth

the West" tale, so when he returned to borrow more food, he brought the youngster books by Alexandre Dumas, Miguel de Cervantes, Emile Zola, and Arthur Conan Doyle. In 1985 Rojas listed as his favorite writers those four, plus Victor Hugo, Honore de Balzac, Rudyard Kipling, Robert Louis Stevenson, Charles Dickens, Bernal Diáz del Castillo, Vicente Blasco Ibáñez, Mayne Reid, Harold Lamb, Bret Harte, Mark Twain, O. Henry, Washington Irving, Jack London, Robert Cunningham Graham, and Howard Fast—a varied group.

If Rojas's style was to a degree polished by his reading, his content directly reflects the *hombres del campo* (men of the land) with whom he rode; it is in his work that the vaqueros have found their collective voice. "I got my material around the campfire and in the bunkhouse on winter nights," he explained. Rojas became a writer following World War II when he was named chairman of a rodeo sponsored by the American Legion post in Bakersfield, then the hub of the San Joaquin's cattle industry. He had opened a stable just outside the town in 1935 ("I called it the 'Bar-O Stable' because I borrowed everything"), a business he continued until 1950, when he would become an equine dentist as well as a horse trainer. The former vaquero approached Jim Day, editor of the *Bakersfield Californian*, seeking publicity for the rodeo. Day suggested that Rojas compose something that could be used as publicity, so he wrote thumbnail sketches of several old vaqueros whom he planned to honor at the rodeo. These sketches subsequently appeared in Day's column, "Pipefuls." *Bakersfield Californian* editorial writer Ralph F. Kreiser, a local historian, encouraged Rojas to continue recording his stories, and Day continued printing them. Rojas could not type so Richard Bailey, director of the Kern County Museum, offered him secretarial services. Before long, his tales were appearing in the newspaper and the local historical society's newsletter under Rojas's own byline.

In the early 1950s Rojas received a letter from noted California historian Monsignor James Culleton, who offered to publish his material in book form at the Academy Library Guild in Fresno, which released Rojas's first three books, all of which were favorably reviewed.

Rojas's books are generally collections of *estampas*, *cuentitos*, and *chismes*–Spanish forms of brief tales that hover on the line between fiction and history. None can be classified as short stories in a formal literary sense; many are like much good folklore, too true to allow facts to interfere with their magic. A man of prodigious memory–itself a characteristic of oral tale-tellers–Rojas wrote of many incidents, no two quite the same. In *Lore of the California Vaqueros* (1958), for example, he recounts the experience of a man who tried to ride a bronco while wearing a pocket watch: "The watch fastened to a buckskin thong dropped out of his vest pocket at the first jump and swung in an arch and hit the buckeroo in the nose. The next jump, the watch gave him a black eye and as long as the horse bucked, the watch swung. If the horse had not quit bucking, the watch 'would have beat me to death,' as the vaquero afterward said. He untied the buckskin thong and threw what was left of the watch as far away as he could."

His books also include a good deal of folk history. In the same volume he writes: "How and when the San Joaquin Valley Indians learned to speak Spanish no one has ever been able to tell me. Probably as soon as they acquired horses. Up to and some time after the coming of the gringo, the aborigines went to school, yet their language flows in a mellow old-fashioned Spanish of simple words without a trace of slang. And to the everlasting shame of all of us, the Tejonenos speak the tongue more fluently than the descendants of the people who taught it to them." Margaret Shedd, writing in the English-language *Mexico City News*, accurately observed that Rojas's own use of Spanish featured "español que no está escrito" (Spanish that is not written); it contains

terms such as "chirrionero caballo pajarero" (a horse that shies at shadows) or "agarrarse del sauce" (literally, take hold of the willow, meaning to grab the saddle horn when riding a bucking horse).

Practical lore is also imparted in Rojas's books, especially in *Bits, Bitting, and Spanish Horses; The Chief Rojas Fact Book about Successful Horse Training and The Proper Use of Equipment* (1970). "To a vaquero," he observed, "a horse was an open book in which his rider's virtues and vices were written for all to see: "He could tell if a horse had had a young or an older rider. A horse ridden by an old man was always quiet, because old men never quarrel with their horses. A young man, on the other hand, will often fight his horse." In the same book he points out, "If a five-pound bit is put in a ten-pound mouth, the horse will disregard it to the extent of bearing on it. On the other hand, if a ten-pound bit is put in a five-pound mouth the horse will suffer from too much bit. It is when the horse is bitted properly and the rider and horse have developed an affinity to each other that the bit becomes a signaling device and ceases being a lever."

It is the unexpected and magical that readers find in Rojas's work. He captured in print a time and a culture whose human qualities would otherwise have been forgotten; underlying his work is the theme that the vaqueros were real men living tough lives, and their accomplishments merit attention. A constant focus is on the people of the West and their unusual lives. He talked to men who claimed to have known legendary California bandit Joaquín Murrieta, those who said they rode camels and ate ostriches on Rancho Tejon, and those who said they had confronted an apparition of the mythical weeping La Llorona in San Antonio, Texas. Of Harry Gillem, a black vaquero in Kern County, he writes: "Seeing that he was bandaged I asked if he had been in an accident. He told me of having been set upon by three men. He had fought them until he had just about whipped all three, when one of them drew a knife and slashed him. Harry was cut badly and spent some time in a hospital. But he carried off the honors of war, however, because he had fought fair and when he was out of the hospital, two of the men with whom he had fought paid him five dollars a piece to not fight with them again." He talks of a lady's experience with the famous *bandido* Tiburcio Vásquez, who was Rojas's uncle: "The bandit met her the night she wore hoop skirts at a dance. The sheriff and

Rojas in 1980

his deputies, hunting the fugitive, surrounded the dance hall, barring all windows and doors. When the sheriff walked in to look over the dancers, Vásquez crawled under Teresa's skirts which hid him effectively. The sheriff, baffled, left empty-handed. She was *muy lunática*." Of various old vaqueros, he writes, "Víctor Ortega would put a dollar on each stirrup and ride a bucking horse without losing either coin. Juan Pérez, nearly ninety, could rope a hundred calves before he missed a throw. Tiny, shriveled old Avelino Martínez tucked a six-shooter into his shirt to command the respect he got from all men. Jesús López sat aching on his horse until all his men had eaten before dismounting to eat himself. Bruno Contrereas picked his old body off the ground when bucked off by the white horse and climbed on again for a repeat performance."

Such samples abound in Rojas's books. If some of his yarns seem apocryphal it must be recognized that particular incidents need not be factual in order for truth to be achieved. There is a veritism in the writing of Rojas that bespeaks a time, a place, and a way of life now passed.

Interview:

Gerald Haslam, "A *MELUS* Interview: The Last Vaquero, Arnold R. Rojas," *MELUS*, 13 (Spring-Summer 1986): 125-133.

References:

Gerald Haslam, "Arnold Rojas, Vaquero," in his *Voices of a Place: Social and Literary Essays from the Other California* (Walnut Creek, Cal.: Devil Mountain, 1987), pp. 65-71;

Haslam, "Arnold Rojas: Voice of the Vaqueros," *The Californians*, 4 (September-October 1986): 36-40;

Haslam, "California's Last Vaquero," *Western American Literature*, 21 (August 1986): 123-130.

Papers:

Some of Rojas's papers are held in the Historical Collection of Kern County, Beale Memorial Library, Bakersfield, California.

Orlando Romero

(24 September 1945-   )

J. Allan Englekirk
University of South Carolina

BOOK: *Nambé–Year One* (Berkeley, Cal.: Tonatiuh International, 1976).

OTHER: "Augustine Primavera," in *Southwest*, edited by Karl Kopp and Jane Kopp (Albuquerque: Red Earth, 1977), pp. 232-233;
"Self-Portrait," in *A Ceremony of Brotherhood, 1680-1980*, edited by Rudolfo A. Anaya and Simón J. Ortiz (Albuquerque: Academia, 1981), p. 132.

PERIODICAL PUBLICATIONS: "Maria Mueller," *De Colores*, 4, no. 1-2 (1975): 75-76;
"Maria & Domingo Machote," *De Colores*, 4, no. 1-2 (1975): 77-79;
"Of Men and Llamas," *De Colores*, 5, no. 3-4 (1976): 104-106;
"Autumn Moons/Lunas de otoño," *El Palacio*, 90 (Fall-Winter 1984): 28.

Orlando Romero

Through his writings Orlando Romero recreates an image of a people whose values and customs may soon be erased, or significantly altered, by forces dedicated to progress. He is one of several young contemporary authors of northern New Mexico to write about his cultural heritage in an attempt to characterize the essential elements responsible for forming his sociohistorical and spiritual identity. His literary efforts attempt to preserve the past for the future, so that succeeding generations may be exposed to those beliefs most basic to traditional Hispanic culture in the southwestern United States.

Born in Santa Fe, New Mexico, Orlando A. Romero grew up in the village of Nambé, a small, rural community tucked among the foothills of the Sangre de Cristo mountains, some twenty miles from the city. The son of José Romero, a machinist, and Ruby Ann Romero, his direct ancestry in this region has been traced to 1598. Three generations of Romeros have resided in Nambé.

He was reared by his mother and his paternal grandfather, Enrique Romero, since his father abandoned the family when Romero was in the sixth grade. In an unpublished 1986 interview Orlando Romero said that, more than any other individual, Enrique Romero was responsible for defining the ideals that would become most important to his grandson as time passed. A man tied to "los tiempos de antes" (the bygone days), the grandfather preferred traditional methods of irrigation, cultivation, and harvest and taught Orlando the value of a slower, more philosophical pace. From Enrique Romero's perspective, innovations in the sciences had not created a better world, but instead, a more fragile existence. Among people of his heritage in Nambé and surrounding villages, he detected a progressive lessening of the sense of unity that had always been so prevalent and vigorous. He lamented the disappearance, or transformation, of long-standing Catholic practices and instilled in his grandson a love for the land and respect for the beliefs most cherished by his Hispanic and Indian ancestors.

It was not until the first year of elementary school in Nambé that Orlando Romero was put into immediate contact with Anglo-American values. The intensity of culture shock was amplified by the linguistic challenge of being forced to learn English in the classroom. The pressures to adopt a new language and adapt to a culture not his own caused him to perceive school, initially, as a hostile environment. He spent his favorite childhood moments with his grandfather in the fields and, in the afternoons, at the mill in Nambé—where his grandfather and other older members in the vicinity would meet to exchange anecdotes from their past. Many of these tales formed the core or provided the impulse for stories Romero later wrote. He was also an avid reader.

During his years in high school in Pojoaque, New Mexico, Romero began to write. His first tentative efforts were poems of less than a page in length on themes that would become constants in his subsequent writings: real or imagined Gypsies, aspects of the harvest cycle, people and events in his village, and thoughts on, or visions of, his grandfather. Though one of his poems about his grandfather was published in the mid 1960s by a literary magazine in Santa Fe, he has discarded the major portion of his production from this period. The act of writing was, even at this early age, a means of revealing or confessing his innermost thoughts. This objective was to be of principal importance to his later prose and poetry also, but as a youth he felt little need or desire to share his ideas with others.

On 10 February 1968 Romero married journalist Rebecca López of Española, New Mexico. In 1969, five years after his graduation from high school, Romero enrolled at the College of Santa Fe. While he was pursuing a degree in English, his readings focused on works of magic realism, philosophy, science, and mythology. Of secondary interest to him were novels about the Southwest. Though no single writer exerted significant influence on his thoughts or literary efforts,

his favorite authors at this time were Pearl Buck, Victor Hugo, and William Faulkner.

The demands of his course work in the humanities made it impossible for Romero to read sufficient literature of his liking, or to dedicate as much time as he might have wanted to carving and sketching—pastimes which he had adopted while in high school, before his first attempts at creative writing. These factors forced Romero to consider the relative value of his academic education. He began to feel that his program of studies was too specialized, too regimented, and that it denied him the chance to continue to acquire the practical information necessary for daily existence, information he had obtained from his grandfather and other elders while in Nambé. He persisted in his classwork despite these misgivings, however, and received his B.A. degree in English in 1974. By this date Romero and his wife had two children, Carlota Bernarda and—the first of two sons—Orlando Cervantes.

Romero's novel, *Nambé—Year One* (1976), was written in a span of four months during his final year at the College of Santa Fe. It was published initially in excerpts by *Puerto del Sol*, a literary journal from New Mexico State University in Las Cruces. After reading the material Romero sent to the magazine, Octavio Romano, the editor of the publishing firm Quinto Sol, requested that he submit a first draft of the entire document. This manuscript, complete with crayon markings drawn by Romero's daughter, Carlota, was accepted with few editorial changes.

Nambé—Year One is written in the form of an autobiography narrated by Mateo Romero, a young man in his mid thirties who resides in Nambé. The events of the text are not ordered in chronological sequence, but rather follow the flow of Mateo's thoughts as he envisions his existence. Though randomly presented, no stage of his life is left unportrayed. The narrative shifts continually among experiences of his childhood, adolescence, early and mid twenties, and the present. The reader must determine from the context when the events transpired because few specific dates are given and the narrator seldom reveals his exact age in depicting individual occurrences. Interspersed among the happenings of Mateo's life are stories based on folklore or related to episodes in the lives of his ancestors or other inhabitants of the region.

The novel is dedicated to womankind: "A la hembra, puerta de los misterios del universo" (To the female, doorway to the mysteries of the uni-

A Little Stories for Little Children

These stories were ~~created~~ made up or created as ~~they were being~~ told ~~to my 3 year old~~ them to my 4 year old. They are regional in the sense that they take place in New Mexico, to make them applicable and meaningful. ~~The Witches Convention~~ I suggest you change the locations to your area

The Witches Convention — a little fairytale for all ages

Once upon a time, in Northern New Mexico, a witches convention and party took place. It was at the edge of a large forrest where a little boy named Bernardo used to gather wood. Well, poor little Bernardo soon realized that all of a sudden witches were appearing everywhere as he stood hiding in the brush shaking in his shoes.

Why there were witches of all kinds, witche with long scrag white hair, witches with pink hair, purple hair, blonde hair witches with no hair. Why there were witche with no teeth, and witches with long broken fangs. There were men witche women witches and some brujas, so ugly, you couldnt tell what they were.

Anyway poor Bernardo was so terrified he didnt dare move fearing what the witche might do to him. In fact the great convention and party had started. Why there were witche on one side of the camp who were giving long winded talks, they had gone to college. In other parts there were witche drinking their own brew and were getting sick. There was

Page from the manuscript for a children's story by Romero (courtesy of the author)

Romero with a sculpture by his son Orlando Cervantes Romero (photo by Orlando Cervantes Romero)

verse). Much of the autobiographical detail describes Mateo's love for a Gypsy woman of enchanting beauty who is present in his life either physically or spiritually from the start. Mateo's grandfather, whom he admires immensely, experienced identical sentiments for a Gypsy woman in his own youth, and Mateo believes that previous ancestors probably had similar loves since Gypsies had wandered through the area for several centuries.

More than the Gypsy's attractive physical features fire Mateo's passion, however. She is mysterious and magical, and her eyes–like those of the grandfather's Gypsy–have hypnotic powers. Beginning at the point of innocent initial contact, a bond is established between Mateo and this special individual: "From that very moment we were bound and chained to each other. It was a golden chain that didn't tie us to earthly bounds and limitations but which transformed our feet to wings." As an enigmatic force in his life, she elicits contradictory reactions from Mateo, but these responses only further intensify his love for her.

Balanced against the protagonist's affection for the Gypsy is his deep-seated emotional attach-

ment to the land and people of his region. The conflict of interests between these two forces confounds the narrator of *Nambé–Year One* and compels him to constant self-analysis. The Gypsy is the symbol of adventure and mystery, but following her would represent for Mateo the abandonment of family, land, and all other elements of his immediate world that form part of his identity. In a vision a giant salamander warns him never to forsake what is most truly his: "I have been summoned by the Earth gods to quench the fire that would remove you from your ancestral bones. With one breath, mortal, I can surround your Gypsy in a prison of watery ice. It is the desire of your soul that will determine her fate, as well as yours." In the final pages of his autobiography, in a letter of farewell to the Gypsy, Mateo accepts that he must live without her, yet, in ending, he states: "I cannot bear it, but I must say goodbye . . . until, perhaps my son or my grandson is afflicted by the same love." The dream that was his will not perish–the illusion that inflamed his spirit will remain and awaken the same strong, yet ambiguous, desires in his children, and in theirs in perpetuity.

Commenting on the process of composition of *Nambé–Year One* in a 28 November 1979 article by Anne Hillerman, Romero asserted: "Like many first novels, it was a matter of confession. It was painful to write. Sometimes I would sit at the typewriter and cry." In the unpublished 1986 interview he said that most of the characters of *Nambé–Year One* represent actual people in his life. The Gypsy is a possible exception. Her portrayal is intriguing because, quite often, Mateo leads the reader to believe that she may be nothing more than a vision elaborated by his imagination: "I would love and dance with the Gypsy, but she would never lie next to me. Maybe she was an illusion, like the Payasos (clowns) and Magicians that traveled throughout these mountains." Whether or not she was, or is, an actual person in the author's life is similarly puzzling, for, in interviews, Romero generally avoids discussing her in specific detail–preferring to leave her somewhere between fact and fiction. Real or illusory, however, she typifies womankind, and she embodies the abstract concept of the unattainable ideal.

Critical reaction to *Nambé–Year One* has been generally favorable. Nasario García (Fall/Winter 1978) acclaimed the novel for its three-dimensional treatment of time. Vernon E. Lattin (in a review in *Explorations in Ethnic Studies*, July 1978) and Beatrice A. Roeder (October 1977) have written on Romero's compelling portrayal of Hispano-Indian life and customs in New Mexico. Charles Tatum also found local color to be an appealing aspect of the novel in a review in *World Literature Today* (Summer 1974), but faulted Romero for repetitive imagery and for excessive attention directed to the Gypsy. Within New Mexico Romero's novel has been well read and well received–with the result that the author has been invited to participate in many symposiums and seminars on Hispano-Indian life and literature of the region.

Most of the literary critics have placed *Nambé–Year One* within the body of writings defined as Chicano letters–a classification with which Romero is not entirely pleased, since he believes that the culture of the Southwest and West is too diverse to be identified by a single phrase: "Chicano culture–you cannot mix together people from California, Arizona, southern Colorado . . . into a homogeneous bottle of milk. Our food is different, our thinking is different–we are united politically under *chicanismo*." Romero asserts that the term *Chicano* has come to be associated far too strongly with politics and that most

Chicano authors of the 1960s and 1970s were not composing literature, but rather, political manifestos oftentimes lacking aesthetic merit. He distinguishes his creative writing from many of these Chicano literary works: "I'm going to write things that are going to last–not things that are going to be meant . . . as manifestos and texts to be studied in some class. I'm going to write literature. . . . I have to write things that I feel strongly about, that have to do with the examination of a people. . . ." He is not attempting to deny his spiritual bond with Hispanic-Americans of the Southwest, but merely to assert his independence as an artist. When asked to define his literature, he prefers to consider it "New Mexican literature."

Romero earned an M.A. in library science from the University of Arizona in 1976. In the preceding two years, he completed several short stories that were published in Chicano anthologies and journals. In 1979, three years after the publication of *Nambé–Year One*, Romero received a Creative Writer's Fellowship Grant from the National Endowment for the Arts. Since his application for the grant had included segments from his novel, the author viewed the award as an achievement of professional importance, stating in a 1979 interview: "The acceptance is even more important to me than the money. It means that someone I have never met can read excerpts from *Nambé–Year One* and like it enough to give me recognition."

After receiving his degree, he returned to New Mexico with more tales in various stages of completion, and the NEA grant afforded him extra time to finish other stories begun in Arizona. Some of these tales form part of a collection to be published under the title "The Day of the Wind." Romero commented in the 1986 interview that the works in this volume will address the theme of "man's questions about self and about God," with special attention focused on portraying "the complex relationship between man and woman in the southwestern United States." His efforts in creative writing have been complemented by work in Santa Fe as a library assistant and research librarian with the New Mexico Supreme Court Library (1969-1974), the New Mexico State Library, Southwest Collections (1977-1983), and the Museum of New Mexico History Library since 1983. Since assuming the position at the museum he has had less time to devote to writing.

Romero is also a sculptor and painter. Since his first attempts in high school, he has carved *santos* (statues, generally from ten inches to two feet in height, representing religious personages) and other traditional figures of southwestern sculpture. He has sought increasingly to evolve freer, more abstract objects–mostly on commission. Though he has used other materials, he prefers wood. Several of his works are on permanent display at the International Museum of Folk Art in Santa Fe.

Romero's grandfather died in 1980, the year of the birth of Romero and his wife's second son, Enrique Alvaro. For a prolonged period he mourned the loss of an individual who had been, at once, his father, grandfather, unofficial confessor, and best friend. A void was created for which he was unable to compensate, and periods of loneliness still plague him sporadically. These feelings are tempered by the sensation that the grandfather is still spiritually present at every moment of his life. With the exception of relatively brief periods of time Romero has chosen to reside in, or near, Nambé, New Mexico. In his writing he has sought to reflect the people and land of his place of birth, and it is these individuals who most thoroughly apprehend the spirit and sentiments his writings transmit. In his literature and his life he is dedicated to sustaining in as pure and complete a form as possible the world that his grandfather taught him to admire.

References:

Nasario García, "The Concept of Time in *Nambé–Year One*," *Latin American Literary Review*, 7 (Fall/Winter 1978): 20-28;

Anne Hillerman, "Nambé Author Awarded Writer's Fellowship," *New Mexican* (Santa Fe), 28 November 1979, p. D1;

Beatrice A. Roeder, "Roots in New Mexico: *Nambé–Year One*," *La Luz*, 6 (October 1977): 18-19, 30-31.

Papers:

Romero's papers are held by the Special Collections Department at the University of New Mexico, Albuquerque, and the New Mexico History Library in Santa Fe.

Jim Sagel

(19 June 1947-   )

Lawrence Benton
California State University, Chico

BOOKS: *Hablando de brujas y la gente de antes: poemas del río chama* (Austin, Tex.: Place of Herons, 1981);

Foreplay and French Fries: Poems (San José, Cal.: Mango, 1981);

Small Bones, Little Eyes, poetry by Sagel and nila northSun (Fallon, Nev.: Duck Down, 1981);

Tunomás Honey (Havana: Casa de las Américas, 1981); bilingual edition (Ypsilanti: Bilingual/ Editorial Bilingüe, 1983);

Los cumpleaños de doña Agueda (Austin, Tex.: Place of Herons, 1984);

Sábelotodo Entiendelonada and Other Stories (Tempe: Bilingual/Editorial Bilingüe, 1988).

Jim Sagel writes about the Chicanos of northern New Mexico's Española Valley. He sees his writing as an attempt to portray their lives–particularly their language–with realistic accuracy. In an unpublished 1985 interview Sagel said that he considers the long New Mexican tradition of oral story telling the strongest influence on his writing.

Born in Fort Morgan, Colorado, Sagel is descended on both sides from grandparents who emigrated from the same village in Czarist Russia. After public school he enrolled in the University of Colorado, graduating in 1969 with a B.A. in English. The turning point of his life occurred that same year, when he moved to New Mexico. There, he said he experienced a sort of déjà vu, "like a dream recognition, almost"; a feeling that he had reached the place where he belonged. He found the *nuevomexicanos* (New Mexicans) to have a compelling sense of cultural continuity and a respect for the past which he greatly admired. Soon after arriving he managed to find work as a high school teacher. In 1970 he met and married Teresa Archuleta. During the succeeding six years he continued his teaching career, built an adobe home, and obtained an M.A. in creative writing from the University of New Mexico. Since 1976 he has held a teaching post at North-

Jim Sagel (courtesy of the author)

ern New Mexico Community College. He also works as a free-lance journalist.

Though Sagel is known primarily as a short-story writer, he started his career as a poet. He first began to submit work for publication in 1976. Several of his poems appeared in such journals as *Puerto del Sol*. Three of his books of verse were published in 1981: *Hablando de brujas y la gente de antes: poemas del río chama* (Speaking of Witches and the People of the Past: Poems of the Chama River); *Foreplay and French Fries*; and *Small Bones, Little Eyes*. Some of the poems of these collections appear in English, some in Spanish, and some in a combination of both languages. A few are lyrical and personal, but most are strongly narrative. They cover a wide variety of topics, from such universal matters as love, old age, and death to themes such as the Chicano youth culture, the clash of nuevomexicano and Anglo values, social justice, and the Pueblo Indian culture.

The work for which Sagel is best known is *Tunomás Honey* (Only You, Honey), a book of short fiction published late in 1981. Cultural dissonance in these stories is expressed through the conflict of generations. The young function as apologists for an essentially secular worldview. The *ancianos* (old ones), by contrast, see life and death in sacred terms. They believe the point of human existence is to live (and die) honorably according to the tenets of their Catholic faith. They thus become a metaphor for the traditional nuevomexicano culture, an emblem of resistance to Anglo ways. All of the stories (with perhaps one exception, "La Junta" [The Meeting]) are essentially studies of character.

"El Americano" (The American), "Chifladera" (Whistling), and "Tunomás Honey" depict bizarre characters in humorous situations. "El Americano" portrays a largely assimilated and somewhat effeminate teenager. His macho father, hoping he will become more masculine, sends him to work on a ranch with his nuevomexicano relatives. The boy's struggles, though hilarious, nonetheless express the dialectic between the two cultures. The other two stories portray Chaplinesque characters whose lives seem little more than a series of slapstick episodes. Alicia, the protagonist of "Chifladera," is a classical gossip, and the character Tunomás Honey is a dirty old man, though he still fancies himself a Latin lover. Despite the utter triviality of their lives, the reader tends to sympathize with the characters in all three stories, perhaps because they emerge as victims of an ersatz culture which adopts the worst values of both nuevomexicano and Anglo.

Three stories in *Tunomás Honey* deal with characters who have physical or emotional handicaps. All are set in institutions and, except for occasional lapses, all are narrated in the first person. The theme of both "El Lupito" (Little Lupe) and "Nosotros, los cieguitos" (We, the poor little blind kids) is the Chicano struggle with Anglo-dominated education. "El Lupito" tells the story of an eighteen-year-old high school student who, though he stands but two feet tall, nevertheless struggles bravely against the insensitivity of his principal and teachers and in the end emerges a

cultural hero. "Nosotros, los cieguitos" chronicles the abuses by students at the hands of their teachers in a school for visually handicapped children. Except for a male nurse who appears briefly in the final two paragraphs, the sole character in "La criada" (The Maid) is Ruth, a mute Chicano girl afflicted with multiple personality disorders. The plot consists of a series of episodes supposedly about four other patients in the mental hospital whose characters differ markedly from each other and who in reality turn out to be the four personalities of the narrator herself. The theme of "La criada," perhaps more than that of any other piece in the collection, could be considered universal, at least in the sense that to some degree it transcends ethnic boundaries. It should be borne in mind, however, that like the dwarf and the blind children, Ruth's life is dominated by an Anglo-run institution.

A third group of stories deals with the elderly. "Vete a jugar béisbol" (Go Play Baseball), "Poco veneno no mata" (A Little Poison Won't Kill), and "La espera" (The Wait) set forth the pain and alienation of old age. "Poco veneno no mata" consists of a monologue in which a lonely old woman talks to her son. She reveals to him her terror of rest homes and her lack of faith in modern medicine. The son turns out to be an illusion, for the woman has never had a child. "Vete a jugar béisbol" describes the painful last hours of an old man referred to only as "abuelo" (grandfather). In a heroic gesture, he tells his grandson not to worry: "Vete a jugar béisbol" (Go play baseball). The grandson obeys, and when he returns to the hospital, his grandfather has died. "La espera" takes place in the waiting room of a clinic where an old man, crippled by rheumatism and reduced to sitting in a wheelchair, dies as he waits to see a physician.

"Conversaciones" (Conversations) consists of three vignettes in which a grandmother tells her grandson stories from her youth. The first of them, "El Valiente Tío Sam" (The Brave Uncle Sam), takes place during World War I. It explores the contradiction between the dreadful poverty suffered by the nuevomexicanos and the flag-waving patriotism they are taught in school. "La Bruja" (The Witch) depicts an evil woman who is killed by a magic stone which had given her wealth and lovers. The third vignette deals with the custom of arranged marriage, common in New Mexico during the early days. In "Me fui con Coche" (I Left with Coche) the grandmother recounts the somewhat antiromantic story of a woman who abandoned her husband on the night of her wedding in favor of the man she truly loved. Unfortunately, the latter turns out to be an idler whom she is forced to support; he eventually murders her.

"La Junta" deals with the conflict between Anglos and nuevomexicanos over land use. The plot–based on an actual incident–revolves around the failed efforts to prevent an Anglo speculator from building on a huge housing tract on a choice parcel of irrigated land. It presents in an almost allegorical way the historical struggle between the rights of native New Mexicans and the expansion of Anglo-American interests. With its stereotypical characters and ambiguous ending, it eschews individual responsibility. The guilt falls not upon any person but upon the economic and political system which has deprived the nuevomexicanos of their birthright.

Sagel's *Los cumpleaños de doña Agueda* (Doña Agueda's Birthdays, 1984) consists mainly of verse, with an occasional piece of very short prose. The Vietnam War, local political corruption, and the new right are the topics covered, but the main focus is old age. As in Sagel's other writings, the old exemplify and validate pre-Anglo culture. One of the prose pieces, "El hambre en la luna" (Hunger on the Moon), uses a play on words "hambre" (hunger) instead of "hombre" (man) to express the contradiction of a society which allows some of its citizens to go hungry so that others may go to the moon. His *Sábelotodo Entiendelonada* (Know-It-All Understand-Nothing, 1988) is a collection of six stories about northern New Mexico.

Sagel's books have been well received, but except for *Tunomás Honey*, there have been few reviews. *Tunomás Honey* was praised by critics for both the English and the Spanish versions. It received favorable accounts in the *San Francisco Chronicle Review* (23 October 1983) and, closer to the author's home, in the *Santa Fe New Mexican* (16 September 1983) and the *Santa Fe Reporter* (14 September 1983). Spanish language evaluations by Arturo Arango Arias (*Revista Casa de las Américas*, March-April 1982) and Nuria Bustamante (*Revista Chicano-Riqueña*, Spring 1984) praised the work, with Bustamante concluding, "There is no doubt that the reading of *Tunomás Honey* will fulfill the dual purpose of providing moments of reflection for those considering the disadvantageous situation of some Chicano sectors, and moments of laughter over the numerous comical situations created and ably expressed by the author." Reviewer Michael R. J. Roth (*Sante Fe New Mexican*, 12 April 1985) praised *Los cumpleaños de doña Agueda*, calling it a rich collection, "as wry and sharp as the people it portrays." Writing for the *Sante Fe Reporter* (14 September 1988), E. A. Mares compared Sagel's latest book, *Sábelotodo Entiendelonada*, to *Tunomás Honey*, praising the author for his ironic humor and penetrating observations.

Jim Sagel's major concern as a writer has been the attempt to clarify personal values within the historical process. In his view, cultural identity must somehow be forged out of the tension between Hispanic tradition and Anglo technocracy. And it is language, the peculiar fusion of English and sixteenth-century Spanish, which can both achieve and legitimize the synthesis: a culture which critically adopts the best of both worlds. His work succeeds not only because he grasps the essential nature of the nuevomexicanos' struggle but because, having mastered their idiom, he can allow them to speak for themselves.

Floyd Salas

(24 January 1931-   )

Gerald Haslam
Sonoma State University

BOOKS: *Tattoo the Wicked Cross* (New York: Grove, 1967);
What Now My Love (New York: Grove, 1970);
Lay My Body on the Line: A Novel (Berkeley: Y'Bird, 1978);
To My Wife To Tell Her Boss What I Do All Day, Poems Needing Print Series Number 23 (Berkeley: Crosscut Saw, n.d.).

OTHER: "Mendocino High School," in *Poetry in the Schools,* edited by Stephen Vincent (San Francisco: Poetry Center, San Francisco State University, 1972), pp. 130-132;
"Romantic, If You Want To Call It That," in *I Write What I Want,* edited by Salas (San Francisco: Poetry in the Schools, 1974), pp. iii-v;
"Dead Time," in *Chicano Voices,* edited by Carlota Cardenas de Dwyer (Boston: Houghton Mifflin, 1975), pp. 126-132;
"Doors in Black Silhouettes," "Color of My Living Heart," in *Word Hustlers,* edited by Salas (Berkeley: Word Hustlers, 1976), pp. 4-10, 41-42;
"There's a Narcotic Hum in the Air," "Great Big Pink Cement Trucks," "For Shirley and All Those Other Black Girls Who Got Fired by Their Bosses," in *To Build A Fire,* edited by Salas (Oakland: Celebration of Writers, 1976), pp. vi, 12-13;
"Steve Nash Homoscual Transient Executed San Quentin Gas Chamber August 21st 1959 For Killing Eleven Men And A Little Boy," in *Calafia: The California Poetry,* edited by Ishmael Reed (Berkeley: Y'Bird, 1979), pp. 287-293;
"A Short Note on Poetics," "To Sergie My Sweet Old Dog Who Died in Old Age," in *The Holy eARTh,* edited by Jerry Kamstra (San Francisco: Peeramid, 1982);
"Pussy Pussy Everywhere," "Exhibit 'A', Censorship, Female Fascism, and Pussy Pussy Everywhere," in *Quilt 4,* edited by Reed and Al Young (Berkeley: Reed & Young, 1984), pp. 126-131, 133-141;

Floyd Salas (courtesy of the author)

Stories and Poems from Close to Home, edited, with contributions, by Salas (Berkeley: Ortalda, 1986);
"Brothers Keepers," in *California Childhood,* edited by Gary Soto (Berkeley: Creative Arts, 1988), pp. 6-18.

Although Floyd Salas has written a fine prison novel, *Tattoo the Wicked Cross* (1967), as well as other lauded prose and poetry, sometimes his political views, his social notions, and his ethnicity have attracted more attention.

Floyd Francis Salas was born in Walsenburg, Colorado, 24 January 1931, to Edward and Anita

230

Sanchez Salas. His father's ancestors originally immigrated to Florida in the seventeenth century, then to Colorado over the Santa Fe Trail in the mid nineteenth century. His mother's family came to the Southwest with Spanish explorer Juan de Oñate in the 1580s and pioneered in New Mexico and then in southern Colorado. Edward Salas moved the family to California when Salas was eight. The Salas family relocated frequently, living in the East Bay area of California and in the area near Shasta Dam in northern California. Salas attended six high schools in four years—"A great education for a future writer. . . . I had to scrap my way up the pecking order each time we'd move." Salas reported in an unpublished 1987 interview that during one fifteen-month period, following the death of his mother, he was arrested five times for brawling. He served 120 days in Santa Rita Prison Farm for spitting in a cab driver's face after a traffic accident, an experience that would influence his first novel: "It taught me to avoid prison at all costs if I want to survive," he said.

Salas evidenced a natural talent for fighting, and an older brother he much admired was an amateur boxing champion who eventually turned professional. In 1956, at the urging of a cousin who was on the team, Salas presented himself to the boxing coach at the University of California, Berkeley, whom he so impressed that he was awarded the first boxing scholarship in that institution's history. In 1958 he won a scholarship to El Centro Mexicano de Escritores, a writing school in Mexico City sponsored by the Rockefeller Foundation.

Salas has never been reluctant to express himself on issues, whether publicly or privately. For example, on 10 May 1968 he challenged Saul Bellow, who was speaking at San Francisco State, over the latter's view that the university should be a haven from vulgarity for writers, this at the very time activists were demanding admissions barriers be lowered so that everyone could benefit from a higher education. Bellow included a version of the incident in *Mr. Sammler's Planet* (1970), according to Mark Harris, who wrote of the confrontation in *Saul Bellow: Drumlin Woodchuck* (1980). Within a month of challenging Bellow, Salas participated in a successful week-long sit-in at San Francisco State; the participants demanded ten new minority teaching positions, a La Raza (Chicano) studies department, a black studies department, and the admission of one thousand minority students. In 1964 Salas won

Cover for Salas's novel about political radicalism in the Bay Area during the late 1960s

the prestigious Joseph Henry Jackson Award for "The Star, the Cross and the Broadsword," an early version of *Tattoo the Wicked Cross*. The following year he was awarded the Eugene F. Saxton Fellowship to continue work on the novel. He wrote seven complex drafts before the completed work was published.

In *Tattoo the Wicked Cross* Aaron D'Aragon, the fifteen-year-old protagonist, is sent to a prison farm for juveniles because he is caught street-fighting and because he is a *pachuco* (an assertive young Latin). Aaron finds the juvenile jail a brutal, inverted world in which those who are tough and who bully weaker boys are made monitors by the warden. Those who are good are respected by no one. Aaron is small but rugged. At first he possesses unyielding integrity and loyalty. He is concerned about Barneyway, a sworn blood brother who had been sent to the prison farm before him. Barneyway has been changed by something that happened to him at the prison dairy, but Aaron does not know what. Then he hears that the dairy is where "they beat 'em up first, then . . . gang-bang 'em, man! Make queens of 'em forever." He cannot believe that rape occurs until it happens to him. The rape turns him into a killer. Aaron poisons his antagonists, committing murder but earning new respect among other inmates for his crime. His brutalization is complete. In an unpublished 1985 letter Salas said of *Tattoo the Wicked Cross:* "I listened to everything I heard in jail. I used what I heard, what I learned, what I felt, what I knew. But it's not the story of my life. I've never been in reform school. I've never even seen one, only juvenile hall for thirty days at fifteen and the county jail farm as a young adult. I invented the story from something an artist friend, who had been sent to reform school as a boy for selling pot, told me."

Reviews of *Tattoo the Wicked Cross* were generally favorable, although some critics echoed the reviewer for *Time* (8 September 1967), who attacked the book as excessive in its depiction of juvenile prison life. C. Michael Curtis (*Saturday Review,* 23 September 1967) said that *Tattoo the Wicked Cross* "may be one of the best and certainly one of the most important first novels published in the last ten years." Donald Stanley (*San Francisco Examiner,* September 1967) observed that the power of the novel "resides in the muscular and realistic language." Walter Van Tilburg Clark pointed out in the *Evergreen Club News* that it is "tough, unflinching writing about a very tough, grim world. But also, in concept, insight, language and form, a work of art. . . ." Roger Sale (*Hudson Review,* October 1967) praised the passion of the novel, saying it is "one of those rare books written not because its author wanted to write but because in the face of his experience he had no other choice."

In 1981 *Tattoo the Wicked Cross* was reissued by Second Chance Press. Writing in *Change: A Juvenile Justice Quarterly* (June 1982), Andrew Vachss noted the verisimilitude of the novel: "Aaron acts in accordance with the inflexible demands of the institutional world, and a high-status killer is born. The boy who entered 'training school' for 'rehabilitation' is now a card-carrying member of

the life-style violent underclass. His orientation is no longer to his community; it is to his new and permanent world–the world of violence." John Lutz, in the *St. Louis Globe-Democrat* (19 December 1981), called the novel "a powerful, ugly, poetic, brilliant, compassionate rendering that even the squeamish should read." Ramón Jiménez, in the *New York Amsterdam News* (8 May 1982), saw the novel as a strong message for reform of the way the law treats minority youth: "If our legislators and concerned community leaders would invest a small sum of money [the price of the novel], they would learn more about the minority experience in juvenile prisons than the sum total of knowledge accumulated to date by the army of 'consultants' and 'experts' paid by our tax dollars. And maybe, just maybe, if they knew something, they would do something."

Salas's short novel *What Now My Love* (1970) traces the journey of three hippies after they are involved in the shooting of a policeman during a drug raid. Miles is a hip teacher of creative writing who dabbles in drugs. Carole is a six-foot beauty who is more concerned with dope than love. Sam is a drug dealer who spouts *Reader's Digest*-style Eastern philosophy. They flee to Tijuana with the intention of hiding in Mexico, but never leave the city because they become involved in Tijuana's drug culture and their own illusions. Miles and Carole become increasingly intimate, but she dies. At the book's conclusion, Sam drifts toward Mazatlán, Mexico, and Miles walks toward the U.S. border to face whatever punishment awaits him, his bitter soliloquy reflecting confused values and bitterness toward the uncomprehending general public, who "supported the laws that made dope illegal in America and forced people like Sam and Carole and I into the underworld. . . ."

In general, Salas's rendering of the drug subculture was received negatively by that culture, but Bay Area reviewer Bob Loomis (*Vallejo Times-Herald,* 8 March 1970), after noting the outrage in the underground press, said, "one suspects that he has accurately depicted the dark side of that lifestyle, the side that mushroomed–you should pardon the expression–out of its entanglement in illegal drug activities."

Salas traveled widely following the election of Richard Nixon in 1968. "I made the world's pot scenes," he explained in an unpublished letter, "following the hippy trail from San Francisco to Marakesh, writing a novel about my radical ex-

Salas in 1980 as assistant boxing coach at the University of California, Berkeley (courtesy of the author)

periences in the Bay Area called *Lay My Body on the Line*."

Salas and his wife Velva Daryl Harris, whom he married in 1948, were divorced in 1970. He taught creative writing at several Bay Area colleges in the 1970s, including Foothill College in Los Altos from 1979. In 1975 he was appointed assistant boxing coach at the University of California, Berkeley. In 1977 he was awarded a Lynch Fellowship at the University of California, Berkeley, where he worked with student writers. He won a creative writing fellowship from the National Endowment for the Arts in 1978. He married Virginia Ann Staley in 1979. In 1980 he was appointed lecturer in creative writing at the University of California, Berkeley. Salas and his second wife were divorced in 1981.

Salas's third novel, *Lay My Body on the Line* (1978), examines the uprisings at San Francisco State University in the late 1960s through the eyes of Roger Leon, an activist, teacher, and former boxer. Leon, descendant of a Spanish family, is haunted by family tragedies and insecurity

caused by perceived government surveillance. Readers cannot be certain whether Roger is slipping into delusions or is, in fact, a victim. He is pressed by forces real or imagined, and the novel grows increasingly tense. The turmoil and adventure of the Bay Area during that time, its political radicalism and hypocrisy, are powerfully captured in the novel.

Roger Leon was perceived by readers as a strongly autobiographical character, for Salas has skillfully laced events from the recent past, some from his own life, with fiction. Salas explained (27 November 1978) to interviewer Mary Walker of the *Daily Cal* that the book was, on the whole, fifty percent autobiographical, but, as Walker noted, "the parallels between Salas and his hero are remarkable and haunting." Asked if he was paranoid during those times, Salas said, "you never knew if you were being watched or not. I treated everything and everybody with skepticism and figured then that I would be safe."

Lay My Body on the Line received mixed reviews. Fred Cody of the *Berkeley Monthly* (23 November 1978) called Leon "an utterly believable narrator, plagued by demons of his past and a persistent susceptibility to paranoia." *San Francisco Bay Guardian* reviewer Stephen Arkin, who taught at San Francisco State during the 1969 strike, said (5 October 1978) that "for all the violent trappings of recent American political history that are invoked to flesh out Salas's book, what comes through is a not very appealing character in search of what sounds like the Sixties' version of happiness." Rita Fink, writing in the *Pacific Sun* (10-16 November 1978), called the book "a driving novel of the uprising of the Sixties, the idealism and activism, the paranoias."

Salas's work has continued to appear in anthologies, and increasingly he finds himself writing more poetry. His subject matter is varied and sometimes controversial. "To Sergie My Sweet Old Dog Who Died in Old Age" is Salas's elegy to a dog he loved. "Steve Nash Homosexual Transient Executed San Quentin Gas Chamber August 21st 1959 For Killing Eleven Men And A Little Boy" seeks to understand the forces which led Nash, discriminated against as a homosexual and as an Okie (native of Oklahoma), to act as he had. In *Quilt 4* (1984), an anthology edited by Ishmael Reed and Al Young, Salas is reported to have told John Bryant, editor of a countercultural newspaper, that he wrote the poem not because he supported Nash's murders or his homosexuality but because he "wanted to let people see *his* side of the story, show that he had suffered and that he deserved at least our compassion, if not our empathy."

Salas remains one of the San Francisco Bay Area's most prominent, controversial authors. His first novel, *Tattoo the Wicked Cross,* has been listed by Linda and Bill Katz as among the neglected great books of the twentieth century (*Writers Choice* [Englewood Cliffs, N.J.: Prentice-Hall, 1983]), and both his prose and poetry continue to appear in anthologies–including *Stories and Poems from Close to Home,* a collection of Bay Area writing he edited in 1986. Salas is currently completing work on a historical novel, "Widow's Weeds," which traces the experiences of a pioneering Spanish family in the American West. He has also begun drafting yet another novel, the subject of which he has not revealed, and he finds himself once more writing poetry. A prominent member of PEN, a teacher of creative writing, and a director of the Foothill Writers' Conference, Salas remains deeply involved in literary life.

References:

Gerald Haslam, "Floyd Salas–Writer on an Ethnic Edge," *California English,* 24 (May-June 1988): 24-25;

Roger Sale, "Good Servants and Bad Masters," *Hudson Review,* 20 (October 1967): 664-674;

Sale, "Unknown Novels," *American Scholar,* 43 (Winter 1973-1974): 86-104.

Luis Omar Salinas

(27 June 1937-   )

Gary Soto
University of California, Berkeley

BOOKS: *Crazy Gypsy* (Fresno, Cal.: Origines, 1970);

Afternoon of the Unreal (Fresno, Cal.: Abramás, 1980);

Prelude to Darkness (San Jose, Cal.: Mango, 1981);

Darkness under the Trees/Walking behind the Spanish (Berkeley: Chicano Studies Library, University of California, 1982);

The Sadness of Days: New and Selected Poems (Houston: Arte Publico, 1987).

OTHER: *From the Barrio: A Chicano Anthology,* compiled by Salinas and Lillian Faderman (San Francisco: Canfield, 1973);

Entrance: 4 Chicano Poets; Leonard Adame, Luis Omar Salinas, Gary Soto, Ernesto Trejo (Greenfield Center, N.Y.: Greenfield Review, 1975).

Luis Omar Salinas was born on 27 June 1937 in Robstown, Texas, to Olivia Treviño and Rosendo Valdez Salinas. Soon after his birth his father, a merchant and owner of a small grocery, moved the family to Monterrey, Mexico, where he opened a store. His mother contracted tuberculosis and died in 1941, causing several changes in Luis Salinas's life. His father returned to Robstown where, after a few months of coping with his family alone, he gave up his children for adoption: his daughter Irma went to live with her Aunt Anita and Luis went to live with Rosendo's brother Alfredo, who had recently married.

Alfredo's family left Texas for California while Salinas was in elementary school, first settling in San Francisco and later in Fresno, where, for the first time, Salinas lived among Anglos who did not embrace the racism of Texas (segregated schools and second-rate jobs). In Fresno, Salinas became a paperboy, a boy scout, and a practicing Catholic. In high school he joined the football and wrestling teams, dated occasionally, and, after his family moved to Bakersfield, California, played trumpet in a six-piece combo. During his senior year in high school he wanted, as he described himself in an unpublished interview (July 1981), to be "a rebel, to be different but not too different." He wore a black nylon jacket and tucked his hands into his back pocket.

In 1956 Salinas entered Bakersfield City College with the intention of majoring in drama. In 1958 he moved from Bakersfield to Los Angeles to live with his father and began attending California State College at Los Angeles. He lived in the barrio of East Los Angeles.

In college he took classes in voice and diction, modern Continental drama, advanced acting, elementary voice, and American literature. But his college career ended abruptly when he suffered a mental breakdown and spent eleven months under observation. After his release from the hospital he lived with his adoptive parents, and, after two years, he returned to California State College at Los Angeles in 1963 to take a history course. He enrolled in his first creative writing course in 1965. His instructor was poet Henri Coulette. Of Salinas, Professor Coulette remembers in an unpublished letter:

> What intrigued me that day back in 1965, when my eye roved over the names on the class roster, was the first time I had had a Spanish name pop up in one of my creative writing classes. The name belonged to a young man whose handsome face looked as though it had been turned on a lathe. Salinas carried himself like a Marine Corps rifleman. At first, I thought he was sullen. A few days later I decided shy might be more accurate, for his eyes were almost always on his folded hands. Later, I thought maybe frightened was the right adjective. In any event, I wasn't prepared for the literary sophistication of those surrealist poems of his that started turning up on my worksheet.

Shortly after he took the creative writing class Salinas and his parents moved to Sanger, California, an agricultural town just outside of Fresno. In 1966 Salinas began writing classes at California State College at Fresno under teachers such as Philip Levine, Robert Mezey, and Peter Everwine. He was hospitalized numerous times in the late 1960s, his mental health strained in part by the cultural and political turmoil of the period. He was involved in teaching in La Raza (Chicano) studies and the movement that started with the United Farm Workers' strikes against grape growers.

Salinas's first book, *Crazy Gypsy* (1970), was rushed into production essentially unedited. Many of these poems are deeply felt, highly imaginative, and psychologically true. The book is nota-

Luis Omar Salinas

ble for its unusual imagery and its major theme, the frightening sense of alienation and loneliness that issues from the death of a mother. Included in this volume are poems that have become favorites of anthologists: "Nights and Days"; "Crazy Gypsy"; "Aztec Angel"; and "Mexico, Age Four"; among a few others. Perhaps the most remarkable poem in regard to its imaginative power and its completeness (several poems in this book are mere jumbled impressions of the world) is "Sunday . . . Dig the Empty Sounds." In it the narrator searches for his mother through a desolate landscape of frightening images such as "the blood of children and the clouds with mouths," to conclude, "I survive the rain/dreaming, lost, frowning/while the shoes of my mother/talk/to the children of Africa/to the crazy dogs/that huddle in corners/starving/empty of sound." Salinas wrote this poem, as well as others in *Crazy Gypsy*, while under a self-induced trance: according to a witness, he had not slept in more than forty-eight hours. Wired on countless cups of coffee and spurred on by conversations with friends, Salinas wrote his best poems.

Crazy Gypsy was a commercial and critical success. Salinas was offered readings throughout the United States and became a presence in the emerging Chicano literary scene. With Lillian Faderman, professor of English at Fresno State College (later California State University, Fresno), he was asked to compile an anthology of Chicano writings published as *From the Barrio* (1973).

In early 1976, after several years in which almost none of Salinas's poems were published, Greenfield Review Press brought out the anthology *Entrance: 4 Chicano Poets*, a compilation of poems by Leonard Adame, Luis Omar Salinas, Gary Soto, and Ernesto Trejo. The book included old and new poems by Salinas. Pleased by his first publication in six years, Salinas began to write vigorously under the editorship of Christopher Buckley, Gary Soto, and Jon Veinberg. His second book of poems, *Afternoon of the Unreal* (1980), can be called a study in extremes. In tone, the poems are utterly happy or miserable. One of the finest poems in the collection is "For Armenia," in which the narrator announces, "I feel enchantment everytime/I enter an Armenian household," and goes on to "drink coffee, eat baklava/and the night air comes in/singing to the tune of dusted/stars, hovering above/like mad gypsies." The narrator concludes, "And what awaits me is the future–/blue ringing of flesh–/as I waltz,/a man like any other,/watching everything emerge/like a crazy wake." The writing is grand, almost theatrical, and most certainly romantic. Typical of the poems in *Afternoon of the Unreal*, in which often the narrator postures not unlike Don Quixote or a traveling bard, is "Until Heaven Gets Tired," which begins, "In this curious mad evening/when the things I invent/are unreal and my life like a cow,/sings crudely, I make the villages/in my brain whistle at the girls./They are drums and flutes,/women milking shadows/in this fleeting residence." Even though the poem is dark, there is wit and a self-effacing humor. It begins with the poet transforming himself one "mad evening" (an inspired moment) into a cow that sings crudely. This device is purposely self-mocking: Omar is laughing at his poetic abilities; instead of transforming himself into a noble beast–horse or Pegasus–he opts for a simple animal of the field. This is followed by the lines "I make the villages/in my brain whistle at the girls." Again this illustrates Salinas's wit and ability to write a fascinating image.

Salinas works in opposites: he is either of the low order of things (the cow is an example) or is part of the high order of things (a vagabond poet filled with the mysteries of life is the example from "For Armenia"). These either/or situations occur in many of his poems and suggest his desire to be "up or down," away from the humdrum existence of everyday life.

Prelude to Darkness (1981) is a collection of love poems in which Salinas is often the object of spurned love. The tone is quiet, tender (at times precious), and often playful. In "Last Tango in Fresno," he walks between a pastrami and a dream, counting his blessings. He wants to seduce a woman, but he can find no lover with whom to scuttle to a motel. Instead, he "waltzes" down the street, carefree as ever, "and bump(s)/into a lesbian friend/who is out of/work and needs a job./I give her five bucks/and feel/that in the next life/I'll get it all back." The title poem to the collection, which is about trying to stay healthy, ends by asking why life can be so miserable: "Who could have dreamed this/agony up? The nuns/with their sorrowful mysteries/and dark beads? Jesus/with a bad memory?" The weakness of this collection lies in Salinas's tendency to posture, that is, to stand cigarette in hand, wind flicking his hair, and sunlight dancing about him as he thinks of "the sweetheart waters of moonlight." Salinas seldom does anything ordinary. The simple act of drinking iced tea becomes momentous as he begins to imagine devils, virgins, and "the lips of death/[that] croon everywhere. . . ." He doesn't walk, but has to "waltz"; he doesn't talk, but must dance while he sings. In short, every gesture enlarges the poet, so that the writing at times emerges stagey and melodramatic.

Darkness under the Trees/Walking behind the Spanish (1982) is to date Salinas's best single collection of poetry. The poems are mature, ambitious in scope, well written, and altogether a convincing portrayal of one man trying to rationalize his unjust fate. The book is in two parts. *Darkness under the Trees* consists of thirty-six poems, most of which are one-page lyrics on themes of death, madness, isolation, and unrequited love. The book's theme is stated in the initial poem, "On My Birth": "What I want to do is/tell you about my wounds/and place a few yellow flowers/on your kitchen table." Salinas's poetry is filled with sorrow and the simple gestures of tenderness. The love poem "You Are Not Here" is a representative example of darkness. It begins with the speaker addressing a lover who, for reasons that are not apparent to the reader, has left him. He re-

Cover for Salinas's most recent poetry collection

members her flesh, her voice, music, and the suggestive moment when "blossoms twirl their tongues." Failed love is placed against a backdrop of nature—love that is tragically sweet, and not loud with recriminations and accusatory reminders of each other's failings: "And the evening walks off, shrugging/its grey shoulders, and I'm on a bench/impetuous as the pigeons pecking/the nothings in my hands, holding/a simple hat for your soul." "The Odds" is a comic poem which begins with serious questions posed about humanity's fate. It ends with an image of self-mocking courage: "Let the dead-mad divide and/ anger the moon, but I prefer/to simply go unadorned/among kings and hold my head/high among the common towns/I come from, unnoticed in my/open coat and summer hat./I've known dogs in my life/who have died gallantly/ with feet straight up in the air."

Walking behind the Spanish, the second part of the collection, consists of forty-one poems that for the most part pay homage to Spanish civil war poets, or those poets and activists influenced by Spanish literature. The narrator in the poems joins these poets, both in the sense of literary influence and sensibility toward a world community, admiring them for their work as well as their stance against fascism, by which many of them lost their lives.

Like Salinas's earlier work, these poems are short, romantic, imagistic, and sometimes surreal. The narrators are love struck, downtrodden but courageous, humorous, and full of compassion for the poor. The titles of the poems are eye-catching: "My Dead Friends Are Hitchhiking"; "A Clever Magician Carrying My Heart"; "I Surrender in the March of My Bones"; "When the Stars Get Angry and Coo Above Our Heads";

"Rosita, the Future Waits with Hands of Swans"; "If You Want to Know Something About Me, Talk to the Clouds For I Am Going There"; and "To the Tavern Where Life Meets the Eye I Turn an Ear and Boast Friendship."

The themes are large but seldom vague: lost love, death, courage, friendship, and family. One of the finest poems in this second section is "My Father is a Simple Man." It begins with the narrator on a walk to the store with his father, and like Aristole and Plato, they are at odds with life and its larger values. The narrator sides with pomegranates (the rich fruits of life) because of their princely jewels, and the older man sides with oranges (the common fruit that grows everywhere) because they are full of seeds and are therefore perpetual. In the end the narrator sides with his father and says, "The truth is, he's the scholar/and when the bitter-hard reality/comes at me like a punishing/evil stranger, I can always/remember that here was a man/who was a worker and provider/who held no pretense." He concludes that when his father is gone, "I shall have learned what little/there is about greatness."

Salinas's *The Sadness of Days: New and Selected Poems* (1987) contains fourteen new poems and a generous selection from each of his previous books. The new poems are similar in construction to the earlier work. They are short, lyrical, and largely imagistic. Unlike that of his previous poems, the tone here is resigned, in part because he is wiser and older. Moreover, the poems are less surreal, less political, less rambunctious, and more steeped in sadness. In "Come Pick Up My Body" he gives himself over to approaching death, and in "Pain" he is "tired of looking/at the unbent trees." Still, in spite of his tiredness, the poems are tender, not bitter, and playful, not stern. *The Sadness of Days: New and Selected Poems* illustrates the progress of his career from a poet of the movement toward Chicano ethnic awareness to a poet who would later receive the prestigious General Electric Foundation Award for Young Writers in 1985. This collection demonstrates that Salinas possesses a powerful imagination, a sensitivity toward the world, and an intuitive feel for handling language.

Reference:

Gary Soto, "Luis Omar Salinas: Chicano Poet," *MELUS*, 9 (Summer 1982): 47-82.

Ricardo Sánchez

(29 March 1941-   )

Joel Hancock
University of Utah

BOOKS: *Canto y grito mi liberación (y lloro mis desma-drazgos . . .)* (El Paso: Míctla, 1971); expand-ed and republished as a bilingual edition (Garden City, N.Y.: Anchor/Doubleday, 1973);

Hechizospells: Poetry/Stories/Vignettes/Articles/Notes on the Human Condition of Chicanos & Pícaros, Words & Hopes within Soulmind (Los Angeles: Chicano Studies Center, University of Cali-fornia, Los Angeles, 1976);

Milhuas Blues and Gritos Norteños (Milwaukee: Spanish Speaking Outreach Institute, Col-lege of Letters and Science, University of Wis-consin, 1980);

Brown Bear and Honey Madnesses: Alaskan Cruising Poems (Austin: Slough, 1981);

Amsterdam Cantos y Poemas Pistos (Austin: Place of Herons, 1983);

Selected Poems (Houston: Arte Publico, 1985).

MOTION PICTURE: *Entelequia*, screenplay by Sánchez, Stazar (Denver), 1979.

OTHER: *Los cuatro*, edited by Sánchez and Abe-lardo Barrientos Delgado, includes work by Sánchez (Denver: Barrio, 1971).

Ricardo Sánchez (Special Collections, General Library, University of New Mexico)

Ricardo Sánchez has written about the many forces–historical, cultural, linguistic, social, political–that have shaped and determined Chi-cano reality. At the same time he expresses con-cerns about the universal human condition and asks questions related to individual existence.

Ricardo Sánchez was the youngest of thir-teen children born to Pedro Lucero and Adelina Gallegos Sánchez. He was raised in the rough dis-trict of El Paso, Texas, known as Barrio del Diablo (Devil's Neighborhood). Stifled by an edu-cational system he would later denounce as being overtly racist, Sánchez dropped out of high school. He enlisted in the U.S. Army, and after-ward he served sentences in Soledad prison in Cali-fornia (he was paroled in 1963) and Ramsey Prison Farm Number One in Texas (from which

he was paroled in 1969). After his release in 1969 he earned a high school equivalency certifi-cate, and, in 1974, sponsored by Ford Foundation grants, he earned a Ph.D. in American Studies and cultural linguistic theory at Union Graduate School in Yellow Springs, Ohio, submitting a dis-sertation entitled "CUNA: The Barrio and the Po-etics of Revolución."

In addition to his work as a writer of poetry and prose, Sánchez wrote the script to the film *Entelequia*, directed by Juan Salazar (1979), and, re-cently, he has worked as a free-lance writer and journalist. He is founder and editor of Míctla Publications (El Paso, Texas); *La Luz* (Denver, Colorado); and *Ins and Outs* (Amsterdam, Holland). He has also edited issues of *Wood/Ibis* (Austin, Texas); *". . . ?" Magazine* (Venice, Italy); and *De Colores: Journal of Emerging Raza Philosophies* (Albuquerque, New Mexico).

Sánchez has held visiting appointments as professor or writer in residence at various universities and has developed successful programs in the arts and in education, such as a long-standing series of readings by Texas poets. He helped found and organize the "Canto al Pueblo" (Chant to the People) festivals in Milwaukee, Wisconsin, and he has worked to improve the health of itinerant migrant workers and involved himself in diverse community outreach projects. Particularly significant has been his work as an instructor in various prisons and his participation in the organization of halfway houses.

Scholarly attention first came to Sánchez in 1973 with the republication of his 1971 volume *Canto y grito mi liberación (y lloro mis desmadrazgos . . .)* (I Cry and Sing My Liberation [and cry my deracinations]). In his preface Sánchez says that the book "gestated in the frenzy of Soledad prison." Most of the forty-four items were written in 1969 and 1970, with a few pieces dated 1963 and 1968. The volume, a mix of poetry and prose, contains a rich assortment of subjects and themes. Sprinkled throughout are expressions of pride and love for the Chicano people, their beauty, and their customs. Sánchez writes as himself in first person; he speaks of basic human dignity and exhorts Chicanos never to compromise their racial identity but instead to resist any efforts of assimilation into the majority. He attacks racist attitudes and practices, which he asserts are present at all levels of government and the educational system. Repeatedly he voices his fear of the attempts to enslave and dehumanize his people. Oppressive conditions demand immediate correction. Although at times he communicates a sense of hopelessness regarding the political situation, he more often is spirited in his call for solidarity in the struggle against white supremacy. Freedom, justice, and self-determination are goals to be attained, and revolutionary activity may be the only means. Thus, in the poem "Chingaderismo" (Screw Job) he admonishes the ruling powers that "if amerika don't change, we shall burn it to the ground."

Numerous pieces in the volume are very personal "machistic self-affirmations," as he labels them in "Existir es . . ." (To Exist is . . .). Sánchez

writes about being incarcerated in the poem "Stream," describing prison as a place where he was forced to retreat into a world of hopes and dreams, only to emerge "lonely, hurting, needing." He finds parallels between his experiences and the general situation of the Chicano, whom he describes as always an inmate in American society. He recounts his activities as a youth, his life in a poor neighborhood in El Paso, the comforts provided by his friends, his feelings while traveling far away from his roots, and the importance of heavily Chicano cities like El Paso, San Antonio, Denver, Albuquerque, and Los Angeles. There are also occasional poems which describe specific events, such as political meetings and rallies. Among his most poignant poems are those which disclose his deep love for members of his immediate family and the strength they offer him, in particular his wife Maria Teresa Silva, whom he married in 1964. "Tere" is a personal and tender poem affirming his love for his wife after six years of marriage.

Most of the poems in *Canto y grito mi liberación* are blends of Spanish and English. Sánchez is particularly successful in the employment of colloquial expressions and adept in using neologisms. His images are vividly visual. Another salient characteristic is the musical dimension of his compositions, which is created by pulsating rhythms, alliterative word combinations, and effective use of occasional rhyme. There is also a marked diversity of tone. In his essays Sánchez articulates his thoughts and arguments forcefully and cogently.

Sánchez coedited and contributed eight poems to the anthology of four Chicano poets, *Los cuatro* (The Four, 1971); the other three contributors were Abelardo Barrientos Delgado, Reymundo Pérez, and Juan Valdez. In the introduction, Sánchez avers that Chicanos will not remain dormant and subjugated. Most of his protest poems advocate resistance, insurrection, and revenge. The tone, befitting the themes, tends to be combative: "It is better to live like a man," Sánchez affirms in "Carnal tras rejos" (Brother behind Bars), "rather than survive on the floor like a servant." The poems are dedicated to Chicanos, to whom he offers his soul in writing. He expresses his ideas aggressively and with anger. The most noteworthy piece in the collection, one he often read at political rallies during the early 1970s, is "Indict Amerika," a synthesis of many of his ideas. In it Sánchez sits in judgment of the

                                                                    en ruinas xicanas
                                                                    arden historias
                                                                    y gritan las voces
                                                                    de los asesinados.
                                                                      San Antonio de Bexar
                                                                        9° de marzo 1988

                                --monde d'chicano--
                                      por el Dr. Ricardo Sánchez

1.

    las pierdas gritan   the rocks cry out
    genocidio enfermo   sickened genocide

    los años vorados   erased years
    vomitan pedazos   vomit out pieces
    de una historia   of a mutilated/tormented
    mutilada/tormentada   history

    nosotros buscamos   we search
    dentro ruinas/artefactos   within shards/artefacts
    endemoniados en nuestras   enraged in our losses
              pérdidas

    hijos desnativizados,   denativized progeny,
    chicanos marginados,   alienated Chicanos,
    el futuro arde   the future smoulders
    en nuestras miradas   in our visages
    y una revolución   and a revolution
    nos invita   bids us welcome

2.

    we walked, o humankind,   anduvimos, o humanidad,
    from the entrails   desde las entrañas
    of sickness   de la enfermedad
    smiting/raping   afligiendo/estrupiendo
    our people's destiny   el destino de nuestro pueblo
    in the vicious diatribes   con los ataques viciosos
    of gringo manifestation,   del manifiesto gringo,
    we burned within   ardíamos dentro
    Amerikan megalomania   la megalomania amerikana
    withstanding an English Only   resistiendo un mandato servíl
    mandate for servility, still   del inglés nomás, pero
    we survive   seguimos sobreviviendo
    on margins   en las márgines
    where our spirits plot   donde nuestros espíritus trazan
    a transformation   la transformación
    to dignify all life...   para dignificar la vida...

3.

    luchamos dentro el amor   we struggle within the love
    que sentimos latiendo   we feel pulsating
    hacia lo humano, somos   toward all human-ness, we are
    granos de la humanidad   grain/strains of humanity
    cantando versos libertadores...   singing liberating poems...

                        copyright: Ricardo Sánchez

Typescript for a recent poem by Sánchez (courtesy of the author)

country and its institutions, and he vents his anger at the oppression of the Chicano people.

Preceded by an introduction and seven essays called by Sánchez "Notes on the Human Condition," *Hechizospells: Poetry/Stories/Vignettes/Articles/ Notes on the Human Condition of Chicanos & Pícaros, Words & Hopes within Soulmind* (1976) contains ninety-seven poems, most of them dated between 1969 and 1974 and often identified as to specific time, place, and circumstance of composition. In one of the notes, "Hechizos: Pieces of Life," Sánchez defines *Hechizospells* as "enchantments/fascinations . . . pieces of life–the hectic skits of action–that everyone must grapple with in order to live and define the world." In the same note he goes on to describe the contents of the volume as a variety of writings that reflect his own interior being: "This book is a series of glimpses at a multifaceted world; seething with anger and discontent; pulsing with love and hope; and inspired by the humanity of those who have shared moments with me."

The preface of *Hechizospells* conveys Sánchez's thoughts on writing and on Chicano literature. Writing mirrors his life and values. It is his response to the many questions and issues that obsess him: ethnic identity, love, justice, and oppression. Art is a political statement, and his own creative production is directed to the struggle for human liberation: "As a human being with a Chicano/cultural/linguistic/historical self-image I affirm, unreservedly, my right to live and express my sense of life, to live and die for my ideals, and to share in the struggle for human liberation in solidarity with all oppressed people everywhere. To do otherwise is to deny my own responsibility as a human being." He views Chicano literature as a universal expression of the struggle for human liberation.

The poems of *Hechizospells* are predominantly political in nature. Many of the poems are in groups with a thematic cohesion (four poems were penned on 5 March 1971, for example). Frequently, poems treating similar subject matter are grouped together, as is the series composed while he was participating in the Frederick Douglass Fellowship Journalism Program in Virginia. Sánchez is adamant in his insistence on liberation and often argues that the struggle may become violent. As he says in the poem, "Confe de Brotherhood Awareness" (Conference of Brotherhood Awareness), "If it takes a river of blood to carve out freedom, then let it be." Among the most personal poems are those which describe

Caricature of Sánchez by El Zarco Guerrero (copyright © 1981 Zarco Guerrero)

Sánchez's experiences growing up in the Barrio del Diablo in El Paso. Other deeply moving poems in the volume include an elegy for his son Pedro and a tribute to his father.

Stylistic form and language in *Hechizospells* is varied. Sánchez mixes English and Spanish and uses rhyme, alliteration, typographical variation, periodic cadences, and onomatopoeic sounds that suggest musical instruments or heartbeats ("ca-tum-ba, ca-tum-ba, tun-tun-pa," "tum-tum-tum, tuuummmmmmmm!"). He invents words or gives them new meaning (a leftist is someone "left behind in leftover barrios"). He joins words together for rhythmic or lexical effect ("canto-grito," "mindsoulbody," "hisemptysocketeyes") and plays with words and phrases for satiric effect ("de/mock/ra/cy/," "Amerika-ga-da," "let us prey"). Spanish pronunciation of English words sometimes serves a humorous and critical purpose (John Wayne becomes "ya buey" [okay ox]). Internal rhyme is used with ironic intent "y las masas con sus grasas" (and the masses with their greases).

In 1977 Sánchez held an appointment as visiting professor at the University of Wisconsin-Milwaukee. *Milhuas Blues and Gritos Norteños* (Milwaukee Blues and Cries from the North, 1980) collects writings related to his stay there. Dedicated to the people of Milwaukee the book contains eleven poems and one essay that is punctuated with verse. A principal theme in the volume is Sánchez's worry over misdirection in the Chicano Movement as typified in the first poem, "Escritura, pintura, ba ba sura" (Writing, Painting, Ga Ga Garbage). The participants in the Chicano Floricanto Festival (1976) are lifeless and headed toward a wasteland, and the art, especially the literature, that is being produced is drivel and garbage. New leaders, Sánchez asserts, are consumed with petty jealousies and are mutilating the humanistic ideals of the movement. In "Re-encuentro" (Re-encounter), one of the last poems of the collection, written upon his return to El Paso, where he was then living, Sánchez admits that no one, including himself, has the solution to the problems plaguing the movement. In the struggle for equality, he claims, people are sometimes hurt and thus begin directing their anger toward each other. Although he was skeptical about the direction of the movement, his commitment to the fight for liberation did not waver. In "La casi muerte" (The Almost Death) he states that every person has the right to enjoy a dignified life and, consequently, urges Chicanos to organize in their fight against enslavement.

Other poems in *Milhuas Blues* are more personal. In "sólo & with remembrances" he combats loneliness by fantasizing about spending intimate, sensual moments with her. Similar erotic experiences are more graphically depicted in "Tóricas a las nichis," the final poem of the collection.

In the one essay included in *Milhuas Blues and Gritos Norteños*, "Arte: Cumbre de lo Humanizante" (Art: Summit of the Humanizing Process), Sánchez describes his work as "slices of thoughts and sentiments." He addresses the subject of the function of art. In the poem that precedes it, "Milwaukee Blues y Gritos Norteños" (Milwaukee Blues and Cries from the North), he identifies the creative process as a liberating experience, a channel through which societal chains are broken and freedom is achieved. Inspired by his 1977 role in the "Canto al Pueblo" festival in Milwaukee, Wisconsin, which focused on Chicano artistic endeavors and accomplishments, Sánchez writes that art is the essence of culture: "one of the truest vehicles for the spiritual/intellectual expression of our humanity." On the personal level, art is an instrument that facilitates self-definition and provides an individual with the opportunity to "thinkfeel." Commenting specifically on Chicano art, Sánchez declares that it has played an important unifying role, helping "to retain our self-image as an integral people." Art offers hope and nurtures those persons living in an "alien/alienating" world, and it offers encouragement in the struggle for survival. It is "the key to our having retained much of our humanity."

In September of 1978 Sánchez attended the One World Poetry Festival in Amsterdam, Holland, an international event drawing poets from all continents. Much like his previously published work, *Amsterdam Cantos y Poemas Pistos* (Amsterdam Songs and Drunken Poems, 1983) is a detailed journal account written in poetry, describing the preparations, impressions, impact, and aftermath of the event. There are thirty-three entries, each preceded by an informative outline listing place, date, and nature of his thoughts and activities.

In the third poem, "Para que" (For What), Sánchez communicates his fear that the European audience would not understand his Chicano perspective. The idea of participating in the international event makes him both nervous and proud of the recognition his accomplishments are receiving. The childhood dreams of traveling around the world have been realized, and he wonders how many of his high school companions have been so fortunate.

Amsterdam Cantos y Poemas Pistos is autobiographical; Sánchez's diary is an introspective travelogue embodying impressions, experiences, and personal thoughts and emotions. He transcribes these thoughts during airline flights, train rides, boat cruises, and as he traverses the streets of the city. He also observes the Dutch people, their manners, and their speech in hotels, restaurants, bars, bistros, and the festival events. With genuine admiration he describes Amsterdam's cosmopolitan atmosphere. Although he raves about Dutch generosity and hospitality, occasionally he views the locality as "the homeland of our oppressor," and senses phantoms of Nazi horrors. He includes poems dedicated to specific people and occasions, such as a tribute to Reidar Ekner, a Swedish poet attending the festival, or his observance of the sixteenth of September (Mexican Independence day) which takes place while he is in the Netherlands.

The trip to Amsterdam proved to be personally significant to Sánchez. Filled with excitement, he declares in the twenty-seventh poem (untitled) that never before has he felt so free, "away from the vitiating viciousness/of the living/in the blandness of the usa." Gone are the daily pressures and confrontations of barrio survival and the struggle for affirmation. In Amsterdam he feels love and the opportunity to hear and see other realities. Each day at the festival is a celebration for him, as he lives for the moment and basks in warmth and camaraderie. As he says in the same untitled poem: "For the first time in 20 years/I could simply/just be/me:/a man sharing poetry." He views the journey to Europe as the opportunity to relax and recoup his strength before returning home to continue the fight for liberation: "for one week/have felt freer/& more irresponsible/than ever before,/a nice luxury/that everyone should have/at least once/in their lifetime/. . . I must return/to plunge/into the pus of social discontent."

During the summer of 1979 Sánchez was writer in residence at the University of Alaska in Juneau and taught a creative writing course at the Lemon Creek State Prison. From his association with the penitentiary, where he also directed a practicum, *Lemon Creek Gold: A Journal of Prison Literature* was begun, with Sánchez as its first editor. During the time spent in Juneau Sánchez also composed poetry. It appeared in the collection *Brown Bear and Honey Madnesses: Alaskan Cruising Poems* (1981), one of his shorter works, containing only eight poems. *Brown Bear and Honey Madnesses* is particularly significant for understanding Sánchez, for it reveals that the new direction he seemed to be taking in *Amsterdam Cantos y Poemas Pistos* had reached fruition: he is now a more mature artist, calmer and less angry. The poems are written almost exclusively in English, and, with few notable exceptions, focus principally on introspective musings. There is little mention of his involvement in the Chicano Movement or of his advocacy of liberation.

The impact of travel and living in a distant land is a subject referred to with great frequency in *Brown Bear and Honey Madnesses*. In the first poem, "Journeys: Praxis and Entelechy," Sánchez declares that travel "elongates thought processes." Throughout the collection he gives evidence that he is at relative peace with himself and the world. He states that he has achieved personal definition and that the labors and struggles of his past have yielded positive results. Free

from past anxieties, he feels tranquil, and thus his writing is more thoughtful and deliberate. As he says in the same poem, "my words now come/slower paced." In the poem "bar banter," he states that he is "no longer tired/nor disgusted with life/. . . I need not/hate humankind/nor shout obscenities." Even in the face of death, as he describes in the poem "Vida o muerte" (Life or Death), Sánchez declares in erotic terms that he will live life to its fullest and always celebrate its sensuous nature.

Sánchez's self-proclaimed growth and change does not mean that he avoids addressing issues of political and social import in *Brown Bear and Honey Madnesses*. Certain things he sees and experiences in Alaska provoke his ire. For example, the "absorbingly frenetic" Alaskan nature is incomparably beautiful, but the nature of the nonnatives who inhabit the land is despicable. In "interminable," for example, he describes the hollow life of invaders from other states who live in trailers and condominiums, eat "pre-fabricated" food, and find entertainment in discotheques. They are inhumane thrill seekers who, while worshiping nature, reject the natural essence of the native people. Sánchez accuses the interlopers and the government of committing genocide: "yes, deny/the eskimos,/aleuts,/athabaskans,/haida & tlingits/their historical/right/to live/as their ancestors/lived/when Alaska/was their land,/kill them off,/Amerika,/now, right now."

Teaching writing in an Alaskan prison–an environment about which Sánchez is particularly knowledgeable and sensitive–gave him the opportunity to repeat his excoriations of the atmosphere of penitentiaries. In "Tinieblas y Prisones: Voyage to Lemon Creek" (Darkness and Prisons: Voyage to Lemon Creek) he is saddened "to view human kind/rampaging/against/itself" in a "steel-cement-iron enclosure" ironically surrounded by Alaskan greenery. Dejectedly, he analyzes his role as a prison teacher, entertaining convicts so they might be liberated for an instant from the dismal reality of their captivity. Sánchez identifies with their imprisonment, feeling that he, too, is "encaged/by the limitations of Juneau/and my own perception of my mortality."

Some occasional poems were written during Sánchez's stay in Alaska. For example, an official visit as a dignitary to attend a book fair in Mexico City caused him great discomfort, as mentioned in "& would that I could." The supplicating beggars of the city bring to his mind the history of the Chicano people and their sevverance from the Mexican nation. An untitled poem written in Alaska on Father's Day recalls the great courage Sánchez's father always displayed, and the poet laments the fact that his father will never be able to read the writings and thus become familiar with his son's anxieties and aspirations. Sánchez reviews militant days spent in the Chicano Movement, and he tells his deceased father that the time they did spend together was important. With great pride he assesses his accomplishments and comments: "I've since written much/published and lectured/from el paso to yale."

Sánchez's *Selected Poems* appeared in 1985. The collection contains twenty-eight poems written predominantly in English. For the most part they are pieces that had been composed earlier and published in other works. However, over one-third are from his 1977 manuscript, "Sojourns and Soulmind Etchings." *Selected Poems* is prefaced with "Ricardo Sánchez" (Sometimes), a long autobiographical poem which highlights his lifelong activities and accomplishments. The first section of the volume, "La Pinta/The Joint," expresses his feelings about incarcerations in California and Texas. Under the heading "Barrios of the World," he communicates impressions gathered while traveling and living in other communities at home and abroad.

The poetry of Sánchez has taken different directions. His initial angry affirmations of political militancy have evolved into a more serene expression that validates life in general as something joyful and replete with meaning. The popularity and critical recognition of Sánchez's work is due to the sincerity of the poet's thoughts and convictions as well as to the rich lyrical nature of the writings, a thought affirmed by Juan Bruce-Novoa in *Chicano Authors: Inquiry by Interview* (1980). Bruce-Novoa summarizes general critical sentiment which identifies Sánchez as a lyrical poet of great talent: "Ricardo Sánchez is one of Chicano literature's most talented creators of poetic narrative . . . , he is the epitome of the artist: incapable of living anything without raising it into an aesthetic experience."

References:

Juan Bruce-Novoa, "Ricardo Sánchez," in his *Chicano Authors: Inquiry by Interview* (Austin: University of Texas Press, 1980), pp. 219-234;

Bruce-Novoa, "A Voice Against Silence: Ricardo Sánchez," in his *Chicano Poetry: A Response to Chaos* (Austin: University of Texas Press, 1982), pp. 151-159;

Cordelia Candelaria, "Abelardo Delgado and Ricardo Sánchez," in her *Chicano Poetry: A Critical Introduction* (Westport, Conn.: Greenwood Press, 1984), pp. 50-58;

Francisco A. Lomelí and Donaldo W. Urioste, "El concepto del barrio en tres poetas chicanos: Alurista, Abelardo Delgado y Ricardo Sánchez," *De Colores*, 3, no. 4 (1977): 22-29;

Charles M. Tatum, *Chicano Literature* (Boston: Twayne, 1982), pp. 145-147.

Papers:

Ricardo Sánchez's papers are held in the Nettie Lee Benson Latin American Collection at the University of Texas at Austin.

Gary Soto
(12 April 1952-)

Héctor Avalos Torres
University of New Mexico

BOOKS: *The Elements of San Joaquin* (Pittsburgh: University of Pittsburgh Press, 1977);

The Tale of Sunlight (Pittsburgh: University of Pittsburgh Press, 1978);

Father Is a Pillow Tied to a Broom (Pittsburgh: Slow Loris, 1980);

Where Sparrows Work Hard (Pittsburgh: University of Pittsburgh Press, 1981);

Black Hair (Pittsburgh: University of Pittsburgh Press, 1985);

Living Up the Street: Narrative Recollections (San Francisco: Strawberry Hill, 1985);

Small Faces (Houston: Arte Publico, University of Houston, 1986);

Lesser Evils: Ten Quartets (Houston: Arte Publico, 1988);

Baseball in April (San Diego: Harcourt Brace Jovanovich, forthcoming 1990);

Who Will Know Us? (San Francisco: Chronicle Books, forthcoming 1990).

OTHER: *Entrance: 4 Chicano Poets; Leonard Adame, Luis Omar Salinas, Gary Soto, Ernesto Trejo* (Greenfield Center, N.Y.: Greenfield Review, 1975);

California Childhood: Recollections and Stories of the Golden State, edited by Soto (Berkeley: Creative Arts, 1988).

Gary Soto

The son of American-born parents of Mexican background, Gary Soto was born on 12 April 1952 in Fresno, California. His father, also born in Fresno, was killed in an accident at work at the age of twenty-seven, when Soto was only five years old. Soto's grandparents, both born in Mexico, made their living in the United States from field and factory work. Soto grew up in the environs of the San Joaquin Valley, a social experience he described in an unpublished 27 May 1988 interview: "We grew up very Californians, like *pochos.* . . . Assimilation was looked upon as something for kids to go through." Upon graduation from high school in 1970 Soto decided to attend Fresno City College because he thought he would not be able to get into California State University, Fresno. At Fresno City College he chose geography as a major, as he put it, "for no articulate reason except that I liked maps. I like seeing the world in print." Although Soto grew up with Spanish being spoken all around him by the family and other older adults, he was never formally taught Spanish. He does not think he came "from a culturally rich family in the academic or educational sense of the word. We had our own culture which was more like the culture of poverty, as I like to describe it."

Soto's decision to give up geography and take up poetry was prompted by the poem "Unwanted" by Edward Field. In Field's poem Soto saw his own alienation from society described and saw that a sense of alienation was not unique to him but rather that "it was . . . a *human* pain," he said in 1988. With the reading of "Unwanted" Soto began to recognize the power of written language to capture experience that is not simply subjective and personal, or indeed, general and social, but existentially universal. Thereafter, Soto's talent and intelligence began to come under strict discipline, with rapid and fruitful effect. In 1972 and 1973 at California State University, Fresno, Soto studied with poet Philip Levine, whom he called "a constant master of the nuts and bolts of how to read a poem–how to analyze and how to critique a poem" (1988 interview). Under his tutelage Soto learned not only the concrete linguistic tools for shaping language into poetry but also that "subject and craft have to go hand in hand. . . . They have to mingle together nicely." In 1974 Soto was graduated magna cum laude from California State University. He married Carolyn Oda 24 May 1975. In 1976 he earned an M.F.A. in creative writing from the University of California, Irvine, spending that year as a visiting writer at San Diego State University. In 1977 he began teaching at the University of California, Berkeley, where he is currently an associate professor in both the English and Chicano studies departments.

In 1975 Soto won the Academy of American Poets Prize and the *Discovery*-Nation Award. The United States Award of the International Poetry Forum and the University of California at Irvine's Chicano Contest Literary Prize were given to him in 1976. In 1977 *Poetry* magazine awarded him the Bess Hokin Prize. *The Tale of Sunlight* (1978) was a finalist for the Lenore Marshall Poetry Award. The recipient of a Guggenheim Fellowship in 1979 to 1980, Soto spent a year in Mexico City writing. He received a National Education Association Fellowship in 1981, and in 1984 *Poetry* awarded him the highly regarded Levinson Award. *Living Up the Street: Narrative Recollections* (1985) won the American Book Award in 1985. In the spring of 1988 Soto was Elliston Poet at the University of Cincinnati.

Clearly, discovering the power of the written word and disciplining his talents and energy have allowed Soto to accomplish much in a short span of time. Since his first poetry publication in 1977, *The Elements of San Joaquin*, Soto has kept up a steady stream of publications. Reviewer Arthur Ramírez (*Revista Chicano-Riqueña*, Summer 1981) points out that Soto's attention to craft and subject matter has taken his poetry into the pages of such well-known periodicals and journals as *Antaeus, Partisan Review, Paris Review, Poetry, Nation, American Poetry Review, North American Review*, and the *New Yorker*. He concludes: "Gary Soto learned by trial and error that the creation of literary works requires craft and work, learning and progress. . . . Life, like literature, requires a great deal of work–this seems to be clear in the life and work of a leading Chicano writer."

Soto's first book, *The Elements of San Joaquin*, proved that he learned the craft of writing poetry quite well. The book, divided into three sections, provides a multifaceted perspective on the currents of life that characterized the Fresno of his childhood. The first section presents a collage of sharply and vividly drawn characters who act out their lives in a Fresno that is hostile and unkind to human life. For instance, the opening poem, "San Fernando Road," paints a bleak and penetrating image of the social reality in which the main character Leonard Cruz moves about:

> On this road of factories
> Gray as the clouds
> that drifted
> Above them,
> Leonard was among men
> Whose arms
> Were bracelets
> Of burns
> And whose families
> Were a pain
> They could not shrug off[.]

Cruz knows the way factory work taxes the humanity of the workers that daily walk into its "ovens." Cruz is homeless and must sleep in cargo. His own pain is so great that it acts as a barrier to the pain of others who are worse off than he: "He did not think/Of the cousin/Spooning coke/Nor the woman/Opening/In her first rape." In the poems that follow, a thief waits for his unsuspecting victim, an elderly man wanders alone through the corridors of a county ward, and a complacent housewife shields herself from the grim social reality that surrounds her. The final poem of the first section bears the title, "The Morning They Shot Tony López, Barber and Pusher Who Went Too Far, 1958." It exemplifies the kind of poetic power Soto's verse is capable of, moving with philosophical eloquence through the universal themes of birth and death. López, a drug dealer, is shot when police enter through the back door of his house and catch him by surprise. Soto takes the reader to the moment López dies, and there, with piercing imagery, he reminds him of the arbitrariness of birth and death:

> When they entered, and shot once,
> You twisted the face your mother gave
> With the three, short grunts that let you slide
> In the same blood you closed your eyes to.

The poetry paints the scene of López's death, and the image of his twisted face tells the story of someone who was born in blood and died in blood; just as his mother's blood let him slide out of the womb to see life, so López closes his eyes in a pool of his own blood to meet death.

Section 2 of *The Elements of San Joaquin* focuses on the San Joaquin Valley. In Soto's poetic terms, the valley is composed of the four universal elements of the Greek philosophers: earth, air, water, and fire. He takes these elements and translates them into the particular sights, smells, and labors of the San Joaquin Valley. Thus, in "The Elements of San Joaquin" the element earth becomes a field and the field the ground of the poet himself: "Already I am becoming the valley,/A soil that sprouts nothing/For any of us." Soto identifies with the valley not to turn it into an idyllic setting but to show how its earth never yields a harvest for the ones who have worked the fields. Air carries the smells of the people who have hoed up and down the rows of cotton. Fire appears as the sun and stars in the same poem: "In June the sun is a bonnet of light/Coming up,/Little by little,/From behind a skyline of pine." In "Hoeing" the four elements of earth, wind, fire (the sun), and water are mixed into a combination of poetic syntax and imagery:

Hoeing

> During March while hoeing long rows
> Of cotton
> Dirt lifted in the air
> Entering my nostrils
> And eyes
> The yellow under my fingernails
>
> The hoe swung
> Across my shadow chopping weeds
> And thick caterpillars
> That shriveled
> Into rings
> And went where the wind went

> When the sun was on the left
> And against my face
> Sweat the sea
> That is still within me
> Rose and fell from my chin
> Touching land
> For the first time[.]

In a striking picture the air stirs up the dust while the sun makes the hoer sweat even before it is mid morning. Earth and air sting the narrator's senses. The shadow cut by the arc path of the swung hoe and the sun hitting the left side of his face show that, while his shadow is still long, the sun has already begun to beat hard.

Critics have tended to focus on the final section of *The Elements of San Joaquin* because of its personal tone. Raymund Paredes (*Minority Voices*, Fall 1977) called the poems in this section "the most poignant and engaging in the collection." Here Soto shows he is capable not only of dispassionate observation but also of intimate disclosure. "Photo, 1957" is about the impending death of Soto's father and the loneliness that will surround his mother, to whom he says, "You do not know/In few months/You will waken alone/And where the rooms go unlighted,/It will be cold." In the poem "Spirit" readers see the emotional depth with which Soto portrays himself, a grieving five-year-old, hearkening to the silent commission of his dead father: "But it was you father/Who sent me across/A dry orchard/Where I pointed/To a thin cloud/And thought/Beyond/That cloud/You lived in Limbo/God's Limbo/And were watching/And soon for/The first time/You would come to me/Calling *son son*." In the closing poem of the book the narrator says, "It's 16 years/Since our house/was bulldozed and my father/Stunned into a coma. . . ."

There is no question that Soto's remarkable ability to write poetry that captures some existential common denominator impressed the critics of *The Elements of San Joaquin*. In closing his examination of the book in *Abraxas* (1978), Christopher Buckley focuses on Soto's blending of literary and social-existential dimensions, saying that what distinguishes it from other first books is "that Soto has something *human* and important to say, and this makes the craft worthwhile, and sets these poems above many." Paredes (*Minority Voices*, Fall 1977) said it was a "work that illuminates, in hard economical language, various aspects of the Chicano experience. . . . Soto works successfully within the boundaries of Anglo-American literary conventions."

The Tale of Sunlight, Soto's second book, is also divided into three sections, each section being thematically unified while at the same time contributing to the whole. In the opening section Soto introduces the reader to Molina, a companion on a journey through a landscape of poverty and hunger. In many ways Molina is an Everyman character. In "The Map" Soto traces his birth to all of Latin America, and in "The Cellar," the closing poem, he identifies himself with this lineage, expressing solidarity with Molina: "I imagined I could climb/From this promise of old air/And enter a street/Stunned gray with evening/Where, if someone/Moved, I could turn,/And seeing through the years,/Call him brother, call him Molina." Emphasis on Latin America gives *The Tale of Sunlight* political overtones. Soto makes consistent use of imagery related to Latin America to create a work that is allegorical in scope.

The final poem of section 2 of *The Tale of Sunlight*, "How An Uncle Became Gray," is dedicated to Colombian writer Gabriel García Márquez, a great influence on Soto. In the unpublished 1977 interview Soto said of García Márquez that he regards *The Tale of Sunlight* as "a poem of praise to him," and considers his *Cien años de soledad* (1967; translated as *A Hundred Years of Solitude*, 1970) "one of the greatest books of our time." García Márquez is perhaps the best-known practitioner of the influential aesthetic and philosophical literary movement termed "magical realism," in which some ordinary image of everyday life is used to portray human existence in magical and extraordinary terms, in effect defamiliarizing a reader with everyday surroundings. "The Manuel Zaragosa Poems," which make up the third section of *The Tale of Sunlight*, have a strong flavor of "magical realism." Soto experiments with imagery that comes from the ordinary aspects of the everyday life of Manuel Zaragosa, Latin American tavern keeper and poetic Everyman, by giving imagery a life of its own. In the opening poem, "The Creature," Soto has Zaragosa speak and describe his existential suffering using the image of a bird and having it refer to the common human experience of a premonition: "This morning something/Perched like a bird/On my shoulder,/And was silent./If I brushed it away,/It reappeared/Like a premonition./If I ran,/It clawed deep/Into my coat/My wool coat,/And closed its eyes–/Or what I thought/Were its eyes." With the poems that follow "The Creature" in sec-

tion 3, Soto shows his reader that humanity, in the shape of Manuel Zaragosa, must wend its way through such existential mysteries and realities as work, sex, birth, love, suffering, and even transcendence. Thus, the final poem in the volume, "The Space," ends in a note of human triumph: "It is enough, brother,/Listening to a bird coo/A leash of parables,/Keeping an eye/On the moon,/The space between cork trees/Where the sun first appears." The bird that once acted like a warning points to parables in "The Space," to new narratives–indeed to Soto's own comprehension of and commitment to the power of language in poetic shape.

The Tale of Sunlight received an enthusiastic critical welcome. Paredes (*Minority Voices*, Fall 1978) compared Soto to T. S. Eliot and of one poem in particular said: "[it] presents an image of the American landscape as desolate as any T. S. Eliot ever imagined." Writing in *New Letters* (September 1979), reviewer Maryfrances Wagner said Soto "offers his reader a well-crafted collection of solid poetry–poems of poverty and courage revealed through the simple lives of strong characters." *Poetry* critic Alan Williamson (March 1980) placed Soto with his former teacher Levine: "Soto still has room to grow as a poet . . . but at his frequent best, Soto may be the most exciting poet of poverty in America to emerge since James Wright and Philip Levine."

In 1980 a collection of Soto's poems that had appeared previously in a variety of poetry journals was published in a chapbook entitled *Father Is a Pillow Tied to a Broom*. *Where Sparrows Work Hard*, published in 1981, contains the images, sounds, people, and urban settings of California and tells the many stories of particular people who live out their hard lives in those settings. Soto's poetic voice is always part of the Chicano community; those with whom he has worked are often the focus of the poems. There are three sections in the work. In "Mission Tire Factory, 1969," a poem from section 1, Soto tells the story of a Chicano coworker injured on the job, poignantly capturing the emotional tenor of the incident:

> All through lunch Peter pinched at his crotch,
> And Jesús talked about his tattoos,
> And I let the flies crawl my arm, undisturbed,
> Thinking it was wrong, a buck sixty-five,
> The wash of rubber in our lungs,
> The oven we would enter, squinting
> –because earlier in the day Manny fell
> From his machine, and when we carried him

Cover for a later printing of the 1985 book that Soto described as "a set of recollections" of his childhood

To the workshed (blood from
Under his shirt, in his pants)
All he could manage, in an ignorance
Outdone only by pain, was to take these dollars
From his wallet, and say:
"Buy some sandwiches. You guys saved my life."

A poem titled "Frankie," dedicated to Frank Torres, speaks of the culture of poverty. Frankie, a young tough, bullies the young protagonist of the poem and inflicts upon others a violence that, from every indication, he learned at home: "He tells me of/About a sister howling/In a locked closet,/About his dog/Slammed against a tree/By a laughing father."

As critic Bruce Weigl (*Poet Lore*, Spring 1982) pointed out in his critical review of *Where Sparrows Work Hard*, this work "represents a crystalization of the stripped down, clear observations which run throughout Soto's canon. Most of his lines are short, seldom more than three beats, and most are enjambed so that there is a

shunting effect as we are forced to pound down through the poems which seem to accumulate power as they move to some chilling inevitability." John Addiego, writing in the *Northwest Review* (1983), compares Soto with Dylan Thomas, stating that the protagonist of "Joey the Midget" "cleaves closer to the bone of poverty."

Soto's poetic diction, mature and confident, displays an unmistakable philosophical resonance in *Black Hair* (1985), which is thematically focused on death and childhood. One of the better poems about childhood is "Oranges," which is about a date the narrator had at the age of twelve. It begins, "The first time I walked/With a girl, I was twelve,/Cold, and weighted down/With two oranges in my jacket." The two walk down to a drugstore, and there the narrator asks the girl if she wants a candy bar. While she picks out a chocolate that costs a dime, he fingers a lone nickel in his pocket:

I took the nickel from
My pocket, then an orange,
And set them quietly on
The counter. When I looked up
The lady's eyes met mine,
And held them, knowing
Very well what it was all
About.

The closing poem of the collection, "Between Words," deals with death in a variation on the carpe diem theme:

Remember the blossoms
In rain, because in the end
Not even the ants
Will care who we were
When they climb our faces
To undo the smiles.

Living Up the Street: Narrative Recollections (1985), *Small Faces* (1986), and *Lesser Evils: Ten Quartets* (1988) are autobiographical prose works which form a thematic continuity. When asked to speak about what prompted the move from poetry to prose, Soto replied in the unpublished 1988 interview that his motivation was curiosity: "I was testing myself and I also like the openness of prose." In a lecture at a University of New Mexico symposium, "Reconstructing The Canon: Chicano Writers and Critics" (6 March 1987), Soto credited prose with two major graces. Compared to poetry, there is "a greater expanse, more territory, more frontier" in prose. He argued that essayists must remain closer to the facts of social reality–they cannot invoke poetic license in writing about social problems. He summed up these two graces under his notion of "cool-headedness," a notion which prescribes that essayists leave behind "a certain poetic verbiage" and in "plain, direct, unadorned" style construct prosaic scenes that are exciting to read. Soto's three prose works are examples of the fact that he practices his own tenets.

Living Up the Street, said Soto in the unpublished 1988 interview, was intended to be "a set of narrative recollections with very little commentary. I would rather show and not tell about certain levels of poverty, of childhood; I made a conscious effort not to tell anything but just present the stories and let the reader come up with assumptions about the book–just show not tell, which is what my poetry has been doing for years and years." Soto fills the recollections with stories of mischief from his childhood, adventures of his adolescence, and the trials of adulthood. Two fragments from the opening recollection, "Being Mean," demonstrate Soto's scheme of showing not telling. The tone of the prose is casual, the structure simple, as he talks about his life as a five-year-old in the summer of 1957: "While we play in the house, Mother Molina just watched us run around, a baby in her arms crying like a small piece of machinery turning at great speed. Now and then she would warn us with a smile, 'Now you kids, you're going to hurt yourselves.' We ignored her and went on pushing one another from an opened window, yelling wildly when we hit the ground because we imagined that there was a school of sharks ready to snack on our skinny legs." The meanness that was part of Soto's childhood is seen in his confrontation with another child: "In turn, I was edged with meanness. . . . I was also hurt by others who were equally as mean, and I am thinking particularly of an Okie kid who yelled that we were dirty Mexicans. Perhaps so, but why bring it up? I looked at my feet and was embarrassed, then mad. With a bottle I approached him slowly in spite of my brother's warnings that the kid was bigger and older. When I threw the bottle and missed, he swung his stick and my nose exploded blood for several feet."

Critics were taken by Soto's first prose work. Geoffrey Dunn, writing in the *San Francisco Review of Books* (Summer 1986), stated: "The twenty-one autobiographical short stories (or, more accurately, vignettes) assembled here recall with amazing detail the day-to-day traumas, tragedies and occasional triumphs of growing up brown in the American Southwest." A reviewer for *Booklist* (August 1985) said, "Poet Gary Soto's first prose work is a pleasure to read," while a reviewer of *Small Faces (Choice,* October 1986) described his prose as a stylistic "blend of naturalism, impressionism, and symbolism." Critic Alicia Fields, writing in the *Bloomsbury Review* (January/February 1987), observed that "Although *Small Faces* contains stories about major events in the author's life . . . , this is primarily a book about small but telling moments." More than one critic expressed concern that Soto's wife, Carolyn, did not appear any more than as a conventional figure; typical was Paredes (*Rocky Mountain Review of Language and Literature*, 1987), who stated: "As he depicts them, the roles are wholly conventional. . . . It is perhaps too much to say that Soto's portrayals of his wife and daughter are offensive but it is significant that his imagination, so finely tuned in other circumstances to the diversity and nuance of behavior, should perform unremarkably here."

Of *Lesser Evils: Ten Quartets* Soto has said in the unpublished 1988 interview that it is about his own Catholicism and that with it he intended to make large statements about life, himself, and the people around him. In the interview Soto acknowledged a deep thematic interest in the Catholic church and called himself a reconciled Catholic. A reviewer for *Booklist* (1 March 1988) noted that the "collection shows a writer who is becoming more reflective as he matures, making sober observations about women, marriage, pets, parenthood, teaching, writing, responsibility." Evidence of his new reflectivity is seen in quartet number 8, which contains the humorous essay "Agreeable." There he writes: "I'm in my 30s. I'm arguing less and less. Let people be right, even if they're dead wrong." In other words, if Soto has always been a keen observer of human nature, now he is also more ironic, more humorous, more subtle. A reviewer for *Publishers Weekly* (4 March 1988) found the strength of *Lesser Evils* in its quartet structure: "While much pleasure arises from Soto's poetic talent for capturing small, telling details of his life, the book's depth lies in its quartet structure. Each of four independent parts engages an essay's theme from a different angle, and together they synthesize new meaning." Writing in the *San Francisco Chronicle* (28 February 1988), literary critic Jonah Raskin summarizes the progression in Soto's three prose books, saying: "The painful, often angry journey that began in *Living Up the Street,* that was continued in *Small Faces,* concludes in *Lesser Evils* on notes of acceptance, domestic tranquility and the felicities of marriage."

Soto's consistent attention to the craft of writing and his sensitivity to his subject matter have earned him an undisputable place in American and Chicano literature. The general critical reception of his work has been overwhelmingly positive. He has earned the respect of critics and reviewers of his work because he represents his experience in a manner that shows his talent at creating poetry and prose that, through simple and direct diction, expresses the particulars of everyday life and simultaneously contains glimpses of the universal. Of the universal aspect of Soto's work Paredes (*Rocky Mountain Review of Language and Literature,* 1987) has written: "In all his work, Soto establishes his acute sense of ethnicity and, simultaneously, his belief that certain emotions, values, and experiences transcend ethnic boundaries and allegiances." Time and again, critics point out that from the well-crafted and gritty lines of *The Elements of San Joaquin* to the direct prose style and ironic humor of *Lesser Evils,* Soto, in the words of Ramírez, "portrays his characters and their patterns of behavior in such a vivid, concrete, sensorial, convincing manner that the Chicano condition becomes one of the forms of the human condition."

Readers can expect a further commitment to poetry by Soto. In the unpublished 1988 interview he said, "I think my gift is really in poetry." It is with a profound and even meditative conviction that Soto stated in the same interview, "This [writing] is my one talent. There are a lot of people who never discover what their talent is . . . I am very lucky to have found mine." Throughout his career Soto has shown himself to be tenacious and unafraid to explore his talent. Whichever genre Soto chooses in the future, there can be no doubt that his gift for story telling will find expression according the most exacting standards of style and subject matter.

References:

John Addiego, "Chicano Poetry: Five New Books," *Northwest Review,* 21, no. 1 (1983): 147-158;

Jerry Bradley, *Western American Literature,* 14 (Spring 1979): 73-74;

Christopher Buckley, "Keeping In Touch," *Abraxas,* nos. 16-17 (1978);

Buckley, "Resonance and Magic," *Slow Loris Reader Three,* 2 (January 1980): 36-43;

Alan Cheuse, "The Voice of the Chicano," *New York Times Book Review,* 11 October 1981, pp. 15, 36-37;

Tom D'Evelyn, "Soto's Poetry: Unpretentious Language of the Heart," *Christian Science Monitor,* 77 (6 March 1985): 19-20;

Alicia Fields, "Small But Telling Moments," *Bloomsbury Review,* 7 (January/February 1987): 10;

Raymund Paredes, "Recent Chicano Writing," *Rocky Mountain Review of Language and Literature,* 41, nos. 1-2 (1987): 126-128;

Jonah Raskin, "Childhood Gone; Mad-Gray Years Ahead," *San Francisco Chronicle,* 28 February 1988;

Alastair Reid, "The Lenore Marshall Poetry Prize," *Saturday Review,* 6 (27 October 1979): 38;

Hector A. Torres, "Genre-Shifting, Political Discourse and the Dialectics of Narrative Syntax in Gary Soto's *Living Up the Street,*" *Crítica: A Journal of Critical Essays,* 2 (Spring 1988): 39-59;

Bruce Weigl, "Towards a Fine Scrutiny of Experience: Contemporary Poetry in Review," *Poet Lore,* 77 (Spring 1982): 44-47;

Alan Williamson, "In A Middle Style," *Poetry,* 135 (March 1980): 348-354.

Papers:

Soto's papers are held in the library and the Chicano Studies Department of the University of California, Berkeley.

Mario Suárez
(12 January 1925-   )

J. Allan Englekirk
University of South Carolina

SHORT STORIES: "El Hoyo," *Arizona Quarterly*, 3 (Summer 1947): 112-115;

"Señor Garza," *Arizona Quarterly*, 3 (Summer 1947): 115-121;

"Cuco Goes to a Party," *Arizona Quarterly*, 3 (Summer 1947): 121-127;

"Loco-Chu," *Arizona Quarterly*, 3 (Summer 1947): 128-130;

"Kid Zopilote," *Arizona Quarterly*, 3 (Summer 1947): 130-137;

"Southside Run," *Arizona Quarterly*, 4 (Winter 1948): 362-368;

"Maestría," *Arizona Quarterly*, 4 (Winter 1948): 368-373;

"Mexican Heaven," *Arizona Quarterly*, 6 (Winter 1950): 310-315;

"Los coyotes," in *Festival de Flor y Canto*, edited by Alurista, F. A. Cervantes, Juan Gómez-Quinones, Mary Ann Pacheco, and Gustavo Segade (Los Angeles: University of Southern California Press, El Centro Chicano, 1976), pp. 26-29.

Though the published works of Mario Suárez are few, his place in the evolution of Chicano literature is important. He was by no means the first Mexican-American to compose fiction depicting the people and customs of a community of Hispanic ancestry in the United States. However, the focus he has employed in his published prose distinguishes his creative efforts from those of most Chicano writers who preceded him. He envisioned in his early short stories a Hispanic-American barrio (neighborhood) typical of the late 1940s. Idealized local color was not his goal. He examined reality with the intent of reproducing it accurately in minute detail, and also of making it comprehensible on more than a superficial level.

Suárez was born in Tucson, Arizona, and spent his early and adolescent years there. His father, Francisco Suárez, originally from Santa Rosalía, in the Mexican state of Chihuahua, had visited the United States on several occasions be-

fore moving to Tucson permanently in the 1920s to continue his occupation as a tailor. Soon after his arrival he married Carmen Minjárez, a young woman from Hermosillo, Mexico. The couple had five children; Mario was the first.

Francisco Suárez encouraged his offspring to develop an interest in literature and music. Suárez acquired a penchant for reading early in his schooling. He attended Safford Junior High and Tucson High School, graduating in 1942. Although he was dedicated to his classwork, Suárez, as he described himself in an unpublished interview, was "no more than an average student."

Upon receiving his diploma, Suárez enlisted in the U.S. Navy and served with a coast patrol stationed in Lakehurst, New Jersey. Near the end of 1943 he was sent to Brazil, where he spent the remainder of his military assignment in various cities. He returned to the United States in 1945, after the end of World War II.

In 1946 Suárez enrolled at the University of Arizona. His studies centered on the humanities, and his appetite for literature grew. Besides works by Mexican and Spanish authors, Suárez expanded his focus to include the writings of several North American novelists, with Ernest Hemingway and John Steinbeck his favorites. The realization that one day he might become a creative writer occurred after his reading of Steinbeck's *Tortilla Flat* (1935). Appreciation for Steinbeck's fictional world and perspective motivated Suárez to try to write similar literature. As part of assignments in his freshman English class taught by Ruth Keenan, Suárez produced two sketches. One depicted El Hoyo (the Pit), the Mexican-American barrio of Tucson. In the other, a short narrative entitled "Señor Garza," Suárez detailed the set of events most likely to occur in Garza's Barber Shop—an establishment within El Hoyo.

Keenan's reaction to Suárez's sketches was positive. She recommended that he enroll in a class on literary techniques offered by an established writer, Richard Summers. Suárez's work for Summers prompted Keenan to suggest that he forward his works to the *Arizona Quarterly* for possible publication. After minimal revision Suárez submitted "El Hoyo," "Señor Garza," "Cuco Goes to a Party," "Loco-Chu," and "Kid Zopilote." *Arizona Quarterly* accepted the pieces, publishing them in their Summer 1947 issue.

The five narratives in *Arizona Quarterly* depict a world known well by Suárez. In "El Hoyo" he precisely describes the barrio, supplying information that enables the reader to formulate a realistic image of both setting and inhabitants: "Its houses are built of adobe, wood, license plates, and abandoned car parts. Its narrow streets are mostly clearings which have, in time, acquired names. Except for the tall trees which nobody has ever cared to identify, nurse, or destroy, the main things known to grow in the general area are weeds, garbage piles, dogs, and kids." He lists the occupations of people that populate the neighborhood—proprietors of small shops, clerks, cotton pickers, railroad workers, general laborers, and truck drivers—and classifies the barrio inhabitants—both employed and unemployed—into types such as "harlequins, bandits, oppressors, oppressed, gentlemen, and bums. . . ." El Hoyo is home to the best and worst elements of society. Suárez shows that even though conflict is frequent and violent, a sense of camaraderie prevails in times of individual crisis. People in trouble or in need receive assistance from other members of the community whether they actively solicit aid or not. At the close of the sketch, Suárez attempts to summarize the nature of El Hoyo and its inhabitants. He asserts that the Chicanos of the barrio possess few common traits other than that they are all people of Mexican heritage residing in the United States. With this in mind, he proposes an analogy between the people and one of their favorite meals, *capirotada*. Like the Chicanos of El Hoyo (or, by extension, any Chicano), the dish is never the same: "It is served hot, cold, or just 'on the weather,' as they say in El Hoyo. The Garcias like it one way, the Quevedos another, the Trilos another, and the Ortegas still another. While in general appearance it does not differ much from one home to another it tastes different everywhere. Nevertheless it is still capirotada. And so it is with El Hoyo's Chicanos. While many seem to the undiscerning eye to be alike it is only because collectively they are referred to as Chicanos. But like capirotada, fixed in a thousand ways and served on a thousand tables, which can only be evaluated by individual

taste, the Chicanos must be so distinguished." Although the fact that Chicanos are a heterogeneous group has often been pointed out by those who have endeavored to define *chicanidad* (Chicanicity), Suárez's "El Hoyo" represents one of the initial efforts made by a Chicano writer to question the validity of the use of a single term for people of varied cultural and socioeconomic origins.

"Señor Garza" focuses on a single person within the barrio setting. The daily routine of the proprietor of Garza's Barber Shop is reviewed, from the opening of the green blinds of the shop in the morning to the latching of the door at night. Garza's barbering is of incidental importance when compared to his other activities during and after business hours. The shop "is where men, disgruntled at the vice of the rest of the world, come to air their views. It is where they come to get things off their chests along with the hair off their heads and beard off their faces. Garza's Barber Shop is where everybody sooner or later goes or should." Garza is a confessor, an arbiter, and a consultant. He willingly shares his money—when feasible—with those suffering hard times. His identity is seldom the same for any two customers: "When necessity calls for a change in his character Garza can assume the proportions of a Greek, a Chinaman, a gypsy, a republican, a democrat, or if only his close friends are in the shop, plain Garza."

Within the barber's daily routine is a chronological sketch which traces Garza's life from birth to the point at which he assumes his present position. A succession of different jobs requiring different skills, his existence might be seen to exemplify the lives of many—but by no means all—in his community. After experiencing several "setbacks" and "conquests," Garza has attained a position of prominence within El Hoyo. Life has not been easy for him, but he has found the peace of mind and self-assuredness necessary to be able to counsel others. For the present, at least, Garza is as much in control of his destiny as anyone might hope to be: "Garza, a philosopher. Owner of Garza's Barber Shop. But the shop will never own Garza."

Not all the inhabitants of El Hoyo, as portrayed by Suárez in the Summer 1947 issue of *Arizona Quarterly*, are as successful as Garza; three stories are about characters who fail in their efforts to integrate themselves into society, and there is little implication that they are willing or able to improve their conditions. "Cuco Goes to a

Party" narrates the plight of a man who is never truly accepted by his in-laws. After the birth of his first child he resolves to leave his wife and return to Mexico. "Loco-Chu" depicts an eccentric panhandler whose day-to-day existence depends solely upon the generosity of other members of the barrio. "Kid Zopilote" is about a young Chicano who returns to El Hoyo as a *pachuco* (zoot suiter) after a trip to Los Angeles. He is rejected by most elements of the community but makes no effort to alter his image.

Excited by the local recognition he received when these works were published, Suárez set off for New York City in July of 1947 with the hope of finding a publisher and learning more about writing. He used "Cuco Goes to a Party" as the basis for a full-length novel–a work which he wrote in three weeks. Macmillan rejected the novel, but its editors encouraged Suárez to continue writing. This response induced him to remain in New York for several months, but financial considerations eventually made it necessary for him to leave.

By September of 1948 Suárez had returned to Tucson, where he re-enrolled at the University of Arizona. Though the trip to New York had not been productive, he remained optimistic regarding his future as a writer. In a course with Summers, Suárez produced a second novel, entitled "Trouble in Petate," which portrays the sad fate of a young Indian who returns to his native town and dies after an unsuccessful attempt to obtain meaningful employment in a large and distant city. Though he was satisfied with the novel, he chose not to seek a publisher because he believed that the work would not be accepted.

In the winters of 1948 and 1950 the *Arizona Quarterly* published three additional sketches, "Southside Run," "Maestría," and "Mexican Heaven." Of the three, "Southside Run" is more reminiscent of Suárez's previous narratives in that, by describing the buildings and people passed by a bus driver on his rounds of El Hoyo, the text records the physical appearance of the barrio and gives readers a general understanding of the socioeconomic forces responsible for determining conflict or accommodation. "Maestría" and "Mexican Heaven" differ in focus from Suárez's other work in that they examine Anglo-Hispanic intercultural contact–an element present but not emphasized in the writer's 1947 publications. "Mexican Heaven" is a positive statement on cross-cultural relations: Anglo Father Raymond, through his own initiative, assimilates so effec-

tively with the Hispanics of the parish that he comes to be known only by his Spanish name, Padre Ramón. "Maestría" laments the disappearance from the barrio of the "maestro" (a true master at a skill or trade) as well as the gradual disappearance of traditional Hispanic values and customs. Technological advances and moneyed interests have irreversibly altered aspects of the Chicano community, and the assimilation of Anglo-American ways has distorted or erased long-endorsed beliefs. The sketch, however, is not so much a condemnation of North American culture as it is a nostalgic comment about a world in the process of change.

Suárez received a degree in liberal arts at the University of Arizona in June 1952 and began to work for a finance company in Tucson. On 19 March 1954, following four years of courtship, he married Cecilia Cortarobles, whose parents, like his, were originally from northern Mexico. The couple's three children were born in Tucson.

Though his work and family life demanded much of his time, Suárez continued to write. Between 1952 and 1954 he composed his third novel, "A Guy's Worst Enemy," which is about a young man who attempts to become a mobster but is eventually killed in his efforts. Rather than seek a publisher immediately, Suárez set the manuscript aside in order to work on other stories that he had left in various stages of completion in the late 1940s. It was his intent to combine the works from the *Arizona Quarterly* with his other texts into a single volume to be entitled "Chicano Sketches." He received a John Hay Whitney Foundation fellowship in 1957 to assist him financially as he worked on the project.

While editing the unfinished El Hoyo texts, Suárez worked as a volunteer for *P-M*–a weekly newspaper first published on 6 December 1957 for the Mexican-American community of Tucson. He wrote articles on events of local importance. The paper suspended publication in 1958 because of lack of money, and shortly afterward Suárez and his family moved to the Los Angeles area.

A series of different jobs in various locations within the area prohibited Suárez from consistent efforts at creative writing. After working for a time with a finance company, he served as a recreation supervisor for the *Los Angeles Times* Boys' Club from 1962 to 1964. During this same period he attended California State University, Fullerton, in order to earn teaching credentials.

The additional schooling made it possible for him to obtain positions as an English instructor, first at a skills center in East Los Angeles and later–from 1968 to 1970–at Claremont College. He left the latter institution in September 1970 to accept an appointment on the faculty at California State Polytechnic University, Pomona. There Suárez has taught remedial English, Mexican and Southwest history, Southwest folklore, Chicano literature, and Spanish. His wife also teaches at the university, directing courses in education.

In 1975 Suárez completed a draft of a fourth novel, "The Kiosk." The novel depicts the experiences of some of the marginal people in the towns bordering Mexico and the United States. The tragic death of the principal female character at the end of the novel underscores the tenuous existence of these figures: survival depends on a favorable blending of wit and good luck. The sense of the text is that few of these individuals are blessed with good fortune for more than a short period of time in their lives. As with some of his previous novels, Suárez took no immediate steps to publish the manuscript. He believes that the draft still possesses several "under-developed paragraphs and rough spots" but is confident that the work will reach the public once he eliminates these weaknesses.

One of Suárez's short stories has been anthologized since his move to Los Angeles. "Los coyotes" (in *Festival de Flor y Canto*, 1976) presents people and events in El Hoyo. Two men amass substantial profits by deceiving inhabitants of El Hoyo while purportedly assisting them through difficult times. More than forty years after the appearance of the initial *Arizona Quarterly* sketches, Suárez continues to write. He readily admits that his more contemporary pieces, novels such as "The Kiosk" and "Mex Mecca" (a novel about Mexican-American life in Los Angeles, a work still in an early stage of development), are designed primarily to entertain readers. Though they portray Mexican-American existence, this factor is overshadowed by the stress on action over character development and description of setting. The fast-paced plot of "The Kiosk" provides easy reading; a sense of relentless movement propels events to a dramatic conclusion.

Anthologies of Chicano literature often include at least one entry by Suárez, and two comprehensive studies of Chicano letters make mention of his contribution to prose fiction of the southwestern United States. Raymund Paredes (*MELUS*, Summer 1978) classified him as "the first truly 'Chicano' writer" and praised him for his ability to capture in detail the complexities of the ambiguous stance of many Mexican-Americans of the post-World War II period with regard to the process of their acculturation into Anglo society. Along with other critics, Paredes made reference to the compassion and understanding with which Suárez portrays the protagonists of his works. Juan Rodríguez in 1979 perceived Suárez as a transitional figure in the development of Chicano literature, representing the first of a more aggressive group of authors whose objectives in writing were not to defend their culture, but rather to define it.

Beginning with Suárez, in the opinion of Rodríguez, Mexican-American authors more consciously and consistently endeavored to write for Chicanos about Chicanos. A need to justify specific and/or unique features of their culture to those of a different ancestry was replaced by the desire to discern this uniqueness more fully and share this comprehension with other individuals of like values and perspectives.

It might be assumed that Suárez's prominent position within Chicano literature would warrant an extensive bibliography of secondary materials discussing his literary efforts. Though several doctoral dissertations include extended segments on his prose fiction, there exists no full-length article dedicated specifically to his short stories. Most often, discussion of his work is limited to several paragraphs on two of the stories published by the *Arizona Quarterly*, "El Hoyo" and "Señor Garza." Because of his pivotal importance to Chicano literature in the post-World War II period, a more prolonged analysis of his fiction is needed. Since well before 1947 Mexican-American authors, essayists, and poets have described the Chicano experience from a multiplicity of vantage points, but few have been as effective as Mario Suárez.

References:

Raymund A. Paredes, "The Evolution of Chicano Literature," *MELUS*, 5 (Summer 1978): 71-110;

Juan Rodríguez, "El desarrollo del cuento chicano," in *The Identification and Analysis of Chicano Literature*, edited by Francisco Jiménez (New York: Bilingual/Editorial Bilingüe, 1979), pp. 58-68.

Carmen Tafolla

(29 July 1951-   )

Yolanda Broyles González
University of California, Santa Barbara

BOOKS: *Get Your Tortillas Together*, by Tafolla, Reyes Cárdenas, and Cecilio García-Camarillo (San Antonio: Caracol, 1976);
Curandera (San Antonio: M&A, 1983);
To Split a Human: Mitos, Machos y la Mujer Chicana (San Antonio: Mexican American Cultural Center, 1985).

OTHER: "La Isabela de Guadalupe y otras chucas," in *Five Poets of Aztlán*, edited by Santiago Daydí-Tolson (Binghamton: Bilingual/ Editorial Bilingüe, 1985).

Carmen Tafolla is among the foremost Texas poets to come out of the post-1960s Chicano experience. With most writers of the Chicano Movement, she shares a deep consciousness of social injustice, an identification with life in the barrio, and a thorough knowledge of her cultural heritage. Her poetry first came to public attention at a Floricanto festival (Austin, 1975) and in the magazine *Caracol*.

Mary Carmen Tafolla was born and raised in the west side barrio of San Antonio, Texas. In unpublished autobiographical notes she said that on her mother's side she comes from "a long line of metalworkers, maids, nursemaids . . . , [and] servantpeople"; on her father's side there were "preachers, teachers, vaqueros (ranch-hands), and storytellers." It is, in part, because of her awareness of her ancestors that Tafolla has developed her clear sense of Chicano identity and of history. Her poetry is rooted in a collective identity: "The people of my family's past, the myths and heroes and characters they painted with their words and with their eyes are alive in me today, as are the people of *my* past and present. . . . They are all still alive in my mind, as they are in the lives of those today who reflect them and their actions. It's not that my poetry is nostalgic—it's prophetic. History is not there for history's sake; it is there to help describe and decipher the present."

Tafolla spent the first eight years of her education in exclusively Chicano schools. She was

Carmen Tafolla (courtesy of the author)

awarded a scholarship to an academically oriented private high school. She has written poetry since she was a teenager. Tafolla earned a B.A. in Spanish and French (1972) and an M.A. in education (1973) from Austin College, Sherman, Texas. In 1981 she completed the Ph.D. program in bilingual education at the University of Texas, Austin. She has taught at both the high school and university levels. From 1973 to 1976 and in 1978 and 1979 she was director of the Mexican American Studies Center at Texas Lutheran College in Seguin, Texas. In 1984 she accepted an appointment as associate professor of women's studies at California State University, Fresno. Her husband, Ernest Bernal, is also an educator and the inspiration for several of her love poems. A woman of versatility and wide-ranging interests, Tafolla has worked as a folklorist, an educational researcher, and a writer for both television and the movies. Her poetry has been included in numerous anthologies.

Among Tafolla's most characteristic and powerful poems are those in which she brings barrio personalities to life using their own voices. She does not purport to speak for Chicanos in an obtrusive or omniscient tone of advocacy or political radicalism. Instead in her poetry the disenfranchised speak for themselves in their own language. Typical figures are a young school dropout, an old woman, a young pachuca (female hoodlum), a mother, and a little boy who has found a dime. Tafolla shows a rare sensitivity toward the registers of barrio speech of persons from various age groups and walks of life.

In addition to poems written entirely in the voices of barrio heroines and heroes Tafolla has written poems in which third-person comments are interwoven with the barrio voices. A unifying thematic feature of this group of poems is the spirit of self-determination in the face of adversity, whether that adversity be the result of racism in the schools, inferior educational programs, economic deprivation, or poor housing. The poems of commentary, among which are "Tía Sofia" (Aunt Sofia), "Esa casa ya no existe" (This House Does Not Exist), and "19 años" (19 Years), center on self-preservation, human dignity, and the maintenance of Chicano values and culture.

Tafolla's belief in the validity of the oral tradition of Chicano literature leads her to question the professed validity and authority of print. The prose poem "Historia Sin Título" (Untitled Story), from *Five Poets of Aztlán* (1985), illustrates the disparity: "Y ya entendí / Que ellos ni sabian lo que taba pasando porque they had learned it de los libros que had learned it de los otros libros y nadie sabia ni pensar" (Now I have understood that they did not even know what was happening because they had learned it from the books which had learned it from other books and nobody even knew how to think).

Many of the poems by Tafolla first published in *Get Your Tortillas Together* (1976), a volume which also includes verse by Reyes Cárdenas and Cecilio García-Camarillo, appear in

Curandera (Healer Woman, 1983) and in "La Isabela de Guadalupe y otras chucas," her contribution to *Five Poets of Aztlán*. For this reason it is difficult to speak of Tafolla's development, but her poetry falls into thematic and linguistic clusters. Closely related in sentiment to her commentary poems–but separated from them by linguistic and imagistic differences–are her many poems of remembrance and recollection which are generally restrained in tone. Human memory, the storehouse for oral culture which is the means of transmission of the collective Mexican, Chicano, and Indian traditions from generation to generation, figures prominently in Tafolla's work as it does among most writers of the Chicano Movement. Many of her poems center around remembrance of ancestors and family elders. Notable examples are "Como un Pajarito" (Like a Small Bird), "Curandera," "Memories," "Tía Sofia," and "Ancient House." In "Ancient House" the spirit of an old dying woman in a house "engraved with the secrets & scars of 5 generations" is absorbed into the young speaker:

In this tall-ceilinged ancient eight-walled house
    owned by cold drafts and volcanic spaces
I breathe in through her onionskin lungs
        and know,
with her eyes too old to need vision to see
        that she
            is
            me.

Similarly, in "Curandera" the speaker physically merges with the world of the wise healer:

Curandera
    te siento arrastrando tus chanclas por los arcos-
        portales
    de mis venas,
    bajando los botes de tu sabiduría del gabinete
    de mi cabeza.

(Healer woman
    I feel you dragging
your worn shoes through the arches-portals
    of my veins,
getting the containers of your wisdom from the
    cabinet
    of my mind.)

Other of Tafolla's poems of recollection define the Chicano cultural heritage through nature imagery. Terms such as *venado* (deer), *coyote*, *cactus*, *mesquite beans*, and *conejos* (rabbits) connote the Native American ancestry of the Chicanos, often present only at the subconscious level, as in the poem "Aquí" (Here):

> He shops the windows, happy,
> Where the stalking once was good
> and his kitchen floor is built on bones
> of venison once gently roasted.
> ....
> He feels the warmth
> and doesn't know his soul is filled
> with the spirit of coyotes past.

Her poem "Dead Lipán Apaches" suggests that the Apaches are merely presumed dead. The Indian heritage is in the Chicano present, even when, as in the poem "Warning," it is denied by "a brown ghost / who keeps starving white / and dying brown." In "Memories" the poem's persona speaks of "lavando la herencia" (washing the heritage) in the life-giving artery of the Medina River. Similarly, in "Caminitos" (Pathways) the "pathways of my thoughts" meander with the Medina River and end up:

> . . . . in the monte, chaparral
> ....
> remembering venado,
>   remembering conejos,
>   remembering
>   where
>   we came from.

Tafolla's intense sense of rootedness in her heritage, however, is in no way indicative of a static view of culture. In the poem "444 Years After" cultural practices are shown as dynamic, in constant transformation and adaptation. Our Lady of Guadalupe—the most revered Chicano spiritual symbol—is worshiped in modern fashion:

> If I gathered roses for you . . .
> ....
>   would my jeans jacket sprout
>   an embroidered vision
>   of the same old Lupe
>   with stars in her cloak
>   but standing on a pick-up
>   truck with melons?

Both historical and personal memory for Tafolla are strongly matrilineal, and a constant in her poetry is the poor woman who succeeds in spite of poverty. Her female figures are not described in intellectualized images; they speak in their own words or are described in a colloquial language that relies heavily on images from every-

day life and various rhythmic effects such as incantational repetition. Even in the most adverse situations–such as impoverishment or prostitution–Tafolla's women generate an indomitable will to endure and survive. Through her women figures Tafolla redefines the concept of strength. Strength is not power over others but is self-directed. It is self-empowerment even if only through spiritual rebellion. The nineteen-year-old prostitute in "19 años" illustrates this concept of power: "Por tanto que me chingan de afuera / no me pueden chingar el corazón" (As much as they may violate my body / they cannot violate my heart).

Another powerful person is La Malinche, the Indian woman Malintzin Tenepal (Hernán Cortés's interpreter, adviser, lover), who is traditionally regarded as a traitor. In "La Malinche" Tafolla has her tell her story in the first person, describing her historical role as that of a visionary of "Another world–a world yet to be born."

"La Malinche" and "La Isabela de Guadalupe y el Apache Mío Cid" are among the few Tafolla poems in which male figures appear as foils addressed by the female poetic persona. In "La Isabela" Tafolla explores the historical unity of opposites found in the sexual union of men and women whose backgrounds, over time, necessarily include mixtures of social classes and ethnicities. Most of the views on women that she expresses in her poetry are elaborated in her prose work, *To Split a Human: Mitos, Machos y la Mujer Chicana* (1985), which addresses problems such as stereotyping, institutional sexism, and racism as they affect Chicanos.

Tafolla's move from her native Texas to the state of California in 1983 has demanded considerable readjustments and has caused some changes in her writing. For the first time she is writing a novel. Its working title is "The Land of the Locos." Her recent unpublished poetry shows a heightened mastery of a colloquial poetics and a more contemplative style. In 1987 her most recent collection of poems, entitled "Sonnets to Human Beings," won the first prize in the poetry division of the annual Chicano literary contest at the University of California, Irvine.

References:
Reyes Cárdenas, "Las Carnalas Poetas," *Caracol* (September 1975): 17;
Cárdenas, "Crisis in Chicana Identity," *Caracol* (May 1977): 14-15;

Santiago Daydí-Tolson, Introduction to *Five Poets of Aztlán*, edited by Daydí-Tolson (Binghamton: Bilingual/Editorial Bilingüe, 1985).

Papers:

Tafolla's papers are held in the Nettie Lee Benson Collection, Latin American Collection, University of Texas at Austin.

Sabine R. Ulibarrí

(21 September 1919-   )

Reynaldo Ruiz
Eastern Michigan University

BOOKS: *Al cielo se sube a pie* (Mexico: Impresora Medina, 1961);

El mundo poético de Juan Ramón: estudio estilístico de la lengua poética y de los símbolos (Madrid: Edhigar, 1962);

Tierra Amarilla: cuentos de Nuevo México (Quito: Editorial Casa de la Cultura Ecuatoriana, 1964); republished as *Tierra Amarilla: Stories of New Mexico/Cuentos de Nuevo México*, bilingual edition, with translations by Thelma Campbell Nason (Albuquerque: University of New Mexico Press, 1971);

Amor y Ecuador (Madrid: Ediciones José Porrúa Turanzas, 1966);

Mi abuela fumaba puros = My Grandmother Smoked Cigars y otros cuentos de Tierra Amarilla (Berkeley: Quinto Sol, 1977);

El alma de la Raza (Albuquerque: UNM Cultural Awareness Center, 197?);

Primeros encuentros = First Encounters (Ypsilanti: Bilingual/Editorial Bilingüe, 1982);

El Cóndor and Other Stories, bilingual edition (Houston: Arte Publico, 1989).

OTHER: *La fragua sin fuego/No Fire for the Forge*, bilingual edition, edited, with foreword, by Ulibarrí (Cerrillos, N.M.: San Marcos, 1971).

Sabine R. Ulibarrí is a short-story writer, a poet, an essayist, a critic, and a university professor who ranks among the best known of today's Chicano writers. He has received both popular and critical recognition for his literary works and for his ability as an eloquent public speaker. Although some may consider him a regional writer,

Sabine R. Ulibarrí

his appeal transcends his native New Mexico. His works have been well received in the United States and also throughout the Hispanic world.

His poems and stories have been widely anthologized in elementary, high school, and college texts. Ulibarrí first achieved literary success in Mexico, Ecuador, and Spain before being recognized in his own country. In fact he is one of the few Chicano writers who writes entirely in Spanish and whose works are translated into English.

Ulibarrí was born 21 September 1919 in Tierra Amarilla, a small village in northern New Mexico at the base of the Sangre de Cristo mountains, the oldest child of Sabiniano and Simonita Ulibarrí. His father (a cattle rancher) and mother instilled in their children a strong sense of pride, honor, respect, and the work ethic. Both parents were college graduates who came from families long established in New Mexico. His was an extended family that included uncles, aunts, cousins, and grandparents. His grandmother was a great influence on him. As he says in *Mi abuela fumaba puros = My Grandmother Smoked Cigars y otros cuentos de Tierra Amarilla* (1977), "I have so many and such gratifying memories of her. But the first one of all is a portrait that hangs in a place of honor in the parlor of my memory."

Ulibarrí's family and the rugged terrain and rustic beauty of the area around Tierra Amarilla helped shape his sensitivity, attitudes, perceptions, and individuality. The environment–the land and the often inclement weather–contributed to his physical and psychological development. Ulibarrí stated in an unpublished interview in August 1985, "To earn a living in that land requires that one struggle with the natural elements. . . . So, in order to struggle with nature, one develops a special kind of character and at the same time one develops a certain love for that land, for that region." Since he was raised on a ranch he had to learn the tasks of a ranch hand. Some of his experiences on the ranch eventually manifest themselves in the stories found in *Tierra Amarilla: cuentos de Nuevo México* (1964; translated in a bilingual edition as *Tierra Amarilla: Stories of New Mexico/Cuentos de Nuevo México*, 1971) and *Mi abuela fumaba puros*.

His father recited beautiful poetry. Ulibarrí remembers many of the poems and stories of his childhood, including those about such stock figures of New Mexican folklore as Don Cacahuate (Mr. Peanut), Doña Cebolla (Mrs. Onion), and Pedro de Urdemalas. In his story "Sister Generose," from *Primeros encuentros = First Encounters* (1982), he says, "Through the long nights of winter my father read us a chapter from some long novel or other. He had a sonorous and mellif-luous voice with all the rhythms, tones, and tempo for bringing to life the text he read and making it vibrant. I was fascinated, captivated. So it was I got to know Don Quixote, Don Juan, the Count of Monte Cristo, the Twelve Peers of France, El Cid, [and] Martín Fierro. . . ." He was a voracious reader before reaching school age.

Ulibarrí was taught through high school by nuns from a midwestern order. He questioned his teachers' adherence to discipline and insistence on learning the basics but also their implacable desire to impose their midwestern values and views. *Mi abuela fumaba puros* contains a few episodes about pranks that he and some other youngsters played on the nuns. An episode that shows his independent thinking even as a youth occurred at a Catholic ceremony of Confirmation when he refused to get in line and kiss the archbishop's ring, though it was customary for the worshipers during Confirmation to do so. He talked about the incident during the interview: "I was sure that when we returned home I would get a whipping, but nothing happened. My parents were very liberal and intelligent."

Among the many books which he read was Charles Darwin's *On the Origin of Species by Means of Natural Selection* (1859), which had a profound impact on him. He claimed in the interview that "I believe that I read it before my time. I wasn't mature enough to assimilate that material that I was reading and I experienced a 'craziness' in me. I became a rebel which made me come in conflict not only with the nuns but also with the local priest." As an adolescent he formed a literary club among his peers in which he organized and led debates on various topics of the day. These debates were one of the highlights for the community. He arranged to have the discussions take place in the formal ambience of the courtroom in the county courthouse; here parents came to watch and hear the club members develop their ideas.

Upon finishing high school Ulibarrí had the opportunity to study at eastern colleges and at Notre Dame, but expenses for travel and room and board were prohibitive. He decided instead to attend the University of New Mexico, from which he had a personal invitation from the president, James Fulton Zimmerman. He was given a scholarship and a job at the university. From 1938 to 1940 he taught in the Río Arriba County schools. Later he obtained a teaching position at the Spanish-American Normal School in El Rito, New Mexico, and taught there until 1942. The

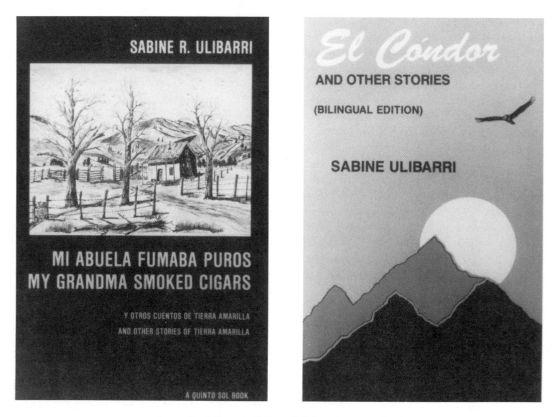

Covers for bilingual editions of Ulibarrí's story collections

summer of 1942 Ulibarrí studied at Georgetown University. As World War II intensified he returned to New Mexico where he joined the U.S. Army Air Corps and married María Concepción Limón from Las Cruces, New Mexico, whom he had met at the University of New Mexico several years before. From 1942 to 1945 Ulibarrí, a gunner, flew thirty-five combat missions over Europe, for which he received the Distinguished Flying Cross.

Immediately after returning from the war in 1945, Ulibarrí, with the help of the G.I. Bill, renewed his studies at the University of New Mexico and graduated in 1947 with majors in English and Spanish. He was granted a teaching assistantship in the Department of Romance Languages and a year later finished his M.A. in Spanish, writing his thesis on Spanish novelist Benito Pérez Galdós. In 1949 Ulibarrí started teaching full-time at the University of New Mexico but interrupted his teaching career for three years in order to pursue a doctorate. He finished his Ph.D. at the University of California, Los Angeles, in 1958, the year his son Carlos was born. For his doctoral dissertation he wrote on the Nobel laureate for 1956, Spanish poet Juan Ramón Jiménez (1881-1958). His dissertation was published in Madrid in 1962. Upon receiving his Ph.D. he returned to the University of New Mexico where he resumed his duties in the Department of Romance Languages.

Ulibarrí's first book, *Al cielo se sube a pie* (One Gets to Heaven on Foot, 1961), contains fifty short poems. It was first published in Mexico and subsequently in Spain. The foundation for the volume was laid years prior to its publication, for Ulibarrí began writing poetry in childhood. Although he was preparing his scholarly study on Jiménez for publication, Ulibarrí felt apprehension about his own poetry and feared that it would not be well received or accepted. In the 1985 interview he explained, "This business of publishing is frightening because publishing is like undressing in public, one is confessing whether one has talent or not. And the fear of publishing something that might make you the laughing stock of everyone . . . ; one just doesn't dare." The major themes in the collection are love, the narrator's awareness of his identity and standing in life, and his incessant drive to reach and merge with the essence of love, beauty, and life. At the heart of the poetry is an intense yearning for communion with the spiritual world; the narrator is always conscious of the duality of the mind and of feelings. While attempting to merge with the spiritual world the narrator creates tension by acknowledging that beauty and perfection are in the eyes of the beholder, who by giving essence and meaning to the outer world gives meaning and life to himself. As Ulibarrí says in his poem "Mujer Imagen" (Woman Image):

> En ti, por ti, no eres nada;
> ansia terrestre en suelo agreste.
> En mí, por mí, lo eres todo,
> en aire nuevo ansia celeste.
>
> (You, by yourself, are nothing
> mundane anxiety of this world.
> In me, by me, you're everything
> a new life, celestial anxiety.)

It is then necessary to live in harmony, to integrate oneself with a higher spirit and live symbiotically. The merging of mind, spirit, and emotions only is realized by facing reality, as it says in "Profesor de pie" (Professor on Foot):

> A los cielos se sube a pie;
> no hay alas ni escaleras,
> no hay ascensor, ni avión, ni tren,
> ni fondas en las fronteras.
>
> (One gets to heave on foot
> there are no wings, nor stairways
> there is no elevator, nor plane, nor train
> nor inns on the way.)

The bold imagery and the absence of detail of Ulibarrí's poetry suggest the influence of the Spanish poets Gustavo Adolfo Bécquer, Juan Ramón Jiménez, Miguel de Unamuno, Federico García Lorca, and Antonio Machado. The strength of the volume lies in its ability to combine the sensual—color, touch, sight, and smell—with symbols, rhythm, and structure.

Tierra Amarilla: cuentos de Nuevo México is the work that has given Ulibarrí the most recognition among Chicano writers and readers. Ironically, this work, which has a regional focus, was first published in Quito, Ecuador. It was well received by Ecuadorians as well as by others in South America. *Tierra Amarilla* provided the opportunity to look at a group of people—*nuevomexicanos*—that has for the past three centuries maintained the Spanish language and a culture distinct from Anglo society. Thelma Campbell Nason's 1971 English translation expanded the readership, and this bilingual edition has had six printings.

The *Tierra Amarilla* stories permit the reader to probe into the soul and spirit of Chicano communities in northern New Mexico. Three of the stories are particularly noteworthy, "Caballo mago," "Forge without Fire," and "Man without a Name." "Caballo mago" (My Wonder Horse) depicts a young boy's maturation as he catches a wild horse that has eluded adults in his community. The horse was a legend. He "always escaped, always mocked his pursuers, always rose above the control of man. Many a valiant cowboy swore to put his halter and his brand on the animal. But always he had to confess . . . that the mystic horse was more of a man than he."

After capturing the magic horse, the boy says, "I drove him toward the town. Triumphant. Exultant. Childish laughter gathered in my throat. With my newfound manliness, I controlled it. . . . It was the ultimate in happiness. It was the pride of the male adolescent. I felt myself a conqueror." "Forge without Fire" presents the meaner side of mankind. Edumenio, the protagonist, and his wife Henrietta (haunted by a bad reputation) are the subjects of ridicule and scorn. As a result, Henrietta leaves Edumenio and both flee the village. Showing sensitivity and compassion for the victims, the narrator underlines man's malevolent nature: "I remember and I weep. I am ashamed of human nature that denied to you Edumenio and to you Henrietta the gift of happiness that God had bestowed upon you. God proposes and man disposes." "Man without a Name" presents man's incessant need to search for his true being, identity, and reality. The plot is complex. It deals with a protagonist writing a book about his father. Ulibarrí contrives a schema that not only presents the multipersonalities but also underscores the notion that man is what he is because he gives meaning to himself and his creations.

Amor y Ecuador (Love and Ecuador) Ulibarrí's second book of poetry, was published in Spain in 1966. His first contact with Ecuador was in the summer of 1963 when he established and served as director of a language institute funded by the U.S. government under the National Defense Education Act. He has directed other language institutes and numerous university programs, living in Ecuador for extended periods of time. He has been influenced by the country's diverse terrain, by the Andes, and most of all by the indigenous people, their culture, and traditions. As the title hints, the book has two sections. The first section is a tribute to Ecuador and its people. In "Idiosincrasia" (Idiosyncrasy) the narrator describes the long and arduous history of the Indio (Indian):

> Tus indios vienen saliendo
> lentamente del pasado
> los ojos, las esperanzas
> en el suelo arrastrando.
>
> (Your Indians are slowly
> coming out from the past
> with their eyes and hopes
> dragging on the ground.)

The imagery is graphic and poignant in these elaborate sketches of the Indian's condition. In other poems the narrator elaborates on the attributes that have helped the Indio endure through the ages:

> Llenas la vena ajena
> y cada hueco humano
> de cariño y belleza
> de respeto y nobleza.
>
> (You fill every heart
> and every empty human space
> with affection and beauty
> with respect and nobility.)

The second section of *Amor y Ecuador* is the story of a search for perfection, the divine, harmony, and the essence of life in love. Tension occurs because of the narrator's hopelessness in not merging with a higher form of love and life:

> Tu imagen fugitiva se desliza
> por el laberinto de mi conciencia;
> huraña se desvanece y esquiva,
> habiendo sido siempre pura esencia.
>
> (Your fleeting image slides by
> through the labyrinth of my conscious;
> shyly and bashfully it dissipates
> having been always just essence.)

Poem forty-nine presents yet another variant of hopelessness:

> Sólo cargo mis pecados,
> sin campanas, por la noche
> por el suelo solitario
> de mi ansia fatal y doble.
>
> (I just carry my sins
> through the night, without fanfare,
> through the solitary path
> of my heavy and fatal anxiety.)

El Cóndor

Por Sabine R. Ulibarrí

Ernesto Garibay estaba solo en
su despacho. Era ya cerca de media
noche. La lámpara iluminaba la
superficie de su mesa, dejándolo
a él y al resto del aposento en
la sombra. El silencio denso e
intenso. Casi se podían oír sus
pensamientos.

Ernesto había tomado una
determinación que le estremecía todo
el ser y el estar. Había llegado
la hora de lanzar una terrible
y turbulenta actividad que había
venido elaborando por años. Su
plan era diabólico, y por eso,
perfecto.

Entre otras cosas, no habría nadie para
recibir el dinero. El dinero se quedaría allí
por ocho días. Entonces, cuando ya estuvieran
seguros, Ernesto y Sofía lo recogerían. No
cuento los detalles porque no quiero que a
algún loco se le ocurra utilizar el
mismo plan.

Antes de las diez empezaron a
llegar los pilares de la sociedad, cada
uno con un bulto bajo el brazo. Los
arreglos se concluyeron como anticipados.
Parecía mentira, de pronto Ernesto y
Sofía eran dueños de medio millón
de dólares. El plan había sido tan
sencillo, casi infantil, que resultó
infalible. Todos los contribuyentes
recibieron una tarjeta de agradecimiento.

El Dr. Ernesto Garibay y su
bella dama, la dueña de sus amores y
sabores, la de las nalgas de oro y de
los ojos espadas, han llegado a Quito.
Están en función de guerra. Escribió
Ernesto por entonces:

de mis antepasados que si usted no
cumple, usted me responderá directa-
y personalmente a mí.

El Cóndor

El Dr. Garibay estaba casi
convencido que el jefe de policía
no le iba a hacer caso. No quería
que le hiciera caso. Necesitaba un acto
violento y dramático, que sacudiera al país, para completar
la imagen legendaria de El Cóndor
como protector del indio y del pobre.
La carta se repartió por todas las
calles de Quito en hojas sueltas.
De inmediato explotó la discusión,
la especulación, el misterio: ¿quién
era? ¿qué quería? ¿a dónde iba todo
esto? Los periódicos, la radio, la
televisión no hablaban de otra cosa.
El nombre de El Cóndor estaba en
la boca y en los pensamientos de todos.
Empezó la larga espera.

Pages from the manuscript for the title story in Ulibarrí's 1989 collection (courtesy of the author)

As in his previous volume of poetry, *Al cielo se sube a pie*, Ulibarrí continues to unveil his soul before the reader, expressing a sense of anguish and torture while searching for spiritual life and divine love. The poetic individuality is that of an honest spirit who desires a communion with the essence of love, life, and meaning:

> Llena el vaso de mis ausencias
> de aromas vitales y tuyas,
> del matiz de tu beso oscuro,
> de luz y vino tibio.

> (Fill my empty life
> with your vital aromas,
> with a hue of your dark kiss
> with light and with tepid wine.)

The narrator pleads to the essence of love for peace and harmony. His pursuit of the ideal and of perfect love are one and the same.

The 1960s were years of remarkable professional accomplishment for Ulibarrí. He established and directed two summer language institutes in Ecuador in 1963 and 1964, and in 1969 was founder of the Andean Center in Quito under the auspices of the University of New Mexico. By 1966 four of his books had been published; he traveled extensively throughout South America and spent a year conducting research in Spain during 1965 to 1966. In 1969 he was elected president of the American Association of Teachers of Spanish and Portuguese. He served in this capacity for one year and for the next five years served as member of the executive committee of that organization. In 1973 Ulibarrí was appointed chairman of the modern and classical languages department at the University of New Mexico, a position he held until 1982.

Ulibarrí identified with and supported the Chicano Movement at its inception in the late 1960s and early 1970s. He knew of hunger, abuse, poor living conditions, exploitation, frustration, discrimination, and the high drop-out rates of Chicanos. In his foreword to the anthology *La fragua sin fuego/No Fire for the Forge* (1971) he states, "The 'We are all Americans' and 'This is America' crowd keeps fighting a pluralistic society and promoting a monolingual citizenry in the most narrow-minded and short-sighted way. Their belief appears to be that being different is unAmerican, that homogeneity (as in milk), that mass production (as in doughnuts), is the great American purpose. I submit that ignorance and stupidity are criminal and infinitely more unAmerican. Human beings are not refrigerators and cannot be forced into the same mold. Viva la diferencia!" He argues that the notion of "Americanization" is not viable for New Mexico's native Spanish speakers because "We never left our native land. New Mexico is our native land, our fatherland and motherland." He elaborates: "we have a language, a history, and a tradition that knit and hold us together in a manner that cannot be matched by any other minority group. . . . The Spanish speaking peoples are known for the tenacity with which they hold on to their traditions. Our roots run deep and sinuous in the land of our forefathers. Our culture is based on the soil. We have a running and ancient dialogue going with the mountains and the mesas, the sunsets and the deserts, the paisano [peasant] and the ponderosa, the wail of the coyote and the lament of la llorona [the wailing woman]. . . ." According to Ulibarrí, it is ironic that in spite of New Mexicans' rich traditions, they still remain outside the American mainstream: "We never set out in search of the American dream. The American dream came to us unannounced and uninvited. For most of my people the American dream remains just that, a dream, unfulfilled and unrealized. The mainstream has marginized us."

Mi abuela fumaba puros is a bilingual collection of ten short stories held together by a dominant theme–the life of the New Mexican in the village of Tierra Amarilla during the early part of the twentieth century. There are ten principal characters, some of whom still form an integral part of New Mexico's oral tradition, such as Don Cacachuate and Doña Cebolla. The point of view is that of a New Mexican child who provides an intimate, vivid, and authentic representation of the beliefs, traditions, culture, aspirations, and perceptions of his people. One of the principal characters in the collection is the child's grandmother. Ulibarrí remembers his grandmother, on whom the character is based, as an imposing lady. Of her he says, "I never saw her bend or fold. Fundamentally, she was serious and formal . . . ; a smile, a compliment or a caress from her were coins of gold that were appreciated and saved as souvenirs. . . ." Uncle Cirilo represents the multidimensional workings of the law. El Negro Aguilar is a free-spirited cowboy who depends on his abilities to make his livelihood, and on his charm and singing talent to coax his admirers and get his way. An Apache symbolizes the harmonious coexistence of and blending of three cultures–the Indian, mestizo, and Spanish. The Penitente Brotherhood underscores the deep religiosity of the people.

Ulibarrí's *Primeros encuentros = First Encounters* is a collection of nine very short stories in a bilingual edition. It deals with characters (locals and strangers) who have had a profound influence on the people of Tierra Amarilla, and, like *Mi abuela fumaba puros*, it explores the people of New Mexico–Indian, Hispanic New Mexican, and Anglo. The stories go beyond superficial notions of cultural pluralism to underscore the benefits of authentic relationships among people of different ethnic backgrounds. The background for the traditional cooperation is traced in the story "Mónico": "The first Spanish colonists who came to the Río Grande Valley established themselves where the Río Grande and the Río Chama meet. They found an Indian Pueblo there. . . . The Indians received the strangers with hospitality and courtesy. They offered them everything they had. . . ." Ulibarrí describes how the Spanish and the Indians helped one another, how they shared their food and shelter, and how both came together to "share the same loneliness in a hostile and violent land." Although there are many cases throughout time in which the Chicano has had negative experiences in dealing with the Anglo, Ulibarrí chooses to develop the positive experiences between Chicanos and Anglos. He presents several stories, most notably "They Got Married," in which Anglos marry successfully into the oldest and most influential New Mexican families. Ulibarrí's most recent story collection, *El Cóndor and Other Stories*, was published in a bilingual edition in 1989.

In 1978 Ulibarrí was appointed by the Real Academia de la Lengua Española (The Royal Academy of the Spanish Language) to serve as a correspondent of the Academia Norteamericana de la Lengua Española (North American Academy of the Spanish Language). In this capacity he judges the use and meaning of neologisms that come into use in Spanish and makes recommendations regarding their incorporation into the language.

Ulibarrí's poetry has not received the critical attention it deserves, and his contributions to the short story have yet to be evaluated fully. Yet he is a writer worthy of attention. In his short stories the narrative appears to be simple, narrowly focused on one area of rural New Mexico. But his characters help readers understand all the peoples of New Mexico through the microcosm of Tierra Amarilla, a place where people of differing languages and cultures can live in harmony and cooperation.

Jorge Ulica
(Julio G. Arce)
(9 January 1870-15 November 1926)

Clara Lomas
Colorado College

BOOK: *Crónicas diabólicas (1916-1926) de "Jorge Ulica,"* as Jorge Ulica, edited by Juan Rodríguez (San Diego: Maize, 1982).

Julio G. Arce, who wrote as Jorge Ulica, was born in Guadalajara, Jalisco. He was the son of a prominent surgeon, Fortunato G. Arce. Although he studied pharmacy he had a preference for journalism. He founded two student newspapers, *El hijo del progreso* (Child of Progress) at fourteen and *El amigo del pueblo* (Friend of the People) while in pharmacy school. After completing his studies he and a friend opened a drugstore in Mazatlán, Sinaloa. There he actively participated, as contributor and editor, in local newspapers and founded the literary review *Bohemia Sinaloense.* Eventually he moved to Culiacán, Sinaloa, where he married and found much support for his journalistic endeavors, principally with the local government's newspaper, *El Occidental.* His government affiliation helped him secure several public offices as well as a position as Spanish language instructor at the Instituto Rosales.

In 1901 Arce organized a small newspaper, *Mefistófeles,* and with it introduced journalism to Culiacán. By 1909 he was editor of the influential Culiacán paper *El diario del pacifico* (Pacific Diary), which he used as an organ of the counterrevolution. Political conflicts that evolved from his advocacy forced Arce to flee. He sought refuge in Guadalajara, where, along with other political refugees, he started *El diario de occidente* (Occidental Diary) as well as "La asociación de la prensa unida" (United Press Association), which provided protection for incarcerated journalists. Arce himself spent two-and-a-half months in jail and was released as a result of political pressure from his colleagues. However, fear for his life forced him to flee the country.

In October of 1915 Arce arrived in San Francisco, California, with his second wife and five children. He soon integrated himself into the Latino

Cover for Arce's posthumously published collection of narrative sketches, written under the pseudonym Jorge Ulica

community, where he found many other Mexican political exiles. Within a month he was working for the then one-year-old San Francisco newspaper *La crónica.* By November 1915 he became editor of the newspaper and in 1919 its sole proprietor under its new name, *Hispano-América.* According to his own account, his objective was to document the news "sin ligas ni compromisos con nadie, juzgando imparcialmente personalidades y eventos" (without ties or commitments to anyone, judging personalities and events impartially).

Both Juan Rodríguez (*La Palabra,* Spring 1980) and Oscar Treviño (*Caminos,* February 1981), in their brief studies on Arce's journalism, assert that he became an influential cultural and political figure who used his newspaper as a forum for the Spanish-speaking community of the Bay Area.

Under the title "Crónica diabólica," Arce, using the pseudonym Jorge Ulica, wrote short narrative sketches of daily events in the San Francisco area. As is characteristic in the *costumbrista* (local color) style of writing, Ulica narrates in the first person an array of anecdotal incidents. Unlike other literary forms published in southwestern Spanish newspapers during the 1920s—which included mostly European literature in translation—Ulica's prose pieces comment on the social and cultural concerns of the San Francisco Latino community, concerns such as the U.S. political and judicial system, U.S. fashions, social institutions, cultural values, customs, and the Latino community's relationship with these.

The various levels of Mexican assimilation into the dominant Anglo-American culture and life-style, or failure to adapt adequately to it, are objects of Ulica's satire. Evident manifestations of social change as a result of U.S. economic and political hegemony—endorsement of eugenic studies, massive immigration to the United States, emergence of unofficial linguistic and cultural expressions, and the woman suffrage movement—are all depicted from the perspective of a middle-class Mexican immigrant who maintains the distant stance of an outside observer; at times, of a participating visitor. For example, in "No vote pero me botaron" (I Didn't Vote But I Was Booted Out) and "Mesican Wine," Ulica caricatures the U.S. political and judicial practices as nonthreatening. American philanthropists and pseudoscientists are satirized in "Touch-Down extraordinario," "Así se escribe nuestra historia!" (Our History Is Written This Way!), and "El Palacio de las Tribus Peregrinantes" (The Palace of the Pilgrimaging Tribes) for their pretentious and insubstantial goodwill toward and knowledge about the U.S. Latino community.

Ulica takes aim at Mexican immigrants also, commenting humorously and critically on the various ways they deal with their new environment. He jeers at the propensity of lower-class immigrants to take advantage of others and their inability to fit into the new social ambience and to perform well, as in "No estamos bastante aptos" (We Are Not Apt Enough), "Los 'parladores de Span-ish'" (The Spanish Speakers), and "Por no hablar 'English'" (For Not Speaking English). Middle-class Mexican women are ridiculed for their inclination to ape American ways. They are depicted readily assimilating the new fashions, customs, foods, and language and accused of trading in their husbands for American ones, as narrated in "Como hacer surprise-parties" (How to Make Surprise Parties), "Repatriación gratuita" (Gratuitous Repatriation), and "Sobre el arte culinario" (On the Art of Cooking). One of Ulica's common objects of mockery is the attempt by women to exercise their civil rights, revealing his hostility to the changing role of women in society. "Arriba las faldas" (Up with Skirts) and "Inacia y Mengildo" are sketches in which he pans women's whimsical yet malicious attempts to take advantage of men. In "Do You Speak Pocho" Ulica especially pokes fun at the preposterous misuse of the English language by such women. He defines the term *pocho* as "Un revoltijo, cada día más enredado, de palabras españolas, vocablos ingleses, expresiones populares y terrible 'slang'" (a jumble, every day more confusing, of Spanish and English words, popular expressions, and terrible slang), mocks the inappropriate use of both standard Spanish and standard English language by Mexican-Americans, and satirizes the misunderstandings that arise.

Although there is contempt, or at least apprehension, on Ulica's part for the use of pocho as a means of communication, he uses it and experiments with it to create humor for his audience—most probably literate, male, and middle-class—who used both languages interchangeably and were confronted daily with similar linguistic phenomena. Part of his humor is derived from the incongruities that develop from the narrator's role as a middle-class Mexican exile. It may be surmised that the audience for which he was writing would be the ones to derive the most humor from his satire.

Critical reception of the 1982 collection of Ulica's *Crónicas diabólicas* has been mixed. This has been primarily due to the fact that, since recovery and republishing of his *Crónicas* have been directly linked to efforts in establishing a Chicano literary tradition, a debate has arisen regarding his place within that tradition. Chicano literary historians such as Luis Leal, Charles Tatum, and Rodríguez consider the recovery of Ulica's prose pieces as representing an important link in the development of Chicano narrative. In "El florecimiento de la literatura chicana" (1977)

Rodríguez refers to the pieces as true jewels and to Ulica as a master. In "Narrativa chicana: viejas y nuevas tendencias" (1985), Leal regards the sketches as rich prose. Tatum (*Revista Chicano-Riqueña*, Winter 1981) asserts that Ulica, along with other writers like him, should "figure prominently in any future reconstruction of Chicano literary history." Some critical response has been adverse. In his review of the *Crónicas diabólicas* (*Revista Chicano-Riqueña*, Spring 1985), Arthur Ramírez seriously questions whether Ulica's columns are in fact literature, Chicano, and humorous, calling them "journalistic and pedestrian," marked by "unhumorous broad farce," and produced by someone who displays "a curious ambivalence toward Americans and Mexican Americans."

Given the biographical data there is on Arce and the treatment in his *Crónicas* of the Mexican community in the United States, it is clear that he was a Mexican journalist and a political exile who wrote from that perspective. Arce as Ulica does not view himself as part of an oppressed minority, and his short satirical pieces reveal more insights about his ideological position than they do about the community he is depicting and satirizing. His influence on the Mexican community as a creative writer and journalist has barely been explored, as may be seen in Treviño's 1981 article in *Caminos*, "Julio G. Arce: un pionero" (A Pioneer). Placing Ulica in a Chicano literary tradition raises important questions of identity, affiliation, and influence which need to be addressed.

As further studies objectively elucidate the complex and dynamic sociohistorical factors which gave rise to the intellectual and literary presence of the oppressed Chicano minority at the turn of the century, it will become possible to precisely situate writers such as Arce in the framework of tradition.

References:

Luis Leal, "Narrativa chicana: viejas y nuevas tendencias," in *Aztlán y México: perfiles literarios e históricos*, edited by Leal (Binghamton: Bilingual, 1985), pp. 111-120;

Clara Lomas, "Resistencia cultural o apropiación ideológica: visión de los años 20 en los cuadros costumbristas de Jorge Ulica," *Revista Chicano-Riqueña*, 6 (Fall 1978): 44-49;

Juan Rodríguez, "El florecimiento de la literatura chicana," in *La otra cara de México*, compiled by David Maciel (Mexico City: Ediciones "El Caballito," 1977), pp. 348-369;

Rodríguez, "Jorge Ulica y Carlo de Medina: Escritores de la Bahía de San Francisco," *La Palabra*, 2 (Spring 1980): 25-26;

Rodríguez, "Julio G. Arce: vida y obra," in Arce's *Crónicas diabólicas*, compiled by Rodríguez (San Diego: Maize, 1982), pp. 9-21;

Charles Tatum, "Some Examples of Chicano Prose Fiction of the Nineteenth and Early Twentieth Centuries," *Revista Chicano-Riqueña*, 9 (Winter 1981): 58-67;

Oscar Treviño, "Julio G. Arce: un pionero," *Caminos*, 2 (February 1981): 43-60.

Daniel Venegas

(birth and death dates unknown)

Nicolás Kanellos
University of Houston

BOOK: *Las aventuras de Don Chipote o cuando los pericos mamen* (Los Angeles: El Heraldo de México, 1928; republished, Mexico City: Secretaría de Educación Pública and Centro de Estudios de la Frontera del Norte de México, 1985).

PLAY PRODUCTIONS: *¿Quién es el culpable?*, Los Angeles, 1924;
Nuestro egoísmo, Los Angeles, 1926(?);
Esclavos, Los Angeles, 8 January 1930;
El maldito jazz, Los Angeles, 1930 (?);
Revista astronómica, Los Angeles, 1930(?);
El con-su-lado, Los Angeles, 1932;
El establo de Arizmendi, Los Angeles, 1933.

PERIODICAL PUBLICATIONS: "En el Vil Traque," *El Malcriado*, 4 (17 April 1927);
"El Repique del Diablo," *El Malcriado*, 4 (17 April 1927).

Daniel Venegas's work is a precursor of today's Chicano literature not only in openly proclaiming a Chicano identity but also in generating a style and literary attitude that would come to typify the Chicano novels of the late 1960s and the 1970s.

Very little is known of the life of Daniel Venegas. He was the founder and editor of the weekly satirical Los Angeles, California, newspaper *El Malcriado* (The Spoiled Child) from 1924 into the 1930s, and prior to this he was a journalist for the newspaper *El Pueblo* (Los Angeles). He also was the author of numerous plays, revues, and a novel. From 1924 to 1933 Venegas's name appeared occasionally in the Los Angeles Spanish-language daily newspapers, *La Opinión* and *El Heraldo de México*, usually in reviews of his plays, in reference to his newspaper or to his theatrical company, La Compañía de Revistas Daniel Venegas (The Company of Daniel Venegas's Revues). Biographical information about him is found in autobiographical passages in his novel *Las aventuras de Don Chipote o cuando los pericos mamen* (The Adventures of Don Chipote or

When Parakeets Suckle Their Young, 1928). Venegas emigrated from Mexico as a laborer, traveling through Juárez, México, and El Paso, Texas. He made his way to Los Angeles by working on the Santa Fe Railroad and, despite his becoming part of the Hispanic cultural elite of Los Angeles, was proud of and identified with his working-class origins. It is clear from newspaper reports that he was a favorite of working-class theater audiences and that his theatrical company catered to workers rather than the elite. The political attitudes assumed in *Don Chipote* are clearly in sympathy with the working class.

All of Venegas's theatrical works have been lost, leaving only a smattering of newspaper reviews for posterity. In a 19 November 1924 newspaper interview journalist Gonzalo Becerra on the occasion of its debut commented that Venegas's *¿Quién es el culpable?* (Who's to Blame?) is "todo un éxito, habría de provocar comentarios extraordinarios que más tarde se traducirán en un triunfo más" (a complete success that should provoke extraordinary commentary and will be acclaimed as one more triumph). His 1926 play, *Nuestro egoísmo* (Our Selfishness), was supposedly "dedicada a la mujer mexicana, a su honor y defensa" (dedicated to Mexican women, in their honor and their defense), according to *El Heraldo de México*, 11 October 1926. However, *Nuestro egoísmo* received a rather harsh rebuff in a playwriting contest, according to an account published in *El Heraldo de México*, 1 June 1928, by one of the jurors and fellow dramatists, Gabriel Navarro: "el jurado crítico condena acremente la libertad del lenguaje" (The jury severely condemns the liberties taken with language), that is, his use of working-class language and Spanglish or *pochismos* (Mexican-American dialect). Of his play *Esclavos* (Slaves) and his musical comedy revues nothing is known more than their rather suggestive titles: *El maldito jazz* (That Darned Jazz); *Revista astronómica* (The Astronomic Revue); *El establo de Arizmendi* (Arizmendi's Stable), after a popular Latino boxer, Baby Arizmendi; and *El con-su-lado*, a title referring to

271

Cover for the 1985 edition of Venegas's novel. The National Library of Mexico holds the only known copy of the first edition, published in 1928.

the Mexican consulate with a wordplay on *lado* (side) meaning satirically the consul's *side* (version of things).

Only one issue of Venegas's satirical newspaper, *El Malcriado*, has been located; it is held in the Bancroft Collection, University of California, Berkeley. The 17 April 1927 ten-page "Semanario Joco-Serio de Caricaturas" (Comic-Serious Weekly of Caricatures), satirizes world and local news, customs, and sports; advertises local businesses; and publishes stories, commentaries, and caricatures. Becerra, in his article "El Cuento del Lobo Joven" (The Story of the Young Wolf), in *El Heraldo de México*, 19 November 1924, commented that it was difficult to relate the mild-mannered young Venegas, author of the beautiful drama, *¿Quién es el culpable?*, to the news-

paper "esas saetillas que a todos nos hieren" (whose barbs wound us all). The extant issue of *El Malcriado* supplies samples of Venegas's various writing styles, his philosophy, and his politics. In some of the pieces he adopts working-class speech. He reports the workers' favorite sport, boxing, and challenges Mexican intellectuals, particularly journalists in exile:

> Los periodistas deben ponerse con su agrupación al frente de las demás sociedades mexicanas, como guiadores hacia un porvenir de afectiva solidaridad y verdadero patriotismo para todas los exiliados.
>
> Es decir, para realizar la dignificación no solamente de los trabajadores mexicanos–también los periodistas son trabajadores–residentes en una tierra extraña, sino por manera muy especial la de la Patria.

(Through their association, the journalists should place themselves at the head of the rest of the Mexican associations as guides toward a future of affective solidarity and true patriotism for all of the exiled.

This must be done not only to endow with dignity Mexican workers–journalists are also workers–who reside in this land, but also to dignify our fatherland.)

Echoing the ideology common among the Mexican elite in the United States, Venegas believed that it was the duty of the intellectuals, writers, and artists to protect and preserve Mexican culture while in exile. And it was the Mexican writer, more than any other type of intellectual, who perceived the threat of Anglicized language and, consequently, who embarked on crusades in their columns and chronicles against the influence of the English language in speech and in writing. But it is noteworthy that Venegas, while advocating the protection of Mexican culture and the Spanish language, chose to adopt Chicano speech in parts of *El Malcriado*, in *Don Chipote*, and in his plays.

Of the two stories by Venegas included in the surviving issue of *El Malcriado*, "El Repique del Diablo" (The Devil's Bell-Ringing) is of little interest, relating in standard Spanish the tragic and sentimental story of a father in love with his daughter-in-law. The other story, "En el Vil Traque" (On the Evil Tracks), is also by no means original, given the popularity of ballads, oral tales, and newspaper chronicles elaborating the theme of Mexicans working on the railroads at this time. The story even closes with the same message as many of the *corridos* (ballads) and one similar to *Don Chipote*'s that the United States is a land of hardship and exploitation for Mexicans: "a los paisas que se quieren venir, voy también a decirles la verdad, porque muchos creen que acá no más llega uno y se pone a recoger los pesos con palas, como si fueran tierra" (And to those compatriots who would like to come here, I shall also tell them the truth, because so many believe that you just come here and start shoveling up pesos as if they were dirt). The real value of "En el Vil Traque" lies in its relationship to *Don Chipote*. The story seems to be a rudimentary plot outline for the novel without, however, any of the spice, humor, and picaresque elements that make *Don Chipote* such a rich literary document. "En el Vil Traque" reveals that Venegas in 1924 had the same concerns for the Mexican immigrant worker as he did in his 1928 novel. In "En el Vil Traque" the protagonist narrates a sad, woeful tale of immigration, hard labor, and disillusionment, while in *Don Chipote* an omniscient narrator–who at times identifies himself with the real-life Venegas–spins the picaresque yarn. In "En el Vil Traque" there is linguistic experimentation with Chicano worker dialect, including Anglicisms like "monises" (money), "troca" (truck), "jaigüey" (highway), "draiver" (driver), "gumorig" (good morning), "juasumare" (what's the matter), and many others.

Las aventuras de Don Chipote o cuando los pericos mamen was published by the Los Angeles newspaper *El Heraldo de México* in 1928; the only known copy is in the National Library of Mexico. The book was reprinted in 1985–with an introduction by its discoverer, Nicolás Kanellos–in a run of thirty thousand copies by Mexico's Department of Education and the Center for the Study of Mexico's Northern Border. In its time *Don Chipote* must have represented an heroic effort to dignify the Mexican immigrant worker and his culture in a novel. Chicano culture at the time was constantly under attack from elite writers who wrote for the Spanish-language newspapers of the Southwest. Under the pretext of correcting the workers' behavior and speech and elevating their culture, they were in reality hiding their shame of being associated with the lower, uneducated classes of Mexicans. What is new about *Don Chipote* is precisely the identification of its author-narrator with Chicanos and his having as ideal readers other Chicanos. Not only does it imply that a good portion of those workers knew how to read but also that those workers, like the au-

thor himself, were capable of producing literature and art.

Las aventuras de Don Chipote is the humorous tale of the trials and tribulations of one Don Chipote who immigrates to the United States from Mexico in order to shovel up the gold from the streets he has heard about and send it back to his family. Spurred on by a slick ne'er-do-well, Pitacio, who has supposedly returned rich to his village, Chipote begins his odyssey, always accompanied by his faithful, although always starving, dog Sufrelambre (a play on words with "Suffers Hunger"). During his journey he picks up a companion, Pluticarpo, who accompanies him as he travels through the underworld of Juárez, Mexico, El Paso, Texas, and Los Angeles, California, as well as lays track through the arid expanses of New Mexico and Arizona. After hearing no word from Chipote for months and after constantly fending off the amorous advances of Pitacio, Doña Chipota and her children leave home in search of father and husband. Chipote, finally recovered after a railroad injury and various short-term employments, takes up with a flapper whose only interest is in his cash. Doña Chipota catches him in a poor theater house in Los Angeles just as he is making a spectacle of himself to impress his tawdry flapper. All return to Mexico where they should stay, for "los mexicanos se harán ricos en los Estados Unidos: cuando los pericos mamen" (Mexicans will only become rich in the United States when parakeets suckle their young), that is, never.

Besides entertaining the reader with the tragicomic situations in which the poor protagonist finds himself, *Don Chipote*'s frank and open intention is to disillusion would-be immigrant workers about the United States and to criticize the social and labor conditions on both sides of the border that workers faced in the 1920s. In the course of the novel Venegas paints a naturalistic picture of the demeaning treatment and conditions of slavery offered Mexican immigrant workers. Besides blaming the gullible workers and those who return to Mexico with glowing accounts of life in the United States, Venegas also indicts the government of the United States: "Casi no se puede creer que las autoridades de los Estados Unidos no se hayan dado cuenta de este robo de que son víctimas nuestros compatriotas . . . ; son cómplices de las sinvergüenzadas de las compañías" (It is impossible to believe that United States authorities are not aware of the victimization of our compatriots . . . ; they [the authorities] are accomplices to the shameless deeds of the companies.)

Although it may deal with the picaresque odyssey of a *campesino* (farm worker), *Don Chipote* is obviously an urban novel, with high interest in the customs, speech, and attitudes of the urban proletariat and the cynicism of the parasites (such as pimps, prostitutes, floozies, flophouse owners, and quack healers) who prey on the poor workers in Juarez, El Paso, and Los Angeles. It is noteworthy that this precursor of the Chicano novel of the 1970s is an expression of the Mexican-American in the city, rather than in the small town as in the works of Tomás Rivera, Rudolfo A. Anaya, and Rolando Hinojosa-Smith.

Moreover the language of *Don Chipote* foreshadows contemporary Chicano literature's use of "caló" (barrio slang), dialects, Anglicisms, and general identification with working-class Mexican-Americans. *Don Chipote* is a rich guide to Chicano lexicon during the years just prior to the Great Depression. Not only is its linguistic value historical but also literary in that the Chicano's language and dialogue become important elements of humor, satire, and irony in the hands of Venegas, who apparently had carried on years of linguistic and literary experimentation in writing *El Malcriado*.

Daniel Venegas and *Las aventuras de Don Chipote* must be considered precursors of today's Chicano literary sensibility in style, language, and class philosophy. The author's life and his creation represent the continuity of Mexican-American art and culture. Mexicans lived in the Southwest long before it was part of the United States. The nature of their relationship with Anglo-America has in great part defined and formulated their recent literary expression. It

should be no surprise that literary form and publication took place not only in the 1920s but even much earlier, certainly since the Mexican American War of 1846-1848. Given the nature of United States expansion west and its conquering and incorporating of different peoples into its empire, it should also be of no surprise that the greater part of the literary and artistic heritage of these peoples in what is today the United States is lost. *Don Chipote* offers readers a glimpse of what that larger literary patrimony must have contained.

References:

Gonzalo Becerra, "El cuento del Lobo Joven," *El Heraldo de México* (Los Angeles), 19 November 1924;

Becerra, "El estreno de '¿Quién es el culpable?' en el Teatro Capitol," *El Heraldo de México* (Los Angeles), 31 August 1924;

"California Dreamin'," *Nexos*, 8 (July 1985): 53-54;

Nicolás Kanellos, Introduction to Daniel Venegas's *Las aventuras de Don Chipote o cuando los pericos mamen* (Mexico City: Secretaría de Educacíon Pública and Centro de Estudios de la Frontera del Norte de México, 1985), pp. 7-15;

Kanellos, "*Las aventuras de Don Chipote*, obra precursora de la novela chicana," *Hispania*, 67 (September 1984): 358-363;

Gabriel Navarro, "Teatrales," *El Heraldo de México* (Los Angeles), 1 June 1928;

Vicente Francisco Torres, "La primera novela chicana," *Revista Mexicana de Cultura*, 111 (16 June 1985): 12;

Patricia Vega, "Las aventuras de Don Chipote, el primer testimonio chicano," *La Jornada* (Mexico City), 13 May 1985.

Tino Villanueva

(11 December 1941-   )

Julián Olivares
University of Houston

BOOKS: *Hay Otra Voz: Poems* (Staten Island, N.Y.: Editorial Mensaje, 1972);

Shaking Off the Dark (Houston: Arte Publico, 1984);

Crónica de mis años peores (Los Angeles: Lalo, 1987).

OTHER: *Chicanos, Antología histórica y literaria*, edited by Villanueva (Mexico City: Fondo de Cultura Económica, 1980).

PERIODICAL PUBLICATION: "Reflections on Poetics," *Denver Quarterly*, 16 (Fall 1981): 101-106.

Tino Villanueva

Tino Villanueva emerged as an important voice of Chicano expression in the early 1970s. A poet and an academic, his personal endeavors as a writer were stimulated by the struggle for sociopolitical emancipation and the heightened cultural awareness that characterized the Chicano Movement of the late 1960s and early 1970s. The poetic voice for him is an existential affirmation of being by which one achieves salvation from silence, chaos, and annihilation.

Villanueva was born on 11 December 1941 in the south-central Texas town of San Marcos, where he lived in a dusty barrio. His parents were migrant field workers, an occupation that Villanueva found embarrassing. In a 1985 interview with Wolfgang Binder he recalled his feelings as a schoolchild: "The teachers would ask, 'What are you going to do, Johnny, during the summer?' And the Anglo kid would say, 'I'm going to visit my aunt in Detroit.' 'And how about you, Sally?' 'We're going to North Dakota to take a trip to the Badlands,' or 'We're going to California.' And I remember that the Chicano kids–the migrant Chicano kids–were too embarrassed to admit that during the summer it was no vacation for them, that they were going to do a lot of stoop labor. So they would essentially lie–it was a half-truth, actually–they would say, 'I'm going to be in Amarillo, I'm going to be visiting

an aunt.' But inside you knew that you were going to Amarillo all right, but you were going to bust your tail off, hoeing cotton . . . I did this until my seventeenth year . . . the caste system was already predicted . . . because the other Anglo kids knew that any brown kid that came [back to school] in the middle of October had to be a cotton picker." He graduated poorly educated from high school, having learned virtually nothing but racial prejudice and Texas history. He failed his college entrance examination and worked in a furniture factory for three years, during which time he began to make up for the gaps in his education. He dedicated himself to self-improvement by studying, for example, the "Increase Your Word Power" section of *Reader's Digest*.

Villanueva was drafted into the U.S. Army in 1963 and spent two years in the Panama Canal Zone, where he was brought into closer contact with Hispanic culture and where he first heard of Nicaraguan poet Rubén Darío and Cuban revolutionary José Martí. When he returned to San Marcos he studied Spanish and English at Southwest Texas State University. While taking a Spanish course for native speakers, he wrote his first published poem, a sonnet, "Camino y capricho eterno" (Road and Eternal Caprice). It appeared in the *San Antonio Express and News* (7 April 1968) and is included in his first collection, *Hay Otra Voz: Poems* (There Is Another Voice: Poems, 1972). His English professors recommended he study E. E. Cummings, T. S. Eliot, and, especially, Dylan Thomas. It was under the latter's influence that he wrote, in this period, one of his best poems, "My Certain Burn Toward Pale Ashes."

After receiving his B.A. in 1968 Villanueva accepted a fellowship at the State University of New York at Buffalo. There he read *El Espejo/The Mirror* (1969), the first anthology of Chicano literature, and became aware of his spiritual and literary alliance with fellow Chicanos. Living away from the Southwest permitted him to take stock of himself and to take into account the injustices perpetrated upon him and his people. He embraced the Chicano Movement and wrote most of the poems, especially the Chicano poems, published in *Hay Otra Voz*. With his M.A. in Spanish from Buffalo Villanueva commenced his doctoral studies at Boston University in 1971. In 1972 he wrote "Chicano Is an Act of Defiance," which he dedicated to Rubén Salazar, the *Los Angeles Times* correspondent killed by the police in the East Los Angeles racial turmoil of that year. In 1980 Villanueva's anthology *Chicanos, Antología histórica y literaria* was published. The book is a result of his interest in Chicano history and literature and responds to the need for a general anthology that could be used in a Spanish classroom. As Villanueva told Binder, "I often used to hear that the English Departments at universities would not teach Chicano literature because the Spanish Departments should do it. The Spanish Departments would ask, 'Where are the books, where is a general anthology that we can handle?' " The anthology claims a literature that begins in 1848 with the conclusion of the United States-Mexican War and the annexation of Mexican territories, whose Hispanic inhabitants thus became American citizens.

After the publication of *Hay Otra Voz* Villanueva published poetry and articles on Spanish and Chicano literatures in various journals and traveled widely, giving readings in the United States and in Europe. He received the Ph.D. in Spanish from Boston University in 1981, and his part-time appointment at Wellesley College was made a full-time position. In 1984 he

began publication of *Imagine: International Chicano Poetry Journal*, which, because it desires to "expand the horizons of the usual poetry journal," accepts texts in any language accompanied by an English translation. He states in the introduction to the first issue of the journal, "*Imagine* transcends the usual circumscribed efforts and self-invested attitude of most poetry journals. In doing so *Imagine* attempts to avoid the perils of inbreeding: the insular self-interest and provincial smugness that regional (or national) literary trends tend to create." In the introduction Villanueva summarizes much of what he published in scholarly journals and in his anthology on Chicano history. One of his most important statements is his assertion that Chicanos are bicultural: "To say they are *angloparlantes* (English-speaking) and *hispanoparlantes* (Spanish-speaking) as well as *angloactuantes* (Anglo-behaving) and *hispanoactuantes* (Hispanic-behaving) is to identify their very essence." Speaking of the code-switching (blending of English and Spanish) that is often found in Chicano poetry, he adds, "In its portrayal of linguistic relationships, the bilingual poetry of Chicanos presents the reader with the challenge of imagining a creative verbal topography without reducing it to a map or to mere language. The immediate reaction is one of a richer notion of aesthetics where the poetic text is deeply infused with imaginative power, a particular inflection of the natural idiom called style, cadences with a native strain, resulting in the unambivalent unity of an artistic identity."

Appearing in 1972 when there were very few journals that gave space to U.S. Hispanic literary expression, aside from very brief mention in New York Spanish newspapers, *Hay Otra Voz* was received without any reviews. With the subsequent publication of Villanueva's poetry in various journals and with his readings in Europe, articles on his poetry and life began to appear in the United States and overseas. In his book *Chicano Poetry: A Response to Chaos* (1982) Juan Bruce-Novoa called Villanueva "an exacting taskmaster of language," saying that his collection "displays one essential vision: certain oppressive forces in life threaten to relegate people to a silent, invisible and anonymous state of nonexistence." The themes that appear in *Hay Otra Voz*, and which continue in Villanueva's second book, *Shaking Off the Dark* (1984), are time, death, and silence, each on a personal and societal level. Societal involvement is seen as a moral imperative, the poet's response as an affirmed human being responsible for himself and his fellow human beings. The goal of self-realization finds its complement in socially committed poetry. Each of the three parts of *Hay Otra Voz* represents a successive stage in the poet-protagonist's evolvement from self to social self. "My Certain Burn Toward Pale Ashes" traces the strivings toward self. Time is symbolized by the daily cycle of the sun measuring the life of the narrator:

> My certain burn
> toward pale ashes is told by the
> hand that whirls the sun; each
> driving breath beats with the quick
> pulsing face.

Time is also expressed by sand, "each/ghostly grain a step in time that/measures tongues." In the inexorable march toward death, the narrator's creative voice is vital to affirm his existence, for silence–even in life–is tantamount to nonexistence:

> My waking light
> began when the fertile lips spun
> my pulse; and I, with muted tongue,
> was drawn destroyed from the making-
> mouth into this mass.

In the second part of the volume, the poet, continuing the birth-growth allegory, becomes an Adamic persona discovering and naming the world, thereby inventing himself. There is "meaning then the word" as he comes into being: "illusions becoming real./To think in images is to be mature,/losing myself in their duration./I become."

There is an almost equal division in *Hay Otra Voz* of poems in English and Spanish, with another group of bilingual poems, reflecting the Chicano's bicultural experience, included in the section "Mi Raza" (My People). One of the best of the bilingual poems is "Day-Long Day." The poem, inspired by the beginning of Native American poet James Welch's "Surviving," presents the theme of social exploitation as experienced in the Texas cotton fields. The migrant workers are caught in a remorseless cycle in which the heat of the sun is oppressive and the sun itself is linked with a master who oppresses his workers:

> Third generation timetable.
> Sweat day-long dripping into open space;
> sun blocks out the sky, suffocates the only breeze.
> From *el amo desgraciado*, a sentence:

> "I wanna a bale a day, and the boy here
> don't haf 'ta go to school."

The poetry resonates with multiple voices: the poet's, the voice of his people, and the landowner's. The voices of the workers and the landowner present two social classes in conflict, with the landowner's southern-English dialect being the language of oppression. A mother in the field complains that it is as if the elements were spitting fire, and the elders, in self-deprecation, tell the youngsters to "Study so you won't be an ass like us":

> . . . Lubbock by way of Wharton.
> "Está como si escupieran fuego," a mother moans
> in sweat-patched jeans,
> stooping
> with unbending dreams.
> "Estudia para que no seas burro como nosotros,"
> our elders warn, their gloves and cuffs
> leaf-stained by seasons.

The poem's final line, which reverses the refrain "Lubbock by way of Wharton," is an expression of timeless and cyclical repetition, understood not only as a work pattern but also as social oppression in all its manifestations. As Villanueva told Binder, "There is a line here that says, 'Lubbock by way of Wharton.' Lubbock is in the north [of Texas] and Wharton is near Houston in the southern part. These are the extreme poles of my experience, and of many other families and children working in the summer around the Houston area during the very hot season, and then traveling north to do the cotton crop there, too. And at the end of this poem it says 'Wharton by way of Lubbock.' The idea that I was trying to convey was that it's a never ending cycle. You go to Lubbock, and when the crop is over, then you return home; but your own home becomes also a stop on the way to Wharton. And the cycle begins all over again."

Villanueva's *Shaking Off the Dark*, forty poems almost all written in Boston, was well received. Reviewer Antonio Olliz Boyd, in *World Literature Today* (Spring 1985), called it "a journey into the semiotic concept of biculturalism. Tino Villanueva alludes to his sense and sensitivity of being Chicano with delicately interlaced poetic imagery." Rafael Castillo, in the *New Mexico Humanities Review* (Fall 1984), affirmed that "Good poetry comes alive with the sound of words, the rhythm of lines, and the juxtaposition of the senses. The new poetry by Tino Villanueva is a masterly achievement by a rising new star in American poetry."

Villanueva's second collection manifests essentially the same structure as his first but with more thematic intensity and range of expression. The initial poem "Much," also the subtitle of the first section of ten poems, conjures up images of prenatal development in an extended allegory of the genesis of poetic creativity. The shaping of the poem, its gestation period, consists of a process similar to the formation of vital organs: "The breath is alive/with the equal girth of words./ This fist, a tougher lung,/takes up the oracular burden. . . ." Writing becomes an act of defiance against destruction: "Fist of my life,/you are now a heart of light/seeking the good."

The title poem, "Shaking Off the Dark," is the poet's reaction against the doldrums of inactivity. Menaced by a hostile world, the "shook heart of the ruined age" can easily be enticed to a passive life and unresistingly go with the flow of time. Conformity with formulas for the comfortable life are "rites of life" which "can waste the wit." The poet rebels against this temptation that would commit him to a wasted existence:

> Yet, a rebellion overtakes the mind,
> the kind that breaks the shadow's hold:
> I ram a fist into the howl of the wind,
> shake off the dark locked
> within the hell of those rare depths.
> The common street
> and shifting sky become a song.

In the thirteen poems that comprise the second section, "Odyssey," the poet emerges in the world outside the self where he encounters scenes and events that parallel his inner struggles. Villanueva's many travels to Europe provided just the context for the dialectic between self and society. In "Now that I'm in Spain" the personal labor involved in breaking silence and affirming existence is seen in a political context, the remembered dictatorship of Francisco Franco (1892-1975) which repressed free speech. The presence of the *Guardia Civil*, the state police, makes a casual stroll along the grand boulevard of Madrid, *La Gran Vía*, repressive: "They have lined my tongue against a concrete/diaphanous wall."

Many of the poems in *Shaking Off the Dark* affirm Villanueva's Chicano heritage. In "History I Must Wake To" the poet's Spanish name and the weight of the history of his people and their condi-

Cover for Villanueva's 1984 collection, forty poems, many of which affirm his Chicano heritage

tion cause him to assume a "conflictive attitude" and become his people's voice. "Haciendo apenas la recolección" exploits the meanings of *apenas* (scarcely), *a penas* (with hardship), and *recolección* (meaning both harvest and meditation and evoking the English word *recollection*) so that the poem deals with cotton picking and, metaphorically, with the gathering of memory:

> For weeks now
> I have not been able
> to liberate me from my name.
> Always I am history I must wake to.
> In idiot defeat I trace my routes
> across a half-forgotten map of Texas.
> I smooth out the folds stubborn
> as the memory.

The poem expresses the poet's "roots-routes" and the hardships of migrant workers, and concludes with the affirmation: "Weep no more, my common hands;/you shall not again/pick cotton." His hands now have a common cause in that he works for the Chicano people, and they will labor over art so as to proclaim the existence of his people. This poem is the realization of what Villanueva considers indispensable in the shaping of a committed poem, as he said in a 1981 article on poetics in *Denver Quarterly:* "In times of social crisis one would hope . . . that the poet would immerse himself so deeply in the historical flux that the so-called committed poems would, instead of being forced out, come naturally from within his whole being. By this act alone the poet would serve as artistic translator of a world which men have created around themselves, and of which he is an organic and inextricable part. So too would the poet lay bare a complete self, the twofold source that he really is: artist by impulse and human being responsible for himself and his fellow beings. Simply put, it is a matter of being answerable to oneself such that the human function of writing becomes a creative act and a civil duty, a verbal-esthetic event and a moral gesture."

One of the most accomplished and moving poems in *Shaking Off the Dark* is "Now, Suns Later," dedicated to the poet's grandmother. It was written in Boston during the winter of 1974-1975, ten years after she had passed away. Villanueva discussed the circumstances of the poem in his interview with Binder: "I had wanted to write about my grandmother. It came to me . . . I guess with the Women's Movement. It made me reflect on how life for a Chicano woman at the turn of the century was like, and how it may have been, had the [Chicano and Women's] Movement . . . occurred then and not now . . . . My question is: 'How could this have changed her life?' Here is a lady who brought nine children into the world and who got up before everyone else did in the morning. The wife of a migrant worker who got up and cooked for everyone, washed the dishes and went on and worked in the fields herself. And then at noontime she had to leave before everyone else, so she could return home and prepare lunch. And the same thing happened in the afternoon. She washed clothes for all these people. That's a terrible life! So I began to think of this experience of hers. Here I was with . . . my own little struggles with academia, teaching here and there, participating in marches and boycotts, and having a rough time financially at the beginning. I would consistently ask myself: 'Who am I to complain? You have it good compared with grandmother.' So all those elements bear on this poem." The poem in-

terweaves light imagery emanating from two sources, the sun and the grandmother:

> And when dawn's colors flooded the lasting
>   fields,
> She walked into light
> finding her place in the arrogant sun:
> she too went tilling the yielding earth.
> And to the blazing wind sparks flew
> from sun-struck stones
> scraped by her quick-thinning hoe.

His "thinking back how much she strained in/ radiant need" provides him with a lesson in patience, dignity, and endurance.

Shaking Off The Dark concludes with the hortative poem, "Speak Up, Chicano, Speak Up," which was first published in Boston as a broadside. Of this poem he told Binder, "I think that poetry is like prayer many times, that perhaps this poem or fragments thereof [can] serve somebody or uplift somebody. I do not expect each Chicano reader to identify with all of the facets of the poem. Sometimes it addresses the students, sometimes it addresses the farmworkers, and sometimes it addresses the urban factory worker. It is a very existentialist poem, too, because of the line toward the end: 'You are *free* to act but you must *act* to be free.' " Anglo society is indifferent, he says,

> And it matters little that you call yourself
> mexicano, Mexican American, mexicanoamericano,
> hispano, Hispanic American, Spanish American,
> Latin American, or Chicano;
> or that you are lighter skinned,
> speak English with utterly divine diction,
> and have won a Congressional Medal of Honor . . .
> To them there is no difference.

The weapons of words must be wrested from the oppressors:

> So arise, Chicano,
> arise from the shadow of Nothingness;
> arise from that neverending *Nada* [nothing] of
>   servitude.
> The problem is we live by other people's words:
> We think we are what *they* think we are.

Although his life experience provides the stimulus and material for much of his poetry, Villanueva's *Crónica de mis años peores* (Chronicle of My Worst Years, 1987) is, in its conception and structure, specifically autobiographical. A verse chronicle of eighteen poems, it relates to his discovery of himself and the revindication of history and his people. With this book, probably Villanueva's best, there is a consciousness of writing that goes beyond the poet's engagement with language. Even more than in his previous books, writing itself is a strategy. Words are not only the means to write the author's text of himself but also the implements to rewrite history and to regain the power from those who hold the dominion of the spoken and written word:

> Se me volvía loca la lengua.
> Quería tan pronto saber
> y decir algo para callar
> el abecedario del poder . . .
> Pero todo era silencio,
> obediencia a la infecta tinta
> oscura de los textos[.]

> (My tongue became confused.
> Quickly I wanted to know
> and say something to silence
> the alphabet of power . . .
> But all was silence,
> obedience to the obscure
> and corrupt ink of textbooks.)

The book is written entirely in Spanish, for Villanueva wishes to revindicate a language that was proscribed in the schools of his youth. The wording is lucid and concentrated, a product perhaps of his study of contemporary Spanish poets. Castilian, American Spanish, and Chicano Spanish are combined to create a powerful and compelling language.

The focus of Villanueva's autobiography is his early childhood, his "education" in the Texas school system and his life as a migrant worker, in which the reader encounters many of the motifs and symbols of his previous books. One of these is the dusty road. Unpaved, dusty streets are emblems of poverty and social injustice. In "Casi bíblica ciudad: Chicago" (Almost Biblical City: Chicago) the poet-protagonist recounts hearing radio broadcasts from Chicago that reach his south Texas town and which induce in him a nostalgic yearning for this faraway paradise. Rather than a babel of confusion, the many languages of the metropolis offer the possibility of self-expression. From the real edifices of the metropolis, conceived as a symbol of hope and freedom, the edifices become a metaphor of the text, self-expression, outlets from his dusty roads to bright boulevards:

> Desde mi aldea del sur
> y desde entonces,
> para alzar este edificio
> de convocadas palabras
> he venido reptando polvorosamente
> desde el hondo tiempo transcurrido,
> izando exactamente la esperanza,
> sintiéndome más hombre
> en las horas de albedrío
> por cada bulevar.

> (From my village in the south
> and since then,
> to raise this edifice
> of summoned words,
> I have crawled dustily
> from the deep passage of time,
> hoisting hope exactly,
> feeling myself more of a man
> in these willful hours
> along each boulevard.)

In "Cuento del cronista" (The Chronicler's Story) the poet convokes other chroniclers, such as the Aztec scribe Tlacuilo, to assist him in his recording:

> Vigila por mí, Tlacuilo venerable,
> ayúdame a ser fiel a mi linaje, las fechas
> castigadas por el sol y lavadas por la sombra.
> Bendíceme, dile a tus dioses que oren por mí.
> Prefiero no olvidar
> la sucesión de sueños rotos, pues sería
> igual que querer quemar la historia.

> (Watch over me, venerable Tlacuilo,
> help me be true to my lineage, to the dates
> punished by the sun and washed by the shade.
> Bless me, tell your gods to pray for me.
> I prefer not to forget
> the succession of broken dreams, for it would be
> the same as burning history.)

Spanish explorer Alvar Núñez Cabeza de Vaca is seen as a symbol of personal survival:

> Tú también, desflechado peregrino castellano,
> Alvar Núñez Cabeza de Vaca, maldito explorador. . .
> enséñame a entender el alfabeto ahora. . . .
> Enséñame a salvarme de aquéllos que con
> mano airada separaron la esperanza germinal
> de mi inicial suspiro e hicieron los días naufragar.

> (You also, errant Castilian pilgrim,
> Alvar Núñez Cabeza de Vaca, unfortunate explorer. . .

teach me now to understand the alphabet. . . .
Teach me to save myself from those who
with an angry hand sundered my germinal hope
from my first breath and made a shipwreck of my
    days.)

With this poem—which also records the poet's mestizo inheritance—Villanueva becomes a chronicler
and places himself within a tradition.

Villanueva is now teaching at Boston University and is working on a fourth book of poetry, inspired by the final scene of the motion picture
Giant, in which the protagonist, portrayed by
Rock Hudson, fights (while the jukebox plays
"The Yellow Rose of Texas") with the owner of a
diner who has refused to serve a Mexican-
American family. Its working title is "Scene from
the Movie *'Giant.'*" If his previous work is any indication his future creative work will show insight
and wisdom.

References:

Wolfgang Binder, *Partial Autobiographies: Interviews with Twenty Chicano Poets* (Erlangen,
West Germany: Palm & Enke, 1985), pp.
203-220;

Juan Bruce-Novoa, *Chicano Poetry: A Response to
Chaos* (Austin: University of Texas Press,
1982);

Bruce-Novoa, "Tino Villanueva," in his *Chicano
Authors: Inquiry by Interview* (Austin: University of Texas Press, 1980), pp. 253-264;

Julián Olivares, "Self and Society in Tino Vi-
llanueva's *Shaking Off the Dark*," *Confluencia,
Revista Hispánica de Cultura y Literatura*, 1
(Spring 1986): 98-110;

Olivares, "Two Contemporary Chicano Verse
Chronicles," *Americas Review*, 16 (Fall-Winter
1988).

José Antonio Villarreal
(31 July 1924-   )

Tomás Vallejos
University of Houston–Downtown

BOOKS: *Pocho* (Garden City, N.Y.: Doubleday, 1959);

The Fifth Horseman (Garden City, N.Y.: Doubleday, 1974);

Clemente Chacón (Binghamton: Bilingual/Editorial Bilingüe, 1984).

OTHER: "Chicano Literature: Art and Politics from the Perspective of the Artist," in *The Identification and Analysis of Chicano Literature*, edited by Francisco Jiménez (New York: Bilingual/Editorial Bilingüe, 1979), pp. 161-168.

PERIODICAL PUBLICATIONS: "The Odor of Pink Beans Boiling," *San Francisco Review*, 1 (Spring 1959): 5-9;

"The Fires of Revolution," *Holiday Magazine*, 32 (October 1962): 82-83.

José Antonio Villarreal occupies a distinct position among Chicano writers. His first novel, *Pocho* (1959), the first known Chicano novel published by a major publishing company in the United States, has been widely recognized as an important work of Chicano literature. Villarreal was born in Los Angeles, California, in the wake of the Mexican Revolution of 1910. His parents, José Heladio Villarreal and Felícitaz Ramírez, were born and raised as peons on an hacienda in the state of Zacatecas, Mexico. During the revolution his father fought in Pancho Villa's army for seven years. The family moved to the United States in 1921, migrating throughout California as seasonal farm workers.

Villarreal recalls his preschool years with delight. In those days his family was still traveling in California, living mostly in tents pitched in the fields. He and his family knew only Spanish and, as he puts it, "lived always in a Mexican enclave." (This and other direct quotes from Villarreal, unless otherwise noted, are taken from "An Interview with José Antonio Villarreal" by Francisco Jiménez in *Bilingual Review*, Spring 1976.) He re-

José Antonio Villarreal

members these years of isolation from North America's mainstream as a time of warmth and security. Because of their closeness and poverty the migrants entertained themselves through story telling. He recalls:

> And so they talked and told tales of their region, and I listened. Long into the night I listened until I dropped off to sleep and my father would pick me up onto his lap as he continued to talk about the Revolution.... And every camp was different, none existing for more than six or seven weeks, then off we would go to the next harvest, where new people would gather and there would be new tales to be told and heard. I knew when I was six years old that the one thing I most wanted from life was to be a storyteller.

Villarreal was able to begin acquiring the necessary tools to be a writer when he reached the age of six. Upon securing steady, year-round employment in Santa Clara, California, his family settled there in 1930, the year he started school. Villarreal relishes the memory of his first year in school. His first-grade teacher, Miss Uriell, did not speak Spanish and he knew no English, but somehow they communicated. By the end of the first year she had him reading English. By the time he was in the third grade he was reading so avidly that he was taken out of class by the principal and promoted to the fourth grade. He taught himself to read in Spanish, which he says made him "the happiest of persons." Villarreal says that he still thinks fondly of his first-grade teacher, who introduced him to the world of the written word and encouraged his interest in reading by giving him books for Christmas up to the time he graduated from high school and left Santa Clara.

Although Villarreal recollects his early years with pleasure, certainly they were not without their measure of pain. His experiences growing up *pocho* (between cultures) in Santa Clara are at the heart of his first novel, which describes, among other experiences, cultural confusion and painful encounters with racism. As Villarreal has related in interviews, being pocho involves linguistic conflict and incongruity. For many years after he began to master English at school, he was forbidden to speak English at home by his parents, who did not know the language and made no attempt to learn it. The acceptance of English into the Villarreal household came only gradually. Nevertheless, the author informs his interviewers that although Spanish is his native language, English is his preferred language. This linguistic conflict is indicative of much deeper cultural, social, psychological, and philosophical conflicts in Richard Rubio, Villarreal's young protagonist in *Pocho*.

Villarreal's experience, as well as Richard Rubio's, is not unlike that of an entire generation of Mexican-Americans, children of immigrants struggling to adapt to life in the United States during the unsettling years of the Depression and World War II. This conflict, which in many ways repeats itself in each generation of American children born to immigrants from Mexico, has given *Pocho* lasting significance as a novel of the Mexican-American "identity crisis."

Besides *Pocho*, Villarreal wrote only two other novels, not a large body of work considering the number of years it spans. He submitted the first version of *Pocho* for publication in 1952. *The Fifth Horseman* was published in 1974, and his third novel, *Clemente Chacón*, in 1984. Villarreal attributes the large gaps between his novels to the difficulties of finding a publisher as well as the circumstances of his life. He received a B.A. in English from the University of California, Berkeley, in 1950. After that he did graduate study at the same university but decided that he had to choose between literary scholarship and writing, and chose the latter. He married Barbara Gentles in 1953 and became the father of three children between the years 1954 and 1958. Villarreal explains that the first priority in his life has been his wife and children, followed by his novel writing. To provide for his family, he has held a variety of jobs, including public-relations work for an insurance company, driving a delivery truck, and working as a technical editor and writer for defense and aerospace industries such as Ball Brothers in Colorado and Lockheed in southern California.

Providing for his family also necessitated moving back and forth between jobs in Mexico and the United States. While in Mexico in 1956, he completed the version of *Pocho* that was finally published in 1959. At that time he also researched his second novel, an undertaking which included returning to the hacienda where his parents grew up and interviewing people who had experienced the Mexican Revolution firsthand. In 1963, eight years after the death of Villarreal's mother, his father returned to Mexico. Ten years later Villarreal became a Mexican citizen, more as a matter of economic convenience than because of any disenchantment with the United States or nostalgia for his father's homeland. Villarreal maintains that he is equally at home in both countries.

The publication of the Anchor paperback edition of *Pocho* in 1970 brought Villarreal recognition as a writer and thus led to a series of jobs more closely related to literature. These included editorial positions, guest lectureships, teaching positions at such institutions as the Stanford Research Institute, the University of Santa Clara, the University of Colorado, the University of Texas at El Paso, the Preparatoria Americana of the American School in Mexico, Pan American University, and California State University, Los Angeles. Five years after he finished his first draft of *The Fifth Horseman* it was published by

Dust jacket for Villarreal's 1974 novel about the
Mexican Revolution

and societies are undoubtedly those Villarreal himself lived through in his formative years. *Pocho*, however, is more than the story of cultural conflict. It is also a bildungsroman, a novel about self-discovery and maturation. Modeled upon James Joyce's *A Portrait of the Artist as a Young Man* (1916), it is about the artist's struggle for freedom and individuality against the forces of tradition, conformity, and materialism that surround him. Villarreal says that he was especially conscious of Joyce, Thomas Wolfe, and William Faulkner.

Pocho begins in Mexico at the close of the revolution, focusing upon Juan Rubio, Richard's father, who throughout the work represents the ideals of the revolution and a stubborn refusal to part with Mexican traditions, especially *machismo*. At odds with his insistence upon male domination and patriarchy is his wife, Consuelo, who eventually rebels, although in pathetically counterproductive ways, for she has no clear understanding of her goals or how to achieve them. Embroiled in this conflict are the Rubio children, who represent the generation in transition between rural Mexican culture and that of the urban United States. Perhaps in even greater opposition to his father's Mexican ideals is Richard's ideal of individualism. The novel realistically concludes on a note of uncertainty and alienation. The Rubio family disintegrates and Richard sets out for military service in World War II, knowing that "for him there would never be a coming back."

While *Pocho* has earned Villarreal widespread recognition, in-depth literary criticism of his work is relatively scarce. Instead *Pocho* has prompted controversy and criticism surrounding its stated and implied socioeconomic and political views. At the center of this controversy is the author himself, who maintains a most precarious status as a Chicano writer. To begin with, he has repeatedly stated that he does not really identify himself as a Chicano, although he does not object strenuously to this term or its application to him. He also openly questions whether there is such a thing as "Chicano" literature, asserting that most Chicano novelists are primarily influenced by the British and American literary tradition and write in English, not Spanish. Of greater importance is the fact that Villarreal found himself at odds with the ideology, rhetoric, and methodology of the Chicano Movement in the late 1960s and early 1970s. Yet he is aware that the movement was responsible for *Pocho*'s resuscitation after a

Doubleday. However, it was largely ignored and subsequently went out of print. In 1974, the same year in which *The Fifth Horseman* was published, Villarreal completed his first draft of *Clemente Chacón*; but because his second novel was not commercially successful, he had to find another publisher. Bilingual Press published his third novel in 1984, several years after it was completed. Villarreal's last novel has received little attention, leaving *Pocho* his most successful work to date and his most important contribution to Chicano letters.

The success of *Pocho* is due in large part to its autobiographical nature. Villarreal's own experiences growing up as the son of Mexican immigrants are depicted through the character Richard Rubio with candor, sensitivity, and realism. The pressures Richard experiences as a result of being caught between two cultures, generations,

decade of neglect following its publication in 1959. More than 160,000 copies of the 1970 Anchor edition have been sold, making it one of the most widely read works of Chicano literature.

The marketing of the 1970 edition was partially responsible for the misguided emphasis placed on its socioeconomic and political content. Ramón Eduardo Ruiz's introduction diverted attention from the work as literature and analyzed it primarily as "a historical piece" reflecting "Mexican American thinking of the time ... the 'assimilitionist' phase that prevailed then." This oversimplification and the subsequent criticism it invited from Chicano activists hounded Villarreal for several years. While teaching at the University of Colorado during this period, he found himself the object of strong criticism from student activists. Villarreal did not approve of the Ruiz introduction, but because of the trend in the marketplace, he acquiesced to Doubleday's decision to include it. The third printing of the book, which appeared in the 1980s, no longer includes the introduction; Villarreal welcomed this change as a vindication of his viewpoint.

As critics have indicated, *Pocho* is not without literary shortcomings. A common criticism of the novel is that Villarreal's attempt to impart a feeling of Spanish speech patterns by applying Spanish syntactical structures to English dialogue results in awkwardness and artificiality. Another frequently voiced criticism is that the protagonist's level of intellectual maturity is inconsistent with his age; that is, Richard is far too precocious to be credible. Critics have also said the work lacks focus. Villarreal conceded in an interview that the novel is flawed as a result of his inexperience and "the fact that I was trying to do something I perhaps lacked the technical ability to handle."

Nevertheless, Villarreal counters that he is not completely dissatisfied with the book. Neither are his critics. Therein, perhaps, lies the difficulty in assessing *Pocho*. With the furor of the movement era more than a decade past, critics can examine the work with greater detachment. Recent critics observe that the novel's most serious shortcomings are not so much its social or political messages, but contradictions between the author's stated intentions and their execution within the work. This critical approach dismisses the earlier simplistic judgment that the novel advocates the rejection of Mexican culture in order to achieve upward mobility in American society. To this effect, Richard is more accurately perceived

not as an American "rugged individualist" but a literary kinsman of Joyce's Stephen Dedalus, who maintains his artistic individuality through exile.

However, the author's stated purpose in writing *Pocho* was "to share my experiences of growing up in an old country traditional way, breaking away from that culture and going on to a new way of life, yet still holding on to the traditional ways that were good and adding to them the new things I liked in the Anglo-American society." Unfortunately, this cultural syncretism presupposes a resolution of conflicts in which the protagonist creates his own identity through cultural eclecticism. This, however, is not the way *Pocho* ends, as critics have observed. Instead, Richard Rubio has been characterized by most critics as lost, confused, and alienated at the end of the novel.

Some critics contend that Richard's confusion is a manifestation of Villarreal's own misconceptions. Rafael F. Grajeda faults Villarreal for promulgating American myths such as the idea that anyone can succeed in this society because the individual is free to control his own destiny and the notion that racial discrimination is "due more to the character of a handful of men than to the wide, almost organized attitude of a society." Grajeda especially takes issue with Villarreal's statements about the novel because the actual experiences he presents contradict such conclusions. These and other contradictions within *Pocho* are observed as problematic in assessing it as literature. Despite the negative criticism *Pocho* has received, it is still considered important by literary scholars and sociologists. Ironically, however, despite Villarreal's insistence that it be appreciated for its artistic merit, it is still more often read for its historical, psychological, and sociological value. Its chief merit, critics agree, is its sensitive, realistic, and honest representation of the conflicts faced by the Mexican-American in transition between cultures.

Villarreal's second novel, *The Fifth Horseman*, has, for the most part, suffered more from neglect than from criticism. It begins on a Mexican hacienda during the regime of President Porfirio Díaz before the revolution. A well structured novel, it is divided into a prologue and three "books": "Hacienda de la Flor," "The Campaign," and "Los Desgraciados" (The Downtrodden). The prologue pulls the reader into the horror and brutality of the revolution, thus clearly establishing the novel's theme. The first book of the novel provides the background of the revolu-

Covers for Villarreal's third novel, set in El Paso during one September day in 1972

tion, presenting the protagonist, Heraclio Inés, as a *jinete* (horseman) working as a peon with his father and four older brothers on the hacienda of Don Aurelio Becerra. The second section recounts the idealistic protagonist's adventures as a cavalryman in the army of Villa. In the final section, Heraclio becomes disillusioned with the senseless carnage and perfidiousness of the revolutionaries. The novel ends with Heraclio realizing that he must leave Mexico, but vowing to return someday in order to "help rebuild his homeland" rather than "to take a part in its destruction."

Villarreal believes that *The Fifth Horseman* is artistically superior to *Pocho*. The critics agree. Reviews outside the circle of Chicano scholarship have been generally favorable, citing the richness of characterization, strong story line, and even the use of Spanish syntactical structures to create the impression that characters are speaking Spanish. One reviewer naively praises the novel as

clever and action-packed, comparing it to a soap opera with its endless series of crises; others describe it as mature and realistic. Judith M. Dimicelli praises its sensitivity in exposing the tyranny of Porfirio Díaz, the ideals of the revolution, and the revolution's failure to find direction and ideological consistency. She applauds the meticulous balance of the plot's events, the symbolic use of clothing, and the allusion to Greek mythology in the protagonist's name.

Chicano critics too have praised the novel's structure and strong story line, as well as its rich descriptions. They have also recognized its historical and mythical allusions to the romantic Mexican bandit Heraclio Bernal, the Greek demigod Heracles, the biblical Book of Revelations, and even the pre-Cortésian Mexican myth of the fifth sun. However, Chicano scholars are less liberal with praise and more negative in their critical assessment of the novel as a whole. What is seen by non-Chicano critics as a clever accommodation of English to a Spanish sentence structure to create the impression of Spanish speech patterns is viewed by Chicano scholars as artificial. More important, while other critics praise Villarreal's characterizations, Chicano critics have found them overly idealized and exaggerated. The emphasis on Heraclio's *machismo* is viewed as excessive and his extraordinary heroism is seen as unconvincing. Heraclio is not considered to be a realistic peon of prerevolutionary times, but an unrealistic super-macho who fails to engage the reader's sympathies.

Furthermore, while some critics accept unquestioningly the historical veracity of *The Fifth Horseman* and Villarreal's handling of Mexican traditions of destiny and manhood, Chicano critics do not. Rather, they conclude that the novel lacks significance on the grounds that it distorts the historical realities it attempts to describe by failing to capture the true essence of the peon. Roberto Cantú says the novel is ahistorical because it creates a hero who is a man of destiny, a man of ominous birth, not a true man of history. He explains frankly that the novel has been overlooked not so much because its return to the theme of the revolution has become trite by now, but because Villarreal's handling of the theme appears trite. Whatever reasons may explain its neglect, *The Fifth Horseman* slipped in and out of the public eye with little fanfare. Although it was republished by the Bilingual Press in 1984, it remains, for the most part, obscure.

With the publication of *The Fifth Horseman*, Villarreal completed half of what he has planned to be a "loose tetralogy." He said that "*Pocho* is an extension of *The Fifth Horseman*. . . . Heraclio Inés becomes Juan Manuel Rubio." The third book, half written in 1975, according to the author, and tentatively called "The Houyhnhnms," was to "have Richard Rubio become Mike de la O." The fourth book is "very far away" and is to be "about Richard, Mike's son. . . ." The last two books have yet to appear in print, although the author has recently repeated that the third book is still in progress and he still plans to write the fourth. When he was interviewed in 1975, Villarreal reported that he had put aside "The Houyhnhnms" to complete another novel, "a change of pace, a short story that got away from me and became a short novel" (*Clemente Chacón*).

While teaching at the University of Texas at El Paso, Villarreal made observations of life on the streets of Juárez, Mexico, just across the bor-

der, and El Paso, noting especially a hard-boiled, cynical Mexican boy whose basic philosophy was, as it is put tersely in the novel, "Anything to survive." Villarreal was intrigued by this little street hustler and began to write a story about him. However, upon realizing that the boy was so adamant in his cynicism that he was not likely to change, except perhaps to harden by slow degrees, Villarreal decided to have him "killed" in his novel. He then shifted his emphasis to another young hustler whose feelings were ambivalent, giving him more potential as a protagonist. Thus was born the character of Ramón Alvarez, who in the novel rises to success in the United States under the assumed name of Clemente Chacón.

An oversimplified summary of *Clemente Chacón* would call it a Chicano variation on the Horatio Alger story, as Villarreal himself blatantly suggests at the beginning: "He, Clemente Chacón, was Horatio Alger, even if he was Catholic and brown." It is the story of a boy who begins life as the illegitimate son of a poor rural Mexican woman forced by circumstances into prostitution. Ramón Alvarez learns survival on the streets of Juárez as a shoe shine boy, pimp, and drug dealer. Later he crosses the border into the United States, where he becomes a successful insurance executive, but at the expense of denying his former identity until the end of the novel. In the process of presenting the rags-to-riches life of Ramón/Clemente, Villarreal provides much insight into the cultural, psychological, societal, and ethical conflicts of an upwardly mobile Mexican-American. Thus the author takes what might otherwise be a trite theme and enriches it with vivid, sometimes startling, descriptions of life in a poor Mexican village and the underworld of prostitution, drug dealing, and survival on the streets of a Mexican border town.

Clemente Chacón is indeed a change of pace for Villarreal. For the first time he employs Spanish liberally in his dialogue and descriptions, giving them more authenticity than they had in his first two novels. Structurally, his third novel is more complex than his other books, the work of a more experienced writer. This novel is not arranged chronologically; it is set in El Paso and occurs, except for the epilogue, within the span of one September day in 1972. It is a momentous day in which Clemente experiences several changes. Interspersed masterfully throughout the developments of the day are flashbacks to his past, which provide the reader with an understanding of Clemente and people from a similar background. The flashbacks also serve to impress upon the reader the futility of trying to forget one's past, and to convey Villarreal's message that while upward mobility is desirable, it need not occur at the expense of one's Mexican identity. Clemente proclaims this discovery near the end: "I am a Mexican and I am an American, and there is no reason in the world why I can't be both."

Villarreal states with pride that *Clemente Chacón* is his best work. To support his contention he cites the fact that it was among the American novels of 1984 selected for exhibition in both the Frankfurt book fair and the Madrid book fair. Certainly it is artistically his most sophisticated work. In addition, some of its minor characters are among the most memorable Villarreal has created. Most notable of these are the cynical street urchin Mario Carbajal and the seedy but almost quixotic Charlie Morgan, Clemente's surrogate father, who is killed for trying to rescue Chacón's mother from prostitution. However, *Clemente Chacón* also contains some of the same flaws as Villarreal's previous novels. The protagonist is a bit too wholesome (he never uses alcohol, drugs, or women throughout his life on the streets) to be credible as a representative of his social class. Some of the characters and plot developments also lack clear focus and purpose in the novel. Villarreal's description of the work as "a short story that got away from me" may ironically ring true, for the plot seems to become overly complicated at the end and at other times it seems bogged down with events and propagandistic dialogue that serve no purpose but to criticize those Chicano militants who gave Villarreal such grief in the early 1970s. As in *Pocho*, seemingly intelligent and progressive characters who are supposed to have arrived at self-understanding may instead be regarded by critics as purveyors of conservative social and political opinions.

Villarreal continues to work on the two remaining books of his proposed tetralogy. His children are grown now, which leaves him more time to write. However, the desultory nature of Villarreal's work history has not changed. His employment status in 1985 was still temporary. Thus the financial stability that is conducive, if not vital, to the production of creative literature

is still missing from his life. It remains to be seen whether Villarreal will produce a work that will gain him greater recognition than *Pocho* or whether he will remain an important Chicano literary figure for being, as Ruiz stated in the introduction to the 1970 edition of *Pocho*, "the first man of Mexican parents to produce a novel about the millions of Mexicans who left their fatherland to settle in the United States."

References:

Juan Bruce-Novoa, "José Antonio Villarreal," in his *Chicano Authors: Inquiry by Interview* (Austin: University of Texas Press, 1980), pp. 37-48;

Bruce-Novoa, "*Pocho* as Literature," *Aztlán*, 7 (Spring 1976): 65-77;

"Cannery Worker Writes Novel About Mexican-Americans' Life," *San Jose Evening News*, 28 October 1959, p. 12;

Judith M. Dimicelli, "A Chicano Twentieth-Century Book of Genesis," *Bilingual Review*, 3 (Spring 1976): 73-77;

Rafael F. Grajeda, "José Antonio Villarreal and Richard Vásquez: The Novelist against Himself," in *The Identification and Analysis of Chicano Literature*, edited by Francisco Jiménez (New York: Bilingual/Editorial Bilingüe, 1979), pp. 329-357;

Francisco Jiménez, "An Interview with José Antonio Villarreal," *Bilingual Review*, 3 (Spring 1976): 66-72;

Luis Leal, "*The Fifth Horseman* and Its Literary Antecedents," in Villarreal's *The Fifth Horseman* (Binghamton, N.Y.: Bilingual/Editorial Bilingüe, 1984), pp. xi-xxvi;

Marvin A. Lewis, *Introduction to the Chicano Novel* (Milwaukee: Spanish Speaking Outreach Institute, 1982), pp. 6-13;

Francisco A. Lomelí, "Vorágine del destino," *La Comunidad* (Sunday Edition), *La Opinión* (Los Angeles), 30 June 1985, pp. 13-14;

Carl R. Shirley, "*Pocho*: Bildungsroman of a Chicano," *Revista Chicano-Riqueña*, 7 (Spring 1974): 63-68.

Papers:

Some of Villarreal's papers are held at the University of Santa Clara.

Bernice Zamora

(20 January 1938-   )

Nancy Vogeley

University of San Francisco

BOOK: *Restless Serpents,* by Zamora and José Antonio Burciaga (Menlo Park, Cal.: Diseños Literarios, 1976).

OTHER: *Calafia: The California Poetry,* edited by Ishmael Reed, includes poems by Zamora (Berkeley: Y' Bird, 1979);
Chicanos: Antología histórica y literaria, compiled by Tino Villanueva, includes work by Zamora (Mexico City: Fondo de Cultura Económica, 1980);
Flor y Canto IV and V: An Anthology of Chicano Literature, edited by Zamora and José Armas (Albuquerque: Pajarito, 1980).

PERIODICAL PUBLICATIONS: "Flexion," *Caracol,* 2 (March 1976): 4-5, 11;
"Our Voice, Our Truth," *El Fuego de Aztlán,* 1 (Spring 1976): 3;
"Andando," *Revista Chicano-Riqueña,* 4 (Fall 1976): 14;
"Notes from a Chicana 'Coed,'" *Caracol,* 3 (May 1977): 19;
"Editorial: Chicanas View Chicanos," *El Fuego de Aztlán,* 1 (Summer 1977): 4;
"Primal Dream," "Lava Beds," "Do You Take?," *El Fuego de Aztlán,* 1 (Summer 1977): 24;
"The Chicana as a Literary Critic," *De Colores,* 3, no. 3 (1977): 16-19;
"Sex as Metaphor," *Mango,* 1, nos. 3-4 (1977): 12-15;
"Review of *The Road to Tamazunchale,*" *Atisbos,* 3 (Summer-Fall 1978): 226-228;
"Vergüenza," *De Colores,* 4, nos. 1-2 (1978): 6-18;
"Archetypes in Chicana Poetry," *De Colores,* 4, no. 3 (1978): 43-52;
"Introduction," *De Colores,* 5, no. 1-2 (1980): 1-4;
"Guillermo Hernández' Canciones de la raza: Songs of the Chicano Experience," *De Colores,* 5, nos. 1-2 (1980): 136-141;
"Preface," *De Colores,* 5, nos. 3-4 (1981): 1-2.

Bernice Zamora's considerable reputation as a poet rests largely on one book, *Restless Serpents*

(1976). Other poems, essays, reviews, and short stories by Zamora appeared in journals and anthologies during the formative years of the Chicano Movement; and these writings, together with papers she has presented and personal efforts to encourage other Chicano writers and artists, have earned her a respected position. Her theoretical work on archetypes has particularly affected others so that her influence must also be a factor in considering her importance. In categorizing her in his 1979 essay "Las poesía chicanas: Una nueva trayectoria," Salvador Rodriguez del Pino concludes that her poetry often goes beyond what is normally thought of as Chicana feminism: "Bernice Zamora ha tenido la distinción o el dudable halago de que su poesía 'parece haber sido escrita por un hombre'" (Bernice Zamora has had the distinction or the dubious praise that her poetry 'seems to have been written by a man'").

Bernice Ortiz was born on 20 January 1938 in Aguilar, a village in the coal-mining region in the mountains of Colorado, and grew up in Pueblo, Colorado. Her father was a coal miner and farmer. The population of Pueblo was a mixture of Chicanos, Italians, Slovenians, and Anglo-Texans; and, according to an unpublished 1985 interview, she did not learn racism there so much as "a dislike for coloration," against which Zamora soon rebelled. Cultural life centered around the Catholic church and its traditions, and Zamora recalled the Latin and morals it taught. She was the oldest of the children, and when she was three years old neighbors took her to catechism classes so that her mother could have time for her other children. The nuns discovered she had learned to read English from cereal boxes and such things, and they encouraged her parents to limit her language learning to English. As Zamora said in 1985, "My parents didn't need to be told that because they had already suffered." Therefore, although Spanish was spoken within the family, Zamora's formal linguistic development was largely in English. She speaks of the delight of finally discovering how Spanish words she had heard were spelled. The family moved to Denver where her father became an automobile painter in a body shop. When a piece of heavy machinery fell on him he became disabled, and Bernice Ortiz's mother (born Valdez) began to work for an optical company.

Bernice Ortiz attended parochial school through eighth grade. In high school she showed an aptitude for art; later she worked at a bank and took courses at night. She read the work of Soren Kierkegaard and Jean-Paul Sartre, although without understanding a great deal. She was stunned when at a meeting of the Knights of Columbus auxiliary, a woman spoke of existentialism. Surprised, Zamora asked her where she had learned about philosophy. The woman, who had eight children, said she had been taking philosophy courses at night. Zamora decided that she could also study. At the age of twenty-eight (by then, married to a man named Zamora, she was the mother of two girls) she began her undergraduate work at Southern Colorado University. She was graduated with a B.A. in three years, majoring in English and French. She speaks of her French studies appreciatively because there was more freedom, more careful examination of texts, and more opportunity to study women writers than in the British tradition.

Although Zamora's marriage was beginning to fall apart in the late 1960s, she does not attribute this to her decision to continue her education. It was her circle of friends from the women's auxiliary who, though they ranted against the women's movement then forming, helped her to analyze her life as a wife and a Catholic.

Zamora pursued her studies of English and French literatures at Colorado State in Fort Collins. She commuted for two years while working on an M.A. degree. There she came to understand the different approaches to thinking which each literature represented and thus became aware of why she was so "divided" in her own bicultural approach to literature. Although she liked English literature (a Shakespearean play, she says, would "spin me on to writing about twelve poems"), she was "absolutely enthralled" with Dante and considered many non-English writers superior to most British writers. Her M.A. thesis compared the poetry of Wallace Stevens and Francis Ponge; she received her degree in 1972. In 1973 she began studies for a doctorate at Marquette University, where she wrote "Sonnet,

Freely Adapted" (published in *Restless Serpents*), a parody of William Shakespeare's Sonnet 116 ("Let Me Not to the Marriage of True Minds").

In 1974, after Zamora spent a year at Marquette, her marriage ended. She then drove west with her daughters Rhonda and Katherine to continue her studies for a doctorate at Stanford University. Increasingly she realized that the classes she was taking in literary history, theory, and analysis were obscuring the original texts that she wanted to read. She compared literary analysis to admiring "a cute little puppy" and then proceeding to kill it by dissecting it to see what made it work. While she was studying, she taught at Stanford, the University of California, Berkeley, and the University of San Francisco. Stanford University awarded her a Ph.D. in English and American literatures in 1986.

In 1976 while at Stanford, together with José Antonio Burciaga, she published *Restless Serpents* in an edition of two thousand copies. The book employs a format which several other Chicano works of the period advantageously utilized; Zamora and Burciaga's two collections are bound as one, dos-à-dos.

Zamora's poetry in *Restless Serpents* explores such topics as Chicano cultural traditions, the experience of women in that culture, language, and the power of poetry. "Pueblo 1950" is the story of a first kiss told from the perspective of an adult remembering that she was punished, but the boy was not punished: "I said shame on me, and nobody / said a word to you." In "Progenitor" the narrator identifies with a wild "padre" (father), a grieving "madre" (mother), a "primo" (cousin) who marries his younger cousin, a reflective "puta" (whore), children, and with "abuelos" (grandparents) whose hope is lessened by the death of their grandchildren:

I am all the children
and I am the abuelos
of dead children
whose resurrections
depend on
resurrections.

"Let the Giants Cackle" mocks those who exercise their power by requiring Chicanos to speak English by comparing them to fattened geese:

Words, words, English words—
turds of the golden goose—
words we picked up, wiped off,
cleaned up, prepared and served

as canapes to the lordly lords
that they might digest–again–
their famished thoughts
to fart their foul days away
    beanfeasting.

"A tropezones en Stanford" (Painfully, at Stanford) is a lament for the decline of Spanish saying "Mañana– / me van a descarnar la lengua" (Tomorrow they are going to take out my tongue). The title poem, "Restless Serpents," repeats the refrain "Lyrics, / lyrics alone soothe / restless serpents" to suggest the transforming power of poetry: "strokes / more devastating than / devastation arrived."

Zamora said in an unpublished 1985 interview that *Restless Serpents* was published for a Chicano community that had been "accused of not being a literate, thinking group." She said the Chicano community was "desperate for texts" and that they deserved as much as young artists and writers could create. Critical reviews of *Restless Serpents* were favorable. Bruce-Novoa's praise in *Caracol* (September 1977) recalls the book's title: "Like those serpents, Zamora's poetry fascinates: inscrutable signs of life and death in beautiful form, capable of demonic possession; gods of mysterious, lost worlds, only accessible to us in the surface of the images they themselves are."

Because it has often been anthologized, the title poem "Restless Serpents" deserves special attention. The poem's beginning lines ("The duty of a cobra's master / is fraught with fettered chores") suggest a wealth of meaning. One may read a socioeconomic relationship into the imagery which shows master and servant inextricably bound together. References to snakes recall "Stone Serpents," an earlier poem from the collection in which this architectural detail ("stone serpents lie carved into the balustrades") identifies a castle or temple in which the "weary wealthy" allow no life. The image of snakes suggests the serpent cult practices in Aztec temples and thus the historic and mythic origins of the Chicano people. However, the snake is also a common symbol in many religions, standing not only for the force of evil but also the perfect union of male and female in a flowing, continuous bisexual form. Here Zamora's use of archetypal imagery draws on her sense of universal mental structures. The poem had its origins in a dream in which a woman nursing a baby suddenly found the baby had become a snake.

In a review of *Restless Serpents* (*Mango*, no. 2, 1977) Lorna Dee Cervantes declared that Zamora, "as evidenced by her tight, carefully crafted poems, proves herself to be one of the most (if not *the* most) outstanding Chicana poets today." Joe Olvera said, "Her poetry is strong and sure of itself, with its future assured" (*American Book Review*, October 1979).

Evidence that *Restless Serpents* is a seminal work are the continuing references to the book and its author in studies of Chicano poetry. The important essay "La poesía chicana" by Rodríguez del Pino observes that her poetry criticizes oppression and nostalgically evokes barrio traditions and values. Elizabeth J. Ordóñez writes in "The Concept of Cultural Identity in Chicana Poetry" (*Third Woman*, 1984) that Zamora engages in "a process of mythopoesis" as she creates identity anew in her poetry; she cites two poems by Zamora not included in *Restless Serpents*, "José el revolucionario" (published in *Mango*, 1977) and "Notes from a Chicana 'Coed' " (published in *Caracol*, 1977). In these poems, Zamora explicitly condemns the Chicano exploitation of Chicanas by mocking the way Chicanos use the rhetoric of the Chicano Movement for purposes of seduction. In "Notes from a Chicana 'Coed' " the narrator says,

To cry that the gabacho
is our oppressor is to shout
in abstraction, carnal.
He no more oppresses us
than you do now as you tell me
"It's the gringo who oppresses you, Babe."
You cry "The gringo is our oppressor!"
to the tune of $20,000 to $30,000
a year, brother, and I wake up
alone each morning and ask,
"Can I feed my children today?"

Although Zamora admits a feminist message in her poetry, she says her primary anger is directed against oppression in all forms. In the unpublished 1985 interview she said, "I never once felt myself to be a feminist–oppressed, yes, but Chicanas' relationship to their men is different [from that of Anglo women]," a subject she explores in "Chicanas View Chicanos," a 1977 editorial she wrote as guest editor for the Summer 1977 issue of *El Fuego de Aztlán*. She says if there is one word which sums up the underlying expression in her poetry it is "rage."

She confesses that the urge to write poetry is overwhelming. She has pulled off the freeway while driving to write a poem; "Situation" was writ-

Asina me dijo mi papá

Beneath the heaving elm
I wait for the horseman.
Thousands of leaves mark time
under a moon moving quickly.

He will touch me, I know,
then continue without
speaking a word.

—Así te va pasar, mija.
No tienes miedo porque tu vida va cambiar.

And so I wait for the horseman
Beneath this heaving elm.
—Asina me dijo mi papá.

Fair copy and illustration by Zamora (courtesy of the author)

ten during an astronomy class. "As long as I'm writing poetry I know I'm healthy," she says. She is acutely conscious of the voices that speak through her, of the Chicanas and Chicanos she has known, who cannot write, whose "heroic" experiences cry out to be recorded. She speaks especially of Chicanas she met while in Texas collecting material for her dissertation who were forced into prostitution to support their children.

Zamora's two published short stories, "Flexion" (*Caracol*, 1976) and "Vergüenza" (*De Colores*, 1978), convey a more absolute sense of oppression and misery than her poetry. In "Flexion," for example, the narrator, an Anglo woman in a state mental hospital, is in love with another patient, a Chicano. The reader understands that in some way their confinement is a result of an impossible institutional experience, hers with a university and his with the military in Vietnam. He has lost his sexual capacity so that there is no possibility of any healthy, productive relationship between them.

At the December 1976 meeting of the Modern Language Association, Zamora read a paper, "Archetypes in Chicana Poetry" (*De Colores*, 1978), based on research for her dissertation. In it she spoke of the oral tradition in Chicano poetry and discussed the problem of knowing. Zamora sees that primordial images which lie at the heart of myth and ritual can provide the basis for a study of Chicano poetry. However, she explains this will be difficult because the Mayan and Aztec mythologies have been complicated in the Chicano experience by the mixture with Greek and Christian myth.

In December 1979 Zamora left Stanford for Albuquerque to help edit the journal *De Colores*. Her contacts with other members of the Chicano publishing community have always been good; in 1975, for example, she regularly hosted a gathering of Chicano writers and artists such as Alurista, Ron Arias, and José Antonio Burciaga and his wife, Cecilia Preciado. They would meet together and read their works, "energizing" one another. Zamora wrote critical articles during this period; "Sex as Metaphor" appeared in *Mango* in 1977, and her review of *The Road to Tamazunchale* came out in *Atisbos* in 1978. In 1980 she and José Armas edited an anthology of Chicano literature from the *Flor y Canto* festivals held in Albuquerque (1977) and in Tempe, Arizona (1978). In 1980 she fell desperately ill in Houston. She returned to California in December 1982. Partly because of her illness and partly because of her desire to avoid contention, she avoided any critical activity in 1985. Although she has continued to write poetry, recently she has refrained from publishing any. She sees her future in writing outside the university system. She has written a play, and she plans a theoretical work on third world aesthetics.

Zamora worries about the consequences of poetry, citing Plato's exclusion of poets from his republic. Translated into Chicano terms, she feels Chicanos should offer one another their best songs, music, food, and poetry. Because she believes isolation is a universal problem for Chicanos (the community feels cut off from its roots by its loss of language, and Chicano writers have no commercial outlets for their works), she said she wants desperately to create a literature for Chicano young people which will allow them "to feel part of the world." From her own experience in school and as a witness to the problems of minority students she understands the value of responding to this need.

References:

Wolfgang Binder, ed., *Partial Autobiographies: Interviews with Twenty Chicano Poets* (Erlangen: Palm & Enke, 1985), pp. v-xviii, 221-229;

Juan Bruce-Novoa, "Bernice Zamora y Lorna Dee Cervantes: Una estética feminista," *Revista Iberoamericana*, 51 (July-December 1985): 565-573;

Bruce-Novoa, "Bernice Zamora" in his *Chicano Authors: Inquiry by Interview* (Austin & London: University of Texas Press, 1980), pp. 203-218;

Bruce-Novoa, *Chicano Poetry: A Response to Chaos* (Austin: University of Texas Press, 1982), pp. 160-184;

Cordelia Candelaria, *Chicano Poetry: A Critical Introduction* (Westport, Conn.: Greenwood, 1986), pp. 146-156;

Parul Desai, "Interview with Bernice Zamora, a Chicana Poet," *Imagine*, 2 (Summer 1985): 26-39;

Joe Olvera, "A Critical Study of Bernice Zamora's *Restless Serpents*," *American Book Review*, 2 (October 1979): 20;

Elizabeth J. Ordóñez, "The Concept of Cultural Identity in Chicana Poetry," *Third Woman*, 2, no. 1 (1984): 75-82;

Tey Diana Rebolledo, "Soothing Restless Serpents: The Dreaded Creation and Other Inspirations in Chicana Poetry," *Third Woman*, 2, no. 1 (1984): 83-102;

Salvador Rodriguez del Pino, *Interview with Bernice Zamora* (Santa Barbara: Center for Chicano Studies, University of California, 1977), videotape;

Rodriguez del Pino, "La poesía chicana: Una nueva trayectoria," in *The Identification and Analysis of Chicano Literature*, edited by Francisco Jiménez (New York: Bilingual, Editorial Bilingüe, 1979), pp. 68-89;

Marta E. Sánchez, *Contemporary Chicana Poetry: A Critical Approach to an Emerging Literature* (Berkeley & Los Angeles: University of California Press, 1985), pp. 214-268;

Sánchez, "Inter-sexual and Intertextual Codes in the Poetry of Bernice Zamora," *MELUS*, 7, no. 3 (1980): 55-68;

Sánchez, "Judy Lucero and Bernice Zamora: Two Dialectical Statements in Chicano Poetry," *Revista Chicano-Riqueña*, 6 (Autumn 1978): 64-73.

Papers:

Zamora's papers are in the Mexican American Collections at Stanford University.

Appendices

Chicano History

Chicano Language

Literatura Chicanesca: The View From Without

Chicano History

Carl R. Shirley
University of South Carolina

In order to comprehend and appreciate any aspect of Chicano existence, including literature, it is necessary to understand some elements of Chicano history, which in turn lead to Mexican and pre-Columbian history. Philip D. Ortego pointed out in the *Nation* (15 September 1969) that "no history of a people has been more obscure, more apocryphal, and so utterly misapprehended by the majority of Anglo-Americans than the history of Mexican-Americans, for they continue to exist in the United States as an 'invisible minority.'" By contrast, Chicano writers and many of their readers have a deep awareness of their past because Chicano lives have been so shaped and influenced by events of the last five centuries that their past is very much an active part of their present (as evidenced by its frequent portrayal in literature). The contemporary Chicano, searching deeply for his heritage, finds its source in ancient Indian civilizations, principally those of the Aztec and the Maya who once flourished in Mexico and Central America.

The stories, legends, customs, and even deities of the Aztec and Maya are frequently significant to the Chicano of today. For example, the Aztec story of the founding of Tenochtitlán (Mexico City), part history and part legend, is in relationship to the Chicano as the stories of U.S. frontier heroes such as Daniel Boone and Davy Crockett are to the Anglo-American. The name *Aztec* is derived from Aztlán (the place of the herons), a mythical land to the north of present-day Mexico which the Indians regarded as the cradle of their race. According to the story, the Aztec, after years of searching for a promised paradise, were finally led by the war god Huitzilopochtli to the shores of Lake Texcoco in Mexico's high central plateau. One of the members of the tribe fell into the water and, while at the bottom of the lake, heard a voice which instructed him to search for a place where an eagle perched on a cactus held a serpent in its beak. The Indians were to construct their city on that site. Later, priests found such an eagle on an island in Lake Texcoco and established Tenochtitlán (near the cactus), which has grown into Mexico City. The story is well-known to many Chicanos who readily recognize the Mexican flag which bears a picture of the eagle, the serpent, and the cactus. The term *Aztlán* is also significant because many Chicanos believe that the "place to the north" was located in what is now the southwestern United States. Aztlán has become a rallying cry, a banner, and a unifying symbol of the deep racial and cultural roots of Americans of Mexican descent. It is a frequent reference in all literary forms, providing the writer and his public with an image reflecting a language, history, and culture significantly different from those of the Anglo.

The Spanish explorer and conqueror Hernán Cortés (1485-1547) invaded the land which is now Mexico and vanquished the Aztec between the years 1519 and 1521, bringing Spanish blood, language, religion, and customs. Cortés and his troops were able to overcome the much more numerous natives partly because of the legend of Quetzalcóatl, a fair-skinned, bearded, and absent god whom the Aztec expected to return at about the time of Cortés's arrival in 1519. Taking the invader to be Quetzalcóatl, the efficient Aztec leader, Moctezuma II (1466-1520), treated Cortés like a god and presented him with silver and gold. Cortés took Moctezuma hostage and ruled through him for a time until forced to withdraw by Charles I, the Spanish monarch. In the absence of Cortés, the Aztec rebelled and Moctezuma was killed. Upon his return a fierce battle was fought on 30 June 1520, called by the Spanish *noche triste* (sad night) because so many of their number died. Cortés attacked again, this time defeating the Aztec and their new leader, Cuauhtémoc (Falling Eagle, 1495-1525), who thus was the last Indian ruler of Mexico and, for that reason, has been revered by Mexicans and many Chicanos. Moctezuma, Cuauhtémoc, and Cortés are names frequently encountered in Chicano literature.

Mexico, including the region now known as the American Southwest, eventually became populated by mestizos, people of mixed Spanish and Indian ancestry. The merging of two peoples to form *La Raza* (The Race), a distinct ethnic group, is an important historical factor which serves to differentiate the Mexican-American from the Anglo-American. On the eastern coast of the United States settlers drove the native Indians out, or else isolated them by placing them on reservations. Usually, entire families came to settle and there was little or no mixing of races. By contrast in Mexico, mostly soldiers and priests came to the newly discovered lands with the intention of taking what they could and returning to Spain. The priests, of course, desired to teach the natives the Catholic religion. The men who remained in Mexico dominated the native peoples with their own culture, language, religion, and values; but they also took cultural elements from the Indians, and thus a blend of the two races and cultures was created. *La Raza* is a term frequently mentioned in Chicano letters. It immediately invokes the Mexican past while at the same time it suggests the values and aspirations of the Chicano people.

Another important historical Mexican symbol seen in many aspects of Chicano life and literature is that of *La Virgen de Guadalupe*, the patron of Mexico. Chicanos are familiar with the story of the miraculous appearance of the Virgin Mary to the Aztec peasant Juan Diego near the hill of Tepeyac in what is now Mexico City in the year 1531. She instructed him to go to the bishop with news that she wanted a church built on that site, which formerly had held a temple in honor of Tonanztín, the Aztec mother of all gods. The bishop refused to believe the peasant, who returned to Tepeyac where the Virgin reappeared and repeated her wishes. Again the bishop sent Juan Diego away, this time with instructions that he bring proof of her existence. On the 12th of December, still a day of celebration in Mexico and among Chicanos, the Virgin once again appeared before Diego and instructed him to climb the hill and cut some roses for delivery to the bishop as proof. Juan, faithful yet doubting that he would find roses because it was winter, and the arid land produced only cacti, complied, and discovered that there were indeed roses. Moreover, he presented them to the bishop wrapped in his *tilma* (cloak), and as Juan opened it, revealing the roses, there also appeared on the *tilma* a full-length portrait of the Virgin of Guadalupe. The bishop took the cloak, complied with the request to build a chapel near Tepeyac, and placed the image in it. This story has been well-known for generations, and there are constant references to the Virgin of Guadalupe in Chicano literature; many Chicanos today have an image of her somewhere in their homes. The shrine in Mexico City is the country's holiest, and all religious Mexicans and many devout Chicanos dream of visiting it.

Mexican Independence Day, 16 September, is also widely celebrated among the Chicanos. It was on that date in the year 1810 in the town of Dolores, in the Mexican state of Guanajuato, that priest Miguel Hidalgo y Costilla (1753-1811), called the Father of Independence, uttered the famous *Grito de Dolores* (Cry of Dolores), call to arms against the Spanish. His words, *"Viva Nuestra Señora de Guadalupe y muera el mal gobierno!"* (Long live Our Lady of Guadalupe and death to bad government), became a rallying cry for independence. The bell from Hidalgo's church, whose ringing accompanied the call to arms, has become a symbol of Mexican freedom. In most large cities in the American Southwest and in many small towns 16 September is a holiday, with celebrations as enthusiastic as those on the Fourth of July.

After finally winning independence from Spain in 1821 Mexico suffered under several poor rulers and increasing problems in its northern region. It was during the first term of president Antonio López de Santa Anna (1794-1876) that the nation began to have serious trouble maintaining its border with the burgeoning United States. Mexico's northern provinces of Alta California, part of Sonora, Nuevo Mexico, and Texas were far removed physically from the capital city. These regions were thus not very involved in or concerned about Mexico's struggle for independence. Residents were pursuing trade and other contact with the United States, especially in Texas. Anglo-Americans, after the Louisiana Purchase from France in 1803, were moving steadily westward and settling in eastern Texas. They were driven and encouraged by the doctrine of Manifest Destiny, a belief that Providence intended that the United States should settle and control the entire landmass between the Atlantic and the Pacific oceans. The settlers' efforts were aided by incompetent rulers in Mexico whose malfeasance was exacerbated by the difficulty of governing a huge geographic area. The sparse Mexican settlement in the north and the Mexican government's encouragement of foreign colonization as a means of solving the problem of underpopulation served to encourage the doctrine's followers. Mexico issued some twenty *empresario* land grants to the United States citizens, who were obliged to recruit settlers. Under the terms of these grants, all people had either to be, or to become, Catholics and swear an oath of loyalty to Mexico. Thus, by around 1830 the population of Texas consisted of only about four thousand Spanish-speaking Mexicans but more than twenty-five thousand Anglos, most of the latter contemptuous of all things Mexican. Fueled by internal conflicts between supporters of federalist versus centralist forms of government in Mexico, matters in Texas grew worse until finally complete independence from Mexico was declared on 2 March 1836. An armed struggle followed which included the battle of the Alamo in San Antonio, Texas, in 1836. Mexican President Santa Anna himself led the army against what his government viewed as a seditious revolt led by traitors and rebels. At the Alamo Mexican troops destroyed 187 Texans fighting under a Mexican flag and commanded by Col. William Travis. Eventually Santa Anna was defeated and captured; this led to the Treaty of Velasco in which he exchanged land for his freedom. Texas thus became a recognized independent government, eventually annexed to the United States in March of 1845.

Meanwhile, President James K. Polk, an aggressive expansionist, had attempted to purchase the areas now called California and New Mexico, but was unsuccessful. He sent Gen. Zachary Taylor to Texas to provoke a war, which broke out in May of 1846. American soldiers landed at Veracruz in southeastern Mexico in March of 1847 and pushed inland to Mexico City under the command of Gen. Winfield Scott. They assaulted the fortress of Chapultepec which was defended by military college cadets, six of whom gave their lives, becoming national heroes known as *Los Niños Héroes* (The Child Heroes). The war eventually ended a year later with the signing of the Treaty of Guadalupe Hidalgo on 2 February 1848, in which Mexico ceded to the United States the territory now forming the states of California, Arizona, New Mexico, Utah, and half of Colorado. For fifteen million dollars Mexico also relinquished any claims it still had on Texas and agreed on the Rio Grande River as an international boundary. In 1853 President Franklin Pierce bought an additional forty-five thousand square miles in Arizona and New Mexico, in what is now called the Gadsden Purchase. Thus, since independence from Spain in 1821, Mexico had lost or sold about fifty percent of her original national territory. Most contemporary Chicanos, certainly those who read the literature or those who are politically active, know the history of Mexico's lost land and the Treaty of Guadalupe Hidalgo.

The eighty thousand people left behind in the new territory were guaranteed certain rights by this treaty. It gave them one year in which to choose between going to Mexico or remaining as U.S. citizens; only about two thousand left. The treaty guaranteed the new citizens the "enjoyment of all the rights of citizens of the United States according to the principles of the Constitution; and in the meantime [they] shall be maintained and protected in the free enjoyment of their liberty and property, and secured in the free exercise of their religion without restriction." The fact that the United States government failed to uphold the provisions of this treaty has long been a problem for Chicanos, and this betrayal has been reflected in Chicano literature. Wayne Moquin and Charles Van Doren discuss the Treaty of Guadalupe Hidalgo in their book *A Documentary History of the Mexican Americans* (1972) and provide the following commentary:

> To say that the treaty had been honored *only* in the breach is an exaggeration, because the religious rights of the Chicano have been fairly consistently protected. But in no other area have their rights been paid much heed. As the only minority, apart from the Indians, ever acquired by conquest, the Mexican Americans have been subjected to economic, social, and political discrimination, as well as a great deal of violence at the hands of their Anglo conquerors. During the period from 1865 to 1920, there were more lynchings of Mexican Americans in the Southwest than of black Americans in the Southeast. But the worst violence has been the unrelenting discrimination against the cultural heritage—the language and customs—of the Mexican Americans, coupled with the economic exploitation of the entire group. Property rights were guaranteed, but not protected, by either the federal or state governments. Equal protection under the law has consistently been a mockery in the Mexican-American communities. Economically, the Mexican Americans have been relegated, both legally and by informal arrangement, to the bottom of the labor ladder. Yet, for all of the inequities perpetrated upon the Mexican Americans, the Treaty of Guadalupe remains the key document for the understanding of the place of this minor-

ity with American society. The fact that most of its provisions remain to be fulfilled is both the complaint and the hope of Mexican Americans, as the movement toward social justice slowly gains ground in the United States among those for whom the rewards of American life have been all too meager.

Since the current status and daily existence of most Chicanos can be linked to the failed promises of the Treaty of Guadalupe Hidalgo, it figures strongly in Chicano literature, both as a historical event and as a commentary on the Chicano's place in American society.

Another event of significance to the Spanish-speaking citizens of the American Southwest was a battle which took place in Puebla, a city southeast of Mexico City, in 1862. Cinco de Mayo (the fifth of May), commemorates a victory of Mexican soldiers over the French who had invaded Mexico in 1861. It was during this troubled period that Benito Juárez (1806-1872), a full-blooded Zapotec Indian from the southern state of Oaxaca, struggled desperately against the French imperialists. Although his government was forced to the northern frontier during Archduke Maximilian of Austria's reign as emperor of Mexico from 1864 to 1867, he was elected president in 1867. Cinco de Mayo has long been widely celebrated among Chicanos, and in many cities there are fiestas and parades, frequently with much support from Anglos. The irony of Anglo participation in this event is discussed by Carey McWilliams in his classic history, *North From Mexico; The Spanish-speaking People of the United States* (1949), which characterizes Anglo celebrations of Mexican holidays as part of a phenomenon he calls "fantasy heritage." He defines this as a romanticization and mythification of the "Spanish" history of a state such as California where mythical grandees are honored on the fifth of May, while their Mexican-American descendants are neglected on a daily basis. When the Chicano celebrates Cinco de Mayo he recognizes the true significance of the French defeat at Puebla: the victory of the masses of Mexico—the lower classes, the downtrodden—over the upper-class Europeans. Another ironic aspect of the holiday lies in the fact that many Chicanos view themselves as oppressed by the majority Anglo culture which has invaded what once was their land, just as the French invaded Mexico. It is important to remember that Benito Juárez came from the very lowest class in Mexico—the Indian—and was able to rise to the presidency of his country. It is no surprise

that his name appears frequently in Chicano literature, often paired with those of Abraham Lincoln or John F. Kennedy, other Chicano heroes.

Porfirio Díaz (1830-1915), after opposing Juárez in his bid for the presidency in 1867 and again in 1871, finally succeeded in the elections of 1876 and held the position of president until forced from office in 1911. Although Díaz is given credit for doing much to modernize his country—he helped develop railroads, industry, communications, the banking system, and waterworks—his rule was dictatorial and he was responsible for the fact that ninety percent of Mexico's citizens remained landless. His programs kept the majority of property in the hands of the wealthy. The poor masses were forced to look elsewhere for a means of earning money or obtaining food, and the country to the north became their principal escape after 1890. Mexicans started coming to the United States in large numbers, a tide of migration which has ebbed and flowed over the years and has contributed greatly to the Chicano population of the Southwest.

During the early years of this century it was quite natural for Mexicans to come to the United States, particularly to the Southwest, because that land had been part of their country for many years. Many scholars have characterized the process of immigration as one of "migration." Unlike European or Oriental immigrants, the Mexican did not leave behind his language, customs, food, and other elements of his culture; he merely moved, physically, to another region, only technically to another country. That region was, in many respects including geography, identical to the one he left behind. McWilliams said that the political boundary between the United States and Mexico is "one of the most unrealistic borders to be found in the Western Hemisphere." Joel Garreau, in his book *The Nine Nations of North America* (1981), calls the United States-Mexican border region *Mexamerica* and states that the "Anglo world is the latest invader of these parts, not the Indian, Mexican and Spanish. It's the borders that have moved, not the founding cultures. There are great numbers of Hispanics in the Southwest who can't be told by ignorant Anglos to go back where they came from. They *are* where they came from."

Mexican and Chicano lives were greatly changed by the events and leading figures of the revolution of 1910. This war was the first great social upheaval of the twentieth century, and it produced several leading figures who are often named in Chicano literature. Among the earliest leaders to voice dissatisfaction with Díaz's social and economic policies were liberals who had fled to San Antonio, Texas. The Flores Magón brothers (Enrique and Ricardo), Antonio Villarreal, and Juan Sarabia published a newspaper there, *Regeneración* (Regeneration), with much criticism of Mexican policies. In the 1910 Mexican presidential elections Francisco Madero (1873-1913) ran against Díaz and was subsequently jailed. After his release he went to San Antonio, Texas, where he planned to invade his country. Meanwhile, the Flores Magón brothers had moved to Los Angeles, California, to organize and lead an invasion of their own. In northern Mexico, Madero's followers, among them Venustiano Carranza (1859-1920) and Francisco (Pancho) Villa (1877-1923), pushed the revolutionary movement southward until Díaz finally resigned and fled to exile in Europe. Madero quickly won the presidency.

In the first phase of the long revolution, Madero was the new president, but confusion and conflict reigned. There was great distrust among the leading figures. Madero was not a good administrator, and in his first four months there were three armed upheavals. The largest revolt was led by Emiliano Zapata (1877?-1919), one of the great leaders from the south. He was not satisfied with Madero's policies and practices; he especially felt that the president did not do enough to restore land to the Indian peasants. Madero sent one of his loyal followers, Victoriano Huerta (1854-1916), to capture Zapata, but to no avail as Zapata simply hid in his familiar mountains. Later, Huerta conspired with Felix Díaz (nephew of Porfirio Díaz), and they eventually forced Madero and his vice-president, Jose María Pino Suárez, to resign. Madero and Pino Suárez were arrested and later shot, ostensibly while attempting to escape. Huerta became president and remained so for seventeen months, an extremely bloody period in Mexical history.

Like Madero, Huerta had plenty of opposition. The first to declare against him was from the northern state of Coahuila, where Venustiano Carranza issued a proclamation called the Plan of Guadalupe which called for the president's resignation. Other northern rebels included Alvaro Obregón (1880-1928), a scientific soldier called "The Centaur of the North," and Pancho Villa, a semi-literate, extremely competent, and popular ex-bandit. All three leaders fought numerous battles, but they were united only by their desire to unseat Huerta. When they finally succeeded the leaders of the three northern factions and Zapata in the south were at odds as to who was to be the new president. Zapata and Villa took turns dominating Mexico City with their troops, but anarchy prevailed and they eventually left. Obregón was supporting Carranza who was eventually recognized by the United States. Villa, defeated finally at the battle of Celaya, by 1915 had retreated to the north where he raided the town of Columbus, New Mexico. Carranza called a constitutional convention in 1917 and sent an emissary to appease Zapata, still not satisfied with land reform. Unappeased, Zapata was later ambushed and killed. Meanwhile, Obregón had been gathering support, eventually mustering enough troops to meet Carranza in battle. Carranza managed to escape, but was killed in May of 1920. Obregón became president and the long and complicated revolution was at last over. This first social revolution of the twentieth century was a monumental struggle with any leading figures. It obviously was significant in Mexico's history, but it also played an equally large role in Chicano history. Its importance cannot be underestimated. Matt S. Meier and Feliciano Rivera, in their study *The Chicanos: A History of Mexican Americans* (1972), summarize:

> The 1910 revolution, a period of great violence and confusion in Mexican history, directly affected the Southwest. An estimated one million Mexicans lost their lives in the decade of fighting, and a large-scale displacement of people took place. Thousands fled from the countryside into the large cities of Mexico, while at the same time other thousands fled from the central portions of Mexico northward to the United States. No one knows precisely how many Mexicans were involved in this great exodus; one estimate holds that more than one million Mexicans crossed over into the United States between 1910 and 1920.

While Anglo-Americans know little about the Mexican Revolution except perhaps the name of Pancho Villa, many Chicanos are well acquainted with all the major participants and causes, since most had relatives involved in the struggle. Because it was a fight for social equality, something many Chicanos feel they still do not have in the United States, the revolution assumes an important role in contemporary Chicano history and is frequently mentioned in literature.

World War I (1914-1918) holds special significance for Mexican Americans because it provided, for the first time, an impetus for them to move away from their transitional jobs in mining, agriculture, and railroads. Government work, usually in construction or factories, provided employment, with many positions in locales outside of the Southwest, notably the Midwest and Northeast. There were also negative effects of the war, among them the Selective Service Act of 1917 which caused many immigrants and their families to return to Mexico. Although a large number of Chicanos served in the U.S. armed forces, they were subjected to much suspicion and discrimination from Anglos, particularly in Texas. This tension was exacerbated by events such as Pancho Villa's raid on Columbus, New Mexico, in 1917 and Gen. John J. Pershing's subsequent invasion of Mexico. There was also the famous Zimmerman letter, in which Germany promised to restore to Mexico the lands lost by the Guadalupe Hidalgo Treaty if they would join forces with them against the United States. Mexico refused, but the offer caused some doubts in Anglo circles about the loyalty of U.S. citizens of Mexican descent and spurred racial disharmony.

It was during the period between the world wars that Mexican Americans first began to organize societies for mutual help and protection. Some associations, such as the League of United Latin American Citizens (LULAC), founded in 1929, were politically oriented and provided leadership in the struggle for civil rights. LULAC was essentially in favor of assimilation, to the point of advocating abandonment of the Spanish language. Nevertheless, the *LULAC News* and similar publications of other organizations, along with the many periodicals and many Spanish-language newspapers that became popular, published poetry, short stories, and nonfiction, thus providing an outlet for aspiring writers.

During the Great Depression many Mexicans returned to Mexico. Prior to the 1930s there had been a scarcity of cheap labor in the United States, and Mexicans had been welcomed. They contributed greatly to local economies, particularly in the agricultural communities of the Southwest. With the vast unemployment in all sectors of society during the Depression, it was convenient to get rid of Mexicans because of job competition. It was quickly forgotten, if it had been recognized at all, that the prosperity in the Southwest in the first three decades of the century was due in large measure to the labor of Mexi-

cans and Mexican-Americans. An increasing Anglo desire to deport Chicano workers stemmed from the involvement of many of them in the labor movement. Because of their attempts to better their working conditions, they were no longer perceived as docile and, as a consequence, became undesirable.

As so well depicted in John Steinbeck's novel *The Grapes of Wrath* (1939), many lower-class Anglos were forced from their homes in the dust bowl or other hard-hit regions, and they headed west in search of any sort of work to support their families. Since the only available jobs were usually agricultural, these new migrants were in search of work traditionally performed by Chicanos or Mexicans. The problem of getting rid of Mexicans was made difficult because of the government red tape involved in deportation of illegal aliens or because many had children who had been born in the United States who were, therefore, citizens. A system was devised whereby Mexicans could express a "willingness" to return and were provided a free trip to Mexico City. It has been estimated that almost fifty percent of those returning to Mexico in the 1930s were American born. Later, when some attempted to come back, they were informed that they were no longer citizens, because they had either voted in a Mexican election or had served in the military.

World War II (1939-1945) brought many Mexicans back to the United States. The booming economy demanded labor just as many men were being inducted into the military. In August 1942 the U.S. and Mexican governments reached a formal agreement whereby Mexican labor could be recruited for work on this side of the border during the war. By the end of 1943 more than fifty thousand of these so-called braceros were employed. What began as a temporary measure lasted until 1965, and in the second phase of what became known as the Bracero Program, from 1948 until 1965, between four and five million Mexican citizens participated. Since the majority were involved in agriculture, the work tended to be seasonal and the wages were low. Living conditions in migrant camps were frequently deplorable, and there were many complaints concerning food and housing. There was also widespread discrimination. Many of the daily experiences and problems of life in pursuit of the crops have been depicted in Chicano literature; indeed, one of the major contemporary themes in prose, poetry, and drama is the migratory experience, and many writers have firsthand knowledge to draw on or have been told of the experiences of their parents or grandparents.

World War II was a turning point in the history of the Chicanos. Over three hundred thousand served in the military, with seventeen winning the Congressional Medal of Honor. Many former soldiers were eligible for the G.I. Bill, which provided them with educational opportunities or business loans. Others had gained experience working with Anglos and had done much to better race relations. Meier and Rivera sum up the positive effects of World War II as follows:

> Education, acculturation and wartime experiences modified the attitudes of younger Mexican Americans but had less effect on the older generation. Spanish-language newspapers, magazines, and radio stations, as well as greater possibilities for travelling to Mexico, all helped to preserve the Mexican life style. Because World War II provided Mexican Americans with new views, needs and desires, they became increasingly motivated to attain higher economic and social levels; toward this end they began to form their own organizations and to seek ways of developing ethnic political power.

The period between the end of World War II and the 1960s Chicano political movement was one in which many people sought to assimilate, to join American society as other ethnic groups had done, virtually stripping themselves of their cultural heritage. In the early 1960s, fueled by the apparent gains of the black civil rights movement, large numbers of Chicanos emerged from the conservative postwar years with new ideas of social and political equality. The Vietnam War, coming as it did at about the same time as the Chicano movement, provided much subject matter for Chicano writers. The number of Chicanos participating in Vietnam and earlier in the Korean War (1950-1953) was far out of proportion to their numbers in the general population. As in World War II, many served bravely and were decorated for their heroism, but they still suffered from social and economic oppression.

Other events of the 1960s provided greater political, social, cultural, and economic gains for the Chicano; this period stirred great literary activity, with the majority of works political and social in nature. In 1962 César Chávez began organizing the first agricultural union in history, the United Farmworkers Union. In New Mexico,

Reies López Tijerina founded the *Alianza Federal* (Federal Alliance) in 1963 with the purpose of regaining lands lost after the Treaty of Guadalupe Hidalgo. In 1965 César Chávez's fledgling union began a grape strike in Delano, California, which prompted dramatist Luis Valdez to organize *El Teatro Campesino* (The Farm Workers' Theater) which kindled interest in and gave birth to modern Chicano theater. At about the same time poet-boxer Rodolfo "Corky" González founded the Crusade for Justice in Denver, Colorado, as a program to provide cultural activities, social services, education, and a base for urban reform among Chicanos. González's epic poem *Yo Soy Joaquín/I Am Joaquín* was written specifically for distribution by the Crusade for Justice. In 1967 *La Raza Unida*, a political party, was formed in Texas to coordinate Chicano civil rights activities in the Southwest. In 1969 the Crusade for Justice met with more than fifteen hundred young people in the First National Chicano Youth Conference and adopted a call for Chicano liberation, *El Plan de Aztlán*. (The next year they met again, this time with thirty-five hundred participants.) Among other important groups established in the 1960s and early 1970s were MECHA (The Chicano Student Movement of Aztlán), and MAYO (The Mexican American Youth Organization). Many of the political organizations published newspapers, in both English and Spanish, as a means of reporting their activities. Along with news and information, these periodicals included literature, principally poetry.

The 1960s were marked by a large quantity of literary material which expressed the assertion of a new cultural and political identity. Chicano literary criticism also took a giant step forward in the late 1960s as literary journals were established. In 1967 *El Grito: A Journal of Contemporary Mexican American Thought* was issued in Berkeley, California. In 1969 *El Espejo/The Mirror*, the first Chicano literature anthology, was published.

Another important product of the political movement was the establishment, beginning in the late 1960s, of Chicano Studies programs at many colleges and universities, mainly in the Southwest, and the inclusion of Chicano-related courses in ethnic studies programs elsewhere. There was increased academic attention to all areas of Chicano life, including the arts and literature. Chicano Studies provided a greater need for printed material, and Chicano publishing houses were created, some small and evanescent, others larger and still in existence. While many of today's major Anglo-controlled firms will issue nonliterary studies on the Chicano, a Chicano novel, book of poetry, or drama collection printed and distributed by these companies is a rare item. The majority of Chicano literature has been sold through Chicano-controlled houses. Outside academic circles, Chicano literature is not generally known to the non-Chicano, nor is it likely to be reviewed or even mentioned by the establishment concerns. Thus a rich and vibrant facet of contemporary American literature has gone and still goes largely unnoticed.

Because of federal programs such as affirmative action, Chicanos of the 1970s and 1980s have made social and political gains, but they still have not achieved full equality. The last census reveals the median Hispanic family income in the United States to be $16,140, seventy-one percent of the median white salary. More and more Chicanos are attending and graduating from college, but their population ratio in higher education is far below that of Anglos. After 1970, according to historian John R. Chávez, the Chicano movement entered a period of consolidation: "Having had many of its hopes and grievances dramatized, the Chicano community was gradually able to take advantage of the advances the movement had attained, especially in education and self-awareness."

The close relationship the Chicano writer has always had with his historical, social, and political situation has been summarized by Rudolfo Anaya and Antonio Márquez in their introduction to a collection of short stories:

Chicano literature has undergone a phenomenal growth during the past two decades. Working both within and outside the context of the social-political movement known as El Movimiento, contemporary Chicano writers have created a body of work that has rightfully taken its place in American and world literature. The Chicano Movement was not only a declaration of Chicanos' right to their heritage within the American society, it was also an avenue for literary creativity. Writers and artists have attempted to give form to the aspirations of the Movement in poetry, drama, story, film, song, and other aesthetic media, and Chicano writers seized the impetus of the movement to forge a contemporary literature. This role required a responsibility and commitment on the part of the writer as he sought to capture the dimensions, nuances, subtleties and paradoxes of Chicano life and culture. The writers of the movement met the challenge, and the literary upsurge brought forth accomplished writers whose unique voices, intrepid visions, and passionate intensity created the literature of El Movimiento.

The Chicano voice, long proud of its culture and history, has begun to be heard, and it is still speaking. Especially in the Southwestern states, Mexican-Americans have asserted themselves politically, and this assertion has caused Anglo politicians to take notice. The history of the Chicano people is intriguing, and the quality of their literature is fine; the increasing impact of the late-twentieth-century Chicano on the American society has become a significant one.

Chicano Language

Erlinda Gonzales-Berry and Shaw N. Gynan
University of New Mexico

Within the Mexican-American community there is an entire range of language varieties. The recently arrived monolingual Spanish speaker from Mexico may live next to a fourth generation family in which the youngest children neither speak nor understand Spanish. The Chicano may speak standard English or what is commonly referred to as Chicano English. The Chicano may come from a family which settled on the land centuries before the arrival of Anglo colonists and may continue to speak a language variety reminiscent of Spanish spoken at the time of the European invasion of the Americas.

This multitude of tongues, the heritage of today's Chicano, also serves as the linguistic medium of expression for writers who wish to capture in their works of prose and poetry the essence and drama of life in the Chicano community. The response to the multifaceted society in which the Chicano writer lives is as predictably complex and polymorphous as is the linguistic heritage.

The continued presence of the Spanish language in the Southwest of the United States today is in part the result of Spanish and then Mexican domination of the area for a period of three hundred years. By the end of the sixteenth century the Spanish conquistadores made their way into what is now New Mexico. In 1610 Sante Fe was established and today holds the distinction of being the first capital city in the continental United States. The Spanish entrenchment in the Southwest resulted in the founding of major Spanish-speaking centers in what is now New Mexico, Texas, and California. The Spanish-speaking population in that region by the time of the Treaty of Guadalupe Hidalgo in 1848 was eighty thousand.

Although the treaty provided certain guarantees of preservation of cultural integrity and individual rights, no specific mention was made of preservation of the Spanish language. Nevertheless, the Spanish language continued to flourish in the Hispanic Southwest. For example, between 1848 and 1900 over sixty-five Spanish language newspapers were known to circulate in the New Mexico territory and legislative sessions of that region were conducted in both Spanish and English throughout this period. In southern California laws were still being published in Spanish as late as 1876. Evidence of abundant Spanish language literary activity during this same period is still being documented.

After the completion of the transcontinental railroad in 1869 Anglo immigration to the Southwest increased, and Chicanos were the minority except in New Mexico; however, at the turn of the century large numbers of Mexicans fled war-torn Mexico and migrated to the Southwest. The continuous flow of Mexicans through the twentieth century has reinforced and nourished Chicano culture and contributed to the continued vitality of spoken Spanish in the Southwest. In more recent years Mexican immigrants have settled in the Midwest, and it is not uncommon to encounter large urban enclaves of Mexican-Americans who continue to preserve Spanish even as they acquire English.

Despite the renewal of the vitality of the Spanish language through immigration, the influx of English speakers contributed to the hastening of the delegitimation of Spanish because English became the language of commerce, government, and education. Certainly the federal government felt similarly about English in the nineteenth century, since it postponed New Mexico's entry into the union until its population demonstrated sufficient English ability. The last Spanish territory to be conquered culturally and linguistically, New Mexico entered the Union in 1912. By that time English had come to be used for all official and public purposes, whereas Spanish was limited to informal situations, among friends and family members. The linguistic concept of *diglossia*, originally proposed by Charles Ferguson to define a situation in which a standard language is superimposed on a local language, has been extended to include those situations in which the local language continues to be used in the face of a superimposed language from conquerers; this is the case with Spanish in the Southwest. Spanish is used to communicate with older members of the household, with friends, and neighbors. English tends to dominate almost exclusively the areas of commerce, education, health care, media, government, and increasingly, religion, though the need for Spanish in these domains becomes more apparent as the Mexican-American population increases with each census count.

Maintenance of Spanish is found in settings where strong family and community ties result in the continued use of the language. Spanish is spoken more often among marginalized populations in which members have relatively little access to the mainstream culture. Thus, Spanish maintenance is to be expected among those communities most isolated or economically marginalized. Regarding the correlation between marginalization and language maintenance Rosaura Sánchez observes, "To the degree then that Chicanos have been isolated or set apart, economically and socially, they maintained ample use of their Spanish language varieties. To the degree that they have incorporated into English-dominant employment categories and moved up the income scale, they have been acculturated, probably moved out of the barrio and into integrated communities and lost significant use of the Spanish language, . . ." Even where the use of Spanish has been maintained (that is, is predominant), language shift has occurred. Language shift refers to the change within a community from one language to another. During the intermediate stage of language shift, when both English and Spanish are spoken in the community, the Chicano may use both, even in the same sentence. This use of two languages is known as code-switching and is a result of and a predictor of language shift.

Despite the rapid shift from Spanish to English that is occurring in some areas, language maintenance is notable in others. Such maintenance is due in part to isolation and marginalization from the economic mainstream and to the constant flow of Spanish-speaking emigrants from Mexico who revitalize Spanish-speaking communities and provide Chicanos with more reasons and opportunities to speak the language. The latest expressions and cultural innovations are imported, and the vitality of Spanish is guaranteed.

In addition to emigration and marginalization, Chicano pride also contributes to maintenance of Chicano Spanish. The Spanish language identifies community membership and serves as a vigorous symbol of cultural identity and loyalty. The imposition of standard Spanish and standard English is resisted with the realization that with increased political power is a right to language and identity. This cultural resistance has caused no small controversy. English-speaking powers often question the loyalty of those who claim their own language and cultural rights, and conservative Mexican-Americans loyal to Anglo-American values sometimes disassociate themselves from the group, viewing it as divisive and dangerous.

Since Spanish in the United States has become virtually excluded from the public domain, the written register of the language has been greatly reduced in comparison with that of English. Chicano Spanish has evolved apart from the influence of a school-supported standard; consequently it is a spoken and informal dialect and like other spoken dialects of Spanish, Chicano Spanish may be characterized by phonological reduction. Phonological reduction refers to a weaker or less tense pronunciation of a particular sound. For example, fricative consonants such as *d* and *b* may weaken to the point of disappearance as in the case of words like *estaba* (was), *usted* (you), *soldado* (soldier), which become *está*, *usté*, and *soldáu*. Complex verb conjugations may have been regularized or simplified. For example, whereas the standard imperfect form of the verb *decir* (to tell) is *decía* (telling) the regularized form often heard in the Chicano community is *dijía*. Regularizations are also found in irregular nouns, as in the commonly heard *la problema* (the problem), instead of the standard *el problema*. These phenomena appear throughout the Spanish-speaking world, but Chicano Spanish is different in that reduction and regularization are more universal, cutting across class lines, since the majority of its speakers have not been educated in Spanish and may not be familiar with the standard language. In other Spanish-speaking areas the phenomenon would occur among rural inhabitants, the less educated, or in informal situations.

Chicano Spanish traditionally contains archaic forms because of the physical isolation of New Spain's northernmost colonies from Mexico City. The generalized lack of formal education in Spanish has allowed certain sixteenth century forms to remain. Spanish in areas which have received large numbers of emigrants from Mexico in recent times does not tend to display this characteristic.

Daniel Cárdenas argues that the base of Chicano Spanish in general has been influenced by several Mexican varieties that can be divided into four subdialectal zones: Texas, New Mexico-southern Colorado, Arizona, and California with "overlapping occurring along the border state areas from the mouth of the Río Grande all the way to Baja California." However, Sánchez observes that it is impossible to isolate Spanish varieties by state or region because numerous varieties are spoken in every region. What is of far greater importance, she says, is the situation within which differing varieties are used. Important is the level of material wealth of the speaker, whether he resides in a rural or urban area, and the speaker's role in relationship to his listener.

Despite the effect of social variables on Chicano Spanish, language norms exist within a given Chicano community. Emigration, which accounts in part for variety, given that emigrants originate in different geographical and dialectal zones of Mexico, also constitutes a standardizing effect. Other agents or events which fulfill standardizing roles are radio and television, church services (where print is available in the form of hymnals or missals), and more recently, Spanish language advertising.

Caló, a subvariety of Spanish has developed among Chicano youth, partly in response to the generally negative attitude of society toward Chicano language and culture. Like other argots it is typically understandable only to members of a group and thus serves as a secret code and group identifier. In his *Social Functions of Language in a Mexican-American Community* (1972) George Barker notes that caló serves to distinguish certain Chicano youth, providing identity where none is forthcoming from the larger Anglo or Chicano communities. Mexican author Octavio Paz, in *The Labyrinth of Solitude* (1961), while hostile to pachuco (Mexican-American hipster) culture, recognizes that the need of Mexican-American youth for an identity was essential to the development of the pachuco movement in the late 1940s through the 1950s. Though caló was most popular in that era, it has continued to thrive. Caló, which derives its vocabulary from such diverse sources as Mexican argot, English slang, and black English, may not be comprehensible to the uninitiated: *gasofa pa' la ranfla* (gas for the car), *Ahi te guacho* (I'll be seeing you) and *¿Quiúbole vato?* (What's happening, man?) are just a few of the more commonly heard examples of caló. Most Chicanos know some caló, and many sprinkle their speech with caló expressions.

Among a substantial number of Chicano Spanish speakers, the influence of English is notable. Code-switching, the changing from one language to another, is posited by some anthropologists to constitute a new language norm. Among Chicanos, change from one language to another may occur within the same sentence, within a given conversation, or from situation to situation. Such switching is not a random phenomenon, but rather follows tacit linguistic conventions and limitations. An affective switch is triggered by topics that are culturally bound, thus requiring a switch to the culturally appropriate language. For example, *We spent the whole day haciendo tamáles at tia Lola's* (. . . . making tamales at Aunt Lola's) or *Te llamo esta noche a las seven thirty, ok?* (I'll call you tonight at . . . .).

Chicano Spanish, code-switching, and Chicano English all have been the object of scorn and derision. Mexicans refer to Chicano Spanish as *pocho* or *mocho*, words that refer critically to the influence of English on the language or to the rustic quality of Chicano Spanish. Code-switching is mockingly labeled *Tex-Mex* or *Spanglish*. Both these terms imply that code-switching is a local, even primitive jargon that does not enjoy the status of a language. English speakers have long made fun of Spanish-accented English, and Chicano Spanish is cast in the same mold. These pejorative attitudes are characteristic of any dominant social group toward the language of people excluded from mainstream society.

Despite the often unfavorable status of Chicano dialects they have survived and continue to flourish today. Chicano writers are exploring and exploiting Chicano Spanish in their creative works, thereby reinforcing the language both formally and as an important medium of expression of the Chicano experience. The sociopolitical activities of the Chicano movement of the 1960s and early 1970s showed the need for a strong sense of emotional and ideological cohesion based on a shared common denominator of ethnic identity and a perceived notion of cultural nationalism. Early in the 1960s poetry and drama became important instruments. Narrative fiction soon followed. The linguistic options available to Chicano writers at that moment were English, Spanish, and code-switching, with caló lending itself to elaboration within all three codes.

Despite the vigorous search of Chicano writers for personal and cultural identity and authenticity, it is perhaps ironic that some of them have written in English, the language that threatens to assimilate their cultural base. In this sense Chicano literature written in English can be compared to the literatures of other colonized peoples who have sought to reveal the evils of an oppressive colonial system and simultaneously to illuminate positive elements of a native culture and its spiritual and philosophical struggles with the dominant culture. Material written in English makes possible the dissemination of Chicano literature to broader audiences, thus enabling it to serve the didactic function of sensitizing those audiences. The use of English seems less of a contradiction in the works of writers like John Rechy, Sandra Cisneros, Ron Arias, Arturo Islas, Gary Soto, Berta Ornelas, Isabella Ríos, and Cherrie Moraga, who embrace issues and themes (homosexuality, magical realism, politics, feminism, the occult) beyond the purely cultural realm.

Those Chicano writers who turn to Spanish as the prime vehicle of expression, among them, Sabine Ulibarrí, Miguel Méndez, Aristeo Brito, Alejandro Morales, Tomás Rivera, Lucha Corpi, and Sergio Elizondo, propose to create at the aesthetic level a link with Hispanic belles lettres. Politically they can be said to seek to reject English and all it symbolizes, turning to Spanish as a means of seeking refuge from their alienation. For them, the use of Spanish must be seen as the appropriation of a weapon in a struggle for self-determination. In an unpublished 1977 letter Chicano novelist Brito commented that his hope for Chicano literature was that it be written in Spanish "for it is in that language that our authenticity lies." Aside from the cultural and political implications of using Spanish as a preferred mode for creative expression, in general these writers contribute to Chicano letters a highly self-conscious aesthetic innovation and experimentation which links them to current Latin American literary tendencies. This is particularly true of the works of Morales, Hinojosa-Smith, Brito, Méndez, Elizondo, and Margarita Cota-Cárdenas.

Notwithstanding the important contributions to Chicano literature of writers who use Spanish, their works constitute yet another contradiction in that the majority of these writers are Hispanists. Professors of Spanish and Spanish belles lettres, they possess the training which allows them to use the native language at a formal level. The fact that few Chicanos are literate in Spanish raises questions about the audience of Chicano writers. It may be said that their work represents an elitist tendency within Chicano letters. Their works are most likely destined to be read by students of Spanish and Latin American literature. Ulibarrí commented in an unpublished 1977 interview that "Chicano writers who write in Spanish are writers without a destiny." The fact that many of these works have appeared in books which include English translations is recognition by Chicano presses of the lack of a broad reading audience for Spanish language works. Literature written in Spanish depends on a community of Chicanos nourished on the cultural nationalism of the Chicano movement, and trained in bilingual programs which would allow them to read literature written in Spanish. The increased number of Chicano students in university Spanish classes seems to be a healthy indicator of increasing Spanish literacy.

The contradictions inherent in the use of English or Spanish disappear in literature written in a bilingual idiom. There exists no doubt regarding the implied audience, for those writers who select a bilingual code obviously write for Chicanos, or for readers who have internalized the grammar of Chicano code-switching. Chicano theater would simply not be credible if the dialogue were not bilingual (note that the effect is one of credibility and not of authenticity). Gary Keller correctly asserts that code-switching in bilingual literature is first and foremost stylistically and aesthetically designed and as such gives the writer license to depart from socially established norms. For example, in Luis Valdez's 1970 play *Bernabé* the Spanish words or phrases effectively open up a sociopolitical connotation: "O, simón! (. . . yeah!) I didn't mean it like that, carnal (brother). I meant you're a Chicano, you know? If people don't like the way you are, tengan pa' que se mantengan!" (. . . . let them try this on for size!). Angela de Hoyos uses code-switches in her poem "Café con leche" from *Chicano Poems for the Barrio* (1975) to mock Chicano males who prefer Anglos. She establishes a cultural framework by entitling and beginning the poem in Spanish. In order to emphasize the magnitude of the treachery, she switches to English, underscoring the cultural as well as personal nature of the betrayal. The code-switch to a Spanish diminutive (*gringuita*) belittles the Anglo accomplice. The switch to English, "all smiles," draws attention to what the poet may view as a foreign, or Anglo, cultural tendency to display one's personal life publicly. In the next stanza, the poetic voice returns to Spanish ostensibly to relieve the Chicano male of guilt for his act; however, the irony of this remark is highlighted by a return to a quasi-scientific examination in English of the cultural implications of his behavior ("Homogenization is a good way to dissolve differences and besides what's wrong with a beautiful race. . . ."). The irony of comments favorable to miscegenation is devastatingly clarified by the final code-switch of the poem: a reiteration of the title in Spanish, "Café con leche," by means of which the sexual tryst is condemned as a supreme act of treason against Chicanos.

In bilingual literature the contradictions inherent in the use of the language of the dominant culture disappear because English is not used according to standard rules. Chicano writers consciously and aggressively manipulate English subjecting the language to norms of the Spanish linguistic system. Those poets and dramatists, and more recently novelists (such as Hinojosa-Smith, Morales, and Cota-Cárdenas), who insist on the juxtaposition of Spanish and English within the same work have appropriated Spanish, the language which represents their cultural patrimony and English, the language which belongs to their political legacy, in order to create a special code. The implications of this process are political (in that it contributes to self-determination and self-definition), cultural (given the affective impact of code-switching on Chicano readers), and aesthetic (given that literary criticism has had to formulate criteria for evaluation).

Caló has likewise enriched the pages of Chicano literature, both in works with pachuco characters and as an influence on Chicano writers as a whole. Méndez, in *Peregrinos de Aztlán* (1974), masterfully re-creates the language of the pachuco, capturing its lexical flexibility, its playfulness, and its unusual expressive function: "La pinchi placa de Los, me apañaba de volada y como les rayaba la jefa, ése, a puro chingadazo me dejaban más boludo que un burro encanicado; me metían al tari por un mezquite. !Esele vato! ¿Qué pasadenas califa, no está mistiendo la birria?

Qué pasiones? (The goddamn L.A. pigs, they'd grab me for nuthin' and since I'd curse their old ladies, they'd beat the shit out of me and leave me swollen up like a horny donkey; they'd throw me in the slammer for thirty days. Hey, man! What's goin' on, ain't you got no more brew? What's happenin'?). In "Homenaje al Pachuco," for example, Raúl Salinas uses a number of linguistic registers; caló, standard English, and English slang are interwoven to present an ironic vision of an idealized discourse which has attempted to obfuscate the social pathos of the flesh-and-blood pachuco, who finds himself interned in prisons throughout the Southwest.

The proliferation of the last twenty years in Chicano literature, is owed in large part to the fact that Chicanos recognized the necessity of becoming involved in the means of production and distribution. With the advent of publishing houses such as Quinto Sol, Justa, Pajarito, Maize, Arte Público, Chicano literature likewise began to flourish. Economic reality, however, has dictated the demise of many of these presses. The same reality has prevented non-Chicano presses from taking advantage of the exciting aesthetic promise of the use of two or more languages in the creation of literature. The most critical and unfortunate issue facing Chicano writers today (particularly those who choose to write in codes other than English) is one of finding outlets for their works.

Literatura Chicanesca: The View From Without

Antonio Márquez
University of New Mexico

One of the aims of Chicano literature and criticism is to counter Mexican-American stereotypes in American literature. To that end the term *literatura chicanesca* is used to describe literary works about Chicanos written by non-Chicanos. The term was coined by Francisco Lomelí and Donaldo Urioste in their annotated critical bibliography, *Chicano Perspectives in Literature* (1976), where they point out that in evaluating the merits of literatura chicanesca "it must be kept in mind that the perspective is from the outside looking in." Cecil Robinson's *Mexico and The Hispanic Southwest in American Literature* (1977) argued that the perspective from outside the Chicano experience has significant value: "All societies need the corrective vision that the outsider, with his greater detachment, can sometimes supply.... American literature dealing with Mexican and Chicano culture now has the advantage of a double vision, the view from within and the view from without." Notwithstanding Robinson's endorsement, the historical record of literatura chicanesca does not give cause for celebration. Save a few extraordinary works, literatura chicanesca has historically perpetuated negative stereotypes. Marked by ethnocentrism, it has largely failed to represent Chicano life and culture honestly and judiciously.

The history of literatura chicanesca is almost as long as the history of American fiction. Timothy Flint's *Francis Berrian, or The Mexican Patriot* (1826), the first work of fiction dealing with Mexican themes published in the United States, appeared less than forty years after the first American novels were being written, at a time when the American connection to Mexico was still tenuous. The distortions and contrivances in Flint's novel augured ill for literatura chicanesca. Flint was never in the northern Mexican provinces he wrote about and relied instead on secondhand information to concoct his melodramatic work. Robert Montgomery Bird's *Calavar; or, The Knight of the Conquest* (1834) and *The Infidel; or, The Fall of Mexico* (1835) were similarly written without firsthand knowledge of Mexico. Replete with anachronisms, inaccuracies, and melodramatic excesses, these early novels now stand as quaint relics of a time when American writers visited a remote, seemingly exotic Mexico only in their imaginations.

The opening of the Santa Fe Trail in 1822, an event that profoundly influenced the history of the American West, had great bearing on United States-Mexico relations. In the 1830s and 1840s Anglo-Mexican commerce continually increased, and American traders, trappers, frontiersmen, and entrepreneurs steadily streamed into the northern provinces of Mexico. Of course, the trail also attracted its share of thieves, cutthroats, and fugitives, who tramped the road from Independence, Missouri, to Santa Fe in search of easy loot. But the historic and larger consequence of the opening of the trail was the meeting of two cultures, a process that tended to itensify antagonisms rather than ameliorate them. American literary images of Mexicans are deeply rooted in political and cultural conflicts that can be traced to the time of the Anglo-American entrance into the Hispanic Southwest. Carey McWilliams's seminal historical study, *North From Mexico: The Spanish-Speaking People of the United States* (1949), describes the rudiments of the clash: "From Brownsville to Los Angeles, the first impressions which the Anglo-Americans formed of the 'native' element were highly unfavorable.... In these early impressions, carefully embalmed, one can find the outline of the present-day stereotype of the Mexican." The seeds of discord planted in early nineteenth-century American literature helped spawn more than a century and a half of stereotypes.

Early American chroniclers and travel writers invariably described Mexicans in exceptionally unpleasant terms. The earliest of these chronicles, *The Personal Narrative of James O. Pattie* (1833), an account of Pattie's travels in the Mexican borderlands between 1824 and 1830, categorizes Mexicans as an immoral lot given to gambling, fornication, and indolence. Mary Austin Holley's *Texas: Observations, Historical, Geographi-*

cal, and Descriptive (1833) justifies Anglo-American expansionism and stresses the Mexican's barbarity: "The Mexicans are commonly very indolent, of loose morals, and, if not infidels of which there are many, involved in the grossest superstition." Albert Pike's *Prose Sketches and Poems Written in the Western Country* (1834) is similarly hostile; Pike reveals strong antipathy toward Mexicans, repeatedly describing them as an ugly, brutish, and backward race. In the same vein, Josiah Gregg, in his *Commerce On The Prairies: Or, The Journal of a Sante Fe Trader* (1844), rails against the corruption and inefficiency of the Mexican government and portrays Mexican citizens as superstitious, priest-ridden, ignorant, and deceitful. George Wilkins Kendall's *Narrative of the Texan Santa Fe Expedition* (1844), a chronicle of the failed invasion of New Mexico by Anglo-Texans, reinforces this disparaging view: "They pertinaciously cling to the customs of their forefathers, and are becoming every year more and more impoverished–in short, they are morally, physically, and intellectually distanced in the great race of improvement which is run in almost every other quarter of the earth."

As exemplified in Kendall's narrative, the literary debasement of the Mexican was often paralleled by an ethnocentric celebration of Anglo-American progress. As mid century approached, American attitudes toward Mexicans were greatly influenced by the ideology of westward expansion. The notion of Anglo superiority served as a partial justification for the militant nationalism of Manifest Destiny. Erna Fergusson, in *Our Southwest* (1940), captured the general attitude of the times: "Texans could not get it out of their heads that their manifest destiny was to kill Mexicans and take over Mexico."

The Mexican War of 1846-1848 was the culmination of the American crusade for the Southwest. The defeat of Mexico cemented an image of Mexicans as a primitive and inferior people in the American mind. The character of literatura chicanesca was now well-defined. Chronicles such as Henry Augustus Wise's *Los Gringos, or An Inside View of Mexico and California . . .* (1849), John W. Audubon's *Audubon's Western Journal: 1849-1850* (1906), and John Russell Bartlett's *Personal Narrative of Explorations and Incidents in Texas, New Mexico, California, Sonora, and Chihuahua* (1854) scorned Mexicans as lazy, rapacious, and cowardly. Wise, for example, admits that he was cordially received by Mexicans but adds that "generally speaking they were dirty, ill-bred persons,

without moral principles, and the greatest liars in existence." Negative images and stereotypes also found their way into fiction of the time. Charles W. Webber's *The Prairie Scout: A Romance of Border Life* (1852) describes the eagle on the Mexican flag as "a dirty, cowardly creature that feeds upon carcass" and proposes it as a fitting symbol for the Mexican character and nation. In fiction was also fixed the image of the "greaser." Jeremiah Clemens's *Bernard Lile, an Historical Romance* (1856) and *Mustang Grey* (1858) offer virulent sarcasm on greasers. *Bernard Lile* includes a lengthy explanation of the term and suggests that it derives from the Mexican proclivity for filth and disorder. *Mustang Grey,* a compendium of stereotypes, is a story of wily bandits, ignorant peasants, lusty wenches, and lecherous priests (the last an indication that anti-Catholicism also prejudiced the American view). The stereotype comes into play in Augustine Joseph Hickey Duganne's ethnocentric potboiler, *Putnam Pomfret's Ward* (1861), which uses the Mexican War as its background and makes the case that "a single yankee could whip a pack o' greasers." George Emery's 1869 short story, "The Water-Witch," published in the widely circulated *Overland Monthly,* portrays "a ragged, dirty Mexican, whose matted hair was a model of a cactus-fence, whose tattered blanket served to make more evident his nakedness, an unmistakable, unredeemed greaser." The Mexican expresses himself in "grunts" and "aboriginal shrugs" and offers his service as a water diviner for the simple payment of *aguardiente* (liquor).

The appearance in the 1860s of the dime novel was instrumental in the dissemination of the stereotypes of literatura chicanesca. Characterized by sensationalism and an unabashed appeal to chauvinism, dime novels expanded the American mythological canon of cowboys, frontiersmen, Indian fighters, and other emblems of Anglo-Saxon righteousness. Invariably, the dime novel presented a racist formula: an Anglo-Saxon hero versus a Mexican or Indian foe. Sam Hall's *Little Lone Star, or The Belle of The Cibolo* (1886) is typical. Hall presents a greaser-hating Texan, extraordinarily skillful with knife, gun, and fists, who rescues a kidnapped "Spanish Lady" from the clutches of a drunken Mexican bandit intent on rape. The Texas kills the "yaller-belly greaser" and wins the senorita's hand in marriage.

The Hall novel also illustrates that ancillary sexist stereotypes have been a feature in literatura chicanesca. Throughout the nineteenth century American society frowned on the eroticization of Anglo-American women in literature, so an outlet was found in Mexican and Indian women. Beginning with Zebulon Pike's *An Account of Expeditions to the Sources of the Mississippi . . . and A Tour Through The Interior Parts of New Spain* (1810), Mexican women were stamped as exotic, voluptuous creatures given to moral laxity: "They have eradicated from their breasts every sentiment of virtue and ambition . . . their whole souls . . . being taken up in music, dress, and the little blandishments of voluptuous dissipation." Enticingly dressed, revealing swelling bosom, shapely hips and legs, and with alluring dark eyes that wantonly invited the attention of Anglo-American men, the exotic and lusty Mexicana became a staple of American literature. The poem "They Wait For Us" (in *National Songs, Ballads, and Other Patriotic Poetry, Chiefly Relating to the War of 1846,* compiled by William M'Carty, 1846) has Mexican women awaiting the Anglo-invasion of Mexico and the boon of Anglo-American masculinity: "The Spanish maid, eye of fire, / At balmy evening turns her lyre / And, looking to the eastern sky, / Awaits our Yankee chivalry / Whose purer blood and valiant arms / Are fit to clasp her budding charms." Many nineteenth-century novels were melodramatic tales of love affairs between Mexican senoritas and Anglo-Americans; two of Edward Carroll Judson's Ned Buntline books, *Magdalena, The Beautiful Mexican Maid* (1846) and *The Volunteer, or The Maid of Monterrey* (1847), mined the exotic attributes of the Mexican woman, giving a racial tinge to romanticism. The stereotype has lingered well into the twentieth century, in ever more explicit form, as for example in Harvey Fergusson's *Grant of Kingdom* (1950) and N. Richard Nash's *Cry Macho* (1975). Both books portray aggressive Mexican females in relationships with white men. For example, in *Grant at Kingdom,* a woman named Consuelo seductively smiles at the Anglo-American protagonist, a total stranger to her, then opens her robe to entice him.

The negative stereotypes of literatura chicanesca were not confined to pulp fiction; they were also grist for influential figures in American literature. Enormously popular writers such as O. Henry (William Sydney Porter) caricatured Mexicans again and again in his writing. In the stories collected in *Heart of the West* (1904), such as "The Reformation of Calliope," "The Caballero's Way" (which introduces the Cisco Kid), and

"An Afternoon Miracle," the Mexicans are villainous buffoons. The most blatant stereotyping occurs in "An Afternoon Miracle," in which the heroine is accosted by "a big, swarthy, Mexican, with a daring and evil expression, contemplating her with an ominous, dull eye." She is rescued by a handsome, smooth-shaven ranger who quickly dispatches the knife-wielding Mexican: "Then he delivered the good, Saxon knock-out blow–always so pathetically disastrous to the fistless Latin races– and García was down and out, with his head under a clump of prickly pears."

Stephen Crane employs stereotypes in some of his fiction that would later become commonplace in Western literature and film: the Mexican bandit and the comic Mexican sidekick. His 1896 story "One Dash-Horses" presents a confrontation between a ranger and his sidekick and just such a bandit: "a certain fat Mexican, with a mustache like a snake, who came extremely near to have eaten his last tamale." José is the ranger's sidekick; he plays the kind of role that would later find wide currency in Pancho, the Cisco Kid's sidekick. The fat Mexican "was insane with the wild rage of a man whose liquor is daily burning at his brain . . . Five or six of his fellows crowded after him." The Mexican and his men kick and pummel José until he scurries to safety behind his master. "A Man and Some Others" (1897) and "The Five White Mice" (1898) offer the same stereotype; a gang of heavily armed Mexicans against a single Anglo-American. The Mexicans are cowardly and tricky, and they capitulate to the Anglo-American's superiority with gun, knife, or fists. Crane's classic "The Bride Comes to Yellow Sky" (1898) similarly presents Mexicans as cowards. When a drunken gunslinger storms into town looking for trouble, "two Mexicans at once set down their glasses and faded out of the rear entrance of the saloon." It is true that in his stories Crane sought to address the ironies of frontier mythology. However, it is also obvious that the Mexican was a negative component of the mythos he portrayed.

Even so, Crane signals a retreat from extreme nationalism in American literature beginning around the turn of the century. The twentieth century saw writers turn toward a more critical and realistic assessment of society. Perhaps due to rising awareness of the problem of social and economic stratification in America, stereotypes tended to be presented in a less offensive manner. In some notable cases the Mexicans were presented in sympathetic terms. Hamlin Garland's "Delmar of Pima" (1902) reverses the stereotype: Delmar, the "greaser sheriff" of Pima, is a courageous man of justice; the Anglos are thieves and cowards. An ironic twist comes when the unarmed Delmar coolly walks in and disperses a lynch mob of seventy-five armed and angry white cowboys. Tellingly, Mexican-American Elfego Baca–probably a more courageous and honorable lawman than Wild Bill Hickok, Wyatt Earp, or Bat Masterson–performed a similar feat but has not received deserved recognition, let alone apotheosis, in the history and literature of the West.

American liberals were greatly sympathetic to the Mexican Revolution of 1910, and some writers, especially those of a socialist bent, portrayed the Mexican as a symbol of the downtrodden. A well-known literary product of this empathy came from socialist Jack London. In "The Mexican" (1911) London romanticized the Mexican Revolution and made protagonist Felipe Rivera a shining model of revolutionary idealism. London's polemic contrasts the corruption of capitalistic American society with Rivera's noble sacrifice in becoming a prize-fighter in the United States in order to raise money to buy guns for the revolution. Lacking boxing skills or the cunning of his Anglo opponents, Rivera wins on sheer fortitude, endurance, and because of the spiritual strength of his cause. "The Mexican" sags from ideas borrowed from Marx and Nietzsche, and the characters are one-dimensional mouthpieces for London's socialist program; but Felipe Rivera, whom London invests with quiet dignity, is at least not a buffoon or bandit.

Despite the lessening of prejudicial stereotypes in some quarters, ethnocentrism continued to color literatura chicanesca. Harvey Fergusson, notable for his prolific writings on the indigenous cultures of the Southwest, demonstrates this failing. Arthur G. Pettit (in the *New Mexico Historical Review*, July 1976) has assessed Fergusson's work as "a classical example of Anglo-American ethnocentricity" and concludes that "the historical value of Fergusson's writings is that they have accentuated the already existing anti-Mexican feelings among the Anglo-Americans." In *The Blood of the Conquerors* (1921), *Wolf Song* (1927), and *In Those Days* (1929), Fergusson advances the thesis that the decline of Hispanic influence and the rise of Anglo-American social and political power was a historical necessity and a source of social progress, due to the fact that the Anglo-American was uniquely gifted to forge his destiny through conquest. Fergusson's work is proof that the racist underpinnings of Manifest Destiny persisted well into this century. His novels are not fundamentally different from the scurrilous dime novels of the nineteenth century.

Ethnocentrism and historical distortion also marred the work of major American writers of the modern era. Willa Cather's *Death Comes for the Archbishop* (1927) is a significant example. Cecil Robinson has celebrated Cather's historical novel as an exemplary product of literatura chicanesca, praising it as "an accomplishment which suggests that one need not have been nurtured on tortillas and beans to respond aesthetically and with comprehension to the indigenous culture of the region." But Chicano cultural historian E. A. Mares (in *New Mexico Magazine*, June 1985) is closer to the mark; he calls the book "tragically flawed by the narrowness of its ethnic and cultural biases" despite its "high literary merit." Cather depicts the Mexican population as quaint, primitive, fanatically religious, and childlike in frequent stereotypical generalizations. For example, the character sketch of Old Marino Lucero, a notorious miser who had accumulated wealth but lived in squalor, concludes, "Thrift is such a rare quality among Mexicans that they find it amusing." Such lapses into stereotype are regrettable but minor compared to the historical distortion that accompanies the novel's major theme: the struggle for ecclesiastical power between Bishop Jean Marie Latour and Padre José Antonio Martínez. The character of Latour is a fictionalization of French-born Bishop Jean Baptiste Lamy, the first bishop appointed to the territory of New Mexico after its annexation by the United States. Martínez is the real name of a Mexican priest. While the substitution of a fictional name for Lamy can be read as an attempt to lend historicity to the character of Martínez, both men are fictionalized. Bishop Lamy was not the saintly figure and Padre Martínez not the scoundrel that Cather makes them. She distorts the Mexican's physical and moral character, giving him an animalistic, savage cast: "His mouth was the very assertion of violent, uncurbed passion and tyrannical self-will; the full lips thrust out and taut, like the flesh of animals distended by fear or desire." More seriously, Cather impugns Martínez's moral character by alleging that, through fraud and exploitation of his office, he acquired lands belonging to Taos Indians, which "made him quite the richest man in the parish." She also alleges that the fictional Martínez exacted tithes from his poor parishioners and had mistresses and fathered children while a priest; the original Martínez had a wife and children before entering the priesthood, and there is no evidence he exacted tithes from the poor Mexicans and Indians of his parish. Martha Weigle's *Brothers of Light, Brothers of Blood: The Penitentes of the Southwest* (1976), Ray John De Aragón's *Padre Martínez and Bishop Lamy* (1978), and Fray Angélico Chávez's *But Time and Chance* (1981) demonstrate that Cather's depiction of Padre Martínez is distorted and defamatory.

In some cases, the treatment of the Mexican in twentieth-century fiction has been because of irony and subtleties of narration. In Ernest Hemingway's 1933 short story "The Gambler, the Nun, and the Radio," Cayetano Ruiz, the gambler, and the three unnamed Mexicans in the story are not traditional stereotypes but, rather, typical of Hemingway's characters of the period. When Ruiz says, "I am a poor idealist. I am the victim of illusions," he announces the thematic crux of the story and surfaces as the Hemingway code hero. Coming close to death from a gunshot wound and peritonitis, Ruiz is a model of self-control and stoic suffering. The Mexicans are the vehicles for his nihilism. The stereotype of the priest-ridden Mexican is overturned; one of the unnamed Mexicans is a Marxist whose interjection–"Religion is the opium of the people"–opens the story. The story closes with bitter irony: the Mexicans "Play the Cucaracha another time. It's better than the radio." "La Cucaracha," the famous song from the Mexican Revolution, serves as Hemingway's symbol for earthiness, rebellion, suffering, and the existential encounter with life and death. Although they are saddled with Hemingway's existentialist baggage, the Mexicans in "The Gambler, the Nun, and the Radio" are striking characterizations; they are contemplative rather than stupid, rebellious rather than resigned, and complex figures rather than stereotypes.

Some modern writers were contradictory in their treatment of Mexican characters. William Saroyan's "With A Hey Nonny Nonny" (1934) depicts the labor struggles and quandaries of Mexican agricultural workers in California. Saroyan's existential story is notable because there is no stereotyping, either positive or negative. He forcefully renders Juan Rivera's anguish and confusion as he struggles to survive in a world without choices, a life without possibilities. Rivera is an existential figure in a world he has not made, can-

not understand, and least of all control: "... it was so much an evil truth to him that he wanted to stand tall on the earth, as tall as a great tree, and shout at all who brought about such things. But he could do nothing and in desperation he turned to the man beside him, and then decided not to speak, since there was nothing to say." Saroyan's story is free of the cheap sentimentality that often accompanies sympathetic views of the Mexican in twentieth-century fiction. It is difficult to believe that the author of the superb "With A Hey Nonny Nonny" also wrote at about the same time the silly "My Uncle and the Mexicans" (1935). This brief narrative concerns a group of Mexican migrant workers who come to the Saroyan farm looking for work. To ease his uncle's apprehension, Saroyan offers the platitude that "Mexicans are noble and simple people." The story then succumbs to stereotype in an exchange between Saroyan and his uncle: "I hear Mexicans do a lot of stealing, said my uncle. They'll take anything that ain't got roots in the earth, I said." Saroyan later qualifies that "The stealing they do never amounts to anything," but the general impression made by the story is that thievery is as natural to Mexicans as raising dogs and eating beans and tortillas. Despite Saroyan's humor the Mexicans in "My Uncle and the Mexicans" are stamped with the trait of incorrigible thievery, a stereotype further reinforced by John Steinbeck.

His *Tortilla Flat* (1935), due to its extensive use in high school and college curricula, has been influential in instilling certain images of the Mexican. In the past two decades *Tortilla Flat* has been reassessed by Chicano and non-Chicano critics, yielding the near consensus that Steinbeck's fable of carefree, happy "paisanos" (peasants) is deleterious stereotyping. The most severe indictment has come from Arthur G. Pettit in his *Images of the Mexican American in Fiction and Film* (1980): "*Tortilla Flat* stands as the clearest example in American literature of the Mexican as jolly savage.... The novel contains characters varying little from the most negative Mexican stereotypes." Indeed, it is difficult to overlook the negative images in Steinbeck's portrayal of Mexicans as childlike primitives reveling in constant drunkenness and unbridled sexuality. *Tortilla Flat* is not a racist book but displays misplaced sensibilities. Apparently Steinbeck sought to romanticize the paisanos' way of life as a sharp contrast to the puritanism and rigid commercialism which he saw as characteristic of American society. He says, "The paisanos are clean of commercialism, free of the complicated systems of American business, and, having nothing that can be stolen, exploited, or mortgaged, that system has not attacked them very vigorously." In effect Steinbeck's paisanos are straw figures for his disenchantment with American society, and verisimilitude and authenticity are sacrificed to that end. Chicano critic Philip D. Ortego offers a pithy distinction: "Chicanos can only conclude that Steinbeck may not have lacked *corazón* (heart) but that he lacked *seso* (brains). To his credit Steinbeck's foreword to the 1937 Modern Library edition offered an apology: "If I have done them harm by telling a few of their stories, I am sorry. It will not happen again." However, his apology, which is rarely taught, does not lessen the vast irony that the most famous and popular novel about Mexican Americans is also a monumental failure of literatura chicanesca.

Few works can be recommended as offering insight into what it means to be a Chicano. Frank Waters's *The People of the Valley* (1941), Paul Horgan's *The Common Heart* (1942), Oliver LaFarge's *Behind the Mountain* (1956), and Eugene Nelson's *Bracero* (1972) are commendable for their overall avoidance of negative stereotypes and for the authors' sensitivity and knowledge of their subject matter. Only two writers are truly exceptional. They are Amado Muro and John Nichols. Both relocated (Muro from Ohio, Nichols from New York) to the Southwest and assimilated into Chicano culture.

Muro was hailed by critic Gerald W. Haslam in *Forgotten Pages of American Literature* (1970) as "one of the most promising Mexican American writers." In the introduction to his anthology *The Chicano: From Caricature to Self-Portrait* (1971) Edward Simmen said "Amado Muro . . . seems to have written more good short fiction than any other young Mexican American." It wasn't until after his death in 1971 that people generally knew that Muro was Chester Seltzer, who had moved to the Southwest in the 1940s and married a Mexican woman, Amada Muro (from whom he took his pseudonym). He had two children by her and lived with his family in El Paso, Texas, between excursions as a hobo and railroad hand, until his death. Seltzer's marriage to Muro, whose culture he adopted, and his many years of travel throughout northern Mexico and the American Southwest provided him with firsthand knowledge of Mexican-Chicano life and culture. His witty, charming, and folksy short stories

stand as the best of literatura chicanesca. Muro works within the oral tradition of the *cuento* (folktale). Although deceptively simple and anecdotal, his stories subtly touch on significant themes. Several of the stories set in the barrio of El Paso, Texas, focus on the Mexican and American cultural duality of Chicanos. They are as authentic and insightful as anything written by a Chicano. "Cecilia Rosas" (1964), his best story and one of the best stories in all of literatura chicanesca, poignantly notes Cecilia Rosas's rejection of traditional Mexican culture and succinctly captures the process of assimilation: "She prided herself on being more American than Mexican because she was born in El Paso. And she did her best to act, dress, and talk the way Americans do. She hated to speak Spanish, disliked her Mexican name. She called herself Cecile Roses instead of Cecilia Rosas." Other notable stories such as "María Tepache" (1969), "Sunday in Little Chihuahua" (1955), and "Mala Torres" (1968) are brilliant in their rendering of cultural background and social atmosphere. Regrettably, the Muro canon is quite small. He never used his unique gifts to produce a major work that matches the achievement of John Nichols's *The Milagro Beanfield War* (1974).

Nichols is by far the most impressive figure in contemporary literatura chicanesca. His trilogy— *The Milagro Beanfield War, The Magic Journey* (1978) and *The Nirvana Blues* (1981)—reveals a remarkable knowledge of the Chicano experience and offers an acuteness and sensitivity that are extraordinary. As Carl R. Shirley has pointed out in "A Contemporary Florescence of Chicano Literature" (in *Dictionary of Literary Biography, Yearbook 1984*), Nichols is "a spiritual cousin to the Mexican Americans of New Mexico" and his comprehension of their language, history, traditions, and customs has "provided him a perspective of the Hispanic community of his region that is not often achieved by Anglos." Nichols lives and works with the Chicano people that he represents in his fiction; he shares with readers their needs, fears, aspirations, and dreams. His vantage point informs his fiction with authenticity.

Nichols's singular role in literatura chicanesca does not solely rest on his ability to dramatize the social, economic, and political circumstances that beset the Chicano; he indicates the decency, pride, honor, love, and other sustaining virtues that are found in Chicano communities but does not romanticize these virtues. He does not minimize divisiveness and discord within the communities, and he shows disreputable, but genuine, Chicanos. *The Milagro Beanfield War,* his best novel and the best *novela chicanesca,* exemplifies his style. Although *The Milagro Beanfield War* is essentially a comic novel, it has serious moments and sober characterizations. Pertinent examples are the portrayals of Carolina Montoya and Linda Bloom (a Chicana who had married an Anglo and tried to deny her cultural roots and identity). Both characterizations are exceptional; Carolina and Linda are individualized as Chicanas and as women. Neither sexpots nor simpletons, they are fleshed-out characters with human weaknesses and strengths. Nichols's achievement is especially noteworthy because, as has been noted, the portrayals of Mexican women in American literature have been exceedingly callous and sexist. *The Milagro Beanfield War* presents lucid and truthful characterizations that encompass individual traits and important facets of Chicano life. The character Onofre Martínez argues against stereotyping: "I don't believe this is a brown against white question. This is only one kind of people against another kind of people with different ideas. There are brown and white people on both sides. . . . The brown and white people on our side are better people because they are on the correct side, that's all." The correct side is formed by those who fight the physical and spiritual devastation brought about by rabid capitalism. Nichols's affection for Chicano people and his admiration for their struggle to maintain their traditional culture can be glossed from *The Milagro Beanfield War:* "But Bernabé understood roots and he understood the fractured culture, loving what was good in the past while refusing to romanticize it, at the same time he admired all of his stubborn neighbors who had survived on a wing and a prayer, on bootleg liquor, on a half-dozen illegal deer a year, and on a hand-

ful of over-grazed alfalfa fields. And any man or woman or half-grown kid, who come hell or high water, had hung onto a piece of land, a ragtag goat, a rifle, and the Spanish language was okay in Bernabé's book." However, Nichols avoids the claptrap that the Chicano people, because of their righteous cause, will emerge triumphant. On the contrary, *The Magic Journey* and *The Nirvana Blues* are progressively bleaker than the first novel. They intimate that Chicano culture will continue to disintegrate from the onslaught of the dominant Anglo culture. For him the destiny of Chicanos—as of all Americans—is imperiled by forces of fascism at large in American society. His stellar position in literatura chicanesca has been earned by his integrity, candor, and keen observations on Chicano life and culture.

More than a century ago Walt Whitman presaged the failings of literatura chicanesca. Writing from New Orleans, Louisiana, in 1848, he commented, "I have an idea that there is much of importance about the Latin race contributions to American nationality in the South and Southwest that will never be put with sympathetic understanding and tact on record." In the great bulk of literatura chicanesca, excepting the extraordinary works noted, the Chicano has been bandied about as cheap literary commodity and encased in simplification, cliche, stereotype, distortion, and falsification. Moreover, the negative images of the Chicano in American literature amount to a chimera, an unreal creature sprung from the imaginations of Anglo writers and shaped by racial prejudice and ethnocentrism. Ultimately, literatura chicanesca—"the view from without"—discloses a vast ignorance about what the Chicano is and has been; it is not capricious to say that most of the Mexicanos-Chicanos depicted in American literature from the early nineteenth century to the present have never existed, not then and not now.

Checklist of Further Readings

Acuña, Rodolfo. *Occupied America: The Chicano's Struggle Toward Liberation.* San Francisco: Canfield, 1972.

Alford, Harold J. *The Proud Peoples: The Heritage and Culture of Spanish-Speaking Peoples in the United States.* New York: McKay, 1972.

Baker, Houston A., Jr., ed. *Three American Literatures: Essays in Chicano, Native American, and Asian-American Literature for Teachers of American Literature.* New York: Modern Language Association, 1982.

Binder, Wolfgang, ed. *Partial Autobiographies: Interviews with Twenty Chicano Poets.* Erlangen, West Germany: Palm & Enke, 1985.

Bornstein, Miriam. "The Voice of the Chicana in Poetry," *Denver Quarterly,* 16 (Fall 1981): 28-47.

Brokaw, John W. "A Mexican-American Acting Company, 1849-1924," *Educational Theatre Journal,* 27 (March 1975): 23-29.

Bruce-Novoa, Juan. "Canonical and Noncanonical Texts," *Américas Review,* 14 (Fall-Winter 1986): 119-135.

Bruce-Novoa. *Chicano Authors: Inquiry by Interview.* Austin: University of Texas Press, 1980.

Bruce-Novoa. *Chicano Poetry: A Response to Chaos.* Austin: University of Texas Press, 1982.

Candelaria, Cordelia. *Chicano Poetry: A Critical Introduction.* Westport, Conn.: Greenwood, 1986.

Chávez, John R. *The Lost Land: The Chicano Image of the Southwest.* Albuquerque: University of New Mexico Press, 1984.

Chicano Theatre One. San Juan Bautista, Cal.: Cucaracha, 1973.

Durán, Livie Isauro, and H. Russell Bernard, eds. *Introduction to Chicano Studies,* revised edition. New York: Macmillan, 1982.

Eger, Ernestina. *A Bibliography of Criticism of Chicano Literature.* Berkeley: Chicano Studies Library, 1982.

Englekirk, John E. "Notes on the Repertoire of the New Mexican Spanish Folk Theatre," *Southern Folklore Quarterly,* 4 (December 1940): 227-237.

Fisher, Dexter, ed. *Minority Language and Literature: Retrospective and Prospective.* New York: Modern Language Association, 1977.

García, Eugene E., Francisco A. Lomelí, and Isidro D. Ortíz, eds. *Chicano Studies: A Multidisciplinary Approach.* New York: Teachers College Press, 1984.

García, Richard A., ed. *The Chicanos in America, 1540-1974: A Chronology & Fact Book.* Dobbs Ferry, N.Y.: Oceana, 1977.

Hancock, Joel. "The Emergence of Chicano Poetry: A Survey of Sources, Themes and Techniques," *Arizona Quarterly,* 29 (Spring 1973): 57-73.

Heisley, Michael, ed. *An Annotated Bibliography of Chicano Folklore from the Southwestern United States.* Los Angeles: University of California Press, 1977.

Herrera-Sobek, María, ed. *Beyond Stereotypes: The Critical Analysis of Chicana Literature.* Binghamton: Bilingual/Editorial Bilingüe, 1985.

Huerta, Jorge A. "Chicano Agit-Prop: The Early *Actos* of El Teatro Campesino," *Latin American Theatre Review,* 10 (Spring 1977): 45-58.

Huerta. *Chicano Theatre: Themes and Forms.* Ypsilanti: Bilingual/Editorial Bilingüe, 1982.

Jiménez, Francisco. "Dramatic Principles of the Teatro Campesino," *Bilingual Review/Revista Bilingüe,* 2 (January-August 1975): 99-111.

Jiménez, ed. *The Identification and Analysis of Chicano Literature.* Binghamton: Bilingual/Editorial Bilingüe, 1979.

Kanellos, Nicolás. "The Flourishing of Hispanic Theatre in the Southwest, 1920-30's," *Latin American Theatre Review,* 16 (Fall 1982): 29-40.

Kanellos. *Mexican American Theatre: Legacy and Reality.* Pittsburgh, Pa.: Latin American Literary Review, 1987.

Kanellos. "Mexican Community Theatre in a Midwestern City," *Latin American Theatre Review,* 7 (Fall 1973): 43-48.

Kanellos. *Two Centuries of Hispanic Theatre in the Southwest.* Houston: *Revista Chicano-Riqueña,* 1982.

Kanellos, ed. *Mexican American Theatre: Then and Now.* Houston: Arte Publico, 1983.

Lattin, Vernon E., ed. *Contemporary Chicano Fiction: A Critical Survey.* Binghamton: Bilingual/Editorial Bilingüe, 1986.

Leal, Luis. *Aztlán y México: Perfiles literarios e históricos.* Binghamton: Bilingual/Editorial Bilingüe, 1985.

Leal, Fernando de Necochea, Francisco Lomelí, and Roberto G. Trujillo, eds. *A Decade of Chicano Literature (1970-1979): Critical Essays and Bibliography.* Santa Barbara, Cal.: Editorial La Causa, 1982.

Lewis, Marvin A. *Introduction to the Chicano Novel.* Milwaukee: University of Wisconsin, Spanish Speaking Outreach Institute, 1982.

Lomelí, Francisco A., and Donaldo W. Urioste. *Chicano Perspectives in Literature: A Critical and Annotated Bibliography.* Albuquerque: Pajarito, 1976.

Márquez, Antonio. "The American Dream in the Chicano Novel," *Rocky Mountain Review,* 27 (1983): 4-19.

Martínez, Julio A., and Francisco A. Lomelí, eds. *Chicano Literature: A Reference Guide*. Westport, Conn.: Greenwood, 1985.

McWilliams, Carey. *North From Mexico: The Spanish-Speaking People of the United States*. Philadelphia: Lippincott, 1949.

Meier, Matt S., and Feliciano Rivera. *The Chicanos: A History of Mexican Americans*. New York: Hill & Wang, 1972.

Meyer, Doris L. "Anonymous Poetry in Spanish-Language New Mexico Newspapers, 1880-1900," *Bilingual Review/Revista Bilingüe*, 2 (September-December 1975): 259-275.

Moore, John W., and Alfredo Cuéllar. *Mexican Americans*. Englewood Cliffs, N.J.: Prentice-Hall, 1970.

Morgan, Thomas B. "The Latinization of America," *Esquire*, 99 (May 1983): 47-56.

Ordóñez, Elizabeth J. "Chicana Literature and Related Sources: A Selected and Annotated Bibliography," *Bilingual Review/Revista Bilingüe*, 7 (May-August 1980): 143-164.

Paredes, Américo. *"With His Pistol In His Hand": A Border Ballad and Its Hero*. Austin: University of Texas Press, 1958.

Paredes, Raymund A. "The Evolution of Chicano Literature," *MELUS*, 5 (Summer 1978): 71-110.

Paredes. "Mexican American Authors and the American Dream," *MELUS*, 8 (Winter 1981): 71-80.

Robinson, Cecil. *Mexico and the Hispanic Southwest in American Literature*. Tucson: University of Arizona Press, 1977.

Robinson. *With the Ears of Strangers: The Mexican in American Literature*. Tucson: University of Arizona Press, 1963.

Rodriguez, Richard. "Mexico's Children," *American Scholar*, 55 (Spring 1986): 161-177.

Rodriguez del Pino, Salvador. *La Novela Chicana Escrita en Español: Cinco Autores Comprometidos*. Ypsilanti: Bilingual/Editorial Bilingüe, 1982.

Rojas, Guillermo. "Toward a Chicano/Raza Bibliography," *El Grito,* 7 (December 1973): 1-85.

Saldivar, Ramón. "A Dialectic of Difference: Towards a Theory of the Chicano Novel," *MELUS*, 6 (Fall 1979): 73-92.

Sánchez, Marta Ester. *Contemporary Chicana Poetry: A Critical Approach to an Emerging Literature*. Berkeley: University of California Press, 1985.

Seator, Lynette. "*Emplumada:* Chicana Rites of Passage," *MELUS*, 11 (Summer 1984): 23-38.

Shirley, Carl R., and Paula W. Shirley. *Understanding Chicano Literature*. Columbia: University of South Carolina Press, 1988.

Sommers, Joseph, and Tomás Ybarro-Frausto, eds. *Modern Chicano Writers*. Englewood Cliffs, N.J.: Prentice-Hall, 1979.

Tatum, Charles M. *Chicano Literature*. Boston: Twayne, 1982.

Tatum. "Some Examples of Chicano Prose Fiction of the Nineteenth and Early Twentieth Centuries," *Revista Chicano-Riqueña,* 9 (Winter 1981): 58-67.

El Teatro Campesino: The Evolution of America's First Chicano Theatre Company, 1965-1985. San Juan Bautista, Cal.: El Teatro Campesino, 1985.

Trujillo, Robert G., and Andres Rodríguez. *Literatura Chicana: Creative and Critical Writings Through 1984*. Oakland: Floricanto, 1985.

Valdez, Luis, and El Teatro Campesino. *Actos: El Teatro Campesino*. San Juan Bautista, Cal.: Cucaracha, 1971.

Vallejos, Tomás. "Ritual Process and the Family in the Chicano Novel," *MELUS,* 10 (Winter 1983): 5-16.

Vassallo, Paul. *The Magic of Words: Rudolfo A. Anaya and His Writings*. Albuquerque: University of New Mexico Press, 1982.

Ybarra-Frausto, Tomás. "The Chicano Movement and the Emergence of a Chicano Poetic Consciousness," *New Scholar,* 6 (1977): 81-109.

Ybarra-Frausto. "Punto de Partida," *Latin American Theatre Review,* 4 (Spring 1971): 51-52.

Zimmerman, Enid. "An Annotated Bibliography of Chicano Literature: Novels, Short Fiction, Poetry and Drama, 1970-1980," *Bilingual Review/Revista Bilingüe,* 9 (September-December 1982): 227-251.

Contributors

John C. Akers ....*North Carolina State University*
Douglas K. Benson ....*Kansas State University*
Lawrence Benton ....*California State University, Chico*
Cordelia Candelaria..*University of Colorado*
Jean S. Chittenden..*Trinity University*
Clark Colahan ....*Whitman College*
Barbara Brinson Curiel ....*University of California, Santa Cruz*
S. Daydí-Tolson ....*University of Wisconsin–Milwaukee*
Patricia De La Fuente...*Pan American University*
Gwendolyn Díaz..*St. Mary's University*
J. Allan Englekirk ....*University of South Carolina*
Annie Olivia Eysturoy ....*University of New Mexico*
Roberta Fernández..*Occidental College*
Nasario García..*New Mexico Highlands University*
Judith Ginsberg...*Modern Language Association*
Erlinda Gonzales-Berry ....*University of New Mexico*
Yolanda Broyles González ....*University of California, Santa Barbara*
Shaw N. Gynan..*University of New Mexico*
Joel Hancock ....*University of Utah*
Gerald Haslam ....*Sonoma State University*
Nicolás Kanellos ....*University of Houston*
Juanita Luna Lawhn...*San Antonio College*
Luis Leal ....*University of California, Santa Barbara*
Marvin A. Lewis..*University of Missouri–Columbia*
Clara Lomas ....*Colorado College*
Francisco A. Lomelí.........................*University of California, Santa Barbara*
Antonio Márquez...*University of New Mexico*
Doris Meyer...*Connecticut College*
Julián Olivares..*University of Houston*
Ernesto Chávez Padilla...............................*California State University, Bakersfield*
Ana Perches ....*California State University, Hayward*
William Rintoul ....*Bakersfield, California*
Margarita Tavera Rivera ....*California State University, San Bernardino*
Joe D. Rodríguez ....*San Diego State University*
Salvador Rodriguez del Pino.............................*University of Colorado at Boulder*
Reynaldo Ruiz ....*Eastern Michigan University*
Jorge Santana ....*California State University, Sacramento*
Carl R. Shirley...*University of South Carolina*
Paula W. Shirley ....*Columbia College*
Gary Soto ....*University of California, Berkeley*
Charles M. Tatum ....*University of Arizona*
Héctor Avalos Torres ....*University of New Mexico*
Donaldo W. Urioste ....*California Lutheran University*
Tomás Vallejos ....*University of Houston–Downtown*
Nancy Vogeley ....*University of San Francisco*
Donald Wolff....................................*Pennsylvania State University at Harrisburg*
Richard D. Woods ....*Trinity University*
Yvonne Yarbro-Bejarano.....................................*University of Washington*

Cumulative Index

Dictionary of Literary Biography, Volumes 1-82
Dictionary of Literary Biography Yearbook, 1980-1988
Dictionary of Literary Biography Documentary Series, Volumes 1-6

Cumulative Index

DLB before number: *Dictionary of Literary Biography,* Volumes 1-82
Y before number: *Dictionary of Literary Biography Yearbook,* 1980-1988
DS before number: *Dictionary of Literary Biography Documentary Series,* Volumes 1-6

A

B

C

Cumulative Index

D

K

L

Y

Z

(Continued from front endsheets)

71: *American Literary Critics and Scholars, 1880-1900,* edited by John W. Rathbun and Monica M. Grecu (1988)

72: *French Novelists, 1930-1960,* edited by Catharine Savage Brosman (1988)

73: *American Magazine Journalists, 1741-1850,* edited by Sam G. Riley (1988)

74: *American Short-Story Writers Before 1880,* edited by Bobby Ellen Kimbel, with the assistance of William E. Grant (1988)

75: *Contemporary German Fiction Writers,* Second Series, edited by Wolfgang D. Elfe and James Hardin (1988)

76: *Afro-American Writers, 1940-1955,* edited by Trudier Harris (1988)

77: *British Mystery Writers, 1920-1939,* edited by Bernard Benstock and Thomas F. Staley (1988)

78: *American Short-Story Writers, 1880-1910,* edited by Bobby Ellen Kimbel, with the assistance of William E. Grant (1988)

79: *American Magazine Journalists, 1850-1900,* edited by Sam G. Riley (1988)

80: *Restoration and Eighteenth-Century Dramatists,* First Series, edited by Paula R. Backsheider (1989)

81: *Austrian Fiction Writers, 1875-1913,* edited by James Hardin and Donald G. Daviau (1989)

82: *Chicano Writers,* First Series, edited by Francisco A. Lomelí and Carl R. Shirley (1989)

Documentary Series

1: *Sherwood Anderson, Willa Cather, John Dos Passos, Theodore Dreiser, F. Scott Fitzgerald, Ernest Hemingway, Sinclair Lewis,* edited by Margaret A. Van Antwerp (1982)

2: *James Gould Cozzens, James T. Farrell, William Faulkner, John O'Hara, John Steinbeck, Thomas Wolfe, Richard Wright,* edited by Margaret A. Van Antwerp (1982)

3: *Saul Bellow, Jack Kerouac, Norman Mailer, Vladimir Nabokov, John Updike, Kurt Vonnegut,* edited by Mary Bruccoli (1983)

4: *Tennessee Williams,* edited by Margaret A. Van Antwerp and Sally Johns (1984)

5: *American Transcendentalists,* edited by Joel Myerson (1988)

6: *Hardboiled Mystery Writers,* edited by Matthew J. Bruccoli and Richard Layman (1988)

Yearbooks

1980, edited by Karen L. Rood, Jean W. Ross, and Richard Ziegfeld (1981)

1981, edited by Karen L. Rood, Jean W. Ross, and Richard Ziegfeld (1982)

1982, edited by Richard Ziegfeld; associate editors: Jean W. Ross and Lynne C. Zeigler (1983)

1983, edited by Mary Bruccoli and Jean W. Ross; associate editor: Richard Ziegfeld (1984)

1984, edited by Jean W. Ross (1985)

1985, edited by Jean W. Ross (1986)

1986, edited by J. M. Brook (1987)

1987, edited by J. M. Brook (1988)

1988, edited by J. M. Brook (1989)